P9-DDR-615

WITHDRAWN
WALLINGFORD PUBLIC LIBRARY
200 North Main St.
Wallingford, CT 06492

WITHDRAWN

ALSO BY MICHAEL SCAMMELL

Solzhenitsyn: A Biography

AS EDITOR

The Solzhenitsyn Files
Unofficial Art from the Soviet Union
Russia's Other Writers

KOESTLER

KOESTLER

The Literary and Political Odyssey
of a Twentieth-Century Skeptic

Michael Scammell

WALLINGFORD PUBLIC LIBRARY
200 North Main St.
Wallingford, CT 06492

RANDOM HOUSE
NEW YORK

B
KOESTLER
SC

Copyright © 2009 by Michael Scammell

All rights reserved.

Published in the United States by Random House, an imprint of
The Random House Publishing Group, a division
of Random House, Inc., New York.

RANDOM HOUSE and colophon are registered
trademarks of Random House, Inc.

Portions of this work were originally published in different form as the following: "Arthur
Koestler Resigns: A Discovery in the Moscow Archives," *The New Republic,* May 4, 1998;
" 'No Revolution Can Be Accomplished Without Morality': Arthur Koestler's Resignation
from the Communist Party in 1938," in *Literature, History and Politics: Essays in Honor of
Thompson Bradley,* ed. Sibelan Forrester and Thomas Newlin (Slavica, 2004); and
"Arthur Koestler in Civil War Spain," *Agni,* Fall 2001.

Library of Congress Cataloging-in-Publication Data
Scammell, Michael.
Koestler : the literary and political odyssey of a twentieth-century skeptic /
Michael Scammell.
p.   cm.
Includes bibliographical references and index.
ISBN 978-0-394-57630-5
eBook ISBN 978-1-588-36901-7
1. Koestler, Arthur, 1905–1983.   2. Novelists, English—20th century—Biography.
3. Zionists—Biography.   4. Political activists—Great Britain—Biography.
5. Philosophers—Great Britain—Biography. 6. Journalists—Great Britain—
Biography.   I. Title.
PR6021.O4Z84 2009
828'.91209—dc22
[B]   2008051108

Printed in the United States of America on acid-free paper

www.atrandom.com

2   4   6   8   9   7   5   3   1

First Edition

Book design by Christopher M. Zucker

For Rosemary

If we can speak about the Central European intellectual at all . . .
it is because of the personality of Arthur Koestler. His Jewish-
Hungaro-Czech origins are a sort of advance warning that explains all his researches and his ambiguity: from Judaism to the
theory of assimilation, from Marxism to the absolute negation of
communism, from the flirtation with eastern spiritualism to its
demystification, from faith in science to doubt of all "closed systems of thought," and from the search for the absolute to serene
resignation in the face of man's critical aptitudes. Koestler's intellectual adventure, through to his *ultimate choice,* is unique even
within the most broadly defined borders of Europe. It contains
the potential biography of every Central European intellectual—
in its radical realization.

— DANILO KIŠ

There are men and women who, in addition to having special
gifts, seem to embody the times in which they live. Somehow
their biographies take on and make more visible to the rest of us
the shape and meaning of the age. Even if Arthur Koestler had
not been a significant writer and publicist, future historians
would be fascinated by his career. It touches, with uncanny precision, on the hopes and nightmares, on the places and events,
which have given the twentieth century its flavor.

— GEORGE STEINER

CONTENTS

PART TWO: FAME AND INFAMY
The Author as Novelist
(1936–1946)

PART THREE: LOST ILLUSIONS
The Author as Activist
(1946–1959)

PART FOUR: ASTRIDE THE TWO CULTURES
The Author as Polymath
(1959–1983)

PROLOGUE

Men are convinced of your arguments, your sincerity, and the seriousness of your efforts only by your death.

— ALBERT CAMUS

ON TUESDAY, MARCH 1, 1983, Arthur Koestler and his wife, Cynthia, entered their sitting room at 8 Montpelier Square, London, sat down facing each other, he in his favorite leather armchair, she on the couch, and poured themselves their usual drink before dinner. Arthur's was his favorite brandy, Cynthia's was scotch. The only difference between this and a thousand similar evenings was the presence on a small table between them of a bottle of wine, a large bottle of Tuinal sleeping tablets, a jar of honey, and some extra wineglasses. Arthur and Cynthia swallowed about half the tablets each, washed them down with wine and honey, then sipped their brandy and scotch. Within half an hour or so they were unconscious, within an hour completely dead, and they remained there, fully clothed, for a day and a half, until their Brazilian maid came to clean the house on Thursday morning.

The suicide was meticulously planned and carried out without a hitch. Several months beforehand Koestler had prepared a handwritten letter. "The purpose of this note is to make it unmistakeably [*sic*] clear that I intend to commit suicide by taking an overdose of drugs without the knowledge or aid of any other person. The drugs have been legally obtained and hoarded over a considerable period." The immediate reason for his decision was illness. He was suffering from both Parkinson's disease and what he called "the slow-killing variety of leukemia." He had lived with Parkinson's for about seven years already, but leukemia was the last straw. "I kept the latter a secret even from intimate friends to save them distress. After a more or less steady physical decline over the last years, the process has now reached an acute state with added complications which make it advisable to seek self-deliverance now, before I become technically incapable of making the necessary arrangements."

"Self-deliverance" was an interesting term for Koestler to use. It echoed the *Freitod* (literally "free death") of his native language, German, with quite different connotations than its grisly synonym *Selbstmord* ("self-murder") or the more clinical *Suizid* ("suicide"). It was a form of death with which he was more than familiar, as a Central European Jew who had grown up in the shadow of anti-Semitism and the rise of fascism. Self-deliverance was also the term favored by the Voluntary Euthanasia Society, of which Koestler was vice president, and he had long ago made it clear that he would kill himself rather than suffer a lingering death. In a preface to the society's controversial *Guide to Self-Deliverance* he had written: "An unknown country to which the only access leads through a torture chamber is frightening. . . . The prospect of falling asleep is not only soothing but can make it positively desirable to quit this pain-racked mortal frame and become unborn again." Noting that animals enter the world and leave it again presumably without pain, he had added: "The conclusion is inescapable. We need midwives to aid us to be born—or at least the assurance that such aid is available. Euthanasia, like obstetrics, is the natural corrective to a biological handicap."

He had not chosen self-deliverance lightly. The variety of leukemia he suffered from, chronic lymphocytic leukemia, was slow acting, and even in combination with Parkinson's was not necessarily lethal, and he had waited eight months after his diagnosis before deciding on the final step. He probably made up his mind for good on Sunday, February 27. Koestler hated Sundays. He was fond of quoting Dostoyevsky: "Even if you are in the deepest dungeon, you always know when it is a Sunday." But the true decision had been made long before, of course.

It was characteristic of Koestler to seek the kind of control over his death that had eluded him in managing his chaotic and crowded life, yet if we regard this death as unavoidably a public act, he failed in one crucial respect, for there was the no small matter of Cynthia. More than twenty years younger than Koestler and in perfect health, Cynthia had no objective reason to die, and so far as we can tell, the decision was not the result of impulse or sudden despair. In a postscript to Koestler's suicide note, she wrote: "I fear both death and the act of dying that lies ahead of us. . . . However, I cannot live without Arthur, despite certain inner resources. Double suicide has never appealed to me; but now Arthur's incurable diseases have reached a stage where there is nothing else to do. Cynthia Koestler."

Double suicide is a rare and titillating event. One has to go back to a slightly older Central European Jewish writer, Stefan Zweig, and his younger wife, in 1942, for a precedent, and that too was regarded as unnatural and shocking. Cynthia's death at the comparably young age of fifty-five startled friends and strangers alike. The popular press had a field day: "Author and Wife Found Dead"; "Koestlers in Suicide Pact"; "Anti-Red Crusader and Wife in Suicide Pact"; "Wife's Tragic Devotion." It was a sensational end to a life that had already seen more than its share of drama, yet there was a certain aptness to it. For Koestler had lived almost all his life in the public eye, amid the glare of publicity, and was no stranger to the scent of scandal that followed him beyond the grave.

PROVOCATION AND CONTROVERSY were meat and drink to Koestler, elements of a tumultuous life in which he rarely experienced peace or quiet. His pugnacious personality was a lightning rod for strong feelings and extreme opinions, and he reveled in the notoriety they brought him. Like many short men (barely five foot six in his stocking feet), he was incorrigibly competitive and relentlessly combative, quick to take offense and slow to forgive. Hungarian in his temper, German in his industry, Jewish in his intellectual ambition, he was never comfortable in his own skin, doomed to oscillate between arrogance and humility, like one of those mercurial Russians in the novels of Dostoyevsky, whom Koestler so admired and wished to emulate.

But there was another side to Koestler that few beyond his immediate circle got to see, an undisguised vulnerability and painful honesty, a self-conscious shyness and morbid sensitivity, that combined with his boyish exuberance and devil-may-care daring made him a magnet for innumerable women. Mamaine Paget, his second wife, found the combination of his fiery, un-English temperament and extraordinary attentiveness irresistible. To the English novelist Elizabeth Jane Howard, who lived with him for a while, he was a noble goblin, addicted to childish jokes, with a "continuous, crackling, almost irritable energy" that made you feel that if you touched him "you would get an electric shock." Several of the women he was passionately involved with remained his friends for life, and Cynthia, his third wife, demonstrated her devotion in the most dramatic way possible when she chose to die with him. But his chronic promiscuity led other women to detest him, and long after his death he was accused of having once committed rape.

What made Koestler so exhilarating and often so difficult to be around was a form of manic depression that caused him to alternate between demonic glee, with an inflated sense of his own importance, and gloomy humility, powered by chronic self-doubt. He could be reckless and impatient at one moment, totally incapable of controlling his volatile temper, yet generous and tender the next. It's no wonder he tended to think and write in terms of binaries and antitheses: yogi and commissar, arrival and departure, insight and outlook, lotus and robot. Alcohol (bolstered by Benzedrine and other pep pills) was his drug of choice, rescuing him again and again from the ravages of recurring feelings of inferiority while deepening his dilemmas and getting him into even more trouble.

Despite his urge to be a Casanova, Koestler just as often preferred the company of men, especially those, such as Dylan Thomas, Henry Green, Albert Camus, and Jean-Paul Sartre, who shared his disregard for bourgeois niceties. More conventional friends secretly envied or despised his drinking and womanizing, according to temperament, and welcomed or resented his forensic skills, depending on task. In Britain, John Strachey found Koestler "unpardonably brilliant," Michael Foot called him the "most pulverizing arguer I have ever met, bar none," and George Orwell regarded him as a staunch ideological friend and loyal ally. In America, he was admired by Mary McCarthy, James Burnham, and Philip Rahv, among others, for his political penetration and dialectical brilliance. Camus described him as "a man of substance" who could be relied upon through thick and thin, and Raymond Aron called Koestler the "greatest of the engaged intellectuals" of the twentieth century.

What these admirers understood was that for Koestler, ideas were never just intellectual playthings but part of his life's blood, more palpable to him than most of the humans around him. His intellectual nerve endings were so finely tuned that he experienced the onset of fresh ideas like orgasms, and mourned their passing as the end of treasured love affairs. He lived for ideas and was ready to die for them, as he showed when incarcerated in a Spanish jail and a French concentration camp, and he insisted on following the logic of his inspirations wherever they led him—which late in life was to some extremely odd places, including a belief in the possibilities of extrasensory perception and the powers of parapsychology.

Born in Hungary, Koestler fled with his family after World War I to Vienna, where he spent his adolescence. After his student years he moved to Palestine and then to Western Europe, and lived for periods of time in France, the Soviet Union, and the United States, "perpetually in search of a country," in Malraux's words, before settling uneasily in England. He was a chameleon, a vagabond, and a pilgrim, constantly changing and reinventing himself, inhaling, as it were, the essence of each place he stayed in, while remaining perpetually alien to his surroundings. Never fully Hungarian, not quite Austrian or German, a Jew who had turned away from Judaism, incapable of being French, definitely not an Englishman, and unwilling to accommodate himself even to the melting pot of multicultural America, he wandered the earth like a modern Quixote in search of a spiritual homeland. As a writer he changed languages not once (like Conrad) but twice, first from Hungarian to German, which he continued to write in until the age of thirty-five, and then from German to English. Knowing so many countries so intimately, he was never parochial or narrow-minded. He understood the complex interplay among psychology, culture, and religion and between competing national interests and political systems as few writers before him or since, and despite his Cassandra-like pessimism, he never abandoned his quest for a better life for mankind.

DURING HIS LONG LIFE Koestler investigated a multitude of political movements, religions, and scientific disciplines, from Zionism to Catholicism and even Buddhism, from anti-fascism to communism and anti-communism, from astronomy and evolution to neurobiology and parapsychology. His literary and political odyssey spawned more than thirty books, among them six novels, four autobiographies, four scientific treatises, four volumes of essays, three nonfiction investigations, and innumerable newspaper articles. And yet the sheer bulk and variety of this output, not to speak of its inevitable unevenness, raise questions about its quality and relevance, for in one sense Koestler simply wrote too much, in too many genres. As a journalist, novelist, essayist, autobiographer, and writer of scientific speculations, as all of which he excelled at one time or another, he's impossible to classify or pigeonhole—and it's hard to fit him into the conventional college courses that guarantee a writer some portion of popularity. In consequence his reputation has worn more badly than it should have, so that the contemporary biographer has to face the question: Why read Koestler now?

The obvious answer is that Koestler's justly famous second novel, *Darkness at Noon,* which has never gone out of print since its first appearance in 1940, is still prized as one of the great books of the twentieth century. In that deeply political and philosophical novel, inspired by the puzzling success of Stalin's show trials of the 1930s, Koestler examined the key problem at the heart of communist and all revolutionary ideology, that of the conflict between individual responsibility and historical necessity and between ends and means, and he enacted the symbolic execution of his former self as a punishment for his sins as a party member. It is a novel of ideas and psychological tension, partaking of the nightmare vision of modernists as varied as Dostoyevsky, Conrad, Kafka, Camus, and Thomas Pynchon, and remains Koestler's literary masterpiece. Together with several essays published in *The Yogi and the Commissar, The God That Failed,* and *The Trail of the Dinosaur,* it also constitutes Koestler's principal contribution to political thought, forming one of the most imaginative and coherently argued indictments of totalitarian ideology and practice available to western readers.

But that's far from all. Although Koestler has often been tagged as an example of that phenomenon he so dreaded and rejected all his life, the one-book wonder, and although other novels like *The Gladiators, Arrival and Departure, Thieves in the Night,* and *The Age of Longing* seem rather dated now, each has passages of imaginative power and intellectual brilliance. The same can be said of the best of his provocative science books, *The Sleepwalkers,*

The Act of Creation, and *The Ghost in the Machine,* to which Koestler brought both a storyteller's eloquence and his characteristic activism, for his urge there, as in all his fiction and nonfiction, is not just to describe the world, but also to change it.

However, the work that guarantees Koestler's continuing importance (besides *Darkness at Noon*) is his literary nonfiction—five autobiographical works and the best of the essays. Alongside Orwell in Britain in the 1940s and early '50s, he poured forth a stream of inspired commentary on some of the most acute social and political issues of the day, and was initially more prescient than Orwell about the totalitarian forces shaping the modern world. Of the autobiographies, Koestler's first work in this genre, and in some respects his best, was *Dialogue with Death,* a piercing memoir about his imprisonment and near execution in civil-war Spain. (Sartre greeted the book as an early example of existentialism.) This was followed three years later by *Scum of the Earth,* a documentary memoir of his incarceration in a French concentration camp and escape from the invading Germans on the eve of World War II, and also a requiem for the anti-fascist left between the two world wars. "Memoirs of a Tightrope Walker," the lead essay in *The God That Failed,* analyzed with unrivaled dialectical verve and penetration his seduction by communism and subsequent disillusionment.

His most ambitious works in this genre were two volumes of straight autobiography, *Arrow in the Blue* and *The Invisible Writing,* in which Koestler fashioned a new paradigm for the genre, treating his life and experiences as a prism through which to examine the extraordinary struggle of mid-twentieth-century intellectuals to comprehend (and survive) two world wars, the Great Depression, and the rise of two seemingly irresistible totalitarian movements, fascism and communism. His response to those movements and their value systems took the form of a lifelong interrogation of the problem of individual freedom and the ethics of choice, and the conflict between collective necessity and individual morality, often summarized as the battle between ends and means.

KOESTLER WAS A ROMANTIC whose quixotic hopes that some variant of the utopian dream might lead to happiness on earth were constantly being shadowed and undercut by a pessimistic acknowledgment of the realities of human nature. He was also a gambler and a provocateur, taking physical and intellectual risks that led him to exciting and dangerous places, and sometimes to important insights ahead of his time. He was a Zionist in Palestine when it was extremely unfashionable to be a Zionist, and an anti-Zionist when Zionism was in its prime. He was a communist before communism became à la mode for western progressives, and an anticommunist at the flood tide of communist popularity during World War II. Later he was in favor of the Cold War and against McCarthyism; he was against capital punishment and in favor of euthanasia; and he wasn't afraid to attack the fortress of neo-Darwinism and defend the shaky premises of parapsychology when the intellectual consensus was overwhelmingly against him.

In the words of a French biographer, Koestler was inveterately "a man against," at his best when challenging truisms, opposing received opinion, and exploring new frontiers, at his worst when pontificating on the obvious. He was often foolish and occasionally cheap, but rarely dishonest and never dull, and the flash of his intellect flickers brilliantly over his best pages.

Late in life, in a burst of self-deprecation, Koestler once referred to himself as the "Casanova of causes," hinting that while his causes were passionately embraced and worthy of devotion, the act of serving them was psychologically as important as the causes themselves. A close reading of his letters, diaries, and books confirms that view, for Koestler's quest for enlightenment was not some arid, abstract sort of search, but a deep instinctual urge, powered by personal unhappiness and psychological frustration, which started early in his life and continued to the very end of his days. This is not to devalue its results, which are there for all to see in his books, but it was the cause of causes lurking behind every other cause Koestler espoused and everything he wrote, emblematic of the twentieth century's own flailings in its search for a workable form of utopia. Koestler was bound to fail in his quest, of course, but the quest itself was the point.

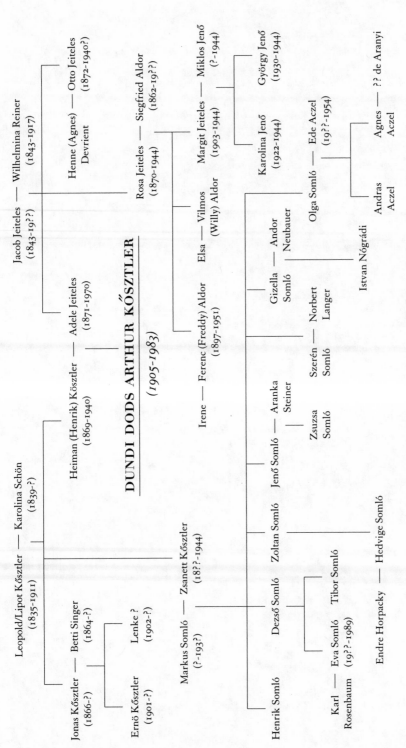

KOESTLER FAMILY TREE

PART ONE

A LONG APPRENTICESHIP

The Author as Journalist
(1905–1936)

CHAPTER ONE

BEGINNINGS

A novelist is someone who hates his mother.
— GEORGES SIMENON

WHEN KOESTLER CAME to write the first volume of his autobiography, *Arrow in the Blue,* he began by casting his "secular horoscope." He took a copy of the London *Times* published on September 6, 1905 (one day after his birthday), and studied its contents to discover what "influences" might have been at work on the global environment into which he was born. Skimming the advertisements and some minor news stories of the day, his eye came to rest on two weightier items: "Fierce Fighting in the Caucasus," about an anti-Jewish pogrom in Baku and the forcible suppression of a strike; and "Disturbances at Kishineff," describing an attack on Russian workmen and Jews attending the funeral of a murdered woman.

The Russian workers' movement and the impending revolution of 1905 were both gathering steam at the time of Koestler's birth, and the situation of the Jews was implicated in both. Equally fascinating to Koestler was a *Times* editorial on the Treaty of Portsmouth between the Russian tsar and the emperor of Japan to end the Russo-Japanese War. The editorial extolled the virtues of the victorious Japanese, their "subordination of the individual to the tribe and the state," and their "monastic discipline," which it contrasted with the "excessive individualism" of the West. For Koestler, who had yet to make his own visit to Japan, the editorial had a sinister ring: "The clock that struck the hour of my birth also announced the end of the era of liberalism and individualism, of that harshly competitive and yet easy-going civilization which had succeeded in reconciling, thanks to a unique kindly-callous compromise, the slogan of 'survival of the fittest' with that of *'laissez faire, laissez aller.'* " After listing some luminaries active in science and culture (Einstein, Freud, Tolstoy, Kipling, Cézanne, and Matisse among others), he concluded pessimistically: "I was born at the moment when the sun was setting on the Age of Reason."[1]

The horoscope was a trick, of course. Looking back, Koestler picked out the events that suited him and arranged them to fit what he conceived to be the essential pattern of his life, yet for his biographer it has its uses. Strikes, pogroms, anti-Semitism, wars, the rise of the "first modern totalitarian state," and the decline of liberal humanism—as well as striking achievements in science and the arts—all were to spark his creativity in the course of his life, while the decline of the Age of Reason became an obsession of his later years. Just as important as the subjects was the nature of the selections he made. Everything Koestler found worthy of inclusion in his horoscope was external, public, social, political. There was nothing inward or intimate in that list, little to hint at the complex psychological life and excruciating personal struggles of the person writing it.

It wasn't that Koestler considered such things irrelevant. Later he paused to consider the two main motives for writing autobiographies, "the Chronicler's urge" and the *"Ecce homo* [behold the man] motive," both intended to transcend the isolation of the self. The chronicler stressed external events, the contemplative stressed internal processes. A good autobiography needed both. Koestler admitted that though he had once vowed to write an intimate autobiography in the tradition of Rousseau and Cellini, he had shrunk from the "process of self-immolation" that their confessions had entailed. Acknowledging the tortured nature of his own psyche, he declined to investigate it closely, preferring not to look too deeply into the convoluted contours of his mind and motives. It was not uniqueness that Koestler sought in his self-examination but universality, confirmed by his description of the two volumes of his autobiography as "the typical case history of a member of the Central-European educated middle classes, born in the first years of our century."[2]

KOESTLER WAS WRITING in a tradition of autobiography that he adapted and improved upon to suit his particular purposes, and that has been all but superseded by the tell-all memoir of our own day, but he didn't ignore his emotional life altogether, particularly when it came to his childhood. Though his narrative is sparse, he lets his guard down freely in places, for, under Freud's influence, he came to regard his childhood experiences as the source of his later unhappiness.

A striking example occurs in the opening of chapter four, where Koestler arrives at the moment of his birth. "I was born in the eighth year of my parents' marriage," he writes, "their first and only child, when my mother was thirty five. Everything seems to have gone wrong with my birth: I weighed over ten pounds; my mother's labor lasted two days and almost killed her. The whole unsavory Freudian Olympus, from Oedipus Rex to Orestes, stood watch at my cradle." Oedipus, be it noted, slept with his mother, and Orestes murdered his, a fair indication of Koestler's conflicted emotions, so perhaps it's not surprising he got the details wrong. He was born in the sixth year of his parents' marriage, not the eighth, and his mother was thirty-four, not thirty-five. Neither error is significant in itself. What is interesting is that Koestler's mother was alive and well at the time he wrote his autobiography, but he couldn't bring himself to consult her. He found it extremely hard to write about his childhood at all, and dreaded her reaction. "The awareness that she is going to read this passage in print has the same paralyzing effect which prevented me as a child from keeping a diary—knowing that wherever I hid it, it would be found and read by her."[3]

Adele Koestler was eighty and Koestler forty-six when he wrote this, but he still feared her every bit as much as in childhood. Her mother love, according to him, was "excessive, possessive and capricious," partly because he was a late and only child, but also because she was plagued by ill health and the extreme changes of mood it brought in its wake. Her loving tenderness would give way to violent outbursts of temper, and vice versa. The son claimed he was traumatized. Tossed constantly from "the emotional climate of the tropics to the arctic and back again," he developed an early conviction of personal guilt and shame that never left him. The very chapter in which Koestler recounts his childhood is called "The Tree of Guilt."

It's hard to say how just this is, or when Koestler started to blame his mother for his later miseries. His few childhood letters to her that have survived are conventionally effusive and adoring, but there are very few from her to him, and her frequent absences from home suggest that she was indeed a cold, egotistical, and selfish person, whom he held responsible for his own mood swings, inferiority complex, rootlessness, and obsessive search for nirvana in the arms of countless women. It has been said of Ingmar Bergman that all his relationships with women were built on a desperate craving for mother love, and the same seems to have been true of Koestler. Daphne Henrion, who lived with Koestler for some years and translated *Darkness at Noon,* said that Koestler thought of his discarded mistresses the way he thought about his mother, and invariably recoiled once he was done with them. Throughout his adult life he remained uniformly hostile to Adele and rarely consented to visit her, though she lived in a boardinghouse for "Jewish Ladies" (for which he paid) only a few miles from his house in London and survived, as if to spite him, to the ripe old age of ninety-nine. Her existence

nist instincts, Eleonore persuaded her high-strung niece to consult a promising young Jewish physician named Sigmund Freud about a persistent tic that was bothering her.

Adele was not impressed. "Freud massaged my neck and asked me silly questions," she complained to Koestler some fifty years later. "I told you he was a disgusting fellow." She told Kurt Eissler, secretary of the Sigmund Freud Archives, that she had visited Freud only reluctantly ("you were held to be half-crazy if you went to Dr. Freud") and had disliked him on sight, mainly because of his black side-whiskers. She said that while massaging her neck Freud had asked her if she had a sweetheart. Shocked, she refused to answer and hurried away as fast as she could. Freud's interest in sex was "scandalous and outlandish," and though her girlfriends couldn't wait to hear about her visit, Adele claimed that no one in her circle took him seriously.[10]

Adele's father, Jacob, was said to have been ruined when one of the Jeiteles girls married a "villainous adventurer" who induced him to endorse a loan and then defaulted on it, causing Jacob to go bankrupt and flee to America. As a companion piece to the story of Grandfather Leopold appearing out of Russia, this account of another grandfather disappearing to America has a seductive symmetry, but Jacob didn't exactly disappear. In 1900 he was living on West Fifty-third Street in New York City, and by 1902 was on East Seventy-first Street, giving his occupation as "president" (although of what isn't clear). He established businesses downtown and uptown, became treasurer of a company called Lispenard, and was last heard of in 1910, living on West 120th Street. In July 1907 he wrote to Adele from the Berkshires, sending her, "in exchange for your beautiful photos," a postcard of himself relaxing in a rocking chair, holding a walking stick and petting a dog. The mystery of why he emigrated and what happened to him remains unsolved, and Koestler was disinclined to unravel it.[11]

The Jeiteles girl who married a "villainous adventurer" was Adele's elder sister, Rosa, and the adventurer was her Hungarian husband, Siegfried Aldor, who lived in Budapest. One result of the financial scandal was that Adele and her mother were forced to move to Budapest to live with Rosa and Siegfried, though it's surprising that they should have chosen to live with the "villain" (if indeed he was) who had been the cause of their misery. As women unaccustomed to work, they probably had no choice, but the move constitutes another mystery that has never been resolved.[12]

IT WAS A PAINFUL LETDOWN for Adele. Like most Viennese, she regarded Budapest as provincial and Hungary as semibarbaric. She had lost her prospects for an advantageous marriage and was marooned in a despised backwater. When she met Leopold's son Heiman, she was twenty-nine and virtually on the shelf, but the well-dressed young businessman made an impression. Starting as a draper's assistant, he had risen to become general manager and junior partner of Sommer and Grünwald and was about to launch his own import business. Adele traded her aristocratic manners and Viennese sophistication for financial security, and it must have been a relief to bid goodbye to prolonged spinsterhood. On the last day of the nineteenth century, possibly under pressure from Adele, Heiman altered his name to the German-sounding Henrik, and on January 25, 1900, the couple were married in the registry office of the Sixth (Theresa) District of Budapest, with Siegfried Aldor (the "villainous adventurer") as one of the witnesses. They then lived with Lipot for a while before moving to 16 Sziv Street and, eleven years later, to a more spacious apartment next door at number 18.[13]

Sziv Street was a spanking-new thoroughfare lined with Baroque apartment houses thrown up in a frenzy of speculation fueled by Hungary's economic miracle, a stone's throw from the sweeping Andrássy Avenue (the Champs-Élysées of Budapest), with its jewel of an opera house, fashionable theaters, Viennese-style coffeehouses, shopping arcades, and opulent apartment buildings. Budapest's new neo-Gothic parliament building and stock exchange were the largest in Europe, and beneath Andrássy Avenue city officials constructed the first underground railway in Europe, the Foldalatti, to commemorate the millennial of the Magyar conquest of Hungary in 896. It had a single line running from the Danube embankment to the zoo, and was the pride and joy of forward-looking citizens such as Henrik.

The entire Theresa District was popular with Budapest's assimilated middle-class Jews, who had little desire to mix with the poorer Jews from the ghettoes of Poland and Galicia living in the Elizabeth District to the east, an uncomfortable reminder of the past and a provocation to the anti-Semitism that still smoldered beneath the prosperous surface of the city. The Elizabeth District housed the vast Moorish-style Central Synagogue, the biggest in Central Europe (Hungarians were addicted to superlatives), where Arthur and his parents would later celebrate the Jewish holidays.

The idea that it was possible to acquire great wealth and acquire it fast had taken firm root among the Jews who flocked to Budapest during the latter part of the nineteenth century. Largely barred from government service and the top echelons of the military and, to a lesser extent, from the universities, they had little choice but to join the professions or go into business. For Henrik it was natural to follow his father into the clothing trade, and the decade before the outbreak of World War I proved a halcyon one for him. Like many short men, he made up with energy and determination what he lacked in physical stature, and his import business was phenomenally successful.

HENRIK WAS SAID to be a natty dresser, invariably sporting a starched shirt and striped pants, with a rolled umbrella and black bowler hat. "His splendid English and German pronunciation, all are vivid in my mind to this day. And the enthusiasm with which he offered his wares," wrote a colleague much later. Henrik and Adele became regular visitors to the opulent Leopoldstadt Casino on the Danube, where high-rolling Jewish businessmen liked to relax and spend their surplus cash. Photographs show them in a variety of restaurants with colleagues or friends, Adele a little plumper and coarser than in her salad days, wearing one of her extravagant wide-brimmed hats, sometimes smoking, sometimes with a drink in hand, and Henrik, with his slicked-down, neatly parted hair and bushy mustache, immaculate in winged collar, carefully knotted cravat, and breast-pocket handkerchief, regarding his wife with benign indulgence.[14]

The couple had five years of this carefree life before their son arrived on September 5, 1905. Adele was thirty-four, old for a first-time mother in those days, and she never forgot the painful ordeal of her son's birth (nor failed to mention it when chiding Koestler later). She swore never to have another child, and never did. They called the boy Dundi Dods Arthur Kősztler, an extraordinary combination of names that joined the folksy Hungarian Dundi (suggesting chubbiness in Hungarian—perhaps a reference to his size at birth) with the more formal German Arthur (pronounced with the stress on the second syllable) and the completely incomprehensible "Dods," which is a mystery to every Hungarian and Austrian I have consulted.[15]

The young Koestler detested his names, Dundi because of its childish sound and Arthur because he was unable to roll his r's in proper German fashion (he was to have trouble with the letter r all his life). He typically blamed his mother for this humiliation, maintaining that she had insisted on it out of contempt for her adopted homeland, for there was no Hungarian derivative or equivalent of Arthur. Adele spoke little Hungarian (the wedding ceremony had been translated into German for her) and insisted on reading only the German-language *Pester Lloyd* newspaper while in Budapest.[16]

In a society where the norm was at least three children (one of Arthur's aunts had seven), Henrik and Adele were unusual in having only one, and Arthur was a chronically lonely child. The rigors of the difficult birth had cast Adele into what sounds like a postpartum depression. No one then knew what that was, and when she took to her bed for days or even weeks at a time, Arthur was handed into the care of nursemaids and maids. These separations induced feelings of profound anxiety and resentment, from which he never recovered. His twelve cousins, all older than he, were uninterested in playing with the baby of the family, and Adele felt they "weren't good enough" or might give him some kind of infection. The only bright spots were those occasions when his mother invited some business colleague of his father to a *jour fixe* (for the ceremonial consumption of coffee, cakes, and whipped cream in the late afternoon), when a wife and child might come along. Arthur would turn into a "frenzied little maniac," showing off his toys and the ingenious games he had prepared beforehand, and then into a "fierce bully who had to have his own way," a pattern of capriciousness that never left him.[17]

He was also subjected to a Victorian system of punishments meted out to him from an early age. Characteristic was the time he was locked in an un-lighted bathroom and crashed headlong into the iron support beneath the washbasin. His screams caused his mother to fling open the door and take him in her arms. As he got older, he was punished by their long-serving par-lormaid, Bertha Bubala, a working-class girl and unwed mother, who pined for the son she'd left behind in the countryside. One way to get revenge was to take out her resentments on Arthur by making him stand in a corner fac-ing the wall or refusing to speak to him for hours at a time if he misbe-haved.[18]

ARTHUR'S MAIN COMPANION during his early childhood was Grandfather Lipot, who lived a few blocks away in Eötvos Street. Lipot seemed com-pletely exotic to the young boy, with his flowing white beard and habit of lift-ing the tails of his morning coat before settling into his rocking chair. He used to take Arthur for walks in the nearby City Park. Like most Jews of his generation, Lipot observed the Mosaic dietary laws and went regularly to the synagogue, but he appears to have had no problem letting Arthur eat ham sandwiches when they were out together.[19]

Koestler later cited this practice as proof that his family was totally assim-ilated and indifferent to Judaism, and it's true that in common with the ma-jority of successful Hungarian Jews, Henrik and Adele regarded Judaism as a faith rather than a mark of ethnicity and were not particularly observant in their daily lives (they didn't keep kosher, for example). But they had been married according to Mosaic law, regularly visited the Central Synagogue on High Holidays, and enjoyed the Sabbath meals organized by Henrik's brother and sisters. Koestler makes no mention of these in his autobiography, nor of the fact that in school he was obliged to attend synagogue every other week to study Hebrew and the Old Testament. He insisted he had been brought up "without roots in the Judaic tradition," but according to two of his cousins, Henrik and Adele didn't ignore or reject Judaism, they simply took it for granted—as did the young Arthur growing up.[20]

In 1911, Lipot died at the age of seventy-six, depriving five-year-old Arthur of a boon companion, and that same year Arthur suffered a shock that was to mark him for life. Adele and Henrik took him by the hand one afternoon and led him around the corner to Andrássy Avenue, where Hen-rik's cousin Dr. Andor Neubauer had a successful practice. Arthur was un-ceremoniously strapped into a chair, had a metal tray fastened beneath his chin, and was confronted by the white-coated doctor and his assistant, who forced his jaws apart. His relative inserted steel forceps into the back of his throat and tore out his tonsils without benefit of anesthetic. The terrified boy choked and gagged and was drenched in his own vomit and blood.

There was no explanation before the procedure and very little afterward, but it left an indelible impression on Koestler. "Those moments of utter loneliness abandoned by my parents, in the clutches of a hostile and malign power, filled me with a kind of cosmic terror. It was as if I had fallen through a manhole, into a dark underground world of archaic brutality. Thenceforth I never lost my awareness of the existence of that second universe into which one might be transported." Koestler later dubbed this feeling the "archaic horror" and was inclined to attribute his adult preoccupation with violence, terror, and torture to the traumatic ordeal at Dr. Neubauer's. He felt that it enabled him to identify all the more vividly with the victims of Europe's dictatorships, especially those of the Holocaust.[21]

Hard as it is to believe, this kind of treatment for tonsillitis was not uncommon at the time. The French novelist Michel Tournier suffered a virtually identical procedure in Paris a quarter of a century later, with identical results. Tournier also had a name for it. He called it "the Aggression, the Attack, a crime that bloodied my childhood and from whose horror I never recovered." Thousands of children must have undergone the operation without suffering such aftereffects, but it seems that for sensitive children such as Koestler and Tournier, the consequences were unfathomable.[22]

The tonsillectomy was Koestler's blacking factory, a devastating experience that darkened his memories of childhood, opened his eyes to a void that lay seemingly beneath his very feet, and revealed the chaos that could result when normal life broke down. In *Dialogue with Death* and in several of the novels Koestler describes torture and physical abuse with a graphic immediacy that shocked his readers at the time and outstripped most writers of his generation, anticipating a major theme in the art and literature of the second half of the twentieth century.

CHAPTER TWO

A BUDAPEST CHILDHOOD

When we are young, the idea of death is intolerable, the possibility of ridicule unbearable.

— ISAK DINESEN

ARTHUR HAD RECENTLY started classes at an experimental private kindergarten founded by Laura Striker (née Polanyi), an ardent feminist who pioneered some of the same homeschooling ideas as Maria Montessori and Rudolf Steiner. Laura's school was modern and progressive, with enlightened rules for behavior, hygiene, and parental support, and emphasized art, music, and dancing as well as the three R's. Arthur refused to take his clothes off to change for dancing at first, but eventually he joined in. When asked by his teacher, "Why do we learn?" he said, "In order to become famous," and when asked at the end of the year what he would do, he replied, "Make stories"—remarkably accurate predictions for one so young.[1]

Laura Striker was from one of Hungary's most extraordinary and influential intellectual families, the Polanyis, whose members were to play a decisive role in Koestler's later life. Her elder brother, Karl Polanyi, had helped found the influential Galileo Circle in Hungary and later became a world-famous economist. Her younger brother, Michael Polanyi, was one of the most brilliant polymaths of the twentieth century and exercised a profound influence on Koestler when both were living in England after World War II. Laura's daughter, Eva, a vivacious, curly-haired little girl when Arthur met her in kindergarten, was to become his lover in Paris, his close friend in Berlin, his host in Kharkov, and his source for some crucial plot details in *Darkness at Noon*. They remained friends until the end of his life.[2]

Laura's kindergarten was followed by the state elementary school in Andrássy Avenue, where the lessons were in Hungarian. Arthur spoke mainly German at home, especially with his mother, but picked up Hungarian from Bertha and his cousins. Hungarian remained the only language in which he could do his multiplication tables and add or subtract with ease. Growing up in a bilingual home seems to have laid the ground for Koestler's later facility with languages, as did the tutoring he received from governesses hired by his parents to teach him French and English. He claimed his first recorded words in French—to a governess at the age of three—were *"Mademoiselle, pantalons mouillés"* (Miss, my pants are wet).[3]

An early short story of Koestler's is about his elementary school and puppy love. "I was six years old when I met my first ideal," the story begins, "a little girl wearing a red dress, with black eyes and a blue ribbon tied in her chestnut-colored hair." The story then takes a more sinister turn, attesting to Koestler's dark vision. "I was about eight years old when I fell in love with my teacher. I was tortured by horrible nightmares. I saw in my dreams how it would feel to stab a knife to the hilt into her armpit (I heard her screaming and I cried silently into my pillow—I was sorry for her)."[4]

As an only child he was a voracious reader, though not without opposition from his parents. True to Victorian notions of child raising, they held firmly to the view that "reading is bad for your eyes," but prolonged bargaining, accompanied by tantrums and tears, extracted permission to read ten printed pages a night before going to bed and "not a page more." As a result of this rationing system, reading for pleasure was indelibly associated in his mind with forbidden fruit, while the need to break off rigidly after every tenth page invested all reading with the tantalizing suspense of a cliff-hanger. "Useful" books, on the other hand, which he was allowed during the day, were exempt from this constraint, so that reading science, history, or reference books became a much more relaxed affair.

In short order he devoured the Brothers Grimm, Hans Christian Andersen, and Struwwelpeter in German, and Rupert Bear in Hungarian. He read the Alice in Wonderland books in both languages, and later, when allowed to read more than ten pages at a time, made his way through *Robinson Crusoe, Gulliver's Travels, Till Eulenspiegel, Don Quixote,* the frontier tales of James Fenimore Cooper, the fantasy westerns and adventure stories of the German writer Karl May, and the science fiction adventures of Jules Verne.[5]

He also developed a passion for mathematics and physics. He adored mechanical toys, construction sets, and all manner of scientific gadgets, and at ten developed a talent for changing fuses and mending simple electrical devices. He built a toy submarine that successfully navigated the family bathtub, and his parents decided he should go not to the classical *gymnasium,* with its emphasis on Greek and Latin and the study of the humanities, but rather a *realiskola,* a high school that specialized in science and modern languages. It was an unusual choice for an upwardly mobile couple with high ambitions for their son, but Arthur shared his father's respect for science and agreed that this was the right path for him.[6]

WHILE STILL A CHILD he was naturally insulated from the grown-up world beyond his home, but Hungary in the years before World War I was changing in unforeseen ways that would threaten the entire future of the assimilated Jews of Budapest, including the Koestlers. Until then the country had been remarkably successful in assimilating its Jewish immigrants into an otherwise Christian population, but in the early years of the twentieth century, the social and political consensus began to crumble. Jews now amounted to more than 20 percent of the inhabitants of Budapest and about 40 percent of its voters. They dominated the financial, commercial, professional, cultural, and intellectual professions, but with nationalism growing everywhere in Europe, including Hungary, there was a sudden rise in anti-Semitism.[7]

Certain clubs began to close their doors to Jewish members, no matter how rich or prominent they were. The distinction between the clienteles of the Leopoldstadt and Country casinos became almost absolute, and there were subtle splits in the universities. None of this spilled into the streets just yet, for the uneasy compromise that kept overt anti-Semitism in check was sustained by the continuing prosperity of the country. But when world war broke out in the heart of Europe, the strains became overwhelming. The first time the nine-year-old Arthur heard about the war was on a walk with his governess, when a bunch of patriotic citizens came swaggering down the street singing the Hungarian national anthem, "God Bless the Magyar," and shouting slogans with an uncannily modern ring to them: "Death to the Serbian dogs! Serbia, you cur, you will never have Bosnia!" Six months later Arthur composed a patriotic ditty for a boys' magazine. "In the month of December Belgrade capitulated / and the Magyar stood on its citadel, elated." This, his first poem, was rejected, but he continued to stick little flags into colored maps of the battlefront as it moved back and forth, until Austria-Hungary's defeats began to outnumber its victories.[8]

The war was a disaster for Hungary, and in particular for businessmen such as Henrik. He was completely cut off from the British textile manufacturers who were his main suppliers and severely hampered in obtaining German imports, and the young Arthur overheard a terrible row between Henrik and Adele one day that taught him, he said, "the anguish of split loyalties." Henrik had a fatal weakness for get-rich-quick schemes that appealed to his gambler's instinct but usually resulted in big losses. Adele, left alone for long stretches of time while Henrik traveled, suffered from both recurrent migraines and their falling standard of living, and decided one day that she had had enough. About a year into the war she insisted they give up the apartment on Sziv Street and move to her hometown of Vienna. To un-

derline her determination, she abruptly decamped with Arthur, to be followed a few weeks later by Henrik, and for the duration of the war they lived
like gypsies in a series of hotels and pensions in Vienna and Budapest, moving, on average, once every three months.[9]

Henrik had business interests in Vienna as well as Budapest and may have
felt it as easy to run them from one city as the other, but the quarrels with
Adele continued, and the cause was almost certainly another woman. It
would appear that, in addition to spending more and more time in bed,
Adele also cut off (or sharply reduced) sexual relations with Henrik out of
fear of getting pregnant again, and that he succumbed to temptation elsewhere. Koestler is ultradiscreet in his autobiography, but he later told a
friend that as a child, "I saw something that I shouldn't have seen, and have
never spoken about since," a Victorian circumlocution that could refer to a
mislaid love letter, or perhaps something more shocking. For all the freedom
of his own sex life, Koestler retained a Victorian prudishness about sex in
print and prided himself on avoiding kiss-and-tell stories of any kind.[10]

In Vienna the family stayed at the exclusive Pension Exquisite on the
Graben, opposite St. Stephen's Cathedral. Arthur was often left alone while
his parents went out to enjoy themselves. One evening he lit some candles,
which fell and started a fire, and was rescued by the French teacher who
lived next door. The fire gutted several rooms before the fire brigade arrived,
but to his astonishment he was rewarded not with punishment but with a
rush of affection from his guilt-ridden parents. Their concern increased
when an operation to remove an abscess from his appendix failed and he had
to go back for a second one. Terrified by the thought of having the ether
mask placed over his face again, he experienced a kind of epiphany, insisting
on holding the mask himself in order to remain in charge of the situation.
When he came around, he experienced a flood of relief, feeling that he had
faced up to his subconscious fears and to the "archaic horror" that had fueled
so many nightmares in the past.

A psychoanalyst might conclude that Arthur's halfhearted attempt at self-
immolation was a desperate device to attract attention in response to feelings
of abandonment by his parents, and that his experiment with the ether mask
was an effort to gain more control. Whatever his subconscious motives, his
ills seem to have succeeded in drawing Henrik and Adele closer for a while
and made them face up to their responsibilities, but it didn't last long, and
Arthur was again abandoned to his own devices for long periods of time.[11]

IN SEPTEMBER 1915, just eleven years old, Arthur returned alone to Budapest to start his studies at the Realiskola, a massive brick structure taking
up half a block on Rippl Ronai (then Bujowsky) Street, just off Andrássy Avenue. The school was spanking new, the first in the country to be lit with

electricity instead of gas, and had the latest word in laboratories and scientific equipment. Not surprisingly, Jews outnumbered Roman Catholics by about three to one, and certainly set the tone of the place. In his first year Arthur got top marks in only three subjects, Hungarian, German, and geometry, but steadily improved until he excelled in all subjects but one. "Dearest Mamuli," he wrote to Adele in Vienna, "at long last I have received your letter and was very happy with it, most of all because I got such a good report, which—to be quite honest—I hadn't at all expected. The '2' in Etiquette is a mystery to me, but it doesn't worry me *at all*."[12]

It's tempting to read the future in Arthur's low mark for etiquette, but it's more likely to have been a side effect of staying with the Aldor family—Aunt Rosa, Uncle Siegfried, and their rapscallion sons, Ferenc and Willy—for the older boys were tearaways who taught Arthur schoolboy tricks and dirty jokes that were well beyond his years. Henrik and Adele also spent some time at the Pension Moderne in Lövölde Place, a tree-shaded small square around the corner from their old apartment in Sziv Street, and it's possible that Arthur stayed there for a while, but his main home was with Aunt Rosa and her boys.

Koestler writes very little in his autobiography about his time at the Aldors' home and in high school, probably because he was unhappy in both places. It seems that he was picked on for his small size and because of his extravagant clothes. Henrik and Adele loved to dress him up in fancy items that Henrik obtained through his textile business and once sent him to school in an English Eton suit, an exceedingly rare outfit in Budapest. Spoiled and pampered at home, regarded as an infant prodigy by doting parents, jealous cousins, and admiring aunts and uncles, he found the rough-and-tumble atmosphere of the school corridors decidedly chilly. "I was an only child and a lonely child," he wrote in one of his rare references to his school years, "precocious, neurotic, admired for my brains and detested for my character by teachers and schoolfellows alike."

There was probably some anti-Semitism at the school because of the high number of Jewish pupils there. Koestler never admitted to it, but later he wrote a short story, "Méta" ("Ball Game"), about a boy who is picked on in a Budapest school playground for being Jewish and persecuted as a result. He later told a friend, Leo Valiani, that he had indeed experienced anti-Semitism in Budapest, while denying that it was a Hungarian phenomenon and insisting it had been imported from Germany—as if that made it any better. But Arthur had his friends, too. A former classmate referred to their class as an "elite" one and mentioned the names of other friends from "the old bunch," and Arthur was master of ceremonies for a cabaret put on in his last year, as well as taking part in a one-act German play, *Braut und Bräutigam* (Bride and Groom), that was part of a concert to benefit war orphans. "If you cannot come," he wrote to Adele, "I would *very, very* much like at least Papa to be there *for certain*. The candies have arrived, thank you very much, they were delicious."[13]

Henrik and Adele's exact movements during this time are a mystery. Henrik still traveled a great deal on business—though no longer abroad—and Adele seems to have shuttled back and forth between Vienna and Budapest, sometimes with Henrik and sometimes without. Arthur wrote to her regularly (signing himself "Dundi" in the letters), and sent her little birthday poems in German. Their tone is forced and jocular, revealing the insecurity of his feelings and oscillating between adolescent cynicism and self-pity. In one he makes fun of himself for writing only from a sense of duty, and wishing her good health only because "medicine is very expensive in war time." One poem ends: "I think these verses should be enough / since you've given me no chocolate or stuff / I beg you to give me some chocolate first / then I will write you another verse." Another wishes his "sweet Mamuken" "a new dress with a nice hat / shoes, stockings, blouses, a wonderful new suit / . . . in short: everything good one can imagine / (and why not? It all comes out of papa's pocket!)." But a year later he is abjectly apologizing to his "dearest, only Mamuli" for a practical joke with a pear. "When I received your letter of the 27th, in which you wrote that you were angry with me, I was so desperate, I can't begin to tell you. I saw the whole thing as a silly joke and found nothing wrong with it. I was very depressed when I got your letter. Just think, Mamuli, I hadn't received a line from either of you for a *whole week*, so that I decided that I wouldn't write to you myself until I had some news from you."[14]

He continued to read voraciously—Shakespeare, Rilke, Goethe, Heine, Byron, and any novel he could lay his hands on—but his four years at the Realiskola confirmed him in the belief that his intellectual loyalties should remain with science. It wasn't a difficult conclusion to reach, for science enjoyed extraordinarily high prestige in early-twentieth-century Budapest (the scientists von Kármán, de Hevesy, Polanyi, Szilard, Wigner, von Neumann, and Teller, all products of "the Budapest miracle," came from the same milieu as Koestler). Arthur was sure that mathematics and physics would help him unlock the secrets of the universe. His heroes were "Darwin and Spencer, Kepler, Newton and Mach; Edison, Herz and Marconi—the Buffalo Bills of the frontiers of discovery," and his "bible" *Die Welträtsel* (The Riddle of the Universe) by Ernst Haeckel, a celebrated German biologist and Darwinist who attempted to apply the doctrine of evolution to problems of philosophy and religion.

Haeckel claimed to have "solved" most of the riddles pertaining to the known universe (conveniently denying the importance of those he couldn't solve, such as the immortality of the soul, the existence of a personal God, the reality of free will). Arthur didn't accept Haeckel's claim but absorbed from him a preoccupation with the moral and philosophical dimensions of science that would reassert itself during the later part of his life. Haeckel, with his wide-ranging theory that tried to explain everything in one go, was probably as much an influence on Koestler's later period as some of the more celebrated thinkers he invoked in his writings.

Arthur's yearnings for a connection with the absolute were spurred by his adolescent reading of Jules Verne. When not quite fifteen, lying on his back on a hill in Buda and staring up at the sky, he experienced a "mystic elation," a vision of an arrow shot into the sky with such force that it would escape the pull of the earth's gravity and travel on to infinity. Maybe he would be the one to solve the riddle of the universe? He interpreted this thirst for the absolute as "a kind of stigma," condemning him never to find satisfaction in the world around him, and he came to think that it was informed by his intense unhappiness as a child, his insecurities, and his search for love and acceptance in a cruel world. "It was the same quest and the same all-or-nothing mentality which drove me to the Promised Land and into the Communist Party. In other ages aspirations of this kind found their natural fulfilment in God."

The thought that his thirst for utopia had roots in an unhappy childhood found its fullest expression in his nature novel *The Age of Longing* and probably owed more than a little to Koestler's reading of Freud, but the image of the arrow flying into infinity remained a potent one, providing the theme for a later poem he wrote, and the title of the first volume of his autobiography, *Arrow in the Blue*.[15]

MEANWHILE HENRIK AND ADELE continued their peripatetic lifestyle without the slightest regard for their son's well-being, keeping him in a state of permanent homelessness and suspense. Paradoxically, in contrast to the growing national misery provoked by the war, Henrik's fortunes rebounded. In 1916 a chemistry professor called Aladar Bedö discovered radioactive clay about a hundred miles from Budapest that turned out to be suitable for making soap. In a time of shortages, with imports cut off, there was a lot of money to be made. Henrik invested heavily and, with Dr. Bedö as partner, built the Frybourg Chemical Works. It was a huge success, manufacturing toilet and kitchen soap, brass and silver polish, and a variety of cleaning powders among its wares. Henrik and Adele could now afford the luxury of living in the best hotels and pensions, as well as indulging Arthur in whatever gadgets, toys, books, and clothes his heart desired.[16]

The war pushed the *Realiskola* to share its quarters with a *Gymnasium*, and classes were now held in two shifts, the *Gymnasium* pupils studying in the morning and the *Realiskola* pupils in the afternoon. The school year got shorter as electricity was rationed and equipment wore out. Teachers (and some of the older students) disappeared into the army, and their replacements were often maimed veterans retired from active service. There were collections for the Red Cross and the Soldiers' Christmas Fund, appeals for books for the men at the front and for subscriptions to war loans. And soon there were grimmer collections—for war graves and war memorials, for newly orphaned children and refugees from Transylvania. By the last year of the war the school was down to sixteen teachers for fourteen grades and was closed for the entire month of January owing to fuel shortages.[17]

As the war ground to its grim conclusion, Arthur went downtown with his father to witness an amazing scene. One of the principal thoroughfares, Lajos Kossuth Street, where his father's office was located, was filled with cheering crowds that blocked the view for as far as the eye could see. A tall, stooping man was addressing them from the flag-bedecked balcony of the Hotel Astoria. He told them that Austria-Hungary had capitulated to the victorious Entente, and he proclaimed the secession of Hungary from the Austrian Empire—after two hundred years under the Hapsburgs. Henceforth it would be an independent democratic republic.

It was November 3, 1918, and the tall figure was Count Mihály Károlyi, leader of the radical Hungarian Independence Party. The Hapsburg empire was collapsing like a house of cards, and Count Tisza, leader of the discredited right-wing government, had yielded power to the newly proclaimed Hungarian National Council, presided over by an assortment of social democrats and other left-wing politicians. Károlyi was an improbable revolutionary, a blue-blooded aristocrat who had spent his life fighting for greater equality and democracy for the masses. After his speech, the crowd in front of the Hotel Astoria burst spontaneously into the national anthem, "God Bless the Magyar," with Arthur and his father singing along. Soldiers with bunches of chrysanthemums stuck in their gun barrels and with red, white, and green rosettes covering their imperial badges were driving through the streets in public utility trucks. "Long live Károlyi!" was on everybody's lips, along with slogans calling for peace, democracy, equal rights, and "land for those who shed their blood." It seemed, as Koestler later wrote, as if "paradise was round the corner."[18]

KÁROLYI'S DREAM OF CREATING the "Switzerland of Eastern Europe" was short-lived. After he had refused to follow the Czechs in sending troops to Russia to fight Lenin's revolutionary forces, the western allies (notably Britain and France) insisted on dismembering the country, causing Hungary's desperate and hungry population to turn against Károlyi's government. But instead of opposing Lenin the Hungarian people decided to join him, and in March 1919 a Communist dictatorship took over from Károlyi, with Béla Kun as its de facto head. Henrik's soap factory was nationalized, but he was kept on as managing director and seems to have adapted to his new situation with typical sangfroid. Not so Adele, who later told her son

that on May Day "we miserable bourgeois no longer dared to show our happiness publicly." The Köstler family was "compressed," and Arthur woke
one morning to find a group of armed soldiers trying to confiscate one of
their two rooms. The redoubtable Adele flew into a fury and the soldiers fled.
But times were hard. The impractical Köstlers found themselves trying to
keep two hens on their balcony, with not the slightest notion how to feed or
care for them.[19]

At school, the first revolution was marked by the arrival of Dezsö Szabó,
author of a celebrated novel about the Hungarian peasantry and a personal
friend of Count Károlyi, as a kind of teacher-commissar. The curriculum
now included economics and constitutional government. Religious instruction was replaced by sociology. A course on history was transformed into a
course on Marxist and revolutionary thinking. Grades and report cards were
abolished, giving way to pass/fail grades, and on May Day that year, one of
the star senior pupils gave a speech praising Danton and Saint-Just. The
speech was "enthusiastically received by the boys and the new masters,"
while "the old teachers listened in acid silence."[20]

The romance of the Károlyi revolution made a deep impression on
Arthur, and he was thrilled by the first May Day under Károlyi's rule. Following Soviet practice, the whole of Budapest was turned into a gigantic fair-
ground, with parades and public performances. Arthur accompanied his
cousin Margit Aldor to some factory meetings and started reading the *Red
Gazette,* learning unfamiliar facts about landownership in Hungary and the
defects of the old regime. Fond memories of that turbulent spring were to
persist well into Arthur's adulthood, exercising a strong influence on his later
decision to join the Communist Party, and they outlasted his disillusionment
with communism itself.[21]

By the summer of 1919, however, the defects of the second revolution had
become all too apparent. The economy collapsed, and the countryside was
roiled by swarms of young "Lenin boys" sweeping through villages, closing
churches, arresting or killing priests, and alienating the largely Catholic
peasantry, while their urban counterparts alienated the middle classes. The
school yearbook for 1920 refers darkly to the "evil we have brought on ourselves" and the spread of "moral decay" under the new regime. The Commune's days were numbered and everyone knew it. The coup de grâce was
again delivered by France and Britain, which tricked Béla Kun's Red Army
into retreating from its gains in the north and allowed the Romanian army to
advance from the Hungarian plain and occupy Budapest. Béla Kun fled, and
a new national government was hastily cobbled together, but real power
passed to a group of counterrevolutionaries in the south of the country, led by
Rear Admiral Miklós Horthy.[22]

Béla Kun was a Jew. More than half his "People's Commissars" were Jews,
and the liberal Hungarian Jewish community had identified with the new

regime's social program. With the tacit encouragement of the western powers, Horthy launched a reign of counterrevolutionary, anti-Semitic terror
that far exceeded in cruelty and scale the repressions of the Reds. Communism was proclaimed a Jewish conspiracy intended to subjugate Hungary to
the Soviet Union, and when Horthy made his triumphal entry into Budapest
in November 1919, he went out of his way to declare his government "Christian and national." He proclaimed Budapest "the guilty city" ("Judapest" in
the lingo of Hungarian anti-Semites) and vowed to cleanse it of revolution.[23]

Arthur's parents didn't linger to watch the White Terror reach its full
fury. As the Romanian troops were entering Budapest, Henrik, Adele, and
Arthur set out for the Austrian border. All normal passenger traffic was suspended. Trains had been requisitioned for troop transports, there was no
gasoline for motorcars, and the countryside was swarming with gangs of
Reds and Whites. The Köstlers had no exit permits and were obliged to bribe
their way out of trouble. After "an adventurous crossing," they arrived safely
in Vienna, where Henrik still had extensive business interests.[24]

The shock of this violent outburst of anti-Semitism and the flight from
Hungary must have made an indelible impression on the family, but the
mature Koestler made only a glancing reference to it in his autobiography,
probably as a result of his later urge to underplay the anti-Semitism he experienced in his youth. It was to be many years before Henrik and Adele made
their way back to Budapest, and many more years before Koestler returned
to visit them. Never again would he live for any length of time in Hungary.

CHAPTER THREE

RISE, JEW, RISE

The Jew is a man whom other men take to be Jewish. His life is only a long escape from other people and from himself.
— JEAN-PAUL SARTRE

THE VIENNA THE KÖSTLERS returned to in 1919 was a far cry from the gay and glittering city Adele had known in her youth. If Hungary was severely shaken and its territory truncated by defeat, Austria was decimated. Denuded of almost all the lands that had made up her glorious, thousand-year-old *Reich,* reduced from a world power to a small landlocked country in Central Europe, the rump state resembled a "mutilated trunk bleeding from every pore." Atop that puny trunk sat the "hydrocephalic head" of Vienna, swollen by refugees to two million inhabitants, a third of the country's population. There was near anarchy in the streets. Most Austrians were forced to subsist on tiny rations of ersatz bread and coffee and rotten potatoes. The city's residents shivered in their unheated apartments and burned furniture to keep warm. Inflation spiraled out of control, wiping out the savings of the middle class, while massive unemployment swelled the ranks of the poor and homeless, leading to a serious increase in crime.

Not everyone suffered equally, though. The rich, for the most part, stayed rich, and the Köstlers were still among the rich. In Vienna, the irrepressible Henrik had set up a new import company, with himself as president. What exactly he imported is not clear, but a photograph from 1919 shows him on board a steamship bound for England. Since Britain was now one of the main providers of aid to war-torn Austria, it's likely Henrik was involved in the reparations trade. Whatever he did, his company proved phenomenally successful. The family occupied a suite of rooms at the Grand Hotel, the very

performance and stoned the members of the troupe all the way to the rail-road station. Koestler's amnesia on this subject is extraordinary in light of the sensitivity to anti-Semitism he was to develop just a couple of years later.[6]

THE WHEREABOUTS OF ADELE AND HENRIK during Arthur's three years in Baden are again a mystery. Adele adored Vienna, but she also liked to travel and spent most of the summers away. In the spring of 1921 she went first to London and then to Karlsbad, to take the waters. Henrik joined her briefly in July, but was back in Vienna by August. For two years running she was away on her birthday, an absence noted wistfully by Arthur, who wished they had an apartment where they could be together again. "Dear sweet Mamuli, I feel like an old bachelor who wishes for a home of his own. Papuli feels like that too. Don't you feel bad about this nomadic life of yours?"[7]

Were these separations an indication of continuing problems between his parents or simply the result of Henrik's work schedule and Adele's restless-ness? And when did Arthur's feelings for his mother change from adoration to resentment and alienation? Perhaps a clue can be found in an incident Koestler divulged to Sir Nicholas Henderson some thirty years later. Walk-ing on Vienna's famous Graben one day, he looked into a fashionable coffee-house and saw Adele being embraced by a stranger. What exactly Adele was up to isn't clear, and Koestler never alluded to the subject again, but Adele's journals show she was aware of her estrangement from her son and that she blamed herself for it. *"Toujours prendre, jamais rendre, de plus prétendre"* (Al-ways taking, never giving, also demanding), reads one entry, beside which she wrote: *"C'est moi"* (That's me). Another entry, addressed to "Dundi," reads: *"Ich lehrte Dich reden, Du lehrst mich schweigen"* (I taught you to speak, you teach me to be silent).[8]

Arthur saw Henrik more often and went with him on a couple of vaca-tions to Hungary. At Lake Balaton he developed an intense crush on a young Budapest girl with fair hair and "laughing blue eyes," the main subject of his first story, "Seeing Her Again." They corresponded for a while and he went back to see her the following year when he and Henrik visited some relatives. A young cousin who met them at their Leopoldstadt hotel was dazzled by the glamorous-looking and fashionably dressed Arthur, who was regarded by his cousins as unpredictable and eccentric like his father, but undeniably smart if he was able to hold his own at an elite school in Austria.[9]

It was after one of these visits that Arthur conceived a sudden yearning for his Hungarian roots and started reading the *Becsi Magyar Ujság* (Vienna Hun-garian Daily), published by left-wing Hungarian émigrés who had fled Hor-thy's terror. He developed a passion for Hungarian poetry and read books by Petöfi, Vörösmarty, and the modernist Endre Ady, whose recent death from syphilis at forty-two had endowed the poet with the halo of martyrdom. He sent a fan letter to the literary editor, Andor Németh, with some poems of his own. Németh didn't care for the poems, but he invited Arthur to stop by, and seems to have been impressed by the boy "still in short pants." Arthur was even more impressed by Németh, the first real writer he had met, and "in that awe-inspiring locale, an editorial office," too. He was flattered by the attentions of this "untidy, bulgy-eyed young man" with dandruff on his collar and a down-at-the-heels look, not least because Németh treated him as an equal despite the ten-year difference in their ages. Their friendship would last nearly thirty years and spawned an unusual literary collaboration in Berlin and Budapest before ending in mutual recriminations in postwar Paris.[10]

Arthur now adopted the pose of a "lonely, sensitive, starry-eyed poet" and withdrew even more from the other students at his Baden school. Intensely self-conscious to begin with, he became preoccupied with "the paradox of the ego-spiral," the hunt for the elusive "I" that constantly recedes the more one seeks to pin it down, as in the formulas "I know; I know that I know; I know that I know that I know; I know that I know that I know that I know"; and so on, ad infinitum. Here, he sensed, was a paradoxical counterpart (and a counterpoint) to the "arrow in the blue." While the arrow went off at a tangent, in search of the infinite, the ego-spiral "curled inward, toward the infinitely close, which was yet as unattainable as the other." He was beginning to think in terms of the antitheses and dichotomies that became a hallmark of his mature thinking and later writings, particularly in the realm of science.[11]

By the summer of 1922 he was ready to take his final examinations. Despite his newfound literary interests, he was aware that the path from the Realschule led not to Vienna University but to the Technische Hochschule (Polytechnic), provided one had matriculated satisfactorily, and in June he took and passed the two-day examination. In a letter to his absent parents he reported that he would have to petition for entry. "I have learned in confidence that it is very difficult to be admitted as a Hungarian and especially as a Jew. However, if you include a recommendation from an engineering firm with the petition you are practically guaranteed entry. So please think about it, dear Papa."[12]

THESE WERE NOT IDLE CONCERNS. Vienna in 1922 was reeling under a soaring inflation rate. Hungry workers had smashed the windows of several luxury hotels, including the Grand Hotel, and tossed the furniture into the street. In June they brought the entire city to a halt with a general strike. Luckily, Henrik and Adele had moved from the Grand by then into the more modest Pension Louisenheim in the Jewish quarter of Alsergrund, just north of the university. Henrik had started a new wholesale business in textiles and was still doing reasonably well, despite the continuing economic crisis, but there was no denying the precariousness of the market.[13]

The polytechnic, too, was affected by inflation. Starved of funds to pay teachers' salaries, buy library books, or heat classrooms properly, it was living on borrowed glory from its prewar days. Rampant unemployment and an influx of refugees from the eastern and southern parts of the empire had led to a veritable siege by applicants eager to secure good qualifications. Courses were more crowded than ever. Jews already accounted for over a fifth of the student body, and official resistance to admitting more was an open secret. Every fall fights broke out around university bulletin boards as applicants strained to see if they had been admitted.[14]

Arthur gained entrance (aided, perhaps, by Henrik and Adele's connections) two months into the school year, when Henrik paid tuition fees of 200,000 crowns for his first semester. His religion was listed as "Mosaic" and his birthplace as Budapest, but—and perhaps this was the determining factor—his "mother tongue" was given as German. The Technische Hochschule, Austria's equivalent of MIT or England's Imperial College, was located about a mile and a half from Arthur's home in Alsergrund, and on November 6 he walked for the first time through the imposing neoclassical entrance gate with its utilitarian motto, "For the Encouragement, Expansion, and Improvement of Industry, Civic Skills, and Trade—Franz I."[15]

Arthur had signed up to major in mechanical engineering, which included classes in mathematics, mechanics, descriptive geometry, and machine drawing, as well as mechanical engineering. He also registered for a class in intermediate English. He sat for only one exam at the end of his first year, and it took him two years to complete the first year's requirements. He switched to electrical engineering and was forced to grapple with the mysteries of hydraulics and steel processing, engine transmissions and drive mechanisms, stopcocks, boilers, steam engines, and fuel tanks, as well as electric generators and hydropower. It was not a diet to satisfy the appetite of either the intellect or the imagination, and his interest in engineering ebbed fast. In 1924 he took exams in only four subjects—physics, mathematics, mechanics, and electrical engineering (out of a possible twelve)—and just managed to scrape through the state's comprehensive exam that year. In 1925 he took exams in just two subjects, steam engineering and electrical engineering (gaining his one and only "very good" in the latter subject), before giving up on examinations altogether. His boredom with engineering studies is reflected in his autobiography, which contains almost no information about his time at the polytechnic and nothing at all on his fellow students or professors—nor on his poor marks (which have been gleaned from the polytechnic's records).[16]

Though he later derived satisfaction from being that rare intellectual who can mend a fuse, Arthur seems to have gained very little from his classes, if only because his mind and body were elsewhere, "in a corner of the University library, reading matters which had no connection whatsoever with my studies." Here he read Freud, Adler, Stekel, and Jung and plunged into psychiatry, experimental psychology, and the psychology of art. He was also fascinated by the revolutionary developments in theoretical physics, which were completely unrelated to his curriculum at the polytechnic.[17]

He was later to argue in his autobiography that the nature of his higher education didn't matter much, that there was no social distinction between students at the polytechnic and the university because engineers enjoyed a higher regard in Austria than in Britain. The latter was certainly true, but only to a degree. Manès Sperber, later Koestler's friend, expressed surprise that Koestler had chosen to study science and technical subjects instead of the humanities, for "anyone who wasn't good at Greek or Latin or ancient history at that time was considered 'second class.'" Ambitious Jewish students were particularly sensitive to such distinctions, for as a key to upward mobility, a doctor, a lawyer, or a professor undoubtedly outranked an engineer.[18]

ARTHUR'S OWN AMBITIONS found satisfaction in the university's library and club rooms, rather than in its classrooms, and then in the exclusive and exciting world of Vienna's student fraternities. His mother had a friend called Dr. Benedikt, a high official in the Treasury and an alumnus of the fraternity Unitas, which was one of only three pan-German Jewish fraternities in existence and the only one that insisted on admitting "only young men of the best society." Adele felt that joining a fraternity would keep her son out of trouble, a patently ludicrous idea. Like all fraternities everywhere, Unitas was a hotbed of binge drinking and hazing. More ominously, it was the only Jewish fraternity that recognized and encouraged dueling.

This Arthur discovered in September 1922, when at the age of seventeen he was welcomed into Unitas by Dr. Otto Hahn, the so-called Master of the Foxes—a fox being the name for a novice. Hahn was also the fraternity's dueling instructor, and before long the diminutive newcomer was brandishing a saber and learning about quartes, reverse quartes, and tierces. It was a notable step for one so young, and Arthur took to this semisecret society and its complicated rituals like a duck to water (some of the most lyrical pages in his autobiography describe his experiences there). He was mentored by another Hungarian student, Jacob Teller, who informed him of the fraternity's more serious purposes and political goals. The Jews needed their own country, said Teller, just like other peoples. Until they got it they were condemned to remain "a sick race, top-heavy, with a disproportionately great number of lawyers, merchants, intellectuals, and with no farmers or peasants—which was like a pyramid standing on its top." Teller talked about the Balfour Declaration of 1917 and the way it had stimulated Jewish fraternities such as Unitas to encourage more Jews to emigrate to Palestine.

Koestler later claimed that he had never heard of the Balfour Declaration,

sex in both *Arrival and Departure* and *Thieves in the Night.* The idea seems to have fascinated and repelled Koestler in equal measure, but one shouldn't read too much into one early story. Arthur wasn't the only youth brought up in the repressive atmosphere of 1920s Vienna (or 1930s, '40s, and '50s Europe generally) who wondered whether a little force wasn't needed, or even expected, as part of the mysterious ritual of sex, and in his story, the attempt is a miserable failure.[3]

Arthur's attitude to sex was fairly conventional for his time. In his autobiography he refers to sexual favors bestowed on him by Mathilda, a maid at the Ehrmann pension, suggesting that it was she who initiated him at the comparatively early age of sixteen. Willing maids are a staple of autobiographies of the period, and the tale seems a little suspect in light of the story written three years later, but the possibility can't be excluded. As a college student, Arthur certainly enjoyed the institution of *Das süsse Wiener Mädl,* the sweet Vienna lass immortalized by Arthur Schnitzler in his plays and stories about prewar Vienna. The lasses were working-class girls (like the Koestlers' maid, Bertha, in Budapest) who were often hungry and therefore cheap, but they could also be risky, and it wasn't long before Arthur was calling on Dr. Rudolf Paschkis to be treated for the clap.[4]

THAT WOMEN WERE INFERIOR BEINGS was an article of faith in Vienna (and not only Vienna) in the early part of the century, as is evidenced by some of Freud's early case studies. Arthur adored Freud, but he was even more deeply influenced by the brilliant and disturbed young philosopher Otto Weininger, who published his celebrated treatise *Sex and Character* in 1903, at the precocious age of twenty-one, before committing suicide in the house where Beethoven died. Weininger was one of the first to try to produce a scientific explanation for the differences between men and women, arguing that there were two opposed psychological and biological types in the world, one masculine, the other feminine. The "masculine idea" embodied perfect rationality and creativity, the "feminine idea" the urge to sexual gratification. Weininger (a Jew who converted to Lutheranism) also argued that Jews were "the women" of the human race. "The Jew" was so saturated with femininity that even the most manly Jew was "more feminine than the least manly Aryan." Communism (as opposed to Aryan socialism) was Jewish, because Jews, like women, had no sense of individual worth. They lacked "a free intelligible ego." They were materialists who had flourished in science, particularly in chemistry and medicine, because they were shallow and didn't understand the concepts of greatness or immortality.[5]

Weininger insisted that his argument was conducted in terms of Platonic "essences" and was not meant to be what we would nowadays call either sexist or racist ("despite my low estimate of the Jew, nothing could be further from my intention than to lend the faintest support to any practical or theo-retical persecution of Jews"). But his views were widely perceived as a classic expression of Jewish "self-hatred" and undoubtedly fed the springs of grow-ing anti-Semitism in Austria.

Meanwhile, the young Arthur wasn't the only one to have his head turned by Weininger. Kafka, Musil, Strindberg, Freud, Wittgenstein, Gertrude Stein, and any number of lesser writers professed their admiration for him. The protagonist of "Seeing Her Again" invokes "poor dead Weininger! If only he had known what a chaotic turmoil he caused in many ferment-ing young heads!" and the whole story can be read as an illustration of Weininger's ideas on puberty. Weininger also crops up in an unfinished story by Arthur called "Phantom of the Daily Round," set during the narrator's "second puberty" (when "not the voice but the soul is transformed").[6]

He went on to write a nine-page essay, "Christianity, the Jews and Weininger," in which he agreed with Weininger that "the sharpest anti-Semites are to be found among the Jews" but argued that this was a conse-quence of Jewish self-irony. "Not to take myself seriously means to mock the Deity that created me and that is in me, it means to mock the Spirit that comes into me in a miraculous way and to destroy the meaning of existence." This self-irony was not to be confused with self-criticism. Self-criticism was honest and painful, for "there is no pain greater than the renunciation of vanity," whereas self-irony was the result of shame and usually ended in cynicism. "Jews lack naiveté, they hold in contempt the goy who sits there with his mouth open, listening self-forgetfully. The Jew lacks this self-forgetfulness, because he stands eternally under the curse of sobriety. It is for this reason that he despises the goy who gets drunk, it is for this reason there are no Jewish murderers."[7]

Arthur blamed the Jewish religion for backing its moral commandments with a system of rewards, and expressed the view that true humility was for-eign to the Jew. Jews disdained the concept of goodness "in the Kantian sense," that is, that actions were good only when taken for their own sake and could "never be a means to an end." Jewish youths made up a high proportion of the best students, but they were for the most part intellectual snobs skating over the surface of knowledge. "All these youths running about with horn-rimmed glasses and the newest books under their arm, who speak so cleverly and wit-tily, haven't a single spark of true *Bildung* [cultivation], in Goethe's sense of the word." For them, he wrote, philosophy was a form of "thought-gymnastics," in which someone practices his wit and skill in argument while "full of admira-tion for his own acuity of mind," without believing a word of what he says.

THERE'S LITTLE DOUBT Arthur had himself in mind in this excoriation ("thought-gymnastics" were to remain a habit throughout his life), and his view that Jewish morality was self-serving and that the Jews were corrupted by irony was to surface in some articles he wrote as a tyro journalist in Palestine some eight years later, and again in *Thieves in the Night*. In his Weininger essay he blames historical conditions for these defects. The Jews had for centuries endured "the feeling of being rejected from the community of men, of being pushed into the only vocation that was open to them, making money. Money was their only happiness on earth, and the instrument of their revenge on the hated goyim." How could people forced to live "like lepers," whose most sacred beliefs were "dirtied by the infernal libel of ritual murder," ever raise themselves up to true culture? The tragic result was "a people with a distorted physiognomy and a distorted character," a people "internally torn" that had "lost sight of itself." The Jews were the "fearful fruit" of a "terrible guilt" that humanity had taken upon itself. They were both victims and pariahs.

Arthur drew the conclusion that if anti-Semitism existed, it was not because the Jews were "worthy of hatred," but because others "hated the Jew in themselves." But at that early age he rejected Weininger's implied ultimatum to the Jews to assimilate or be destroyed, for he believed that assimilation had been tried and found wanting. "The foreign culture that the Jews wolfed down was not digested and stayed as a solid mass in their stomachs." After a long period of "vegetating deep in the ghetto, the Jews had emerged all too suddenly into the light" and had been blinded by it, so that they had lost their way in the wilderness.

Weininger's views obviously represented a particular challenge for Arthur. They mirrored and magnified the anti-Semitic prejudices of the Aryan majority, and reflected the inner struggle of an assimilated Jew to find an honorable place in a suddenly hostile world. Weininger concluded that the Jew's first task was to "free the Jew of Jewishness," which was also the goal of Unitas members, but whereas Weininger rejected Zionism as "an impractical idea" and "the negation of Judaism," which could express itself only through the diaspora, Unitas was suspicious of the diaspora and embraced Zionism as its official policy.

IT'S CLEAR THAT the young Arthur witnessed much more anti-Semitism than the mature Koestler admitted. It was certainly on his mind when he saw the Yiddish theater in Baden, and in Vienna he was confronted by the violent anti-Semitism of the German students, whose crude prejudices proved more insidious than he perhaps realized. Whereas in Baden he had thrilled to the sight of Galician Jews on the stage and to the sound of their lilting Yiddish idioms, now (if his later claims are to be believed) the language repelled him, and Yiddish literature made him squirm. "I read some tales of ghetto life translated from the Yiddish and felt even more estranged. They exhaled a stale air, saturated with the smell of narrow streets, of unventilated bedding, mental inbreeding and tortuous ways; they were spiced with over-ripe, self-deprecatory humor. There was in this literature a mixture of servility and spiritual arrogance, of cunning and sentimentality, of mysticism and cupidity, which gave me a feeling of claustrophobia, of wanting to break a window and let the fresh air in."[8]

There is an echo here of another Viennese sage, Karl Kraus, the corrosive editor of *Die Fackel* (The Torch) and author of the Cassandra-like epic *The Last Days of Mankind*. Koestler liked to quote Kraus's ironic dictum that "the impartial observer finally discovers that there is only one partisan anti-Semitic lie: namely that all Jews are clever people." Kraus, a Jew and a secret convert to Catholicism, attacked the corruption of Jews and Christians with equal fervor, but it was widely felt that at heart he was another "anti-Jewish Jew," holding the members of his race to standards that few could attain. It was an exacting form of elitism, but also exhilarating, accompanied by a Jeremiah-like pessimism in the face of reality that set a potent example for Arthur. His later role as a political Cassandra owes more than a little to Kraus's example.[9]

It seems that both Weininger and Kraus had a profound influence on Arthur, and between them set the parameters for his mature beliefs on Judaism. He was on his way to becoming, in Kraus's memorable oxymoron, a Jewish anti-Semite. Koestler's contemporary and later friend Manès Sperber probably got it right when he said that Koestler became a Zionist "not because of his Jewishness but *against* it. It was a kind of Zionism that wanted to prove that the Jews were Gentiles, that is, non-Jewish. What those young people were trying to prove was not that they had the courage to be Jews, but that they had the courage to be like everybody else. Koestler's path to Zionism seems so very odd because it was a flight away from his Jewishness."[10]

ARTHUR'S DISCOMFORT HAD more local causes as well. Some of his new friends in Unitas turned out to be observant, and he found himself questioning the way they carried out their religious obligations. They seemed driven by what he regarded as an empty Talmudic scholasticism, and their religious observance seemed to consist in "cheating the Lord and one's own conscience" by sharp practices. These obvious displays of Jewish faith only provoked more anti-Semitism, and while this redoubled his belief that the answer lay in a national home for the Jews, it was getting harder and harder to make the endless appeals for cash needed for the Jewish National Fund, the Jewish Reconstruction Fund, the Hadassah Hospital, the Hebrew University, and so forth. Though Arthur had volunteered to work in the offices of Keren Hayesod, dedicated specifically to supporting settlements in Palestine, where he was said to be "very smart, successful, and reliable," this unro-

ently, was perfectly at home in Hebrew and the Hebrew alphabet (even if he did advocate its Latinization), and was steeped in Hebrew culture—unlike Arthur. Koestler's later version of Jabotinsky had a great deal of Koestler in him.[17]

Jabotinsky gave a speech at Vienna's Kursalon in the city park, which was filled to capacity, and Arthur was transfixed: "I have heard many political speakers since, but no one who could cast a similar spell over his audience for three solid hours without ever resorting to cheap oratory. There was not a cliché in his speech, delivered in a German worthy of the traditions of the Imperial Hofburg Theatre; its power rested in its transparent lucidity and logical beauty." Not so long before, Arthur had been reading a Revisionist pamphlet about the Arab riots of 1921, with appalling details of Jewish settlers being blinded and castrated and children put to death, and the refusal of the British authorities to let the Jews arm themselves. As in childhood when disturbed by some setback, he had seethed and choked with such rage that he had difficulty breathing. He was overcome by a burning desire to lash out blindly at his enemies and exact revenge for these atrocities. When the sense of outrage subsided, it left him with a fierce determination to devote his life to the cause of the persecuted "as a fighter and a writer of books," just like Jabotinsky.

The reading of the pamphlet and its aftermath proved to be a key moment in Arthur's life. Immediately after reading it, he picked up a book on Einstein's theory of relativity and was carried away in a different sense, transfixed by Einstein's vision of a universe contemplated from such a great distance that human suffering and earthly struggles "shrank to microscopic insignificance." His sensation of choking was at once relieved, giving way to a serene, "self-dissolving stillness" that was both physiological and emotional and brought him an ineffable inner peace. It was a moment he never forgot and that he later recognized as simultaneously dramatizing the innate duality of his nature and offering a path out of his continuing inner conflicts. Unwilling to embrace a spiritual explanation for his experience, he turned to Freud's psychological terminology of the "oceanic feeling" to describe it, but it was in essence a religious vision, almost mystical in its intensity—though Koestler struggled all his life to resist any organized form of faith. It undoubtedly played a role in reinforcing his Zionism (a secular religion in many ways) and illustrated a pattern that was to play out in various ways at future turning points in his life.[18]

Jabotinsky recognized the quality of noble wrath in Arthur and invited his young acolyte to accompany him on a tour of Czechoslovakia. It was a welcome break from Arthur's increasingly boring studies, and he set off without a qualm. Returning, he joined Norbert Hoffmann, then editor of a Jewish literary magazine, and three radical Zionists, Paul Diamant, Joseph Herrlinger, and Benjamin Akzin, in starting an Austrian branch of Jabotinsky's youth movement, Betar, for which he and some of his colleagues helped to design a new uniform.[19]

would return to work in Austria. Henrik and Adele sent their blessings from London, and he left Vienna on April 1. "The entire *Burschenschaft* turned out in 'full colors' and sang the Zionist anthem on the platform while I stuck my beaming face out of the third-class compartment window. Then came the loveliest music to the ears of a young man heading for adventure: the whistle, puff and jolt of the train pulling out of the station." Three years after turning Zionist, Arthur was on his way to the promised land.[32]

CHAPTER FIVE

A RUNAWAY AND A FUGITIVE

To know serenity the dove must fly far from its dovecote.
— RAINER MARIA RILKE

IT'S NOT AT ALL CLEAR what Arthur expected from his trip to Palestine. It took him nearly a month to make his way by train and ship to the Palestinian port of Haifa, and he had plenty of time to think about it. Ostensibly he was going out to become a pioneer and join a settlement, because that's what immigration visas were for, but this ran completely counter to his Revisionist philosophy, which despised the agricultural labor of the kibbutzes and emphasized urbanization as the true purpose of Zionism. A clue to his real state of mind is to be found in his comment to Ellen Delp that he was going to Palestine to become a writer. What he vaguely hoped for, it seems, was to join the settlers and write about them, rather than share in the day-to-day labor of building compounds and working in the fields.

Haifa, a deepwater port perched at the foot of Mount Carmel at the southern end of Acre Bay, turned out to be remarkably cosmopolitan for its small size. Jews constituted less than half its population of thirty thousand inhabitants, but they came from a great variety of countries. The Arabs, too, came from all over the Middle East, along with Turks, Greeks, and Armenians. Arthur loved it, and the day after his arrival called on Abraham (Abram) Weinshall, brother of the Jacob Weinshall he had met in Paris the previous year. Abram was originally from Baku in Azerbaijan. Slim, tall, and boyish, with a shy manner, he revealed his fiery temperament only when he got onto the subject of Jabotinsky and Revisionism. Arthur was fascinated by Abram's brilliance and charmed by his heavy-lidded Russian wife, Zinaida (Zina), a dancer and poet who regularly published her verses in Jabotinsky's Russian-language newspaper, *Rassviet* (Dawn).

The Mediterranean climate of Haifa also worked its magic on the pale young European. He drank in the palm-lined, sandy beaches of Acre Bay, plunged delightedly into the pungent Arab bazaar, and reveled in the unmatched view of the harbor from Weinshall's hilltop villa. But his true destination lay inland, at the pioneer settlement of Hephzibah in the Jezreel Valley. Hephzibah had been founded as a *kvutsa,* smaller than a kibbutz, a few miles south of Haifa but had moved inland to the lower slopes of Mount Gilboa as part of a general Zionist advance into the interior. Jewish immigration to Palestine had recently jumped to more than 30,000 a year, and the Jewish population had doubled during the 1920s to about 140,000. Zionism was on the march, and had crowned its success with the opening of the Hebrew University in Jerusalem in 1924.[1]

THE VALLEY BASIN through which Arthur had to travel was a stony desert, punctuated by malarial swamps infested with mosquitoes and flies. Arab villages dotted the lower slopes of the mountains to either side, their mud walls blending into the dun-colored landscape, and the valley floor was scattered with the ugly concrete cubes of new Jewish settlements. The latter stood out starkly against the bleak terrain, like building blocks dropped from an alien planet, and he formed an instant distaste for them. It took him a full day in a bone-jarring horse-drawn cart to make his way along a narrow, rutted track winding tortuously from one settlement to another before he arrived at Hephzibah, forty sweaty miles from Haifa.

Though his journey was exhausting and depressing enough, it still didn't prepare him for the shock of arrival. "I found myself in a rather dismal and slumlike oasis in the wilderness consisting of wooden huts surrounded by dreary vegetable plots. The huts were not the log cabins made familiar by illustrations of the American pioneering age, but ramshackle dwellings in which only the poorest in Europe would live, as an alternative to the discarded railway carriage. The only buildings made of concrete were the cowshed and a square, white house where the children of the settlement lived together, separated from their parents. I don't know what I had imagined the settlement would look like; but certainly not like this." Arthur joined the *kvutsa* members at their trestle tables in the communal dining hall. Most were still under thirty, but they looked twice their age, exhausted by physical labor. Their faces showed the yellowish tint of malaria, and the women's features had been made hard and coarse by the hot sun and the stress of life in the wilderness.[2]

Koestler later drew on his experiences at Hephzibah for a romantic description of a new Jewish settlement in *Thieves in the Night,* but at the time of his arrival, the physical squalor of the settlement overwhelmed him. The young frat boy suddenly realized that the city suit and half-dozen white shirts nestling in his suitcase were totally ridiculous in his new surroundings. He asked to speak to Dr. Hans Gütig, an old boy of Unitas who had arranged his invitation, but Gütig was in bed with malaria. After a largely silent supper of onion soup, goat cheese, and olives, he got into conversation with his neighbor Dr. Löbl, explaining that he had come with the intention of joining the community. "For good?" was Löbl's laconic response. Arthur lamely replied that he might like to stay for a year or two, and then perhaps move to Tel Aviv and go into politics.

It was the wrong answer, and Löbl's stony silence spoke volumes. Migration to the land was a sacred mission, like entering the priesthood or a monastic order. Arthur had suppressed this thought when persuading Unitas to procure the immigration certificate for him. Faced with the stark reality of the commune and Löbl's disapproving expression, he understood that the role of Zionist settler he had envisaged for himself while in Vienna, even for a short while, was a total illusion. He had escaped one unholy mess only to land himself in another.

He was assigned a bed in a hot, stifling room with two other men. A married couple lived in the other half of the hut, and through the partition he could hear every word and movement, however intimate. Communal showers and a communal latrine, with their total lack of personal privacy, were a further source of embarrassment, and work was no different. The day after his arrival Koestler was assigned to clear stones from an arid, rock-strewn slope, the future site of a vegetable garden, and when he failed at that was dispatched to pick fruit, which was also too much for him. When he inquired after more interesting forms of work, he was told that they were the privilege of older, more specialized members of the collective. Young men were expected to stick to manual labor.[3]

Most of the settlers spoke German as well as Hebrew and prided themselves on their devotion to German culture. If ever there was a commune where Arthur might have settled, this was it. But it was obvious to Elke Unger and Margit Kraus, two young women who got to know him during his brief visit, that staying was out of the question. Margit climbed Mount Gilboa with him, where "he lay on an antique sarcophagus and gazed at the wonderful landscape," but he objected to learning Hebrew. He was turned down by the members' assembly as unsuitable for settlement life, a blow to his pride but also a relief, and he was left with the shaming thought that he had wasted a precious immigration certificate for Palestine.[4]

KOESTLER WRITES THAT he stayed at Hephzibah four or five weeks, but judging by a later letter to Abram Weinshall, he lasted barely ten days—and he left Hephzibah in a tearing hurry, walking most of the way back to Haifa and lugging his heavy city suitcase with him, despite an embarrassing attack of dysentery. This time it took him three days to reach the coast, where Weinshall welcomed him like a long-lost son. The Weinshall brothers were legendary for their Zionist fervor. Abram, still in his early thirties, was a prominent lawyer and chief of the Haifa Revisionist Party. Jacob (Yasha), in Tel Aviv, was a surgeon and the author of several novels and biographies on Jewish subjects, and Eliezer (Ilyusha), also living in Tel Aviv, was a civil engineer and surveyor. All were passionate followers of Jabotinsky and close friends of Wolfgang von Weisl, who was running the Revisionist Party in Jerusalem. Arthur soon felt very much at home and could truthfully say he had influential friends in all three of the main cities of Palestine.[5]

"Red Haifa" was dominated at the time by the Labor Party, a situation Abram Weinshall was determined to change. His first inspiration for putting the Revisionists on the map was a league for the defense of the rights of Palestinian Jews, Ze'chutenu (Our Right), designed to provide legal assistance for Jewish immigrants encountering problems with the British authorities. Abram was a past master at baiting the British and defending his fellow immigrants against the colonial authorities, and Koestler later used him as the model for the lawyer Weinstein in *Thieves in the Night.* Another Weinshall venture was the grandiosely named Sokhnut Medinit Le'umit (National State Agency), or Semel for short, a press service intended to supply European newspapers with information about Palestine with a Revisionist slant. This was the improbable vehicle that launched Arthur's career as a journalist. He told Benjamin Doeg, a Revisionist acquaintance, that he had "a duty as a Jew" to launch his career in Eretz Israel and had come there to become a journalist and a wanderer; a rationalization, perhaps, but not a bad prediction of his immediate future.[6]

Semel was a flimsy affair, consisting of about ten pages of news and comment, which Arthur typed out on stencils, mimeographed, and mailed to some fifty Zionist periodicals in Europe and the United States. Only two paid subscriptions materialized, one from Latvia and the other from Czechoslovakia, though he occasionally heard of material being reproduced without acknowledgment. He took to journalism with enormous enthusiasm, showing a capacity for the hard work, thorough research, and polemical zeal that were to become the hallmarks of his later career. In addition to the news agency, Weinshall had started a Hebrew weekly, *Ha-Tzafon* (The North). Arthur's Hebrew wasn't good enough to help edit the paper, but during the summer and fall of 1926 he published at least half a dozen articles in it translated from his native German. In them he promoted the program of his hero, Jabotinsky, and was heavily influenced by von Weisl's Revisionist tract *Struggle for the Holy Land,* which had appeared in Germany just a few months earlier.

His subjects ranged from customs tariffs (replete with detailed facts and figures on exports, imports, and other arcana of international trade) and the urgent need to encourage Jewish industry in Palestine to ringing editorials reviling the British and moderate Zionists. Some of his pieces were reprinted in Jabotinsky's Russian-language *Rassviet,* and he got a full-page article on Revisionism into the mainstream Zionist newspaper *Jüdische Rundschau* (Jewish Observer). The article was a rebuttal of a column by the Viennese Zionist Adolf Böhm on "The Revisionist Mentality," which sounded the alarm over Revisionism's growing popularity among moderate Zionist youths. Arthur pilloried Böhm and his allies as conformists and cowards, and sharply attacked them for seeking compromise with the British and not confronting them with the demand for an independent state. In another article, "Dreamers and Skeptics," he defended the Revisionists against their critics in the Jewish Agency, asserting that the "old illness of belittling one's value and self-image" was the traditional curse of the "ghetto Jew" and the result of fatigue, timidity, and mistrust.[7]

He cheekily signed his articles "Engineer Arthur Köstler" (awarding himself the degree he had failed to earn in Vienna), but since the only typewriters he could find in Palestine were English and didn't possess an umlaut, "Köstler" had to be rendered as "Koestler," thus spawning one of the most famous bylines of the twentieth century.

ALL THIS HUFFING AND PUFFING made Engineer Koestler sound fully established and about twice his age, especially since he employed the multisyllabic political vocabulary and rolling periods of his models in Vienna. But he was living an extremely precarious life in which he could barely make ends meet and was often forced to rely on his wits. Abram had agreed to pay him a pound a month until he could get on his feet, plus a 10 percent commission on any advertising he could obtain for *Ha-Tzafon,* which was almost none. For several months he went hungry, cadging cigarettes from a sympathetic Viennese architect and constantly changing rented rooms. During this period he worked briefly for an Arab developer and once tried selling lemonade in the bazaar. For a while he shared a room with a Russian policeman and his sister, then slept on the concrete floor of a paint shop and on a leather sofa in a dentist's surgery (which he had to vacate during the day). He also camped out for a while at the one-room Revisionist Club—of which he was the honorary secretary—on Allenby Street in downtown Haifa.

When Benjamin Doeg ran into him again he noted that Koestler's suit had completely lost its shape and was badly faded, with yellow spots all over it. "His face was pale and pinched. He had nothing to eat and nowhere to sleep (not counting the beach)." Doeg sensed that Koestler was too proud to mention his situation, but "when you saw his dulled pupils and the way they brightened from time to time, it wasn't difficult to guess." Koestler found himself leading a peculiar double life, enduring agonies of embarrassment while refusing second helpings at the Weinshalls' or at the home of the wealthy St. Petersburg–born architect Samuel Rozov (Rozov, a former schoolmate and close friend of Vladimir Nabokov, was now a leading Revisionist in Haifa). When Koestler was invited to meet Benjamin and Rosa Zuckermann, two prominent Zionists then working for Baron Rothschild, their youngest daughter, Dora, immediately saw through his pose: "He was pale, thin, sickly looking and yet very charming. I was attracted to our visitor and wanted to get to know him. Was he epileptic, I wondered, or just feverish? Why was he shaking like that? My mother, always very understanding and compassionate, offered him food and drink. He later confessed he had not eaten for several days."[8]

Not long after this he ran into the son of the Baden chief rabbi with whom he had studied Hebrew and the Old Testament during his boarding school days. The son informed him that an article of his had recently been printed on the front page of Vienna's *Neue Freie Presse* and that he was now "famous." The article in question was a travel piece on Acre that he had sent his parents. Adele knew the proprietor and had pulled some strings on her son's behalf, but Koestler saw it as an omen, a promise of greater things to come.[9]

IF GREATNESS WERE TO COME, however, it wouldn't happen in Haifa. He decided to move to the "Jewish capital" of Tel Aviv, walking the sixty miles down the coast to save money. He continued to compile his newsletter and to write for *Ha-Tzafon,* but money was still short and he lived like a hobo again for the next few months. Tel Aviv, built on sand dunes north of the Arab port of Jaffa, with its crooked streets and gimcrack houses, reminded him of the ghettos of Central Europe rather than the modern city he had expected to find. He later described it in *Thieves in the Night* as "a frantic, touching, maddening city which gripped the traveler by his buttonhole as soon as he entered it, tugged and dragged him around like a whirlpool, and left him after a few days faint and limp, not knowing whether he should love or hate it, laugh or scorn."[10]

Koestler was welcomed by Abram's brother Yasha, a surgeon by day and compulsive writer by night, churning out biographies and historical novels (written in Russian and translated into Hebrew) that featured Jewish heroes and notable exploits from Jewish history. Like Abram, Yasha had a Russian warmth and expansiveness that soothed Koestler's battered ego and overcame his feelings of insecurity. Together with his wife, Mala, a former beauty queen, Yasha organized and presided over a Revisionist discussion club, and soon introduced Koestler to the other members. They were an odd bunch, and Koestler was quickly attracted to a skinny, balding psychoanalyst called

Moshe Har-Even, also from Russia, with pronounced Mongolian features. Har-Even, a follower of Freud's disciple Wilhelm Stekel, had virtually no patients in Tel Aviv but turned down Koestler's offer to act as a guinea pig for analysis. He told his young friend to return to Vienna and finish his degree. "If you don't finish your studies, you will remain a vagabond. No matter how successful you are, you will always be a runaway and a fugitive on earth, and all respectable people will smell out the tramp in you." The pleasure Koestler took in quoting this prediction underscores its remarkable prescience.

Koestler was also befriended by the Hungarian-born poet Avigdor Hameiri, a short, stocky man with a volcanic temper who wrote avant-garde verse in Hebrew and lived with his wife and daughter in a tiny apartment among the sand dunes. Koestler slept on Hameiri's floor and shared meals of bread, onion, and hot tea with the poet and his family whenever he had nowhere else to go. Hameiri had known Koestler's idol Endre Ady in Hungary before World War I and had spent three years in the Soviet Union after the October Revolution. In his poems he described the tragic dilemma of the Jewish soldier fighting wars that were not his, and castigated Palestinian society for not living up to its ideals. In his pessimism he was a kind of pro-Jewish Karl Kraus, one of the few Hebrew writers of the period to depict Jewish heroes who were men of energy and action, and undoubtedly influenced Koestler.

Hameiri tried to start a political cabaret at the Hungarian Café, a popular spot with Tel Aviv's homegrown bohemians, which provided Koestler with the grist for an article on Jewish humor—which couldn't exist in Jewish Palestine, according to Koestler, but only in the diaspora, because it depended on the Jews being an oppressed minority. "It turns out that you can make Jewish jokes in every language except Hebrew." A Hameiri lecture to the Menorah Club provided material for an article, "Europe and Us," in which Koestler raised the problem of what the Jews should take from Europe. They should accept its science, technology, medicine, and legal system, but not the spiritual world of Europe. "Life in the ghettos made us ridiculous, not only because of our isolated and secluded way of life, but because we stopped worshipping God according to our belief, and started imitating our surroundings, unconsciously becoming 'monkeys,' distorting the Jewish religion, concentrating on its external expressions, on the commandments between person and God, rather than maintaining its most important element—interpersonal commandments." It was an extension of his student essay on Weininger, and he added that the Jews ought to continue "the war between Rome and Jerusalem, between Homer and Esau and Ezekiel, and this war should be fought with the civilized tools of the latest scientific achievements."[11]

Hameiri inspired another long and admiring article in the *Jüdische Rund-*

schau, "An Attempt at a Synthesis," accompanied by translations of two of Hameiri's poems. Koestler's theme this time was Palestine as a "test tube," in which the most disparate elements were fermenting and struggling to crystallize out of a primeval chaos. In literature, "no ethical system was thinkable without Sinai," but it was essential to consider "extra-Palestinian and quasi-prehistorical" influences on modern Hebrew writers as well. In Hameiri's case, his Hungarian upbringing was critical, and Koestler identified the work of Ady as the determining element in Hameiri's career. Hameiri's example also suggested a way out of the inner conflict Koestler felt between the contemplative and activist sides of his nature. Contemplation that led to narcissism was all too familiar a temptation, and was rarely justified unless combined with the divine lyric gift of an Ady, which he didn't feel he possessed. He could identify with Hameiri precisely because of the latter's dynamic temperament and ethical passion, and because he, too, had found an exit from his youthful narcissism by embracing Zionism.[12]

Hameiri may have been the inspiration for Koestler to write "Méta," his story about the small boy victimized at school for being Jewish, and two fairy tales improvised for Yasha Weinshall's son, Eri, when Koestler was staying with them. Yasha urged him to write them down: "Tel Aviv needs fairy tales. We have no folklore. What is a nation without fairy tales?" Despite their fancy titles ("The Tale of the Crocodile, the Fair Rachel and the Fifty Kittens" and "The Sad Tale of the King Who Couldn't Stop Laughing") they were Zionist parables rather than fairy tales, early examples of Koestler's didactic intellectual style. They were published in the Prague-based *Jüdischer Almanach* (Jewish Almanac), whose contributors included Sholem Aleichem, Max Brod, and Arnold Zweig, but didn't lead anywhere, and Koestler continued to exercise his journalistic muscles in *Ha-Tzafon.*[13] In one article he attacked the Hebrew University for refusing to allow Jabotinsky to speak during a whirlwind tour of Palestine in October 1926. Koestler met Jabotinsky when he came to Tel Aviv and was present at a huge open-air meeting where Jabotinsky spoke for three or four hours, "his silhouette outlined against the darkening sky and later against the stars. There was a recurrent refrain in that speech, a quotation from Cicero's *In Catilinam,* probably *quo usque tandem,* which had a chilling and terrifying effect. It was not a speech—it was an earthquake sustained for several hours."[14]

KOESTLER ALREADY TOOK his writing very seriously. The Zionist writer Gavriel Zifroni, then an errand boy for Tel Aviv's first European bakery, was amazed by the way Koestler "worked like a laborer" over his articles. Rising at seven, Koestler would take a cold bath, breakfast on baguettes or bagels, and be at his desk by eight. For four hours he sat over a big accountant's book writing out his stories in longhand. After lunch and a siesta, he worked again

the mayor of Hebron by mentioning the four-thousand-year pedigree of his city, all he replied was: 'Yeah, yeah, time flies.'" Koestler describes an extraordinary journey through "a labyrinth of narrow, virtually tunnel-like back alleys, through cellar-like courtyards, darkness, smells, noise, dirt, and swarms of urchins" to a tiny synagogue where Abraham allegedly appeared to nine pious Jews in the Middle Ages to rescue them from calamity. "Above the synagogue a staircase of forty steps leads up to the mosque that constitutes the second story of Machpela. For six hundred years, non-Muslims had been forbidden to go higher than the sixth step, obliging the Jews to cluster and pray there, and to thrust their rolled-up pieces of paper with prayers on them into cracks in the wall."[3]

KOESTLER DID ALSO WRITE tongue-in-cheek travelogues with titles such as "City of Fountains and Mosques" (Damascus), "The Cafe of a Thousand and One Nights" (Baghdad), and "The Trollops of Lebanon," in each of which he undercut romantic tourist images of the Levant with descriptions of the squalid reality, but he also filed twice-monthly reports on political, social, and economic developments in the Middle East. Even then Koestler was fascinated by foreign policy, but the most surprising thing about his dispatches is their revelation of how little seems to have changed in the Middle East in the three quarters of a century since he wrote. What also stands out is the Revisionist spin he was allowed to put on the contest between Britain and France for domination of the region after the defeat of the Ottoman Empire. As an Austro-Hungarian Jew writing for a mainly German audience, he took a detached view of this variant of the Great Game and wrote with considerable sympathy of Arab efforts to wrest independence from their colonial masters. Oddly, it was his Zionism that prompted him to identify with the Arabs as underdogs and to express a healthy contempt for British policies in the Middle East. These views were later to resurface in *Thieves in the Night,* in which Koestler showed sympathy for both militant Zionism and Arab nationalism, and in *Promise and Fulfilment,* his chronicle of Israel's war for independence.[4]

Further evidence of how little has changed is to be found in Koestler's 1928 articles on the rise and fall of the Egyptian nationalist leader Nahas Pasha, whom the British seemed to tolerate but worked secretly to undermine. He devoted two dispatches to the discovery of major oil deposits in Mosul, Iraq, and the intense international bargaining among Britain, France, the Netherlands, and the United States over whether to develop the field or not and where the pipeline was to go. In other articles he signaled the arrival of Soviet emissaries in the Middle East and analyzed the "virtuosic cunning and flexibility" of the British in matters of foreign policy. But the British, he thought, would never match the deviousness of the Arabs. The fact that King

Ibn Saud had signed a treaty with Britain by no means guaranteed that he would be able to extend his influence over the countless independent tribes and sheikhs between Riyadh and Mecca. "The British influence doesn't go deep and doesn't touch the national roots of the countries within its sphere of influence—it is a thin enamel crust made from a mixture of gold and gun-metal, just durable enough to withstand the demands made upon it by England's need to impose its wishes on the raw material that lies beneath the crust. This raw material, however, is incalculable dross from the political point of view: warlike, fanatical, nomadic, and divided into tribes, each with its own interests in Arabia; Levantine, corrupt and devoted to following family interests in the Arabian part of Palestine; Levantine, corrupt, but nevertheless slowly wakening to a sense of nation in Egypt."[5]

Two months later Koestler described the Wahhabis' takeover of Arabia as a "coup," comparable to the Bolshevik Revolution in Russia, "with its dictatorial form and revolutionary transformation of the everyday life and outlook of its subjects" (the Ikhwan Brotherhood played the role of the Communist Party). This accounted, among other things, for Ibn Saud's attempts to spread his influence under the guise of defending Islam and to promote the candidacy of his son Feisal for the Syrian throne (much to the discomfiture of the French). In a later article Koestler reported on a call by the Wahhabi sheikhs and mullahs for a jihad against the "hereditary foe," Iraq, and described the Wahhabi faith as a form of fanatical puritanism.[6]

Koestler's Revisionist message was that the Arab Middle East offered "no partner for a major power—in either the positive or negative sense," for the Arabs were too nationalistic, too "Oriental," too untrustworthy to do business with. There was another group in the Middle East that was both trustworthy and European, however: the Jews of Palestine, and it was infuriatingly obtuse of the British, Koestler thought, not to be able to grasp that simple point.[7]

KOESTLER'S ARTICLES ON PALESTINE were written against a political and economic background that was darker and more depressing than the one Koestler had encountered as a dewy-eyed optimist in 1926. At that time Zionist immigration had been on the rise and the country had looked as if it might prosper, but in 1927 and 1928 the economy crashed, unemployment soared, and it seemed that more Jews were leaving the country than immigrating. Worse still from Koestler's point of view, many of those who did immigrate were the dreaded "ghetto Jews" from Poland and Galicia, who struck him as having little of the idealism of the early Zionists and none of the noblesse oblige of Jabotinsky's followers. Koestler held both the British and Weizmann's Zionist Executive Committee to blame for this parlous state of affairs. The British were imposing unreasonable tariffs and exploiting the wealth of the local Jews to balance the national budget, while mainstream Zionists were at fault for not demonstrating that "the Zionists need England and England needs a Jewish Palestine, but only a financially sound and vigorous Palestine. No one does business with bankrupt partners."[8]

In common with other Revisionists, Koestler was convinced that the local authorities only pretended to impartiality, and in fact favored the Arabs. A particular bugbear was the behavior of the local police, who were formally under the jurisdiction of the British but seemed much readier to protect Arab interests than Jewish ones (this had been an issue for Abram Weinshall's Jewish Defense League in Haifa the previous year). In the summer of 1928, there was an alarming rise in the number of rapes of Jewish women (and some young men) by Arabs, some of which had been committed by the Arab policemen whose job it was to prevent such outrages. Koestler pointed out that although Jews constituted a majority of the population of Jerusalem, the police force was entirely Arab, and most of its members spoke neither Hebrew nor any European language. Punishment of Jewish prisoners, including flogging, was carried out by Arab policemen (albeit in the presence of a British officer), which only "sharpens local bitterness against the Mandate government, which makes no allowances for the unique nature and complicated problems of this land."[9]

By the fall of that year Koestler himself was growing restive with the unique problems of living in the Promised Land. During his first months in Jerusalem he had been extremely happy. For the first time since leaving Vienna he had regained a degree of social respectability and earned a decent income, and he was friends with a small circle of immigrant professionals from Central Europe. The Jewish population of Jerusalem was still small, and it was possible to get to know all the middle-class families there without much difficulty. There were dinner parties in Talpioth, horseback rides in the Judean desert, jolly family picnics in the picturesque environs of Jerusalem. On weekends he would visit Har-Even and Hameiri in Tel Aviv or the Weinshalls in Haifa, or go on trips to Galilee, for Palestine was small and it didn't take long to get to these places.

Among his newer friends was the Viennese-born novelist and fellow journalist Moshe Yakov Ben-Gavriel. Ben-Gavriel, a socialist and a Weizmann supporter, held that the Jews should turn their backs on Europe and work with the Arabs to found a unitary state and a Middle Eastern form of socialism. Considerably older than Koestler, Ben-Gavriel found Koestler naive and childlike, pugnacious and yet "extraordinarily trusting," and though he regarded Koestler's Revisionist ideas as "primitive and superficial," he also thought of his younger colleague as "provocative and endearing." Koestler's loudly voiced diatribes earned him the nickname in Jerusalem of "Chief Rabbi of Transjordan" (a reference to the Revisionist belief that Jews should settle both sides of the Jordan River), but Ben-Gavriel tolerated Koestler's overblown rhetoric as the natural outcome of youthful excess.[10]

In his autobiography Koestler says little about his social life in Jerusalem. He complains that there were no cafés, nightclubs, or cocktail parties where a young man could relax or let his hair down and suggests that life there was claustrophobic. On a brief visit to Budapest he proposed marriage to a former girlfriend, but lost out to a dentist. As a consolation he took a German shepherd puppy back with him for company. Jessica (or Jessy as she became) was the first of a long line of aggressive dogs that Koestler was to keep and breed throughout his life, and her bad behavior (chewing up carpets, biting strangers, desecrating a mosque, vomiting in someone's bed) appealed to the perverse delight he took in breaking rules and causing scandals. A further perversity was that dogs were regarded as unclean animals by devout Muslims, and Koestler lived in a Muslim quarter of Jerusalem. This earned him the nickname of Abu Kalb, "Father of the Dog," but hardly endeared him to his neighbors.[11]

THE FALL OF 1928 was unusually hot and turbulent in Jerusalem and was notable for two signal events: a notorious riot at the Western Wall and the return of Jabotinsky to live in the Holy Land. News of the rioting reverberated worldwide after the Arab police waded in with clubs and fists to disperse Jews praying at the wall on the holiest holiday of the Jewish year, the Day of Atonement. In his report on this affair Koestler tried to explain the arcane intricacies of the dispute, which had to do with chairs brought by Jews for the elderly and infirm (which the Arabs interpreted as an attempt to establish squatters' rights) and with the screens separating men from women (which the Arabs insisted on regarding as makeshift walls). Koestler blamed the British, as usual, but modified his views when a British member of Parliament, Colonel Josiah Wedgewood, suggested dominion status for Palestine, with a Jewish majority population. Jabotinsky seemed in favor, and Koestler concluded it might be time to abandon the Balfour Declaration for something that sounded better.[12]

Jabotinsky himself arrived in Jerusalem in October 1928—after much haggling with the British—and assumed editorship of a small Zionist newspaper, *Doar Hayom* (The Daily Mail), with the goal of making it the Revisionists' official organ. Koestler, the Weinshall brothers, Avigdor Hameiri, Uri Zvi Greenberg, Moshe Har-Even, and David Melamed all ended up on the editorial board. Koestler's contributions had to be translated from German, and most of them consisted of reprints of articles published in Germany and Austria, but his proudest achievement—despite his sketchy knowledge of Hebrew—was the invention of the Hebrew crossword puzzle, which was

CHAPTER SEVEN

HELLO TO BERLIN

A man must make his opportunity, as oft as find it.
— FRANCIS BACON

WHEN KOESTLER ARRIVED in Paris in July 1929, he had no idea what his new job would be or how long he would stay. The main thing was to get back to Europe and make a new start. He had every reason for optimism, for Paris still felt like the center of the civilized world. He rented a room in a small hotel, just behind the Church of the Madeleine, and was soon taking his lunch in the rue des Mathurins, where the *patron* delighted him by keeping a napkin ring with his name on it. Every evening he rode the Métro to the stock exchange to drink an aperitif at the Café Vaudeville, play billiards with colleagues, and eat dinner at a prix fixe in the rue des Petits-Champs. It was a far cry from the hot and dusty Street of the Prophets, and Koestler reveled in the civilized orderliness of French life.[1]

His job, however, proved to be insufferably menial and boring. He worked three shifts in the Ullstein bureau at 23 rue Pasquier: from nine in the morning until one; from three to seven in the afternoon; and from nine to eleven at night, which basically ate up his whole day. He later exchanged the morning for the dawn shift, but the effect was the same, the difference being that he now worked part of the time in the Salle des Journalistes beneath the stock exchange, a smoke-filled, airless basement with ink-stained desks and nine long-distance telephone booths from which the lesser foreign journalists in Paris phoned dispatches to their respective newspapers or agencies. At a few minutes after four each morning, a messenger would bring in the sixteen major dailies published in Paris, and Koestler would have to read, digest, and condense their political contents into not more than a thousand words in just over an hour and a half. It was here that he learned to "read with his thumb," a form of speed-reading that consisted of running his thumb down the middle of a column and absorbing whole paragraphs at a time. It was a useful technique for an unendurable chore and one he was to use throughout his life—but it also got him into trouble. In one five a.m. phone call he mistakenly reported that the French government "was tottering" and almost lost his job over it.

Koestler knew virtually no one in Paris and led a lonely life there. He had a brief romance with the office secretary, Ingeborg Seidler, a literate and high-spirited Viennese girl who had run away from home and was looking for fun (one of her favorite occupations was to fabricate news stories for the human-interest columns of Ullstein's tabloids). Ingeborg was much too intelligent to be a secretary and had a wicked sense of humor, belied by an innocent baby face that earned her the nickname of Bébé. In anticipation of Koestler's arrival she had scribbled on the wallpaper behind her desk: "Today arrives the prodigy from the Wailing Wall, now all will be well," and Koestler was soon taking Bébé to late-night cafés and for Sunday joyrides in the diminutive used car he had bought.

Their affair was intense but short-lived, and left him feeling lonely again. He couldn't sleep between his evening and early-morning shifts and became a night owl, prowling the all-night brasseries and bars of Montparnasse, or watching produce being unloaded at Les Halles. He was fascinated by the street women, with their promise of easy sex and forbidden fruit, and especially the sadomasochistic relationships that bound them to their pimps. The pimp, he concluded in his autobiographical musings on the subject, was "the false Messiah of the fallen woman, who makes her suffer without offering redemption." Somewhere in his subconscious Koestler identified the pimp with other types of oppressor (like the murderers of the Jews in Palestine), and the prostitute's guilt feelings with his own unaccountable yearnings for punishment and atonement.

HE WAS RESCUED from his preoccupation with prostitutes and brothels by the arrival in Paris of Eva Striker, whom he hadn't seen since their kindergarten days in Budapest. Eva had gone on to become a potter, and had worked in Hamburg before becoming a ceramics designer in Schramberg in the Black Forest. Her Schramberg employer had sent her to Paris to find out about the latest trends in design, and her mother suggested she look up Koestler and ask him to help her get settled.

They arranged to meet in a Métro station. The signal for recognition was to be a bunch of German newspapers under Koestler's arm. "I can remember him standing motionless on the platform," said Eva later. "When he recognized me, he quietly lifted his elbow, letting the large bunch of newspapers fall, which instantly spread into an impressive pool by his feet. When I quickly bent down to pick them up, his first words to me were: 'Leave them.' This was my surprise introduction to Arthur." Eva was entranced by this boyish prank, and by Koestler's mischievous ways, which matched her own impulsiveness. Soon after they met, he wrote a story for Ullstein about a thirty-foot-high tidal wave. "How do you know how high the wave was?" she asked. "That doesn't matter at all," he replied. "I could write an article with false facts from beginning to end, and no one would notice as long as it was interesting."

Eva wasn't conventionally beautiful. She had a strong, handsome face with a high forehead and deep-set blue eyes, but she radiated vivacity and intelligence, and it wasn't long before they became lovers. She took a room in his small hotel, a badly lit, noisy establishment occupied almost exclusively by journalists coming and going at all hours of the day and night, and shared Koestler's high jinks whenever he had some free time. "We often went to dark little night spots and sat for hours in the Café du Dôme," Eva recalled. "We also went to fine restaurants, because he liked to put on airs and eat well." One night he abandoned her in an expensive restaurant while he drove from friend to friend until he found one who could lend him some money to pay the bill. On another occasion Koestler wondered if some rotting leaves in the forest of Fontainebleau would burn, and lit a leaf with his lighter. Suddenly they were surrounded by a ring of blue flames and were forced to beat a hasty retreat, leaving a cloud of smoke behind them. Guilt-ridden, Koestler sought out a psychoanalyst friend for advice. "I'm the sole support of my mother," he said, with considerable exaggeration, "a foreign journalist in this hospitable country. How could I have done such a thing?" The psychiatrist consoled him with the thought that no fire had broken out, but according to Eva, he continued to brood over this prank for many weeks.[2]

KOESTLER TRIED TO COMPENSATE for the aridness of his job by writing feature articles in his spare time, some dozen of which appeared in *Voss* during the year he stayed in Paris. They were mostly human-interest stories, with some art criticism thrown in. The few political pieces he wrote showed him moving well to the left of his Palestine days and gradually losing interest in Jewish affairs. After the Hebron and Jerusalem riots and the stabbing of von Weisl, he had dashed off a furious article accusing the British of collusion in the Arab pogroms, and a few months later he was the keynote speaker at a gathering of the French Jewish fraternity Hasmonaya. He also took Eva to watch a parade of Betar, the Revisionist youth movement he had once belonged to, and to listen to a speech by Jabotinsky. Eva disliked Jabotinsky's strident manner and his comparison of the Jews in Palestine to passengers entering a crowded railroad car, who should "use their elbows" to make room for themselves. She found his followers "unhealthy-looking and ugly," and felt that Koestler silently agreed with her, for he made no comment on the scene. Though Eva was also Jewish, Koestler never once discussed Zionism or Revisionism with her, and though the Revisionists' headquarters were in Paris, he seems to have kept his distance. A few months later Eva left for Berlin, and their affair ended as casually as it had begun.[3]

It was now that Koestler started publishing some articles on popular science. Their most curious feature was that, whereas in his art criticism Koestler downplayed the emotional and psychological impact of the works he saw and strove to supply them with a theoretical framework, in the scientific pieces he brought a sensory response and imaginative creativity to his descriptions that greatly animated and enlivened the dry theorems he discussed. This was especially true of "The Mystery of Light" (which appeared over the byline "Engineer Arthur Koestler"), a lyrical description of the work of the Duc de Broglie, who had just been awarded the Nobel Prize in physics for his theory of light. Koestler saw the item in a news flash, and in a rare departure from custom was allowed to leave the office to interview the physicist in person. De Broglie was impressed by Koestler's knowledge of physics and the two men talked excitedly for several hours, after which Koestler stayed up all night writing about de Broglie "in a state of exaltation."[4]

His article caught the eye of the senior partner in the Ullstein Trust, Dr. Franz Ullstein, who made a point of meeting Koestler on his next business visit to Paris and singled him out for praise. Franz's young wife, Countess Rosie Waldeck, also took a shine to Koestler, which soon made for complications. When a fight broke out between Franz and his younger brother Hermann over how to run the firm, the countess was accused of working for some unspecified foreign government and meddling in personnel matters. She was "pushing her favorites," including "that Koestler-fellow, who she says is such a great talent." The quarrel divided the firm's employees into two hostile camps: the "Franciscans" (supporters of Franz) and the "Bernardines" (supporters of the powerful editor of the *Vossische Zeitung*, Georg Bernhard, who sided with Hermann).[5]

The power struggle was won by Franz, forcing Bernhard to depart. The paper's science editor, Professor Joel, was due for retirement, and Franz insisted that the post be given to Koestler. Reading between the lines of Koestler's autobiography, it's clear the appointment was unpopular with his colleagues. Professor Joel, like other specialist contributors to the *Vossische Zeitung* (and many of its correspondents), had a doctorate, whereas Koestler hadn't even managed the equivalent of a bachelor's degree—a fact he kept well hidden from his superiors. On the other hand, he undoubtedly knew how to write about science in a stimulating way, and Franz Ullstein sum-

pole and (for the media climax of the expedition) headed for a rendezvous not with an American submarine surfacing from beneath the ice cap (as Hearst had envisioned) but with the Soviet icebreaker *Malygin,* cruising with the Italian Umberto Nobile and other scientists on board. The airship landed on the sea about two hundred feet away from the icebreaker, a boat came over from the *Malygin,* and the fellow polar explorers, Ellsworth and Nobile, managed to shake hands. Owing to danger from floating icebergs, the airship took off again only thirteen minutes after its arrival, and the flight back was an anticlimax, except for the few moments when Eckener allowed Koestler to take the helm.[18]

Upon his return Koestler found himself a celebrity. His dispatches from the Arctic were hugely popular and had been syndicated in several countries. He took a leave of absence from Ullstein and embarked on a six-week lecture tour of Germany, Denmark, Sweden, and the Netherlands, equipped with a set of lantern slides to show to audiences. His first engagement, at the planetarium of the Berlin Zoo, consisted of a week of lectures entitled "The Arctic Through the Zeppelin's Windows," and was such a popular success that its run was extended for a second week. For his Hamburg lecture (in the "House of Curiosities") he was billed as "Doctor" Arthur Koestler. Audiences were informed that he would personally describe the dramatic meeting between the *Graf Zeppelin* and the *Malygin* in the Arctic Ocean and show slides of the "historic" handshake between Ellsworth and Nobile. "You will also hear how the Zeppelin landed on the sea, and will see slides that illustrate more vividly than any words the *colossal difficulties* of the whole enterprise."[19]

Back in Berlin in the fall of 1931, Koestler was promoted to foreign editor and assistant editor in chief of *B.Z. am Mittag,* while retaining his position as science editor of *Voss.* He became a member of the Ullstein *Fürstenrat,* or "Council of Princes," the influential inner circle of editors that met to discuss policy and decide the Ullstein line, a rising star in the firmament of Berlin journalism.[20]

TOP JOURNALISTS AND EDITORS in 1930s Berlin were like today's television anchors and movie stars. They turned heads in the street, had their own clubs and coffeehouses, their own legends and folklore, and were sought-after guests for receptions and dinner parties. Koestler was no exception. After the *Graf Zeppelin* expedition he moved into a comfortable apartment in the West End of Berlin, drove a sporty red Fiat convertible ("Theodore"), and dressed more elegantly than ever. With a cigarette in one hand and a glass of whisky in the other, he was the epitome of the sophisticated young man about town and bon vivant. Yet inwardly he was still wracked by insecurity and self-doubt. He felt that he still looked like an adolescent and was convinced that many of his colleagues despised him, tolerating him only because he was a protégé of Franz Ullstein.

He was still addicted to "mental gymnastics" and still loved talking about politics, religion, and art, the staples of intellectuals everywhere, but discussion rarely remained just a discussion with him. It was transformed into a gladiatorial struggle, in which the goal was to wrestle your opponent to the metaphorical floor and pin him there with your conclusions. Koestler also loved games and contests. A pronounced chess addict, he was thrilled by the clash between white and black, and he played highly competitive weekly games of poker with his journalist colleagues Axel Eggebrecht, Heinz Kahn, and Lothar Stammreich. Like his father, he relished the gambler's thrill of playing for high stakes, and liked to intimidate his opponents by risking large sums of money on the turn of a card or the throw of the dice.

The future novelist and critic Manès Sperber, who met Koestler at around this time, noted the paradox at the heart of his character. Sperber was the same age as Koestler, had studied psychology with Adler in Vienna before moving to Berlin, and had a lot in common with Koestler, including aspirations to write fiction. Sperber noted Koestler's boastfulness and the perverse pleasure he seemed to take in provoking antipathy in those around him. It was as if he challenged people to dislike him, and it took Sperber a while to realize that Koestler's "clumsy, overcompensatory self-dramatization" was the ploy of a sensitive man "who hoped that his mockery would guard him against any hurt. Even people like me, who appreciated his wit and cynical repartee, often had a hard time taking him seriously." Only with time did Sperber understand that this "young dandy" was serious at heart, "filled with a thirst to find out what was concealed beneath the mask of the familiar and behind the outward guise of reality."[21]

Alfred Kantorowicz, whom Koestler had followed from Ullstein's Paris office to Berlin, took a more negative view of his young colleague's antics. In his thinly veiled fictional portrait of Koestler as the young journalist "Kosterlitz," Kantorowicz described him as subject to bouts of sentimentality and romantic pessimism and agonies of cosmic depression and self-doubt, punctuated by fits of neurotic rage. Kantorowicz felt that Koestler was dimly aware of his complexes, but couldn't seem to help himself. Koestler confirms the nature of his split personality in his autobiography. "The problem wasn't that I wore a mask," he comments about this period, "but that the mask didn't fit."[22]

In the Berlin of Herr Issyvoo and Sally Bowles it was normal to try on new personalities and masks and to change them when you felt like it, and Koestler's brittle cynicism was certainly in style. Sperber saw a "new fatalism" in the self-image of advanced intellectuals. Personal difficulties were attributed (thanks to Freud) to traumatic experiences in early childhood. Neurotic and not-so-neurotic individuals hoped that, by tracing their failures to past actions by other people, they could open the way to "unfettered free-dom." Wilhelm Reich, Freud's disciple and Koestler's friend for a while, maintained that the key to that freedom was sex, and that unlimited satisfac-tion of the sex drive would result in perfect happiness. Koestler was a true be-liever, and by his own admission was fanatically promiscuous in Berlin.[23]

The reigning metaphor for all this frenzied sexual activity was dancing. Anton Gill called his Weimar memoir *A Dance Between the Flames*. Victor Weisskopf attended gala balls at the Academy of Arts that "invariably degen-erated into orgies," and Sperber notes that every Saturday in winter he at-tended a fancy-dress ball, where hundreds of young men and women "improvised their love life practically devoid of inhibitions, determined to se-duce and be seduced." Koestler was a regular at these balls. Ruth Ludwig, a tango partner at one of the press balls, scolded him for being too free with his hands, and Koestler was the main rival of the fashionable painter Ferdinand Bruckner for the affections of Marianne Oswald, a sensational redhead who later became a nightclub singer in Paris.

For Sperber, a male friend, Koestler was "an adolescent who manages to sneak into the bed of a desirable woman, or seduces all the women in a harem in a single night" and then brags about it, but Eva Striker, who had moved to Berlin shortly before Koestler, saw him rather differently. In her view he was "adventurous, reckless, ambitious and boisterous," but also "romantic, chari-table" and "loving." It's worth mentioning that to one dance partner, Lotte Jäger, who was very young when he seduced her, Koestler continued to write letters from the *Graf Zeppelin* during his Arctic expedition, and she was to see him off at the station when he left for Russia the following year. Ilse Schreiber, the "Nefertiti of the Kurfürstendamm" (who playfully called him "My Little Turk"), also remained on good terms with him, and Helga Bruck became a close friend again when he moved to the United States in 1950.[24]

Looking back, Koestler rationalized his behavior as a "phantom chase" in search of "the perfect physical and spiritual union." Each new conquest seemed to promise happiness, but the bliss of the union never lasted long, and when it wore off, "the phantom-quest started anew." It was an addiction be-yond his conscious control. "Mix in the mortar an acute sense of loneliness with an obsessive search for absolute values; add to them an aggressive tem-perament, sensuality, and a feeling of basic insecurity that needs constant re-assurance through token victories: the result will be a fairly toxic potion."[25]

CHAPTER EIGHT

IN THE GALE OF HISTORY

"And what do you think will happen in Germany now?" I asked.
"Is there going to be a Nazi putsch or a communist revolution?"
— CHRISTOPHER ISHERWOOD

KOESTLER LATER LIKENED his lust and frenetic love life to his obsessive search for a knowing guru and his yearning for a form of utopia, a condition he diagnosed as "absolutitis." This absolutitis had been in remission since his disillusionment with Zionism. Belief in scientific progress offered an intellectual substitute, and the chase after women promised emotional relief, but neither generated the euphoria that his nervous system craved, nor offered the expiation demanded by his devouring sense of guilt. The vacuum was filled by politics, which, in Weimar Berlin, was not easily ignored. In the general elections of 1931 the Nazis polled 6.5 million votes and increased their number of parliamentary seats from 12 to 107. The Communists also did better than expected, though with 23 seats they lagged far behind the Nazis. The moderate center parties retained their majority but were increasingly beset by the clamor from left and right, particularly after Chancellor Heinrich Brüning decided to govern by emergency decree.

Brüning's regime was neither a democracy nor a dictatorship. It was a kind of desperate holding operation by a bunch of frightened conservative politicians unable to withstand the pressures generated by competing interest groups in German society. Throughout most of 1931 an enfeebled President Hindenburg was reduced to signing one Brüning decree after another. Banks and businesses collapsed in ever increasing numbers, and unemployment rose from three million at the end of 1930 to double that number a year later. The "poverty, the agitation, the propaganda, witnessed by us in the streets

the street. They were mostly anti-Bolshevik Russians, of course (one of them being Vladimir Nabokov), but as the twenties turned into the thirties, the concept of "Russian" merged more and more with that of "Soviet," and the signal achievements of Russia's modernist movement helped blur the picture. Russian influence on the Bauhaus, on German expressionist movies, on Erwin Piscator's avant-garde people's theater, on the populist plays and musicals of Bertolt Brecht, Kurt Weill, and Hanns Eisler, made it seem all-pervasive, while Willi Münzenberg's International Workers' Relief Trust rammed the message home to the masses in newspapers, popular books, films, and exhibitions, all devoted to the simple proposition that western capitalist society was rotten and dying, and that the future lay with Soviet communism.

A highly popular book by the American newspaper correspondent H. R. Knickerbocker, *Germany—Fascist or Soviet?*, exercised a strong influence on Koestler's thinking and starkly posed the burning question of the hour. Its suggestion of no middle ground neatly echoed Communist assertions that the middle-of-the-road Social Democrats were "worse than the Nazis," since they were splitting the working-class vote, and strongly appealed to Koestler's taste for black-and-white political solutions.[6]

Reading and thinking about capitalist excesses accelerated his conversion to Marxism in the same way that reading about Arab atrocities had hastened his conversion to Zionism. "Indignation glowed inside me like a furnace. At times I thought that I was choking from its fumes; at other times I felt like hitting out, and shooting from a barricade or throwing sticks of dynamite. My seething indignation had no personal target; it was directed at the system in general, at the oily hypocrisy and suicidal stupidity which were driving us all to perdition."[7]

One curious feature of Koestler's account of his Berlin years is, as von Weisl noted, his silence on the Jewish question. It's true that he met with Jabotinsky and his son Eri when they visited Berlin in 1930, and had come up with a madcap scheme to plant a Zionist flag on an uninhabited island during his airship voyage, but he never joined in when Weissberg and Sperber got into arguments at Eva's studio on the subject of assimilation (which both opposed). Eva was surprised, and von Weisl wondered why Koestler's broadsides against the Social Democrats in his autobiography weren't accompanied by similar attacks on Nazi anti-Semitism. Koestler excused himself in *Arrow in the Blue* by saying feebly that "of course" he hated and feared the Nazis, "but it was a cold hatred, without the emotional glow which only intimacy with the hated object can provide."[8]

KOESTLER'S MOVE TOWARD party membership was encouraged by two new acquaintances who initiated Koestler into the mysteries of dialectical materialism. One was Otto Bihalj-Merin, born in the Hungarian town of Zemun before it was transferred to Serbia and technically a compatriot of Koestler's, though Bihalj-Merin was as rootless as Koestler (and later settled for living in Serbia). A student of painting at the Berlin Academy of Fine Arts, Bihalj-Merin had joined the party as early as 1924, and taught art history at the Marxist Workers' College while turning out art and literary criticism and trying to become a painter himself. He was a leading member of the German branch of the League of Proletarian Revolutionary Writers, affiliated with the Comintern, and one of the editors of the league's theoretical journal, *Die Linkskurve* (Left Turn), for which he wrote under the abbreviated name of Otto Biha, or sometimes just "Bi."

Koestler greatly admired Biha's articles and one day picked up the telephone to compliment him. Of all the socialist writers he had read, he said, Bihalj-Merin was the most persuasive, and Koestler wanted to talk to him about becoming a Communist. When they met, Koestler took an immediate liking to his new acquaintance. Otto had thin lips and a high forehead, but his most prominent feature was his goggly eyes, "whose luminous gaze, without being aggressive, outstared you with their radiance of sheer brotherly love." Otto was short like Koestler but leaner and wirier, and had the fanatical stare and ascetic demeanor of a true apostle. He was the very type of the selfless revolutionary, with a conspiratorial nimbus that excited Koestler's curiosity and hinted at the unknown risks of a life devoted to communism.[9]

Koestler's other mentor was a self-educated former plumber's apprentice whom Koestler knew only by his party nom de guerre, "Karl." Karl regularly heckled the Nazis at their meetings and was just as regularly beaten up and thrown out. He was also a successful political writer (Koestler never mentions his real name, which remains a mystery), but it was the image of the educated proletarian that attracted Koestler. Otto's and Karl's exhortations were reinforced by Koestler's reading of the classics of Marxism-Leninism. By the time he had finished with *Feuerbach* and *State and Revolution*, "something had clicked in my brain which shook me like a mental explosion. To say that one had 'seen the light' is a poor description of the mental rapture which only the convert knows. The new light seems to pour across the skull; the whole universe falls into pattern like the stray pieces of a jigsaw puzzle assembled by magic at one stroke. There is now an answer to every question, doubts and conflicts are a matter of the tortured past—a past already remote, when one had lived in dismal ignorance in the tasteless, colorless world of those who *don't know*."[10]

The imagery is typical of Koestler. He loved to see his life in terms of burned bridges and leaping off cliffs, blinding revelations and psychological revolutions (he had described his conversion to Zionism in almost identical terms), but no one has conveyed better than he the emotional intensity of conversion to a new creed, and there is little doubt that this is how he experienced it. It was another semimystical experience, religious in all but name, and promised the same sort of relief from inner tensions as had Zionism some six years earlier. By the end of 1931 he was ready to make the leap. On the last day of the year, he wrote a letter to the Central Committee of the German Communist Party applying for membership and about a week later was requested to go to the Schneidemühl paper mill to meet "our representative, Herr Schneller." Ernst Schneller was a member of the Central Committee and head of the Department of Agitation and Propaganda (agitprop), who also ran a Communist intelligence organization in Germany called the N Apparatus. Koestler was told to stay with Ullstein (just as Weissberg had advised) and to try to influence his newspaper to be more favorable to the Communists, while passing on any information that might be helpful to the cause. His membership in the party should remain a secret, and he would report to a comrade called "Edgar" (aka Fritz Burde). Conspiratorial nicknames were a venerable tradition of the party dating back to tsarist times, and Schneller informed Koestler that he would need a pseudonym too. Koestler chose the half-Russian, half-Jewish "Ivan Steinberg."[11]

KOESTLER LOST NO TIME in busily organizing a caucus of left-wing sympathizers at Ullstein, and every week dictated notes about the meetings to Edgar's assistant, Paula. In his autobiography he suggests that news of these meetings was leaked to the management and was the reason he was fired in the spring of 1932, but he told the British police in 1940 that his departure was a result of Ullstein's disapproval of his handling of the Japanese invasion of Shanghai. The latter may have been a white lie to cover up his earlier Communist affiliations, but the public reason given for his dismissal was that the circulation of his newspaper, *B.Z. am Mittag,* had fallen catastrophically and Ullstein could no longer afford him. Though offered a large severance payment and the chance to continue as a freelancer, Koestler accepted the former and declined the latter. He also gave up his fashionable apartment and moved to the famous "Artists' Block" (also known as the "Red Block") in the southwest corner of the city, a group of apartment houses situated just off Laubenheimer Platz in Wilmersdorf. According to the novelist Gustav Regler, even though it was cheap, "scarcely one of the occupants was able to pay his rent," and "many of the apartments contained no furniture other than a mattress on the floor. People ate their meals off packing cases covered with newspaper. But none starved; each man helped his fellow."[12]

Koestler had wheedled Burde into letting him join the block's Communist cell while still at Ullstein, but only now was he able to enter into the life of the cell in earnest. Better off than most of the other residents, and still in possession of his little red Fiat, he took a two-room apartment at 9 Bonner Strasse. His Ullstein colleague Alfred Kantorowicz lived on the ground floor. His poker crony Axel Eggebrecht lived in the next building, with Susanne Leonhardt and her son, Wolfgang, just above. The cell met once or twice a week and had about twenty active members, with several sympathizers and hangers-on.

Like all such cells, it was led by a triumvirate of loyalists, consisting of a political secretary, an organizing secretary, and a secretary in charge of agitprop. The first organizing secretary was the novelist Regler, a man of immense charm and persuasiveness, who recruited Kantorowicz to be political secretary. When Koestler arrived, Kantorowicz persuaded him to be the secretary of propaganda. Half a head taller than Koestler and with a pronounced squint, Kantorowicz ("Kanto") acted as a kind of elder brother in the cell, more sympathetic to Koestler's sudden mood changes and more tolerant of his obsessions than he was later to suggest in his roman à clef.

In a fresh general election in April 1932, Hitler made his first run for president, getting thrice the number of votes of the Communist candidate, but was defeated by an aging and enfeebled Hindenburg. The following month, state elections registered strong gains for the Nazis. Hindenburg dismissed Brüning and appointed the reactionary Franz von Papen in his place. Von Papen proceeded to worsen the situation by dissolving the government of Prussia and ruling the state personally as "Commissioner of the Reich." Finally, in national elections to the Reichstag at the end of July, the Nazis stunned the opposition by doubling their number of votes to thirteen million and emerged as by far the largest party in parliament. Hitler was still not able to wrest the chancellorship from von Papen, but the Nazis now held a stranglehold on the dying republic.

The period of these elections coincided with Koestler's most intense involvement in the Red Block cell. As secretary for agitprop, he churned out hundreds of broadsheets and pamphlets on every conceivable aspect of party policy, ranging from the perfidiousness of the Social Democrats to the inevitability of the World Revolution. One leaflet about the workers' movement in Shanghai earned him an accolade from the district committee. His zest for argument, his love of mockery, his newfound mastery of dialectics, and his immense facility with words all made him an ideal choice for the job. According to Wilhelm Reich, Koestler used to shut himself up alone in his room and write his broadsides at top speed, handing the pages to a printer's devil, who would rush them to a waiting compositor. He wrote "faster than most people could have transcribed that quantity" and, according to Reich, produced "well over half a million words."[13]

Though the description of Koestler's working methods is convincing, the productivity claim sounds extravagant: if there are half a million words (or even half that number) by Koestler somewhere in the party's files, no one has succeeded in tracking them down. What's clear is that working in the semi-clandestine world of the party appealed to Koestler's romantic temperament. He loved the mystery of it all and found again the "warm comradeship" he

they had talked about writing a detective novel together, based on an idea suggested by a Budapest psychologist named Dr. Gyula Baron. Németh went ahead and wrote it as "At the Club of the Cockeyed Cat" and sent it to Koestler in Berlin, who reworked it and retitled it "The Mango Tree Miracle," which he sold under his and Németh's names to the *Münchner Illustrierte Zeitung* (Illustrated Munich News) for a fairly large sum. It appeared in the form of a slender book in May 1932 and holds a certain interest as one of Koestler's earliest literary compositions. Its construction is out of Conan Doyle by way of Agatha Christie, and the story, which begins in a nightclub called "The Cockeyed Cat," is imbued with a phantasmagoric atmosphere reminiscent of German expressionist movies, complete with a sinister hypnotist, Professor Nikolitsch (modeled on the real-life Eric Jan Hanussen), and a Sherlock Holmes–like detective called Sanda Kondor.[20]

Németh came to Berlin to claim his share of the royalties and stayed in Koestler's Bonner Strasse apartment for a while. "The Mango Tree Miracle" attracted the attention of the UFA film studios, and Koestler and Németh were invited to submit a treatment. They produced two synopses, one ("What Happened on December 9"; alternative title, "Song of Death") a Hollywood Gothic, the other ("The Jinxed Lorelei") a more sedate affair set in contemporary Berlin and Paris. According to Németh, UFA dropped the movie idea when it learned that Koestler was a Communist, but it seems just as likely that UFA didn't like the synopses (which have survived among Koestler's papers). The first is pure kitsch, the second anemic. Both dispense with the colorful and cinematic figure of Professor Nikolitsch, along with the theme of misdirected psychoanalysis and Kondor's Holmes-style deductions, thereby losing much of the original story's charm and suspense.[21]

A curious detail of the rewrites is the way Koestler endowed one of the characters, a Gypsy violinist, with an "almost pathological inferiority complex," and made another character "pathologically jealous" of the violinist's charm. Jealousy was the theme of a second thriller that Németh and Koestler attempted (also from an idea by Dr. Baron), about murder by a poisoned dental filling, which never found a publisher. Koestler attempted a movie script on the same subject, this time set in Paris, called "Murder at the Odéon Theatre," but that too went nowhere, and his brief career as a thriller writer was soon over.[22]

He was again at a dead end, and his financial situation was worsening by the day. He continued to go on sorties with his Red Block comrades, sometimes taking Németh along, but had decided that his main goal now was to visit the new Zion, the Soviet Union, as soon as possible. For months he watched as friends and acquaintances made the trip, some just to visit, others to stay and work. Alex Weissberg went to work for the Ukrainian Institute of Physics in Kharkov. Eva went out to join him in January 1932, taking a job with the Ukrainian State China Company. They wrote fascinating letters about their life there, saying the only thing they missed was a car. Koestler and Weisskopf shipped them a car, which sat in the garage for lack of spare parts. Manès Sperber went out for three months in the fall of 1931; Otto Bihalj-Merin went to Moscow to "rest" after being voted off the board of *Linkskurve* by the "Left Opposition"; and Weisskopf joined Alex and Eva in Kharkov to give physics lectures at Weissberg's institute.[23]

It seemed to Koestler that almost everyone but he had either been to the Soviet Union already, was there still, or was planning to go, and he was eager to see the land of miracles for himself. The problem was how. After talking it over with friends he conceived the notion of going as a bourgeois journalist with supposed anti-Soviet prejudices, who would write a series of articles chronicling his "conversion" by the Soviet miracle. He still had a big reputation in Germany, and few beyond his inner circle knew of his conversion to communism. He signed a contract with Carl Duncker Verlag to write articles that would be syndicated in some twenty newspapers in Germany, Austria, France, Italy, and England and then collected as a book, *Russia Through Bourgeois Eyes*.

Koestler justified his deception with the Marxist maxim that the end justified the means. Bourgeois wheels ground much faster than Soviet wheels, however, and by midsummer he was still without a visa. He turned to Becher for help, and Becher asked the International Organization of Revolutionary Writers (MORP) in Moscow to sponsor Koestler's visit. "It is of the greatest political interest to us that this comrade be allowed to see everything he needs and has the best conditions for his journey, since he is one of the few still able to publish here." Becher indicated that Koestler's book and articles might be published in the Soviet Union as well, and added a handwritten request for assistance with "all financial aspects of the visit, and with accommodations and provision of the necessary permits."[24]

The letter was well timed. MORP had begun to reexamine its hostile attitude to writers from bourgeois countries and was trying to be more cooperative. The Soviet State Publishing House agreed to advance Koestler three thousand rubles for the Russian rights to his book, and he was told to contact Comrade Gopner, the head of agitprop for the Executive Committee of the Communist International (EKKI) in Moscow, after his arrival. Becher's letter was sent on July 21, 1932. Ten days later Koestler was on his way. The few belongings that couldn't be fitted into a suitcase were distributed to friends, and his little red Fiat was taken over by Becher in the name of the Red Block collective. By a strange coincidence, Koestler ran into Moses Slutzky, a Unitas fraternity brother, in the Intourist office, also on his way to Moscow. But there was no send-off as in Vienna when he had left for Palestine. Only the faithful Lotte Jäger still came to the station, hoping he would marry her some day. He pressed two silver coins into her hand to pay for their last meal together, and she mockingly curtsied as the train pulled away from the platform.[25]

CHAPTER NINE

RED DAYS

We have established the principle of socialism in all spheres of the economy by expelling capitalism from it.

— JOSEPH STALIN

KOESTLER'S VISION OF RUSSIA had been formed by images of gigantic construction projects in Münzenberg's propaganda magazines, and by pictures of jolly workers transforming the country into an industrial paradise. In this rosy view of Soviet progress, the collectivization of the peasantry was a triumph of social engineering, Stalin's revolution from above was succeeding far faster than anyone had imagined, the five-year plan was ahead of schedule, and the Soviet Union would outstrip America in just a few years. So attached was Koestler to this version of Soviet reality that he was primed, if he should encounter evidence to the contrary, to overlook or deny it. Like most visiting foreigners, he had little inkling of the reality behind the facade or of Stalin's iron grip on the levers of power, nor, as a Communist, would he have been able to accept that the plan's figures were faked, industrialization was halting, and collectivization was being accomplished by mass deportations of the peasants and the creation of a devastating famine—especially in Ukraine, his destination.

Luckily it was the custom to allow friendly foreign writers and journalists to travel in the Soviet Union with little or no supervision, which meant that Koestler was able to go straight to Kharkov. Mindful that he was supposed to "change trains for the twentieth century" at the Soviet frontier, he was disconcerted when the actual train halted for half a day to allow a thorough search of each compartment and every scrap of luggage. He was further puzzled when the train's windows were blacked out as they crossed a river bridge, and astonished to see the train beset at every station by crowds of ragged peasants holding up potbellied children and offering icons and clothing in exchange for bread. He was told by the other passengers that the bridges were military objectives and that the wretched individuals besieging the train were kulaks who had resisted the redistribution of the land and were being punished for their opposition to socialism.[1]

Kharkov turned out to be little more than "a huge village of seven hundred thousand sleeping souls," despite its status as the capital of the second-largest republic in the union. None of his advance telegrams had been delivered, but he easily found Alex and Eva in their modern three-room apartment at the Institute of Physics. Eva's mother (and Koestler's former kindergarten teacher), Laura, was also there, having come on the condition that Eva and Alex marry for propriety's sake, and Koestler now made a fourth. Alex was still his boisterous and excitable self, still reciting poetry, still adept in all the nuances of Marxism-Leninism and the twists and turns of Soviet policy. He had recently founded the Soviet Union's first academic journal for theoretical physics and was a powerhouse in his fast-growing institute.

Weisskopf came over for a jolly reunion, and Koestler was introduced to the Soviet theoretical physicist Lev Landau and a visiting English physicist, Martin Ruhemann. He felt instantly at home in this company and immediately donned the bifocals that would allow him to make Marxist sense of the contradictions that confronted him at every turn. The bright new factories he visited, with their well-equipped schools, clubs, and hospitals, their own apartment complexes, fleets of buses, grocery stores, and sometimes even farms and market gardens, struck him as models of socialist planning. For foreigners there was Insnab, a special store stocked with quality food and household items at reasonable prices, while Intourist hotels and restaurants were equipped with European menus. These islands of prosperity coexisted with the dirty, teeming streets of the old city and a population that was largely excluded from their benefits, but Koestler barely noticed at the time.

In Berlin he had crammed a Russian vocabulary of upward of a thousand words and was self-confidently fluent in an ungrammatical way. Venturing onto the only form of public transportation available in Kharkov—a fleet of rickety streetcars with passengers packed like sardines and clinging to every conceivable handhold outside—he quickly lost his wallet, his fountain pen, and his cigarettes, all without feeling a thing. Weisskopf told him that he had returned to his room one day to find it stripped of all personal possessions (Alex had miraculously gotten them back for him—the police knew exactly who had done it), and his knapsack had been filched from beneath his head while he was using it as a pillow on a train. But there were comforting explanations for these violations. Poverty was the result of "temporary setbacks" and "difficulties on the collectivization front," and Koestler accepted the convenient fiction that backwardness and crime were either a legacy of the bour-

geois past or an accidental by-product of mistakes made by overzealous officials. If these arguments weren't convincing enough, shortages could always
be blamed on the hostility of the surrounding capitalist powers.[2]

Koestler had thought up a snappy new title for his book, *White Nights and
Red Days,* and his plan was to describe the Soviet Union from its most
northerly to its most southerly point, from the Arctic to the frontiers with
Iran and Afghanistan. Part one would incorporate material he had written
about his *Graf Zeppelin* expedition, part two would depict the achievements
of the five-year plan in Russia and Ukraine, and part three would describe
the successful Sovietization of the backward regions of the Caucasus and
Central Asia. Parts two and three would also form the basis of his articles for
the German news agency.

Traveling to Moscow to get his credentials, he found he needed two documents essential to success: a letter of introduction from the chairman of the
Comintern's agitprop department, an open sesame to the party organizations
along his route; and a declaration from the Commissariat of Foreign Affairs
accrediting him as a bourgeois journalist. The latter guaranteed access to Intourist hotels, the "soft" class on trains, and shopping at the coveted Insnab
stores. Like most western visitors at the time, he saw nothing wrong with this
arrangement. Friends reminded him not to show his journalist's documents
to party officials (for fear they would suspect his bourgeois motives), nor to
reveal his Comintern credentials to hotel and restaurant managers (in case he
lost his bourgeois privileges). He developed a system of keeping the two documents separate: the letter identifying him as a bourgeois journalist nestled
in his right-hand pocket, while the Comintern letter stayed on the left.

HIS FIRST EXPEDITION was down the Volga to visit the cities of Yaroslavl
and Nizhny Novgorod (later Gorky). His goal in these ancient centers of
Russian civilization was not to view the Yaroslavl churches or the famous
Nizhny marketplace but to study S.K.1, the "first factory in the world for the
mass production of synthetic rubber," and "the Russian Detroit," site of the
largest automobile factory in Europe. Both inspired him to lyrical descriptions of retorts, furnaces, condensers, pipelines, conveyor belts, lathes, and assembly lines in his best Ullstein manner, and also gave him an opportunity to
strengthen his ideological convictions. A pilgrimage to the Soviet holy of
holies, the Dnieper Dam, stretched his poetic powers to the limit. "In the
shrill light of the August morning the white semicircular dam offers a supernatural sight. The savage river rears and foams in the throttling grip of this
cement lasso, but in vain: it is overwhelmed, deflected, forced to race through
the pressure chambers where nine flaying turbines drain its accumulated
fury and transform it into electric power." The turbines, he noted, were considerably more powerful than the world's next largest at Niagara Falls, and

the energy they produced would "transform rural Ukraine into an industrial base of the Red Continent, second only in importance to the Urals."[3]

Koestler wrote six such articles while staying at the Hotel Regina in Kharkov and traveled to Moscow to show them to MORP for its approval— he saw nothing wrong at this period in his life with submitting to MORP's oversight and censorship. Otto Bihalj-Merin was the new organizing secretary of MORP, but Otto was absent, and Koestler was taken by Paul Dietrich to meet Sergei Tretyakov, the celebrated author of *Roar, China* and MORP's new chairman. The tall, austere playwright was on record as favoring a more open and welcoming attitude to bourgeois writers but was not impressed by the young journalist from Berlin. Koestler's articles were too romantic for his taste, and too politically naive. They needed more discipline and dialectics.

One reason for Tretyakov's hostility was his dislike of Koestler's patron, Johannes Becher, who had attacked Tretyakov in *Linkskurve* for "formalism" (five years later, Tretyakov would become a victim of the purges and be sent to his death in a labor camp). Koestler stiffly accepted the verdict and, after exercising Bolshevik self-criticism, resubmitted the articles to MORP for approval. This time they were returned without comment, and he took the more moderate ones to the Commisariat of Foreign Affairs to be censored before dispatch to Germany. The head of the press department, Konstantin Umansky, a smooth and ambitious young diplomat, was more welcoming than Tretyakov. He approved the articles with minor cuts and laughingly told Koestler to stay away from the zealots at MORP and stick to his role as a bourgeois correspondent. Life would be easier that way.[4]

KOESTLER'S GOAL WAS TO VISIT the Caucasian republics of Georgia, Armenia, and Azerbaijan and then to tour Central Asia. Along the way he would describe Soviet successes in modernizing and industrializing the more backward regions of the country and draw the necessary political conclusions. In Georgia, the breathtaking beauty of the Caucasus Mountains and the generosity of its people almost swamped his political agenda. Good food, good wine, good scenery, and beautiful women were much more interesting than tractors and collective farms, and it was only when he got to Armenia that he sobered up. In Yerevan he read about the Armenian massacres after World War I, which reminded him of the fate of the Jews in Palestine. Blaming both on "imperialism," he welcomed the coming of Soviet rule as a triumph of progress, "when nationalism was buried on one sixth of the earth."[5]

His last and longest stop in the Caucasus was Baku, the capital of Azerbaijan, where a perplexing romance and a brush with the secret police were to have unforeseen consequences. Koestler knew of Baku as the site of some of the richest oil fields in the world and a famous bone of international contention. It was revered by Communists as the place where Stalin had made his name as a Bolshevik leader and where the Baku commissars had been anointed Communist martyrs after their execution by the British. The city had a proud tradition of rebellion and revolt. Its medieval walls and minarets, moldering casinos and opera houses, palm-lined boulevards and balmy climate signaled Europe crossed with the Middle East, a place thick with mystery and intrigue.

His misadventures began on the train, where he picked up a young woman called Nadezhda Smirnova. Nadezhda had the classic profile and regal posture of a Caucasian princess. She was the niece of a former diplomat, a member of the disgraced upper classes, spoke fluent German, and lived with the diplomat's widow (her aunt) in Baku. Though now a lowly clerk at the Baku waterworks, Nadezhda wasn't shy about being seen in the company of a foreigner, and they launched into a passionate affair. One day, at the Insnab store, Koestler was accosted by an ingratiating young German immigrant called Paul Werner. Werner was crippled, with one shoulder higher than the other and jerky movements, and told Koestler about clashes with the Nazis and a murder he had been involved in as a working-class activist in Germany. The reasons he gave for being in Baku were unconvincing, and Koestler suspected him of spying for the GPU, the secret police. This gave him the notion of trying to do a story on the GPU. He naively went to the GPU headquarters to request an interview but was repulsed by a bulky, unsmiling commissar with a shaven head. Just as Koestler was preparing to leave, a tall, slim officer entered the room, saluted, and treated Koestler to a smile as he gave the first officer some letters to sign. The newcomer's manner was in striking contrast to the other's Prussian stiffness, and he seemed to study Koestler while waiting for the letters to be returned.

When Koestler told Werner about his fruitless visit, Werner laughingly explained that the GPU had played a routine trick on Koestler. The tall officer was the real boss, but had pretended to be a subordinate in order to get a look at the unsuspecting foreigner. Now convinced that Werner worked for the police, Koestler told him about his affair with Nadezhda and tried fishing for information about her elderly aunt, the diplomat's widow. Werner informed him casually that the aunt was "an old spy" and that Nadezhda was under surveillance. After a telegram from Germany was mislaid, Koestler jumped to the conclusion that Nadezhda was to blame and asked Werner to find out more. Perhaps Nadezhda was a foreign agent? Werner returned with the puzzling suggestion that Koestler take Nadezhda with him as an interpreter on the next leg of his journey, but Koestler feared a setup. Was Nadezhda supposed to keep an eye on him? Or he on her? When he refused the offer, Werner responded enigmatically, "You have been tried and found wanting."

Koestler brooded on the incident as he crossed the Caspian Sea by ferry, and wondered if he had in effect betrayed his lover by asking questions about

her. As the day wore on, he became aware of a fiery itch in his groin. It was
the clap, caught from Nadezhda. That such a lovely, refined creature should
be suffering from such a vulgar disease seemed further proof of the malig-
nancy of fate, and he nursed his humiliating affliction as a proper punishment for his betrayal. The incident fed his paranoia and haunted him for
years afterward. It became one of the inspirations for *Darkness at Noon* and
the subject of a fascinating chapter in *The Invisible Writing*.[6]

KOESTLER'S NEXT DESTINATION was Ashkhabad, ostensibly the capital of
the still-new republic of Turkmenistan but little more than a dusty garrison
town squeezed between the Kara-Kum desert and the Iranian border. Its few
amenities didn't include a hotel, and Koestler was whisked off to a GPU
guesthouse for visiting officials. The sole item of furniture in his bedroom
was a steel trestle bed. The room's walls were stained with the corpses of
crushed bedbugs, and it was filled with acrid fumes from a stinking latrine
outside his door. Plunged in deep gloom, he gradually became aware of a familiar sound filtering through his wall. It was jazz—Sophie Tucker belting
out "My Yiddishe Momme"—and seemed so unreal as to border on a hallucination.

Going next door, he encountered the black American poet Langston
Hughes, crouched over his portable Victrola and a collection of jazz records.
Hughes had come to the Soviet Union to make a movie about segregation in
America. The film, *Black and White,* was to have been produced by Willi
Münzenberg's Mezhrabpom company under the auspices of the Comintern,
and Hughes was supposed to write the script, but the project had been
blocked (allegedly by the American government), and Hughes had decided
to write a book about "Soviet negroes" instead. The "negroes" were the dark-
skinned Uzbeks and Turkmens of Central Asia, whose experiences since the
revolution compared so favorably with those of segregated blacks in America. Contrary to what Koestler later wrote, it was Hughes's own idea, not
something fobbed off on him by the Soviet authorities, and he had a contract
that would support him until October. Nor was Hughes as financially desperate as Koestler describes him in *The Invisible Writing,* for the contract supplied him with plentiful funds.[7]

Hughes was as astonished to see Koestler as Koestler was to see him. "The
door opened and an intense-looking young white man, in European clothing, with a sharp face and rather oily dark hair, stepped through the door.
'Excuse me,' I said in Russian as I jumped up, 'I thought you were someone
else. I don't believe I know your name.' 'Arthur Koestler,' he said in English." The two men continued in English, and over camel sausage and
vodka discovered they were in Ashkhabad on similar missions, though with
different agendas and different work habits. Hughes had been in Ashkhabad

book and began writing. Like Mercury, neither dust nor sandstorms kept him from his appointed rounds. I admired Koestler." They ate a meal with the local Baluchis, after which a nurse informed the visitors that 90 percent of the population had syphilis. Back in their guesthouse, Koestler launched into a fury of washing while Hughes crawled into bed. "Syphilis!" Koestler exploded, looking at Hughes. "Ninety percent syphilitic! Why didn't they tell us what we were running into?"[13]

In Bukhara, situated at the center of the huge plain known as the Turanian Basin (the supposed original homeland of the Hungarian people), Koestler was reminded of *Travels in Central Asia* by the famous Hungarian explorer Armin Vambéry, and was himself greeted as "the second Hungarian to visit Central Asia." What most astonished Hughes was Koestler's indifference to the large Jewish population in Bukhara. Intrigued by the Orthodox Jews, with their curled sideburns and black caftans, Hughes enlisted Koestler's help in visiting the old Jewish quarter, so that he could interview rabbis and take notes about Jewish life. Koestler, for once, took no notes at all—a reversal of their usual practice. It seems that that the Bukhara Jews reminded Koestler of the Galician "ghetto Jews" he had so despised in Vienna and Palestine, and it's noteworthy that he doesn't mention them at all in his own descriptions of Bukhara.

An incident described by Hughes but not by Koestler illuminates another aspect of Koestler's attitude toward his fellow Jews. A young Jewish journalist had begged Hughes for his last American pencil as a souvenir, offering a Soviet pencil in return. The Soviet pencil proved useless, and Hughes laughingly complained about it to Koestler. "That's just like a Jew!" exclaimed Koestler. "He tricked you. I'm ashamed. Ashamed! Langston, I'll get your pencil back for you." Although this was his last day, Koestler stormed off, and a few hours later returned with the pencil. "As a negro," Hughes wrote, he identified with Koestler. "I can understand how a member of any race can feel ashamed of his blood brothers' sins before another. But, on the other hand, why should any of us be ashamed to be what we are?"

After traveling apart for a while, Koestler and Hughes met up for the last time in Tashkent. It was November and already cold when Hughes tracked Koestler to his hotel room. Koestler shared his camel sausage with Hughes and again complained about the dirt and the poverty. "People are starving here," he said, "there's a famine." Hughes replied that it couldn't be as bad as Permetyab. Koestler smiled wryly and said: "At least I didn't see a jail there. Here in Tashkent the jails are full of people." "Don't you think some of them belong in jail?" said Hughes. "Not so many," said Koestler. "Not all. Maybe none." Hughes was surprised. He had taken Koestler for a Soviet loyalist, unaware that Koestler saw some parts of the truth quite clearly, even if his bifocals stayed firmly in place.[14]

CHAPTER TEN

ANTI-FASCIST CRUSADER

In exile beds are different.

— MANÈS SPERBER

WITH ALL HIS GOOD INTENTIONS, Koestler's year and a half in the Soviet Union had ineluctably planted the seeds of change. Just as his failed movie script and apprentice play signaled an ambition to look beyond mere journalism in his writing, so did his new subjects—the nature of utopia and the prospects for human happiness—reveal an instinctive dissatisfaction with Soviet reality. During the next few years he would fumble and experiment in a variety of genres (another play, a children's story, a novel) as he explored aspects of morality, truth, and human happiness that would lead him ultimately to Rubashov and the apostasy of *Darkness at Noon*. In the short term, however, he was distracted by the looming threat of fascism. It was a blessing in disguise. The sheer repulsiveness of the Nazis made it easier to set aside his doubts about communism, and he rejoiced at the prospect of throwing himself into the anti-fascist struggle.

Returning to Europe, he began by testing some old networks. In Vienna, he had a nostalgic reunion with his Unitas mentors, von Weisl and Otto Hahn. Ever one to dress the part, Koestler materialized on Hahn's doorstep in Soviet-style knee breeches and cavalry boots, looking for all the world like a commissar returning from a dangerous assignment. Hahn was amused by this fancy dress. Not so von Weisl, who was eager to inform Koestler about the latest feats of construction in Palestine. Koestler dismissed them as "trivial" in comparison with the gigantic new subway system in Moscow. "What a pity you can't see it!"[1]

With the chance of making money off *An Improbable Occurrence* now gone, Koestler and Németh turned to the kind of detective story they had earlier written in Berlin. Working back-to-back at neighboring tables in the Café Japan, Koestler writing in German and Németh in Hungarian, they composed first "The Red Kimono," set in London's Chinatown during the war between China and Japan, and then "The Blue Soap Bubbles," also set in London, about the theft of a diamond ring and its concealment in a bar of blue soap. Both were published in popular booklet form, with only Németh's name on the title page. Their unpublished Berlin story, "Next Customer, Please!" appeared in the same series under Németh's name, followed by a fourth story, "Document 313," which seems to have been by Németh alone. None of these potboilers had the seriousness of *An Improbable Occurrence* or *Mbo Mba,* nor did they contain any threatening political ideas, but they helped Koestler stay afloat financially and were useful exercises in constructing a narrative.[9]

Koestler brought back one other thing from his Budapest visit, picked up at a late-night soirée given by József's analyst, Rappaport. Rappaport quoted a joke from Bergson's book on laughter and asked everyone present to explain why it was funny. Thinking hard, Koestler surmised that the humor resulted from the collision of two distinct frames of reference, when a certain kind of activity was viewed through the framework of a completely different one. It was his first inkling of the concept of bisociation, which became the kernel of both *Insight and Outlook* and *The Act of Creation,* written some fourteen and twenty-four years later, respectively.[10]

KOESTLER LEFT FOR PARIS in September of 1933 and rented a room in a cheap hotel at 54 boulevard de Belleville before starting to work for Willi Münzenberg. There had been a sea change in Europe while Koestler was in the Soviet Union. Not long after Hitler achieved full power in Berlin, the Reichstag had burned to the ground, leading to wholesale reprisals. Hitler held the Communists responsible for the fire and used it as a pretext to ban the German Communist Party, forcing many of its members to go underground. Thousands of them scattered to Moscow, Prague, Vienna, London, New York—and to Paris, where the indefatigable Willi set up an elaborate anti-fascist operation and attempted to rebuild his media empire. Willi's "Trust" had gone from being the third-largest media company in Germany to a mere shadow of its former self, but he was determined to fight back.

The stocky, rough-hewn man who greeted Koestler in his office in the rue Mondétour looked to Koestler more like a lumberjack than a media tycoon. He was no taller than Koestler, but his broad shoulders, powerful head, and shock of unruly hair gave Koestler the impression that bumping into him would be like "colliding with a steamroller." Willi's face had "the forceful simplicity of a woodcut." His Thuringian dialect suggested humble origins, and his flashing gray eyes signaled a man not to be crossed. At forty-four to Koestler's twenty-eight, he was not quite old enough to be Koestler's father, but old enough to seem so, and had a magnetism that swept Koestler away as surely as Jabotinsky's a decade earlier.[11]

Münzenberg was in the midst of unleashing an enormous propaganda barrage to expose Nazi excesses. An extraordinary collection of articles, newspaper clippings, and stolen documents, *The Brown Book of the Reichstag Fire and the Hitler Terror,* published by Willi, had charted in convincing detail the Nazis' suppression of the German trade unions, the banning of the Communist Party, the drive to control education and culture, the infamous book burning of May 1933, the persecution of the Jews, and the establishment of the first concentration camps. The book was intended to undermine the forthcoming trial of a Dutch workman, Marinus van der Lubbe, and four prominent Communists, who were accused of setting the fire, and Münzenberg's World Committee Against War had launched an international committee of inquiry that became the first political countertrial of the twentieth century. Münzenberg was now preparing a second *Brown Book,* and put Koestler to work clipping articles from the British press, tracking debates in the House of Commons, and translating material from English into German.[12]

Willi's offices were a sort of transit camp for German political émigrés. During the next few months, Koestler ran into several of his comrades from Berlin—Manès Sperber, Gustav Regler, Max Schroeder, Hanns Eisler, Alfred Kantorowicz, Bruno Frei, and Bodo Uhse—all of them now working for Münzenberg in one capacity or another. Koestler also met Münzenberg's aristocratic common-law wife, Babette Gross, the daughter of a Potsdam brewer, and her sister, Margarethe (Greta) Buber-Neumann, who had married the German Communist leader Heinz Neumann and gone to Moscow with him after the Nazi crackdown. Babette and Greta were legendary for their beauty and intelligence, two of the many upper-class young women who had turned their backs on their bourgeois families and now endowed the Münzenberg enterprise with a touch of class.[13]

Another such touch was provided by Koestler's editor, Otto Katz, alias André Simon, a Czech Jew and "propagandist of genius." The son of a rich factory owner, the mysterious Otto claimed to have been Marlene Dietrich's first husband. He was Münzenberg's right-hand man and chief of publishing operations, smooth, cosmopolitan, fluent in French, German, English, Russian, and his native Czech, and, if rumors were to be believed, the Comintern's choice to watch and report back on Münzenberg.[14]

Koestler immediately took a liking to the world-weary, cynical Katz, whose devotion to communism went with a towering ambition, not unlike Koestler's own. Katz was of medium height, with a large, "slightly cadaverous" head, sad eyes, a sweet smile, and an intangible air of mystery. He was also, according to Koestler, an "unconscionable flatterer," the sort of man who would take you by the shoulders, lean his head close to yours, and speak in a whisper, as if imparting confidential information, even if the subject was what he'd had for lunch. He was a famous ladies' man, and, unlike Koestler, already a successful author. Oozing self-confidence and charm, he immediately diagnosed Koestler's insecurity. "We all have inferiority complexes of various sizes," he told Koestler, "but yours isn't a complex—it's a cathedral." It was a remark Koestler never forgot, quoting it in his autobiography as a badge of his own sincerity.

The Second Brown Book appeared only weeks after the end of the Reichstag trial and was a masterpiece of black propaganda. Münzenberg's team had created a seamless account of events before, during, and after the trial, and a watertight case for a Nazi conspiracy. An ingenious chart depicted Hermann Göring as the evil genius behind the conspiracy, and an appendix listed "seven hundred and forty-seven proved cases of murder of defenseless persons in Hitler-Germany," most of them in the wake of the fire. Koestler's contribution was a chapter of clippings devoted to press reactions from around the world.[15]

IT WAS A HUMBLE START, and Koestler hoped for better things to follow, but the best Münzenberg could do was ask him to take his clippings and set up an "Anti-Fascist Archive" at the newly established Free German Library. He was rescued from this boring task by the two Hungarian cousins in whose home he had stayed as a schoolboy, Willy and Ferenc Aldor. The suave and unscrupulous Ferenc (Feri to family and friends) had married the daughter of a Hungarian stationer, and had parlayed the stationer's mail-order business into a successful publishing house selling sex manuals on subscription. His big breakthrough had come with Theodoor Van de Velde's *Ideal Marriage: Its Physiology and Technique,* which had sold well over half a million copies and made his fortune. Feri now wanted to publish an encyclopedia of sex and needed a skilled journalist to compile it from existing sources. Would Cousin Arthur like to take it on?

Cousin Arthur would. The project bore a striking similarity to Koestler's work for Münzenberg, only now he would be digesting sex manuals instead of political propaganda, a not unpleasant prospect. The flat fee of three thousand francs was extremely welcome, and the enterprise appealed to his vanity. As a science editor in Berlin he had spent a considerable amount of time at Hirschfeld's Institute of Sexology (which happened to be next door to where Münzenberg lived). His articles on Hirschfeld for *Voss* had been spiked as too risqué for publication, but Koestler retained his fascination with the subject—bolstered, no doubt, by his practical experiments in the field. He proposed a sequel in the form of an "Encyclopedia of Psychic Research" (being even then interested in paranormal phenomena), but Feri's mail order inquiries revealed little interest and the idea was dropped.

Drawing on his knowledge of Freud, Jung, Adler, and Stekel and his reading of Paolo Mantegazza's *Die Hygiene der Liebe* (The Hygiene of Love), Koestler buckled down and finished his part of the book in an astonishing two months. The final product was divided into six parts: the evolution of love, sexual intercourse, procreation, the imperfections of love (homosexuality), sexual aberrations, and venereal diseases, with two appendices on the history of prostitution and "the white slave trade." Koestler was responsible for parts one, two, four, and five. A German specialist, Dr. Levy-Lenz, wrote on procreation and venereal diseases, and Willy Aldor, who was Feri's middleman in Paris, compiled the two appendices. The entire volume was edited by Willy and published in late 1933 as *L'Encyclopédie de la vie sexuelle* (The Encyclopaedia of Sexual Knowledge) by Drs. A. Costler (*sic*) and A. Willy (*sic*).[16]

In his autobiography Koestler dismisses the book as out of date and the English version as "oily and whimsical," betraying the sober German of his original. But he is too hard on himself. For its day, the encyclopedia was bold and progressive, setting out to dispel "the deceit and hypocrisy that burden the physical and spiritual relations of men" and "to tear the veils from false modesty, and to make way for a natural outlook on natural phenomena." Direct personal traces of Koestler's writing in the book are hard to find, except perhaps in the reference to "unfortunate Don Juans whose insatiable desires urge them on from one woman to another" and the insight that during lovemaking, "an ironical remark, whether deliberate or not, can spoil a whole life by inducing a sense of inferiority or neurotic anxiety," a crucial plot point in Koestler's 1946 novel, *Thieves in the Night*. Similar traces can be found, perhaps, in the vivid descriptions of biological principles and physiological processes, to which the experienced hand of the science reporter imparts a verisimilitude beyond the reach of most medical specialists, and in the myriad case histories cited to illustrate the different topics discussed. It was these lubricious tales that presumably drew the Aldor brothers to the subject in the first place and accounted for their enormous sales. As in all such works, the hair-raising accounts of marathon masturbators, insatiable fornicators, bravura transvestites, and ingenious fetishists read like fantastic tales brought back by an intrepid anthropologist from the farther reaches of the South Sea islands, while the sad stories of impotency, frigidity, voyeurism, masochism, pedophilia, and necrophilia, which form a melancholy counterpoint, sound as if directly transcribed from a city doctor's casebook or a psychiatrist's journal.[17]

KOESTLER'S WORK AT THE Free German Library was doubly dull by comparison with this racy subject matter. The library had opened on May 10, 1934, on the first anniversary of the infamous burning of the books by the Nazi regime, with Alfred Kantorowicz in charge. Heinrich Mann was honorary president; H. G. Wells, André Gide, Romain Rolland, and Lion Feuchtwanger figured among its international sponsors. The library's purpose was partly symbolic—to show that there was a German cultural center outside the Nazis' control—and also practical: It was a club where exiled German writers could meet to talk and keep up with the latest gossip.[18]

Bored with his clippings and disappointed that he was no longer working directly for Münzenberg, Koestler began to languish. Being around German émigré writers wasn't much comfort, for to them he was a nonentity. He had attempted to sell Red Days to French publishers without success. He had also recast An Improbable Occurrence in the form of a story and submitted it for a literary competition, but again in vain. No one was interested in his work, and in his own eyes he was even more of a failure than ever. Then Münzenberg, once again, reached out and moved him on his anti-fascist chessboard. One of Willi's many projects was a home for refugee children in Maisons-Laffitte, a suburb just north of Paris. Some thirty children between the ages of two and sixteen were housed in a villa donated by a charitable Frenchman, but the home was chronically short of money, and Münzenberg asked Koestler to visit the place and write a fund-raising pamphlet to be distributed to sympathizers.

Koestler wasn't thrilled by this prospect. He knew nothing of children, and when he arrived at the bleak villa on the edge of the forest, an epidemic of diphtheria was ravaging its undernourished charges. The home was run by a spectacularly incompetent, multinational staff of five, with no training in social work or education, who were greatly relieved when the diphtheria outbreak subsided without their intervention. In the casual way of such institutions, Koestler was asked to stay on and lend a helping hand. His heart was touched by the plight of the sick and neglected children, and since he had nowhere else in particular to go, he enlisted as a temporary teacher. His duties were to hold a class for the youngest children and put them to bed, edit the weekly wall newspaper, teach Russian to the two eldest boys in the home, and take his turn with the cleaning and cooking.

The French authorities had been told that this was a simple home for German refugee children of all kinds. In fact they were the children of Communist activists in Germany, some of whom had already died in action. Other activists were operating clandestinely under false identities. For security reasons, the children were not allowed to use their own names but had aliases, prefixed by the appellation "comrade," as did members of the staff. Koestler reverted to his party name of Ivan Steinberg and was known to everyone as "Comrade Ivan." The home was modeled on the Soviet orphanages of the twenties made famous by Anton Makarenko's celebrated memoir *The Road to Life*. As in Makarenko's orphanage, adult staff members were known as "Chaldeans" and played a mainly advisory role. Discipline among the children was maintained by a collective of the older students, which met every day both as an administrative unit and as a kind of court sitting in judgment on children who broke the regulations. Koestler had never seen anything like it before, but was captivated by the phenomenon.

> Children were a new and fascinating discovery for me; I was thrown into their alien universe, with its private laws of logic and subterranean sensitivities, like a traveller in Mbo-Mba-Land, without dictionary or guide, reduced to making contacts by gesture and grin. But contact was made easier by the fact that I had actually lived in Russia where none of the other "Chaldeans" had been . . . and also by my own infantile streak and passion for inventing games, which a frustrated childhood had left behind.[19]

Koestler saw an opportunity in his experiences to revive his literary dreams, and and spent about two months taking notes and creating a rough outline, before writing *Die Erlebnisse des Genossen Piepvogel und seine Freunde in der Auswänderung* (The Adventures of Comrade Dickybird and His Friends in the Emigration), a young-adult novel in three parts and twenty-one chapters. Like everything else he had written so far, the work was heavily influenced by the tenets of socialist realism, which mandated a plethora of realistic social detail and an uplifting progressive message. As part of his documentary technique, Koestler incorporated pages from the home's wall newspaper as well as autobiographical essays by some of the children.

The novel has survived in typescript among Koestler's papers and is interesting for its development of some of the themes adumbrated in *An Improbable Occurrence* and *Mbo Mba*. The novel chronicles the experiences of a young Jewish boy, Peter Pochevsky (the "Comrade Dickybird" of the title), whose family has placed him in an orphanage after fleeing the Nazis. Peter is socially eclipsed by a clever and insecure young cynic called Ullrich, who becomes the mouthpiece for some of Koestler's doubts about collectivism and the Communist utopia. Ullrich questions every decision made by the administrative committee and pours scorn on the conformity of his fellow boarders. Piet, the sixteen-year-old son of a Hamburg stoker killed by the Nazis, stands up to Ullrich and succeeds in getting him temporarily expelled. Piet is the voice of the proletariat, strong, self-confident, and politically correct. Ullrich is an individualist from a bourgeois background, self-doubting and insecure—with many of his creator's characteristics: "At times I feel literally stifled and choked by loneliness. For instance, I am sitting alone in a room reading a book. The others are playing in the garden. Suddenly I stop reading. The air around me begins to vibrate. The whole room trembles with loneliness. It is saturated with loneliness like a chemical solution. My nerves swell with it like capillary tubes. It penetrates into my stomach and heart like an acid. It pumps tears into my eyes like acrid fumes."

This is from Ullrich's journal. Other entries reflect both the youthful and the more mature Koestler. "It drives me mad that my mother must be right after all. She's right, I don't belong to them. I feel an alienation that can't be overcome. Before someone answers a question I already know the answer, and everything else he will say after that. I don't despise them after learning about Marxism, but they bore me to tears. They think so slowly that you can hear the wheels turning as in an old steeple clock, whereas I go tick-tock like a chronometer." Another passage in the novel shows Ullrich wrestling with some of the same riddles as the youthful Koestler. A diary can never be free of play-acting, he concludes, because the author is both "writer and reader at the same time," and he knows that his words are intended to be read by others. "Self-knowledge is like an algebraic progression that converges in infinity."

Ullrich's doubts are provisionally resolved by Assistant Professor Moll, a sociologist, who is an orthodox Marxist. "The bourgeoisie faces backward," he tells Ullrich, whereas members of the proletariat are automatically born with their faces turned toward the future. "The future of history belongs to the others, not us." "But what about justice?" asks Ullrich. "Justice is nothing other than the projection of the next stage of history into the past," replies the tutor glibly. "The moral truths of the prophets come not from heaven, but from anticipation of the future."[20]

Koestler seems to have written the novel to try to resolve his doubts about the Communist utopia. He submitted it to a competition organized by Emil Oprecht, who ran a kind of German Left Book Club in Switzerland, and to a left-wing German publisher in the Netherlands. He also arranged to read excerpts to the recently formed Association of German Writers in Exile. The association was supposed to be politically neutral, except for its obvious opposition to Hitler's fascism, but in a pattern pioneered by Münzenberg and increasingly endorsed by Moscow, its policy was heavily influenced by a secret caucus of Communist writers, who held their own separate meetings in order to "steer" the organization in the right direction.[21]

This caucus included most of Koestler's Berlin comrades: Kantorowicz, Regler, Schroeder, Bihalj-Merin, Eisler, Frei, Uhse, Balder Olden, Alfred Kurella, Egon Irwin Kisch, and the beautiful Anna Seghers, looking for all the world like "an Indonesian farmer's wife," according to Bihalj-Merin.

Koestler's friend Johannes Becher and the Comintern representative, Willi Bredel, also attended the caucus meetings from time to time, and the elusive Brecht occasionally dropped in from his hideout in Copenhagen.[22]

The reading took place in the basement of the aptly named Café Mephisto, a bistro on the boulevard St.-Germain, with huge gilt mirrors on the walls and silver-blue soda siphons arrayed on the counter. As fumes of coffee, brandy, and cigarette smoke circulated through the cavernous room, the youthful-looking Koestler read nervously from his manuscript, seemingly unaware of the ominous silence in the room. The following day he was summoned to a caucus meeting and informed that his book contained "ideological errors." Otto Abusch, the Central Committee's official delegate to the caucus, rightly smelled autobiography in Ullrich's bourgeois complaints about the proletariat and was not convinced by Moll's ingenious recipe for self-transformation. There was too much Freud and not enough Marx in Koestler's analysis of the social evils of capitalism. His multiple references to adolescent sexuality (a fruit, perhaps, of his encyclopedia reading and writing) offended Abusch's puritanical instincts, while the book's playful treatment of conflicts between the children was "frivolous" in the context of the struggle between the international working class and fascism.

Koestler's shaky self-confidence collapsed in the face of this onslaught, and though he tried to reject the accusations, no one spoke in his defense. Kisch argued for tolerance on the grounds of Koestler's ideological inexperience, and Koestler was humbly grateful to the older man for defending him. He was unaware that Kisch fully shared Abusch's negative view of the novel. "He's a bourgeois and no Communist," Kisch had said to his comrades after the reading. "But he's conceited and very touchy about it, and you have to be very careful around him." The association's chairman, Hans Dammert, said the novel's distortions were so serious that they would have to be referred to "higher instances." The Swiss book club awarded Koestler a small prize in the competition it was running, but there was no offer of money or publication; and if the party was against the book, there was no chance of anyone in Paris accepting it either. It was a foretaste of things to come.[23]

KOESTLER WRITES THAT he was so upset by this rejection that he made a halfhearted attempt at suicide. The scene he describes (an open gas tap, a book falling onto his nose) is suspiciously reminiscent of a failed suicide attempt in the fictional *Comrade Dickybird,* but, according to Koestler, it was a rare instance of life imitating art. Koestler's depressive temperament made him vulnerable to uncontrollable mood swings, and that summer he was feeling personally rejected as well. While working in the Free German Library he had fallen for a chestnut-haired typist with an oval face and bluishgreen eyes called Dorothee Ascher. Like Babette Gross, Dorothee came from a well-to-do family and had turned against her privileged upbringing. She had a diploma in social science from the Berlin Academy of Politics and Social Sciences and was trained in Freudian psychology, with a specialty in family welfare and child guidance, but it was impossible to do this work now, and since the ascent of the Nazis Dorothee was content to serve the cause in any way possible.[24]

It's likely that Koestler met Dorothee through Otto Bihalj-Merin, who was married to Dorothee's elder sister, Liselotte. Koestler was intrigued by Dorothee's reserve and self-control, yet sensed in her coiled manner a boldness and mischievousness that was not immediately apparent to others. Dorothee, apart from the physical attraction, warmed to Koestler's passionate commitment to ethical values and was impressed by his formidable knowledge of Marx and Freud. Added to his fiery temperament and extraordinary charm, it made him irresistible to the shy and cerebral social worker.[25]

They had a number of things in common: a bourgeois upbringing that both had rejected, difficult relationships with their mothers, and a complex and critical attitude toward their Jewishness, Dorothee because she had been raised as a Christian after her father converted to Protestantism, and Koestler because he had recoiled from Zionism without finding a Jewish substitute. Both, of course, had found an emotional and intellectual refuge in the party, and both looked to communism to resolve their psychological and political dilemmas. Dorothee moved into Koestler's hotel room for a while and was paying the rent for both of them, but he proved so difficult that she soon moved out again, leaving Koestler penniless and apparently suicidal. Fifty years later, Dorothee couldn't remember the incident of the attempted suicide, but she did remember hearing Koestler say he wanted to die. She thought he was being melodramatic and didn't believe him.[26]

It wasn't long before Koestler was homeless as well. He was rescued by the German novelist Georg Glaser, who took him back to his tent in a nature colony in Meudon-Val-Fleury, just south of the city, owned by a wealthy Swiss eccentric and Communist sympathizer whose code name was "Paul." Koestler then migrated to a bed in a hayloft on the property and was saved from starvation by the providential arrival of Otto Bihalj-Merin from Moscow.[27]

Otto informed Koestler conspiratorially that he had been charged with running a new organization, the Institute for the Study of Fascism (INFA), and that he was no longer known by his old nom de guerre of Otto Biha, but as Peter Merin. The subterfuge struck Koestler as needlessly theatrical, but Otto was leading a semiunderground existence as a functionary of the Comintern and needed some sort of cover. That INFA was a Comintern enterprise was a secret, and the institute was expected to raise funds within France to finance itself. There was no money for salaries, but the party would take care of Métro fares and offer free lunches in the institute's kitchen. Otto asked Koestler to direct the publications program.[28]

INFA's offices, next to the Jardin des Plantes, were furnished with cheap trestle tables, folding chairs, and a number of ancient typewriters and were never as grand as the name "institute" suggested, though its ambitious goals included "ideological struggle against the threat posed to civilization by fascism" and "a systematic study of all fascist movements with regular publication of its results." The staff consisted of Otto, Koestler, a children's book author named Kurt Kläber, a translator named René, and three young German women, spearheaded by a banker's daughter, Ilse Schreiber, whose exotic features quickly earned her the sobriquet of "the Nefertiti of the Kurfürstendamm" (her name for Koestler was "My Little Turk"). Walter Benjamin lectured on "The Author as Producer" under the auspices of INFA shortly before Koestler got there, and it may have been where the two men met before they became neighbors. Koestler was supposed to be responsible for publishing a "weekly bulletin, published in several languages," along with press releases, brochures, lectures, and books on fascism's "racial theories, economic foundations, religious policies, ideology, and relations with democracy." So far as can be determined, he managed just four issues of the bulletin in his two years there, plus one book and one brochure.[29]

Part of the reason for this low productivity was that Koestler was obliged to write most of the contents of the bulletin himself. In one he provided an analysis of the "social and national problems in Yugoslavia" that reads as if it had been written yesterday; another contained an analysis of "science and fascism," accusing the German scientific community of "prostituting itself" and "committing suicide" by refusing to oppose the Nazi regime. More significant was a series of six articles he wrote for the felicitously named French daily *L'Intransigeant* (The Intransigent). A note identifying the anonymous author as "a German opponent of National Socialism who cannot be named without exposing him and his relatives to even worse repression" was a convenient lie in the spirit of Red propaganda and well beyond what was allowed in the INFA bulletin itself.[30]

Koestler set out to convince his readers that there was a vast "Underground Germany" (the collective title of the series) that was seething with the spirit of revolt and insurrection against the National Socialist government. The leaders of this insurrection were Communists, whose illegal methods of operation dated from as early as 1931–32 (that is, when Koestler himself was still in Germany). Unlike the Social Democrats, who insisted on using only legal methods, the Communists had been prepared when the Nazis came to power and therefore enjoyed "uncontested hegemony in the underground," as well as the silent support of "millions of passive allies" inside Germany and "the sympathy of the entire world."[31]

In three following articles, "What a Conspirator Needs to Know," "The Illegal Press," and "Conspiratorial Techniques," Koestler described the organizational and propaganda methods of the party as it was supposed to be operating inside Germany. Drawing freely on internal party documents, he displayed a stunningly convincing attention to detail, implying that he was letting readers into the inner workings of a truly secret world. The "documents" were genuine, in that they had been produced by the party in Moscow, but they were the products of wishful thinking, for the Communist Party in Germany had been decimated by the Nazis and was barely able to function. Moreover, the "huge, passive majority" of ordinary Germans was moving not left but firmly right and into the Nazi camp.

Koestler was thoroughly enjoying himself and exuded boundless political optimism at the time. "Georgie," he said patronizingly to Glaser, "it's time for you to rejoin the party." Later, after the "night of the long knives," when Hitler liquidated Ernst Röhm and his brownshirts, Koestler exclaimed, "Georgie, in one or two years we'll be home." Manès Sperber was brought into INFA at this time as its "ideological leader" and was amazed by Koestler's ardent communism. In Berlin he had taken him for a dilettante and still knew nothing of Koestler's Soviet visit. But he soon saw through Koestler's public bravado. "His boyish face was unchanged, but for the first time I noticed his lips, which were by turns sensually parted and then mockingly or anxiously pinched. His lower lip invariably trembled after he had made an especially aggressive or deprecating remark about someone. There was a contradiction in his blue eyes as well: they reflected mockery and self-irony, and then, suddenly, an uncommon sensitivity and fear of deception and disappointment, fear that a pain one cannot prepare for could destroy one's strength to bear it."

It was the start of a genuine friendship between the two men. Sperber came to prize Koestler's instinctive honesty and candor. "After he had given up dramatizing himself for at least an hour, his real nature, no longer blocked, became visible, and with it his striving for inner integrity, to use a phrase alien to him but hard to replace." And Koestler appreciated Sperber's levelheadedness and analytic temperament, regarding him as the only friend he could trust enough to confide in.[32]

KOESTLER'S DAYS WERE LONG. He would rise in Meudon-Val-Fleury at seven thirty in the morning and walk the three kilometers to the Métro terminal to save the fare. After a ten-hour workday, he returned the same way, purchasing bread and lard on the way home with the money he had saved. He was kept from starving by the thick, nourishing soups, plentiful ham and cheese, baguettes, and cheap red wine and coffee dished out in INFA's spacious kitchen. Although the conspiratorial Otto insisted on everyone having pseudonyms (Koestler was again Comrade Ivan, Kläber was Comrade Max, and Sperber was Comrade Paul), the atmosphere was extremely casual. People ate standing up or sitting down or walking about. The talk was intense and mostly political, and would continue far into the night.[33]

Koestler proposed holding an international anti-fascist exhibition in one of the huge pavilions of the annual Paris fair at the Porte de Versailles, with public rallies, lectures by internationally famous writers and intellectuals, and a standing exhibition of books, documents, and displays illustrating the horrors of fascism. The project was absurdly ambitious, and though INFA set up an organizing committee to approach French intellectuals for help (including André Malraux, whom Koestler met for the first time), few actually gave money, and an emissary arrived from Moscow to close the project down.[34]

In his autobiography Koestler suggests that INFA had become too unorthodox for Moscow to tolerate, and blames the Moscow emissary "Comrade Jan" for setting out to tame it. There was some truth in this. Comrade Jan was Hans Meins, alias Jan Jansen, secretary-general of the League of Proletarian Freethinkers and a cofounder of INFA with Bihalj-Merin. He was a strict organization man sent to introduce some modicum of discipline and financial rigor into INFA's freewheeling ways. Plodding and dour, he had little in common with the philosophical Sperber, the sprightly Bihalj-Merin, or the emotional Koestler, and was excluded from their passionate discussions after hours. With the authority of the party behind him, however, he instituted regular meetings and tried to tighten discipline. In the interest of efficiency, he took the exhibition project away from Bihalj-Merin and Koestler, and Koestler resigned in a fit of anger.[35]

Soon afterward INFA closed its doors, but Meins was not quite as crude and dogmatic as Koestler painted him. He was later recalled to Moscow and ended up in a labor camp. The fact was that INFA duplicated the work being done by Willi Münzenberg and his associates, and there are grounds for thinking that it had been deliberately established by the Comintern to weaken Willi's influence. But Willi had outmaneuvered the Comintern, and it was probably he who was responsible for getting INFA closed. Although Willi's star was beginning to wane, it would be another five years before he experienced his own reckoning with Moscow.[36]

CHAPTER ELEVEN

MARKING TIME

Lying to ourselves is more deeply ingrained in us than lying to others.

— FYODOR DOSTOYEVSKY

RESIGNING FROM INFA wasn't hard for Koestler. He was back with Dorothee Ascher, and she was now willing to support him. She was working for Münzenberg as a part-time librarian in his Free German Library, and she also received a modest monthly allowance from her mother. Koestler was still practically penniless, earning only an occasional honorarium as a freelance, and they rented a room in the rickety Hôtel de la Paix on the Île St.-Louis, poor but evidently happy. Their closest friends were Bihalj-Merin and Sperber, and Dorothee remembered long, happy nights over cheap carafes of wine arguing endlessly about politics and the anti-fascist cause. Their sense of solidarity was sealed by the "radical indifference" of the surrounding French population, whose attitude Koestler described as "impersonal and chilling." Sperber took a more cheerful view, feeling that their joint isolation engendered a "peculiar holiday mood" and guaranteed them "a personal freedom that was hardly known elsewhere."[1]

It wasn't long before Koestler went back to work for Münzenberg himself. Willi urgently needed an emissary to the Saarland to help the Communists influence a plebiscite on whether the region should join Germany, join France, or remain a protectorate of the League of Nations. Koestler spent about a month there editing and writing a satirical weekly, *Die Saar-Ente* (The Saar Duck), so called in homage to the famous Parisian satirical paper *Le Canard Enchaîné* (The Chained Duck). Only one issue actually appeared—on January 6, 1935—with a caricature of Joseph Goebbels on the front page and a mixture of cartoons, doggerel, and satirical articles inside. Koestler wrote an article, "The Sphinx of Saarbrücken," for Leopold Schwarzschild's progressive but non-Communist *Das Neue Tagebuch* (The New Diary), predicting that the plebiscite would produce a two-thirds majority against the Nazis, but he was totally deluded. With a turnout of nearly 100 percent, 90 percent of the electorate voted for reunion with Germany. There was a huge Nazi victory parade on the Sunday following the vote, and the Communist activists in the protectorate, including Koestler, were obliged to run for their lives.[2]

He and Dorothee then set off for Switzerland. Dorothee's brother, Ernst, had been refused a residence permit by the Swiss authorities because of his membership in the Communist Party and was moving to the Soviet Union. Ernst told Dorothee that she and Koestler could live in his Zurich apartment rent-free until the lease ran out if they moved fast. Dorothee was able to use her allowance for their fares, and Koestler persuaded Willy Aldor to pay him one hundred Swiss francs a month for twelve months as an advance against a novel he had just started.[3]

The novel, a distant sequel to *An Improbable Occurrence* and *The Adventures of Comrade Dickybird,* was the fruit of Koestler's continuing to brood on the nature of political revolutions and the conditions necessary for their success. His subject this time was Spartacus and his celebrated slave revolt in the first century B.C. Spartacus had raised an army of seventy thousand men and had repeatedly defeated the Roman army before being overwhelmed and crucified after two years of warfare. Koestler was hardly the first to have his imagination fired by this story. Jabotinsky had translated an Italian novel on Spartacus into Hebrew, and Brecht had started a play on the subject as early as 1918. Spartacus was an obvious subject for students and lovers of revolution, and was a particular favorite with artists and writers who supported the Russian Revolution of 1917.

The advantages of the project for Koestler were that they grounded him in a particular historical era and subject matter, while allowing him the requisite distance from his own experiences (unlike in *Comrade Dickybird*) to tell the story impersonally and concentrate on its political meaning. For months now he had been spending his free days at the Bibliothèque Nationale, researching political and economic conditions in the Roman Empire during the first century B.C., and had discovered vivid parallels with his own century: mass movements and social unrest, rapid economic development, high unemployment, a corrupt and decadent ruling class, and colonialism. But the central question that fascinated him was why the uprising had failed to bear fruit. Why had Spartacus failed where Lenin, say, had succeeded?

Koestler supposed that Spartacus's primitive socialism must have sprung from utopian longings, and wondered if there was an intellectual link between the dreams of the Spartacists and the messianism of the Hebrew prophets—perhaps through Syrian intermediaries (though Koestler's Zionism was in abeyance, it still surfaced in odd ways). In formulating his approach Koestler was inspired by the historical novels of Lion Feuchtwanger and Thomas Mann, and especially by Alfred Döblin's *The Three Steps of Wang Lun,* about a mythical uprising in China.

THE ZURICH APARTMENT proved positively luxurious by Paris standards, and Koestler settled down to write. He had been warned not to seek formal contact with the Swiss Communist Party, for the Swiss police were much stricter than the French in supervising suspicious foreigners—as the treatment of Dorothee's brother demonstrated. But Bihalj-Merin was already there, and Koestler was quickly introduced to the "Humm circle," a group of radical intellectuals meeting weekly at the home of the left-wing Swiss novelist Rudolf Jakob Humm. Humm had founded a literary society called the New Russia, and people who read there included Erika and Klaus Mann, Bernard von Brentano, Bihalj-Merin, Hans Marchwitza, a young Hungarian playwright called Julius Hay, and Ignazio Silone. Silone was a celebrity due to the publication of his first big novel, *Fontamara,* but came irregularly, owing to his tuberculosis. Koestler admired *Fontamara* and was looking forward to meeting Silone, but found him "kind, but very reserved" and very much "wrapped up in himself, surrounded by a soft but impenetrable cloud of melancholy and depression." He was unable to establish any kind of rapport with Silone, a failure that was to be repeated when the two men met again after World War II.[4]

Unable to see the irony (after his experience at the Café Mephisto), Koestler joined Bihalj-Merin and Hay in forming a party caucus within the Humm circle, gathering separately to hammer out their "line" before each meeting. Koestler liked the tall, dark Hay very much. The son of wealthy Hungarians who had lost everything in the Hungarian revolution of 1919, Hay had taught agitprop at the Marxist Workers' College in Berlin and had briefly met Koestler there. Hay was now writing a play set in the Hungarian countryside and frequently consulted Koestler about his literary problems, while Koestler sought Hay's advice on the political conundrums posed by his treatment of first-century B.C. Rome. Hay was also the person Koestler consulted when he and Dorothee decided to get married.[5]

The wedding was held on June 22 in the Zurich town hall and was a double-barreled affair. Hay's girlfriend, Micky, was pregnant, and they decided to marry at the same time. The only other people present were Humm and his wife, Lilly, who lent first the Hays and then the Koestlers their rings for the wedding ceremony. Koestler later maintained that his marriage was a matter of pure convenience. He had married Dorothee, he said, to help replace her German passport with a Hungarian one. "To save our self-respect, the marriage had to remain a reluctant passport affair." But the reluctance was all on Koestler's side. Dorothee was deeply in love with him and thought he felt the same about her. Well aware of his earlier promiscuity, she expected him to change after marriage and looked forward to a normal, mutually supportive relationship with children ("four," she specified in a later interview), but Koestler was dead set against having children. Fixated on the unhappiness of his own childhood, he perversely insisted he never wanted to be the cause of grief in another child.[6]

In other ways Koestler was a traditionalist in marriage. A woman should devote her time to typing, cooking, and looking after her husband's needs, and give up all idea of a separate career. To have children in such a marriage would seem entirely logical, but Koestler was adamant. He also argued that he was "unable" to change from the sexually voracious and promiscuous skirt chaser that he had been at twenty-five. Significantly, he interrupts the brief account of his marriage to Dorothee in his autobiography to reminisce about the "gay and irrepressible Nefertiti" of his INFA days, who turned up in Zurich that summer. Another digression concerns a "striking" and "beautiful" young woman called Helena, which has all the hallmarks of a Freudian slip. His and Dorothee's marriage (unlike that of the Hays) was not a success. Koestler resented her independent ways, while Dorothee resisted his demands that she subordinate herself to him.[7]

KOESTLER SOON GOT AN EXCUSE to run off again. Willy Aldor came to Switzerland to tell him the deal for the Spartacus book was off but they would pay him the same sum to write another sex book instead. The subject this time was "sexual anomalies and perversions," and it would require a trip to Budapest. Koestler went willingly enough, and was happy to renew links with József and Németh. József was getting psychiatric treatment for depression and would sometimes stare wildly and uncomprehendingly at Koestler, but Koestler never suspected that within months of their parting he would commit suicide. Németh had married Judit Szegő, one of his many mistresses, and opened a copy shop. He published a popular biography of Empress Maria Theresa, and Koestler exhorted him to write something more serious, but sensed that "with all his sloth and indolence," Németh lived closer than he to "the things that really mattered" and that, "in some devious way, his passive acceptance made more sense than my kickings and strugglings in the net."[8]

Koestler spent most of his time in his hotel room in Budapest dictating the entire text of Sexual Anomalies and Perversions at breakneck speed to the pretty young wife of a Budapest psychiatrist. Repelled by the distasteful nature of the subject matter, he got none of the vicarious pleasure he had experienced in writing the sexual descriptions for his earlier encyclopedia, and his young typist skillfully deflected his advances. It was a tense, frustrated, and virtually penniless Koestler who traveled not to Zurich, to be reunited with Dorothee, but to Lugano, to spend a month as the guest of Maria Klöpfer. Maria was the daughter of a wealthy Rhineland industrialist and former wife of the German movie star Eugen Klöpfer, a wealthy fellow traveler who made generous contributions to Communist causes and liked to invite impecunious Communist writers to her luxurious lakeside villa to assuage her loneliness. Bihalj-Merin and Becher had both stayed there, and Koestler's plan was to take advantage of her hospitality to work on his Spartacus novel.

The chapter that Koestler devotes to his stay with Maria in *The Invisible Writing* reads like a first-rate short story in itself. Maria gave Koestler the upper floor of her small villa, and they met for meals, walks, and excursions to a local trattoria. In the early mornings Koestler and Maria would have swimming races to an island in the middle of the lake and lie panting side by side to get their breath back. Koestler had mentally written off Maria sexually because of her age and unattractive face: the braces on her teeth canceled the lure of her lean, sinewy body lying a few inches from his, though he was agonizingly aware of her breasts, and of the long, suntanned limbs emerging from her bathing suit. Maria paid all Koestler's bills, even for toothpaste, postage stamps, and other sundries. She also paid for their drinks at the trattoria, and Koestler got it into his head that the local residents regarded him as a gigolo. He told Maria she should give him a sum of money in advance and allow him to pay the bill, thus preserving his amour-propre, but she lost her temper and told him he should be above such prejudices. "You have the vanity to give, but you lack the generosity to take."

Maria told Koestler that she had been sexually abused by an uncle when a small child, which had caused her to suffer hallucinations and several nervous breakdowns, and to divorce her first husband when he, too, started mistreating her. Koestler concluded that Maria was in love with him, and toyed with the idea of responding, but still couldn't get past her physical unattractiveness. Meanwhile, they argued incessantly about free will and determinism. Despite her sympathy for Marxism, Maria was superstitious. She dabbled in Buddhism and Eastern mysticism, believed in poltergeists, and persuaded a reluctant Koestler to join her in psychic experiments, such as table lifting. Outwardly he was scathing. He was a scientific materialist who saw the world as "a clockwork mechanism which, once it had somehow been wound up, would forever follow its course predestined by Newton's laws." But he recognized that Maria was emotionally wiser than he. She had at once seen through "the smirk and the brilliantine" to Koestler's inferiority complex. "You have been kicked about so much that your whole inner surface is raw and sore, and when something touches you, you wince," she said on one occasion, though Koestler later concluded that his extreme sensitivity to their arguments owed more than a little to the fact that his materialist faith had also begun to crumble.

The tension between them exploded after Maria asked him to forget his work for a while and go swimming with her during the day, a favor she usually did not ask, for she was an extremely proper and polite woman and rarely impinged on him. Koestler complied, but complained so much about it that they descended into a raging quarrel about free will, during which Koestler worked himself up into such a "frenzy of resentment, vulgar envy, meanness and cruelty" that he threatened to throw her beautiful soup tureen through a plate-glass window. If she admitted that there was no free will, he said, he would put it down; if not, he would smash both tureen and window.

Maria backed down, but the atmosphere between them grew so tense that Koestler persuaded her to invite Németh to join them on the pretext that he and Koestler could continue with their detective stories. Németh arrived and the situation only got worse: Koestler grew insanely jealous of Németh and abruptly announced his departure. Trembling and weeping, Maria put her long, thin arms around his neck and kissed his temple in farewell, sending a surge of relief through him, as if she had forgiven him. Some weeks later she suffered another hallucination and a seizure worse than any before and was committed to an insane asylum. A few months later she was dead.

Koestler felt that he had failed her in her hour of need. "Maria was fighting what seemed to be a winning battle against the powers of insanity. I did not realize it at the time, and I was unaware of the part that I was playing in it. I thus missed the opportunity of saving her. For a brilliant and hyper-sensitive young man, I was remarkably stupid where others were concerned." Maria came to stand beside Nadezhda in Baku as an example of a woman he had needlessly deserted and betrayed. His capacity for self-flagellation undoubtedly contributed to his sense of guilt, but the real tragedy lay in his incapacity for unconstrained love and spontaneous generosity. Twenty years later, he still thought of the relationship in terms of cause and effect: his coldness as the cause, and Maria's death as the effect. In truth, the episode encapsulated both his imprisonment inside a capricious ego and his almost total inability to reach out emotionally to another person, even when that person was in distress.[9]

KOESTLER TOOK THE TRAIN back to Paris to meet up with Dorothee (who knew nothing of this latest adventure), and moved with her to 6 bis rue du Chevalier de la Barre, a steep, narrow street leading up to the famous Basilica of Montmartre in the Eighteenth Arrondissement. The unfamiliar task of writing a historical novel proved difficult, and he was constantly distracted by the need to earn extra cash as a freelance. In the course of the next few months he turned *An Improbable Occurrence* into a novella, wrote a chapter on Paris for a British travel guide, translated an English novel into German for Münzenberg, and prepared news digests for an obscure press agency run by a Hungarian exile named Alexander Rado. Rado, a short, rotund man with an absentminded, scholarly manner, had an obsession with maps and cartography that successfully concealed his true work as director of the Red Army's European spy network in Switzerland. He was dispatched to the Gulag after World War II, but survived to return to Hungary and write a book about his experiences.[10]

Koestler had continued to write occasional book reviews for *Das neue Tagebuch.* In an article on Julien Green's *Le Visionnaire* (The Dreamer), he weighed the merits of an individualistic, psychological approach to art (as practiced by Green, James Joyce, and Marcel Proust) against the virtues of social realism. Citing Malraux's revolutionary paradox, "A man's life is worth nothing, but nothing is worth a man's life," Koestler insisted yet again that it had to be possible to reconcile the two extremes, that individual psychology had a meaning, but only in the context of history. In another review Koestler reformulated the problem as art versus propaganda. Were they mutually exclusive, or was it possible to have both? Koestler cited Piscator as having "assimilated the great art of highlighting the microscopic detail while not losing sight of the whole." The great Russian movies had shown that "an avalanche was made up of glittering individual molecules" and that each molecule was a part of the avalanche.[11]

Profiling Kisch (and obviously still unaware of Kisch's part in his censure by the party), Koestler compared the "racing reporter" to the "best of the bourgeois reporters," H. R. Knickerbocker. Koestler admired Knickerbocker's recent attack on the Soviet Union's five-year plans, *The Red Trade Menace,* not because he agreed with it but because the methodology was so beautifully worked out. Like Kisch, Knickerbocker was promoting a message, and his strict discipline in interpreting it was what made his work so persuasive. Kisch also understood that there was no such thing as objective reportage: "Facts are only the reporter's ocean; in making his voyage he needs the compass of a logical imagination." It was true that a good reporter needed to have a working knowledge of politics, economics, psychology, and history, but without a weltanschauung, a firm point of view, he would simply swim with the tide and entertain the reader. This was Koestler's credo, and would inform all the nonfiction he wrote from then on.[12]

KOESTLER WAS STILL STRUGGLING FINANCIALLY. *Comrade Dickybird* had earned him an honorable mention and a small monetary prize from the Gutenberg Book Guild but had not been chosen for publication, and he would have run out of money again had Münzenberg not come up with an other commission. Münzenberg had admired Koestler's satirical talent in *Die Saar-Ente* and asked him if he would like to try his hand at a sequel to *The Good Soldier Svejk*, setting it this time in a future war triggered by Hitler. *Svejk* was a highly popular work in Communist circles. Brecht had helped dramatize the novel for a sensational production by Piscator in Berlin in 1928, and a Russian translation in three volumes was enjoying enormous success in the Soviet Union. With the advance Münzenberg paid him, Koestler and Dorothee moved for the summer to the Belgian seaside town of Bredene, "a cheap resort where you can get away from it all," according to Stefan Zweig, and extremely popular with the German exile community.

Kisch himself turned up, fresh from a triumphal visit to Australia (since Kisch had been a drinking companion of Jaroslav Hašek in Prague, this seemed like a particularly good omen). Joseph Roth was there, along with Hanns and Louise Eisler and Irmgard Keun, most of them staying in the Pension Aurore. According to Louise Eisler, Koestler was very popular. His witty paradoxes, ironic asides, and love of a good argument got him lots of attention, and he basked in the approbation of his distinguished fellow guests, whereas Dorothee kept in the background and was mostly silent.[13]

Koestler quickly got down to work and wrote nearly two hundred pages in a few short weeks. Unfortunately, he never finished the novel, so it's impossible to say whether it would have succeeded, but what has survived is much funnier than anything else he wrote. Koestler's "Schweik" is recognizably the earthy Czech peasant of Hašek's World War I original, now bumbling his way through a series of misadventures in German-occupied Czechoslovakia, where he is supposed to act as an interpreter for the Czech prisoners in a German concentration camp. The story includes some farcical interrogations on the subject of racial purity, and Schweik manages to save the Czech wife of a Jew by getting her a job as camp cook. A rabbi is hauled in for miscegenation because his bride is Jewish but he himself is non-Semitic, being descended from the Khazars—the first mention in Koestler's work of the theme of *The Thirteenth Tribe*. Schweik rescues the rabbi and his bride with some quick talking, and in his clumsy way manages to frustrate the intent of the racial laws at every turn.

Schweik's other task is to mingle with the prisoners in the camp and report back on subversive political opinions, allowing Koestler to poke fun at both the Nazis and their Communist prisoners. "How would you characterize the situation in Germany as a whole, comrade?" asks a Marxist called Bretschneider. "The situation is full of shit," replies Schweik. "Are you referring to the shortage of raw materials, the mood of the workers, or the discontent of the peasants?" asks Bretschneider. Schweik: "Everything. When arseholes are in charge things are always full of shit." Schweik later reports back to his superiors: "The prisoner agreed with me that the Führer is an arsehole and the whole situation is full of shit."[14]

Koestler was still working on the book when General Francisco Franco launched his revolt against the Spanish Republican government in July 1936 and civil war erupted in Spain. Like all his friends, Koestler had been following events there with avid interest. It was the first country in which the new Communist policy of joining forces with other socialist parties (instead of fighting them), under the slogan of the Popular Front, was put to the test, and it seemed to be working: the socialist Republican Party had won the elections and taken power. Spain was suddenly the antithesis of Germany: the socialists were in power and the fascists were the insurgents. Left-wing intellectuals flocked to Spain from all over Europe to defend the cause of socialism, and Koestler wanted to be among them. Returning to Paris, he went straight to Münzenberg and volunteered his services. He said his goal was to join the Spanish Republican Army, but it's likely his motives were closer to Orwell's when setting out from England (and his own when he went to Palestine). He wanted to be closer to the action and would also fight if he had to, but above all he wanted a ringside seat at what promised to be the definitive battle between left and right for Europe.

CHAPTER TWELVE

PRISONER OF FRANCO

*What's your proposal? To build the just city? I will. I agree. Or
is it the suicide pact, the romantic Death? Very well, I accept,
for I am your choice, your decision. Yes, I am Spain.*
— W. H. AUDEN

BACK IN PARIS, Koestler found Münzenberg in the thick of an international campaign to get a pact on nonintervention signed by the major powers. Germany and Italy were already sending planes and soldiers to help Franco, and France was secretly helping the Republicans. If this continued, war might explode across the whole continent. Willi didn't expect his own side to observe the pact, of course: the goal was to hamstring the fascists and keep the Republicans in power. His Moscow patrons had done a masterly job of concealing their real intentions until now and were poised to intervene behind the smoke screen of the pact.

Willi was predictably skeptical of Koestler's military aspirations. Taking note of Koestler's Hungarian passport and *Pester Lloyd* press card, he came up with a better alternative. How would it be if Koestler took a little trip to Franco's headquarters in Seville to look for evidence of German and Italian interference in Spain? Everyone knew the fascists were up to something, but since Franco granted access only to right-wing journalists, there was no way to prove it. *Pester Lloyd* was a conservative paper in a semi-fascist country friendly to Franco. It was a perfect cover, and if Koestler could find evidence of foreign forces, it would make a huge impact on the nonintervention debate.

The cloak-and-dagger nature of the assignment greatly appealed to Koestler's romantic temperament. Entering the lion's den of Franco's headquarters was not without its dangers, but as a tiny fish in the Communist pond, he felt certain he was unknown to Franco's small intelligence service. A bigger problem was credibility. *Pester Lloyd* wasn't rich enough to send a correspondent to Seville. Otto Katz contacted Norman Cliff, the foreign editor of the liberal *News Chronicle* in London and a party member, and asked if Koestler might report for the *News Chronicle* as well. It was an inspired choice that was to have major consequences for Koestler's future in Spain, perhaps even for his life. And when Cliff learned that all the expenses were to be paid by Münzenberg, he accepted with alacrity.[1]

With a fresh suit of clothes and several new shirts in his suitcase, Koestler embarked from Southampton on the SS *Almanzora,* bound for Lisbon. It was August 22, 1936, barely a month into the civil war, and he found Lisbon awash with Spanish Nationalists. Within thirty-six hours, like the good newspaperman he was, Koestler had found proof of Portuguese collusion with Franco and successfully penetrated to the heart of the enemy establishment. He also obtained a safe-conduct pass to travel through rebel territory to Seville and a personal letter of introduction to the commander of the Seville garrison, General Gonzalo Queipo de Llano.

It was only when he boarded a ferry to cross the Tagus that it occurred to him that he was in effect a Communist spy, and his bravado began to crumble. To get his safe conduct and letter of introduction he had lulled the Hungarian consul in Lisbon into thinking he was a Franco supporter, but what if the consul had seen through the deception and was setting a trap? He recalled his betrayal of Nadezhda in Baku and his feelings of insecurity as a child, and though he was able to pull himself together sufficiently to continue his expedition, this subterranean fear dogged him the whole time he was in Seville and eventually precipitated his sudden departure.[2]

In *Spanish Testament* Koestler describes how, after checking into the Hotel Madrid, he contacted the head of the press department, a dapper aristocrat named Captain Luis Bolin, and had a frustrating noninterview with General Queipo de Llano, who proved to be unconscionably vain and craftily evasive. It wasn't until Koestler visited the Hotel Christina the next day that he struck gold. Four officers dressed in the white uniforms of the Spanish air force were sitting in the almost empty lounge and speaking German. Koestler's heart beat faster. Here was the evidence of intervention Willi was looking for. But he almost gave himself away. When their companion in civilian clothes got up and walked past Koestler's table, Koestler recognized him as a former Ullstein colleague, Fredrik Strindberg (the son of the celebrated playwright), and flew into a panic. What if Strindberg was a Nazi and informed on him?

Standing up at his table, Koestler called Strindberg by name and pretended in characteristic Teutonic fashion to be insulted by the latter's refusal to acknowledge him. A German pilot asked Koestler to identify himself, which increased his paranoia tenfold, and he found a pretext to rush away without answering. Convinced that he had been unmasked, Koestler grabbed his belongings from the Hotel Madrid, dashed to the general's headquarters to obtain an exit permit, and got a cab to Gibraltar. From there he excitedly cabled a story to the *News Chronicle* about his exclusive interview with General Queipo de Llano and his narrow escape from the Nazi pilots, turning disaster into triumph. In a later article, he expanded at length on the Nazi presence in Seville and the general atmosphere of brutality, without, of course, saying a word about his mission for Münzenberg.[3]

IT WAS A NOTABLE journalistic coup, even if Koestler had quaked in his shoes the whole time he was in Seville and needlessly cut short his visit (it turned out that he had misunderstood Strindberg's silence and almost certainly misjudged him). The Seville adventure made the front page of the *News Chronicle,* and when Koestler went to England from Gibraltar, he found himself newsworthy. For the first time since his Ullstein days he was a person of consequence again, and strangers wanted to shake his hand. In Paris, Münzenberg's staff welcomed him like a conquering hero, but Willi was already planning Koestler's next move. He wanted Koestler to return to London to work with his latest creation, the Commission of Inquiry into Alleged Breaches of the Non-Intervention Agreement in Spain. It was the usual kind of front organization, made up of unsuspecting public figures of the left, right, and center who abominated fascism and were unaware of the guiding hand at the wheel. Few knew who was behind the commission, and those who did didn't care.

But the British secret services knew, and they did care. Otto Katz had been Willi's first choice to go to London, but MI5 had blocked his visa and obliged Willi to find a substitute. It was Koestler's first extended visit to London, and he thoroughly enjoyed it. These were the heady months of the summer of 1936, when the Popular Front was finally coming into its own, and the British people's sense of fair play and sympathy for the underdog made them easy targets for manipulation. Koestler reveled in helping to organize the commission's hearings and offering his own heavily slanted testimony about his Seville visit. The commission was chaired by Eleanor Rathbone, the radical Labour MP for Liverpool, assisted by, among others, Katharine Stewart-Murray, the "Red Duchess" of Atholl, a Scottish Unionist Party MP and member of another Münzenberg front, the Committee for Spanish Relief. Koestler charmed both women with his easy manner and mastery of the political situation, unaware how useful both would prove to be to him in the future (or that his presence at these hearings was noted and recorded by MI5).[4]

When the hearings were over, Münzenberg recalled Koestler to France to start a new assignment. Otto Katz, alias André Simon, was in charge of establishing a Spanish Republican press agency in Paris. He took Koestler to tea with the Spanish foreign minister, Julio Álvarez del Vayo, who told him that after Franco's rebellion had failed in Madrid, a number of right-wing politicians had fled, leaving confidential files and archives behind. They were thought to contain proof of German collusion in Franco's rebellion, but the files were lodged in offices since occupied and shared by Anarchists, Socialists, and Communists (the three main parties in the Republican government), none of whom trusted the others or would give up the documents to a rival faction. What was needed was a foreigner who could go there, comb the archives, and extract the relevant documents. Koestler's success in Seville suggested he was the right man for the job.

It was another Scarlet Pimpernel operation, less dangerous than Seville, and would take him to the Republican side of the lines this time. Katz produced a fake Spanish passport and Koestler left the next day for Toulouse, where he hopped on a rickety old Potez plane to fly into Madrid, which was under siege by Franco's rebels. In the Spanish capital, the Soviet embassy provided him with an enormous Isotta Fraschini limousine, custom built and outfitted for the former prime minister of Spain, with lavender curtains, a control panel in the glassed-in rear compartment, and seats that reclined to form a couch for assignations. Knowing of Koestler's reputation as a Casanova, some of the correspondents in Madrid kidded him mercilessly. "Never had a smaller man traveled in a bigger car."[5]

It's possible that the ridicule Koestler endured in Madrid accounts for his extraordinary silence in his autobiography about the details of his trip. This was the time of Franco's infamous aerial bombardment of the capital, and of Madrid's desperate defense under the ringing slogan *"No pasarán"* (They shall not pass). But whereas Koestler's thirty-six hours in Lisbon and two days in Seville take up twenty-three pages in *Spanish Testament* and twelve pages in his autobiography, his month in the capital is dismissed in a couple of pages, most of them devoted to his car. "I shall say nothing about life in Madrid under the bombardment," he writes, because "the subject has been covered in a number of books from every conceivable angle."[6]

This is odd. Madrid was filled with celebrated writers and journalists of the left at the time, including "Colonel" Malraux, Ernest Hemingway, and Martha Gellhorn, all at the Hotel Florida. Among the Communist writers in town were Pablo Neruda, Rafael Alberti, Ilya Ehrenburg, Mikhail Koltsov, and Louis Aragon and his wife, Elsa Triolet. Gustav Regler arrived in a battered propaganda truck with movie equipment sent by exiled German writers, and others included John Dos Passos, Lillian Hellman, Louis Fischer (with his beautiful Norwegian girlfriend, the correspondent Gerda Grepp), and Claud Cockburn. Even Otto Katz was there for a while, accompanying the British MP Ellen Wilkinson and other British notables. There was hardly a prominent liberal author of the time who hadn't somehow made his or her way to Madrid, and while Koestler knew some of them personally, he never mentions them.

One possible reason is that while Malraux, Hemingway, Regler, Fischer, and others were to behave with varying degrees of heroism in and around Madrid that summer, Koestler left prematurely. Francisco Largo Caballero's Republican government had already gone, and the Soviet embassy staff (Koestler's support system) was about to leave too. "The capital was considered lost. We expected from hour to hour the Moors to appear on the Puerta del Sol. Those who knew how matters stood were terrified, including myself, and made hasty arrangements to follow the government to Valencia." Koestler may also have been "terrified" because the Soviets had helped him get his hands on two suitcases of sensitive documents, many of them originating in Germany and stamped with swastikas. Rumor had it that the Anarchists were blocking all roads to Valencia, requisitioning vehicles, and arresting or shooting their owners. Luckily, his friends at the embassy found a wounded pilot from the Malraux Squadron who needed to be evacuated to France. Koestler took him in his car, escorted by two other airmen, racing over the perilous mountain roads at speeds of up to ninety miles per hour. Only when they arrived in Valencia did Koestler learn that, thanks to the heroic efforts of the International Brigades, Madrid had been temporarily saved from Franco's siege and that he had missed the whole thing.[7]

IN PARIS, Koestler turned the documents over to Otto Katz for use in a new propaganda work, *The Nazi Conspiracy in Spain*. Encouraged by Katz's example and by the success of his earlier newspaper articles on Seville, Koestler retired to his apartment to embark on a propaganda work of his own. He was no longer living with Dorothee. Their marriage had foundered on his continuing proclivity to sleep with every pretty woman who came his way, and she had told him to leave. He moved into a large and comfortable party apartment at 10 rue Dombasle that Katz had recently vacated.[8]

Koestler planned to write a short history of the civil war, based on the material he had collected in Madrid and on documents supplied by Münzenberg and the Comintern. What emerged was a highly colored work of propaganda, *Menschenopfer unerhört* (Unprecedented Human Sacrifices), underlining the abuses perpetrated by landowners, the aristocracy, and the Catholic Church leaders who supported Franco, and denying or playing down the excesses of the Republicans and their supporters. To bolster this line, Koestler cited eyewitness reports of reprisals and torture, and included a photographic supplement containing horrific pictures of the bodies of children killed when a Franco bomb hit a school in Madrid. Other pictures showed the charred corpses of prisoners said to have been burned alive, and of others being led to execution. Such graphic pictures were to become the common currency of propaganda by both sides during the civil war, but they were relatively new at the time and were accompanied by a text that Koestler later acknowledged to be "hectic" and "almost bloodthirsty." He insinuated that he had composed the book this way at Münzenberg's insistence, but he completely shared Willi's hatred of Franco, and the work was mostly his own.[9]

Menschenopfer unerhört was published by Willi's Éditions du Carrefour in January 1937, and the French translation came out a month later as *L'Espagne ensanglantée* (Blood-soaked Spain). The book sold between 2,000 and 3,000 copies in the French edition, which wasn't bad at such an early stage in the war. In his autobiography Koestler disparages it as little better than Communist propaganda, but it was the first book to document Franco's atrocities in convincing detail, and its dissection of his propaganda machine was pioneering in its way. By exposing the Nationalists' myth that they were embarked on a "holy crusade" rather than a campaign of terror, Koestler was well ahead of his fellow writers on Spain, blazing a trail that others would follow in the months and years to come.[10]

OTTO KATZ HAD FINALLY succeeded in putting his news agency together, and asked Koestler to return to Spain to report on the southern front in Málaga. Koestler left Paris by train on January 15, 1937, and traveled to Toulouse, where he caught a plane to Barcelona. There he met up with the English journalist William Forrest, also a party member, who had been assigned by Katz to cover Madrid. Both were accredited as special correspondents of the *News Chronicle* in London, which had no chance of getting any of its own reporters into Nationalist territory owing to its fierce opposition to General Franco. Like Orwell, Koestler was startled to see the chaos, the terrible food shortages, and the long lines outside the stores in Anarchist-controlled Barcelona, but whereas Orwell was thrilled by the revolutionary methods of the Anarchists and joined POUM under the naive impression that it didn't matter which anti-fascist party you fought for, Koestler understood the dialectics of the situation better. POUM was a "Trotskyist" front and to be avoided by a true Communist at all costs. He hastened on to Valencia, where POUM was weak and the Moscow-backed Communists were firmly in control.[11]

Koestler and Forrest had been told to report to Mikhail Koltsov, officially the *Pravda* correspondent in Spain but also a high official in the Comintern. Koestler knew Koltsov from Moscow and Paris and was pleased to see him again, especially when Koltsov allowed him and Forrest to sleep on his hotel-room floor, for Valencia was packed to the bursting point. Just as they were dozing off, Koltsov made a strange announcement. *"Attenzione, Agence Espagne,"* he said in a joking tone of voice. "Tomorrow, in Moscow, starts the trial of Piatakov, Radek, Sokolnikov, Muralov, and accomplices; we are all expected to report the reactions of the Spanish working class."[12]

The news was anything but a joke, and in the semidarkness of the hotel room, Koltsov's statement jolted Koestler awake. It had been two years since the first batch of party leaders had been arrested and tried for murdering their popular colleague Sergei Kirov, and a second trial (the first of the big show trials) had been held when Koestler was on his way to Seville. Whatever twinges he might have felt at the time had been suppressed in the interest of party loyalty, but Koltsov's new message had an unsettling effect. Karl Radek was a specialist in German affairs and a close friend of Münzenberg. Koestler had talked with him in Moscow and been impressed by his knowledge of German politics and culture (and was later to incorporate aspects of Radek into his portrait of Rubashov in *Darkness at Noon*). If Radek was under arrest, who in Moscow was safe?[13]

Absorbed by the distractions of Valencia, he forgot about the trial almost at once. The cabarets closed at nine, and he was dismayed to see the dancers wearing G-strings and brassieres in deference to Communist morality. The local newspapers were down to four pages as the result of a paper shortage, while censors vetted every word he wrote and listened in on his calls to London, but Valencia still managed to maintain the air of desperate jollity that seemed to hover everywhere behind the lines of the Spanish Civil War. Koestler ran into Hanns Eisler and Kantorowicz, the latter now a political commissar in the German division of the International Brigades. He met W. H. Auden at a crazy party in the Hotel Victoria and found Koltsov there too, with the English writer Basil Murray and Gerda Grepp—sans Louis Fischer. Auden left Spain after a couple of months but saw enough to understand the magnetic attraction that war-torn Spain exerted on men such as Koestler and Orwell. Auden's line about the "conscious acceptance of guilt in the necessary murder" was fraught with extra meaning in the context of the Soviet purges, but for most readers, including Koestler (and Auden himself), it achieved its full import only much later.[14]

Gerda Grepp's sweet, kittenish face and opulent figure snared Koestler as surely as they had Fischer before him. Grepp was part Italian and part Norwegian, irresistibly attractive, and surprisingly feminine for a war correspondent. As they traveled south in Koestler's official car, he fussed and worried over her and helped her write her dispatches. They arrived in Málaga just at sunset on January 28, but the magnificent harbor and elegant streets of this Mediterranean resort presented a pitiable sight. Rampaging workers had demolished the fashionable district of Caleta, along with numerous churches and a large portion of the cathedral. There were sunken ships in the bay, and Franco's air force had started bombing the city with impunity. "Darkness, entire streets in ruins; deserted pavements, strewn with shells, and a certain smell which I know from Madrid," wrote Koestler in his notebook. "Fine chalk dust suspended in the air mixed with shell powder and—or is it imagination?—the pungent odor of burned flesh. Madrid after the great air attack and artillery bombardment was a health resort compared with this town in its death throes."[15]

Koestler and Grepp registered with the Republican propaganda department and ran into a farcical obstruction: no censor had been appointed, ergo, no dispatches could be sent. They found a young officer for the job, then got permission to visit the front lines north and south of the city. Colonel José Villalba Lacorte, Málaga's commander, seemed out of touch with reality. His garrison was in shambles, and Grepp's sudden appearance among the soldiers caused a sensation. When Koestler asked the soldiers what they would do in the event of a tank attack, they replied that they would "strangle the enemy with their bare hands," then admitted they had never seen a tank.[16]

Filled with righteous indignation, Koestler gave Villalba an earful the next day on how to improve his garrison and prepare his troops. Then he called on the acting British consul in Málaga, Sir Peter Chalmers Mitchell, an eminent biologist and the founder of Whipsnade Zoo, at his mellifluously named Villa Santa Lucia, high on a hill overlooking the northern suburbs. Sir Peter, seventy-six years old and a wealthy aristocrat with Communist sympathies, treated Koestler with great warmth, especially after Koestler presented him with a copy of *L'Espagne ensanglantée*. There was still a sense of calm in the air, leading Koestler to file an optimistic story with the *News Chronicle* predicting that there would be no rebel attack on Málaga after all.

A day later, nine battalions of Italian tanks and troops converged on the city from the north and an equally large force of Nationalist troops advanced from the south, while Franco's warships began bombarding the coastal roads all around it. The censor appointed with Koestler's help clamped a complete news blackout on the city, and Villalba ordered a general evacuation. Chalmers Mitchell refused to leave, wanting to stay on in Málaga as a "neutral" witness, to observe what happened after it fell to Franco's forces, and Koestler decided he should stay on too. After escorting Grepp a little way north on the road to Valencia, he scribbled a hasty note to the *News Chronicle* about the fall of Málaga and returned with his driver down a road densely packed with refugees fleeing in the opposite direction.[17]

The scene was like Madrid a few months earlier, only worse. The civilian population had completely lost their heads and were streaming out of town in total disarray, accompanied by panicked militiamen who had abandoned the front to avoid being caught. At Republican headquarters, Villalba and his deputy, Colonel Alfredo, were getting ready to leave in Alfredo's car. Koestler went a short distance with them, but then changed his mind and walked back to the city center. Pondering his reasons later, he concluded that it was a reaction to his earlier cowardice in Madrid. He wanted to be braver this time, and was disgusted and humiliated by the failure of the Republican army to stand and fight. Like Chalmers Mitchell, he would "stay and face the enemy rather than flee with the deserters."[18]

THERE WAS SOME TRUTH to this statement, but Koestler's motives were mixed. One trivial but compelling reason to stay was his persnickety reluctance to leave his belongings behind, including papers, manuscripts, and his prized portable typewriter. Another was the dim sense of obligation he felt to Sir Peter, fueled by shame at the thought of his earlier impulse to leave and the faint hope that the British flag might protect not only the consul but also the correspondent of a British newspaper. If it did, he might get the scoop of a lifetime. He would be the first left-wing journalist to witness the capture of a Republican city, and that would eclipse his exploits in Seville.

He momentarily thought of buying a revolver to shoot himself in case of capture, but Sir Peter disabused him of the idea, pointing out that to be found with a weapon would invite the Nationalists to treat them as armed enemies. To calm Koestler's fears, the consul dug out two syringes and two tubes of morphine tablets he had brought from England and showed Koestler how to use them. In case of real danger, Koestler could inject himself into oblivion. They dined on a meager meal of bread and sardines and some scraps that Koestler had filched from his hotel. From the villa's terrace high on the hill, they watched the lights of the invading army as they approached Málaga and, from a neighboring ridge the following day, observed Franco's troops streaming into the city, with no opposition in sight.[19]

At around eleven a.m. on Tuesday, February 9, Koestler was in the library drinking a shot of brandy to calm his nerves when he heard the sound of men entering the front door. He tried to run up the back stairs, but a voice yelled in Spanish: "There goes the hare." He was ordered to halt and put up his hands. He turned to find three officers aiming pistols at him. It was Captain Luis Bolin, General Queipo de Llano's press officer from Seville, and two of his colleagues. Bolin didn't recognize Koestler and realized who he was only after searching his pockets. Another officer, Joaquin "Pim" Vazquez Torres, tied Koestler's hands in front of him with a telephone cable and pushed him into the front seat of Bolin's car, where Sir Peter already sat in the back. There was a tense standoff when the car was halted by a crowd of soldiers brandishing weapons and calling for the heads of the two prisoners, but Koestler's worst moment came when they stopped outside a police station and he was ordered to stand in the middle of the road with his hands bound together. Pim Vazquez took several photographs of him full face and in profile, while a hostile mob jeered and threatened him. He felt a rush of fear that he might be lynched, and Sir Peter fed him cigarettes to calm his nerves.[20]

Bolin drove off with Sir Peter in a cloud of dust, returning a couple of hours later to have Koestler properly searched. He confiscated Koestler's wallet, hypodermic syringe, needles, and typewriter, and insisted (over Koestler's strenuous objections) on giving his fountain pen to Vazquez (Vazquez later claimed that Koestler had given it to him out of gratitude for good treatment, but Koestler said it was stolen). Koestler was put in a truck with five armed men and driven away, convinced that he was to be executed. A soldier scoffed at his fears and said things weren't that simple. When they arrived at Málaga Prison, Koestler understood why. His arrest warrant lay on the table, describing him as a *caso internacional* (international case). He was locked in a bare and forbidding cell in a moment evoked with chilling precision in *Dialogue with Death*. "A cell door cannot be shut except by being slammed to. It is made of massive steel and concrete, about four inches thick, and every time it falls to there is a resounding crash just as though a shot has been fired. But this report dies away without an echo. Prison sounds are echo-less and bleak."[21]

Málaga was the first of at least a dozen cells that Koestler was to occupy over the next five years, marking the start of a precipitous descent into the twilight world of ideological outcasts and political prisoners that would define his outlook for the rest of his life. But for now, as a novice, he could think of nothing better to do than make a mental inventory of the iron bedstead, the washbasin, and the WC that defined his new domicile. He tried to pull himself up by the iron bars of the high window to look outside but predictably failed, covering his suit with white plaster as he fell back. He made a resolution to do exercises every morning, learn a foreign language, and not let his spirit be broken, but at that moment he caught sight of something that drove away all thoughts of resistance and filled him with dread. An eye was glued to the spy hole in the center of the door, "goggling glassily, its pupil unbelievably big." It was an eye "without a man attached to it, and for a few moments the prisoner's heart stops beating."[22]

The fall of Málaga was a major milestone in the civil war. For the Republicans it was a huge setback whose reverberations were felt by Orwell as far away as the trenches of Zaragoza. Responsibility for the collapse was laid at the door of the Anarchists, which gave the Communists a convenient pretext to seize more power from their rivals in the Republican government. The Nationalists' reprisals were carried out not only on the beaches and streets of Málaga but also in the prisons. From his solitary cell, Koestler heard the nightly roll call of condemned men and listened to the melancholy shuffle of dragging feet as up to fifty prisoners at a time were hustled down the corridors to meet their end. Theoretically his status as a foreign national protected him from immediate punishment, but he feared that in the sheer chaos of the occupation he would be swept away by the terror. When a disfigured young prisoner was thrown into his cell and summarily removed again, presumably to be shot, Koestler felt sure his last hour had come.[23]

*   *   *

WHILE KOESTLER'S FEARS were real enough, it's hard to say how justified they were. A few days after his arrest the *News Chronicle* published a brief item stating that a hastily summoned court-martial had sentenced him to death as a spy, and that in response to international public opinion, General Franco had intervened with a reprieve. The story was neither confirmed nor denied by the Nationalist forces, and the truth has never been established. Koestler was kept in ignorance of his status throughout the entire time of his imprisonment in Spain—perhaps because of the sheer confusion generated by the civil war, but more likely to punish and intimidate him. He was never informed about a death sentence, but it was never denied either, and he feared that if his role as a Communist emissary were known, he might well be executed—or handed over to the Gestapo, which would be worse. The title of his memoir on the subject, *Dialogue with Death,* expresses his plight perfectly. He faced the prospect of a death sentence without ever knowing if it had been pronounced or would be carried out.[24]

After a few days in the Málaga cells, Koestler was transferred to the Central Prison in Seville. Situated in the eastern suburbs of the city, the Central Prison was brand new and a model prison in 1937, with ornate wrought-iron entrance gates and a tropical garden that greatly impressed Koestler the first time he saw it. Koestler's cell, number 41, fourth on the right down the cavernous central corridor that ran the length of the main building, was large and spacious (it now holds two prisoners instead of one), containing a washbasin, a WC, a steel table and chair, and a bunk with a straw mattress and woolen blanket.

Koestler has described the three months he spent in the prison in some detail in *Dialogue with Death.* For most of that time he was kept in solitary confinement, and for the first six weeks wasn't allowed to leave his cell at all. To keep track of time he scratched marks on the wall with a piece of wire and set up a schedule of mental lessons: "English from nine to ten, then German, then French poetry, then Mathematics." He scratched a series of equations, and was elated by his ability to recall Euclid's proof that the number of prime numbers is infinite. Meanwhile the food turned out to be bearable, most of the guards were civil, and one of them, Don Ramón, seemed almost friendly. After a couple of weeks he obtained library privileges, and a brief hunger strike produced toiletries and pencil and paper. From March 3, after just under a month in jail, he was able to keep a diary, in which he reconstructed his Málaga experiences from memory and kept a record of his daily activities. It is a measure of those more easygoing times that he was allowed to take the diary with him when he was finally released.[25]

His material conditions were thus relatively good, but psychologically his situation was worse than it now sounds. Even today, to enter the giant gates of that Seville prison as a visitor, and to hear the hollow reverberation of locks clanging, bolts banging, and doors closing, is to sense the hopelessness that must have been induced in those incarcerated there. For Koestler, no matter how comfortable his physical conditions, solitary confinement at the mercy of unpredictable guards was a form of torture, and the uncertainty of his fate inflicted intense emotional suffering. The first symptoms were vertiginous changes of mood. Small alterations in his conditions would lead to instant euphoria or instant depression, and he was deeply oppressed by his isolation. From his window he could see other prisoners in the exercise yard, but they were forbidden to acknowledge him, and his sense of being quarantined was intensified by the almost complete silence of his guards.

As fastidious as ever about his personal appearance, Koestler was further oppressed by the ragged and filthy condition of his shirt, his underwear, and the suit he incongruously still wore. All pleas for soap, comb, and towel were initially ignored, not to speak of his requests for a shave. When the cell door unexpectedly opened to reveal the prison barber, he almost broke down from the shock. He "precipitated such an earthquake in my feelings that I literally had to clutch on to the water tap so as not to fall down. I felt, *horribile dictu,* my eyes grow moist."[26]

His first cigarette, his first library book, and his first bath brought similarly exaggerated rushes of gratitude. He noted their insidious effects in his diary and stored the information away for future use.

> Despite all my feelings of self-respect, I cannot help looking on the warders as superior beings. The consciousness of being confined acts like a slow poison, transforming the entire character. This is more than a mere psychological change, it is not an inferiority complex— it is, rather, an inevitable natural process. When I was writing my novel about the gladiators I always wondered why the Roman slaves, who were twice, three times as numerous as the freemen, did not turn the tables on their masters. Now it is beginning gradually to dawn on me what the slave mentality really is. I could wish that everyone who talks of mass psychology should experience a year of prison.[27]

KOESTLER MEDITATED on the nature of power. He had never believed that a dictatorship could maintain its ascendancy by the sword alone, but was amazed to observe the role played by psychology. "Don Ramón has the key and I am in the cage; Don Ramón, as well as I, looks upon this state of things as entirely natural and is far from regarding it as in any way an anomaly. And if a crazy agitator were to come and preach to us that all men are equal, we should both laugh him to scorn; Don Ramón with all his heart, I, it is true, only half-heartedly—but all the same I should laugh."[28]

The realization of this dynamic became one of the seeds of *Darkness at Noon.* When Rubashov finally confesses to his captors, it is not so much physical suffering as a consciousness of psychological dependency that brings him to his climactic downfall. In the novel there are many motives at work, but it was in Seville that Koestler first glimpsed the complex chemistry of masters and slaves that smoothed the way for Stalin's show trials. On one occasion, he blurted out to Don Ramón that he wasn't "a *rojo* [Red] any longer," an act of self-abasement that made him burn with shame for years afterward, comparing it to his betrayal of Nadezhda in Baku. On another occasion he was visited by an elegant young woman in Falangist uniform who told him she was a stringer for Hearst Newspapers. He again denied he was a Communist, this time out of calculation, but defended the Republican government against her charges. She told him spitefully that he had been condemned to death as a spy, but that General Franco was "considering" a reprieve. If he was lucky, his sentence might be commuted to life imprisonment.[29]

After about six weeks, Koestler was transferred to cell 40, and on March 27 he received his first short letter from Dorothee. She expressed guarded hope for his release, asked for a reply "in his own handwriting" (from which he deduced that she didn't know if he was alive or not), and enclosed a hundred pesetas, which transformed him into an instant millionaire in prison terms. He was able to order cigarettes, matches, sardines, figs, cheese, sausage, eggs, chocolate, and a much prized toothbrush from the commissary, later extending his purchases to a new shirt, socks, and some wine. Dorothee's letter also signaled the end of his solitary confinement. He was allowed into the prison yard for two hours a day to exercise with a small group of other prisoners, and in mid-April had his first visit from the British consul in Seville.

Among Koestler's four companions during his first day's exercise was a young peasant called Nicolás, who had been sentenced to death. Others under death sentence had continued as before, so Koestler thought nothing of it, but when he emerged for exercise the next day, Nicolás was gone. He had been shot overnight, and the shock to Koestler was unbearable: a living, breathing person had disappeared before his very eyes. Nicolás was one of seventeen soldiers shot that night to mark the anniversary of the proclamation of the Spanish Republic, but Koestler never forgot him. He dedicated *Dialogue with Death* to Nicolás, and the implacable opposition to capital punishment born in Koestler's Spanish jail led eventually to *Reflections on Hanging* and his successful campaign to end the death sentence in Britain some twenty years later.

Koestler's revulsion was strengthened by things he began to hear now that he had never noticed before. The critical hours for executions were between midnight and two a.m., and on the second night he deliberately stayed awake and heard the low tolling of the Sanctus bell. A priest murmured prayers as the guards moved slowly down the broad corridor, unlocking the cells one by one. Weeping men called to their mothers as they were dragged out for execution. The procession reached the second cell to his left, then the next cell to his, and suddenly he heard the priest fumbling at his own door. "Not him," said one of the guards, and the procession passed.

He later woke to feel his bed shaking, "as though in an earthquake." It was "my own body trembling from head to foot. The moment I awoke my body grew still; the moment I fell asleep the nervous trembling began again." That night eight prisoners were shot. The next night, nine. And so on. In the space of five days forty-seven more men were executed, and Koestler now heard it all: the ring of the telephone in the chief guard's office at ten o'clock, the names read out and confirmed one by one, the slow midnight procession, the helpless protests of the prisoners. He feared that his trembling would become permanent, like shell shock.

But the executions ended just as suddenly as they had begun, and the prison returned to normal, though Koestler's fear did not abate, particularly after a sixteen-year-old youth was removed from the adjoining cell and shot. At the end of April he wrote an SOS to the British consul and started a hunger strike. Soon afterward, he received a second letter from Dorothee and a second visit from the consul. He learned that questions had been asked about him in the House of Commons and that the British government had made representations to Franco. But Dorothee still didn't know where he was and was still asking for a handwritten letter of reply. The consul told him that his case was officially still sub judice, which meant that at least there was no death sentence—but there was no reprieve either.

Everything still seemed possible. He was moved into cell 17, which he had to share with a prisoner called Carlos, then the two of them were moved to cell 30. He kept up his hunger strike by giving his meals to Carlos, and at the beginning of May the prison doctor at last started to take an interest in him. On May 8, a military investigator questioned him for two hours about his journey to Seville, his propaganda book on Spain, his reasons for remaining behind in Málaga, and the nature of "the secret wire-pullers of the Red Propaganda in England." Luckily the investigator didn't seem to know of Koestler's Communist Party membership, nor of his closeness to Katz and Münzenberg, and Koestler concealed the origin of the documents on which he had based *Spanish Testament*.[30]

The charge against him was aiding the Loyalist armed forces, which strictly speaking was true. He had lectured the Republican commander in Málaga on what to do, and a Nationalist spy had probably reported him. Nevertheless his spirits lifted. He was no military man and could hardly be charged with changing the outcome. Four days later a courtly stranger in a black shirt stood and bowed when Koestler entered the room, and told him he could go free if he signed an assurance not to meddle in the internal affairs of Spain. Koestler signed at once and was told to fetch his belongings. The stranger led him out of the prison, drove him to a nearby airfield, and shepherded him into the backseat of a small open monoplane. The stranger then climbed into the pilot's seat and the two of them took off. Their destination was the small town of La Linea on the frontier with Gibraltar. There Koestler was jailed for forty-eight hours, until the British consul came to identify him. On Friday, May 14, three Spanish guards escorted him across the no-man's-land that separated Spain from Gibraltar and handed him to a British detective inspector, from whom they demanded a written receipt.[31]

"God Save the King!" exclaimed Koestler melodramatically as he stepped across the border. A correspondent who saw him arrive at the Rock Hotel reported imaginatively that Koestler sported a "50-day-old beard, his hair had not been cut for three months," and his suit had been reduced to rags. His luggage was said to consist of a piece of comb, a broken toothbrush, and "a few crushed cigarettes." It's true that he was in poor physical and mental shape, but he was not yet the scarecrow described in the newspaper article. Once at the hotel he dispatched two telegrams. One was to his parents in Budapest: "Free, healthy, happy." The second, to Communist Party headquarters in Paris, cited Schiller: "*Seid umschlungen, Millionen* [I embrace thee, ye millions]," to which Koestler added cryptically, "cured of all bellyaches." *Bellyache* was party slang for ideological doubt. Koestler evidently meant it, but he was further along the road to apostasy than he realized at the time.[32]

CHAPTER THIRTEEN

TURNING POINT

Never send to know for whom the bell tolls; it tolls for thee.
— JOHN DONNE

GEORGE ORWELL SAID that Spain had been a turning point in his life, and that "every serious line" he wrote after 1936 was a result of his experiences there. The same was true of Koestler. His months in Spain marked "the most decisive period in my life, its spiritual crisis and turning point." For Koestler the transformation was gradual and unconscious, and took years to play itself out, but it is also true that every line he wrote after Spain, beginning with his account of his experiences in *Dialogue with Death,* was different in quality and spirit from his writings before. It would become infinitely harder, and then impossible, for him to dissimulate after his experiences in Spain, especially in the name of the cause for which he had suffered. Henceforth in his work he would commit sins of omission but would rarely play fast and loose with facts or bend the truth as he saw it, and *Dialogue* itself would prove to be virtually devoid of propaganda. Such sentimental and romantic touches as there were—in the scenes he wrote about the death of Nicolás, for example, or about his own sufferings and humiliations—were humanitarian and ethical rather than ideological in inspiration. [1]

Subconsciously or not, Koestler was faithful to the lesson André Malraux was to draw from his Spanish experiences and express in his novel on the Spanish Civil War, *Man's Hope.* "All forms of action are Manichean," Malraux wrote, "because all action pays a tribute to the devil; the Manichean element is most intense when the masses are involved. Every true revolutionary is a born Manichean. The same is true of politics, all politics." Before Spain,

Koestler had been the very type of the Manichean (and was never fully to escape this tendency), but in Seville he discovered another reality, a reality that brought him much closer to Malraux's description of the true intellectual as "anti-Manichean" by definition, "a man of subtleties, interested in absolute truth and in the complexity of things."[2]

In Spain, Koestler began to recognize that revolutionary violence was highly questionable, and that the sanctity of life was not to be taken lightly. Malraux and Orwell came to similar conclusions. But Koestler's experiences were radically different from those of other writers who went to Spain. Hemingway, Dos Passos, Auden, Spender, Rolland, and Ehrenburg displayed considerable personal courage in visiting the troops in their trenches and reporting from the front; others, like Malraux, Orwell, Regler, and members of the International Brigades, actually fought (and some of them, like John Cornford, Christopher Caudwell, and Julian Bell, died), but none went to jail or sat in what they imagined to be a condemned cell facing the prospect of imminent execution. Koestler was the only significant writer to stare death in the face in Spain and return to write about it.

In fact he was burning to write about it, and his very first attempt took the form of an emotional letter to Thomas Mann, written from Gibraltar immediately after his release. He was still under the vivid impression of having escaped death by a miracle, and he wrote Mann a long letter of thanks for the inspiration Mann's writing had given him during his ordeal.

> The point is that during those three months [in jail] I was an almost daily eyewitness of the executions of my comrades and awaited my own execution at any moment (I beg you to take this sentence literally), so that during those months, hard up against the boundary of what was psychically bearable, I had you to thank that I never overstepped that boundary. The problem was how to come to terms with the constant imminence of one's own death, how to arrive at a modus vivendi with death, to ward off the temptations of self-betrayal and guard against backsliding. I also had to gain some distance from my own fate and deaden the hypertrophic proliferation of my vital instincts. In the course of making these efforts, I found that the recollection of certain passages from "Buddenbrooks" (the brief scene in which the Consul, before his death, discovers Schopenhauer ... certain motifs from "The Magic Mountain," the Lübeck speech and the essay on Plato) helped me more than any other spiritual resource, with the sole exception of Freud's "Beyond the Pleasure Principle."

The book read by the Consul was Schopenhauer's *On Death and Its Relation to the Indestructability of Our Essential Selves,* which argued that death wasn't final but a transition to another, impersonal form of existence in the

All-One. Schopenhauer was one of Koestler's favorite authors—*The World as Will and Representation* was the only book Koestler took to Palestine with him in 1926—and Schopenhauer's ideas were to exercise great influence on his later writings. But Schopenhauer's reappearance in his life via, as it were, Thomas Mann, at a moment of extreme crisis, struck Koestler as providential.

Sitting in Gibraltar, his emotions still churning, Koestler excused himself: "I share your aversion to overexuberance and am therefore making every effort to find the right formulation; the lack of clarity stems from my state of exhaustion, which makes me temporarily incapable of being more precise." He then added, half apologetically, half humorously: "To put it baldly, I believe I have you to thank for the fact that I'm still alive, or, at least, that I still have my wits about me (I witnessed how my cell neighbor, an Andalusian peasant, was driven crazy, and Andalusian peasants are much tougher than *Voss* editors). I would never have thought it possible that art could exercise such a drastic influence on real life."[3]

KOESTLER WROTE THE LETTER during the week he was forced to languish in Gibraltar waiting to be cleared by MI5, which had started watching him after the Münzenberg hearings in London the year before. Unaware of his newfound celebrity in Britain, he was stunned when Dorothee met him off the boat at Tilbury Docks, accompanied by a jostling crowd of reporters and photographers. He still walked unsteadily, with a slight limp, but the razor-sharp parting was back in his closely trimmed hair, and he looked decidedly dapper as he posed for pictures in a new tweed suit, with a pipe grasped theatrically in one hand. Koestler was in fact one of the first journalists to be made the subject of an international campaign for his release, setting a precedent that helped spawn an entire industry of human-rights organizations in the second half of the twentieth century.[4]

Koestler's case also set a precedent for the infiltration of such organizations by the Communist Party. Publicly Koestler gave the credit to Dorothee, the "shy and inhibited" young wife who had gone to London and tirelessly collected signatures, lobbied MPs in the House of Commons, and engineered petitions and protest resolutions, for which Koestler expressed his gratitude most profusely in *The Invisible Writing*. "Her tongue-tied manner achieved more in England than eloquence could ever have done; her sincerity was instantaneously convincing; the fact that she spoke as the distressed wife of a husband in prison was more effective than any political argument. There were many who helped, but it was Dorothy who saved my life."[5]

But Koestler's picture of Dorothee badgering Otto Katz to send her to London and evading the party bureaucracy is highly misleading. It's true that Dorothee was sincere and by nature shy, but far from bypassing the bureaucracy, Katz had enlisted the considerable resources of the party to pay for Dorothee's expenses and connect her to the party network in England, and Dorothee had sent weekly reports and letters on her activities to party headquarters in Paris. From these it emerges that it was Sir Peter Chalmers Mitchell who first sounded the alarm with a cable to the *News Chronicle* from Gibraltar: "Do everything to save Koestler." The *News Chronicle* had mounted a major campaign through newspaper and diplomatic channels that extended as far as the Vatican and the pro-Falangist press in Britain. Even Hearst joined other press lords in insisting that Koestler's incarceration was an "unacceptable infringement of the rights of journalists to carry out their profession." In France, both Prime Minister Léon Blum and Foreign Minister Yvon Delbos were pressed to urge the British government to intervene on Koestler's behalf, and the French representative to the League of Nations in Geneva promised to raise the case with the Committee for Prisoner Exchanges.[6]

All this information—and more—had been presented to the party on March 1, 1937, in a detailed "Preliminary Report on the Case of Arthur Koestler," compiled by Dorothee. "All actions taken up to this point," she wrote, "have been centralized by the Agence d'Espagne and Otto Katz, who has been kept informed about everything through the English branch of the Agency and has exercised leadership. I am making this report because Otto Katz is not in Paris." Only then did Dorothee move to the Royal Hotel in London, avoiding her mother's comfortable apartment in the West End to emphasize her solitary status and conceal her party connections. She certainly looked the part of the distressed wife: short and slight, with disheveled brown hair and no makeup. She had never been in England before, which added to her air of helplessness, and her halting English, delivered with a pronounced German accent, marked her out as a pitiable foreigner.[7]

These appearances, of course, were deceptive. Dorothee had quickly contacted the party network through Norman Cliff at the *News Chronicle,* and Chalmers Mitchell put her in touch with Eleanor Rathbone, the Duchess of Atholl, and other supporters of the Spanish Republican cause. He also helped her meet officials in the Foreign Office, and soon a formidable lobbying effort was under way that extended well into the Conservative Party and included the Spanish Republican embassy in London. Word came back that it was "impossible" to release Koestler, because he had "played a role in the 'Red Soviet of Málaga.'" This was an exaggerated reference to his conversations with Villalba, but Dorothee played her cards with great skill. She hounded the Italian and Hungarian embassies to get the Vatican involved, tried to work on Hungarian public opinion through a descendant of the great Hungarian explorer Vambéry (who happened to be visiting London at the time), and enlisted a number of prominent women politicians in her cause, including Lady Violet Bonham-Carter, Lady Astor, Sylvia Pankhurst, Lady

Hilton, and Lady Young. Meanwhile she established contact with some well-known Conservative MPs, including Harold Nicolson, Lord Vansittart, and Winston Churchill.[8]

Perhaps her biggest achievement was in appealing to the British sense of fair play and noblesse oblige, and invoking the rights of journalists to freedom of expression in such a way as to completely blot out the idea of Koestler as a left-wing troublemaker. At its annual general meeting over the Easter holidays, the National Union of Journalists passed a resolution calling on the British government to secure Koestler's release, and soon afterward, Lieutenant-Commander Reginald Fletcher, a Labour MP, asked the foreign secretary in Parliament if he would now act. The secretary, Anthony Eden, replied that although Koestler was not a British subject, the government was "concerned" and trying to obtain more information. Shortly afterward, fifty-six MPs, twenty-two of them Conservatives, signed a letter in support of Koestler, and it was as a result of this continuing pressure from the British government that the consul in Seville had been allowed to visit him.[9]

Though Dorothee's energy and perseverance were outstanding, the stream of letters going out in fluent English was drafted in her native German and translated by other party members. And she did not have a free hand. She had to coordinate her activities with Hans Stammreich, an official in the Comintern, and ran into problems when her goal of getting Koestler out of jail as quickly as possible conflicted with the party's policy of extracting maximum political capital from the case. Dorothee's task called for confidential contacts and negotiations through private channels, whereas the party wanted a huge publicity campaign to put Franco on the defensive. Dorothee thought that Franco would never allow himself to be seen as bowing to public pressure, whereas Stammreich suggested that since Koestler was a minor figure in the greater scheme of things, he might be sacrificed for the greater good of the cause, that is, victory in Spain.[10]

Fortunately Stammreich's suggestion wasn't followed, and success came when the Comintern suggested getting Koestler out through the medium of prisoner exchanges. Negotiations involved the League of Nations in Geneva, the Red Cross, Álvarez del Vayo (the man who had sent Koestler to Madrid), and the Vatican, and reached their climax when General Queipo de Llano told the Red Cross he would offer twenty-one Republican prisoners in exchange for a single hostage, the beautiful and aristocratic Señora Haya, the wife of a top Falangist air ace, who had been captured during the fall of Málaga and was under arrest in Valencia.[11]

When the Red Cross negotiator, Dr. Marcel Junod, presented the offer to José Giral, the Republican foreign minister, Giral replied: "Queipo would like to tempt us, but I'm not playing. I'm interested in one man. He's not a Spaniard, but he's a friend of the Republic. His name is Koestler." Junod had never heard of Koestler but concluded the deal anyway, and while Koestler waited at La Linea, Señora Haya was escorted to a British warship in Valencia harbor. The courteous pilot in black who flew Koestler to La Linea was the señora's husband, Carlos Haya. A week after being reunited with his wife, he was shot down and killed in the Battle of Teruel.[12]

KOESTLER MUST HAVE KNOWN something of the party's role in his release when he stepped off the boat at Tilbury, but it didn't lessen his gratitude to Dorothee. Indeed, without her he might well have been sacrificed for the "greater good" of the Communist cause. Meanwhile, the knowledge that Koestler was in mortal danger had softened Dorothee's resentment of his earlier behavior and rekindled her feelings for him. "In my heart," she wrote in one of her early letters, "I do not only hope but feel sure that our seperation [sic] cannot last much longer and I am always thinking of the day when I shall have you back again and when I can give you all the love I feel for you. Ever, ever yours, my darling! Dorothee."[13]

Despite his gratitude, Koestler's feelings for Dorothee hadn't changed at all, and he was too honest to conceal the truth from her. Away from the glare of the cameras, he moved into the Arundel Hotel off the Strand, instead of to Dorothee's hotel. Later they moved together to the grand house of Lord Layton, the proprietor of the *News Chronicle,* in Putney, where Koestler spent his waking hours describing his prison experiences in five articles for the paper, and then to a small Victorian house by the Thames at Shepperton, where Koestler recast the articles into a book, adapting and expanding parts of *L'Espagne ensanglantée* to accompany his narrative. Though not admitted to the marriage bed, Dorothee was pressed into service as a typist, and Koestler dictated the two parts of his book to her in German. They were translated into English by Phyllis and Trevor Blewitt, and the book was sent to Victor Gollancz for the Left Book Club as *Spanish Testament.*[14]

Koestler was now at loose ends. The *News Chronicle* had no further obligation to him. He was a freelance, not an employee, and he couldn't return to Spain because of the undertaking he had signed as a condition of his release. But the *News Chronicle* couldn't be seen to drop him either. The editor, Gerald Barry, considered sending him to Moscow, then changed his mind and dispatched him to Greece and Palestine instead. En route Koestler stopped off in Paris, where Otto Katz met him at the station with an enormous bunch of flowers. Koestler was debriefed in a Left Bank café by the German Communist leader Paul Merker and an unknown party official, and felt decidedly queasy recalling his admission in Seville that he was "no longer a Red." He said nothing, but noticed that after the interview his hand was still shaking.[15]

His next stop was Locarno, in Switzerland, to meet Thomas Mann, who had been very impressed by Koestler's letter, especially the sentence about not having believed before that art could have such an influence on life. "Nor I, before this," Mann noted in his diary. He also remarked on an extraordinary coincidence that he informed Koestler about in his letter of reply. He hadn't reread the Schopenhauer book in thirty years, he said, but had taken it off his shelf and opened it just hours before Koestler's letter arrived. Koestler had come to regard coincidence with a sort of superstitious awe as "the language of destiny," and Mann's letter had led him to fantasize about a mystical bond between himself and the great German author, but he later claimed that Mann had been formal and distant, and gloomily concluded that he had made a fool of himself.

The latter conclusion appears to be true. Having arrived at Mann's hotel on the afternoon of September 20, 1937, and arranged a meeting for the following morning, Koestler worked himself up into frenzy over the fact that he'd used a vulgar bourgeois cliché when speaking to the great man. The next morning and at lunch he was on tenterhooks, and although they talked throughout, seems to have heard only half of what Mann was saying. In his later account Koestler describes Mann as self-absorbed, distant, and incapable of a close human connection with his inferiors, but neglects to mention that Mann also invited him to dinner and talked at length about subjects he thought Koestler would find interesting. In his diary afterward Mann characterized Koestler as "*sympatisch*," but found him "strained and out of sorts,"which made Mann pull back as well. Koestler's disappointment was more the fruit of his own self-consciousness and his pathological need to make a good impression than any disregard on Mann's part.[16]

Leaving Locarno depressed and in a bad mood, Koestler went to Belgrade for a rendezvous with his parents. At sixty-eight, Henrik was looking very old and had lost his sparkle. "His voice had a pathetic ring, and his eyes often shone with the sad tortoise-wisdom of our race." Though still battling to restore his business fortunes—his latest plan was to export bauxite to Sweden—Henrik wasn't making much headway and the project would never come to anything. He may also have been suffering from the stomach cancer that eventually killed him. Adele was her energetic and assertive self, triggering all Koestler's old hostility as she fussed over his health and appearance. According to Koestler she resolutely refused to discuss his imprisonment, but Dorothee had kept Adele and Henrik regularly informed about Arthur's plight and Adele had written to Dorothee the day after his release. "My dearly beloved Dörte, last night we got the wonderful news that our precious scamp is in Gibraltar. . . . I cannot describe the happiness I have been feeling since last night, and the fact that *you* are there overjoys me and doubles my happiness. . . . You must obviously be feeling very happy as well. My dear Dörte . . . you are such a true consolation to me in these difficult times, you have so bravely fought and won, so let me thank you, my darling child, and wish you every happiness. From your ever loving Mother Köstler." Adele hoped that Koestler and Dorothee would get back together again and undoubtedly told him so in no uncertain terms, increasing his resentment; and he may have sensed that this would be the last time he saw his father. The last glimpse he had of Henrik was of him standing forlornly on the platform and waving as Koestler's train pulled out of the station.[17]

KOESTLER CONTINUED ON to Athens and Palestine, where he spent six weeks visiting old friends and reporting on the political situation. He found Revisionists such as the Weinshalls sadly diminished by their political frustrations and demoralized by the near collapse of the Palestinian economy, which aroused conflicted emotions in him. He no longer shared their belief in the messianic promise of Palestine, nor in its future as an inspiration for mankind. He felt more strongly than ever that his roots were firmly planted in Europe, and endorsed the communist line that the "irksome Jewish question" would be solved by the global triumph of socialism. But he was still a Jew. He couldn't forget that millions of Jews in Europe might not be able to wait much longer and had no choice but to come to Israel or be oppressed. "In this limited, resigned and utilitarian sense, I was still a Zionist."[18]

Koestler also saw more clearly than his Zionist friends that the Arabs hadn't resigned themselves to the Jewish presence, nor had they been subdued. Jews were still being stabbed as they walked in the streets, homemade bombs were exploding in buses and trains, the oil pipeline from Mosul was set on fire, Lydda Airport was destroyed—all in the short space of time he was there. In his dispatches he described "two incompatible peoples" struggling over one small patch of land: Jews, who were sons of the twentieth century, and Arabs, who resided somewhere in the Middle Ages. He unexpectedly obtained an interview with Emir Abdullah of Transjordan, who expressed enthusiasm for the recent Peel Commission recommendation that Palestine be partitioned, but when Koestler showed the text of his interview to Sir Henry Cox, the British Resident in Amman, as required by the regulations, Cox severely censored it. "I hope I persuaded him to cut out the dangerous stuff he was thinking of communicating to his paper," he reported to MI5. Koestler told a member of the British Press Bureau in Jerusalem that he was "very depressed by what he had seen and heard," and that, too, was reported to the secret services.[19]

Returning to London, Koestler wrote three long articles for the *News Chronicle* on Palestine's problems. Though he no longer had any desire to live in Palestine himself, he felt a duty to his Jewish confrères and insisted that the need for a Jewish homeland was more urgent than ever. In "Palestine, the Melting Pot," he argued that the Jews were in Palestine mainly as a result of the Balfour Declaration and that it would be unjust not to recognize their claims. True, they were a pain in the neck, but that was because Europe had a bad conscience about them, and a bad conscience was usually experienced as a pain in the neck. In his second and third articles, "This Is an S.O.S. for Palestine" and "Partition—the Only Solution," Koestler publicly abandoned his earlier support for the Revisionist goal of establishing Eretz Israel on both banks of the Jordan River and advocated partition. It would be unjust to both Arabs and Jews, he wrote, and would be immensely difficult to implement, but it had one simple advantage over all other solutions: it was the only way out of an otherwise hopeless situation. "The implacable savagery in this petty guerrilla war threatens to destroy a historically unprecedented experiment. Britain must act, and act quickly. This is an SOS for Palestine."[20]

Interestingly, Koestler's articles openly contradicted the Communist Party line. In Moscow's view, the Arab-Jewish conflict was less important than the class struggle. Arab and Jewish proletariats in Palestine were supposed to find common cause in overthrowing their bourgeois and landowning oppressors and opposing the imperialist designs of the British, but as Koestler pointed out, there was virtually no proletariat in Palestine. His Jewish sympathies now trumped his Communist convictions again, another sign of his increased desire to be true to himself.

KOESTLER RETURNED TO BRITAIN just in time for the publication of *Spanish Testament* by the Left Book Club at the end of 1937, with an introduction by the duchess of Atholl. It was a book that perfectly mirrored the turning point in his writing from polemics to a more considered and more personal form of expression. Its first half was a toned-down and shortened version of *L'Espagne ensanglantée,* which, despite its character as propaganda, showed a distinct advance in objectivity over the earlier work. Gone were the atrocity photographs and inflammatory chapter headings. The raw materials of newspaper clippings and eyewitness accounts were folded into the main story and recast as a first-person narrative. This made a better fit with the second and more important half of the book, *Dialogue with Death,* Koestler's first foray into autobiography, which described his prison experiences in Seville.

The initial version of *Dialogue with Death* had its weaknesses. Koestler retained some of his old socialist-realist urge to wrap the particular in the general and to merge personal with collective experience, and his description of the the fall of Málaga still verged on the apocalyptic in places (the translation into English also left something to be desired), but the resulting narrative represented a quantum leap for Koestler's writing. He had stumbled across the form that was best suited to his talents, the autobiographical memoir. In *Red Days and White Nights* (a quasi-memoir) and in the first half of *Spanish Testament,* propaganda had overshadowed fidelity to personal experience, but in *Dialogue with Death* the reverse was true: the dramatic and personal nature of the subject matter—his capture, imprisonment, fear of dying, liberation—summoned a psychological intensity and exacted an artistic discipline that had hitherto been lacking. It was clear that a first-person narrative allowed him the space and flexibility to comment and digress in his own voice, in addition to exercising his considerable talents as a reporter, while the underlying form of a diary, with its dynamic interplay between the present and past tenses, lent the prose an urgency and immediacy that startled his readers and has a surprisingly modern feel to it.

Koestler recognized the work's distinctiveness a few years later, and in 1942 published an edited and tightened version of *Dialogue with Death* as a separate book, without the first half. Whereas the original text began with the fall of Málaga ("They came on Monday afternoon . . ."), the later version starts with Koestler's departure from Paris. In both, the description of the city's collapse rivals the many set pieces of war writing that were to emerge from the Spanish war. However, it is with the scenes inside the Seville prison that Koestler comes into his own. The combination of exact physical observation with merciless analysis of his mental and psychological responses carries complete conviction. "Permit me, O Lord, to continue to be discontented with this existence, to curse my work, not to answer my letters, to be a trial to my friends. Am I to swear to grow better if Thou lettest this cup pass from me? We both of us know, Lord, Thou and I, that such extorted oaths are never kept. Do not blackmail me, Lord God, and do not try to make a saint of me. Amen. Then the bugle blast woke me up."[21]

Koestler contemplates the effects of doubt and fear on a prisoner's mind and considers what kind of antidotes exist to neutralize this fear. In his own case it consisted of recalling passages from Mann and Freud and scratching Euclid's theorem on the wall. He feels that the solution is to merge "my individual misery with the biological misery of the universe; just as the vibrations and tensions of a wireless receiver are conducted to earth, where they disperse; I had 'earthed' my distress." These mental exercises can act as either narcotics or stimulants, but if practiced enough, they will automatically come into play at the moment of death.

> Thus I had actually no fear of the moment of execution; I only feared the fear which would precede that moment. But I relied on the feeling I had experienced on the staircase in Sir Peter's house, while waiting for Bolin's shot; that dream-like feeling of having one's consciousness split in two, so that, with one half of it one observes oneself with comparative coolness and aloofness, as though observing a stranger. The consciousness sees to it that its complete annihilation is never experienced. It does not divulge the secret of its existence and its decay. No one is allowed to look into the darkness with his eyes open; he is blindfolded beforehand.[22]

Elsewhere, after describing the nightly executions of his fellow prisoners, Koestler meditates on the peculiar state of mind of a person faced with the prospect of imminent death. "The constant nearness of death weighed us down and at the same time gave us a feeling of weightless floating. We were without responsibility. Most of us were not afraid of death, only of the act of dying; and there were times when we overcame even this fear. At such moments we were free—men without shadows, dismissed from the ranks of the mortal; it was the most complete experience of freedom that can be granted a man."[23]

IT WAS PASSAGES like these that prompted Sartre to praise the book as an early example of existentialism. George Orwell, fresh from writing *Homage to Catalonia,* was impressed by Koestler's ethical stance. Orwell immediately spotted the difference in quality between the two halves of *Spanish Testament,* guessing that the propaganda part had been "edited for the benefit of the Left Book Club" (he was wrong—the book had been toned down for the Left Book Club) but recognizing *Dialogue* as "of the greatest psychological interest" and saying that it was "probably one of the most honest and unusual documents that have been produced by the Spanish war." Thomas Mann also felt that the book was "splendidly written," and Walter Benjamin called it "a very good book indeed."[24]

Koestler was changing from Malraux's Manichean revolutionary into "a true intellectual," "a man of subtleties" whose meditations on the "absolute truth" of his experiences in Spain were in a fresh key for him, more religious than political, as he realized when he came to write the second volume of his autobiography some fifteen years later. Having had time to absorb the meaning of his imprisonment, Koestler concluded that his hours spent by the prison window scratching equations had brought mystical insights into another realm of being. He was filled "with a direct certainty that a higher order of reality existed, and that it alone invested existence with meaning." Koestler likened it to "a text written in invisible ink; though one could not read it, the knowledge that it existed was sufficient to alter the texture of one's existence," and elsewhere compared it to Freud's concept of the "oceanic feeling," an overwhelming intuition about the infinite and the eternal that was the essence of religious faith.[25]

Koestler had earlier used Freud's expression, of course, to describe his state of mind shortly before his conversion to Zionism, and had used similar phrasing about his embrace of Communism. Now too he was careful to emphasize that he had by no means experienced an instantaneous death-cell conversion to religion. He had arrived at this magical moment of truth through a rational analysis of a mathematical theorem and by way of an "articulate verbal insight," which "evaporated at once, leaving in its wake only a

wordless essence, a fragrance of eternity, a quiver of the arrow in the blue."
There were more moments of this kind in jail, and they continued intermittently after his release until they tapered off and stopped, but he was too
dazed and shocked at the time of writing *Dialogue with Death* to make much
sense of them, and even fifteen years later found it difficult to verbalize his
experiences. Those months in a Spanish jail, however, were to prove crucial
to his intellectual and spiritual development and to influence every major
book he was to write thereafter, up to and including his late works on the occult and parapsychology.[26]

PART TWO

FAME AND INFAMY

The Author as Novelist
(1936–1946)

CHAPTER FOURTEEN

THE GOD THAT FAILED

Whoever thinks a great deal is not suitable as a party member,
for he soon thinks himself right through the party.
— FRIEDRICH NIETZSCHE

THE SELECTION OF *Spanish Testament* as a monthly choice of the Left Book Club represented a breakthrough for Koestler. A jury of three, Victor Gollancz, Harold Laski, and John Strachey, made the selection, and it guaranteed him an enormous sale for that time of upward of sixty thousand copies, bringing much-needed financial stability and reinforcing his sense that at last he was a writer of some significance.

Unfortunately, his newly recovered sense of his own importance went to his head. The émigré Viennese novelist Paul Frischauer used to hold an informal salon at his home in Kensington Gardens in London, where regular guests included fellow émigrés Robert Neumann, Stefan Zweig, and H. G. Wells's mistress, Moura Budberg. After being invited, Koestler went out of his way to contradict Budberg on the subject of writers in Berlin and got into fierce arguments with just about everyone he came across, prompting Neumann to dismiss him as a "talented hysteric from that breed of superjournalists who are too clever by half." But Koestler got on well with Frischauer, whose all-night bridge sessions were a great attraction, and who was every bit as truculent and competitive as Koestler. On one Sunday drive in the country, the two men argued so violently that they stopped the car to settle their differences with a fistfight. The moment Koestler put up his fists, Frischauer jumped into the car and drove off, leaving Koestler to walk the three miles to the nearest railroad station in blazing heat. (Frischauer returned later to mock the enraged and humiliated Koestler as he tramped along the empty road.)[1]

Koestler's behavior in the public sphere was somewhat better, though it was hard to drop old habits. On a month-long lecture tour of Britain, prompted by his celebrity as a former prisoner of Franco, he noted that the British passion for fair play and sympathy for the underdog that had made it so easy for him to manipulate the Commission on Non-Intervention six months previously still worked to his advantage—and made it childishly easy for him to maintain the fiction that he was a liberal and an independent journalist. When the duchess of Atholl asked him (before agreeing to write an introduction to *Spanish Testament*) if he was a Communist, he lied to her and said no, and when questions were asked about POUM, which was especially well known in Britain (though Orwell had yet to publish his defense of the party in *Homage to Catalonia*), he justified Moscow's description of POUM as "Trotskyist" and "Franco's Fifth Column" with the explanation that any faction causing a split in revolutionary unity was "objectively" aiding the enemy and by definition hostile.

For the first time, however, he began to experience novel twinges of guilt for trying to take advantage of "bourgeois" gullibility, and he qualified his condemnation of POUM by saying that even if its leaders had made mistakes, they didn't deserve a death sentence, contradicting the Moscow line. Seeing how unimpressed his audiences were by his sophistry on this subject, he reflected on the clash between "the world of straight, intellectually limited, unimaginative decency, based on traditional values" that was England and "the twisted world of ruse and deceit in the service of Utopia" that was his accustomed milieu.[2]

Returning to Paris, Koestler was forced to grapple afresh with that milieu when he learned about a new show trial taking place in Moscow. The defendants this time included some of the most prominent leaders of the Soviet Communist Party: Nikolai Bukharin, Alexei Rykov, Nikolai Krestinsky, and Genrikh Yagoda. The trial represented a reductio ad absurdum of the argument that he had just been making in Britain about the culpability of POUM. The defendants were said to be guilty not of any concrete crimes per se but of the crime of omission, that is to say, of omitting to express full support for the policies of Stalin and the Central Committee and "objectively" encouraging others to commit much worse crimes against the state.

This particular piece of sophistry had first surfaced in the wake of the murder of the Leningrad party boss Sergei Kirov in December 1934. A month later, two famous old Bolsheviks, Grigory Zinoviev and Lev Kamenev, had been sentenced to prison for allegedly forming an illegal opposition to Stalin. Theirs had not been a show trial, since it was held behind closed doors, nor were the two leaders held directly responsible for the murder (as we now know, Stalin himself had planned and engineered it). They were found guilty instead of being "morally and politically responsible," which was a rehearsal for things to come. Eighteen months later, in August 1936, they were tried again, this time in the first big Soviet show trial, where they confessed in open court to plotting terrorist actions against Stalin and his associates at the behest of Trotsky.

The scale of the crimes involved, and the abject confessions of their perpetrators, created an unprecedented sensation. If the defendants were to be believed, Trotsky's allies had organized a vast opposition within Russia, penetrating all levels of the party, and were preparing to unleash a reign of terror. It seemed totally surreal, but so little was known of the inner workings of the Soviet state, and of Stalin's paranoid personality, that the confessions were widely accepted as genuine, especially since the presence of western observers and journalists in court seemed to guarantee the integrity of the proceedings. The death sentences pronounced on the defendants were widely accepted by liberal and progressive circles in the West, as they were again six months later, when a third trial was held with Radek and Pyatakov in the dock (this was the trial Koltsov had referred to in Valencia).

Koestler had been too distracted by his adventures in the Spanish Civil War to pay much attention to the 1934 trial, and by the time of the second trial was in jail himself. In the summer of 1937, while he was writing *Dialogue with Death,* there had been a huge purge of Red Army generals ending with more executions, and this was quickly followed by the arrest of Lenin's "darling of the Party," Bukharin, along with Rykov, Yagoda, and hundreds of other leaders (there was poetic justice in Yagoda's arrest, since it was he who had organized the earlier show trials as head of the NKVD). The alleged crimes of the accused included "espionage, wrecking, undermining Soviet military power, provoking a military attack on the USSR, plotting the dismemberment of the USSR, overthrowing the social system in favor of a return to capitalism," and "poisoning Maxim Gorky." Bukharin, one of the original members of Lenin's Politburo, was accused of having plotted to assassinate Lenin as early as 1918.

The blatant absurdity of these accusations was matched only by the allegation that it was again Trotsky who had planned the entire campaign, but public opinion inside and outside the Soviet Union had been softened by the earlier trials, and the well-oiled machinery operated like clockwork. During the first ten days of March, Bukharin, Rykov, Krestinsky, and other defendants confessed to the most hair-raising crimes imaginable. Following the script of the earlier trials, Bukharin denied that he had ever committed overt acts of terrorism, while confessing that he was "objectively" responsible for them. He had degenerated, he said, into an enemy of socialism, and he explicitly attacked western commentators for suggesting that his confession wasn't voluntary. He deserved to be executed as a lesson to those who were wavering in their support of the USSR and its leadership.[3]

*   *   *

NOT SO LONG BEFORE, Koestler would have swallowed these accusations and confessions out of loyalty to the party, but now he was among the waverers. In Moscow, he had admired Bukharin as a model of rationality and moderation. Now he felt personally threatened. Indeed, the widening ripples of the purges had spread outward to the point where they were beginning to touch his own life. From Dorothee he learned that her brother, Ernst, had been arrested in Saratov on charges that he was a saboteur—as a doctor he had supposedly injected his patients with syphilis. Ernst's wife and young daughter had no idea where he was and were later sent into internal exile as well. Dorothee herself was fired from Münzenberg's Free Library on the grounds that she was related to an enemy of the people.[4]

Then Koestler learned to his astonishment that Eva Striker was in Vienna after being expelled from the Soviet Union as an undesirable alien. She was staying with her mother and Koestler helped them leave on the very day Hitler invaded Austria. In London, Eva unfolded to Koestler the perverted workings of Soviet justice. About a year and a half after his visit, Eva had been made director of design of the Dulevo porcelain factory near Moscow, and in May 1936 (around the time that Koestler was released from Seville) she had been arrested and incarcerated in the Lubyanka before being transferred to a prison in Leningrad and placed in solitary confinement. After weeks of isolation she was confronted by an interrogator and charged with plotting to assassinate Stalin. A visitor from Germany was alleged to be a sniper, and she was accused of meeting with Stalin's enemies during a vacation in Paris.

The charges were fantastic. To stay sane, she played mental chess with herself and practiced conversations in French. She composed poems in German and recited them as she paced her cell. As the weeks passed, she learned how to communicate with the other prisoners by knocking on the wall in code, a time-honored practice in Soviet prisons. She learned that she was to be charged with Trotskyism, and that a gun had been found inside a sewing machine in her apartment (the gun belonged to her Hungarian landlord, not to her). Her young interrogator seemed friendly and sexually attracted to her, and told her he would drop the gun charges and get her released if she signed a false confession. She relented and signed, at which point the interrogator turned on her and called her "a stupid bitch" for believing him. Shattered by this betrayal, Eva tried to cut a wrist artery with a piece of wire but failed to find the right spot. She wrote countless letters to the authorities, including one to Stalin, and when she was called from her cell to be shown a document, she thought it was her death warrant. It turned out to be a warrant for her release, and in September 1937, after eighteen months in jail, she was given a new passport and put on a train to Vienna. Her armed escort told her that the crafty young interrogator had been swallowed by the system and was now himself in jail, but this was scant consolation for her suffering.[5]

Koestler was astonished by the parallels with his own experiences. While he had paced his cell in Seville doing mathematical equations, Eva had been pacing hers and composing poetry. He had thought of killing himself with a hypodermic syringe; she had tried to commit suicide with a piece of wire. He had been accused of fomenting a military rebellion; Eva had been accused of conspiracy and a plot to commit murder. The only external difference between them was that he had been in a fascist cell and she in a Communist one, and this coincidence was the most astonishing thing of all.

Eva told him that Alex Weissberg had also been charged with counterrevolutionary sabotage and was in jail, and Koestler vowed to get him out. He composed a letter to the Soviet Union's chief prosecutor, Andrei Vyshinsky, which was signed by three French winners of the Nobel Prize, among them Irène and Frédéric Joliot-Curie, but his attempts to get British scientists to sign came to nought. Martin Ruhemann, Alex's former colleague, flatly refused to have anything to do with the matter, and Ruhemann's wife said Alex was guilty. Michael Polanyi persuaded Einstein to write to Stalin on Alex's behalf, but nothing came of these petitions for a very long time.[6]

Eva's disturbing news was followed by other developments. A young Anglo-German couple of Koestler's acquaintance in Paris were denounced as spies. Emissaries from Moscow brought instructions to exiled German writers at the Café Mephisto to "write the truth" (translation: toe the party line) and insisted that "every Bolshevik must be a Chekist" (that is, a secret policeman). The implication was that writers should police one another to promote the interests of the party. Johannes Becher, now a permanent resident of Moscow, brought stories of German party leaders living in the Hotel Lux in a state of chronic suspicion, terrified of one another and of their Soviet bosses. "Everyone hears the rumble of thunder and ducks his head. He tries to shrink to the point of invisibility, and hopes that lightning will strike his neighbor's place instead." Koestler happened to be living in Becher's old apartment in the rue Antoine Chantin, a stone's throw from the Porte d'Orleans, and must have wondered why on earth Becher didn't stay in Paris to keep out of harm's way. Becher, however, was a party loyalist and insisted on returning to Moscow.[7]

THANKS TO HIS Spanish adventures and the success of his book, Koestler had become a much more prominent figure in the German Writers' Association than before and was asked to give a public talk on Spain. A party official asked him to be sure to denounce POUM, but Koestler decided he would refuse. He knew that POUM's leaders had been arrested and accused of treason, but repeated his view that they didn't deserve a death sentence (he was too late—even as he spoke they had already been liquidated by Moscow). He had in mind, among other things, a phrase from Malraux's *The Conquerors* that kept coming back to him in Seville (he had used it as an epigraph for *Dialogue with Death*): *Une vie ne vaut rien, mais rien ne vaut une vie*—a life is worth nothing, but nothing is worth a life.

Koestler delivered his talk in the hall of the Société des Industries Françaises in Place St.-Germain-des-Prés, before an audience of two hundred to three hundred German exiles. After giving his usual speech on Spain, he ended with three sentences that he had carefully prepared and written down beforehand: "No movement, party or person can claim the privilege of infallibility." "It is as foolish to appease the enemy, as it is to persecute the friend who pursues the same end as you by a different road." And: "In the long run, a harmful truth is better than a useful lie." This last statement, a quotation from the revered Thomas Mann, clearly flew in the face of party policy in the Soviet Union, and the first two contradicted the party's policy in Spain.[8]

There was a long silence from the Communist half of the audience, and Koestler knew that he had overstepped the mark. As he made his way out of the hall former comrades avoided him, and over the next few days he wrestled with his conscience. He knew that loyalty to the party line was supposed to be absolute, and divergence was a betrayal. Moreover, the party had just rescued him from prison and he seemed to be repaying it with black ingratitude. A last chance to mend fences came in early April, when Alexander Abusch summoned him to explain himself. Why had Koestler taken the initiative to protest against the arrest of Weissberg (and to involve British liberals in the process) instead of going through party circles? Why had he refused to speak out against POUM in his speech on Spain? And why was he so reluctant to submit himself to party discipline?

Though deeply shaken by Eva's revelations and still trying to process his Spanish experience, Koestler was desperate to square the circle and preserve his position in the party. He claimed that he was undergoing a psychological crisis (which was true), but tried to lie his way out of trouble by saying that he hadn't written the Weissberg letter and had not intended to excuse POUM, only to protest against its punishment. He added that he respected the party and appreciated Abusch's concern for his welfare, but also insisted on his right to speak out about the Moscow show trials. "Koestler made it clear he simply didn't understand the trials," wrote Abusch in his report to the Central Committee. "He said he couldn't understand why so many arrests were being made in the Soviet Union, couldn't understand the purges," and "couldn't believe the reports and explanations in the party press." Abusch told Koestler to consult with his comrades more often and listen to the party, and observed in his report that Koestler was under the influence of British liberal opinion and Trotskyist arguments. He was "extremely sensitive, quick to jump to conclusions, and had never mastered Marxism-Leninism," but he was also "sincere and no enemy of the party," though "very uncertain and confused."9

A couple of days later Koestler had a bruising encounter with another party stalwart, Kurt Kesten, who was incensed that Koestler had gone to Heinrich Mann and other party sympathizers to collect signatures for his Weissberg letter. Kesten told Koestler that there was absolutely no chance of his work appearing in the *Deutsche Volkszeitung* (German People's Daily) until he had cleared this matter up with the party, and he wrote a letter to Moscow to inform the party of his action (he asked not to be named if steps were taken against Koestler). Aware of his precarious position, Koestler asked Abusch if he could be excused from attending party cell meetings and said that if he were going to be expelled from the party, he hoped it wouldn't be done publicly.

IT SEEMS HE HAD COME to the conclusion that he was bound to be expelled sooner or later. Recantation was out of the question, and party discipline was tighter than ever, so he resolved to anticipate the expulsion with a preemptive strike. On April 22, 1938, he wrote a brief letter to the Writers' Association party caucus announcing his resignation. He was taking this step, he wrote, not in order to join any oppositional group, and not out of disillusionment with the Soviet Union (he wasn't ready to admit that yet), and he asked his comrades to keep his defection secret, since it would "harm the party's cause in England." His argument was that conservatives and liberals had campaigned for him on the express understanding that he was not a Communist. If the truth came out, "a whole lot of people who are important to us would feel used and betrayed, and would refuse to support us in the future." The letter was halfhearted in its attempt to break away and dishonest in its appeal to party solidarity and plea for secrecy. The "irreparable damage" of disclosure would be inflicted not just on "our movement" and "our comrades in Spain" but on Koestler personally, and he further hedged his departure by begging his colleagues to continue to regard him as an ally.10

Written in haste, the letter was both ethically dubious and confused in its reasoning, and Koestler promised to write another letter setting out his argument in greater detail. This he did a week later, accompanying it with a request to Kisch either to read it aloud at the next caucus meeting or to see that his fellow writers got to read it privately. "It is meant exclusively for them, for I think I have the right to acquaint my comrades with the exact reasons for my decision." This second letter, consisting of five single-spaced typed pages, is a remarkable document, much clearer and more rigorous than the first, and demonstrates how thoroughly Koestler had grasped the corruption and degradation of the party and how far ahead of his comrades on the left he was in understanding the consequences for European and world politics. It was one of the most momentous steps of his life, and he took it boldly, with his eyes wide open and regardless of the consequences.[11]

His main reason for leaving the party, he wrote, was its moral degeneration, a degeneration that had begun "long before 1933" and that was now seriously affecting the international arm of the movement. Two former general secretaries of the Comintern had been denounced as "spies, traitors, and mad dogs" and summarily executed. The Moscow trials were not isolated phenomena, affecting just the upper echelons of the party, but were "manifestations of a sickness embracing the entire movement, which has penetrated through the middle ranks right down into the individual cells." For years the Comintern had been dismissing, denouncing, arresting, and even executing its loyal functionaries, most without the benefit of proper proceedings. "It is a logical contradiction when with uncanny regularity the leadership sees itself obliged to undertake more and more bloody operations within the movement, and in the same breath insists that the movement is healthy. Such an accumulation of grave surgical interventions points with much greater likelihood to the existence of a much more serious illness."

Koestler dismissed the claim that the movement had been infiltrated by German, Polish, Hungarian, and Italian agents and tainted with fascist ideas, and pointed out that "spy mania" and "the psychosis of denunciation" were undermining the fraternal roots of the movement. "For years we have been wading knee-deep through a swamp: bitten, browbeaten, covered with filth, blind to reality. They console us by saying that this is the fate of all émigrés. But it was like that in Germany already. And worst of all, it's like that at the front—in Spain. The stink reaches all the way to the front lines, and even with a bullet in his belly a man is not free of the despicable clutches of this inquisition."

Koestler went on to offer his own analysis of the theory and practice of communism, pointing out that revolutionary ethics were nothing more than "a dialectically dressed-up version of the old Jesuit adage that the ends justify the means." The leadership's actions were automatically held to serve the objective interests of the Communist movement—and of human progress in general—while whoever criticized the leadership was "objectively helping communism's enemies" and ipso facto "an enemy of the people himself." Signing off, Koestler spoke nostalgically of the seven years he had spent in the party. He had gambled his livelihood on it and lost, but he had never regretted it, not even in his cell in Seville. "But now I feel I am being suffocated by you, and I have the elementary need to breathe, to think, and to write freely again, and to speak my mind. I don't know if I am going to regret this step. I can see no other way before me. But I know that yours is a dead end."[12]

Koestler delivered the letter personally to Kisch, leader of the party cell, aware that it amounted to ideological suicide. He knew that many party members shared his views in private, but very few were prepared to make the break as early as 1938, even with the evidence of the purges before them. Spain and anti-fascism were the twin pillars of the party's support in Europe, the two causes that legitimized it and blinded potential dissidents to the true nature of the Soviet regime. The Soviet Union itself was far away and inscrutable, and for all its shortcomings, it retained its glamor as a distant ideal that inspired millions of otherwise honest people with a fanatical loyalty—to which Koestler himself was still not wholly immune.

"What's left?" Koestler asked himself rhetorically in his letter.

> The Soviet Union is left. Not Stalin, but the Soviet Union. It's the only hope offered by this miserable century. It's the foundation of the future. Whoever goes against the Soviet Union goes against the future. But whoever presents it, afflicted as it is by all the flaws of transition and by the adolescent growing pains of Stalinism, as a finished prototype of the future, is offering us a caricature of the future. The Soviet Union is the most precious thing we have at present, but it is no prototype. For its *politics* we must defend the Soviet Union at all costs. But for its *theory,* it is an object of study, and study without criticism is unthinkable.

Koestler's description of Stalinism as "adolescent" would not have endeared him to the apparatchiks in Moscow, to whom the letter was forwarded, nor did it appeal to his fellow writers in the party caucus. At a meeting to discuss the letter, they "unanimously" endorsed a written response by Kisch, which would be published "in the event Koestler dared to attack the Party publicly." Koestler's betrayal was clearly the result of Trotskyist influences and "careerism." Koestler should be treated as an enemy from now on and all personal connections broken. Perhaps glad to be rid of this "bellyaching" gadfly, they did observe Koestler's request not to publicize his resignation, and despite the ostentatious hostility of some, he continued to number party members among his friends, and to remain within the Communist orbit, for at least another two years.[13]

CHAPTER FIFTEEN

NO NEW CERTAINTIES

Every revolutionary ends up becoming either an oppressor or a heretic.

— ALBERT CAMUS

THE TWO QUESTIONS that tormented Koestler in the summer of 1938 were how to reconcile the ends-versus-means riddle with Mann and Malraux's insistence on a place for morality in revolutionary practice, and how to account for what he was later to call "the tragedy of our age," the success of the fascists in mobilizing mass support for their regimes against all (as it seemed to him) reasonable expectations. If Communist theory was correct, the masses should have responded to the economic miseries of the Depression by embracing revolution—a development he had been eagerly anticipating in Germany ever since 1933. But the German, Italian, and Spanish masses had refused to oblige. The Communist parties and their supporters were decimated, and nothing seemed to stand in the way of Hitler, Mussolini, and Franco grabbing ever more power for themselves.

These were some of the issues Koestler had set out to examine in his book about Spartacus and his rebellion. Writing the *Svejk* sequel for Willi had interrupted him, but the success of *Spanish Testament* persuaded Jonathan Cape to sign a contract for what was to be his first full-length novel. Cape's advance of 125 pounds allowed him to complete the work by the end of July 1938, and to pay a young German-Jewish student living in London, Edith Simon, to do a translation. Its initial title, *Der Sklavenkrieg* (The Slave War), became *The Gladiators,* and it was published in Britain in the spring of 1939.[1]

The novel follows Spartacus's life from the time he escaped from gladiators' school in Capua with a band of seventy followers to his leadership of a major slave rebellion against Rome at the head of seventy thousand (or, according to other sources, ninety thousand) rebels. The slaves occupied a large chunk of southern Italy and defeated the Romans four times in battle before finally succumbing to the vastly superior forces of the Roman army. Influenced by a little-known Italian writer, Etiani Cicoteo, Koestler speculated that Spartacus had been a forerunner of later revolutionaries in history and was inspired by a kind of primitive socialism. Spartacus founds a utopian colony called Sun City, embraces the values of liberty, equality, and fraternity, and operates according to the socialist principle of "from each according to his abilities, to each according to his needs."

The description of Sun City echoes some of the utopian ideas Koestler first explored in *An Improbable Occurrence,* and when the experiment fails, Koestler again ascribes the breakdown to the rebelliousness of the population (in this case Spartacus's revolutionaries) and to Spartacus's inability to act with the necessary ruthlessness. Spartacus is helpless because he refuses to obey "the law of detours," according to which he should have temporarily subordinated ends to means and insisted that the rebels be executed, thus saving the revolution from defeat. By acting according to the ethical precepts advanced by Mann and Malraux, Spartacus sacrificed his noble ends because the means were repugnant to him.

Spartacus in the novel resembles Lenin (and to a lesser extent Jabotinsky) in that he is prepared at first to employ almost any measures to attain his goals, but he lacks Lenin's ruthlessness in a crisis. It's possible that Koestler also had in mind Brecht's controversial 1930 play, *Die Massnahme* (The Measure Taken), in which a young Russian Communist is killed by his three comrades because he has inadvertently betrayed their mission to the enemy. Koestler was a close student of Brecht. A typescript of the play figures among the papers confiscated by the French police, though in his later incarnation as an anti-Communist, Koestler went out of his way to attack the play for its immoral message.

In truth, Koestler was still confused in his attitude to revolution and its aftermath. While condemning the fanatical ruthlessness that had led to the Soviet show trials, he seemed to think that a "moderate ruthlessness" was still in order and that it could be turned on and off as needed. It was essential for exerting control over the masses but shouldn't be deliberately encouraged or allowed to get out of hand, as was the case in fascist countries. It's noteworthy that this idea is first raised by a member of the Jewish sect of the Essenes, Spartacus's informal "mentor and guide," who early in the narrative invokes the prophetic visions of Daniel and Isaiah and the imagery of the Psalms to describe the utopian (biblical) society that Spartacus should strive to create. It is the unnamed Essene, bald and aging and with a "bullet head," who first articulates the law of detours and urges his leader to be more ruthless and is, in effect, a stand-in for the author, showing that, at a time when he seemed to have forgotten or suppressed his Jewish heritage, Koestler was acutely aware of it, and leaned on it for a crucial part of his novel.

The Essene's musings are taken up later in the novel by a chronicler called Fulvius, who was outwardly modeled on Andor Németh but is clearly another voice for the author. Fulvius becomes obsessed with the refusal of the slaves to join Spartacus and rise against their owners, and writes a treatise, "On the Causes Which Induce Man to Act Contrary to His Own Interests," in which he concludes pessimistically, "The century of abortive revolutions was completed, the Party of Justice had lost its strength. He whose grasp is the most brutal can now rise to untold heights: dictator, emperor, god. Who will be the first to reach the winning post?"[2]

When the novel appeared in the spring of 1939, it was Koestler's Cassandra-like pessimism that most struck reviewers. The book "looks down on humanity with age-old eyes and discovers with a kind of cynical joyousness that the man-eating pattern of history is a timeless design," wrote one critic. The novel also has problems of language and construction. It is static and talky, with characters holding forth on power, politics, morality, religion, and a dozen other subjects that interested Koestler; and Koestler employs three distinct voices in the narrative: a biblical pastiche for the Essene and the chronicler Fulvius, a contemporary idiom for the narration of the action, and a colloquial street language for much of the commentary. The pastiche was deliberate (Koestler told a correspondent that these voices were meant to imitate the style of German translations of Cicero) but ultimately unconvincing, and the way the voices mix in other parts of the novel create an unfortunate sense of bathos. Perhaps the translation into English could be held responsible for some of the confusion, but Koestler always maintained that the translation was excellent.[3]

The novel sank without a trace in the anxious months before World War II, but after the war, and the success of *Darkness at Noon,* it was reissued to a more sympathetic audience. Some later readers were tempted to interpret Koestler's first novel as his *Animal Farm,* in which Rome stood in for the history of the Russian Revolution and the main characters were allegories. Koestler was certainly headed that way, as he had shown in *Mbo Mba,* but he hadn't arrived there in 1938 (nor had Orwell, of course). Some years later, V. S. Pritchett, an exacting critic of Koestler's fiction, judged the novel (somewhat perversely, one can't help thinking) Koestler's "most impressive" book. George Orwell remarked on Koestler's pessimism and felt that it hadn't been fully earned. He compared the novel unfavorably to Flaubert's *Salammbô* (itself a compliment of sorts) and pointed out that whereas the dilemma of the conflict beween ends and means was presented clearly enough, Spartacus's motives were left obscure. "If Spartacus is the prototype of the modern revolutionary—and obviously he is intended as that—he should have gone astray because of the impossibility of combining power with righteousness. As it is, he is an almost passive figure, acted upon rather than acting, and at times not convincing. The story partly fails because the central problem of revolution has been avoided, or, at least, has not been solved."[4]

ORWELL WAS WRITING some six years later and with the benefit of hindsight, but he was right about the "central problem." In the summer of 1938, Koestler was still struggling to find a way to reconcile power with righteousness and was exploring entirely new territory for him. After resigning from the party he felt like an "unfrocked priest," or a "veteran acrobat" who has "fallen from the tightrope and lost his dialectical balance." The sense of weightlessness was exhilarating, and he discovered while working on *The Gladiators* that writing for him was a form of "occupational therapy," a release from the feelings of guilt and anxiety that had become his daily companions. At last, it seemed, he had found a viable profession. "Before the break, I had thought of myself as a servant of the Cause, and of writing as a means of serving it. Now I began to regard myself as a professional writer." It was a new beginning, attended by the elation of discovery, and since ideas were what he lived and breathed for, he felt an urgent need to work out a new intellectual platform to replace the old one.[5]

Koestler had modeled parts of *The Gladiators* on Alfred Döblin's novel *The Three Steps of Wang Lun,* about an imaginary mass rebellion in China ("*Wang Lun* was my literary bible"). Döblin, according to Koestler, had "one of the most original and independent minds of the Left," and Koestler and Sperber (still a party member, but also wavering) started visiting Döblin in his cramped apartment just off the avenue de la Porte d'Orléans. The elderly novelist was a bitter, cynical, and witty man, an older version of Koestler himself. He derided Marx's idea that being determines consciousness and warned Koestler to pay more attention to the subjective side of human nature.

The psychic self, he said, was just as much an objective reality as the social and economic order, and consciousness had to be taken into account as much as social and economic relations. The fascists understood this perfectly. They had replaced the dreariness of the old order by filling the masses with a sense of permanent intoxication. It wasn't true that the workers had nothing to lose but their chains. The workers were consumers as well as producers ("as even the stupidest capitalist understands") and were deeply committed to their families, their nation, and their state. The fascists had given the workers a false sense of belonging to the state. The Russians had absorbed the workers into the state, without allowing them to influence or "proletarianize" it in any way. The state had become all-powerful, but there had to be another way.[6]

Döblin's analysis struck Koestler as a much more convincing explanation of Hitler's successes than any Marxist interpretation he had heard, and his growing skepticism about Soviet policies was strengthened when he ran into

Münzenberg again. Willi was also disturbed by the Moscow purges, not least because he was a prime candidate for liquidation himself. He had been one of the first to warn Moscow that the Popular Front policy in Europe was collapsing, but the party preferred to blame the messenger. In the spring of 1938, the German Central Committee had expelled Willi from its ranks for "negotiating with right-wing bourgeois circles" and attacked his book *Propaganda as a Weapon* for overestimating the success of the Nazi propaganda machine. Willi wrote a formal reply but kept its contents secret, not wanting (like Koestler) to break publicly with the party. But never one to stay idle, he had immediately formed the Friends of Socialist Unity in Germany, with the goal of uniting all the non-Communist, anti-fascist exiles into a single movement, and launched a new magazine, *Die Zukunft* (The Future) as its organ. The name was typical of Willi's flare for publicity, trumping the name *Forward* favored by so many Communist publications by suggesting that Willi already knew what the future held in store.[7]

DELIGHTED TO FIND Willi moving in more or less the same direction as he was, Koestler became *Die Zukunft*'s founding editor and helped plan the magazine's contents. One of his first steps was to enlist the independent left-wing novelist Ludwig Marcuse as literary editor. The bookish Marcuse had been living and writing peacefully in a German enclave in the south of France and was bewildered by the dazzling variety of left-wing sects he found among the exiles in Paris, but he instinctively warmed to Koestler. "When he was in the mood he could be absolutely bewitching, which didn't come across as calculated. He was a melancholic who displayed enormous vitality when he wanted to win someone around. He was brilliant in argument, not just in writing and not just in debate, but also when shooting from the hip." Marcuse approved of the way Koestler jousted with party faithfuls such as Katz and Kantorowicz, whom Koestler still considered his friends, and outargued them on points of ideology.[8]

The first number of the magazine appeared on October 12, 1938, with the slogan "A New Germany, a New Europe" on its masthead. It was presented as a left-wing counterweight to the Soviet-backed Communists, and a brief editorial expressed the pious hope that there would be "no German group in exile, no German colony, no union of German-speaking people in any country that does not read *Die Zukunft* and help promote it." Prominent contributors included Marcuse, Münzenberg, Döblin, Stefan Zweig, and Joseph Roth. Koestler wrote a brief article for the third issue, but devoted most of his energy to editorial matters and to putting together a special Anglo-German number to appear at the end of November.[9]

Contributors included E. M. Forster, Aldous Huxley, Kingsley Martin, Lord Robert Cecil, Harold Nicolson, and Lady Violet Bonham-Carter on the

English side (Koestler tried, and failed, to get Winston Churchill and Anthony Eden), and Thomas Mann, Heinrich Mann, Lion Feuchtwanger, and the Austrian novelist Paul Frischauer for the Germans. Getting Thomas Mann to contribute was tricky, since Mann had moved to Princeton and was suspicious of the German exile community. Koestler sent the great man a long, flattering letter reminding him of their meeting in Locarno, and saying that the magazine's aim was to "bring Europe's voice to those living behind the Chinese wall." Mann obliged with a short, sharp article attacking Chamberlain's appeasement policies, and Koestler then had the delicate task of toning it down (which he did without consulting Mann) because the editors had to make allowances for "English sensibilities."[10]

The Anglo-German issue gave Koestler an opportunity to visit another hero of his youth, Sigmund Freud. Shortly before the annexation of Austria, Freud and his family had moved to Hampstead in northwest London, and Koestler called on him to get a contribution. Freud, then eighty-two, had already contracted the cancer of the mouth that was to kill him within the year. Koestler tiptoed into the great man's presence like a frightened schoolboy but was relieved to find Freud easier and friendlier than Mann. Freud graciously agreed to send an article for the special issue. It consisted mostly of a long quotation from a German author explaining why Christians had a duty to support the Jews and oppose anti-Semitism, with an innocent request for the source. It wasn't exactly a statement by Freud, but its intent was clear.[11]

Freud had good reason to sound a warning. Nazi troops had just marched into his native Vienna to proclaim the *Anschluss* between Germany and Austria, and for Jewish exiles the writing was on the wall. Koestler helped Eva extricate her mother to London, and sometime afterward the entire Striker family, including Eva, traveled by ship to the USA. Six months later came the Munich Pact. In Paris the atmosphere grew heavy and oppressive. Lights were dimmed, the streets went dark, an air raid seemed possible at any moment. But when Daladier returned to Paris and Chamberlain to London, waving their pieces of paper with Hitler's signature on them, the majority of French and British people emitted a huge sigh of relief. As much as they despised Hitler, they feared him more, and dreaded the slaughter war would bring. "Anything, even the most cruel injustice, was better than war," wrote Simone de Beauvoir, and even Sartre, who knew better, told Raymond Aron, "We can't dispose of the lives of others." The French and British weren't prepared to die for Czechoslovakia, a faraway country of which they knew nothing, and still didn't understand that their cowardice would lead to the deaths of many millions more in the years to come.[12]

The German and Austrian exiles understood, however. Some of their friends had died already, and more would follow. In Paris they conducted their feverish debates in isolation from most of the French intellectuals around them. It was at this time that Sperber joined *Die Zukunft* and drew close to Koestler again. The same age as Koestler (thirty-two) and also short, with dark, flashing eyes, a pale oval face, an intense manner, and a vanity in argument that rivaled Koestler's own, Sperber was better educated than Koestler, with a higher degree in Adlerian psychology, and the more logical dialectician of the two. He had also resigned from the party recently, and the two felt they had shed all their earlier illusions.

Sperber noticed that since Spain, Koestler had rid himself of much of his earlier "inner distress." He had emerged from the death cell outwardly unchanged and "had no new certainties," but "he was resolved from then on not to settle for half-truths. We agreed on all essential things, though we continued to differ in matters of taste and lifestyle." (Sperber was a teetotaler and monogamous, and Koestler was the direct opposite.) They were like rock climbers, said Sperber, "who are exposed to the same enticements and dangers and expect no less from each other than they do from themselves. No matter how depressing the events of the day might be, the Jewish wit and the gallows humor that each new day provoked determined the tone in which we expressed our hopes and fears. In fact, we felt more bitterness than is required to hate one's own life and all one's contemporaries, and yet we had a lot of fun when we were together and could often be heard laughing heartily."[13]

Münzenberg organized regular editorial meetings in *Die Zukunft*'s offices and fund-raising events at the plush town house of Olof Aschberg, a Swedish millionaire who was also his chief backer. Food and wine were plentiful and the guests well-heeled. The magazine's well-researched reports on Nazi concentration camps and persecutions of the Jews, and articles by H. G. Wells, Franz Werfel, and other luminaries, were beginning to make an impact. Such was Münzenberg's sleight of hand that for over a year the Gestapo never guessed his role in it.

IN MARCH 1939, Koestler decided he had had enough of *Die Zukunft*. The Spanish Civil War had ended in complete defeat for the Republicans and the installation of a Franco government in Madrid. The first great battle against fascism had ended in utter disaster, and Koestler felt personally affronted. More to the point, he had conceived an idea for a new novel and was eager to get on with it, but had run out of money. Once more the Aldor cousins came to the rescue with a commission to write yet another sex book. This one, *L'Enyclopédie de la famille* (Encyclopedia of the Family), on the psychology of marriage, was to be written jointly by himself and Sperber (drawing on Sperber's experience as a psychologist). The idea of Koestler as an expert on marriage was farcical, to say the least, and it's not at all clear which parts, if any, he wrote unaided (since fewer than fifty of his and Sperber's pages were retained in later editions, it's impossible to tell). The book enjoyed considerable success in France, and later in Britain and America, where it was translated as *The Practice of Sex*. For two months' work Koestler got the equivalent of about forty pounds sterling, which was enough to pay his expenses for another five months. Royalties were promised by the irrepressible Feri Aldor, but never materialized, which was a great pity. Sixty years after its compilation, a revised American edition of the book was still in print and going strong.[14]

Koestler's own attitude to sex and marriage hadn't changed much over the years. He continued to regard his union with Dorothee as a pure formality, but since he made it a point to include very little on his love life in his autobiographies, not much is known about other women he might have seen during these years. There was Gerda Grepp for a time, and in Paris he ran into Dora Zuckermann, the young girl he had tried to court in Haifa when she was sixteen. This time, according to Dora, she was swept off her feet by Koestler's "magnetism." Koestler liked to whisk her off to the poorer and more colorful districts of Paris in his beige Ford roadster, and one day abandoned her for several hours in a dimly lighted apache bar near the Bastille. She was furious and ended the affair, convinced that he was playing games with her.[15]

In the summer of 1939, he was powerfully attracted to a twenty-two-year-old English sculptor by the name of Daphne Hardy. Raised in Holland, where her father worked for the International Court of Justice, Daphne was fluent in several languages, including German. When introduced to Koestler, she had just arrived in Paris on an art scholarship and was on the rebound from an unhappy love affair. Lonely, rudderless, and unattached, she was far from favorably impressed by this pushy Hungarian. To her cool English eye he seemed gauche and awkward, perpetually on the defensive and liable to drop a brick at any time. He was neither tall enough nor handsome enough to satisfy her taste, and he dressed outlandishly in a long, voluminous raincoat and baggy pants that trailed on the ground, looking as though they would trip him up. But there was something pathetic and endearing about this Hungarian oddball that caught her imagination. He was another lost soul like herself, and Daphne agreed to his suggestion to meet again.[16]

Totally unaware of the poor impression he was making, Koestler pursued the distant young Englishwoman with his usual ardor. He liked the tilt of her high forehead, the piercing look of her deep-set brown eyes, and the thrust of her strong chin. She was different from his usual girlfriends in having a strong sense of independence, an interest in art and sculpture, and a complete indifference to politics. Her dry reserve also contrasted sharply with his Hungarian ebullience, though that reserve masked a feeling of insecurity every bit as debilitating as his own. Soon they were meeting regularly, and it was only a matter of time before she moved into his apartment on the top floor at 10 rue Dombasle. (This seven-story house was filled with German left-wing émigrés and fellow travelers, as well as some party members.) As he continued to work on his novel, Koestler decided it would be cheaper for them to spend the summer on the French Riviera. This wasn't nearly as absurd as it sounds now. In the late 1930s the south of France was a bargain—and chock-full of exiled German writers, ranging from Heinrich Mann, Arnold Zweig, Bertolt Brecht, and Ernst Toller to Erwin Piscator, Franz Werfel, Friedrich Wolf, and Ludwig Marcuse, to name just a few.[17]

Daphne had nothing to lose, and she and Koestler traveled south in Koestler's old roadster, accompanied, it seems, by one of the Aldor brothers as far as the Riviera. After searching the coastline for a suitable place to stay, they stopped in the seaside hamlet of Roquebrune, near Menton, a favorite with impecunious German authors, where they were joined by Gerda Grepp. Daphne wasn't happy sharing Koestler with his former girlfriend, but it turned out Gerda had contracted tuberculosis and was visibly dying. The two women became friends, and Daphne sculpted her head before Gerda left for Paris again.[18]

Koestler was infatuated with Daphne. "Either my neurosis has suddenly vanished—though I wonder if such a thing is possible—or else I'm getting old," he wrote to Sperber. "Or perhaps she is simply the first woman who is right for me. We've been living together for nearly two months now and I'm still not browned off with her, which is an absolute miracle." The key to his feelings, he wrote, was that he respected her. "She is working here and she's really good, and having this respect is something new for me."[19]

CHAPTER SIXTEEN

DARKNESS VISIBLE

Wounds heal and become scars. But scars grow with us.
— STANISŁAW LEC

ONCE SETTLED IN ROQUEBRUNE, Koestler got to work on the new novel which he had tentatively entitled "The Vicious Circle." The seed for it had been planted by Leopold Schwarzschild, the editor of *Das neue Tagebuch,* who had remarked in Koestler's hearing about the hypocrisy of the Communists and the huge disparity between their publicly proclaimed virtues and their private sins. The idea germinated into a story about a group of prisoners sentenced to death who reevaluate their lives on the brink of extinction. Each concludes that he is guilty not of the crimes of which he is accused but of the sin of sacrificing morality to expediency, that is, of subordinating means to ends in the name of promoting human happiness. They are therefore guilty of sinning against their own beliefs, and they conclude that their deaths are necessary for the good of the greater cause. They have no argument with which to oppose the verdict against them and are caught in a vicious circle of their own making.[1]

The origins of the story in Koestler's Spanish experiences are easy to see, but Koestler had only the vaguest notion of a plot when he started out. He wanted to take his examination of the conflict between ends and means beyond where he had left it in *The Gladiators.* What if Spartacus had grasped the nettle and been more ruthless in imposing his ends regardless of the means? And what if he had executed his enemies and imposed the enlightened laws of his Sun City by force? Wouldn't he then have been following the law of detours, which Koestler (via Fulvius) had described as necessary to revolutionary success?

Koestler wanted, this time, to emphasize the contemporary importance of his ideas and to set the novel in the recent past, not long ago. The only character firmly established in his mind was the figure of an Old Bolshevik, an amalgam of Leon Trotsky and Karl Radek in appearance, whose way of thinking was loosely modeled on Bukharin's at his recent trial. His first name, like Bukharin's, was Nikolai, his patronymic was Salmanovich (a variation on Solomonovich, "Solomon's son," indicating his Jewish parentage), and his surname was Rubashov, which evoked the Russian word *rubashka,* meaning a shirt. Only later was Koestler reminded that Nikolai Salmanovich Rubashov was also the name of the editor of *Dvar,* the Labor Party's daily Hebrew newspaper in Palestine. Koestler acknowledged this in his autobiography, but omitted to mention that Rubashov was a famously bitter opponent of Jabotinsky and Revisionism. Koestler's subconscious had thrown up the name of an old enemy without his realizing it.[2]

The work flowed easily at first. "Once the opening scene was written, I did not have to search for plot and incident; they were waiting among the stored memories of seven years, which, while the lid was down on them, had undergone a kind of fermentation. Now that the pressure was lifted, they came bubbling up. I did not worry about what would happen next in the book; I waited for it to happen with fear and curiosity." The opening scene describes the arrest of Rubashov, asleep and dreaming of an earlier arrest in an enemy country (clearly Nazi Germany, though the country is not specified). Awakened roughly in the early hours of the morning, Rubashov can't tell whether he is still dreaming about Germany or awake and in his own country (the Soviet Union, also not named, but obvious from the context), a symbolic conflation of the two dictatorships that signaled one of the novel's underlying themes. This conflation must have been subconscious on Koestler's part, for he still consciously supported the Soviet Union and had never before thought to compare it to Nazi Germany. Other characters that sprang to life as he wrote were based on people he had met in Baku. Nadezhda Smirnova became Rubashov's secretary, Arlova; Paul Werner became Little Loewy; the "good" commissar at GPU headquarters became the "humane" interrogator, Ivanov; and the "bad" commissar turned into Gletkin, the ruthless interrogator who forces Rubashov to confess. Themes of secrecy, party loyalty, betrayal, and personal inadequacy began to swirl in Koestler's head as he surrendered to memories of his years in the party, and autobiography intruded more and more into the portrayal of Rubashov.[3]

Always a disciplined writer, Koestler worked furiously every day, and within weeks had completed 230 pages of his first draft. "R[ubashov] has just capitulated," he wrote to Sperber in Paris, "and I have the feeling that the continuation is better than the beginning, for when you look at his statement, his conduct strikes me as so obvious that I'm beginning to wonder why all the trial statements seemed so incomprehensible; no doubt it was because we used to single out *one* isolated motive and exaggerate its importance, whereas when all the incidental and subsidiary motives are taken into consideration, the procedure turns out to be natural and intelligible."[4]

Koestler's preoccupation with the character of Rubashov marked an important change in novelistic strategy for him. From being an account of the behavior of several leaders undergoing trials, *Darkness at Noon* became the story of Rubashov alone. Most of the action now took place inside Rubashov's head, in the form of long internal monologues, and the other characters were refracted through Rubashov's thoughts and imagination. It was a major breakthrough for Koestler's fiction. The single point of view and first-person voice freed him to range widely and digress at will, while still preserving unity of action.

ROQUEBRUNE PROVED TOO BUSY and distracting for Koestler, and he and Daphne retreated to the small Alpine village of Roquebillière, described in the opening pages of *Scum of the Earth,* a sleepy hamlet in the steeply sloping valley of the Vésubie River. They rented a cheap chalet from a local family, and Daphne sculpted while Koestler settled down to finish his novel. But in late August his peace of mind was shattered when he stumbled across an inconspicuous item from the Havas news agency buried on page three of the local newspaper: Nazi Germany had signed a nonaggression treaty with the Soviet Union. The news that the socialist motherland had come to terms with its number-one enemy shocked him more deeply than he could have imagined. Here he was in the south of France, writing a novel to expose the corruption and unscrupulousness of the party, and had just completed a speech in which the interrogator, Gletkin, admits: "We did not recoil from betraying our friends and compromising with our enemies to preserve the Bastion," yet he was stunned to find these words put into such stark practice. (Not so Daphne. "I always thought Stalin was capable of such idiocy," she later said. "I was surprised by Arthur's surprise.")[5]

For seven years Koestler had opposed fascism with every nerve in his body, and even after breaking with the party had seen the Soviet Union as the only hope for a socialist future, but that illusion was now shattered. "While I was reading that Havas notice," he wrote later, "I was not depressed, only excited; but I knew that I would be depressed tomorrow and the day after tomorrow, and that this feeling of bitterness would not leave me for months and perhaps years to come."[6]

Breaking off his work on the novel, Koestler, with Daphne in tow, hastened back to Paris via Toulon and Aix-en-Provence. A general mobilization had been announced in France and their journey was slow and difficult. A complete blackout prevented the use of headlights by night; by day the roads were jammed with military convoys. Nearer to Paris they encountered hordes of frightened families streaming out of the capital for fear of an aerial bombardment. The Germans had just invaded Poland. France and Britain had declared war. For the first couple of nights after their return they stayed with friends in the suburbs, and they moved back to the apartment on the rue Dombasle only when they knew the coast was clear. Antiaircraft balloons flew overhead. Gas masks were distributed in the schools and at places of work. You needed an identity card to make a phone call. Shopkeepers with German-sounding names put up notices that their businesses were French-owned. The streets were lit with dim blue lamps, and every window had to be curtained before the lights were turned on. It was the start of the *drôle de guerre,* the phony war, which was to last ten months before the German invasion, though no one expected it to go on so long.

Koestler's exile friends were desperate. The French government had decreed that all German and Austrian refugees were undesirable aliens and were rounding them up and sending them to internment camps on the grounds that they constituted a fifth column. Communists were particularly at risk, since they were judged to be working for two enemy countries at once: Germany and the Soviet Union. If they were Jewish, their situation was still worse. French anti-Semitism was on the rise and being freely exploited by the Daladier government to divert attention from its own inadequacies. Sizing up the situation, Koestler scrambled to clarify his status, tramping from police station to police station, and from one government office to another, to get his papers in order. He felt he should have been safe. He had a Hungarian passport in his pocket (Hungary was officially neutral), he had left the Communist Party a year and a half earlier, and he planned to go to London with Daphne just as soon as he could get a ticket.[7] But he had been under surveillance by the Paris police ever since his arrival in 1933, and as far as they were concerned he was a potential Soviet agent, whatever his party status. The same held true in Britain, and his application for British visas for himself and Dorothee was turned down by MI5, also on the grounds that he was still a Communist. He impulsively volunteered for ambulance service, absurdly suggesting to the clerk at the Red Cross that Daphne could be "the person sitting next to the ambulance driver" (the Red Cross said no). The French police renewed his identity card but refused to guarantee his safety, and he returned home to work on his novel, keeping a bag packed by his bedside just in case.[8]

On the morning of October 2, 1939, after three distracting weeks of writing, he opened the door to two policemen, leaving a pale-faced Daphne standing in the street as he disappeared with them around a corner. For three days he was held at the district police headquarters, spending his nights locked in a filthy coal cellar with about eighty other prisoners. He wasn't told the reason for his arrest, but later learned it was because of his continuing association with Münzenberg and Katz and his membership in the Friends of Socialist Unity in Germany. The French police believed that Koestler "belonged to the secret propaganda apparatus of the Soviet Union" and considered him "dangerous to the security of France." The question arises as to why the French police arrested Koestler for associating with Katz and Münzenberg while leaving the latter two at liberty, and only recently has it emerged that Münzenberg and Katz were double agents, who worked both for the Soviets and for the French Ministry of the Interior. Katz failed to "give satisfaction," however, and shortly after Koestler's arrest was presented with an ultimatum to leave France or be arrested. He sailed for New York on January 7, 1940.[9]

UNAWARE OF ANY OF THIS, Koestler and a couple of dozen other prisoners were herded into a police van and taken to the Roland Garros tennis stadium, where Koestler spent a tense nine days waiting to learn his fate. The nights were unusually cold and wet for October, and the prisoners slept on concrete floors covered with a thin layer of straw. Space was so tight that they had to sleep like sardines in a can, head to toe, to avoid one another's breath. Rain dripped from the ill-fitting steps of the terraces overhead, and sanitary conditions were primitive. During smoke breaks, Koestler recognized several friends from his Münzenberg days, including Münzenberg's secretary, Willy Schultz, and the novelist Gustav Regler, now an ex-Communist like himself. He also met a fellow leftist and disillusioned former Communist, Leo Valiani, who would become a friend for life. Valiani, who had grown up in Trieste, spoke fluent Hungarian as well as his native Italian and had spent years in Mussolini's jails.[10]

After learning they were being sent away to internment camps, Koestler wheedled permission out of the commandant for Daphne to visit him, and bribed a guard to fetch her in a taxi. She said she would stay in Paris until he was released, and he gave her a string of names of people to contact, including Babette Gross and Malraux, and urged her to do everything she could to get him out. The prisoners were loaded onto a train and taken south to the internment camp of Le Vernet, southwest of Toulouse and thirty miles north of the Spanish border. The camp had been built to house refugee militiamen from the Spanish Civil War. By mid-1939 it had been virtually emptied, but was now pressed into service to hold "undesirable aliens," who included both Spanish veterans and the German and Austrian refugees suspected of being Communists. When the five hundred or so new prisoners were unloaded at the tiny station of Le Vernet, they found themselves in the middle of a flat, featureless plain, and as they were being marched off under armed escort, they got a sudden glimpse of what they feared would be their future: a ragged band of about thirty veteran prisoners marching at the double, urged on by whip-wielding guards.[11]

There were no whips in Koestler's immediate future, but there was head shaving, a humiliating procedure that infuriated him—not even in Seville had they shaved the prisoners' heads. With Regler and Valiani he tried to organize a collective protest, but it fizzled when they discovered that only the Communists were willing to join them. When the time came for Koestler to be cropped, he wrenched the scissors from the barber's hand and began to chop away at his thick black hair himself. "I've been wanting to do this ever since I was a child," he yelled, before submitting angrily to the shearing.[12]

Le Vernet was enormous, covering fifty acres in all. When Koestler arrived it housed about a thousand prisoners of dozens of different nationalities, and by the time he left the number had doubled. It was encircled by barbed wire and trenches, and a loudspeaker proclaimed that whoever went within two yards of the fence would be shot. Other barbed-wire fences divided the compound into three sectors. Sector A was for aliens with a criminal record; B was for political prisoners, including the Communist survivors of the Spanish Civil War; C was a catchall for prisoners with no clear political or criminal record but under suspicion as undesirables.[13]

Koestler and his companions were placed in sector C, hut 34. They slept on straw-covered boards, fifty men to a row, two hundred per hut. There were no windows, just square holes in the walls, and there was no heat of any kind. There were no blankets (unless you had brought your own), no items of furniture, and no lights. The food consisted of a daily ration of eleven ounces of bread, a cup of unsugared coffee in the morning, and a pint of thin soup at midday and in the evening. There were also a few pieces of boiled beef in the midday soup, but "of such a bad quality that only the hungriest would eat it." Since there were no tables, dishes, knives, forks, or spoons to eat with, this fare had to be consumed from makeshift containers made from used cans and scooped up with sticks or bare hands.[14]

The prisoners were divided into squads of thirty men each and set to work with pick and shovel to level the exercise yard. As in Palestine, Koestler turned out to be hopeless at physical labor. József Román, a Hungarian carpenter, tried to teach Koestler how to malinger, but Koestler couldn't get the hang of it. "I felt my eyes starting out of my face and every heartbeat resounding in my chest like a hollow drum." At the end of a six-hour day, with a short break for lunch, he felt "a dense fog" in his brain, "impenetrable to any coherent thought, except the dull obsession of counting the minutes—an aching state of semi-consciousness and dumb idiocy."[15]

Koestler resorted to a trick of his own. He complained of a heart condition, citing his jail experiences in Seville as a possible cause, and asked to be excused from hard labor. The young medical lieutenant who checked his blood pressure probably guessed the truth, but he recognized Koestler's name and promptly exempted him from physical work. Koestler became a sort of "housekeeper" to the working prisoners, shaking out their blankets while they were away, cleaning their straw, and tidying their belongings. He bribed the cooks in the kitchen for hot water and other goodies and soon began getting food packages from Paris, which he shared with his friends.[16]

Despite its nickname as the "French Dachau," Le Vernet was lax by modern standards. Bribery was the order of the day, and Koestler, with money and food soon arriving from Paris, quickly acquired a makeshift table and five stools, and got shelves installed for food and books. He arranged for five palliasses to be sent from Paris, which he stuffed liberally with straw, and he fashioned two lamps from sardine cans filled with oil and a wick suspended from a hook. It was a creative outlet for his obsessive neatness and desire for order in his life. To crown it all, he got permission from the commandant to continue his writing, sitting outside under a large umbrella when it got hot, much to the envy of Regler and the other prisoners. He was able to resume, and almost finish, "The Vicious Circle," and Valiani became his first reader.[17]

POLITICS WAS INEVITABLY the main topic of conversation, and Koestler enjoyed considerable authority as a result of his Spanish book and his international reputation, despite the fact that his critical view of the Soviet Union made him highly unpopular with the Communists and fellow travelers in the camp. Instead, he had gone far ahead of most leftists in his thinking. "Perhaps the truth is that real leftism today can only be anti-Communist," Koestler said to Valiani, Román, and another Hungarian named Tamás Aladar one day. "Communism isn't what sprang from our little student brains. Communism is the Soviet Union. They are building the omnipotent reign of a human god and the domination of the world by the most cruel dictatorship ever seen." Bolshevism, he added, probably with his novel in mind, created fanatics ready to make any sacrifice for the sake of the party, even to say that they were traitors. Stalinism wasn't Marxism. It ignored the teachings of Marx in *Das Kapital,* and its biggest crime was that it had substituted rule by decree for the laws of society.[18]

Some Paris-based humanitarian committees asked Koestler and Regler to distribute gifts of blankets, shoes, and clothing to needy prisoners in sector C (the Communists refused such gifts on principle). Surrealistically, Koestler continued to write his novel by the light of his sardine-tin oil lamp until one day he was abruptly recertified as "fit for all duties." He was assigned to the latrine squad, spending two hours a day emptying brimming barrels, and almost fainted from the overpowering stench. On the first two days he vomited incessantly, but he got hold of a pair of gloves and managed somewhat better after that.[19]

For some reason he was in the unusually privileged position of being able to write and receive two letters per week, and he used the opportunity to instruct Daphne on how to get him out, but poor Daphne was a novice at political intrigue. When she visited Babette Gross the day after Koestler was sent south, Babette looked at her icily and said: "What took you so long? I expected you yesterday." Münzenberg wrote personally to President Léon Blum and the minister of the interior to intercede for Koestler, Regler, and Willy Schultz, but the government's wheels ground slowly and there was no response. Schooled in the rules of conspiracy, Koestler asked Daphne to number her letters so that he could check if all were getting through, but she mixed up the numbers and spoiled the whole scheme, driving Koestler into a frenzy over her incompetence. At his direction, she spent endless days haunting the offices of deputies of the French parliament, writing letters in a vain attempt to get the Ministry of the Interior to explain the reasons for Koestler's arrest, and wrestling with the bureaucratic obstacles that were thrown into her path. She contacted Jonathan Cape in London, who in turn approached the Foreign Office and the Hungarian legation and got Cecil Day-Lewis and the English PEN Club to appeal in the name of English writers. She wrote to the *News Chronicle,* to the duchess of Atholl, and to Edgar Mowrer, and got the last to ask Harold Nicolson to take an interest in the case and to request the French government to let Koestler go to Britain.[20]

It was in many ways a repeat of Dorothee's campaign to get him out of his Seville jail, but without the backing of the party machinery, and Daphne was no Dorothee: she was a political neophyte and hopelessly at sea when it came to pulling the right levers. Appropriately enough, it was Dorothee herself (guided by Münzenberg) who effected Koestler's release. Her key contact was a deceptively languid and flabby-looking young British diplomat called Paul Willert. Tall and handsome, with receding fair hair, Willert had worked for Ullstein in Weimar Berlin and had dallied with communism, getting to know Regler, Münzenberg, and Otto Katz in the process. Later, while working for Oxford University Press in New York, he had employed Whittaker Chambers as a translator, and was Katz's host when Katz went to visit Chambers to persuade him not to defect from the party. Like Katz, Willert was something of a Pimpernel, always in the right place at the right time, and like Katz, he too had changed his spots. He was working for MI5 and monitoring anti-fascist Germans in the emigration.[21]

Willert lived in a luxurious apartment on Place Dauphine with his wife, Brenda (a member of the wealthy Pearson family), and their pet poodle. He knew all about Le Vernet, and he knew quite a lot about Koestler as well. He and Brenda helped Dorothee send packages of food and clothing to Le Vernet, and Willert persuaded Malraux to get involved. Malraux promised to get visas for Regler and Koestler to move to Mexico. He called Daphne and told her that when Koestler got out, he should send his passport to the

Mexican embassy. When Regler was released he did get a visa, but when Koestler applied, he was informed the embassy had never heard of him.[22]

Koestler escaped Le Vernet before Regler, however. Returning from emptying the latrine barrels one day, he was called to the commandant's office and told that the Ministry of the Interior had ordered him to be freed at the request of the minister for information, Jean Giraudoux. This was not entirely fortuitous. Giraudoux was a personal friend of Willert's secret service boss, Noël Coward. Harold Nicolson, now deputy minister of information in the British government, had also lobbied for Koestler's release. Koestler was one of fifty prisoners let out of Le Vernet in January 1940, and several dozen more followed in March, including Regler and Aladar. The rest were left to languish until the Germans overran France a few months later and set up the Vichy regime.[23]

RETURNING TO PARIS, Koestler attempted to set his affairs in order. He questioned Daphne closely on who had helped him, then raced off to see and thank Dorothee before she left for work in the morning and to call on Willert, Malraux, Münzenberg, Sperber, Joliot-Curie, and Henri Membré, secretary of the French PEN Club. He also wrote thank-you letters to everyone who had intervened on his behalf and tried to find out the reasons for his arrest and his release. After innumerable frustrations, he was told the truth by a Detective Inspector Sadovsky. It was his association with Otto Katz. Sadovsky drily added that it wouldn't be long before all the Communists in Paris were stood up against a wall and shot, and asked Koestler if he would become an informer. Koestler refused, but he did write a report on his relations with Katz and give it to the British embassy, in the hope that it would improve his chances of getting a visa.

Not long afterward he learned that he was on a list for rearrest, and on March 12, 1940, his apartment in the rue Dombasle was raided again. The police turned the whole place upside down and carried off half his books and manuscripts, overlooking the typescript of *Darkness at Noon* that lay in full view on his worktable. Fearing a return to Le Vernet, he packed his overnight bag and made further attempts to get a visa for Mexico or Britain. The duchess of Atholl and Lord Layton of the *News Chronicle* lobbied the British government on his behalf, but they were told there were no special reasons for this "alien" to be admitted to Britain and that if Koestler wished to help the war effort, he should join "one of the French units which are open to foreigners."[24]

Weeks flew by. Cape was awaiting the manuscript of his new novel, and Daphne was translating it into English virtually as Koestler wrote it. "After breakfast each day we would draw the curtain which partitioned the apartment in two. He would sit at his table in the bigger room with the bookcases, I would sit on the edge of the divan working at the round table (with the colored matting top which came from Bokhara). I would be imprisoned there until lunch time, feeling rather restricted, while he worked with concentrated fury about ten feet away, on the other side of the curtain, sometimes leaning over the table until he was half lying on it, or even kneeling in complicated positions in his chair, sometimes coming to squint at me and see how I was getting on."[25]

The central heating broke down, the water boiler ceased to function, the elevator stopped running, and finally the telephone was cut off. Koestler and Daphne felt marooned and adrift on the seventh floor, descending the stairs only for hasty meals in a local bistro before rushing back to work on the manuscript. The English translation had to be done at express speed, and Daphne was inexperienced as a translator. She had never attended a British school and was unsure of the finer points of punctuation and grammar. Koestler was baffled and frustrated by her insecurities and demanded she capture every nuance of the original. The English version was mailed to London on May 1, 1940, and they celebrated with some fellow Hungarians over a couple of bottles of champagne.

Rarely can a major novel have been written at such breakneck speed or under such conditions of chaos and fear, with arrest and persecution a palpable threat and whole chapters written inside a concentration camp. No wonder it reeked so claustrophobically of prison and paranoia, and no wonder Koestler entered so effortlessly into the thoughts and dreams of a trapped official doomed to execution. If the Gestapo caught up with him now, he would share the fate of Rubashov, albeit without the luxury of pretending his death might serve a larger cause. After its dispatch to London, the novel was safe. The same could not be said of its author.[26]

CHAPTER SEVENTEEN

SCUM OF THE EARTH

What is the minimal portion of a country, what is the dose of
roots or hearth, that a human being requires?
— JEAN AMÉRY

TEN DAYS AFTER KOESTLER sent off his novel, the German army invaded France. Paris was filled with rumors of impending disaster, leading to another exodus of frightened citizens. Koestler has told the story of what happened to him in *Scum of the Earth,* the second of his autobiographical memoirs, where he describes his second arrest, release, and dramatic escape to the south of France in considerable detail. Koestler based part of his narrative on a diary he had kept, and though his account is largely confirmed by Daphne Hardy's much slimmer diary, it's apparent that some episodes were omitted or rearranged. The picture that emerges is of a Koestler on the run and almost at the end of his tether, but recognizably himself: at times courageous, resourceful, and imaginative, at others indignant, bitter, and self-pitying, riding an emotional roller coaster that repeatedly jolted him from hope to despair and back again.

When news of the invasion arrived, Koestler was preoccupied with trying to help the comrades he had left behind in Le Vernet, particularly Aladar and Valiani. Another imprisoned friend sent his wife, "Primavera," to ask Koestler for help in smuggling some poison to him—just in case. She had acquired some potassium cyanide from a friendly photographer, and Koestler arranged to get it past the guards at the Roland Garros stadium in exchange for half the dose. "Thank God I've received the aspirin you sent me," wrote her husband. "Now I don't care whatever happens. I'm a happy man." Some have concluded that "B, the German author of European fame," as Koestler refers to him in *Scum of the Earth,* was Walter Benjamin, but he was the German novelist Balder Olden, who emigrated to Argentina after the war.[1]

Koestler's own liberty was threatened almost immediately. On the morning of May 22 he answered the door to find a policeman standing there with a fresh warrant for his arrest. While dressing and packing he offered the policeman a drink, but the man refused, explaining that he had to arrest ten more people before lunch. Glimpsing the list, Koestler saw a couple of familiar names and told the policeman that one of them was already in jail and another in a distant part of Paris: he had only eight to go. The policeman relaxed and allowed Koestler to ask Walter Benjamin, his neighbor on the seventh floor, to fetch Daphne from the local post office. Benjamin was still in his pajamas and spilled his coffee at the sight of the policeman. He fetched Daphne without incident, and Koestler was able to instruct her on what to do after he left for the police station.[2]

Koestler was taken to the Buffalo Stadium just south of Paris. Buffalo was not for "suspects," as was Roland Garros, but for full-blown "enemy aliens," whose fate was likely to be a great deal harsher. Noting the Buffalo receptionist's surprise at seeing his Hungarian passport (Hungary was still a neutral nation), Koestler invented a cock-and-bull story about having been accidentally arrested during a roundup in the street, leaving his identity card at home, and needing to attend a government press conference at five o'clock. Within a short space of time he was on his way back to Paris by taxi. He didn't dare return home and sought refuge with Henri Membré, who let him spend the night in the French PEN Club's offices.

Membré took him to see Adrienne Monnier, owner of the Left Bank's most famous bookshop, La Maison des Amis des Livre, and well known for helping German refugee writers in trouble (Walter Benjamin was to be another beneficiary of her sympathy). Monnier hid Koestler at her apartment in the rue de l'Odéon for the night, together with the German photographer Gisèle Freund, who played chess with Koestler and took a haunting picture of him in his room. There was a curious moment in the apartment that night, remembered by all present, when Koestler lay on the couch reading Stendhal's *The Red and the Black* and a four-leaf clover fell out of the book and onto the spot between his eyes. Monnier kissed the spot and said it meant that he would escape to safety.[3]

MONNIER WAS ON GOOD TERMS with Henri Hoppenot, director of refugee affairs at the French Foreign Ministry, and persuaded Hoppenot to issue Koestler a travel permit to go as far as Limoges, where a friend, Hannah Grünwald, lived. From there he hoped to make his way to England with Daphne, who certainly planned to leave for England too but wasn't sure she wanted to go with Koestler. She had stumbled across a small notebook containing a list of "between a hundred and two hundred" names of all the women he had slept with. She wasn't on the list yet, and she remembered Andor Németh's remark that she should be grateful for Koestler's internment in Le Vernet, because he would never have stayed with her so long if he had been free (nor she with Koestler, she said later). When she talked of going to London on her own, Koestler accused her of "spitting on our relationship" and insisted he needed her help to get to Limoges and the south of France. Yielding to his anger, she meekly packed their personal belongings, including her sketches and artist's materials and Koestler's manuscripts and books (including the manuscript of the future *Darkness at Noon*), and arranged to meet him at the station.[4]

In the interim, Koestler had a tense meeting with Dorothee in a Paris café. She was shocked to hear that he was bolting south with Daphne, leaving her behind. Though she had started divorce proceedings, she was still his legal wife (his and Daphne's pet name for her was "Our Wife"), and in fact was still emotionally attached to him. She felt that in view of everything she had done for him while he was in Le Vernet (not to speak of when he was in Spain), he owed it to her to help her escape too. Koestler was guiltily apologetic but unbending, and in a later letter sought to excuse himself. "You probably thought that I got away to Limoges legally and left you in the lurch; whereas the truth is that I got a phony traveling-permit which was only valid for me (without wife), and Daphne could join me because, as a British subject, she needed no permit." The explanation was true as far as it went, but also disingenuous. Koestler had insisted on Daphne accompanying him and hadn't asked for a permit for Dorothee (though he had vainly sought a British visa for Dorothee earlier).[5]

Koestler later described his and Daphne's flight south in *Scum of the Earth,* and Daphne's diary throws additional light on the panic and near hysteria that overcame him at several moments during their journey. In Limoges the police refused to extend Koestler's residence permit because it had not been stamped with permission for him to leave Paris, driving him close to despair. Then came the news that the French government had capitulated and the Germans had entered Paris. It was clear that France would be either totally occupied or forced to install a fascist, pro-German regime, and it would be impossible to reach the coast and make it across the channel to England in time, even if they could could find a way. Koestler was trapped.

As he listened to Marshal Philippe Pétain announcing the capitulation of France on the radio, however, he recalled a film starring Jean Gabin, in which Gabin had signed up for five years in the Foreign Legion in order to evade a police hunt. In a flash he decided to do the same. With luck he would be sent to North Africa, and Daphne could make her way legally to England and wait for him there. A Swiss member of Hannah Grünwald's staff offered Koestler his papers, and Koestler took them to the recruitment office and signed up as Albert Dubert (the name of the police chief of Limoges), allegedly a former taxi driver from Bern. He was given marching orders and a travel voucher to go to Lyons, but he knew that Lyons was in the direct line of the German advance and asked if he might change the order to go to Marseilles instead. "Never mind about your order," said the officer. "All railroad traffic in France was stopped an hour ago. And tonight they'll arrive at Limoges. Good luck."[6]

Returning to Grünwald's place, they found that calm and competent woman weeping in her office. The police commissioner had orders to round up all the Germans in Limoges, and she was worried sick about the fate of her baby son. Daphne gave Hannah her birth certificate and advised her to flee, just as she and Koestler were doing. Daphne and Koestler repacked their belongings into two suitcases and three bags and left his manuscripts—including "The Vicious Circle"—with their landlady for safekeeping.[7]

THEY HITCHHIKED SOUTH to Périgueux, where Koestler found a Foreign Legion barracks and formally enlisted. The depot was in chaos. His uniform consisted of castoffs picked out from a pile of worn clothing in the stores. There were no roll calls, no parades, no duties to speak of, and he was able to sneak out and help Daphne find a local French family to stay with by simply climbing the fence. After a few days, a friendly lieutenant gave him a set of false papers belonging to a former French legionnaire and told him to head for Bordeaux, which was a free zone. Boats were still leaving for abroad, and he might be in time to catch one.[8]

Leaving yet more baggage behind, at the Hôtel de Commerce in Périgueux, Koestler and Daphne set out to hitchhike again. By now the relationship was beginning to fray under the strain of their flight. Koestler complained bitterly of Daphne's passivity, impracticality, and naiveté and said she was chipping away at his self-confidence and undermining him. Daphne felt guiltily superfluous and out of place. It was Koestler's life that was in danger, not hers, and she was in the way. Yet each time she tried to leave, he refused to hear of it. They finally decided to part in Bergerac, with Koestler resigned to being caught and arrested. "Tell the world how my life ended," he told her melodramatically. As a Jew and a revolutionary, he was on the losing side of history, and death was inevitable. Every ideal he had fought for had been destroyed.[9]

They talked of joint suicide. Daphne said she didn't have the expertise or willpower. Koestler said he had the expertise, but he didn't have the willpower either. His curiosity was stronger than his despair, his fear stronger than his determination, and he still possessed the "irrational hope" that he would survive. The next morning they caught a bus to Bordeaux. Koestler donned Daphne's overcoat to conceal his uniform and they arrived without incident, though there was a tense moment when they ran into a couple of Hungarian journalists from Paris. "Koestler, how are you?" said one of them, while the other stood back in the shadows. "I'm sorry," replied Koestler, "you are mistaken. I am not Arthur Koestler," and walked away.[10]

An armistice was signed between Germany and France. A Nazi-controlled occupation zone was to be established in the northern half of the country and a so-called free zone set up in the south, with a fascist French government based in Vichy. German troops were already marching toward Bordeaux. Koestler made frantic efforts to find out if any boats would be leaving for Britain, but the last had left that morning. The British consulate had closed and moved to Bayonne, 110 miles to the south. At the American consulate he ran into Edgar Mowrer of the *Chicago Daily News,* who said he might be able to offer Koestler or Daphne a lift to Saint-Jean-de-Luz, on the border with Spain. Feeling guilty now for having dragged Daphne with him instead of letting her go to England, Koestler told her she should go with Mowrer to the Spanish border and he would stay behind.

Daphne persuaded a reluctant Mowrer to take the two of them along, but Koestler collapsed on a marble counter in a nearby market and grew incoherent. Sobbing, he begged Daphne to go without him, saying he hated this to be her last memory of him. He had always tried to be manly, had never failed for money or erections (*sic*) when he needed them. But now he had no more control over his physical being. He was sick and tired of begging favors, of having no say over his life, and couldn't put up a false front any longer. "But I don't want you to think I'm weeping over my own fate. It's world history I'm weeping for. I won't allow it, won't allow them to come here to this place."[11]

After a long argument, Daphne persuaded Koestler to go with them. They got as far as Biarritz but were stopped by a street patrol, and Koestler was arrested and confined to barracks in Bayonne. Lying on his palliasse, he heard that the Germans were almost in Bayonne and under the terms of the armistice were extraditing all refugees back to Germany. According to another rumor, the last ship sailing from Saint-Jean-de-Luz to Britain had been sunk by a torpedo with the loss of all aboard. Daphne and Mowrer were probably on it and had perished. In a fit of despair he swallowed the potassium cyanide that Primavera Olden had given him. His stomach went into convulsions and he was violently sick, but he quickly recovered. He had vomited up the cyanide before it could take effect. It was his second (or third if one counts the fire when he was a schoolboy in Vienna) attempt at suicide, this time more serious than before, although luckily it again ended in failure.[12]

KOESTLER SPENT THE FOLLOWING WEEK drifting into and out of a drunken stupor on his bunk. His new regiment set out on foot to reach the

French-controlled zone thirty-six miles to the east, and the march was sheer agony. Koestler's feet were so swollen he had to stop to get them bandaged, and he was saved by cadging a lift for the last part of the way. His company was camped in a hamlet just inside the French zone, and for the next six weeks he hung about with his fellow soldiers, living in barns, eating execrable army food, and stealing apples from a nearby farmer. In his pocket diary he concluded that he was a "manic-depressive." At moments he longed for Daphne, at others he felt sure he would never see her again (and tried to persuade himself that he didn't love her). He meditated on the "essentially tragic nature of his life as opposed to trivial everyday life" and decided that, while it was no remedy, his goal should be to remain "eternally conscious not only while suffering, but also while melancholic or even when totally stupefied." Repelled by the brutishness and stupidity of his fellow soldiers, he decided that it was his fate to be "always frantically searching for fraternity while remaining always the outsider," and that "fraternity is an illusion like any other."[13]

His main diversion was arguing with a smiling young Dominican priest called Father Piprot, who in peacetime ran a convent near Marseilles for ex-prostitutes and former women convicts. Piprot was both witty and knowledgeable. "*Le bon Dieu est un metteur-en-scène raffiné* [The good Lord is a sophisticated director]," he commented after Koestler said how glad he was to meet him. They argued at length about the relative merits of socialism and Christianity. Koestler was impressed with Piprot's skill as a dialectician, but felt that Piprot was like the Communists in Le Vernet—*too* logical and *too* rational. "Perhaps deepest cause of Socialists' failure," he noted in his diary, was "that they tried to conquer the world by reason. Perhaps Hitler's genius is not demagogy, not lying, but the fundamentally irrational approach to the masses, the appeal to the prelogical, totemistic mentality (Jung's archetypes). If human brains functioned like clockwork, Utopia would be reached in a year. The right image is not clockwork but several overlapping magnetic fields."[14]

Koestler consoled himself with the thought of writing a book called "Permanent Defeat," on the current situation in Europe. "What I find revolting is the sense that the majority of people are able to negotiate the deluge that has overwhelmed me and Daphne and our friends, while hardly getting their feet wet. Without that I might be happy to swim myself, happy to have saved my life, and perhaps find peace, the nice peace of resignation." The nucleus of *Scum of the Earth* was first sketched in the Foreign Legion barracks outside Marseilles.[15]

In early August, Koestler and half a dozen other enlisted foreigners were sent to Fort Saint-Jean-de-Luz in Marseilles to be demobilized. Marseilles was teeming with refugees struggling to escape France and avoid capture by the Gestapo. Koestler ran into several Paris comrades—Kantorowicz,

Mehring, Werfel, and Benjamin. The latter asked him if he had "anything to take" in case of disaster, and showed him sixty-four tablets of morphine that he had carried with him since his 1933 expulsion from Germany. After using up the potassium cyanide, Koestler had nothing, and Benjamin gave him half the tablets. Benjamin was on his way to Spain, and a few days later committed suicide after crossing the border. The Spanish police had arrested him and threatened him with deportation back to France, but by the time the police came for him he was dead.[16]

Koestler learned in Marseilles that several other refugee writers had also committed suicide. Willi Münzenberg had been sent to a concentration camp in Savoy but had escaped before the arrival of the German army and was presumed missing or dead, perhaps also by suicide. If dead, it meant that two of the most important men in Koestler's life had died within weeks of each other, for Jabotinsky had gone to America to raise a Jewish legion to fight on the side of Britain and had just died there. "One great friend less," Koestler wrote in his journal. "There are not many left, at liberty and undamaged." In his pocket diary he added: "I feel pain, but also a kind of consolation. I won't be the only one to live the tragic life, to suffer and to die."[17]

The German noose was now tightening around continental Europe, and it's not surprising that many of those caught in its coils preferred death to capture by the Gestapo. Koestler hoped that he might be on one of the lists compiled by Varian Fry's newly formed Emergency Rescue Committee, designed to pluck distinguished intellectuals from France before their capture by the Germans. He wasn't prominent enough to make the cut, however, and decided his best bet was to try to get to neutral Lisbon and go on from there. He fired off a telegram to Daphne's address in England to see if she had survived and could help, and was delighted when she cabled that she was safe. She had left Saint-Jean-de-Luz aboard the British merchant ship as planned (it had not been torpedoed) and had crossed the Bay of Biscay in a flood of tears, dreading what might have happened to him. She was ecstatic to hear that he was alive, but helpless as ever to assist him in any way.[18]

As enterprising as ever, Koestler picked up word that about sixty men from the British Expeditionary Force were also interned in Fort Saint-Jean-de-Luz, and that some of the bolder spirits were planning to escape to French North Africa. Koestler persuaded them to let him go along as their interpreter. He was already acting as a regimental messenger and managed to bribe a Port Commission official to issue the men false Foreign Legion papers and get them some uniforms. The papers would reclassify them as unfit for service and due for discharge, and show the place of discharge as Casablanca in French Morocco.[19]

The day before he left, Koestler encountered Sperber in a crowded street. Sperber was experiencing the same kind of hopelessness as Koestler. His name wasn't on any of the lists, and with his second wife, Jenka, he was desperate to get out of France. Koestler offered him a portion of Benjamin's precious morphine tablets, but Sperber took only one, and the two friends embraced before going their separate ways.[20]

KOESTLER AND THE FOUR BRITISH SOLDIERS became the Yugoslavs Popovich, Jovanovich, and so on, allegedly with no knowledge of French, and on September 3 they boarded a tramp steamer to Oran. From Oran they traveled by train to the frontier town of Oujda, where a French adjutant ordered them to transfer to a military train. Koestler knew their fake papers would never pass muster with an experienced officer, so he plied the adjutant with red wine and persuaded him to let them take the train to Casablanca. They might well have been extras in the movie of that name (Koestler, with a cigarette dangling from his lower lip, bore more than a passing resemblance to Humphrey Bogart), especially when they were contacted in Casablanca by an exquisitely mannered and mysterious man in his late forties called Mr. Ellerman. "Tall, elegant, dignified, charming, sophisticated and aristocratic," in Koestler's words, he spoke impeccable English, and it was years before Koestler discovered he was in reality Rüdiger von Etzdorf, a German baron working for the British intelligence service.[21]

Ellerman got the British soldiers emergency visas and added them to a group of about fifty other servicemen due to leave for Lisbon aboard a Portuguese fishing boat. Koestler, with his Hungarian passport and French identity card, didn't qualify. Throwing himself on Ellerman's mercy, he told him his life story, and Ellerman got him a certificate on the basis of his Palestinian passport of 1928. Koestler promised that he would admit everything to the authorities once he was on British soil.[22]

After four days in heavy seas (Koestler was seasick throughout), evading numerous German U-boats in the Atlantic, the 220-ton *El Mar Azul* managed to deposit the escapees in Lisbon. The four British soldiers were welcomed at the British consulate and flown to England, but Koestler, despite his sincere request to join the British army, was turned away. Ellerman tried to persuade Koestler to return to Marseilles and work for the underground railroad there, but Koestler was too scared. He had no stomach for being anywhere near the Nazis.

Meanwhile, Lisbon, though also crammed with refugees, was at least an improvement on Marseilles. Koestler later evoked the atmosphere in *Arrival and Departure:* sidewalk cafés crowded with residents sipping tiny cups of black coffee, bootblacks scampering from table to table, and the refugees huddled in little groups, feverishly discussing politics, prison camps, passports, visas, and steamer tickets. Arms merchants and military men strutted up and down as if they owned the place, and spies seemed to lurk around every corner.

There is evidence that Koestler had a brief, stormy affair with a married American woman called Ellen Hill, but essentially he was alone and frightened. His months in Lisbon were "worse than anything that went before, worse even than Le Vernet," he said later, mainly because he feared the Portuguese would hand him over to Franco. Luckily, he had obtained some funds from Macmillan, his American publisher, and was able to take a room in the Pension Leirense. He sent volleys of telegrams and letters to friends in Britain and America, asking for help with visas. Lord Leighton at the *News Chronicle,* Rupert Hart Davis at Jonathan Cape, and Harold Nicolson from the Ministry of Information all lobbied on his behalf, but the British Home Office was adamant. "Although Koestler now claims to love this country," ran a secret service memo, "he is, or was until recently, a member of a Group (Friends of Socialist Unity in Germany), which requires its members to regard Britain and France as imperialist countries which must be attacked and thrown into chaos as soon as his particular Group has ousted Hitler." If admitted to the United Kingdom, Koestler would "add to the duties and responsibilities and public expenses of the security service and police who would have to supervise his activities."[23]

Koestler had learned from Erika Mann that his name was indeed on one of the lists of "outstanding intellectuals" to be rescued by Fry and wrote to Eva Striker for help. Three long weeks went by while Ellerman also tried everything in his power to get the British to accept Koestler's emergency permit, warning them that Koestler might create bad publicity for them if he were forced to go to the United States instead, but MI5 continued to insist that Koestler was "an undesirable alien" barred "for security reasons." On the last day of September Koestler ran into Babette Gross, who told him of Münzenberg's disappearance in France and Benjamin's suicide in Spain, presumably using the morphine tablets he had shared with Koestler.[24]

Koestler decided to follow Benjamin's example. Being Koestler, he jotted down some "Notes for Benno Lévy (half for their scientific interest, so to speak)," describing how he took a first dose of four tablets just before one a.m. and began to monitor his pulse and heartbeat. "No fear, slight (manic) agitation. Curiosity (what comes next has always had something mystical about it). *Before* I swallowed the pills I accidentally saw myself in the mirror and had a moment of panic. Now nothing of the kind, not even self-pity. It's hardly natural, I still can't believe that this whole thing is irreversible."

By the end of the first hour he had taken twenty pills, still without the desired result. He was aware that sitting at the table taking notes was helping to keep him awake, but he needed it as "a defense against self-pity and sentimentality" and in order not to be left alone with himself. He had a momentary bout of agoraphobia before floating outside himself to congratulate "old Koestler" on his strong nerves. "But," he added, "when he gets up the courage to stop writing, it will go badly with him." A bit later he tried to imagine his own death mask and the "unappetizing shindig" that would be raised in the Pension Leirense when they found him.

At ten minutes past two he decided to swallow the rest of the pills, making thirty-one in all, and to lie down. Before doing so, he wrote out the text of "Autumn Poem," by Rilke, with its ominous opening phrase, "Sir, it is time," and its last stanza, beginning "Who has no house will build himself no more, / Who lives alone will stay alone forever." At half past two, he wrote a last note before going to bed. "It's funny, I don't know whether tomorrow morning I'll wake up dead. But it worked for Benji—and he too died in the early morning. All right, heads up, things are bound to get worse. Goodnight, old Koestler." But the next morning he did wake up, and vomited up the last of the pills. Either they were too old or he had made a mistake in taking them gradually instead of all at once. He never did discover which.[25]

Recovering from his death wish, he went back to his endless quest for a way out of Lisbon, his hopes periodically encouraged by good news from the British consulate, then dashed again by more refusals. He wrote Daphne that he was thinking seriously of emigrating to the United States. "We go to America together or I won't go at all. Nothing means anything for me, in [the] present or future, without you." Daphne agreed by return of post, but by the time her letter arrived Koestler was gone.[26]

He was saved by the same combination of luck and chutzpah that had got him into and out of the Foreign Legion, out of Marseilles, and into Lisbon. Months earlier he had applied for a ticket on the British airline BOAC, which had never removed him from its waiting list. When news of an available seat came through, the British consul general, Sir Henry King, was persuaded to bend the rules and validate Koestler's emergency permit. Koestler wrote out two statements, one, intended for the British immigration authorities, describing his desperate situation as a fugitive and the reasons for his illegal entry into Britain, and another (designed to cover King) outlining his complicated citizenship and falsely confessing to having deceived the British consul general in Casablanca. He persuaded Babette to deliver copies of both to the British consulate in Lisbon after his departure and left the city on November 6, 1940. When the plane landed at Whitchurch Airport in Bristol, Koestler asked the immigration officer if he had a message for him. "No, I'm afraid not," said the officer. "In that case," said Koestler dramatically, "I'm afraid you will have to arrest me." He had fifty dollars, some personal effects, and a bunch of papers in his suitcase, and handed copies of his Lisbon statements to the official to read. He had kept his word to Ellerman and King.[27]

CHAPTER EIGHTEEN

DARKNESS UNVEILED

They meet with darkness in the daytime, and grope in the noon day as in the night.

— JOB 5:14

KOESTLER TOLD HIS FIRST BIOGRAPHER, Iain Hamilton, that after a night in a police cell, he was escorted to London by train by a kindly policeman, Detective Inspector Parker, who bought him cigarettes and treated him with great consideration. This was true, but the impression it conveys of a benevolent officialdom treating him with polite respect is misleading. According to the police report of his interrogation in Bristol, he came within an ace of being deported straight back to Lisbon, for he was regarded by the immigration officer with extreme suspicion. "Apart from his political views and his adventurous nature," runs the officer's report, "he appears to be undesirable; he admitted he is an opium addict, a bottle of opium being among his possessions. Further he carried enough veronal to—in his own words—kill a horse." Koestler told the unbelieving officer that if sent back to Lisbon, he would use the veronal to poison himself. He also informed the officer, a Mr. J. N. Owen, of his unsuccessful suicide attempt with the morphine tablets, but "some doubt was felt as to whether it was a serious attempt as he appears to be given to arranging romantic settings to color his adventures."[1]

Owen added a postscript to the effect that Koestler was "unreliable and thoroughly undesirable, and I intended to return him to Lisbon," but the airport's commanding officer urged him to send Koestler to London for further questioning. "Koestler is almost certainly a Jew," wrote Owen, "but in view of possible repercussions in the *News Chronicle,* the question was not put." In a handwritten addendum he rejected Koestler's claim to qualify for a British visa on the grounds that he had once held a Palestinian passport (Palestine being administered by Britain), for "Palestinians are aliens."[2]

Koestler must have understood the official doubts about his status, for the first thing he did upon arriving in London was hammer on his cell door and insist on a speedy interrogation, declaring that he would go on a hunger strike to resist being deported. The British bobbies at Cannon Row were nonplussed; they had made him ham and eggs for breakfast, but Koestler steadfastly turned his back on the food, and did so again the next morning. Koestler soon got his way and was confronted by a man in a black hood with two slits for eyes. The interrogator was a German national working for British intelligence, and he questioned Koestler about his past. Koestler gave him a largely truthful but somewhat sanitized version of his life up till then, playing down his Communist sympathies and suppressing the true story of his escape from Marseilles, but freely admitting to party membership, his visit to the Soviet Union, and the tricks he had pulled to get into the Foreign Legion and out again.[3]

The interrogator reported that there was sufficient information in Koestler's story for it to be checked and that although his story sounded "somewhat fantastic," it was "plausible." He was "not unfavorably impressed" by Koestler, despite the latter's "communist tendencies" and the disreputable nature of some of his associates. A secret-service observer in the room also found Koestler's account "fantastic," especially Koestler's contention that he had taken the morphine tablets and lived, whereas "Dr. Benjamin" had died from them, and he doubted Koestler's claim that the bottle of opium was for his "indigestion." "My analysis of Koestler," he wrote, "is: one third genius, one third blackguard, and one third lunatic." "He is of interest to us," he continued, "as he has a wide knowledge of [union] officials and other Left-Wing politicians in France. I am not prepared to say he is 100% all right, but I cannot imagine it would be possible for him to do any harm whatsoever." But because Harold Nicolson had been instrumental in freeing Koestler from Le Vernet, he recommended that Nicolson be asked to keep an eye on him, since Koestler was "liable to write sensational stories about his adventures in France" that might harm British prisoners in the occupied zone. The *News Chronicle* and *Daily Express* should be warned not to publish Koestler's articles without referring them to the Ministry of Information for clearance.[4]

THE INTERROGATOR INFORMED KOESTLER that he was no longer in danger of expulsion. Sure enough, he was transferred to cell 40 in Pentonville Prison, where he spent the next six weeks as prisoner 8539. He was entitled to two letters and one visitor a week, and he lost no time in sending Daphne the bittersweet news that he was in England and could see her in the prison visitors' room, separated by a pane of glass. Daphne was upset by her first visit, and Koestler, his self-confidence restored, sent her a tender letter. "Darling, I hope you are recovering from the shock of the meeting in that monkey cage. Of course I had thought out before a lot of lovely things to tell you, and of course they were all gone. I felt like one of those penny slot machines when you shake them and the inscription 'tilt' appears and all those nice red and green lights go out." By the time of his next letter he was all business again, listing the people she should see—lawyer, publisher, editor of the *News Chronicle,* press attaché at the Hungarian legation—and the things she should say to them.[5]

Koestler described Pentonville as a "three star" prison, "the most decent jail I have been in, though the plumbing leaves much to be desired." He was referring to the time-honored British practice of "slopping out"—standing in line each morning with a stinking pot of urine and excrement in your hand, waiting, with dozens of others, to empty it into a fetid latrine tank—which didn't seem to have changed since Oscar Wilde was in Pentonville half a century earlier (Seville, by contrast, had had fully functioning water closets). Koestler also hated being locked in his cell for thirteen hours in total darkness because German air raids made a blackout necessary, but the incident that made the deepest impression on him was the hanging of a German spy. "I don't know how we knew about it but the whole prison became a house of death. The warders went round with faces as in a mortuary. There was something like vibrations in the air, and then we knew, and then it was over and we all started breathing and living again." It was not as horrible as the executions in Spain, but it hardened his conviction that all executions were a form of judicial murder and that capital punishment was an abomination.[6]

The British had declared all Germans and Austrians in the country to be "enemy aliens" and had classified them into three groups. Those suspected of being agents or spies were interned in detention camps, the most notorious being on the Isle of Man. Aliens judged safely anti-fascist were left free, while a third group was subject to further investigation. Koestler hoped he was in the second group, but had a bad scare when two members of MI5 came to his cell and started asking about the other prisoners. He refused to answer them and redoubled his efforts to be freed, sending Daphne to several prominent people for help, including his publisher, Rupert Hart Davis, who sent him a hundred cigarettes, saying he would deduct the cost from Koestler's royalties. Koestler also instructed Daphne to contact his parents in Budapest and Dorothee's mother in London (he had just sent Dorothee fifty dollars) and to give Paul Willert, now serving in the Royal Air Force in England, a list of German refugee intellectuals who had committed suicide in occupied France.[7]

Daphne's mixed success at her various tasks had already led to a terrible row between them, for which Koestler blamed both himself and his "prison psychosis." The prison routine was "a chain of permanent humiliation," he told her, and Daphne's "sweet and pathetic" inability to defend herself had made things worse. It "induced me to go on torturing you. Sadism is sometimes a sort of inverted pity (golden words)," which to Daphne meant that he was punishing her for the weaknesses he feared in himself.[8]

One result was that Daphne now found it harder to deliver the news that his novel about Rubashov had gone through page proofs and was about to be printed. Actually, she also shrank from telling him because she had changed the title without Koestler's knowledge and felt sure he'd explode. Cape didn't like "The Vicious Circle" as a title, she said, and had chosen "a much worse one" of its own, "Darkness at Noonday." This was a white lie: the title was Daphne's. She had written to him in Lisbon about it, but the letter had never reached him, and now she had to tell him in person. When she stammered out the new title, now metamorphosed into *Darkness at Noon,* he surprised her by giving his approval. Koestler thought the title was a quotation from Milton's *Samson Agonistes*—"Oh dark, dark, dark, amid the blaze of noon," an attribution that has persisted to this day—but Daphne's inspiration had been the Book of Job: "They meet with darkness in the daytime, and grope in the noonday as in the night."[9]

Darkness at Noon, a bleak book about a prisoner in solitary confinement, was published in December 1940, while Koestler was in solitary confinement in Pentonville. The irony wasn't lost on its author. Having written much of it in a detention camp, he had come to feel that prison was the perfect metaphor for Europe in 1940, and also, for too many, a brutal reality. The claustrophobic jail smell that clings to every page of *Darkness at Noon* and contributes so richly to its overpowering atmosphere of doom was the fruit not just of Koestler's imagination but of his bitter experiences in French and Spanish jails.

ON THE LITERAL LEVEL, *Darkness at Noon* is about the personality, experiences, and thoughts of a veteran revolutionary leader, Nikolai Rubashov, languishing in jail and being harshly interrogated on charges of treason. After lengthy confrontations with two different interrogators and a period of self-examination in his cell, he decides to make a full confession of guilt, knowing all the while that his alleged crimes are the invention of his investigators and that he is innocent. He knows that his sentence will be death, but finally agrees to it because it is a logical conclusion of his lifelong belief in revolutionary ideals, and the last service he can perform to demonstrate his loyalty to the party.

On a metaphorical level, *Darkness at Noon* is an image of life in the Soviet Union (though the name of the country where the action unfolds is never mentioned) and of the life that was promised Europe if either the Communists or the fascists came to power. Koestler's inspiration was the Soviet show trials, of course, and one of the questions he set out to answer was, how did the party do it? How could such prominent party leaders as Kamenev, Zinoviev, Radek, and Bukharin be brought to the point where they confessed to the most fantastic crimes in open court and in the full glare of publicity? His answer, controversial to this day, was that it was a matter not simply of physical coercion (though Koestler was aware of that dimension too) but of intense psychological pressure, backed by the threat of coercion. This more subtle pressure drew on the prisoners' deepest beliefs in the revolutionary cause and in its flag bearer, the party, to undermine their personalities and break their will. It was an early form of brainwashing (the term had not been invented yet), and Koestler was one of the first to recognize its importance in Soviet political practice.

In the course of the novel, the interrogator Ivanov (Rubashov's former friend) seizes on Rubashov's disillusionment with party policy to show that Rubashov is "objectively" an enemy. "You openly admit that for years you have had the conviction that we were ruining the Revolution; and in the same breath you deny that you belonged to the opposition and that you plotted against us. Do you really expect me to believe that you sat watching us with your hands in your lap—while, according to your conviction, we led country and Party to destruction?" Rubashov is trapped by his own words and by his former actions as a party leader. Ivanov reminds Rubashov that Rubashov is responsible for the deaths of two activists, Comrade Richard and Little Loewy, and indirectly responsible for the arrest and death of his former secretary and lover, Arlova. What is one more death—his own—in the service of historical inevitability? Good cop Ivanov is replaced by bad cop Gletkin (modeled on the GPU officer Koestler had seen in Baku), who brutally insists that Rubashov confess in excruciating detail to instigating a plot to assassinate "No. 1." The whole thing is a fiction, and Rubashov is appalled by the naked cynicism of the demand, but through sleep deprivation and confrontations with an alleged assassin he is brought to admit that "objectively" he is guilty too, for (in a Dostoyevskian flourish) the putative assassin is Rubashov's "logic made flesh." Rubashov meekly signs the elaborate confession drawn up for him by Gletkin, is tried publicly, and is sentenced to death.

Though ostensibly a composite of Bukharin, Radek, and Trotsky, Rubashov also incarnates the Koestler of 1938–39. He is the party zealot who suddenly awakens to the fact that his iron faith has been based on a lie, that the ideals to which he has clung have been betrayed, and that the utopia he sought can never be realized by the movement to which he belongs. Koestler's imagination transposes his flounderings in Baku, his doubts in Kharkov, and his vacillations in Spain into a powerful intellectual thriller about loyalty and betrayal, and symbolically accepts the logic of Franco's supposed death sentence on him as morally justified by his own revolutionary sins. By reenacting these events in the novel, he pronounces a death sentence on his own ideological past and ideals.[10]

Koestler drew not only on his experiences in Seville but also on Eva's account of her prison experiences in Moscow. One aspect of Eva's story that Koestler used to powerful effect was her account of tapping clandestine messages on cell walls (in the novel it is on the water pipes). In one particularly harrowing scene (drawn in part from Koestler's memories of Seville) the prisoners listen in horror as a tortured comrade is dragged, whimpering, on his way to execution, and they communicate this emotion first by tapped messages and then by a sustained drumming on cell doors; and this tapping starts up again in the final moments before Rubashov himself is led off to execution.[11]

Throughout the novel, Koestler's personal anguish, his profound desire to recant and repent his sins, infuses the narrative with a confessional force that is totally appropriate to its subject matter, while Rubashov's descent into hell has a terrifying logic that is irresistible. He is like the hero of a Greek tragedy, condemned by his own character flaws to die. There is no way out. Yet, in a work where there is virtually no uncertainty about the outcome, the suspense is astonishing. It is the suspense of not knowing how Rubashov will arrive at his end, accompanied by the hope that he will somehow, miraculously, evade the bullet. Koestler's inspiration here was the Dostoyevsky of *Crime and Punishment* and *The Brothers Karamazov,* and he even imported some of Dostoyevsky's Christian imagery into his narrative.[12]

On publication, the novel struck Koestler's more astute left-wing readers with stunning force. "Who will ever forget the first moment he read *Darkness at Noon?*" wrote Michael Foot later. "For socialists especially, the experience was indelible. I can recall reading it right through one night, horror-struck, overpowered, enthralled. If this was a true revelation, a terrifying shaft of darkness was cast over the future no less than the past." Wickham Steed regarded it as "the most devastating exposure of Stalinist methods ever written," and Kingsley Martin, in the *New Statesman,* pronounced it "one of the few books written in this epoch which will survive it." A pro-Communist critic, John Strachey, finding the book's message "a bitter pill to swallow," said he was overwhelmed by its terrifying logic. R. D. Charques (anonymously) in the *Times Literary Supplement* was one of the few at the time who perceived the underlying theme of the "growing likeness between the Soviet regime and the Nazi regime."[13]

Orwell thought the book "brilliant as a novel and a piece of prison literature," but was more interested in it as an explanation of the Moscow show trials and as an excuse to attack western leftists for accepting the trials as genuine than as a work of literature (it was to be another four years before Orwell concluded it was "a masterpiece"). Other reviewers were puzzled by the novel's unusual form. "The book is long drawn out, full of repetitions and marred throughout by its obscenity and irreligion" was one's verdict. The book had few characters, most of them with no first names, and, apart from Rubashov, none was described in any detail. It wasn't exactly a psychological novel, nor an allegory, nor a satire, and the plot was hard to follow. It was that unfamiliar thing in Britain and America at the time, a novel of ideas and a moral fable, with an unfamiliar dialectical method of argument—and very little love interest of any kind.[14]

BRITONS IN PARTICULAR had more to think about in the winter of 1940–41 than revolutionary ethics. German armies were sweeping across Europe and into Russia, German bombs were raining down on London, and England was reeling under the Blitzkrieg. There was serious talk of what to do if German armies crossed the channel. "Enemy aliens" like Koestler were still being rounded up and sent to internment camps, and it looked as if the nation might go under at any time. By the end of its first year in print, *Darkness at Noon* had sold 2,500 copies and seemed destined for literary oblivion. But six months later it appeared in the United States, which had still not entered the war, and the Book-of-the-Month Club made it one of its monthly selections, guaranteeing it a large circulation. Whittaker Chambers, then an obscure journalist at *Time* magazine (but one who had reason to understand the book), called it "the most exciting novel of the season," written by someone who "knows Russia and the deep places of the human mind," and other critics echoed his high opinion. "From then onwards," said Koestler later, "my financial troubles never became pressing."[15]

Koestler was released from Pentonville shortly before Christmas 1940 and moved with Daphne into a modest little house in Bute Street, South Kensington, belonging to her mother. In no time he had rearranged the furniture, supervised the purchase of food and other items, and taken charge of the kitchen. "He was a much better cook than I was," Daphne said later. "Even if I started something, he would criticize me for getting it all wrong and finish the job himself." Koestler also persuaded Daphne to give up her auxiliary nursing job to help him with a new book.[16]

Still seething from the insults, humiliations, and hardships he had endured in France, Koestler was bursting to tell the world about the perfidy and ignominious defeatism of the French ruling class, which he seemed to take personally (as if the French had caved in to the Germans to spite *him*). Relying on his and Daphne's diaries for the details, he planned a book along the lines of *Dialogue with Death,* a work of reportage with a moral message, with himself and his experiences at the center. He had started it in Lisbon already, knowing he had a first-rate story to tell, and now, with a modest advance of sixty pounds from Jonathan Cape, he settled in and wrote for two months at white heat. It was his first book written entirely in English, and the leap from German was huge. "A language serves not only to express thought, but to mold it," he later wrote, and the adoption of a new language by a writer means "a gradual and unconscious transformation of his patterns of thinking, his style and his tastes, his attitudes and reactions." Koestler made a vow to read only in English from now on, and he and Daphne switched from German to English in their daily conversation. However, a heavy accent, part Magyar, part Teutonic (and unconsciously comic), survived to torment Koestler for the rest of his life, and became the butt of an extraordinary number of jokes and anecdotes.[17]

Daphne carefully checked Koestler's English original, and Paul Willert edited it, before it was sent to Cape. "You have evolved your English style as you go on in a really remarkable way," wrote Willert, adding that the narrative style of the book, its diary passages, the descriptions of places and people were all excellent. It was only when Koestler came to politics that his language faltered. He had a tendency to use too many abstractions for English taste and a habit of falling back on Marxist jargon. Willert, who remembered France quite clearly from his time there, offered some mild criticisms of the content as well. Shouldn't Koestler have mentioned a few good Frenchmen among the bad? Was Pétain personally to blame for the capitulation to the Germans, or had it been the fault of his advisers?[18]

KOESTLER WAS UNMOVED. He changed the book's title from "French Apocalypse" to *Scum of the Earth*, a favorite phrase of the French press to describe the foreign refugees swept up by the French police before the war. "A few years ago we were called the martyrs of fascist barbarism and defenders of liberty," ran the epigraph, "now we had become the scum of the earth." Koestler aimed to tell the story of the German and Central European left-wing refugees caught between the hammer of fascist invasion and the anvil of a weak but vindictive and collaborationist France. Their story was also his story, and he used it to construct a miniature epic, showing a nation in its political death throes, collapsing in the face of German aggression while venting its rage and shame on the "scum" who had sought refuge in France in the mistaken belief that they would be safe.[19]

There was enough drama in Koestler's experiences to make a fine escape story, not to speak of the psychological interest of his attempts to commit suicide and the vicissitudes of his relationship with Daphne. Yet these elements occupy surprisingly little space in the final text. Although he took the fall of France as a personal insult, Koestler's goal was political: to destroy the myth of a brave and victimized France crushed by a brutal Germany and reveal the cowardice of a ruling class that had thrown in the towel. The book was shadowed by two tragedies, both presented as rebuffs to a disillusioned lover. There was the tragedy of a decadent France: "We had never loved France as we loved it in those late August days. We had never been so achingly conscious of its sweetness and decay." And the debacle of the German-Soviet Non-Aggression Pact (with which the book opens): "Our feelings towards Russia were rather like those of a man who has divorced a much-beloved wife; he hates her and yet it is a sort of consolation for him to know that she is still there, on the same planet, still young and alive. Now she was dead."[20]

The theme of unrequited political love is played out in the book in a thousand variations as the refugees are repeatedly rebuffed, betrayed, and punished by the unworthy object of their devotion. Koestler likened the refugees to the crusaders of the Middle Ages, the majority of them "men of good faith, with a mentality combining contradictory elements of enlightenment and sectarianism, brotherliness and intolerance, charity and ruthlessness, enthusiastic self-denial and mercenary selfishness." Half the world, wrote Koestler theatrically and with typical exaggeration, "adored them as heroes and saints, the other half loathed them as madmen and adventurers." All were threatened with extinction in the "holocaust" that was sweeping Europe. Koestler must have been one of the first to use the word *holocaust* in this context, unaware of the sinister meaning it would acquire in the next few years.[21]

It was a requiem for the European left (Koestler dedicated the book to six political refugees who had lost their lives, including Walter Benjamin), during which the narrator undergoes a "re-education" as he undertakes the journey from "agony" (the title of the first chapter) to "apocalypse" (chapter three). In the course of the book Koestler comes to realize that his leftist ideals are not completely tarnished but rather misplaced. He still values (and idealizes) the working class, as seen in Le Vernet and the French Foreign Legion, and has realized Rubashov's dream of putting the individual before the mass. Encamped in the Basses Pyrénées with his fellow legionnaires, Koestler had noted in his journal, "I had imagined I knew the proletariat— now I realise that those I met at Party meetings, in C.P. cells, etc., were exceptions, a selected vanguard, entirely untypical. In three weeks here I have learned more about mass psychology than in seven years of Communist busybodying. Good God! In what an imaginary world we have lived. Have to start quite afresh—all of us."[22]

Of the two principal narrative lines in *Scum,* the collapse of France and the collapse of Koestler's revolutionary faith, it was the former (the "French apocalypse") that attracted most attention from readers. Harold Nicolson (to whom Dorothee had gone in tears when Koestler was in his Seville jail) vetted the book for the Ministry of Information and asked the author to cut only one passage: a Vichy poem describing Churchill as "syphilitic." Nicolson was impressed by the clarity and eloquence of Koestler's writing but, like Willert, was appalled by Koestler's gloomy assessment of France's moral collapse. "In reading your book I felt that you had lost all confidence in the French people and there seemed to be no ray of hope in anything you write. You may be justified in this pessimism but I do really believe that we shall live to see the day on which some recrudescence of the French national spirit is able to galvanise their virtues."[23]

Scum of the Earth appeared in a Left Book Club edition in July 1941 and was formally published by Cape in September. It introduced Koestler to a much broader segment of the British reading public than *Darkness at Noon* and was far more commercially successful than the novel, selling as many copies in a month as *Darkness* had in a whole year. The reviews were unanimously positive. The book combined "the best qualities of the journalist and of the novelist—brilliant objective 'reportage' and probing analytical introspection." It was "an exile's book, and a bitter book," but Koestler's attitude was constructive and even idealistic. His appeal was to "the conscience of his age and generation." He possessed a "genuine modernity of idealistic temper," but whereas the idealism of the contemporary left was "merely a form of egotism, of romantic and irresponsible self-exhibition," there was "nothing romantic and nothing conceited in Mr. Koestler's vision of a saner ordering of human affairs."[24]

In America the book's reception was if anything more rhapsodic. *The New York Times Book Review* called *Scum* a "personal narrative of intense power and poignancy" and said that Koestler had "written a book so moving that it invites the use of the most extravagant adjectives." The key to Koestler's "astonishing vision" was his identification of the problem of the era as being "the ancient one of ends and means, of doctrine and practice, of thought and action, of absolutely conceived programs and the richness of life itself." *The New Yorker* called it "one of the most extraordinary books of its kind ever written," and *The Christian Science Monitor* praised Koestler's "righteous indignation," mellow "philosophical irony," and "authentic literary mastery."[25]

Such praise was music to Koestler's ears, and made up for the fear and humiliation he had endured during his last year in France. It was especially satisfying that his preoccupation with ends and means had come through so strongly in a work of nonfiction, for until now he had treated it only in fictional guise. The readiness of the critics to acknowledge both his novelistic and his reportorial skills in a single work also justified his choice of a form that was still unusual in English letters. Best of all, he had exploded onto the British and American literary scenes with such force that he immediately established a solid reputation for himself as a fresh and urgent voice with a great deal to say about a world in the grip of a mortal crisis.

CHAPTER NINETEEN

IN CRUMPLED BATTLEDRESS

It is easy to talk and arrange another person's life for them.
— ELIZABETH GASKELL

BY THE TIME *Scum of the Earth* appeared in bookstores, Koestler was a soldier in the British Army. When his call-up papers had come in early February, Cape had asked for a deferment until April 15 so he could finish his book. "I am in receipt of your letter of the 11th instant," wrote a major at one of London's recruitment centers. "As requested, I am postponing Mr Koestler's calling up, and would suggest that he calls at this Centre when he is at liberty to join His Majesty's forces." Having read this remarkable document, Koestler joked, "I was more than ever convinced that England must lose the war."[1]

It was in the cavalier spirit engendered by this letter that Koestler presented himself at the No. 3 Training Centre of the Aliens' Pioneer Corps in the seaside resort of Ilfracombe. He was surely the only recruit in the company to arrive with a portable typewriter, a supply of paper, a stack of unanswered letters, and the immediate goal of locating a hotel for his girlfriend. This genteel holiday resort on the north coast of Devon struck him as "much better than the Côte d'Azur," but he was bewildered by the uproar after he spent the night with Daphne in her hotel. He didn't know that in Britain one needed a marriage certificate to do such a thing—this wasn't the Côte d'Azur, in more ways than one.[2]

The Pioneer Corps was a peculiarly British institution. Its emblem was a crossed pick and shovel, and its motto *labor omnia vincit* (work conquers all). Most of the corps was made up of World War I veterans too old to fight, and a few companies had been cobbled together from men with mild mental and physical handicaps. The rest were made up of "aliens"—mainly Germans and Austrians, but with a scattering of Czechs, Hungarians, and Romanians—who couldn't be trusted to fight. Koestler's company, the 251st, was the last to be formed, and consisted in large part of former members of the French Foreign Legion who distrusted de Gaulle's Free French forces (Koestler himself had considered joining the Free French before opting for the British Army).[3]

The motley collection of European lawyers, accountants, architects, doctors, journalists, and engineers who assembled to march and drill on the windy promenade of Ilfracombe must have comprised one of the most bizarre units in the British Army, and these pipe-smoking, chess-playing intellectuals now found themselves exposed to the full rigors of British basic training, a relentless regimen of physical exercise, rifle practice, and spit and polish that made Koestler's indolent sojourn in the French Foreign Legion seem like a picnic. He survived without in the least coming to resemble a British squaddie, his uniform forever unpressed, his gaiters unblanco'ed, his cap perched at a perilous angle on his head. When it was all over, 13805661 Private Koestler was ordered to pick up his badge and embark for Avonmouth, the site of the naval docks at Bristol. The British had devised one of their ingenious schemes to deceive the German air force, by digging huge shallow craters, filling them with oil, and setting them on fire as German planes arrived to bomb the fuel dumps. The pilots were to think that they had hit their targets and head home, dumping their surplus bombs in the Irish Sea.[4]

The digging was backbreaking work for Koestler, worse than lugging stones in Palestine or leveling the exercise yard at Le Vernet. The German planes arrived regularly at just after nine o'clock each night, and the members of 251st Company were also required to turn out and help fight the fires raised by German bombs. Koestler complained to Daphne that he was totally exhausted. There were "twenty one privates, three N.C.O.s and a radio" in his barrack hut, the latter blaring so incessantly that it was virtually impossible to read, write, or even think effectively. He asked Daphne, now back in London, to correct the proofs of *Scum of the Earth,* since he was too tired to concentrate on them.[5]

In June the company was posted to the picturesque region of the Cotswolds and housed in comfortable modern barracks (still twenty to a room) in the Regency spa of Cheltenham. His new job was digging tank traps, but Koestler was fed up with digging and went to his commanding officer, Major McKay, with an ingenious scheme to write a book about the Aliens' Pioneer Corps. He was aware of the APC's reputation as a dumping ground for foreigners not dangerous enough to be interned in concentration camps (though dangerous enough, in British eyes, to corrupt the real army), and he wanted to show, as he had done in *Scum of the Earth,* that those who had valiantly resisted fascism in Germany, Austria, and Spain were men of great intellectual and moral distinction and a needlessly wasted resource.

Major McKay, a huge man with a bristling ginger mustache and sideburns, a hawk nose, several chins, an exaggeratedly military bearing, and a monocle in one eye, towered over the diminutive Koestler. He had been a hero in World War I, winning a Military Cross and bar, and had been shot through the throat, which left him with a hoarse, deep voice that he had put to excellent use between the wars as an actor. For a military man he was unusually literate, and he was keenly interested in Koestler's idea, not least because Koestler had craftily invited McKay to write the opening chapter. Koestler contacted Allen Lane at the Penguin Press and proposed a Penguin special on "The Regiment with No Traditions," a "collective account of the birth, life and achievements of an Alien Unit serving somewhere with His Majesty's Forces somewhere in Britain." Penguin had just reissued *Dialogue with Death* in paperback, and Koestler cast the project in terms of its social utility. "Its political value is this: I have a feeling that the British public is rather fed up with pitying the refugees, and the refugees are rather fed up with being pitied." The book would show the aliens as good soldiers doing their bit for the country, and would produce friendly reactions "even in readers of the 'intern-the-lot-of-them' type."[6]

Koestler was granted the coveted privilege of sleeping in the company's "library-plus-sports-store room," surrounded by boxing gloves, cricket bats, old volumes of *Punch,* and a Jewish holy shrine containing two "Thora [*sic*] rolls wrapped in gold and velvet," which he later shared with a fellow Hungarian named Francis Szedö. He was granted periodic exemption from physical labor and permission to make research trips to Oxford and London. He was filled with enthusiasm until Sir Arthur Willert (Paul Willert's father) recruited him to give lectures about the European situation for the Army Educational Corps. MI5, in granting permission, had changed its tune, now referring to Koestler as "a very decent man" and commenting that he would be a "good lecturer" for the army. Soon he was happily traveling up and down Britain to talk on such topics as "Inside a German Concentration Camp," "The History of the Fifth Column," and "The Eastern Front," a repertoire that was later expanded to include "The Mysteries of Inheritance" (on genetics and the Nazi race laws) and "With the *Graf Zeppelin* to the North Pole."[7]

KOESTLER WAS ASTOUNDED to discover that the audiences he had once praised for their common sense and desire for fair play were actually pretty ignorant and isolationist. The working-class men and women he spoke to had only the faintest grasp of how their electoral system worked and no idea what fascism was. This strangely passionate little man in the baggy battledress seemed like the man in the moon to them, and some of them wondered aloud why an enemy alien had been allowed to join the British army in the first place. Why, after all, would anyone want to fight against his own country? "I find again and again," he wrote to Paul Willert, "how totally ignorant we are" (about the feelings of the masses). "If we survive this war, we should all sit down modestly on our arses for a few years and shut up and learn the ABC of human thinking and feeling." If his experiences in the French Foreign Legion had begun his education about the "proletariat," these forays expanded it. "For me," he said later, "it was an eye-opener. I was shocked."[8]

In Cheltenham he was introduced to the wealthy Michael Sadleir, the author of *Fanny by Gaslight,* who let Daphne stay at his place for six weeks (until Koestler upset the arrangement by parking a stray mongrel among Sadleir's pedigreed dogs). Another Cheltenham acquaintance was Cecil Day-Lewis, and a third was the literary lawyer and amateur playwright Harold Rubinstein, who became Koestler's legal adviser. The lives of these well-heeled Cotswold grandees were on a plane of luxury unimaginable to the people who made up most of Koestler's audiences, and Koestler began to think that, in class terms, Britain had progressed remarkably little from the "two nations" of Benjamin Disraeli's time. "As a result of all these experiences in the Pioneer Corps and lecturing to Army units," he wrote to Paul Willert, "I became a fervent supporter of the Labour Party." The once convinced continental Communist became a fervent English-style Social Democrat.[9]

There was a certain irony in Koestler addressing his thoughts on the proletariat to Willert. Willert's father was a knight occupying a high position in the Foreign Office. His wife, Brenda, was a scion of the Cowdray family, one of the wealthiest and most aristocratic in England, and Willert himself was a typically languid product of Eton and Oxford. It was to Willert, now training to become a navigator at an RAF camp, that Koestler confided the surprising news that he welcomed the recent entry of the Soviet Union into the war against Germany, though for reasons far removed from those of his British confrères. Everyone he talked to, he wrote, "regards the German-Soviet war as an episode in the Battle of Britain." No one seemed to realize that "huge issues" were at stake. Stalin was the "Russian Chamberlain," a shortsighted "appeaser" whose idiotic pact with Hitler was responsible for leaving his country to fight alone. "Stalin and his bureaucracy will disappear. The great question is, what will come after?" In the case of a Russian victory, "the rebirth of all our hopes, and not only hope but fulfillment." In the case of defeat, the establishment of "some sort of Asiatic Soviet Republic" east of the Urals.[10]

But the Red Army performed much better than Koestler expected, and he began to wonder if Soviet military successes disproved the thesis about Stalin he had advanced in *Darkness at Noon.* The Soviet advance was "hard to explain," wrote Willert. "I suppose they were always better than they let even people like you see." But "I am rereading *Darkness at Noon*. I do not think you will feel like changing anything that you wrote because of the success of No. 1. And what is more important, you should not change anything."[11]

KOESTLER'S LECTURE JAUNTS kept him increasingly away from tank-trap digging, and also from his proposed book on the Pioneer Corps. Major McKay, still awaiting an invitation to write chapter one, grew restless over his absences, and when Koestler asked for a week's leave to participate in the International PEN Congress in London in September 1941, he turned him down twice. Koestler appealed to powerful friends at the War Office and went anyway. He cut quite a figure at the congress in his crumpled uniform, and fellow writers now paid attention when he entered a room. But Koestler's absence proved to be the last straw for Major McKay. With three hundred men in his company laboring for twelve hours a day, the thought of Koestler absconding to gallivant around the country, dining with the rich and famous in London, and having his book reviewed in all the important papers was too much to bear. The major forbade all further trips out of camp, even for lecturing, unless Koestler was officially transferred to the Royal Army Educational Corps. Until then, he would have to perform the same backbreaking duties as the other men.

Whether by accident or design, Koestler immediately sustained an injury to his left arm. His report to the medical officer said, "While unloading large wooden boards at Pittville Camp, I stumbled against a stack of wood and a heavy board fell on my left arm." The injury was slight, some bruising at most, but the medical officer recommended he be put on light duties. Koestler was now in open conflict with Major McKay and thoroughly disgusted with military service. It wasn't at all as he had imagined it, and he came to share the widespread sentiment, later articulated by Goronwy Rees, that in Britain at that time, "for an intellectual to be a soldier was in some way beneath his dignity and a waste of his talents. To enter the civil service, the Office of Information, the B.B.C., was in some way or another to serve one's country usefully and intelligently, without lending oneself to the more brutal arts of war." The arts of the Pioneer Corps weren't so much brutal as brutish, and Koestler asked some influential friends to try to get him out.[12]

After a second visit to London in early November (for which Koestler received a special waiver from the Foreign Office), Koestler got into an argument with Quartermaster Sergeant Bratt over the exchange of a pair of suspenders, and Bratt accused him of insolence. Koestler demanded to be put on a charge, fully expecting to clear his name, but the sour Major McKay ordered him confined to barracks for two weeks for insubordination. McKay also deprived Koestler of the use of the storeroom, reiterated his decree that

no further lectures or trips away from camp would be allowed until Koestler
got a transfer, and put Koestler on fatigues from six in the morning until ten
at night. Two nights after hearing this edict, Koestler suffered a dramatic collapse and was rushed to the emergency room at Montpellier Hospital in
Cheltenham.

The exact cause of his collapse was never clarified. Koestler said he had
suffered a nervous breakdown, but Robert Ringel, the company's medical
corporal at the time, suspected Koestler of overdosing on codeine pills he had
stolen from Ringel's room. "He was alone in the barracks that night, because
everyone else was at the Warship Week dance. He knew the layout of my
room because of all the times we had played poker there."[13]

Ringel's conjecture has the ring of truth to it, and Daphne Hardy also
guessed that Koestler had taken an overdose but felt that the nervous strain
on him was cumulative and genuine and that he had acted out of real desperation. For two days he remained dazed and semiconscious, and the doctors
had the greatest difficulty diagnosing his condition, suspecting (not unrea-
sonably) that it might be due to alcohol poisoning. In the end he was described as suffering from "nervous collapse" and transferred to a civilian
hospital to get some rest.[14]

As soon as he was able, Koestler dictated a letter to McKay volunteering
for wireless duties overseas. He also petitioned the War Office for an official
transfer to the Army Educational Corps on the grounds that he was physically unfit for manual labor. But salvation came from another quarter. After
an enormous number of letters had flown back and forth, he was offered the
choice of working either for Military Intelligence or the Ministry of Information and had no hesitation in choosing the latter.[15]

As the wheels of the government bureaucracy turned with their usual
slowness, Koestler enjoyed a delightful convalescence in Cheltenham. He
asked the nurse in charge of his ward if he might use his typewriter, to which
she replied, "All right, you can have your typewriter, but on one condition:
you must give me your word of honor you won't do any Fifth Column work
on it." He spent Sundays discussing politics and poetry with Day-Lewis and
Frank Halliday. Daphne rushed down from Oxford to see him in the hospital and bumped into a young woman called Philippa Whittington on her way
out, unaware that Koestler had been having an affair with her. The meeting
with Daphne was nevertheless very tender, and after Christmas he announced that his depression, including his "martyr-complex and worrying
and mental untidiness," was gone. "I discovered I was wrong in the things I
did and the attitude I adopted since we parted in France. In fact I found that
I had been in a nasty psychological cul-de-sac."

On March 10, 1942, Koestler was classified as "permanently unfit" for service, putting an end to a brief and inglorious military career that had lasted
less than a year. He exchanged his itchy battle dress and army pay book for a

utility suit, some clothing coupons, and a ration book and set out to find a place to live.[16]

DURING HIS ELEVEN MONTHS in the army, Koestler's double life had grown increasingly surreal. At the London PEN Congress, attended by H. G. Wells, Salvador de Madariaga, Jan Masaryk, Thornton Wilder, and John Dos Passos, among others, Koestler had delivered a paper entitled "The Novelist's Temptations," expanding his ideas on the opposition between social realists and modernists and throwing in his lot with the realists. "I do believe there is a main road leading from *Eulenspiegel* and *Don Quixote* to *War and Peace, The Magic Mountain,* and *Fontamara.* And I also believe that *Tristram Shandy, Wuthering Heights, Swann's Way,* and *The Waves* are masterpieces at dead ends." Too much complacency about the outside world amounted to "passive complicity," and the task of the artist was to expose the full truth and "create the emotional urge for healing."[17]

Koestler's paper led to a brief correspondence with E. M. Forster, who was highly impressed with *Scum of the Earth* but took issue with Koestler's comment that writers ought to be able to "see the chimney stacks" as they wrote. "It is an ethical problem. I'm unconvinced of the necessity of that 'ought.' No doubt it is morally shocking today to write like Jane Austen, and also extremely difficult, but if anyone can succeed in doing so, where, technically, is the weakness?" Later, after praising *Darkness at Noon,* Forster returned to the problem. "I'll fight you as long as you like on this question of variety of outlook, but I think you are fighting for it yourself."[18]

George Orwell invited Koestler to tea at his apartment in Canonbury Square, where Koestler found him bathing and changing his baby son. Koestler admired Orwell's tenderness with his child but found the tall, stooping Englishman "rather intimidating" when it came to adults, "a real Burmah police sergeant." That feeling hadn't stopped him from pouring out his troubles to Orwell, who noted sympathetically in his diary, "What appalling stupidity, when you have a youngish, gifted man who speaks I do not know how many languages and really knows something about Europe, especially the European political movements, to be unable to make any use of him except for shoveling bricks." Koestler couldn't have agreed more.[19]

After being discharged from the army, Koestler had nowhere to live and was taken in by Cyril Connolly until he found a place of his own. Connolly had published an excerpt from *Scum of the Earth* in *Horizon* and on one of Koestler's jaunts to London had exchanged novels with him, Connolly's *The Rock Pool* (which Koestler didn't much like) for Koestler's *Darkness at Noon* (which Connolly did). Connolly had also thrown a big party where Koestler met Stephen Spender (tall and handsome in his dark blue fireman's uniform), Louis MacNeice, Philip Toynbee, John Lehmann, and other luminaries of the literary scene. Spender and his friends deeply admired *Spanish Testament* and *Darkness at Noon,* and were thrilled to meet the hero of Málaga and Seville. The fact that this hero, with his short, stocky build, cropped hair, creased battledress, and heavy Hungaro-German accent, looked and sounded more like the good soldier Svejk made no difference at all. His hair-raising tales of Spain and Paris, and of his skin-of-the-teeth escape from France during the German occupation, were absolutely fascinating, and he impressed everyone with his electric energy, sharp intelligence, and infectious enthusiasm.[20]

Friendship between the legendarily languid Connolly and his intensely neurotic contributor seemed just as unlikely as Koestler's friendship with Forster, but the Connolly connection proved more durable. Connolly was strangely taken by the Central European firebrand, and Koestler, despite their later differences, remained forever grateful to Connolly for his patronage and interest. New to English literary life, Koestler was prey to more self-doubt and insecurity than he cared to admit, and Connolly helped him overcome it. "Cyril took me under his wing. Instead of spending my time in loneliness and isolation, like so many exiles, or confined to an émigré clique, I was welcomed into the *Horizon* crowd. I wouldn't say I was exactly an insider, more a strange bird on the periphery, but the important thing was that I felt at home." The indebtedness was not all one way either. "There is no doubt that we are very necessary to one another," Connolly wrote to Koestler, "at least you are to me—not as a catalyst but as an oxygen tent." There was also the minor matter of hard cash. Connolly was chronically hard up and was in the habit of borrowing twenty pounds or so from Koestler to tide himself over in difficult times—a habit Connolly persisted in almost until the end of his life.[21]

Connolly shared a duplex apartment at 102a Drayton Gardens with his girlfriend, Lys Lubbock, and the poet and critic Peter Quennell. The apartment belonged to the Paget twins, Mamaine and Celia, who didn't live there but liked to mix with their literary tenants. It was a bohemian setup, in which you never quite knew who you would meet at breakfast in the morning. Natasha Spender (who had recently celebrated her wedding with Stephen there) remembered dropping around one day to find Koestler propped up in a huge double bed, surrounded by newspapers containing reviews of *Scum of the Earth,* and talking to his publisher on the telephone, while Daphne stood at an ironing board in the corner, pressing Koestler's shirts.[22]

Quennell and Koestler took an intense dislike to each other and soon quarreled over who should use the bathroom first. Quennell, the senior resident, claimed to find the sight of Koestler in his Continental hairnet "revolting." Their competitiveness came to a head when Quennell began to spread rumors about the hairnet. "I was alleged to have told a girl we both knew," wrote Quennell afterward, "that in bed he wore a hairnet; and he protested that I had gravely injured his chances of securing her affections." The "girl" in question was the glamorous Barbara Skelton, who mischievously informed Koestler that people were giggling behind his back. Koestler wrote an angry letter to Quennell, and Quennell sent an elaborately mocking apology back, saying that "the apparition of a foreign man of genius rushing hair-netted towards his bath" in the mornings had made an "alarming" impression on him. "I take your word for it that it is proper attire at that time of day for 'any civilized continental.' But it's also a fact that, from the hidebound anglo-saxon point of view, the hair-net is still a slightly comic garment." Koestler burned the hairnet the next day and never wore one again (and got his revenge with the kittenish Skelton).[23]

KOESTLER'S CONTINENTAL WAYS and strange accent made him an easy target for his upper-class English friends. Connolly, who made fun of everybody, had guessed the secret of Koestler's early release from the Aliens' Pioneer Corps and teased him mercilessly about his commanding officer and Koestler's supposed susceptability to breakdowns. In Connolly's view, it was the officer who should have had a breakdown, not Koestler. Connolly also made fun of Koestler's heavy accent and his inability to pronounce a British *w*. "Who is more important," Koestler is alleged to have asked one day, "Orvell or Fyvel?" (In another version he asks about Orvell, the writer T. R. Fyvel, and the British general Vavell.) Like the hairnet, this story had a long life, but David Astor, who knew the latter version, thought that Connolly had made it up. Astor likened Koestler's accent to "a hacksaw" but felt it had its positive side. "He wasn't at all an actor or a poser, he was very much himself." The "harsh accent" was part of who he was.[24]

Koestler's English friends were genuinely taken aback, however, by his single-minded pursuit of women, a pursuit that differed from that of Connolly and Quennell mainly in its ruthless intensity. Koestler was immensely attractive to certain women. "Women either loved him or hated him," according to one of his friends of that time. Those who loved him were attracted by his elaborate manners, the candor with which he expressed his admiration, and a mischievous exuberance that made a bracing change from British modesty and understatement. He appealed to women's vanity, their imagination—and their lust, with a directness that was beyond most of his English competitors. Female interest and approval also brought out the best in him. Timidity was banished, a masterful self-confidence took its place, and he loved to show off his connoisseurship of good food, good wine, good music, and good sex.[25]

Not surprisingly, his crude advances and predatory belief that coercion added spice to sexual intercourse also alienated many women. Among his papers (along with the numerous love letters and notes for assignations he collected from this period) he preserved several angry letters from women who rejected his advances, including a scorching missive from one of Daphne's friends. But he adamantly clung to the hoary adage that "all's fair in love and war" and despised what he saw as British hypocrisy and reticence. To a certain extent, Koestler's extreme behavior was fostered by the artificial conditions of life in London during the Blitz, which reminded him of Weimar Berlin, Republican Barcelona, and prewar Paris—and represented a welcome change from his chilly exile in the Aliens' Pioneer Corps. He thrived on the tension and unpredictability of it all, and the gladiatorial contest of competing egos. Michael Foot recalled a drunken night at the Gargoyle Club with Koestler, Dylan Thomas, and the American correspondent Joseph Alsop. After Koestler had routed Alsop in a furious political argument, the others repaired at four in the morning to Foot's bachelor pad, where Koestler trounced Foot at chess while Thomas wandered the room taking books from the shelves and making derogatory comments about their authors. When he got to *Darkness at Noon,* he wrote a rude message on the flyleaf. Koestler snatched it back and wrote an answer. Thomas grabbed it back and wrote another insult. Regrettably, Foot lost the book during the war.[26]

Koestler soon moved from Connolly's apartment to a small, shabby studio in Chelsea. Daphne was marooned in Oxford, but Koestler was able to pull strings through Richard Crossman, then running the German section of the Political Warfare Executive, to get her transferred to the Ministry of Information in London. Not long afterward, they rented a terrace house on three floors at 23 Tryon Street in Chelsea. For a while it was a haven of cozy domesticity. Daphne left for work each morning and returned home eight hours later, while Koestler spent the day writing on the top floor. In the evening, they would make dinner together or entertain.

Their guests included many journalists and politicians associated with the Labour Party. Some, such as Victor Gollancz and John Strachey, had been virtually Communists until disillusioned by the Ribbentrop-Molotov Pact, and others, such as Crossman, Foot, and Aneurin Bevan, had experienced the magnetic pull of Marxism and been hypnotized by the successes of the Soviet Union. Repelled now by Soviet realpolitik, they were trying to build a coherent program that was staunchly anti-fascist and socialist, yet distinct from communism. Their main organ was the weekly *Tribune,* edited by Bevan and another Labour MP, George Strauss, whose private wealth subsidized the magazine. Orwell, a regular contributor, would soon become literary editor.

The author of *Darkness at Noon* appeared to many members of this group as little short of a prophet. Michael Foot had met Koestler at the Savoy Hotel when Koestler was still in the Aliens' Pioneer Corps and "fell an immediate swooning victim to his wit, charm, and inordinate capacity for alcohol." Strachey found the "rumpled figure in a battledress" a brilliant thinker and a wonderfully lively conversationalist. When Strachey's Communist wife, Celia, reacted violently to *Darkness at Noon*, however, Strachey rang Koestler and said, "Arthur, I'm afraid that my nightly visits to you will have to stop. Celia cannot stand you, and you see that I'm really in a position of having to choose between you and her."[27]

Koestler had lost none of his old dialectical skill in argument and still tended to treat discussion as a form of intellectual warfare. Stephen Spender was stunned one day at the Café Royal when Koestler said, "Don't say any more, don't say any more, because I can predict everything that you are going to say in the next twenty minutes." According to Foot, "Others might be said to wield a rapier, a bludgeon or some such old-fashioned instrument. But Koestler got you in a corner, with all escapes blocked, and machine-gunned with fact, analogy, the superabundant debating skill. Sometimes his passion and logic would consume themselves and everyone in sight, in mounting, insensate, satanic virulence."[28]

As with his sexual adventures, there was a disagreeable side to these all-out offensives. Writing in a contrite mood to Willert after an uncomfortable evening at the latter's home in Halsey Street, Koestler made fun of his schoolmasterly manner and pedagogical intensity, "giving lectures to everybody like a wandering, post-Freudian, post-Marxian prophet in the desert." Later, in another apologetic letter to Willert, he offered an excuse for his outbursts. "There is a certain mental type to which we both belong, and which the psychologists call 'emotionally unbalanced.' To speak metaphorically, the person affected by this state walks through life as if balancing a full water-tank on top of his head. A slight nod, a gentle inclination left or right, forward or backward, and schnupp, a massive jet spurts out, which is quite out of proportion with the stimulus that occasioned it. A normal person would only have spilled a few drops of emotion."[29]

This theory of "emotional inflation," as Koestler labeled it, was self-serving, of course, but Koestler's irony, his self-knowledge, and his ability to mock himself redeemed his aggressiveness in the eyes of most friends. The young David Astor, captivated by Koestler's "no-nonsense style," liked the fact that although Koestler could be sarcastic and very funny, "he was always direct, and there was something a little boyish about him too. He was alive and didn't conceal his feelings at all." Koestler's arrival in anxious wartime London was "a great stimulant." "Here he was, full of confidence and vigor—but coming, unbelievably, from a French concentration camp." For the idealistic Astor, "Koestler was the embodiment of an uncompromised, unafraid, international idealism. This small passionate man, with his excruciating accent, his self-mockery, and his devotion to his political friends in Europe whom he called 'The Scum of the Earth,' seemed almost as miraculous an apparition, at a different part of the political spectrum, as Churchill himself."[30]

CHAPTER TWENTY

THE NOVELIST'S
TEMPTATIONS

The best cause needs a good pleader.

—DUTCH PROVERB

KOESTLER'S EUROPEAN PERSPECTIVE and explosive personality made him an unusual figure on the British literary scene. With one foot planted on the Continent and the other in England, he was intimately affected by the fascist occupation of Europe in ways his British friends could hardly imagine, and he continued to brood over the friends and relatives he had left behind and on ways to mitigate their plight.

A piercing reminder of the increasingly unbridgeable chasm between himself and occupied Europe came in the form of a letter from his mother welcoming an end to the "six agonizing months" of uncertainty she had endured after his disappearance from France but bringing bad news of her own. His father had been taken to the Jewish Hospital in Budapest in July and operated on for cancer. "Papa felt so good on the Saturday that he said to me: 'You'll see. I shall earn some money now, just let me get out of this place first. We'll have a couple of happy years with the boy yet.'" But ten days later Henrik died after a massive hemorrhage. "He went peacefully, as was his nature, without pain, and I think at times even resigned to his fate. And then the terrible truth came home to me—I am alone, left alone and deserted by both of you, who have always cared for me so lovingly. I was numbed by pain and surprise, without hope or support, finished and ready to end it all."

Adele's comment about her son's loving care for her was either an illusion or a bourgeois fiction, but he was genuinely saddened to hear that his irrepressible father was dead. He also understood the meaning of Adele's melo-dramatic remarks. His cousin Dezsö Somló had paid the funeral expenses, and Adele was staying with another cousin in downtown Budapest, ashamed of her dependency but hoping that her "dear son" would save her from this "untenable and unworthy situation." Koestler arranged for Adele to be sent regular sums from his royalties in America and for Cape to send her a cable once a month assuring her he was well. But when the USA and Hungary entered the war on opposite sides, Koestler was hard put to send her any money at all. After losing contact for a while, he wrote again to assure her that he was deeply grateful for the family's help and would repay them at the first opportunity. "Be patient and don't despair. Every misery has an end; and there is a room waiting for you in the little country house in which I live" (a polite fiction, matching Adele's fiction, that Koestler felt was justified under the circumstances).[1]

An unpleasant reminder of more family problems came from another cousin, the black sheep, Feri Aldor, who had been interned on the Isle of Man as an "enemy alien" and was pleading for help. Feri's situation was obviously serious, since the overwhelming majority of internees had been released and by this time only a hard core of a couple of thousand were left. But Feri's letter put Koestler on the spot. A couple of years earlier, when he had been a prisoner in Le Vernet and their situation was reversed, Koestler had asked Aldor for some royalties from *The Practice of Sex,* and Aldor had put him off on the pretext that he was moving his business to London. Koestler had had to sue for the money, and now his cousin was asking him to use his influence to get him out of internment.[2]

It turned out that during his two years as a publisher in England, Feri had brought out a whole string of propaganda works with titles such as *Dachau, the Nazi Hell; Poland, Germany's Death Space;* and *I Was an Altmark Prisoner,* most of them written by himself. He had also continued his line of sex books: *The Practice of Sex, Women's Experience of the Male, Sexual Life During the World War,* and *Sexual Life in England Past and Present.* He had been arrested not just as an enemy alien but on suspicion of also being a pornographer. Koestler sent food packages and cigarettes and offered to find Feri a lawyer and to pay his legal expenses, but Feri wasn't satisfied. He wanted Koestler to fly up to see him. Feri then tried to bribe one of the officers in his camp and was brought to London for investigation. Koestler went to see his once rich cousin and found him in a pitiful condition: unshaven, in a collarless shirt and stained suit, with a look of desperation in his eyes. His black hair had turned white, his eyebrows met over his nose, he had shrunk in size, and he looked for all the world like an unhappy troglodyte. In his rapid-fire voice he tried to cajole Koestler ("I'll make you rich") into working for him and helping him restore his publishing business. Koestler, no longer the protégé but reflexively feeling guilty all the same, refused Feri's offer, uneasily shook hands, and departed.

When he came to describe this meeting in *The Invisible Writing,* Koestler wrote that Feri then "vanished from my life" forever. This was a literary flourish, not the truth. Koestler wanted to rid his life story of Feri because "there was a good deal of him in myself," an uncomfortable truth that was hard for Koestler to face. One of Feri's typists described him as such before his imprisonment. Feri had green eyes and black hair, and was "small and stocky, with a square face." He had the "confident air of someone magnetic and irresistible, as did Koestler of course." With his propaganda books, promiscuity, financial juggling, and miraculous ability to land on his feet, Feri was Koestler's dark double, an uncomfortable reminder of his own less savory instincts. But this was not Feri's last appearance in his life. They were to be linked by the disaster that struck their family two years later, when the Nazis overran Slovakia and Hungary and rounded up the Jews, including Feri's sister, Margit, and her family. Koestler was to remain in reluctant contact with Feri until the latter's death in 1951.[3]

MORE BAD NEWS came from Dorothee, now marooned in Marseilles. Koestler had sent Dorothee money and tried to get her a visa for the United States, but the Americans were skittish, allotting only fifteen hundred visas for the thirty thousand refugees clamoring to get out of France. In November 1941 Dorothee had been issued a Cuban visa, and Koestler had authorized payment of $1,500 from his American royalties, but she had never made it. She had fallen down some steps, smashed her shoulder, and had to be hospitalized. With great difficulty, Koestler had managed to transfer some money to pay for the operation and for Dorothee's living expenses during her six-week convalescence. It looked as if a second operation would be required, and this time Koestler had to obtain permission from the Trading with the Enemy Branch of the British Treasury to send her regular payments of twenty pounds a month. No second operation took place, but for months after the first one, Dorothee was laid up with her arm in plaster and unable to work. In June 1942 her Cuban visa was canceled, and Koestler applied for a British visa for her, but before she could use it, the Germans occupied the whole of France and closed the borders. Dorothee and her new partner, Hans Müller, went into hiding, and Koestler lost touch with her.[4]

Babette Gross wrote from Lisbon that the decomposing body of Willi Münzenberg had been found in some woods near Grenoble. The cause of death was said to be hanging, and all sorts of rumors were circulating among the exiles. "No need to tell you that I'm almost crazy and paralyzed. After some terrible weeks I have begun to believe in his death, but I could never believe it was suicide. However, recalling our discussions and your own experiences, perhaps even that is possible." Gross eventually made it to Mexico, as did Regler and Valiani. Koestler sent money to Valiani, and to Andor Németh in France, until Németh and his wife also went into hiding.[5]

Koestler was cast into a severe depression by the bad news streaming in from occupied Europe. It seemed at times as if his entire family, all his closest friends, and his comrades in arms were being abandoned to the Nazi wolves with virtually no one paying attention. After his own experiences in France, he could vividly imagine their feelings and spent a huge amount of time writing letters, lobbying publishers, and giving financial help whenever he could. The success of *Scum of the Earth* suggested that there might be more sympathy for Europe's stranded fugitives than he had formerly thought, and while still in the Aliens' Pioneer Corps he had devised an ingenious quarantine plan. Acknowledging that it was impossible to rescue all hundred thousand refugees still trapped in unoccupied France, he proposed that up to ten thousand of them—those who had taken up arms against fascism and been forced to flee their own countries—deserved special consideration as the "first casualties in the world struggle for liberty." The United States, the only country with the wealth and power to do so, should take these refugees and establish a "quarantine station" for them somewhere on American-controlled territory but outside the continental United States—for example, in the Virgin Islands. This would provide "a temporary waiting room where the hunted men of Europe could wait in bodily safety until the end of the war," after which they would be repatriated to Europe.

The beauty of this scheme was that it got around the increasingly severe American restrictions on immigration and didn't threaten American isolationism, which was at its height as the United States dithered over whether to enter the war. The refugees would engage in "public works" to defray the expenses of the scheme and would all return home without ever having entered the United States at all. One extraordinary stipulation was that the Jewish factor shouldn't be made a criterion for choosing whom to bring, since even if a haven were to be found for many of them, "the German authorities would be delighted to re-fill the French camps with Jews exported from the occupied countries." It was a somewhat dubious argument, stemming perhaps from Koestler's desire to preempt anti-Semites from seizing on this factor to defeat the plan. He was aware, of course, that a full 90 percent of the refugees stranded on French territory were Jews, so they would inevitably make up a huge proportion of the saved.[6]

Having presented his plan in vain to the American ambassador in London in November 1941, Koestler revisited it in two articles for Lord Beaverbrook's *Evening Standard*. His arguments were eloquent and impassioned, but all attempts to arouse British readers and public opinion (and through them, the Americans) fell on deaf ears.[7]

IN THE SPRING of 1942, Koestler was able to give vent to his feelings when he started work at the British Ministry of Information. His job was to write anti-Nazi propaganda programs for the Home Service of the BBC—a return to the kind of job he had once done so well for Willi Münzenberg. His first effort was a forty-minute radio play, *Protective Custody,* which opened to the sound of prisoners singing the "Dachau Hymn," followed by an announcement that the author, "because of his anti-fascist convictions, spent the major part of the last years in the prisons and concentration camps of various European countries as Hitler's night gradually descended upon them." Koestler still couldn't resist a useful fiction for propaganda ends, justifying it on the grounds that the enemy's propaganda was far worse (though it contradicted his dictum that the ends shouldn't justify the means). The play drew on Koestler's experiences in Le Vernet but described a far more brutal environment of forced labor, systematic starvation, and torture than he had personally experienced.[8]

Koestler then wrote two scripts for the Home Service's "Black Gallery" series, one on the notoriously anti-Semitic editor of *Der Stürmer,* Julius Streicher, the other on the recently assassinated head of Hitler's security service, Reinhard Heydrich. He also wrote "Portrait of a German Youth" and "Night of the Long Knives" and branched out into writing for Crossman's disinformation and black propaganda unit at the War Office. Crossman's first wife, Erika Gluck, had been working as a courier for Willi Münzenberg when Crossman met her in Berlin, and Crossman was also busy applying some of Willi's methods to British propaganda. He felt a natural affinity with Koestler, and the two liked each other from the start. Koestler wrote eight scripts for Crossman featuring the adventures of "Kurt Kokorniak," which were broadcast by the German service of the BBC. He also wrote a highly imaginative exercise in futurology that offered a detailed picture of how the Third Reich was bound to collapse in the not too distant future.[9]

Koestler liked to dream up stunts in the spirit of Münzenberg. One was a suggestion that the BBC try to start a coughing campaign inside Germany by telling ordinary Germans to sniff, cough, and clear their throats whenever they heard Nazi propaganda. Another suggestion was that Crossman's unit distribute a leaflet inside Germany called "Victorious unto Death," showing a staircase sketched by the *Daily Express* cartoonist Walter Goetz, in which each step was labeled with the name of a European capital conquered by the Nazis and the figure of an exhausted German soldier climbing ever higher. Beneath the sketch would be a list of German losses in each country, culminating in the huge losses of the Russian campaign. Crossman seems to have liked Koestler's ideas (though he never actually used them), and it may have been he who introduced Koestler to Dick White, the new head of MI5 (Koestler had come a long way since he was the object of MI5's suspicions). White was an ardent advocate of getting writers and intellectuals to help his agency, and over a game of croquet one day he asked Koestler and two academics, Victor Rothschild and Herbert Hart, for help with anti-Nazi propaganda "to make Goebbels sit up." Three such individualists found it impossible to agree, however, and after a few weeks the project "broke up in terrible disarray" and "bitter quarreling."[10]

Koestler's most ambitious project during this period was a film for Basil Wright's Documentary Film Unit, *Lift Your Head, Comrade* (a line from the Dachau Hymn), about a day in the life of an aliens' unit of the Pioneer Corps. A recap of his earlier proposal to Major McKay, the film was inspired by an occasion in Cheltenham when Koestler and some fellow soldiers from 251st Company had been invited to relate their experiences to an audience of Home Guards and civilians. The film introduced a cross section of the lawyers, professors, accountants, doctors, and other professionals who made up a typical unit in the Pioneer Corps. Employing exotic-sounding names that the British commanding officer was unable to pronounce, Koestler emphasized that these strange birds were just as loyal to the Allied cause as their British hosts and should be trusted. And he included some Jewish escapees from Dachau to make clear to the British public what was happening under the German occupation. "For the common people of Britain, the Gestapo and concentration camps have approximately the same degree of reality as the monster of Loch Ness," he wrote, and that was part of the problem.[11]

Hoping to pay off his debt to Major McKay and his comrades, Koestler proposed that the film feature several of the men in his old unit and that it be introduced and narrated by McKay, but his suggestion was vetoed. The film was shot in Weymouth on the south coast of England, directed by Basil Wright, with professional actors playing the parts. When released it was described by the *News Chronicle* as telling the story of the continental Pioneers "quietly and well," and was one of the few British propaganda films to be chosen for showing in America.[12]

IN NOVEMBER 1943, the ministry asked Koestler to submit an outline for a second film, this time on "Race Theory." Koestler produced a thirty-one-page script treatment, complete with suggestions for sets and a sound track. The script was a loose reworking of some of the themes raised in his unproduced 1934 stage play, *Mbo Mba on the Road,* and shows Koestler's continuing preoccupation with the plight of the Jews. Like the earlier work, the radio play was set partly in Africa. Hitler was portrayed as a kind of witch doctor, screaming about *Lebensraum* and the superiority of the Aryan race, while newsreels of fascist rallies were intercut with scenes of cannibalism in the jungle. The message was not that blacks were savages but that stigmatizing and persecuting other peoples was a form of savagery. After quoting and refuting Nazi ideologues on race, Koestler slipped in an interesting comment on what he thought it meant to be a Jew. The Nazis had selected for persecution "a group that is less of a race than any other. A group that is not a nation, not a people. A group that has no country and no language. It cannot protest because it has no diplomatic representatives. It cannot fight because it has no army—and no frontiers to defend."

The assertion that the Jews were "a group" with "no country and no language" represented a considerable departure from Koestler's earlier Zionist positions and foreshadowed his later, highly controversial views on Jewish assimilation. At this time, however, he wasn't quite sure where he stood, and the script ended with a curious elision of race and class that seemed like a feeble attempt to reconcile his Zionist past with his political convictions: Let us have "no more splits into so-called races, so-called nations. No more splits into a slum race and a leisure race."[13]

George Orwell asked Koestler to contribute to a series of booklets that he and T. R. "Tosco" Fyvel were editing, called Searchlight Books. The goal was to provide a left-wing political rationale for the war against Hitler, and Orwell himself wrote the first in the series, "The Lion and the Unicorn," one of his most celebrated essays, in which he optimistically discussed the prospects for a peculiarly British form of socialism. Koestler's contribution was to be called "The Streets of Europe" (subtitled "Five Men on Five Streets"), describing views on Britain and the war from the "man in the street" of five different countries: Germany, Russia, France, Spain, and "the Old Monarchy" (Austro-Hungary). The project was cut short when the series' printing works was bombed by the Germans, but a shadow of the idea surfaced in a column that Koestler started to write for the Evening Standard in the summer of 1942.[14]

Koestler devised a man-in-the-street character called Bertie Blush, an underwear salesman in a department store, who was to ruminate on the war as he traveled home each day ("the idle thoughts of Bertie Blush, your neighbour in the homeward rush"). The combination of underwear and "blush" was thought to be too risqué for Evening Standard readers and was replaced by "the idle thoughts of Sidney Sound, your neighbour on the Underground."

Sidney Sound offered serious comments on British propaganda techniques, mixed with asides on the Spanish Civil War, fascist excesses in Europe, and the German advance on Russia, but his creator's "Continental" sensibility soon got him into trouble. Objecting to the custom of lodging bombed-out members of the London poor for long periods in Underground stations, Koestler pictured Sidney Sound stumbling over "a row of chamber pots" with "property of London Transport" printed on them "like the tea-cups in hotels." Koestler also introduced the motif of shy Sidney lusting for "the blonde A.T.S. corporal" he sometimes encountered on the train and made fun of Churchill's cigars and inflated status as an unassailable British hero. "Within weeks," said Michael Foot, who had commissioned Koestler, "he had ruptured my relationship with proprietor, management and, as they alleged, a considerable chunk of the reading public." The *Standard*'s English readers were not amused by Sidney Sound, and the column was cut after its fourth appearance.[15]

Koestler continued to think about what the future might hold after the war and about the issues of progress and revolution raised by Orwell in both "The Lion and the Unicorn" and a companion piece, "On Fascism and Democracy," in which Orwell exploded the myth of a non-Soviet form of communism. Koestler responded with several essays of his own, starting with "The Yogi and the Commissar," published in *Horizon* in June 1942. In this essay, Koestler moved the discussion from sociology to psychology and returned to the "two-front war" he had been waging with himself since his Spanish prison experiences, first against the "concise, rational, materialistic" approach to life that was his habitual mode of thinking and second against the temptation to creep back into "the protective womb of faith." As in "The Novelist's Temptations," Koestler suggested that what was needed for ratio-nal political change was a synthesis between the yogi and the commissar. Commissar change led (as Orwell had shown) inexorably to the Moscow purges, while change exclusively from within, as practiced, for example, by Gandhi, led to passive submission to violence, to "villages without sewage and septic childbeds and trachoma." Artists were of no great help in this mat-ter because they were inclined by nature to yogi-type solutions, and even sci-entists, under the influence of quantum mechanics, had become seduced by the idea that scientific progress was irrational.[16]

The New York Times Magazine asked him to write an article, "based on personal experience, on what gives men faith to fight to the end for the demo-cratic way." In "Knights in Rusty Armor," Koestler offered a dusty answer. No one was dying for anything as abstract as the democratic way anymore. Some of the greatest victories over fascism were being scored by the decid-edly undemocratic Soviet state, while other opponents of fascism were fight-ing not for democracy but for national liberation, and the British saw the war as a war for national survival, "in defense of certain conservative nineteenth century ideals." Koestler might have added, but didn't, that some of those conservative ideals had found their way into Orwell's English socialism. The "knights in rusty armor," by contrast, were those like himself who dreamed of "a unified, fraternal, socialist Europe," but they were "standing in no-man's-land, with a well-thumbed handbook of Marx-Engels quotations" as their sole guide, and their cause seemed almost hopeless.[17]

In a second article for *The New York Times Magazine,* the "knights in rusty armor" became "a fraternity of pessimists." Koestler was now more sanguine about the war but less hopeful about the aftermath: "In this war," he began, "we are fighting against a total lie in the name of a half-truth." We had declared that we were against racialism and in favor of democracy, yet racialism still flourished and our mightiest ally was a dictatorship. Looking back, he found that the outstanding feature of international politics was "the collapse of all horizontal structures," which indicated a fundamental flaw in liberal and socialist thinking. "To talk of 'ups and downs' is self-deception; we are not on a mountain railway but in a blind alley. Today we are farther than twenty years ago from the realization of a truly new human climate." Surprisingly, his conclusion brought him closer to Orwell again, with an endorsement of British conservatism: "If I have to choose between living under a political commissar or a blimp, I unhesitatingly choose blimp. He will treat me as an annoying kind of oddity and push me about from sheer lack of imagination; the imaginative commissar will politely shoot me because I disagree with him."[18]

KOESTLER'S MOST COMPLETE EXAMINATION of the dilemma facing political radicals came in the form of his third novel, *Arrival and Departure,* which he worked on from July 1942 to July 1943 and which was published in the same month (November 1943) as "The Fraternity of Pessimists." He had started to write a sequel to *Darkness at Noon* called "The Constant Defeat," based on his experiences as a Communist in Berlin during the early thirties, but that project petered out, and he turned to another period of his life for inspiration. The new novel featured a twenty-two-year-old revolutionary activist called Peter Slavek, who arrives in nonbelligerent "Neutralia" after escaping from a fascist prison in an unnamed Slavic country. In his homeland he is legendary for his heroic resistance to torture, but once in Neutralia he is faced with a choice that he finds agonizingly difficult to make. He can either return to his country to continue the struggle against fascism, move to Britain and enlist in the only Western European army still fighting the Germans, or accept a proffered visa for the United States. There he will be reunited with Odette, a young Frenchwoman with whom he has fallen in love, and will be able to retire from the fray.[19]

In the best part of the novel, Peter suffers a psychosomatic crisis, brought on by the news that his American visa has been granted, and loses the use of one leg. Dr. Sonia Bolgar, a psychoanalyst, undertakes to cure him and in a series of intense psychoanalytic dialogues, reminiscent of the interrogations in *Darkness at Noon,* strips away the layers of Slavek's personality to show that his revolutionary ardor springs from a deeply rooted sense of guilt and a desire for martyrdom. He recalls the people he thinks he has "betrayed" in his life, ranging from revolutionary workers and comrades to a group of Jews whose execution his mother forced him to watch as a child, forerunners of a trainload of Jews he witnessed on their way to execution by the Germans. But these are only on the surface. Digging deeper, Sonia forces him to remember that his sin of sins, repressed until now, was personal: an attempt to blind his baby brother with a boat hook when he was a small boy and consumed by jealousy of his sibling.

By the skillful use of her "confessional psychology and dream surgery," Sonia convinces Peter that all his revolutionary activities have been prompted by a search for atonement for his childhood guilt. She persuades him that convictions, values, and causes are "mere pretexts of the mind, phantoms of a more intimate reality," and history "no more than a chain of accidents." Prophets and crusaders try to deny the true ends of life, but the enemies they strike at are inside themselves. As for Peter's physical courage, even that is little more than a personal accident, "a matter of glands, nerves, patterns of reaction conditioned by heredity and early experiences. A drop of iodine less in the thyroid, a sadistic governess or over-affectionate aunt, a slight variation in the electric resistance of the medullary ganglions, and the hero became a coward, the patriot a traitor. Touched with the magic rod of cause and effect, the actions of men were emptied of their so-called moral contents as a Leyden jar is discharged by the touch of a conductor."[20]

At the end of his therapy Peter is "cured." He regains the use of his leg and prepares to follow Sonia to America. "Let the dead bury their dead. For him, Peter Slavek, the crusade had come to an end." But before he can leave, he has a tense encounter with a young fascist and fellow patient of Sonia's called Bernard, who attempts to seduce him to the fascist cause. Bernard is very persuasive. The differences between fascism and communism, he says, are less important than their similarities: "I could even point to a number of similarities between your No. 1 and our No. 1." Both are riding the wave of historical inevitability, but it is fascism, rather than communism, that will point the true way to the "post-individualist, post-liberal era."[21]

At the last moment, Peter is introduced to a badly disfigured young British pilot called Andrew, who persuades him that continuing the war cannot be justified on rational grounds and doesn't necessarily need a "cause" to justify it. "To die for a perfect cause—what luxury! But you can't expect to be pampered by the gods to that extent." Andrew plans to return to England to fight not for the sake of a cause but in response to an ethical imperative too deep to be explained or ignored, and Slavek vows to follow suit. At the end of the novel, he is seen taking to the air (like Andrew) and parachuting back into enemy territory on behalf of his British allies, solely because his conscience tells him to. He has concluded that Dr. Bolgar's cure was a sham.[22]

The genesis of the novel in Koestler's experiences in Lisbon is obvious, and most of the characters had real-life counterparts. Peter Slavek is a fictional variant of Koestler himself, with the physical characteristics and manner of a young Hungarian poet then living in London, Endre Havas. Odette is probably modeled on Ellen Hill, with some character traits borrowed from Sonia Brownell (later Orwell), and Bernard, the fascist, has been given the physical and psychological attributes of Koestler's Communist controller in Berlin, Fritz Burde. Interestingly, Koestler's newly dim view of psychoanalysis had been prefigured in *Dialogue with Death*, where he recalled his old friend Németh after analysis, looking like "a wounded horse dragging itself across a bull ring," and described analysts as preoccupied with "spiritual sewage cleaning," but it is expressed even more vehemently in the novel, suggesting that for Koestler, Freud's version of cause and effect is now no closer to the truth than Marx's. *Arrival and Departure* is also in the venerable tradition of "what-if" novels. What if Koestler had been captured and tortured in occupied France? What if he had truly suffered a nervous breakdown and been "cured" by analysis? What if he had joined a real fighting unit instead of the Pioneers?

It was also his first novel written in English, a fact barely remarked upon at the time. In fact, surprisingly little has been made of Koestler's feat in changing literary languages twice: once from Hungarian to German in his youth and the second time from German to English at the comparatively advanced age of thirty-five.

Koestler had welcomed and embraced the switch to English, and once suggested it had been easy. English was a very "elastic" language, he told a German interviewer, but unlike in German, you couldn't lard your sentences with "on the whole" and "actually," nor could you talk about the "inner logic of events," because there was no such thing as an "inner" and an "outer" logic. English had a very simple grammar and was a language with "no fat, only muscles." He later qualified his view of how easy it had been, however. Changing languages, he said, was "an immensely complex process of metamorphosis, especially for the writer." It was difficult to describe, because most of the changes "occurred gradually below the level of consciousness." In the first phase you "translated" your thoughts from your original language into the adopted one. Then you found yourself thinking in it, and eventually, if you were lucky, you dreamed in your new language. It's fair to say that Koestler's English doesn't exhibit the rich sonorities of Joseph Conrad, nor the Baroque virtuosity of a different sort of prodigy, Vladimir Nabokov, but his style is clear, vivid, and witty, and the absence of comment may reflect a rare modesty in Koestler, for he seldom alluded to it himself.[23]

ARRIVAL AND DEPARTURE was welcomed by British critics as "a striving, impassioned and at times profound novel" with "something of the atmosphere of *The Possessed*." Koestler's "taut and sombre power" was recognizably "Russian or possibly German, or at any rate continental"—anything but British—and Michael Foot called Koestler "the greatest foreign novelist since Joseph Conrad paid us the compliment of writing in the English tongue." In America, Clifton Fadiman called Koestler "the one first class imaginative writer" thrown up by the war, with "a vision deeper than that of any other writer I can recall. If Koestler develops, he may quite conceivably become the great writer of our generation." And Saul Bellow exclaimed that Koestler was "one of the very few living novelists who attacks the most troubling issues of public and private morality."[24]

Several critics, however, drew a distinction between aspiration and achievement. Koestler's "emotions and sympathy, though strong, lag somewhat behind his intellect and imagination." The novel was deprived of "the emotional overtones and wider references of the very best novels," and though the psychoanalytical sessions offered a clear parallel with the interrogation scenes in *Darkness at Noon,* they were less convincing, because unlike Rubashov and Gletkin, neither Slavek nor Dr. Bolgar was the best representative of their ideology. There was also Koestler's besetting sin of a certain kind of journalistic glibness in some of his formulations.[25]

Though excellent in parts, the novel is certainly weaker than *Darkness at Noon.* Orwell brutally characterized it as "a tract purporting to show that revolutionary creeds are rationalizations of neurotic impulses." He feared that Koestler's disillusionment, combined with a rational disgust for the "welter of lies, hatred, cruelty and ignorance" still at large in the world around him, had led him into a political dead end. Koestler was unable to abandon his lingering belief in an "earthly paradise," assuming (mistakenly, according to Orwell) that the object of life was happiness. "There is," wrote Orwell in a much quoted phrase, "a hedonistic strain in his writings, and his failure to find a political position after breaking with Stalinism is a result of this."[26]

But *Arrival and Departure* is far from a "tract." It is Sonia Bolgar's thesis that revolutionary creeds are the product of neurotic impulses, not Slavek's, and Slavek rejects it by returning to his native country to fight. It is true that Koestler had failed to stake out a new political position in his novel and that while he retained his lingering belief in the possibility of a just, socialist society, its content was impossibly vague. Koestler grumbled with some justification, though, that Orwell showed little understanding of the human dimension of his work and that what Orwell labeled hedonism could also be described as his love of life. "You did not realize that my armor was a Nessus shirt dyed in gaudy colors," he wrote in his diary long after Orwell's death. "[I was] an ascetic and an exhibitionist. You were a saintly repressed sadist, so why resent those chinks?"[27]

The main objection to Orwell's argument, however, is that it conflates and confuses two quite different types of hedonism, the personal and the political.

Koestler was an extreme type of hedonist in his personal life, a fact undoubtedly known to Orwell, but his search for some kind of political path to happiness was not just a personal predilection; it was a reasonable response to the misery and cruelty being inflicted on his comrades in Europe by the twin ideologies of fascism and communism. For all his empathy with the oppressed, Orwell spoke from within the impregnable walls erected by British justice and devotion to freedom of the individual, whereas Koestler had experienced the savage methods of totalitarianism at first hand, and if despair hampered his search for a viable political response, it was a hard-earned despair that deserved a more sympathetic response from the English writer whom Koestler admired and esteemed above all others.

CHAPTER TWENTY-ONE

IDENTITY CRISIS

A fugitive and a vagabond shalt thou be in the earth.
— GENESIS 4:12

ARRIVAL AND DEPARTURE was an attempt to explore the implications of Rubashov's comment at the end of *Darkness at Noon* that he and his comrades had been "sailing without ethical ballast" and was replete with religious imagery, much of it Jewish but even more of it Christian, reflecting Koestler's confusion at the time. The Christian imagery was linked mostly to the disfigured British pilot, Andrew, who was based on a celebrated Battle of Britain pilot named Richard Hillary. Hillary was a genuine hero, a prototypical public school boy who had left Oxford at the age of nineteen to join the Royal Air Force and been badly burned when his Spitfire was shot down in flames in the fall of 1940. After months of agonizing surgery and rehabilitation, Hillary wrote a promising autobiographical novel, *The Last Enemy,* that became an instant best seller, and Koestler had been introduced to him by their joint editor at Macmillan, Lovat Dickson. Hillary was fascinated by Koestler's tales of the Spanish Civil War, and Koestler was deeply affected by Hillary's accounts of bravery in combat and by his stoic determination to overcome his injuries at all costs. In Hillary he saw the sort of instinctive bravery and submission to an unnamed ethical imperative, grounded in Christianity, that seemed to offer a way out of the impasse to which his loss of revolutionary faith had brought him.

At the time Koestler met him, Hillary's face was a contorted mask of badly grafted skin; his eyes stared grotesquely from beneath artificial lids, and the fingers of his hands had fused into birdlike claws, with almost no motion in them. These deformations he brushed aside with the bravado of one of "the finest," and a few months later, although far from fit to fly a fighter plane, he bamboozled a medical board into letting him return to the air. Just over a month later, in January 1943, he was killed on a night training flight.

Koestler had interrupted his work on *Arrival and Departure* to write an essay for the April issue of *Horizon,* "The Birth of a Myth," in which he tried to analyze Hillary's reasons for returning to flying and to interpret the myth already crystallizing around Hillary's brief but glorious career and tragic death. He concluded that Hillary combined two potent but disparate elements in his personality. One was the "indomitable spirit and skill" he had displayed as an outstanding sportsman and aero ace; the other was the disillusioned skepticism of a member of the "Lost Generation" of the thirties, influenced by the pessimism of Auden, Isherwood, and Spender. Koestler compared Hillary to Antoine de Saint-Exupéry, Silone, B. Traven, Malraux, Hemingway (and, by implication, Koestler), "airmen, revolutionaries, adventurers, men who live the dangerous life, with a curious alfresco introspection and an even more curious trend of contemplation, even mysticism."[1]

Years later Koestler pronounced the essay "sentimental," but it caught the national mood, and *Horizon*'s readers voted it the best of the year. Koestler's extensive citations from Hillary's letters to his fiancée, Mary Booker, led to a painful rupture with the family, however, several of whose members claimed that he had misused them. Meanwhile Hillary's physical disfigurement found an echo in the controversial scenes devoted to Slavek's torture early in the novel.

Koestler had been fascinated and repelled by torture ever since his incarcerations in Seville and Le Vernet. In his radio play *Protective Custody* he had given vivid descriptions of Nazi torture, and in *Arrival and Departure* he forced his readers to contemplate the true nature of what the Nazis were up to in occupied Europe with graphic descriptions that had not been seen in English literature for many a long day. Even admirers flinched, while Raymond Mortimer (decidedly not an admirer) asserted that Koestler could "breathe only in the climate of violence" and V. S. Pritchett called the torture scenes "pornographic."[2]

Even more upsetting for readers were Koestler's graphic descriptions of the workings of the "Final Solution." The impetus for these scenes came from another extraordinary individual, the Polish resistance fighter Jan Karski, who had infiltrated the Nazi concentration camp of Belsen and witnessed mass executions of Jews. Polish underground leaders had sent him to London to carry his message to the British and American authorities, who by now knew of the Final Solution from intelligence sources but were maintaining a policy of silence.[3]

Koestler was introduced to Karski by the Polish émigré artist Feliks

Topolski, best known for his sketches of London during the Blitz but also a trusted agent of the Polish government in exile. Koestler took Victor Gollancz and Eleanor Rathbone to Topolski's studio, and the three of them listened in stunned silence as Karski described the mass slaughter in horrifying detail. Gollancz was reduced to "near hysteria" and soon after suffered a nervous breakdown. Rathbone was moved to ask a series of leading questions in the House of Commons—all of which were carefully parried by the government—and she went on to establish a National Committee for Rescue from Nazi Terror, with Koestler as a founding member. Koestler, meanwhile, wrote a powerful talk for the BBC's European service that opened with the words "My name is Karski" and ended "The latest estimate of the number of Jews executed by these methods, in the systematic carrying out of Himmler's orders, is two and a quarter million. I have nothing else to say."[4]

The broadcast, and its subsequent publication in a pamphlet called "Terror in Europe, the Fate of the Jews," published by Rathbone's committee, led to a serious row with Karski, who accused Koestler of blowing his cover and objected to a line in the script, "I was, in fact, one of the executioners," which he felt implicated him directly in the killings. Koestler protested that his script had been a rough draft and that he had left security considerations to the BBC and the Polish government in exile, a claim borne out by a letter he had written to the BBC accompanying the script. As for the line about being "one of the executioners," Koestler pointed out to Karski that this was meant as picturesque imagery and not to be taken literally.[5]

Koestler had borrowed some details of Karski's experiences for Slavek in the novel, but their chief reflection came in chapter seven, on "mixed transports," trains that were "scheduled on no time-table" but running all over Europe, with "ten or twenty closed cattle-trucks, locked from outside, pulled by an old-fashioned locomotive." The passengers included deported laborers, political prisoners, Gypsies headed for sterilization, women rounded up to act as prostitutes, and "in the last seven carriages," an entirely novel kind of cargo. Two cars of "useful Jews," who were being taken to dig fortifications, and five cars of old and sickly "useless Jews," who were destined for liquidation. Koestler described in nauseating detail how the Jews were packed into the railroad cars until they could barely move and how contingents of "useless Jews" were marched from their suffocating cattle cars, crammed into specially designed vans, and then gassed to death.[6]

SINCE 1943 WE HAVE BECOME hardened to descriptions of the workings of the Holocaust far more graphic than Koestler's, but *Arrival and Departure* was the first, if not the only, novel of its time to deal with this gruesome subject, and when chapter seven appeared separately in the October 1943 number of *Horizon,* readers were sharply divided. The well-informed applauded him and hoped that the excerpt would help to "decrease anti-Semitism" in Britain, but others reacted differently. Osbert Sitwell wrote to Connolly to ask if "this rigmarole of Koestler's [is] intended as fact or fiction?" Sitwell said that it reminded him of the false atrocity propaganda put out about the Germans during World War I, and bet Connolly five pounds that Koestler had hoodwinked him.[7]

Sitwell's response reflected both a lingering philo-Germanism and a smoldering anti-Semitism. Lord Shelbourne, head of Britain's Special Operations Executive, had used the World War I analogy when questioning Karski about his story, and a few months prior to Koestler's article, a mass stampede at Bethnal Green tube station during an air raid had been blamed on "Jewish panic" (Jewish shopkeepers in Britain were routinely accused of hoarding and profiteering). Koestler answered his critics with a blistering open letter. "Had I published a chapter on Proust and mentioned his homosexuality, you would never have dared to ask whether my information was based on fact, because you consider it your duty 'to know.' But you have the brazenness to ask whether it is true that you are the contemporary of the greatest massacre in recorded history."[8]

He followed up with an essay for *The New York Times,* "On Disbelieving Atrocities," which began, "There is a dream which keeps coming back to me at almost regular intervals; it is dark, and I am being murdered in some kind of thicket or brushwood; there is a busy road at no more than ten yards distance; I scream for help but nobody hears me, the crowd walks past laughing and chatting." Koestler likened his dream to the plight of the Jews of Europe and cited a recent poll in the United States showing that nine out of ten American citizens believed that allegations of Nazi atrocities were "propaganda and lies." The problem was one of proximity versus distance and of degrees of suffering. "A dog run over by a car upsets our emotional balance and digestion; three million Jews killed in Poland cause but a moderate uneasiness."[9]

Koestler's lurid imagination and weakness for exaggeration were a deliberate provocation to English conservatives such as Sitwell, and they served to alienate some natural allies as well. Yet Koestler was much closer to the heart of the matter than either skeptics or opponents allowed, and he was well ahead of his time in grasping the enormity of what was happening in Europe. In an attempt to explain the disparity in people's responses, he alluded to an idea that had first occurred to him in Spain, and that he had explored in his Hillary essay, namely that every individual lives in a state of "split consciousness": "There is a tragic plane and a trivial plane, which contain two mutually incompatible kinds of experienced knowledge. Most of our lives are lived on the everyday, trivial plane, but in moments of elation or danger, we find ourselves transferred to the tragic plane. The latter, with its cosmic perspective, drowns out for a while the shallow frivolities of life, but they always return, and sometimes the two perspectives coexist."[10]

SHORTLY BEFORE THE PUBLICATION of *Arrival and Departure,* Koestler and Daphne had left their modest terrace cottage in Tryon Street for the grand mansion of George Strauss in "Millionaire's Row," otherwise known as Kensington Palace Gardens, next to Hyde Park. Strauss, a wealthy businessman and backer of the left-wing journal *Tribune,* was living virtually alone in his huge house while his wife sat out the war in America. Wartime regulations required him to have some tenants, and after Aneurin Bevan and Jennie Lee moved out, Strauss asked Koestler if he and Daphne would like to take their place. Koestler accepted with alacrity. The rent was only two pounds per week. They would eat with Strauss and be pampered by his servants, leaving Koestler more time to concentrate on his writing, but Daphne was aghast. She loved their cozy life in Tryon Street and suspected (rightly) that Koestler was eager to end it. The intimacy of their cottage routine was making him claustrophobic—and putting an unwelcome brake on his philandering.[11]

Their living quarters consisted of a large bedroom upstairs and a sitting room downstairs. During the day, Daphne worked at the Ministry of Information as an archivist of war photographs, while Koestler sat in the bedroom and wrote, with the curtains tightly drawn to shut out the light. In the evenings there were dinner parties with Labour Party lions such as Foot, Strachey, Crossman, and Bevan or left-leaning writers such as Connolly and Spender. Orwell, the new literary editor of *Tribune,* disliked such gatherings and came rarely, parading his proletarian manners in Strauss's opulent dining room as a provocative point of principle.

Koestler had started drinking heavily again and turned into a complete party animal at night, raising the stakes at poker and blackjack too high for even the wealthy Strauss and beating everyone hollow at chess. On one occasion he persuaded the Strausses and an incredulous Orwell to take part in a body levitation experiment—which was a complete flop, of course. He could be fiendishly charming to any pretty woman present, but when offended by a careless remark, he would push his chair back from the dinner table and ostentatiously sit with his back against the wall until some sort of amends was made. Daphne, who was not in the least flirtatious or even very sociable in large groups, suffered agonies through these evenings, and hated Koestler for his selfish tantrums.[12]

Koestler's erratic behavior presaged a major depression that was to afflict him throughout the fall of 1943 and a large part of 1944. Bouts of agonizing introspection alternated with outbursts of manic aggression and heavy drinking, leading to remorse and guilt that triggered the whole cycle again. At first he put it down to health problems. In the two years since his Pioneer Corps meltdown he had suffered a series of stomach disorders, culminating in a duodenal ulcer. He had then been treated by a noted Hungarian specialist, Dr. Egon Plesch, who had persuaded him that the origin of his pain was psychosomatic and got him to try psychoanalysis.

Koestler's scathing treatment of psychoanalysis in *Arrival and Departure* should have been a warning. Disillusioned with Freud, he had come to regard psychoanalysis as a closed philosophical system, designed to reduce emotional and spiritual phenomena to infantile psychological impulses— much as Marxism reduced complex political and economic forces to class interests. In desperation, he submitted to Plesch's suggestion, hoping that the trained analyst might be able to overcome his reservations. Very soon, however, Koestler brought the sessions to an abrupt end, having concluded that the treatment would interfere with his creativity and "deprive him of his drive to unique self-expression," a fear that he later expanded on in "The Yogi and the Commissar—II." "In theory," he wrote, analysis ought to help the artist sublimate his complexes, but "this externally induced sublimation does not express itself in artistic creation but in rationalizations and in diminishing or destroying the generating tension. I have never heard of a neurotic becoming an artist by learning to sublimate on the analyst's couch."[13]

His fear was not entirely unfounded. One of the impulses that had driven him to analysis was the bitter experience of a new problem for him—writer's block. In November 1943 he commenced a sequel to *Arrival and Departure,* describing Peter Slavek's mission after being parachuted into occupied Europe. By the spring of 1944 he was experiencing a recurrence of his stomach troubles and the continuance of problems with his writing: "Work block still lasts," he wrote in his diary. "Terrible depression." Shortly after this came "a Bordeaux-like nervous breakdown" and then: "Am rather in despair about inability to work."[14]

His depression was brought on in part by the deterioration in his relationship with Daphne. Returning late one March night from a dinner with Michael Foot, he had answered Daphne's reproaches with a volley of insults. It was impossible for them to go on living like this, he said, and flung in her face the names of all the women he had slept with since they had been together, including several of her friends. Calming down (according to his diary), he was "torn between love, pity, exasperation." But Daphne was devastated. It was a replay of her experience in Paris on finding his little red notebook. But she was also relieved: "It was like the bursting of an abscess." She had suspected something of the sort for months, and now she knew the worst.[15]

Her first impulse was to pack her bags and walk out, but she had nowhere to go. Their relationship limped on for a few more weeks, punctuated by more rows ("D. again hysterical. No good."), until in mid-May Daphne moved in with a German graphic designer, Frederick Henry Korn, who had adopted the French surname of Henrion to disguise his German origins. "Henri," as he was generally known, was a patient, kindly man, deeply in love with Daphne and happy to take her in, though she herself was still unsure of her feelings. Koestler noted her departure with a mixture of relief and gloom. "On the surface it leaves me cold and rather relieved, but can't fathom what's going on within me; she was, I thought, the real and lasting thing, but neurosis keeps butting in."[16]

Despite his domestic difficulties, Koestler was still able to produce the occasional essay. In November 1943 he had written a witty, satirical piece called "The French 'Flu," for Orwell at the *Tribune,* poking fun at the sentimental Francophilia of literary critics such as Connolly and Mortimer. The term *French 'flu* became a popular catchphrase and neatly captured that peculiarly British worship of all things French characteristic of London's literary set. Indeed, not a month passed before Connolly brought out a collection of aphorisms, literary quotations, and journal notes, heavily influenced by Gallic models, that seemed to exemplify Koestler's observations. *The Unquiet Grave,* published in a limited edition by *Horizon* in December 1944, was saturated with nostalgia for *la belle France,* without a word about politics or war.[17]

In another essay, "A Reader's Dilemma," Koestler attacked the British class system, but his best essay of this period was "The Intelligentsia," which Connolly published in *Horizon.* Citing the *Oxford English Dictionary's* definition of *intelligentsia* as "that part of a nation that aspires to independent thinking," Koestler traced its history from the French Encyclopedists of the eighteenth century to the Russian intellectuals of the nineteenth (who invented the term) down to his own day. In Koestler's description, the term *intellectual* was subtly elided into *progressive* and then into *revolutionary.* There was no room in his scheme of things for "right-wing" or even "liberal" (in the European sense) intellectuals, but it is a sign of the pinkness of his readers that this aspect of the essay went entirely unnoticed. The essay was admired by Orwell, among others, who, in his next "London Letter" for *Partisan Review,* complained about the "successive literary cliques which have infested this country" because they were not "true intellectuals." "It is just because I do take the function of the intelligentsia seriously that I don't like the sneers, libels, parrot phrases and financially profitable back scratching which flourish in our English literary world."[18]

IN EARLY 1944 GERMAN air raids on London were assuming a new intensity. It was not quite a replay of the 1940 Blitz, but people had to scurry repeatedly into their air raid shelters, and nerves were stretched to the breaking point. Koestler noted that while the raids lasted he felt "moderately scared," but in between he found himself "looking forward" to them, "like a drug." The worst moments were when he could hear the planes dive, followed by the whistle of the falling bombs. The rest of the time his fear was repressed until the raid was over, when suddenly it overcame him again. This was particularly so the night a bomb blew out all his windows. Koestler tried to help the war effort by becoming an air raid warden and spent six months going out twice a month as an ambulance driver. Driving an ambulance was "much more fun" than fire watching, but it meant that he couldn't drink while on duty, and the physical condition of the people he picked up was more upsetting than he had anticipated.[19]

He continued to maintain a frantic schedule of lectures and public appearances. In the course of 1944 he gave talks to the Churchill Club, the Fabian Society, the Canadian Legion, the British Council, the Oxford Union Socialist Club, the Anglo-Palestinian Club, the PEN Club, the Friends of Free Hungary, the Oxford and Cambridge Club, the Jewish Committee for Relief Abroad, the Girl Guides Association, the London School of Economics Students' Union, and the Progressive League. He continued to lecture indefatigably for the army's educational service and, after exhaustively covering the Greater London area, asked if he might make a tour of the West Country. He also volunteered to help the Society of Friends' Committee for Aliens and Refugees and Vera Weizmann's Youth Aliyah movement.

This frantic activity did little to relieve the smoldering depression that now settled on him, brought on, it seems, by a severe identity crisis. In a fit of self-disgust he drew up a "list of miseries." Number three on the list was "lack of self-confidence," followed by "guilt," "hunt for father image," and "collapse of *Lebensplan* (Daphne)." Since the list included a welter of other accusations against himself, ranging from "lack of personality" and "impatience" to "vanity, jealousy, drink, sentimentality, rudeness, vulgarity," and so on, its self-flagellation (though not entirely inaccurate) shouldn't be taken too literally, but the collapse of his relationship with Daphne did seem to have large implications. In breaking with her he felt he was decisively abandoning an old identity while unable to find a new one. During the tumultuous six years he had spent with her, he had experienced his first great surge of creativity and completed the three novels on which his reputation rested: *The Gladiators, Darkness at Noon,* and *Arrival and Departure.* Coming to England, he had established himself as a memoirist (*Scum of the Earth*) and essayist with a special knowledge of that mysterious place known to all British people as "the Continent" and had written regularly for such influential publications as *Horizon, New Statesman and Nation, Tribune, The Observer,* and *The New York Times.*

It was an impressive enough list of achievements but now meant little to him, for it was thoughts of the future that turned his knees to jelly. Separating from Daphne implied a symbolic turning away from his European past, but how British could he become, and how assimilate to this baffling, insular culture? Joining this new club would be the severest test yet of his chameleon-like ability to change his manners and language, adapt his personality, and write in a completely new idiom.[20]

The problem of roots and identity wasn't to be resolved overnight, of course, and he wasn't entirely ready to turn his back on the past. Soon after his arrival in London he had established links with a variety of Hungarian refugees, some in the Hungarian PEN Club in Exile (it was as a representative of Hungarian writers that he had spoken at the PEN Conference), some in the London Hungarian Club (despite its Communist leanings), and some in the New Democratic Hungary Movement, headed by Count Károlyi (whose proclamation of Hungary's secession from Austria he had witnessed as a schoolboy in Budapest). Károlyi's wife, Catherine, had reviewed *Darkness at Noon* for *Horizon,* and Károlyi asked Koestler if he would ghost the second volume of his memoirs. Koestler declined but was initially attracted to Károlyi's non-Communist form of socialism until he stirred up a hornet's nest with a talk about the "bankruptcy"of the traditional left and said it was time to abandon utopian dreams and build "oases" in the moral desert. Karl Polanyi's wife, Ilona Duczynska, wrote an impassioned letter to the count, urging him to invite a speaker from the Soviet embassy to counter Koestler's pernicious influence, and the friendship with Károlyi withered on the vine.[21]

More important to Koestler's sense of identity was his status as a Jew. Since renouncing Zionism and a life in Palestine, he had gone out of his way to ignore his Jewishness, but the meeting with Karski and the facts he had learned about the Final Solution had shocked him into a renewed awareness of his responsibilities and prompted him to get in touch with the London-based patriarch of the World Zionist Organization, Chaim Weizmann. They met for the first time in 1943, and Koestler fell under the spell of the old man's "mesmeric charm." "Isn't he a wonderful-looking man?" he said to David Astor, who had accompanied him. "Just like a prince or a priest."[22]

In February 1944 Koestler joined the Palestine Luncheon Club, whose members included Michael Foot, Israel Sieff, Kingsley Martin, David Astor, and Guy de Rothschild, a dapper French banker who had returned to London from the USA to work for the Free French. Rothschild stayed with Koestler for a few days and was astounded when Koestler served him breakfast in bed. With his "receding forehead, thick black hair slicked back and a nervous, twitching face," he struck Rothschild as "not very imposing at first sight," but Rothschild was moved by Koestler's concern for the plight of the Jews trapped in Europe, and they worked together on several committees. Under Koestler's influence, Rothschild even entertained the idea of starting a left-wing political journal in Paris after the war, but it remained a pipe dream.[23]

Koestler also attended meetings of Weizmann's Anglo-Palestine Committee, and it was there that Rothschild introduced him to Isaiah Berlin, then a
British diplomat in Washington. "When Isaiah began to talk, dazzling as always, Arthur, to my surprise, either didn't know how or didn't care to meet
the challenge and remained stubbornly silent." Koestler was nervous and
tense in Berlin's presence and seemed to find the latter's odd combination of
loquaciousness and diffidence intensely irritating. Berlin was "unpleasant"
and "oily," Koestler wrote in his diary, and "makes a virtue of awkwardness."
It's likely that Koestler was jealous of Berlin's impeccable Establishment credentials and fluent English, though he wasn't the only committee member to
be put off by Berlin's manner, for Blanche Dugdale and Lewis Namier also
thought him "supercilious," "cynical," and "desiccated."[24]

The committee's main goal was to oppose the British white paper of 1939
that had set a limit on Jewish immigration to Palestine of seventy-five thousand over the next five years. Given the reluctance of the United States to accept Jewish refugees and the murderous policies of the Nazis, the effect was,
in the eyes of the Zionists, to condemn large numbers of their people to the
gas chambers. Weizmann told Koestler privately that while Churchill favored helping the Jews, the pro-Arab Colonial Office would frustrate him in
every way possible. Weizmann was optimistic, however, that after the war
the British would permit either partition or a Jewish canton in Palestine,
with unrestricted Jewish immigration.[25]

THE IMMEDIATE AND MOST pressing problem for the committee, however, continued to be the gas chambers, and Koestler's growing sense of desperation was compounded by the fact that so many friends and members of
his family were now threatened. Dorothee and Hans, the Sperbers, and the
Némeths had all disappeared in occupied France. His uncle Otto had committed suicide in Berlin, and his other uncles and aunts and cousins, not to
speak of his mother, who had looked to be safe in neutral Hungary, were
suddenly exposed to a new threat themselves. In March 1944 Nazi troops
marched into Hungary and occupied the entire country. Adolf Eichmann
lost no time in planning a Hungarian Final Solution, and in the course of the
next two months, hundreds of thousands of Hungary's Jews were stripped of
their property, herded into ghettoes, and forced to wear the dread yellow star
on the left breast of their outer garments. The country was divided into six
zones, and in April, the first trainload of Hungary's Jews left for Auschwitz.[26]

Koestler's hopes were momentarily raised by news of the Brand mission, a
fantastic top secret proposal by Eichmann to exchange Hungary's Jews for
ten thousand trucks, two million bars of soap, eight hundred tons of coffee,
two hundred tons of cocoa, and eight hundred tons of tea. The Germans
added that they would guarantee to use the trucks "only on the eastern

front." The Allies appeared to take the offer seriously, but when Weizmann asked the British Foreign Office about saving a million Jews from the gas chambers, an official responded, "What am I going to do with a million Jews? There's a war on." Eventually the talks were broken off on the grounds that the whole idea was a ruse to split the Allies from the Russians.[27]

Shortly after hearing about this conversation, Koestler received a copy of a secret telegram from "somewhere in Poland" decoded by the Nationalities Department of the Foreign Office. It reported that "since the second half of May thirteen trainloads have been arriving daily at Oswiecim (Auschwitz), averaging 45 wagons, each carrying Jews from Hungary. They are being killed simultaneously by gas in two chambers, each holding 1,000 persons. The corpses are burned in 4 crematoriums and in piles." Just at that moment Feri Aldor sent news from his wife in Switzerland that Feri's mother (and Adele's sister), Rosa, her daughter, Margit, and her two grandchildren had been taken from their home in Kalna and interned in a transit camp. Margit's husband had died mysteriously a few weeks earlier, and the women had been left to fend for themselves. Two weeks later Koestler learned that Adele had been staying with Rosa and Margit when the Germans arrived and was presumably in the transit camp as well.[28]

This grim piece of news finally melted Koestler's hostility toward his mother and cast him into a further depression. Until now he had exchanged brief messages with Adele through the Red Cross in New York, so that if she were ever questioned by the authorities she could deny any contact with him. Now even that tenuous thread was broken, and he found it virtually impossible to go on working or to write anything at all. The tragic fate of the Jews in Europe was catching up with him in the starkest and most personal way possible.[29]

CHAPTER TWENTY-TWO

COMMISSAR OR YOGI?

Writing is really filling in the blank spaces in existence, that nullity which suddenly yawns wide open in the hours and the days, and appears between the objects in a room, engulfing them in unending desolation and insignificance.

— CLAUDIO MAGRIS

KOESTLER HAD EXPLAINED his separation from Daphne as the product of his "neurosis," a portmanteau word he tended to use for almost all his emotional problems, but in this instance the breakup had been precipitated by the appearance of a potent new rival for his affections, one of the twins who owned Connolly's apartment. Mamaine was one of the stars of war-torn London's somewhat tattered social scene. She and her equally beautiful identical twin, Celia, had been much photographed debutantes in the late thirties, and Mamaine had modeled for Harrods.

Koestler had first met her in January 1944 at one of Connolly's parties and was immediately entranced by her pale oval face, delicate features, diamond-bright blue eyes, and slightly pouting red lips. Slender and petite, Mamaine had an air of physical fragility about her that instantly aroused protective instincts in the men she met, but she was no social butterfly. Though lacking a university education, she was impressively well read, played the piano, and was an expert bird-watcher and a high-spirited mimic. She also spoke fluent French and German, and had recently turned the head of Edmund Wilson (who wrote a dithyramb to her beauty in one of his *New Yorker* columns).[1]

Koestler christened Mamaine "Mermaid" in his pocket diary, and she took note of their meeting in a diary of her own. They turned out to have friends in common, and soon were bumping into each other at a variety of social gatherings. Mamaine was working at the Ministry of Economic Warfare, and sent him snippets of information about the machinations of the Germans in the occupied countries. Her dry, sometimes droll manner was well calculated to keep importunate male admirers at bay, and Koestler was frustrated in his hopes for a quick conquest. "Party for Paul [Willert]," he noted in his diary for mid-March. "Mermaid unpleasant as usual."[2]

About a month later, however, Koestler was able to write in his diary: "Dinner and uneasy seduction of Mermaid." This laconic formula was amplified in a painful letter to Mamaine in which he tried both to apologize for his behavior and excuse himself. "I know that I behaved in a rather swinish way. I got you to allow me to make love with you by the usual old tricks and cunning—but I still believe that is permissible if the result is enjoyed by both. Without an element of initial rape there is no delight."[3]

"Rape" was an overstatement, but it shows Koestler's awareness of the dangers of his behavior, and there is no doubt that he subscribed to the belief that a little force added spice to sex. In *Arrival and Departure,* Peter Slavek takes Odette by force but is forgiven by her, and they embark on a passionate affair. And so it was with Mamaine, who seems not to have regarded the incident as at all out of the ordinary. The day before their fateful encounter, Koestler had taken Celia out to dinner and "made a terrific pass," according to Celia. When the two sisters, who enjoyed a total empathy and shared their innermost feelings with each other, compared notes, Mamaine asked Celia, "What did you do?" Celia said, "I said no." "Well," said Mamaine, "he was the same with me last night and I slept with him. But I wasn't sure whether to tell you or not."[4]

The next few weeks were a time of exuberant mutual discovery, as evidenced by their two diaries. Koestler's, as usual, is laconic and factual, packed with brief notes about lunches, dinners, lectures, committees, and meetings of all sorts, while Mamaine's is more discursive. Typical are their entries for the last day of May.

Koestler: "Hemingway-party: drunkenness, row, unpleasant."

Mamaine: "Cyril Connolly's for dinner. Cyril was giving a party for Hemingway, but wasn't sure if Hemingway would come or not. So we started dinner without him. Soon Hemingway arrived, a bandage round his head from when he had had an accident in a car, and with a huge beard; he sat next to me at dinner. After dinner lots of people came in, mostly rather unpleasant intellectuals, American poets who were said to be famous but looked pretty awful. Cyril gave us all some awful drink he'd made. The party was from the first a terrible flog. A.K. got very drunk on Cyril's drink and insulted everybody—I left before him which caused violent protests from him."[5]

MAMAINE'S INDEPENDENT SPIRIT was good for Koestler, and it even seemed his writer's block was melting. "Worst of crisis seems to be over," he noted, "novel slowly progressing." But a couple of weeks later there was a regression: "No, worst ever crisis on full blast."[6]

The novel in question was the planned sequel to *Arrival and Departure,* which Koestler had been inspired to write by Vera Weizmann's Youth Aliyah program to rescue abandoned Jewish children from occupied Europe and resettle them in Palestine. Koestler particularly approved of the fact that some members of Youth Aliyah had returned to Europe to fight on the side of the Allies and wrote several chapters portraying Slavek in Europe and his relationship with a poor priest (Father Zlatko) who secretly harbors two Jewish children whom he has saved from the gas chambers. The priest informs Slavek of a scheme to smuggle the children to safety, but when Slavek returns to the "mist-covered Lotusland" of England, he finds it impossible to interest the authorities in his scheme.[7]

It was the first time Koestler had tackled an explicitly Jewish theme and is further evidence of how World War II forced him to confront his Jewish loyalties once more. The saga of Father Zlatko was based on a true story, and the novel was planned as an allegory of the tragedy of the Jews in Nazi-occupied Europe. His notes for the novel included the terse comment "This is frankly an *Ideen-Roman* [novel of ideas]; to hell with Flaubert," but although the plight of the Jews was overwhelming Koestler's imagination at the time, he experienced the greatest difficulty in linking the theme of suffering to Slavek's search in England for a rational response to the crisis. As the novel progressed, it grew increasingly autobiographical, and the theme of the stranded Jews began to fade into the background.[8]

It's evident from Koestler's diary that the manic mood swings and growing sense of self-pity that he described as belonging to Slavek mirrored his own condition in the summer of 1944 and that an excessively close identification between author and character was one of the sources of his writer's block. After one periodic crisis he again turned to a psychiatrist for help, though he hadn't intended to. Karl Theodore Bluth was a Prussian Protestant and a former friend of both Brecht and Heidegger, as well as a literary critic of some renown, who had left Germany as early as 1934 in protest against the Nazi takeover. When Bluth called one day to talk about a mutual acquaintance, he casually opined that he could completely cure Koestler of his "work-inhibitions." Koestler was doubtful. Bluth was "the devil in person," one of the "most horrifying" addicts he knew, but he was also tempted. "What if we make a pact with Mephisto? For five D[arkness] at Noons I'd do it. But my petit-bourgeois commonsense rebels."[9]

He must have changed his mind, because by the beginning of June he was calling on Bluth to get some "drugs to make me work." What these drugs were he doesn't specify, but the day after he took them was the day of the Allied invasion of Normandy, and Koestler noted in his diary that "everything" was better, though whether it was the drugs or the invasion that produced his improvement is not clear. By the end of the month he was off the drugs again but not free of Bluth's attentions. The doctor informed him that the novelist Anna Kavan was suffering from acute paranoia and had conceived a terrible fear of Koestler after Koestler had criticized two of her articles in *Horizon*. A volley of letters passed among Bluth, Koestler, Connolly, Kavan, and Cape in an attempt to sort out the mess, but less than two weeks later, Kavan made her fifth unsuccessful attempt at suicide. After she recovered, she became friends with Koestler, telling him about the miserable life she had led and the sexual abuse she had suffered as a teenager. In a burst of fellow feeling he sent her to Plesch, who proved unsympathetic. Plesch was simply "too neurotic," Koestler decided, to care about the plight of others.[10]

Koestler broke off his novel on page 79 and never resumed it. He found himself thinking with greater intensity than ever about his mother. After one of Weizmann's gloomy bulletins about the latest atrocities against Jews, Koestler noted in his diary, "Mother is growing on me; all consciously repressed, but growing, growing." In the first week of July, Weizmann reported that 400,000 Jews had been deported from Hungary and 100,000 killed. By then Koestler had successfully applied for certificates for his mother and Aunt Rosa to go to Palestine (with a further request for Margit and her two children in the pipeline), and Weizmann wrote to say that "the necessary steps are being taken to obtain their release from Hungary." But was it too little, too late? In a fit of remorse, Koestler decided that he should renounce his frivolous way of life and attempt some form of mourning.

AS A FIRST STEP, he decided to give up alcohol and fine dining. This farcical-sounding gesture was more serious than it seemed, for Koestler was well down the road to alcoholism and more dependent on his daily intake than he was prepared to admit. When forced to stop drinking the year before to cure his stomach ulcer, he had "suffered hell," but now he felt confident he was embarking not on "self-punishment" or "masochism," as Plesch averred, but a voluntary renunciation. "The obsolescence of mourning rites" was "a sign of degeneration," he noted in his diary. The black robes of Victorian widows were "ridiculous" because they were an externalization of grief, but it was also "degrading" to walk "from an open grave straight to the pub." He felt there was no excuse for leading a debauched life "while my people are slaughtered by the thousands per day, Mama among them."[11]

In his grief, Koestler strongly supported a Jewish Agency plan to bomb Auschwitz in a last-ditch effort to disrupt the Nazi extermination machine, even if it led to the deaths of the Jewish prisoners there, and he prepared a memo for Strachey setting out the arguments in favor. Grim thoughts of Auschwitz brought back memories of early childhood, some of which he jotted down in his diary (they eventually found their way into *Arrow in the*

Blue). "As a child, the idea that mother should die seemed a cosmic catastrophe; I prayed not to survive her. According to a JTA [Jewish Telegraphic Agency] report, Jews deported to Oswiecim die by a new gas manufactured in Hamburg, thrown into death-chambers by SS-men wearing gas masks; the victims (circa 1,000 at a time) are stripped naked under pretext of having bath; it takes appr[oximately] 3 minutes. Or, if sick, phenol injection over heart. So that is how mama died, or is dying in this minute, or shall die."[12]

To bolster his resolution, Koestler told friends not to invite him to parties anymore, suspecting himself of an "exhibitionistic desire" to parade his suffering even as he asked them. A much harder problem was what to do about Mamaine. He felt that their whole relationship was based on wining and dining and sleeping together, in other words the pleasure principle, and should be stopped. But it wasn't easy. There was a powerful sexual chemistry between them, which abstinence from alcohol seemed to strengthen rather than dampen. Continuing to see Mamaine was "cheating his vow," but he was also, to his dismay, falling in love, and his diary for the next few days gives the clearest possible picture of what this meant for his tortured psychology.[13]

One day Mamaine confided in him about the difficult childhood she and Celia had endured after the death of their mother when they were a week old. Their father had been subject to bouts of melancholia and had died when the girls were only twelve, a loss from which they had never recovered. Both had experienced repeated bouts of bronchitis, pleurisy, and pneumonia and were lifelong sufferers of asthma. They had been sent to a series of expensive boarding schools, presented at Court, and been expected to find rich husbands but found society life "a huge bore." She also told Koestler about her affair with the legendary Richard "Dick" Wyndham, a World War I hero, amateur flyer, and accomplished writer, painter, and photographer. Wyndham was more than twenty years her senior, twice divorced, elusive, and promiscuous, and though Mamaine had given him up for another lover, she was still finding it hard to get over him.[14]

Her confession acted on Koestler like an aphrodisiac. He felt he now understood the "glittering hardness" of her social manner—which was in such puzzling contrast to that of her twin sister, Celia—and was overjoyed to find that it was "a superficial defense mechanism." Her defenses were down, and the way was now open for him to truly fall in love with her. His ability to love "past pure desire," he told his diary, was "always born out of pity." He recalled other women who had inspired him with this "pity-love": his mother, Dorothee, Daphne, Gerda Grepp, Helga Bruck. Their appeal lay in their childlike joy or equally childish grief. Buoyed by this discovery, a wave of tenderness poured over him and he felt gloriously happy.

The following Sunday they met for "tea and coitus," and Koestler experienced another surge of "pity-love." They discussed the possibility of moving in together, but that night he sat up until the small hours composing an agitated letter in which he renounced Mamaine. He had acted "like a cad" in seducing her and in "blackmailing" her to stay with him, but he couldn't help himself. "You once said something about us being 'frightfully sophisticated.' My foot! I am thirty-nine and feel about you exactly as sophisticated as I would have felt at nineteen. I would like to cry and bite my knuckles and bite big chunks out of the flesh of your body and gulp them down."[15]

The real reason he was giving her up, he wrote, had nothing to do with her but was because of what was happening in Europe. "My people are slaughtered by the thousands. I know the details, they are unspeakable. If I happened to be among them I would have to die. If, from over there, I could see with my mind's eye a fellow called A.K., making money and a reputation out of describing their sufferings, and making merry on it, I would vomit before walking into the gas chamber. Wouldn't you? And don't you see that my reaction is more *normal* than the reactions of those who shut their eyes to reality and act as if what happens outside our immediate view were not true?"[16]

The letter was classic Koestler, filled with genuine remorse and emotion yet suggesting that he had been looking over his own shoulder as he wrote. He had composed it in a fever of agitation, then spent the next morning correcting and typing it out (not forgetting to make a carbon copy), which led to a curious psychological drama that he recorded with brutal honesty in his diary. After finishing his fair copy he went out to buy some phonograph records as a parting gift to Mamaine. When he returned, he found a note from George Forbat, a former business partner of his father's, saying he had news of Koestler's family. Koestler's first reflex was a dishonorable fear that they were all right and that he had broken with Mamaine in vain. In his diary he wrote, "this at first unconscious, but dragged it immediately into consciousness—a thought shamelessly grinning with toothless mouth." He rang Forbat and was told that his whole family was in a concentration camp or perhaps deported already, a supposition that was confirmed by a fresh cable from Irene Aldor. The shock was followed by a sharp image of SS men in gas masks, and he added a postscript to Mamaine reflecting his despair. "This is later. Just as I was about to dispatch this, a wire arrived from Zürich: 'whole family in concentration camp, probably already deported Poland.' Oh, darling, this is very bitter. I still hoped against hope."

Throughout the rest of the day Mamaine continued to haunt his thoughts as the "most unneurotic girl I know." In the evening he settled down to write in his diary and found "the facility of diary-writing an easy outlet." He asked himself how much of what he was thinking and writing centered around its real source, his mother, and answered: 10 percent. How much was about himself? Fifty percent. The rest was about Mamaine. Then his thoughts reverted to his mother again. "Mother dying or dead—cerebral torture without emotional amplitude. Tears pressed out on lonely shore with one spectator, myself. Mermaid, very alive, dining somewhere—enormous amplitude. One would say she is being poisoned and mother only temporarily dead. I can't blame myself. Still, if somebody spat into my face in public, I would feel grateful and relieved. I'm going to sleep. I feel deprived of the desire to die, feeling those unwritten books in me, and not knowing whether I can write at all."[17]

KOESTLER SOUGHT A TEMPORARY RESPITE in more meetings of the Anglo-Palestine Committee. Word came from Hungary that Miklós Horthy had ordered a pause in the deportations at least until mid-August and had told Swiss diplomats that all Jews possessing entry permits for other countries, including Palestine, would be permitted to leave. In desperation the committee dreamed up a scheme for Koestler and G. Kuhlman, the deputy high commissioner for refugees, to go to Budapest and negotiate for Hungary's Jews to be brought under British protection pending their transfer to Palestine, but the Foreign Office wasn't interested.[18]

Paralyzed by indecision and overcome by feelings of oppression, Koestler fled to Strauss's summer home in Slaugham, Sussex. There, in isolation, he gradually achieved some peace of mind and was confirmed in his conviction that the dissipated life he had been leading in London was a terrible mistake. Solitude was what he needed, and it required an abrupt leap into the unknown to achieve it. "Proves once more that only radical breaks, against commonsense, can cure me. That's how I dragged myself out of every crisis: engineering; to Palestine; [out] of Palestine; into C.P.; to Russia; to London; to Spain; in Málaga; out of journalism; out of Party; into Foreign Legion; into and out of P[ioneer] C[orps]; away from Doerte and Daphne; and now away from alcohol, parties, Mermaid. A succession of jumps into cold water, of self-destructive suicide symbols, as Plesch would call it. When commonsense becomes corrupted, one can only live against commonsense, against the lazy, slothful habit-current. Don't drift any more. No more guilt feelings."[19]

He felt that he had "practically forgotten Mamaine" and was numb even to the fate of "the primary cause of this all," his mother. Was he made of stone? he wondered. Were his feelings of love for her simply buried, or had they "burnt themselves out" in childhood? Was he capable of love at all? He thought that the "incest-dreams" that got in the way had stopped about a year ago, when he had "faced and dissolved them." Yet as late as June he had listed "incest barrier" as number one in his "List of Miseries" and had linked it explicitly with number two on his list, "devaluation of partner." If he got too fond of a woman, it seemed, it was difficult to regard her as a sexual partner. It was necessary to degrade her. Perhaps there was a connection here with his peculiar theories about "initial rape"?

Within days he was beginning to change his mind about Mamaine again. "Strange," he confided to his diary, "how the tentacles of the hydra nostalgia fasten now on Daphne, now on Mermaid or Doerte. The glue is pity. At other times it may be desire. The whole thing is called falling in love." He wondered how it could be possible to spend decades with one woman but decided that "affection" was the "tougher connecting tissue" that took over in such cases. A week later he wrote to Mamaine to explain that he was sending her a "filthy copy" of *Scum of the Earth* (which she had once asked for) that he had found at Slaugham and to apologize for the "horrible pompous letter" he had written her before his departure. He felt he was too "un-English" in not being able to control his feelings and hoped she would not "loathe" him, as his psychology textbook told him she would.[20]

Mamaine answered that of course she didn't loathe him and didn't think at all that he had behaved badly toward her. They might have been very happy together, and "it certainly isn't your fault that we can't be now. I didn't for one moment think you were morbid or priggish or anything like that— oh God, I am unhappy for you, for both of us." She wasn't unhappy for long, however. Koestler soon found an excuse to make an excursion to London and they spent the night together, after which Mamaine went down to Sussex for the weekend. There she found him in an excellent mood. A telegram had come from Irene informing him that his mother had survived after all. Adele had returned to Budapest from Kalna shortly before Margit and her children were taken away and was living in town with one of her nephews. This didn't mean she was safe. She was trapped in the Budapest ghetto and Eichmann was still plotting his Final Solution, but at least she wasn't dead. The news made him "happier than I had expected."[21]

FOR THE FIRST TIME in his life, Koestler had begun to think of writing as a form of therapy and to imagine a life for himself divided between long periods of monastic immersion in serious work and short bursts of pleasure and self-indulgence. To test out his theory, he devoted his first weeks in Slaugham to the relatively easy task of revising and rewriting *An Improbable Occurrence*, the play he had started at the Hotel Metropole in Moscow and completed in Budapest. He also changed its name again, from *The Ultimatum* to *Twilight Bar*.

The play was a throwback in terms of Koestler's literary and political development. It was as if, before fully renouncing his Communist past, he felt an irresistible urge to revisit it one last time. The new version still featured two aliens, who arrive on Earth and issue their ultimatum to earthlings to find happiness in three days or face annihilation by "Delta-rays." Now, however, when the government resigns, it is the newspaper columnist, rechristened "Glowworm," who assumes power and is charged with introducing a regime of universal happiness. After a couple of days he seems to succeed. Money is abolished, authority is overturned, taboos and inhibitions are done away with, and a "natural" order asserts itself. But on the third day it is revealed that a serious robbery has taken place, and the two "aliens" are arrested as suspects. As they are led away to jail, the old order is restored and everything returns to normal.

Koestler was in a cheerful mood when he dispatched the play to his new agent, A. D. Peters. Peters, the very model of an English gentleman, had actually been born in Germany and knew what it meant to be a foreigner in a strange land. He had been interned as an enemy alien during World War I and understood Koestler well enough to become a sort of father figure to him, part counselor, part literary critic, and always a loyal friend (sending cigarettes, cigars, and boxes of typing paper at a time when rationing was at its worst). Peters's colleague Margaret "Stevie" Stephens also mothered Koestler, so that in them he acquired a sort of surrogate family. Peters quickly established his worth by persuading Macmillan to publish the play and pay a generous royalty, and Koestler had high hopes for a movie contract. Alexander Korda (a fellow Hungarian) had taken an eight-week option for MGM on Koestler's next five novels and plays, but he wasn't keen on the play. Nor was Ealing Studios or Columbia Pictures, and though Peggy Ashcroft agreed to read it for the stage, nothing came of the plan to stage it either.[22]

The play's main contribution to Koestler's career was its role in unlocking the door to a fresh burst of creativity, leading to the publication of his first collection of essays, *The Yogi and the Commissar,* in which he definitively bid goodbye to his Communist past. For months now, as the war shifted in the Allies' favor, he had watched with growing anxiety as the United States and Britain drew closer to Russia. Pictures of "Uncle Joe" Stalin and articles about the glorious victories of the advancing Red Army were in the newspapers almost every day. Politicians in Britain were beginning to speak of the need to "reward" the Russians for their contribution to the war with the postwar partition of Germany, and in February Koestler had watched a House of Commons debate on foreign affairs with a distinct sense of foreboding. "This was the historic debate when the U.N. charter was torn up and Europe handed to Russia," he wrote in his diary. Nobody seemed aware that "the future frontiers of Soviet Poland" would run "only a few miles east of Berlin. In two years it will be a natural deduction. If I said it aloud today, nobody would believe me and I'd probably be interned."[23]

Koestler's prediction was astonishingly accurate, but none of his Labour Party friends would listen to him, leading his Cassandra itch to return with full force and in July his resolve to write something was reinforced when Orwell sent him the manuscript of *Animal Farm.* "Envious congratulations," Koestler wrote back. "This is a glorious and heart-breaking allegory; it has the poesy of a fairytale and the precision of a chess problem. Reviewers will say that it ranks with Swift, and I shall agree with them." That was, if the reviewers got to see it, for Orwell's novel immediately collected rejections from Victor Gollancz ("I could not possibly publish a general attack of this nature"), Jonathan Cape ("I think the choice of pigs as the ruling caste will no doubt give offence to many people, and particularly to anyone who is a bit touchy, as undoubtedly the Russians are"), and T. S. Eliot at Faber & Faber ("the positive point of view, which I take to be generally Trotskyite, is not convincing; your pigs are far more intelligent than the other animals, and therefore the best qualified to run the farm").[24]

"Intelligent pigs" was a reasonably accurate description of Stalin and his henchmen, and it would have been hard to convict T. S. Eliot of pro-Communist sympathies then or at any other time. It was the tenor of the times to feel good about Russia and to wish not to offend these indispensable allies who were helping the West to win the war. Such a view of the matter, mixing hardheaded self-interest with sentimental idealization of the Russian "proletarian" army, was virtually universal in Britain and was like a red flag to Koestler. Much as he had welcomed Russia's entry into the war, he was convinced the leopard would never change his spots and felt he understood the animal far better than his British colleagues did. He planned an essay of about "ten to fifteen thousand words" on the subject and finished the first ten pages in a day and a half: "My bones ache from writing 12 hours per day, can't sleep. Got diarrhoea, and this is happiness."

Within a matter of weeks the essay had expanded to three: "Anatomy of a Myth," "Soviet Myth and Reality," and "The End of an Illusion." In the first (autobiographical) essay, Koestler described his infatuation with the "Soviet myth" (defined as the "psychological reflection in the European left" of events in the Soviet Union) as if it were the experience of an entire generation. In the second and third essays, he documented the way the Soviet system had evolved from a radical experiment in socialist revolution into a classic case of reactionary imperialism. Thirty years before Aleksandr Solzhenitsyn, he described Stalin's mass deportations from eastern Poland and the Baltic states, the forced-labor camps (the term *Gulag* hadn't come into use yet), and a "new Chinese wall" (the phrase *iron curtain* also hadn't been coined) between Russia and the rest of the world. "Human rights and moral traditions which fifty years ago we took for granted are abolished in large parts of the world and in the process of abolition in others. *Habeas corpus,* freedom of speech, civil law, respect for individual life, the unwritten code of certain minimum decencies of conduct—how stale and ridiculous these appeared at a time when utopia seemed at hand, and how desperately important they are now, when we stand with our backs to the wall!"[25]

THE ESSAYS TRACED an arc that corresponded to Koestler's own development: infatuation with the myth, experience of the reality, and disillusionment with the outcome, yet he reaffirmed his touching faith in socialism. "The age of enlightenment has destroyed faith in personal survival; the scars of this operation have never healed. There is a vacancy in every living soul, a deep thirst in all of us. If the Socialist idea cannot fill this vacancy and quench our thirst, then it has failed in our time. In this case the whole development of the Socialist idea since the French revolution has been merely the end of a chapter in history, and not the beginning of a new one." For Koestler, the psychological dimensions of the myth were as important as the historical, and writing about them was an exercise in catharsis.[26]

In his last essay for the planned volume, with the unfortunate title "The Yogi and the Commissar—II," Koestler embarked on a wide-ranging survey of science and ethics that expanded on some of the ideas expressed in his opening essay of that title. In between came his *Horizon* essays on Richard Hillary, the French 'flu, and the intelligentsia, and a selection of his political pieces for *Tribune* and *The New York Times.* Jonathan Cape, his publisher, raised no objections to the anti-Russian material (perhaps feeling guilty over his rejection of *Animal Farm*), and Veronica Wedgewood worked with Koestler to get the historical and social detail straight. Koestler urged Cape and his American publisher, Macmillan, to publish the book quickly, for he still hoped, however quixotically, to influence the postwar settlement.

The Yogi and the Commissar was published in May 1945 and, despite its later neglect, remains one of Koestler's best books. On its appearance, Koestler was greeted as "a brilliant writer and often a profound thinker" who had the "rare merit of being able to think important thoughts and to clothe them in words which reveal rather than conceal their importance." He was also "a man of acute feeling who has suffered long and intensely. He knows that suffering alone does not produce wisdom; and yet the great dividing line now is between those who have suffered and those who have remained relatively untouched." The strongest pieces were agreed to be Koestler's tribute to Richard Hillary, his essay "The Intelligentsia," and the three long pieces on the Soviet Union at the end of the book. The Soviet articles composed a "brilliant lawyer's brief drawn almost entirely from evidence freely submitted by the accused."[27]

The book's title soon achieved proverbial status. *Yogi* and *commissar* became shorthand for the terms of a political debate that was to continue for many years, a signal achievement for a nonnative writer of English. Hannah Arendt (who liked most of the book) felt that in his title essay, Koestler wrote about freedom "as though nobody before him had ever taken it seriously," but the response of prominent fellow travelers showed how much Koestler's book had hit home. Koestler wasn't a man, wrote Eric Bentley, but "as Nietzsche said of Wagner—a disease. Mr Koestler has raised ex-communism to the status of a glamorous and almost Byronic career, and I find Koestlerian young men talking of their entirely mythical communist past merely to seem more interesting." Harold Laski voiced the fear that Koestler had become "the unconscious instrument of the very reaction he was once so anxious to destroy," and Kingsley Martin responded to Koestler with a classic apologia for Stalin and the Soviet Union in a full-page editorial in the *New Statesman*.[28]

Martin was answered by Orwell in his essay "The Theory of Catastrophic Gradualism," in which he supported Koestler's *Yogi* essays and denounced Martin's obscurantism. Orwell's acute ear, however, had noticed that Koestler still dated communism's ills from Stalin, whereas "the seeds of evil were there from the start," but he thought Koestler was right to call for a period of contemplation and a change of direction. "In the minds of active revolutionaries the longing for a just society has always been fatally mixed up with the intention to secure power for themselves." Koestler's desire to see a new "fraternity," "sharing the life of the masses but voluntarily debarring themselves from power," was not as utopian as Koestler feared. But Orwell thought it wouldn't happen without a change of heart. "To that extent, though no further, the Yogi is right as against the Commissar."[29]

Connolly published a review of the essays in *Horizon* but indiscreetly informed Mamaine that he admired the book more than its author. The next day he rang to say that he hadn't really meant what he said, only that he had been insulted by Koestler so often that he couldn't resist the temptation to retaliate. Connolly's true opinion of Koestler was probably expressed in a letter to Edmund Wilson shortly before Koestler's book came out. "I am not a friend of Koestler's," Connolly told Wilson somewhat misleadingly. "I endure him out of loyalty to literature. As a person I think he is insupportable (like Marx); as a writer he is perhaps only a journalist of genius, but I am afraid he is much more, a dynamo generating just the energy which the enlightened left had almost despaired of. Like everyone who talks of ethics all day long one could not trust him half an hour with one's wife, one's best friend, one's manuscripts or one's wine merchant—he'd lose them all. He burns with the envious paranoiac hunger of the Central European ant-heap, he despises everybody and can't conceal the fact when he is drunk, yet I believe he is probably one of the most powerful forces for good in the country."[30]

CHAPTER TWENTY-THREE

RETURN TO PALESTINE

Wherever we go, whatever we do, self is the sole subject we study and learn.

— RALPH WALDO EMERSON

BY THE FALL OF 1944 the Allied armies had liberated France and were at the German border, and the Red Army had overrun East Prussia and much of Poland. Koestler was outraged when the Soviets halted their troops outside Warsaw and let the Poles stage their suicidal last uprising against the Nazis alone, but Strauss refused to let him write an article for *Tribune* for fear of offending the Russians. The great race for Berlin was now on, with the right to decide Germany's new boundaries as the prize. Farther south, Soviet armies had invaded Romania and Hungary and looked as if they might soon be in Budapest. Irene Aldor sent word that Adele was, thankfully, safe and living with Betti Singer, her sister-in-law, in the Budapest ghetto. Adele had no money of her own, however, and was living off the charity of Betti's son, Ernö. Koestler learned that she was ashamed and humiliated by her situation and was constantly fighting with her sister-in-law, but all attempts to contact her or send money were frustrated by wartime regulations.[1]

The worst of it was the uncertainty, for Budapest's Jews were living on a knife-edge. Crammed into overcrowded apartment houses marked with enormous yellow stars, allowed into the streets only with a yellow star sewn to their clothing, they were hungry, cowed, and frightened. Hungary's own fascist army, the Arrow Cross, continued to march Jews off to the firing squads, and it was impossible to know who their next victims would be. The Hungarian government had indicated that foreign visas and certificates of entry for Jews in Budapest would be honored, and Koestler hoped that Adele's Palestine certificate would also allow her to leave, but the future was completely uncertain.[2]

The news from France was better. Dorothee and Hans Müller had survived the war and were living in Paris with false papers, he working as a journalist and she as a typist, under the assumed name of Nicole Gadiot. Her shoulder had completely healed, and for the latter part of the war they had been active with de Gaulle's branch of the French Resistance. "We were homeless much of the time," she said later, "and slept wherever we could get a bed. We had to stay underground until the end of the war. It was doubly dangerous for me because Arthur was on the French police's wanted list. We helped a lot of people escape from France, and we sent information to England about German troop movements."[3]

"A stone fell from my heart," Koestler wrote to Dorothee in Paris, "to hear you are sane and safe." He had heard about Hans, he wrote, and if the two of them wanted to marry, "you can at any time start divorce proceedings against me, and I shall of course take the blame." He himself was in no hurry to remarry. "Daphne and I are great friends, *mais c'est tout*. I thought this news would in some feminine way cause you some satisfaction and cheer your heart. Anyway, I'm going to remain a bachelor for the rest of my middle-aged days."[4]

Tactfully he made no mention of Mamaine, whom he was seeing more often than ever. His days and nights were again filled with bibulous lunches and argumentative dinners—though he no longer drank to excess or exploded into senseless rages. His diary for this period comes to an end on August 25, but Mamaine chronicled their busy schedule and lists a familiar cast of characters: the Willerts, Strachey, Foot, Plesch, Korda, Sylvester Gates, Anna Kavan, and Dr. Bluth. Two new members of their circle were Henry Yorke (better known as the novelist Henry Green) and the philosopher A. J. "Freddy" Ayer, whom Koestler had met at Willert's at the start of the war. Ayer, like Willert and Korda, was connected with the British intelligence service and had just returned from spells of duty in America and North Africa. A worldly and sophisticated intellectual (and a gifted philosopher), Ayer shared Koestler's left-wing politics and roving eye for pretty women, which was to make for a wary and competitive relationship between the two, especially when Ayer had an affair with Celia.

Ayer soon left for newly liberated Paris, to be followed by Orwell (in the unaccustomed role of war correspondent for *The Observer*), Philip Toynbee, Connolly, and Evelyn Waugh. Koestler, with characteristic contrariness, decided to head in another direction. Europe, he thought, could look after itself. What most mattered now were the terrified survivors of the Nazi Holocaust. Untold numbers of Jews had perished in the concentration camps, but their very deaths posed the question of a homeland for the survivors, and Koestler still believed that that homeland should be Palestine. Since the British government disagreed and was turning Jews away, Koestler realized that the coming struggle would be intense, and he wanted to be a part of it.

Ever the romantic, he even toyed with the idea of moving to Palestine. His thoughts were "more and more centered around Palestine," he told Michael Polanyi late in the war, and for reasons that curiously resembled his reasons in 1926. "Apart from the *Gesinnungs* [sentiment] aspect, the idea fascinates me to write some kind of 'Rougeon-Macquart' series of novels" that would culminate in Palestine. Two years before, he had inquired of Norman Bentwich, a former attorney general of the government of Palestine, whether he might get his citizenship back. Technically he was still stateless. The Hungarians had canceled his citizenship when he joined the British army, and though his service in the Aliens' Pioneer Corps automatically qualified him for British citizenship, he had postponed his decision because he disapproved of British policy in Palestine. To become a Palestinian citizen now would demonstrate solidarity with the persecuted Jews.[5]

He still had to find a way to get to Palestine, however. All exit permits from Britain had been abolished for the duration of the war. One way to go was as a foreign correspondent, and though he had "no intention of returning to professional journalism as a way of living," he concluded a deal with the *New Statesman* to go out as its "special correspondent" and with *The Times* to write two fifteen-hundred-word "unsigned and objective articles" on the Middle East and on Palestine. He also tried to get Lewis Namier at the Jewish Agency to give him financial support for a novel on Jewish-Arab relations. Namier referred him to Weizmann, who secured for Koestler both a passport and a "priority passage" to Palestine, but no money.

Weizmann had an ulterior motive in helping Koestler. Weizmann's supporters in the Haganah favored partition, but they were being fiercely opposed by the Irgun, the successor movement to Jabotinsky's Revisionist movement. The Stern Gang, loosely affiliated with the Irgun, had recently launched a campaign of terrorism and had assassinated Britain's colonial secretary, Lord Moyne. The British were outraged, and Palestine was in turmoil. Weizmann knew of Koestler's sympathy for the Revisionists, but also that Koestler was in favor of partition, and felt he might have a contribution to make. "Talk to those *meshuganeh* [mad] friends of yours," said Weizmann, and make them see reason.[6]

KOESTLER SET OUT from Liverpool on December 20, 1944, on the SS *Exeter,* one of a convoy of ships bound for Alexandria. His triumphal arrival in Jerusalem three weeks later was like the return of the prodigal son. The *Palestine Post* announced his visit in its "Social and Personal" column, and the *Post*'s editor, Gershon Agronsky, threw a huge party on his first night there.

A few days later Koestler addressed a packed audience of journalists at the Café Fink, informing them of his joy at returning to his political roots, and gave a press conference at which he announced that he had come to study the political situation and gather material for a novel. Like Hemingway, the gatherer of news was news himself (one correspondent actually made the comparison), and his mission had a decidedly thirties ring to it. His goal was to write a novel (or novels) that would be socially useful fiction based on fact, just as he had recommended in "The Novelist's Temptations."[7]

The flood of letters and phone calls to his hotel (felicitously named the Hotel Eden) made it seem as if he had indeed gone to heaven and was watching a replay of his life. Former girlfriends wrote to recall salad days in Vienna and Berlin. Puttl Rauchwerger joyfully invited him to meetings of the Palestine branch of Unitas. Ernst Gütig informed him that the Hephzibah settlers who had found him unworthy of *kvutsa* life would welcome him back after twenty years. Noemi von Weisl sent a note to the *chevalier sans reproche* to come visit old friends; and at an enormous party thrown by Moshe Shertok he encountered former Ullstein colleagues, exiled Budapest writers, French Resistance survivors, Spanish Civil War veterans, Revisionist activists, and ex–Communist comrades in arms who besieged him with reminiscences and smothered him with invitations to revisit the past.[8]

After two weeks of parties, receptions, and reunions, he wrote Mamaine that unlike the last time he had been there, he felt "sinfully happy" in Jerusalem. "This is a town which acts like a drug, a thing of such incredible and tragic beauty that every time I look down from my balcony I go all soft and shaky inside." Teddy Kollek, second in command of the Haganah's intelligence service, had invited Koestler to celebrate a seder at his kibbutz of Ein Gev, a fishing village on the eastern shore of the Sea of Galilee. Koestler insisted on dragging along Guy de Rothschild, who was in Jerusalem on behalf of the Free French. To get there involved a romantic journey by boat across the southern end of the lake, and the visitors were welcomed by the kibbutzniks in a large tent at the water's edge, where the festive meal was eaten. That night the Eastern European kibbutzniks danced the hora, a "stamping and swaying round-dance, a savage ring-polka" that Koestler memorably described in his novel when he came to write it.

> Joseph stood by the door, watching the dancers. Their faces, thrown back and turned towards the ceiling, were covered with sweat; many of them had closed their eyes. When they stopped racing round to shout out the refrain, the three magic syllables of *hag-al-il* burst from their lips like savage barks. When they resumed their circular race, their mouths remained half open in a self-forgetful, panting rapture. Thus transfigured, they no longer appeared to Joseph ugly and reptilious, but like some stylized Assyrian or Sumerian carving come to

life in the flickering light of the candles. His feet had begun to stamp out the torrential rhythm of the dance, his body began to sway, he longed to be swallowed up in the swirling eddy.[9]

Joseph was a stand-in for Koestler, of course, and that evening he felt that he had truly come home. It was a feeling that stayed with him as he embarked on a tour of kibbutzim in Galilee to seek a location for his novel, stopping off at Hephzibah one night for a party in his honor. "When I neared the kibbutz, I felt that, despite the darkness, I had returned to the specific location in the homeland that I could refer to as home." But he freely admitted to the assembled members that he had been a failure as a settler, unwilling to accept the primitive conditions of life on the kibbutz and unable to meet the exacting standards of the founders. In the end it had been best for him to leave, since he could never have achieved success had he stayed to live that kind of life.[10]

To gather material for his novel he elected to spend two weeks at the larger kibbutz of Ein Hashofet, perched in the Menashé Hills a few miles south of Hephzibah. A lot of his time was spent questioning the kibbutzniks on their way of life, how and why they had come there, what their views were about the British, about the Arabs, about partition, and about the various political parties in Palestine, but the high point of his stay was an expedition to the summit of an arid hill some miles away to plant a new settlement. An advance party went in the dead of night to scout the territory and set up a ring of guard posts. Around two in the morning, a convoy of ancient trucks with doused headlights ground its way over dried-up streambeds to the desired location. The trucks bore everything that was needed to build a watchtower and erect the first two communal huts in one swoop. These were quickly surrounded by a hastily fashioned stone wall topped with a barbed-wire fence, so that by the time the sun rose the next morning, the surrounding Arabs were presented with the impregnable nucleus of a new settlement. Koestler loved every moment and was thrilled by the tension and the risk, taking away with him an album of photographs recording this feat and the idea for the title of his future novel *Thieves in the Night* ("But the day of the Lord will come as a thief in the night").[11]

THE HOSPITABLE KIBBUTZNIKS were flattered to be featured in Koestler's next novel, but their relations with him were complicated. The kibbutz had been founded by members of Hashomer Hatzair, the militantly socialist youth movement formed by Jews from Central Europe (Manès Sperber was a former member), and Soviet Russia was a sacred socialist icon to them. They were strong supporters of Weizmann's Jewish Agency and the Jewish Labor Movement and hostile to the Revisionists. Koestler's passionate arguments against Stalinism and his defense of Revisionism (which also found their way into *Thieves in the Night*) fell on deaf ears. Revisionism's heirs, the Irgun and Lehi (better known as the Stern Gang), were "Jewish fascists" in the eyes of the Labor Party, and the two wings of Zionism were irremediably polarized. Koestler's quixotic desire to somehow straddle the differences and bring about a reconciliation would dog him for years.

The full seriousness of the split between the two wings of Zionism was brought home to him when he moved to Tel Aviv. Yasha Weinshall and the beautiful but faded Mala still held court at some of the best parties in town, but they and their Revisionist friends now struck Koestler as political dreamers straight from the pages of a nineteenth-century Russian novel. Quarrelsome, sentimental, and unself-conscious in their pursuit of epicurean delights (in other words, not unlike Koestler himself), they presented a striking contrast to the buttoned-up discipline of members of the Haganah and the austere life of the kibbutzniks, whose monastic habits and abhorrence of alcohol made Koestler feel like a sinner in their sunny midst. It was at one of Mala's tumultuous soirées that he met a pretty twenty-three-year-old Czech refugee and aspiring journalist named Anny Bauer, wide-eyed and innocent, a sitting duck for Koestler's cosmopolitan charm. She became his girlfriend for the duration of his stay in Palestine and would remember this episode for the rest of her life.[12]

Tel Aviv's dreamers were also a far cry from the hard men now leading the Irgun and the Stern Gang. Gabriel Zifroni put Koestler in touch with David Friedman-Yellin, only thirty-two and the brains behind the assassination of Lord Moyne. He was a bitter man, having lost his mother and three brothers to the Holocaust; his wife was being held hostage in a British jail and he himself had gone underground. But Koestler had a weakness for the concept of an armed Jewish resistance. He saw the young gang leader as a "tragic killer with the expression of Abraham sacrificing Isaac" and accepted Friedman-Yellin's definition of the Stern Gang as more like the French Resistance or Tito's Partisans than the "terrorists" they were called by the British and by their Jewish opponents.

Koestler also interviewed Menachem Begin. The Irgun leader had altered his name to Israel Sassover, had grown a thick beard, and was moving from safe house to safe house to escape detection. He knew of Koestler's meetings with Weizmann, rightly suspected him of unofficial links to the British secret services, and was unsure whether to trust him. Koestler had to change cars five times and eventually had to speak with Begin in a pitch-dark room. Koestler told him that after the war, the British Labour Party would probably come to power and was much more friendly to Zionism than Churchill's war cabinet. Labour would allow 100,000 Jews to enter Palestine during a ten-year transition period, and would probably support the Jewish Agency's plan for partition. Begin was not impressed. He would continue to fight for unlimited immigration, and recited all the biblical reasons why the Jews should get the whole of Palestine on both sides of the Jordan River. "There was no rapport between us," Koestler later wrote, for Begin "had no conception of realpolitik or compromise."[13]

Kollek told Koestler that the Haganah had turned over lists of the Irgun leaders' names and addresses to the British authorities because they were convinced that terror was counterproductive (without revealing to Koestler his personal role in the denunciations). Koestler strongly disapproved of Jews denouncing other Jews, especially since Kollek's Haganah was also a semiunderground movement, but made a last attempt to broker a compromise when Weizmann arrived in Palestine and he and Koestler were honored guests at the twentieth-anniversary celebrations of the Hebrew Technical College in Haifa. Koestler visited Weizmann at his palatial home in Rehovoth to report on his meetings with the Revisionists and offered to introduce Weizmann to von Weisl, but Weizmann declined. He felt that Koestler was still too close to the Revisionists and didn't trust him. He may have been right, for when Koestler visited the Jabotinsky Institute with his Hebrew translator, Joseph Nedava, he inscribed in the guest book (in French): "One always returns to one's first love."[14]

KOESTLER, AS EVER, was caught in the middle, trying to be all things to all people and convincing none, and this stance extended to the Arabs as well. As a good reporter, he tried to learn about the Arab point of view. In Jerusalem he got to know the moderate Arab nationalist leader Musa al-Alami and made a point of visiting Arabs in the countryside. "I divide my time between Arab villages and Jewish settlements," he wrote to Mamaine, "and my sympathies are so split that in the end I shall develop schizophrenia." Oddly enough, when Koestler talked to young Arabs in the cities, they preferred discussing communism and the thesis of *Darkness at Noon* to talking about the future of Palestine. As he contemplated the huge social and economic divide between the poor Arab fellahin and their feudal, absentee landlords, many of whom were selling the land from under them at exorbitant prices, Koestler's socialist sympathies came into play. The landlords were rich exploiters in the classic mode, hypocritical and corrupt, without a shred of principle. But as much as he sympathized with the dispossessed Arab peasants and proletariat, he still couldn't rate their interests above those of the persecuted Jews.[15]

Koestler also hobnobbed with British colonial officials in Palestine, starting with the high commissioner in Jerusalem. Most of the British had a sneaking admiration for the Arabs in a T. E. Lawrence sort of fashion and responded positively to the Arabs' innate conservatism, their traditionalism, and their attachment to the land. They were much more like the "natives" in the rest of the empire than were these upstart Central European Jews—pushy, demanding, ungrateful, and now openly rebellious—who looked down on their colonial bosses every bit as much as the bosses looked down on them.

Koestler's impatience with British attitudes came out at a dinner party given by Agronsky. When he got into a heated argument with a British official named Ronnie Burroughs, who was making the case for evenhandedness between the Jews and the Arabs, Koestler burst into an impassioned denunciation of British indifference to the fact that the Jews of Europe were dying like flies for lack of a place to go. "He thundered like an authentic Old Testament prophet, demolishing the other man's position," according to the young American correspondent Saul David, who was present. "Ronnie murmured something about the unfairness of Koestler's argument. Koestler apologized, but said it was impossible to be cool about such matters 'when your mother has been baked in an oven in Lublin.'" The shocked silence that followed this statement ended all argument then and there. Later a more knowledgeable bystander commented that "Koestler was right, but his mother wasn't baked anywhere. She is alive and well."[16]

Koestler enjoyed a modest fame among the British officials, but they were suspicious of his intentions as "a bloody Jew," and Koestler had suspicions of his own. Drawing on old experience in the Communist underground, he insisted that his correspondents in Britain number their letters so that he would know if one went astray, and he was careful to number his own. He fully expected to be followed and reveled in the cloak-and-dagger aspect of it all. On the very night he was whisked away to see Begin he had been entertaining the head of the Jerusalem CID to drinks. This man, Richard Catling, had a reputation for "third-degree methods of interrogating terrorists," but Koestler felt it necessary to find out what the police thought as well and was flattered by the idea of being taken into Catling's confidence.[17]

In readiness for writing his new novel, Koestler rented an apartment on the top floor of the Schiller House in Talpioth, the suburb where he had lived some twenty years before. The house had a flat roof overlooking Jerusalem, on which he sunbathed during the day and worked at night. A cleaning woman came in for an hour a day, and he cooked all his own meals. "Sometimes three or four days pass without my seeing a soul," he wrote to Mamaine, "except the char and the Arabs who come in to sell eggs and fruit." And Anny Bauer (whom he didn't mention), who regularly made the short trip from Tel Aviv to Jerusalem to spend weekends with him.[18]

His mood while writing swung from euphoria to self-doubt and back again. "What a country for a writer," he wrote to Daphne Hardy. "I can't understand that Hemingway and Co haven't discovered it yet. The problems of a continent concentrated within the area of a country. You scrape the earth and out come pottery and coins from Nebuchadnezzar's days; you scrape a

human being and out come all the archetypal conflicts—racial, religious, social, ethical—which in Europe one only gets in a thin, diluted state. Everything is concentrated here, over-spiced, over-salted, over-heated—like the
Dead Sea." But the novel was "fantastically difficult to write."[19]

After the failure of part two of *Arrival and Departure,* Koestler was doubly
nervous about tackling Jewish themes. If he succeeded in focusing on "only a
fraction" of what he had observed in Palestine, he told Lovat Dickson, it
would be "the book of my life. I feel humble and rather frightened." To Mamaine he wrote, "If it comes off—touch wood—I shall perhaps get rid of my
surplus of guilt feelings and get absolution for some of my sins." The book
was the "most damned difficult task I ever faced." Bound up with this apprehension was the realization that his fond dream of staying on in Palestine was
unrealistic. "When I came out I toyed with the idea of perhaps settling here;
after a month I find that I love this country more than I ever thought—the
incredible beauty of the landscape more than anything else—but that living
here would mean to abdicate as a writer." His friends, he discovered, were so
wrapped up in local problems that they were losing touch with Europe. They
knew it, and they couldn't help it. "But the main obstacle is the language
question: my English is (as you know) a very tender plant, which would soon
dry up in a foreign environment."[20]

KOESTLER'S RELATIONSHIP WITH MAMAINE remained ambiguous.
They had ostensibly agreed to part. "I wish I had had the sense never to let
you touch a drop of drink. Did we ever go to a party together and not quarrel?" wrote Mamaine in one of her letters. Yet she invariably addressed him
as "my darling Nyuszi" (Hungarian for "uncle") and gave free rein to her
loneliness and depression. "It was bloody awful when you went away. You
were so incredibly sweet to me and made me so very happy, that is why I was
so miserable when you left." "I miss you like hell, darling, I don't think I have
really laughed properly since you went away." "You are impossible to write
to because (unlike most men) you understand everything so well that there
seems no need to say it at all." She slyly let him know she was still in touch
with Dick Wyndham, who was in the Middle East as a correspondent for
The Sunday Times, and asked Koestler jokingly if he had gotten himself an
affreuse juive (frightful Jewish girl). "I hope she is very *affreuse* if so."[21]

Before leaving Britain, Koestler had taken Mamaine with him to northern
Wales to look at a house he planned to rent, and he asked her to monitor
some alterations: a hot-and-cold shower for guests, a cold shower for himself,
and sundry other amenities. Whether or not this was a "joint project" was
left unclear and became a running joke between them. "I would like to live
there with you if you weren't such a Branch Street kid," wrote Mamaine,
"but anyway I will come and stay with you perhaps and cook you lovely post-

war meals." To which Koestler responded, "Sorry to bother you so much with this—but this house is a kind of common enterprise of ours and I can't imagine moving in without you, at least for the first few weeks. Should you by then have developed—how does one say it without shocking the censor—other ties, I shall nevertheless kidnap you for a few weeks." The implication was clear. Despite their "official" separation, each was regretting it, strongly suggesting that things were not over between them.[22]

Mamaine applied for a job with the British press attaché in Jerusalem and was bitterly disappointed when she didn't get it. Never mind, wrote Koestler. "This country is only bearable for people who have very strong emotional ties with it—otherwise the climate is hell and the provincialism of life would bore you to death." In her "bitter and gloomy" letter reporting her failure, Mamaine reproached him for discussing her with Wyndham, a frequent visitor to Jerusalem in his capacity as Middle Eastern correspondent. Wyndham was fiercely pro-Arab and jealous over Mamaine, but neither man could resist the lure of getting together to argue politics and exchange taunts with his hated rival.[23]

At the end of April, Edmund Wilson resurfaced in London as a third contender for Mamaine's affections. In one of his pieces for *The New Yorker* he had devoted several pages to "G," a young woman who was "astonishingly beautiful in a feminine way" and, unlike American women, didn't try to compete with men. Mamaine was amused and flattered, and when Wilson bombarded her with letters from Italy and returned to London laden with gifts and a proposal of marriage, she temporized—"I miss you a lot—nobody I know here is half as much fun to be with as you"—but she didn't wish to commit herself. In June, forced to respond by Wilson, Mamaine told him, "I don't think I can marry you or indeed do anything to make our relationship fit any conventional pattern, if it doesn't do so anyway. I don't think you know me very well either."[24]

Early May had seen the long-awaited German surrender, signaling the approaching end of World War II. London exploded in VE Day celebrations. Mamaine pushed her way through the crowds thronging Piccadilly Circus and Leicester Square "with the aid of a rattle that made a noise like a machine gun and a sailor's hat with HI YER BABE written on it." She drove around London to see the public buildings newly lit up—a dazzling sight after nearly five years of blackout—and went to dozens of parties but still felt empty inside.

Then came the general election in June, ending in a Labour landslide, which seemed to signal the start of the social revolution Koestler and Orwell, and so many others, had been waiting for. Many of Koestler's friends were elected to office—John Strachey, Michael Foot, George Strauss, Dick Crossman, Aneurin Bevan, and Francis Noel-Baker—and Mamaine was ecstatic. "Now we can all cock a snook at all the people we've hated and despised for years," wrote Mamaine. "Already the stock market has gone right down and it looks as if there might be a terrific slump."[25]

Reading between the lines, it's easy enough to see that Mamaine was still in love with Koestler and he with her, though both maintained the pretense that if they shared Bwlch Ocyn, the house in Wales, for a while, the relationship would be platonic. But not all was well with Mamaine. She was being invalided out of her job at the Ministry of Economic Warfare, and she was suffering from "anxiety neurosis." "Nyuszi, I look 104! You will not like me at all when you see me. My character has become worse and worse too, as I am almost the most frustrated woman in England and that is very bad for one, so I look sour as well as plain." The truth was that her asthma had become worse and she needed rest. Never physically strong, she found that too much excitement and strain invariably had physical repercussions for her.[26]

Koestler flew back to England on August 12, 1945, having obtained a flight (for "urgent press affairs") at short notice. Anny Bauer drove him to the airport. Picking up the latest issue of the *Jerusalem Post,* he read with astonishment about the dropping of the first atom bomb and the dreadful devastation visited upon Hiroshima. The war was clearly over, and he pondered the political implications for the future, barely remembering to say good-bye to the tearful young woman by his side. The loyal Anny drove back to Jerusalem, cleared out his apartment, and transferred it to Eri Jabotinsky, Jabo's son, who was soon to be Koestler's publisher in Palestine. It was a bitter moment for her. Koestler was her first serious lover, for whose sake she had had an abortion (three years later, married to someone else, she wrote wistfully to Koestler, "I often wish I had not done away with the prospective junior"). By the time Koestler apologized (three months later) for his behavior, she was philosophical. "In your way you were as much to me as you could be to anybody at the time—and who can ask for more?"[27]

Mamaine awaited Koestler in London "sick with excitement" and found him tanned and cheerful, with a bag full of arak and cognac to fend off the miseries of liquor rationing in war-torn Britain. Over dinner they discussed the future. "A said he would like to marry me," she wrote in her diary, "but (a) cyclic neurosis (b) refused to have children; I said I would like to too but refused not to have children." Mamaine wondered to herself whether "normal relations are possible with A; don't particularly want to sleep with him, but everything to do with him is so important to me." She went ahead and proposed marriage anyway, but he refused, insisting in the same breath, however, that she go to Wales with him.[28]

In the course of the next couple of weeks Koestler embarked on a frantic round of lunches, cocktail parties, dinners, and uproarious late-night drinking sessions with just about everyone he knew in London. High on the list of people he sought out were his newly successful Labour Party friends—Strachey, by now a junior minister, Crossman, Foot, Strauss, and Baker, all of whom had to be briefed on the Palestinian situation and enlisted in support of the Jews. But he was still his old quarrelsome and unpredictable self, which meant that Mamaine's days and nights were spent on an emotional roller coaster: quarrels followed by tears followed by reconciliations followed by passionate bouts of lovemaking. She had given up another man she had been seeing, but there were other admirers in the wings, most of whom Koestler managed to insult and drive away. After an evening of listening to Koestler hold forth on Palestine, however, Mamaine felt "more than ever devoted to K and how right he is about most things."[29]

CHAPTER TWENTY-FOUR

WELSH INTERLUDE

It takes patience to appreciate domestic bliss; volatile spirits prefer unhappiness.

— GEORGE SANTAYANA

AT THE END of August 1945, Koestler's Slaugham dream of getting away from it all was realized when he set off for the remote farmhouse of Bwlch Ocyn in the mountains of North Wales. In terms of distance and isolation, it had nothing on the island of Jura, where Orwell was soon to settle, but it was far enough, and was dramatically different from the cities where he had spent most of his life. Luckily, Mamaine had agreed to accompany him. She loved the countryside and knew what it took to make a life there, whereas for Koestler the country was a romantic and exotic locale in which you spent vacations but didn't stay when the weather got bad. In any case, he lived for most of the time inside his own head. His physical surroundings, even when they were as dramatic as in Snowdonia, were simply scenery, a backdrop to the intellectual and emotional storms that whirled inside him.

Bwlch Ocyn was perched in the upper reaches of the Vale of Ffestiniog, between the lush, Italianate seaside resort of Portmeirion and the grim slate-mining town of Ffestiniog. It was an old Welsh longhouse, originally built in 1620, with walls of solid granite and a roof of locally quarried slate. Though located on the south side of the valley, it sat sufficiently high that it could be reached from the road only by a steep, narrow driveway, which became impassable when it snowed. Today the house is surrounded by a luxuriant garden filled with trees and flowers, but when Koestler and Mamaine arrived after a three-day odyssey from London, it was virtually open to the surrounding sheep meadows. Across the vale reared the bare peaks and wide valleys of the Moelwyn Mountains, the panorama that had so attracted Koestler's attention in the first place.[1]

The farmhouse had once belonged to the family of Clough Williams-Ellis, the architect and creator of Portmeirion, and the rugged building had been remodeled in the Italianate Portmeirion style by Williams-Ellis himself. It had a spacious drawing room with a high, barrel-vaulted ceiling and a raised gallery, a huge inglenook fireplace, and a large picture window looking out on the mountains. The cozy oak-paneled dining room beside it became Mamaine's study, "next to the kitchen with a communicating door, so that I can, so to speak, read in it while stirring the stew with one hand," and Koestler chose to work in a small bare room tucked behind the fireplace. This monastic cell had a sloping ceiling, two small windows with a view of the fields, and its own small bathroom. Koestler invariably took a cold bath or shower every morning, no matter how late (or drunk) he had gone to bed the night before.[2]

Within a couple of weeks they had acquired a Welsh collie puppy, Joseph (soon to be followed by Dina and Nellie), a clutch of chickens (a great luxury in the days when eggs were still rationed), and some plants for the garden. "We started planting bulbs," noted Mamaine in her diary, "me putting them in willy-nilly as I've forgotten which are which, K digging up the weeds and most of the plants. Said he didn't know what daffodils, narcissus or crocuses were." In a letter to Edmund Wilson, Mamaine wrote that "nobody could be more surprised than I" by this latest development in her life and that she didn't expect it to be long-lasting. Since Koestler refused to have children, "there seems no chance of getting married and not much point in doing so." To Celia, however, she reported that "relations with K could not be better." In a repeat of his earlier words to Daphne, and with his usual talent for self-deception, he told her he had never lived so well with anyone else and couldn't imagine anything going wrong with their relationship. Her health, always fragile, was not helped by the damp Welsh climate, and when she took to her bed with a cold, she found that "K now treats me as if I'd had double pneumonia." In December she was ill for two whole weeks—a harbinger of things to come—and their part-time housekeeper was also ill, "so poor K had to do all the housework and cooking as well as looking after me and trying to finish his novel. All this he did with great efficiency and was very sweet to me and really looked as though he didn't mind having to do so much when he was trying to work."[3]

WILLIAMS-ELLIS AND HIS WIFE, Amabel, had formed quite a colony in their corner of North Wales, with a regular stream of interesting visitors. Amabel was John Strachey's sister (and Lytton Strachey's niece). Tall, aristocratic, highly cultivated, and a former Communist like her brother John, she had a habit of getting deep into conversation with her guests as she drove them around the hairpin bends and narrow lanes, looking carelessly over her shoulder to see if they were listening (Michael Polanyi swore that she changed gears to punctuate each point in her conversation). Bertrand Russell and his fellow philosopher Rupert Crawshay-Williams lived nearby, and the novelist Storm Jameson, president of English PEN, with her husband, Guy Chapman, was also a frequent visitor.[4]

Koestler's own visitors that fall included Daphne, still resentful of the abrupt way he had left her. After seeing Koestler drunk, she wrote, "I saw you as many others have probably seen you all along, as quarrelsome, ill-behaved, self-centered and boring, and thought to myself 'Good Lord, is that how he really is, and all the time I didn't see it?' I hope you have not yet circumcised the unfortunate Welsh puppy—or reduced him to a chronic alcoholic like yourself."[5]

The big social event of their first few months was a visit by George Orwell and his baby son, Richard, for Christmas. Koestler and Orwell had drawn closer during the past couple of years, offering parallel messages about the Soviet threat and picking up on each other's themes in their political essays. Orwell had recently invited Koestler to review for *Tribune* and later asked him to take over his reviewing job at the *Manchester Evening News,* which Koestler declined. Orwell had also introduced him to David Astor at *The Observer* and eventually handed over his monthly "Letter from London" for *Partisan Review.* The two men were obvious allies. "He was a pessimist and so am I," Koestler said much later, "so I found it stimulating, not depressing, to be with him." Both men also carried heavy loads of personal and social guilt, felt a visceral hatred of all forms of oppression, and had experienced political epiphanies in Spain. It was natural to feel they understood each other.[6]

It was also an open secret that since the sudden death of his wife, Eileen, Orwell had been looking for a successor and a mother for his adopted son, and, given that Celia had recently separated from her first husband, Koestler and Mamaine thought they'd invite her for Christmas too and try their hand at matchmaking (such romantic notions of a family tie took little account of Orwell's notoriously stubborn character or of Koestler's legendary prickliness). Koestler got a taste of Orwell's unbending character on the day of the latter's arrival. Koestler's play *Twilight Bar* had been published in August to less than rapturous responses—and Orwell's review in the December issue of *Tribune* had been the least rapturous of all. "The drama is not Koestler's line," Orwell began, and ended, "The dialogue is mediocre, the play demonstrates the gap that lies between having an idea and working it up into dramatic shape." The day after reading the review, Koestler accompanied Mamaine to Llandudno to meet Orwell and Richard off the train and drive them back to Bwlch Ocyn. Koestler wondered why Orwell hadn't mitigated his harsh remarks with a single redeeming phrase and was expecting Orwell to say something in the car, but Orwell said nothing and they rode in silence. Finally Koestler blurted out, "That was a bloody awful review you wrote, wasn't it?" "Yes," said Orwell, "and it's a bloody awful play, isn't it?"[7]

Koestler thought that Orwell's rigidity had a lot to do with his uphill struggle with his illness. A stern self-discipline made him "ruthless toward himself," and the extension of that ruthlessness to friends was a form of compliment. "The closer somebody was to him, the more he felt entitled to treat that friend like he treated himself." It was a harsh code but one that Koestler could grasp and respect, and in the days ahead the two crusaders achieved a comfortable modus vivendi. One day when they were taking a stroll outside, Koestler was to glimpse another side of Orwell's ruthlessness, a quality that perhaps explained the controversial torture scene in *1984*. They were discussing Freud, and Orwell said, "When I lie in my bath in the morning, which is the best moment of the day, I think of tortures for my enemies." "That's funny," replied Koestler, "because when I'm lying in my bath I think of tortures for myself."[8]

The week was a success. George liked Celia, and Celia liked George. Celia and Mamaine christened Orwell "Donkey George"—after Benjamin in *Animal Farm*—and were impressed by the skillful way he carried Richard on his hip and bathed and changed him with total confidence. Koestler was less enamored of the baby, who drove him to distraction by clambering over him in smelly diapers, then crawling about the house and turning everything upside down. He felt that Orwell was too lenient with the child. But when the baby woke one morning while the exhausted Orwell was trying to sleep (he and the baby shared a room), Koestler spent an entire hour making faces through the bars of Richard's cot so Orwell could get some rest.[9]

KOESTLER'S INVITATION TO ORWELL was not entirely social. In the first months after the war there was a lot of ferment among British intellectuals about how to exercise their influence on the power politics of the postwar world. It was a great time for voluntary organizations such as the Freedom Defence Committee, the National Council for Civil Liberties, the League for the Rights of Man, the International PEN Club, the British Centre against Imperialism, and groups of a similar sort, many of which Koestler had been approached to join. He refused most of them, however, because they were either virtual front organizations for the Communists or else moribund or ineffectual.

He proposed to Orwell that they start a successor to the old League for the Rights of Man, which in France had been taken over by the Communists and in Britain was dormant. Orwell, though already vice chairman of the Freedom Defence Committee, was enthusiastic and agreed to draft a manifesto, which he completed in less than a week. Its starting point was that while "liberty without social security is valueless, it has been forgotten that without liberty there can be no security." The majority of the people in Britain were little interested in their democratic rights and took them for granted, while "a considerable section of the intelligentsia has set itself almost consciously to break down the desire for liberty and to hold totalitarian methods up to admiration." The new league's task would be to "redefine democracy" and work for a synthesis between "political freedom on the one hand and economic planning and control on the other," and it would oppose "infringements against the rights and dignity of man" wherever they occurred.[10]

Koestler liked the draft, and the two of them set to work to enlist others. Orwell was turned down by Tom Hopkinson and Barbara Ward on the grounds that the organization would be too anti-Russian, but he had better luck with Michael Foot. Koestler had two near neighbors he thought would take an interest: Crawshay-Williams, on the Portmeirion estate, and Russell, who lived in a converted schoolhouse across the Vale of Ffestiniog with his third wife, Patricia, and their eight-year-old son, Conrad. Crawshay-Williams had the same reservations as Ward and Hopkinson, but Russell was very interested. The anti-Russian part didn't bother him at all, but he felt that it was too late to start a purely ethical movement, since the world was already on the brink of atomic war. "Russell thinks that it is up to the USA to state fully and explicitly what they would regard as a *casus belli* and let the rest go," Mamaine wrote in a letter to Edmund Wilson. Russell also thought it was fine for the United States to intervene in Spain and China to prevent undemocratic governments there, "even if they intervene about other things which they shouldn't (e.g. to preserve capitalism in England)." Russell suggested a conference of about a dozen influential people with international expertise to discuss "how to prevent an atomic war" and promised to take part himself.[11]

This was rather different from what Orwell and Koestler had proposed, but it was important to have the support of someone as distinguished as Russell, and Koestler felt sure he could find a way to bridge the gap. Celia was now working for Humphrey Slater, the editor of *Polemic,* and Koestler persuaded her to arrange a meeting for him with Slater and his wealthy Australian backer, Rodney Phillips. Koestler planned to hold a conference at the nearby Oakley Arms hotel at Easter time, and he booked accommodations for twelve people, informing Orwell that he could host a further "six to ten" people in the guest rooms of his farmhouse. Participants would include Russell and Crawshay-Williams, and they would be joined by Orwell, Foot, Gollancz, Sperber, perhaps Malraux or Silone, and "an American" to be brought in by Orwell. The whole thing would be paid for by Phillips, and the league's eventual secretary would work out of *Polemic*'s offices for a while.[12]

What this meant for *Polemic* became clearer when Koestler wrote from Wales with a list of four tasks for Phillips to perform and a postscript asking for copies of the draft petition "when it is typed out." This was wholly in Koestler's style, to galvanize an individual or an organization with his energy and rhetoric and then to turn over the day-to-day chores to someone else. But Slater and Phillips weren't playing. Theirs was a "purely theoretical" journal, above the political fray, and they were alarmed by rumors circulating in London that *Polemic* was to become the league's house organ. Ayer, a key contributor to *Polemic,* was skeptical about the league and threatened to jump ship if Phillips and Slater agreed to Koestler's proposals. Slater wrote an apologetic letter to Koestler, and the idea of the conference was dropped.[13]

KOESTLER WAS FURIOUS over this weak-kneed "betrayal" and wrote to Celia that her boss was "an ass," but he didn't lose interest in the larger project. Russell had sent him a powerful essay, "The Atomic Bomb and the Prevention of War," in which he called for a world government to prevent a third world war. Partly under the influence of this document, Koestler and Mamaine drafted a petition to accompany (or replace—the intention is not clear) Orwell's original manifesto. The new document took up several of Russell's themes, including the problems caused by political differences among the western powers and Russia and the dangers of a third world war if tensions weren't resolved (Churchill had just given his famous speech in Fulton, Missouri, about an "iron curtain" descending across the continent of Europe). Koestler's new contribution was a call for "psychological disarmament," which would entail the free exchange of newspapers and periodicals between the two blocs, the modification of censorship regulations, the abolition of travel restrictions, and the free circulation of ideas across frontiers.[14]

As usual Koestler was light-years ahead of his time: It wasn't until the 1950s and '60s that this idea became popular, but he wasn't entirely alone in his thinking. Besides Orwell there was another old ally, Victor Gollancz, whom Koestler was eager to involve for his sure political instincts and organizational dynamism. "I know nobody else with your drive and experience who could take the initial steps." Gollancz hesitated. Unlike the other objectors, he felt that Koestler's "intellectual disarmament memo" was, if anything, too pro-Russian, rather than pro-American, but he was willing to give it a try.[15]

In late April, however, the collaboration with Russell exploded. The official version of the rift is that Russell's wife, Patricia (known to friends as "Peter"), misrepresented Russell's views to Koestler, Koestler verbally attacked her, Russell backed his wife, and relations between the two families soured. This certainly happened. Russell was spending a lot of time in Cambridge, where he had a fellowship at Trinity College, and had asked Peter to act as an intermediary in ironing out the text of the manifesto. When Peter objected to some of the wording, Koestler called her "stupid" and they had a blazing row, which Russell used as a pretext to withdraw. "Writers do better work as individuals than by collaborating in groups," he told Koestler and suggested the latter proceed on his own.[16]

But there was a subtext to this "explosion." Russell had renewed an affair with an old flame of his, the actress and novelist Colette O'Neil, while in Cambridge, which Peter bitterly resented. Peter herself was a striking woman, with a fine head of copper-colored hair, parchment-white skin, and a tall, slender figure that attracted widespread admiration, and she compensated for her humiliation by constantly talking about sex and the number of men who were in love with her. Koestler, it seems, drew the logical conclusion and acted accordingly. According to one source, Peter returned home one night after visiting Koestler (when Mamaine was away in London), burst into Russell's study, and announced dramatically, "I've just been to see Koestler and he tried to rape me." "Oh yes," said Russell, and went on working. A few days later the same thing happened again, and Russell responded, "I have often heard of women being raped, but seldom twice in one week, and seldom by the same man."[17]

The story is probably apocryphal, but Peter did write Koestler a stinging letter of reproach. It was about their manifesto differences, and her account has the ring of truth to it. It must have been due to the "intense individualism of the artist," she wrote, that Koestler found it impossible to cooperate with others. But "is it really necessary, among people who have the best will in the world to like you, to be so combative? To turn everything from the most casual conversation to the most serious public affairs into a struggle for absolute personal dominance? This attitude doesn't aid human relations—it makes you exhausting even when genial, and intolerable when morose. It blinkers your acute powers of perception. Worst of all, it ruins your intellect." Twisting the knife in the wound, Peter accused Koestler of never having lost his old Communist habits of thinking. "I know the etiology of all this, but that never helps so much as it should. In practice people are offended by offensive behavior, however much they can explain it." If Koestler didn't take steps to break his steamroller habits, she added prophetically, he would be surrounded by people too inferior to notice how inferior he thought they were.[18]

Koestler apologized to Russell about the misunderstanding, and the contrite Peter sent Koestler a gushing note of regret, ending with "Love to Mamaine—yours affectionately in spite of everything—Peter." There was a fuller rapprochement in the summer. Koestler said it was because Russell had a crush on Mamaine, and sure enough, Russell made a pass at her, "to the extent of holding my hand and saying over and over again how glad he was to be coming to Ffestiniog so as to be able to see more of me, etc." Quite apart from his appreciation of Mamaine's beauty, Russell must have been looking for revenge against his rival, but Mamaine found his advances "rather horrifying," and shortly afterward another clash with Peter virtually ended the re-

lationship. Looking back on the matter, Koestler described Russell as "imp-
ish, waspish and donnish," and commented that "for a champion of so many
humanitarian causes [he was] strangely lacking in human warmth." Much
the same could have been said of Koestler, of course. The two men were too
alike to be able to work together.[19]

WALES WASN'T AT ALL GOOD for Mamaine's asthma, and she went on a
short trip to France and Switzerland to recuperate. She crossed the channel
with Pietro Nenni and Ignazio Silone. The latter hadn't read either *Darkness
at Noon* or *The Yogi and the Commissar* but introduced Mamaine to his Paris
friends as the wife of *"un des grands esprits revolutionnaires* [one of the great
revolutionary spirits]." The French translation of *Darkness at Noon* had just
come out in Paris, and Mamaine was an instant celebrity. Simone de Beauvoir ("she talks a lot, hardly listens to anybody else, and dresses badly")
wanted to know what else Koestler had written and told Mamaine she would
like to serialize his forthcoming novel about Palestine in the journal she
edited with Sartre, *Les Temps Modernes* (Modern Times). Mamaine met
Camus for the first time and was instantly attracted but flirted by proxy with
a composer suitably named Casanova.[20]

Tristan Tzara tried to seduce Mamaine in Geneva. He was "a sweetie,"
she told Edmund Wilson, but also "a Stalinist of the deepest dye," whose
ideas were "completely mad." She informed the still-hopeful Wilson that she
had changed her mind about how long she and Koestler might stay together.
"He is not altogether easy to live with, because he has a violent and emotional
temperament, which carries him to extremes in both directions; but he is
never mean or selfish, and never boring. Also he is really fond of me and
looks after me wonderfully. So you see I don't think of marrying anybody
else and don't suppose I ever shall." Mamaine added that she had "never expected to be able to live with Arthur for 5 minutes" but now would find it
"very difficult to live without him."

Back in Wales, she found Koestler "his sweet and usual self again" and
that summer broached the idea of marriage again. "I suggested to K that he
and I might get married," she confided to her diary, "if he could ever divorce
his wife, and he said he would if I really wanted to (though poor soul he hates
the idea of marriage). But after all we do what he wants about most things of
importance, such as not having children, so I didn't feel too bad about saying
I would like to be married, though it did rather go against the grain, and I
wouldn't have felt capable of insisting if K had shown great reluctance. I do
hope it will come off. I suddenly feel very strongly about it."[21]

But soon enough she started to change her mind. Koestler began nagging
her about the untidy state of the house and her failings as a homemaker,
while taking it for granted that she should copyedit his novel on Palestine (at

the rate of twenty-five pages a day), correct his English, and type his correspondence. Later, when he began to tackle the huge and unwieldy scientific treatise that was to become *Insight and Outlook,* he insisted on Mamaine's sitting beside him and taking dictation. "The more he nags, the more hopeless I become, in spite of fervent resolutions to improve," Mamaine told her diary. She was unnerved by the black moods that seemed to descend out of nowhere and settle over him like an impenetrable cloud, making him impossible to be around.[22]

In the summer of 1946, Mamaine confided to Celia that she was in despair after a discussion "along well-known lines" about her function in Koestler's life. Was it that of a mistress or wife, "of whom K may after a bit get bored as people do with their spouses," or was it that of "a full-time secretary and assistant who he will always want to have around because she shares his work, which is the most important thing in his life?" Koestler had complained about her obvious dislike of secretarial work and said it made life more difficult for him. "It is not a question that I am bad at it, for I am by now fairly efficient, but apparently my face when K is dictating to me is so filled with loathing, boredom and despair that he simply can't bring himself to do it. He said, as he has said 1000 times before, that what a writer wants to be married to is somebody who will consider his work THE most important thing in life, and who will be willing to do any boring chore 24 hours a day 365 days a year, if by doing it she can further the interests of one of his books. He said I know I am offering you very little and asking the impossible, namely, that you should be attractive and a good hostess and cook and at the same time a good and full-time collaborator. Well, I said, I guess you are. All I can say is that I will try to adapt myself, and as I have already made progress in this direction I may make more; but I don't altogether like the idea, and what's more I'm afraid that if I do as you suggest you will get to think of me only as a secretary in the end. K said, that's very possible."[23]

THEIR DOMESTIC NEGOTIATIONS were interrupted and complicated by the arrival in July of Koestler's mother from Budapest. From Koestler's point of view, Adele was a vivid example of what family life was all about and a reminder that his aversion to marriage (and certainly to having children) was inspired by unhappy memories of his childhood. It seems that it was Plesch who, in the course of his analysis, finally convinced Koestler that Adele, with her migraines and alternating bouts of coldness and smothering love, was responsible for the guilt and insecurity (his "neurosis") that oppressed him as an adult. So when the news came that she was able to leave Budapest and was on her way, his relief was mixed with adolescent feelings of apprehension and dread.

Plesch tried to convince Koestler that he was crazy to bring Adele to

Britain at all. What was the point of uprooting a seventy-four-year-old woman and setting her down in an alien country where she knew no one and didn't speak the language? Koestler couldn't have agreed more but felt he had no choice. Adele was alone and, as she saw it, abandoned in Hungary, where she still had problems speaking the language. Her husband, brother, sister, niece, and niece's family had all died or been lost to the Holocaust, and she was frantic to get away from the hellhole of the Budapest ghetto. Eichmann had come within an ace of blowing it up before he left town, and though it had been liberated by the Soviet army after fifty-three days and nights of vicious street battles (in one of the bloodiest campaigns of the entire war), the Russians had spirited away the Jews' last champion in Budapest, Raoul Wallenberg, and Koestler was certainly not going to leave his mother in Soviet-occupied territory.[24]

Adele had sent several letters to Koestler via Irene Aldor, alternating syrupy declarations of maternal love with angry denunciations of his indifference to her and crammed with minute descriptions of her diet and health problems and precise demands for food and medicine. In one, written in English and addressed to "Dear Arthur," she pretended to be a friend. "Harry's widow beg me to inform you of her address—Wesselenyi utca 17 III 1. She is in the greatest misery and beg you to find a way to send her pounds or dollars as quick as possible. She is weak and cant nourish herself. The Family where she is living till now ask for money and her situation is wors from day to day. She is without shoes stokking linnen etc (and the worth) and her teeth ar in the greatest disorder and wants new fals teeth. In spite of all sufering she is by good health, only anxious to hear of either you can make her come to you (her greatest wish) or you com her. My dear Arthur I hop you ar in the best state of health. With best regards your old friend Peter Hopkis."[25]

The letter was funny and heartbreaking. Koestler sent her a soothing letter back, explaining his reasons for not writing (he was convinced the Soviet occupation forces would intercept his letters and refuse her a visa) and assuring her he would take care of her. "Only a little more patience, dearest, and we shall be united again. Don't let yourself go; everything depends on one's own will. My books have been fairly successful here and in America, and I shall be able to give you all the comfort which you have so long and so bitterly missed." Soon afterward a member of the British mission in Budapest confirmed that Adele was undernourished and having problems with her eyes and teeth but was otherwise in reasonable health. "Although she is living in a house where Russians are billeted, she has had no trouble at all on account of anything you have written."[26]

At the beginning of 1946 Pál Ignotus, who was now living and working in London, went to Hungary to deliver some lectures, and Koestler asked him to take a can of sardines and a bar of chocolate for his mother. Ignotus proposed sending her a postcard to inform her of his arrival, but Koestler was aghast. Didn't Ignotus know about the postal censorship and the secret police? After some argument, Ignotus agreed to visit Adele in person but was startled at the end of his first lecture when an elderly lady in black stood up, waved her arms, and called out in German, "*Ich bin die Mutter von Koestler! Sie müssen mit mir sprechen!* [I am Koestler's mother! You have to speak to me!]" Ignotus learned that Adele was famous in Budapest for touring newspaper and government offices, and even storming into the Soviet military headquarters, to announce that she was the mother of a famous Hungarian author and should be allowed to go to Britain. Far from having the police shadow her, as Koestler feared, Soviet officials in Budapest had no idea who she was and would have been glad to get rid of her. Alone with Ignotus the next day, Adele complained loudly about Koestler's silence and denounced his excuses for not writing. There was no stopping the onward rush of her bitter indignation, but she eagerly accepted the tea, chocolate, and sardines Ignotus had brought her and reported on the meeting in great detail in her next letter to Koestler.[27]

When news arrived that Adele had finally received her exit visa and was on her way, Koestler rushed down to London. According to Mamaine, he was deeply depressed at the prospect of seeing his mother again. It had been eleven years since their last meeting, and the very thought made his knees buckle. There was also the pressing question of what to do with Adele when she arrived. He had told the immigration authorities that she could live with him. Worse still, he had said the same to Adele, and in her letters she chattered about seeing him every day, "if only for a little while." But now he felt it was out of the question. He rationalized that she was old and sick and would need the sort of treatment that would be difficult to get in cold and windy Wales, but the truth was that she would undoubtedly drive him insane if they lived under the same roof. He rented a room for her in a nursing home for Jewish refugees at Ashtead in Surrey, run by a family friend of Adele's, Dr. Berliner.[28]

For ten days Koestler hung around London, expecting his mother to arrive at any moment, but she arrived over two weeks late, when he was already back in Wales. Dashing to London, Koestler spent three days taking her out to restaurants, going shopping at Harrods, and introducing her to Dr. Plesch. She went gladly to Ashtead, to stay with her "dearest friends from Vienna," but soon a reaction set in. "My soul is sick, is that why my body is sick, or is it the opposite?" she noted in her diary. She longed to be with her Dundi, not convinced by his excuse that Bwlch Ocyn was too far from civilization and lacked the medical and social services she needed. If she stayed in the London area, she would be as alone in Britain as in Budapest.[29]

CHAPTER TWENTY-FIVE

THE LOGIC OF THE ICE AGE

The tree of liberty must be refreshed from time to time with the blood of patriots and tyrants. It is its natural manure.
— THOMAS JEFFERSON

DURING THE YEAR that had passed since the end of World War II, Koestler had had to spend more time than he would have liked sorting out his tangled literary affairs. As he irritably pointed out to Wren Howard at Cape, whereas *Darkness at Noon* had been a Book-of-the-Month Club choice and had sold hundreds of thousands of copies in the United States, Cape had managed to sell only 7,600 copies in four years in Britain. He was worried that *The Gladiators, Scum of the Earth,* and *Arrival and Departure* had been allowed to go out of print, and feared the same would happen to *The Yogi and the Commissar.* "The relation between publisher and author is very like that of husband and wife. When it becomes a cat and dog life, it is time to end it." Howard replied defensively that his hands were tied by paper rationing and that Koestler was overstating the problem. *Arrival and Departure* and *The Yogi and the Commissar* were still in print, and *Yogi*'s print run had been a respectable 10,000 copies. He promised instant reprints of *Darkness at Noon* and *Arrival and Departure* and a new edition of *Scum of the Earth* when paper and labor permitted, and said that Penguin Books had signed to produce mass-market paperback editions of *The Gladiators* and *Darkness at Noon,* the latter in an edition of 250,000. It sounded good, but Penguin later dropped *The Gladiators,* and *Darkness at Noon*'s print run was reduced to 80,000.[1]

The war had of course been bad for most literary careers, but for Koestler it had been close to a disaster. He had come to maturity as a writer just as the war broke out, and his books had been virtually swallowed up by the global catastrophe—and if publication in English was a headache, the position with regard to translations was a nightmare. Owing to the breakdown of civil society on the Continent, British publishers had started issuing their own translations in French and German. Penguin's proposed titles in French, for example, included both *Darkness at Noon* and *Arrival and Departure.* Koestler hired Émile Delavenay to work with him on *Darkness,* paying him out of his own pocket, and Delavenay translated the book in a tearing hurry. Even then, though the translation was completed by the end of 1944, it was to be over a year before it appeared in France.[2]

The situation with the German edition of *Darkness at Noon* was even worse. Though written in German, the original manuscript had been lost. Koestler had miraculously recovered a piece of it after the war but was obliged to translate the rest of it back into German from the English version. It was printed by the British publisher Hamish Hamilton nearly two years later, in 1946, but the British High Commission banned its distribution in Germany for fear of upsetting the Soviet Union and was to maintain its ban (while also preventing republication by a German publisher) for another year and a half. Meanwhile, Koestler had gotten himself into an unholy mess over *Arrival and Departure* by granting Irene Aldor the Swiss and German rights to his new novel in gratitude for her help with his mother, only to find that this conflicted with Hamish Hamilton's rights for its German-language series. Worse still, Irene's translation for Artemis Verlag turned out to be a catastrophe. In the course of the recriminations that followed this debacle, none other than Irene's estranged husband, Koestler's old nemesis Ferenc (now Francis) Aldor, appeared out of the blue to make an offer for the German rights to *Arrival and Departure* and *Darkness at Noon*. It turned out that after having been released from the Isle of Man just before the war's end, Aldor had restarted his old publishing firm in London, and was ostensibly trying to help his ex-wife out of a hole. Astounded by his tenacious cousin's effrontery, Koestler was obliged to devote more precious time and energy to blocking his offer, by which time Hamish Hamilton had abandoned their German series entirely.[3]

In the interim, Koestler's sole published play, *Twilight Bar,* was optioned and staged in the United States by the prominent director George Abbott, who planned a top-flight production, with Burgess Meredith in the leading role, Leonard Bernstein composing the music, and Oliver Smith doing the sets. Meredith and Bernstein dropped out, and when he got down to basics, Abbott found himself struggling to interpret the meaning of the play. Was the whole thing a dream of Glowworm's that remained entirely in his head? Koestler said no and asked Abbott to maintain the illusion that the aliens were genuine. Abbott also had problems with the ending. How defeatist should it be, and how probable was the annihilation of mankind by the Delta-ray? Koestler couldn't really answer him and opted for ambiguity.[4]

The play opened in Baltimore in March 1946, with Luther Adler in the lead as Glowworm, and got a lukewarm reception. Adler had "a tendency to rant and rush" and was unable to do justice to the play's intellectual argument, while the third act (the love story between Alpha and Omega) seemed like an anticlimax. Abbott moved the play to Philadelphia, where the critics and the audience pronounced the fantasy scenes boring, leading Abbott to close it before running the risk of going to Broadway. Koestler generously consoled the director, and Abbott was grateful. "My admiration for Koestler is so limitless that I was really depressed at the play's failure," he told A. D. Peters. "And it was a great relief to me to receive not only his very understanding letter, but also this note from you."[5]

MEANWHILE KOESTLER CONTINUED to follow developments in Palestine with his usual close attention and to write and lobby for a better deal for the Jews. In the first of his two articles for *The Times* he defined the main problem in Palestine as a conflict between the Jewish desire for modernization and traditional Arab nationalism. The Zionists argued that Arabs would be better off with modern institutions, but the Arabs insisted that no nation would sell its "aspirations to independence and sovereignty" for the sake of hospitals, schools, and metal roads. "We want neither their honey nor their sting" was the Arabs' favorite saying, and the result was political deadlock. In his second article Koestler analyzed the military situation, concluding that the forces of the newly formed Arab League would be no match for the highly trained troops of the Haganah (he had watched them at their secret maneuvers in Palestine and been highly impressed with their discipline and skill). The longer Palestine remained closed to the survivors of the German massacres in Europe, the harder it would be for the Haganah to restrain its forces from open revolt, and Koestler argued for partition as recommended by the Royal Commission's report of 1939. The displacement of populations would be "small" compared with what was happening in Europe, and after a transition period with a "reasonable amount of rioting," the two partners would, "according to oriental habit, in all likelihood accept the inevitable and settle down to make the best of it."[6]

The two articles, coyly billed as "From a Special Correspondent Lately in Palestine," created a considerable stir in London. *The Times* had never before endorsed partition, and this looked liked a change of heart. Koestler was discreetly invited to appear before the highly influential Royal Geographical Society, but before he could do so, Dick Wyndham, still smarting from his loss of Mamaine, unmasked *The Times*'s correspondent as a "notorious Zionist," and the Royal Geographical Society withdrew its invitation.[7]

On the face of it, Wyndham's accusation was unfair. Koestler had bent over backward to be judicious in his *Times* articles, but in a third article,

"Land of Broken Promise," commissioned by *Life* magazine, he took the gloves off and openly defended the heirs of Jabotinsky ("the Trotsky of Zionism"), namely the Irgun and the Stern Gang. Koestler had smuggled out a comprehensive collection of their leaflets and documents and used them to trace the "profound misery and despair" of the Jews over the British white paper of 1939, "another Munich," as Churchill had characterized it, which had ignored the recommendations of the Royal Commission and firmly closed the door to further Jewish immigration to Palestine. "Only a nation of eunuchs," wrote Koestler, "could have been expected to hold its peace under this continuous strain of provocations," and it was no wonder they had turned to terrorism.[8]

The article, the closest Koestler had yet come to defending terrorism, was turned down by *Life,* and also by *Collier's, This Week, Reader's Digest, The Atlantic, Harper's,* the *Yale Review,* and *The New York Times.* Even for Americans, its nationalistic, pro-Jewish message was too incendiary. In Britain, it was scooped up by an aspiring young editor (and former member of Koestler's old fraternity, Unitas, in Vienna), George Weidenfeld, who was starting a small internationalist magazine called *Contact.* The magazine was so small, however, that Koestler's article was barely noticed at the time.[9]

In common with most Zionist supporters, Koestler had placed his hopes in the Labour Party and was outraged when the Clement Attlee government (despite President Truman's urging) refused to budge on immigration. Weizmann was invited to put the case to Labour backbenchers, and Gollancz asked Koestler for help in briefing him. Koestler, still in Palestine, replied that his relations with Weizmann were strained after their recent meeting "because I reproached him with political quietism and our deplorable shortcomings in the field of propaganda and public relations." Koestler also thought that Weizmann resented his friendship with Jabotinsky, but he nevertheless sent Gollancz a lengthy memo to help bolster Weizmann's case. He astutely characterized the Labour government as torn between conflicting imperatives: a will to help the Jews versus the fear of doing injustice to the Arabs; the reluctance of the left to support a dwarf state based on ethnicity; and a socialist government's fear of "presiding over the dissolution of the Empire." On the other hand, "not even the most perfect policy could have breached the chasm between two peoples rooted respectively in the 19th century and the 20th century." If nations with a common history, such as the French, Belgians, and Dutch, not to speak of the Czechs and Slovaks or Serbs and Croats, found it next to impossible to federate, such a dream for Jews and Arabs was utopian.[10]

Koestler felt that the Weizmannists were insufficiently hardheaded, and that it was in Britain's self-interest to establish a strong Jewish presence. The Arabs had been heavily influenced by anti-Semitism and fascism in their ideologies, but it wasn't only the Arabs, and Koestler sent Gollancz some microfilms of a secret British military intelligence handbook (stolen by the Irgun) to prove his point. "A start [should] be made by purging the CID Political Dept, the majority of whose officials are Black and Tans, and the police, which is ridden with ex-Mosleyites." Koestler wanted Gollancz to organize a Jewish march "from Whitechapel to Whitehall" and a simultaneous demonstration outside the British consulate in New York. Perhaps it could be "a kind of hunger march or Sacco-Vanzetti demonstration" that would carry banners reading "4,000,000 Jews were killed in Europe—open the doors of Palestine to the survivors" or "We want a home like any other nation." He added, "Please do not think me cynical if I say that if clashes with the police occurred, it would do no harm in view of the terrible harm which threatens us in Europe and Palestine. Ten Jewish injured in London hospitals appeal more to the imagination than one million dead in Poland."[11]

Koestler was again ahead of his time—it wasn't until the fifties that such marches and demonstrations became popular. Gollancz declined to follow up on the idea, but he did pass on Koestler's memo and letter, with the personal passages omitted, and Weizmann used it in making his speech. It was a great success with the MPs and seems to have contributed to the government's reluctant decision to join the Americans in appointing a commission of inquiry into the Palestinian situation. But Koestler's correspondence with Gollancz had attracted the attention of MI5. A Jewish informer told British intelligence in Jerusalem about Koestler's possession of confidential CID files and alleged that he was planning to write about them on his return to London "to discredit the British authorities here." Koestler did in fact discuss with Gollancz the idea of publishing a short political book on Palestine but dropped it to concentrate on his novel.[12]

MI5 didn't lose interest, however. Koestler's microfilms of the secret handbook mysteriously disappeared from the office of Bert Locker, the head of the Jewish Agency in London, to whom Gollancz had forwarded them, and were never found again. Recently declassified documents show that anguished memos and letters passed back and forth within the intelligence service on whether to prosecute Koestler or not or whether to try to blackmail him (and Gollancz) into not publishing, but the officials rightly concluded that pursuing Koestler would probably bring them more trouble than it was worth, since Koestler was bound to go public with it, so the matter was dropped. Neither Koestler nor Gollancz ever learned of it.[13]

THE COMMISSION OF INQUIRY went to Palestine and returned with ten recommendations, one of which backed Harry Truman's earlier call for the immediate issue of one hundred thousand certificates of admission into Palestine for "the victims of Nazi and fascist oppression." Dick Crossman, one of its members, had gone out convinced that Zionism was a "spiritual concentration camp" and that the idea of a Jewish national home was a "dead-end" but was "completely converted by the time of his return." Truman endorsed the recommendations, but Attlee sidestepped them, and Ernest Bevin crudely inquired of Crossman if he was circumcised, adding that the Americans favored Jewish immigration to Palestine because "they don't want too many Jews in New York." Crossman was incensed and concluded that Bevin had double-crossed the commission by setting it up and then ignoring its recommendations.

At the beginning of June, Crossman, Foot, and Koestler gathered at Crossman's country home to compose an angry pamphlet, "A Palestine Munich?" (Churchill's phrase), for publication by Gollancz at sixpence a copy and distribution at the forthcoming Labour Party annual conference, with Crossman and Foot named as authors. The bulk of the text was written by Koestler, who basically repeated his earlier arguments from *The Times* and accused the Labour Party of reneging on its promises. But even as he wrote, Koestler's prediction of violence and chaos was being fulfilled. British soldiers rounded up three thousand leading members of the Haganah and the Irgun (including von Weisl), and herded them into a concentration camp at Latrun. Von Weisl declared a hunger strike, and Noemi wrote to Koestler for help in gaining his release. "Black Saturday," as it came to be called, was a British riposte to Jewish sabotage of the colonial infrastructure, especially the destruction of eight road and railroad bridges linking Palestine to its neighbors, but it led in turn to one of the worst atrocities of the entire British Mandate, the blowing up of the King David Hotel in Jerusalem by the Irgun. Although it seems that both the Haganah and the Irgun had sanctioned the operation—and the Irgun had phoned in a warning to the British, which was apparently not acted upon—the hotel was not evacuated and the carnage was almost inconceivable at the time: ninety-one British and Arab dead, forty-six badly wounded.[14]

The attack caused outrage in Britain. The press unanimously condemned it as an act of despicable terrorism, and the Zionist cause was dealt a tremendous blow. Herbert Morrison, chairman of the British cabinet's Palestine Committee, came up with a scheme for a federation of Jews and Arabs, but the United States squashed it, insisting on partition instead. In August 1946, Crossman and his second wife, Zita, went to spend a week with Koestler and Mamaine in North Wales. The four got on famously, and Koestler took the opportunity to "educate" Crossman further on the Palestinian problem. Though he deplored the loss of life, he was not in the least deflected by the King David disaster from his sympathy for the Irgun. He gave Crossman the proofs of *Thieves in the Night* to read, and these influenced Crossman in the writing of his own book, *Palestine Mission,* about his experiences with the commission of inquiry.[15]

Crossman was followed to Wales by Teddy Kollek, who strongly favored partition and wanted to know how to keep up the pressure on the Labour government, despite the soured atmosphere. Koestler arranged for Kollek to meet with Harold Macmillan of the Conservative Party, and with Aneurin Bevan and other members of the left-wing *Tribune* group, including Crossman. Kollek hoped to influence cabinet discussion of the issue and drew about a hundred backbenchers to an informal meeting on Palestine. "I did start with an anecdote and I kept your general line," he wrote to Koestler, but then he had to answer a lot of tough questions. The MPs grilled him about the King David affair but in private surprised him with a different response. "People (Englishmen) react funnily. Most of them say 'smart work.' "[16]

IT WAS AN APPROPRIATE MOMENT for *Thieves in the Night* to appear. Faithful to his promise to stay close to his raw material, Koestler had incorporated a great deal of what he had seen and experienced during his recent visit to Palestine. Ein Hashofet and the planting of the new kibbutz went in, as did Kollek's kibbutz of Ein Gev and the hora, Abram Weinshall's court battles, von Weisl's military exploits, and the interviews with Friedman-Yellin and Begin. Koestler transposed parts of his youthful self into the figure of Joseph, the half-English, half-Jewish protagonist, whose progress through the novel ends with him reluctantly embracing terrorism, but he didn't intend Joseph's development to end there. He still thought of the novel as the first in a series, probably a trilogy, but felt that *Thieves in the Night* was sufficiently unified to publish first. Among other things, he fervently hoped it would influence the political debate.

Curiously enough, he had just offered a hostage to fortune in the form of an article for John Lehmann's symposium "The Future of Fiction" (published in *New Writing and Daylight*), in which he set out some of the ideas that had inspired him in writing his fourth novel. All fiction rested on archetypes, he wrote, but was bound to express the period in which it was written. He wishfully forecast a trend toward "three Rs: Realism, Relevance, Rhythm." Rhythm was shorthand for artistic economy, and relevance spoke for itself, but it was Koestler's definition of realism that said most about his own practice. Realism meant striving to approach the reality of the human condition with "an open mind and a disregard of convention" and taking in "new extensions of the visible range" of subject matter offered by psychology, the social sciences, the evolution of language. This required an ability to master new fields so completely that no residue of the study or the laboratory remained visible.

As an example of new fields to be mastered Koestler mentioned sex. In the Victorian novel there was "a gap in the spectrum" where sex should have appeared. Today some aspects of this subject were admitted to fiction, but they were far from covering "even the most recurrent unmentionable thoughts and emotions of real people." Even a courageous writer was still not able to handle this subject with grace and ease. He added, prophetically, that it would take another half century for the novel to digest the discoveries of Freud. No writer so far, not even Hemingway, had depicted "the most fundamental act of reality, procreation," with anything like conviction.[17]

What this meant for his own work emerged when *Thieves in the Night* appeared in the fall of 1946. Koestler had acted on his threat to leave Cape and had switched to the British branch of Macmillan, with Lovat Dickson as his new editor, and Dickson was worried by "the physiological honesty" of Koestler's sexual references. These, as Koestler had intended, were unusually frank for the time, and Koestler refused to alter them, even when Peters intervened on the side of Macmillan.

The particular scene Dickson had in mind describes the experience of the novel's hero, Joseph, the son of a Jewish father and English mother, when he is humiliated by the first woman he has ever slept with. She is much older than he, a neo-fascist, and recoils in horror from "the sign of the Holy Covenant on his body, the stigma of the race incised into his flesh," that is to say, his circumcised penis. "The incident," as it is somewhat ponderously labeled, is crucially important to the novel's plot, for it drives Joseph to rediscover his Jewish origins. He emigrates to Palestine, joins a kibbutz, and participates in the forcible planting of a new settlement close by. He also falls in love with a young German woman called Dina, who cannot return his love (physically, at any rate) because of the torture she has endured while trying to escape from occupied France.

Part two of the novel, presented in diary form, gives Joseph's account of the daily life of the kibbutz a year later. The reader is introduced to the main political players in Palestine: patronizing British bureaucrats, devious Arab leaders (notably a village elder called the Mukhtar), cautious Jewish Agency officials (personified by the upright kibbutz secretary, Reuben), and the disciplined activists of the Haganah. The two most interesting characters are the anti-fascist Viennese veteran, Bauman, loosely modeled on von Weisl, and Simeon, a bitter young intellectual (with a bit of Koestler and a lot of Friedman-Yellin in him) who preaches the Old Testament doctrine of an eye for an eye and a tooth for a tooth.

As the novel unfolds, the reader is familiarized with the three-way struggle among the British, the Arabs, and the Jews for control of Palestine. Bauman resigns from the Haganah and leaves the kibbutz to form an illegal militia (loosely based on the Stern Gang), soon to be followed by Simeon. Joseph vacillates until Dina is brutally raped and killed one night (allowing more frankness about sex and violence) after secretly visiting a cave containing the bones of "Joshua the Ancestor." Joseph asks Simeon for help, and a week later the Mukhtar is found dead in the same spot, with twenty-seven stab wounds (the same number as Dina) and a typewritten note in Arabic pinned to the body: "Vengeance has been taken and the shame done away with." After this, Joseph decides to join Bauman and is led to his secret headquarters, much as Koestler was led to see Friedman-Yellin and Begin, and the implication is that Joseph has joined the Jewish terrorist movement.

MACMILLAN KEPT ITS PROMISE to produce much larger British and American editions of the novel than Koestler was used to, and did an excellent job with advance publicity. When it appeared at the end of October 1946, after delays in Britain occasioned by the paper shortage, the novel got lead reviews in all the important newspapers and magazines, and within two weeks was on the best-seller list of *The New York Times*. Orwell, Connolly, Isaiah Berlin, Guy de Rothschild, and Harold Macmillan all praised it after reading advance copies, and Sperber wrote from Paris to say that it was the most suspenseful, most informative, and most important book about Palestine that had yet been written. Teddy Kollek, while rueful over the treatment of Zionist officials like himself, found it a "great joy to read," and Eric Mills, the head of the Palestinian Immigration Office in Jerusalem, agreed that Koestler had written a book "of penetrative insight," though his descriptions of British officials were "unfair." "I do not think that you will be loved for the book."[18]

As it turned out, the initial sex scene skewed much of the response to the novel, not because of its frankness but because it betrayed Koestler's ideal of realism. Koestler claimed that Joseph's dismissal by his lover was a true story, based on something that had happened to "somebody I knew" (most likely himself and most likely in Germany). But Peters put his finger on the problem in a funny note before publication to say that "no young lady, however versatile" would discover that Joseph was circumcised in the novel's circumstances "because an uncircumcised penis looks and feels exactly the same as a circumcised one when erect. It is true I have never compared the two; but I cannot believe that any penis could look barer and more skinless than mine (uncircumcised) when ready for action." Equally to the point, "I believe that more young Englishmen, of anything but the lowest class, are circumcised than uncircumcised."[19]

Koestler revised the scene to imply that the penis was no longer erect in the crucial scene but insisted on keeping the incident, although Peters was right: circumcision was common in Britain for hygienic reasons. Neither then nor later did anyone point to the real weakness of the scene—that in the age of the Holocaust, it was an extraordinarily feeble motivation for such a momentous change in Joseph's life (Koestler's insistence on sticking to the sexual slur suggests that it was indeed autobiographical in origin). A similar motivational weakness attends Joseph's embrace of terrorism. The rape and murder of Dina are acts with even more powerful sexual overtones, and although Joseph explicitly denies that her death is the cause of his conversion, its placement in the section of the novel called "Days of Wrath" contradicts that assertion.

The novel was called "impassioned and arresting" on publication, as well as "shocking, bitter, painful" and "sardonic, probing and introspective." Koestler was "the most brilliant of those modern writers who try to diagnose the ills of our society." His study of Jewish character fitted into a tradition running "from Shylock to Hyman Kaplan." He resembled Steinbeck and Dos Passos in his reforming zeal, and his book recalled crusading works such as Uncle Tom's Cabin and Ten Days That Shook the World. He was also compared with Malraux and Silone for having written "a masterpiece of propaganda" that was "full of the psychological insights which are the only things that make history intelligible and the writing of it a humanistic art."[20]

But there were some familiar problems as well: haste, a certain cheapness of phrasing, oversimplification. "He is master of the epigrammatic flash," wrote one critic, "the instant generalization which seems to point to a conclusion, even if, on afterthought, it is shown to have led nowhere." It was undoubtedly "an unforgettable document," said The New York Times, but was it a novel, "when narrative, characterization and plot are so nakedly sacrificed to argument?" Like Arrival and Departure, the novel failed to live up to the impossible standard Koestler had set for himself in Darkness at Noon, and also like its predecessor, its best parts (its evocation of life in Palestine, the establishment of the new kibbutz, the unusually sympathetic portrait of the Mukhtar and the Arab villagers, Joseph's progress toward terrorism) proved to be better than the whole. But its best parts are extremely good indeed, and Thieves in the Night remains Koestler's best novel after Darkness at Noon.[21]

Thieves not only fulfilled Koestler's promise to himself to write a "Jewish novel" but was also, among other things, his first sustained meditation on what it meant to him to be a Jew. There are flashes of Weininger's musings on Jewish self-hatred in the text, as when Joseph, with his "intelligent monkey face," is struck by the "ugliness of the faces around him as they were lit up in the intermittent ghastly flash of the searchlight." Here are the "thick, curved noses, fleshy lips and liquid eyes" of anti-Semitic propaganda, along with references to the "masks of archaic reptiles" and an "over-ripe race." Joseph takes consolation in the fact that Dina is different, but then "Dina only half-belonged to them like himself." This half-in, half-out stance suited Koestler's novelistic purposes rather well, but it also expressed his lifelong ambivalence about his origins. Shortly before the novel appeared, Dickson wrote to say that readers in the United States were asking Macmillan whether Koestler was a Jew or a Christian. Koestler replied that he was "half-Jewish by descent," which was not even a half-truth. Was he literally confusing himself with Joseph, or was it an example of wishful thinking? If the latter, the timing was distinctly odd, for it coincided with the period of his maximum identification with Palestine.[22]

The most controversial aspect of the novel, of course, was Koestler's conditional defense of terrorism, highlighted at the novel's climax by a Dostoyevskian dialogue between Joseph and Bauman that recalls Rubashov's dialogues with Ivanov in *Darkness at Noon* and Slavek's with Sonia Bolgar in *Arrival and Departure*. "You are a flabby Machiavelli," says Joseph in response to Bauman's arguments in favor of certain kinds of terrorism. "It is the logic of the Ice Age," replies Bauman. "We have to use violence and deception to save others from violence and deception." This is not much more than a variation on Soviet (and Stalinist) arguments, and it's extraordinary that Koestler couldn't see the parallel. When it came to Jewish affairs, he tended to lose his moral bearings, perhaps blinded by a sentimental loyalty to Jabotinsky and the Revisionist fervor of his youth.

In the novel, Koestler shows Joseph wrestling with his conscience but reluctantly agreeing with Bauman, even as a "wave of disgust" engulfs him. "He was too weary to argue about ends and means—for that was what the whole question boiled down to. This was no time for soul searching. Who was he to save his integrity while others had their bodies hacked to pieces? In the logic of the Ice Age, tolerance became a luxury and purity a vice. There was no way to escape the dilemma. To wash one's hands and let others do the dirty job was a hypocrisy, not a solution. To expose oneself was the only redeeming factor."[23]

Even before publication Connolly commented that the book's subtitle might have been "the making of a terrorist," and Orwell wrote tersely to Mamaine, "You know my views, or at any rate Arthur knows my views, about this terrorism business" (not writing to Koestler directly was a way of registering his disapproval). Crossman pointed to the obvious—that Bauman's "logic of the Ice Age" was a "justification for Communism, Fascism and every other philosophy" that chose Joseph's "easy way out." Did Koestler mean that states and world philosophies must reject totalitarianism but that a small people deprived of its state is justified in using terrorism in defense against an empire?[24]

Koestler stubbornly chose not to answer his critics in public or private until Daphne Hardy accused him of abandoning his earlier convictions. He had never said that the end could never justify violence, he replied; "you can look it up in the Yogi if you like." It was a question of proportion and circumstances. "If one accepted the total Yogi attitude, one would have to reject all revolutionary movements including the French, the Russian, all the maquis, etc." Whether they had done more harm than good was a purely utilitarian question. "On the whole I think that acts of sabotage with due preliminary warning, passive and active resistance against the prevention of immigration, and even retaliation for floggings may be historically justified, whereas indiscriminate assassinations cannot be justified either on ethical or utilitarian grounds."[25]

Readers of *The Gladiators, Darkness and Noon,* and *Arrival and Departure* might have been forgiven for agreeing that Koestler had reneged on his earlier convictions, but perhaps it was not so. George Orwell, for one, had noted that while Koestler was "generally assumed to have come down heavily on the side of the Yogi," he was "somewhat nearer to the Commissar's end" of the scale. In fact Koestler was trying to elaborate a different sort of principle, one that Crossman had fished for and missed in his *New Statesman* review and that came down in essence to a defense of the underdog. In the case of contemporary Palestine, both his socialism and his Zionism led him to a similar conclusion, namely that revolutionary movements per se were fine and even to be encouraged, if they enabled the oppressed to overcome injustice and secure their own place in the sun. In the service of opposing tyranny even violence was allowable, as he had suggested in *The Gladiators* with his "law of detours." The problem arose when violence became an end in itself, especially when it became the violence of the strong against the weak. This was the issue at the heart of both *The Gladiators* and *Darkness at Noon.*[26]

In Palestine, he was describing the violence of the underdog, "passive and active resistance" against an unjust colonial regime, and in that regard, and to that extent, he was prepared to accept it. What he was unwilling, or unable, to explain was how and when the defensive violence of the weak turned into the oppressive violence of the strong.

PART THREE

LOST ILLUSIONS

The Author as Activist
(1946–1959)

CHAPTER TWENTY-SIX

ADVENTURES AMONG THE EXISTENTIALISTS

*Man is nothing else but what he makes of himself. Such is the
first principle of existentialism.*

— JEAN-PAUL SARTRE

SHORTLY BEFORE *Thieves in the Night* was published, Koestler made plans
for a long-delayed visit to France. It had been six years since his desperate
flight in a legionnaire's uniform, and his immediate pretext was an invitation
from Jean Vilar to watch the rehearsals of *Twilight Bar* and attend the first
night. But his real reason for going was his newfound celebrity in France.
Darkness at Noon, translated as *Le Zéro et l'Infini* (Zero and Infinity), was enjoying an unheard-of success. Published by the venerable firm of Calmann-
Lévy, it had sold 7,000 copies in the first month alone. Lines formed outside
the publisher's office waiting for the books to come off the press, and second-
hand copies were changing hands at seven or eight times their original price.
By April 1945 it had sold 50,000 copies, by June 100,000 copies, and by the
time Koestler decided to make his trip in the fall of 1946, it had sold 300,000
copies. It went on to sell more than half a million copies in two years, a record
for a serious novel in France and Koestler's greatest publishing triumph anywhere.[1]

This unparalleled success was due in part to its timing. Humiliated by defeat in war and compromised by the German occupation, postwar France
was in a state of moral, political, and economic turmoil. De Gaulle had
headed the postwar provisional government (with Malraux as his minister
of information and Raymond Aron as Malraux's chief of staff, both friends of
Koestler's), but the Communists were the largest single party in the Con-
stituent Assembly and, with the support of the Socialist Party, had engi-

neered de Gaulle's ouster, hoping to take power themselves. Their wartime record as leaders of the Resistance had earned them broad popular support, and in their view, the nation most responsible for the overthrow of Hitler was not the United States but the Soviet Union. The Russians (fellow Europeans and "socialists") were the French people's natural allies in the face of Yankee imperialism.

In this context, Koestler's novel about the Soviet show trials and the logic of Communist ideology exploded with shattering force. As sales boomed, a copy of the novel was spotted on de Gaulle's night table, and the Communists were obliged to defend their Soviet sponsors. Rumors flew of a Communist delegation visiting Robert Calmann-Lévy to demand he cease publication, and of the party dispatching members to bookstores to buy up all the available copies and burn them; and it was said the French translator had removed his name from the title page for fear of being personally assaulted. None of these rumors was strictly true, but their sheer persistence (many are still current today) bore witness to the passions aroused by Koestler's opus.[2]

French enthusiasm for the novel also stood in sharp contrast to British indifference and represented a sort of poetic justice. Written in France at a time of extreme moral and political crisis, when war was about to break out, *Darkness at Noon* had appeared at a time of fresh crisis, when the conflicts at the core of the novel—free will versus predestination, ends versus means, morality versus ideology—were again the center of intense debate. Koestler's themes also chimed with the "existential ethics" being worked out by Sartre and Camus, and they echoed some of the ideas expressed in Malraux's 1937 novel, *Days of Hope,* about the Spanish Civil War. *Darkness at Noon* powerfully illustrated the existential loneliness of the individual facing the inexorable forces of history, and was imbued with a revolutionary philosophy that made it that much harder for Communists and their supporters to dismiss out of hand. It had a Bolshevik for a hero and by no means endorsed a reactionary message. On the contrary, Gletkin's incisive arguments in favor of the party were said to have prompted some young Frenchmen to join the party under the spell of Gletkin's (that is to say, Koestler's) logic.[3]

Ironically, the French Communists were at first taken unawares by the power and popularity of *Darkness at Noon*. Forced to acknowledge Koestler's "incontestable talent," they accused him of "bad faith" in dredging up the "old subject" of the Moscow trials. "Without the Moscow trials would France now be free? Would England be free?" Jews, including Calmann-Lévy, the book's publisher, owed the Russians a debt of gratitude for delivering the victims of Auschwitz from Hitler's clutches. Koestler was publicly denounced by Professor Joliot-Curie (his former ally in support of Weissberg) and was dismissed as a traitor to the party, a Trotskyist, and a petit bourgeois decadent. He was described in party literature as a "typically German writer who had always been considered German," a writer of potboilers addicted to sentimental kitsch, a producer of popular pap for housewives with no intellectual or political significance. But when a constitutional referendum was held in France in May 1946, the Communists were defeated 52 percent to 48 percent, and the noted novelist François Mauriac opined what many were thinking—that the most important factor in tipping the vote against the Communists had been the publication of *Darkness at Noon*.[4]

While all this unfolded Koestler was sitting at a safe distance in Wales, getting reports on the French situation from Sperber and other friends. Sperber informed Koestler about the sharp polarization of the French intellectuals and warned him against taking sides. Although the success of *Darkness at Noon* had "opened all doors to him," some (by this Sperber meant some right-wing doors) were not worth going through. It was important to remain politically neutral, and Sperber was upset that Koestler's article "Challenge to Russia: Lift the Iron Curtain" had been reprinted on the front page of the Gaullist newspaper *Carrefour* (Crossroads), on the eve of the referendum.[5]

Koestler couldn't exactly control his publications in France. He had sold syndication rights to his fellow Hungarian (and fellow Jew) Paul Winkler, the owner of the French news agency Opera Mundi, aware of Winkler's right-wing leanings. But two of his books, *Scum of the Earth* and *The Yogi and the Commissar,* had been acquired by a young left-wing publisher from Algiers (and friend of Camus's) named Edmond Charlot, and Koestler was perfectly happy with the connection. Unfortunately, Koestler was such a hot property that Charlot insisted on bringing out both books at once, whereas Koestler wanted them staggered. A former Hungarian friend was also capitalizing on Koestler's fame by bringing out an unauthorized translation of *The Gladiators* and was rushing to bring out *Twilight Bar* as well—this time with Koestler's permission. Koestler managed to persuade Calmann-Lévy to hold back the French editions of both *Arrival and Departure* and *Thieves in the Night,* but this was at the cost of not acquainting French readers with his latest work.[6]

KOESTLER STILL HAD to overcome French police objections that he was an "undesirable alien," but he was finally granted a visa in October 1946 and returned to Paris not as a hunted émigré but as a literary lion and conquering hero. Most of his first week was spent visiting old friends and attending rehearsals of *Twilight Bar* with Vilar and his crew. Vilar was full of enthusiasm for Koestler's play, calling it "a great satirical comedy" in the tradition of Aristophanes, in which he planned to take the star role of the journalist himself. But the rehearsals were a mess, there were cast changes at the last minute, some of the backers dropped out, and when the play opened in the tiny Compagnie du Théâtre on the Left Bank it was an even bigger disaster than in the USA. The Communist literary journal, *Les Lettres Françaises,* castigated it as "a pitiful burlesque, sinister, cynical and odious," and not even supporters could find much good to say of the play. Koestler watched the first night from his box in semidisguise, with his hat brim pulled low over his face and a pipe clenched between his teeth, and was forced to admit that the play was a mediocre relic of an earlier period in his life, which he should retire for the foreseeable future.[7]

One distinguished visitor who sat wrapped in his overcoat in the unheated auditorium was the elderly André Gide, who had read Koestler's works in English. "I have rarely read books that went more directly to my heart than his," he wrote in his journal. "I feel very close to him as I cannot put down anything he writes." He sent word that he would like to meet Koestler, but though such a meeting seemed logical (it had become routine to compare *Darkness at Noon* with Gide's *Return from the USSR*), Koestler declined. He had harshly criticized Gide's *Imaginary Interviews* in his essay "The French 'Flu" and felt it would be hypocritical to call on the eminent French writer under the circumstances. He was unaware that Gide had admitted the justness of Koestler's criticisms and still wanted to meet him.[8]

Koestler was of two minds about his reception in Paris. "The first three days were heaven," he wrote to Mamaine, "but then I got rather depressed. To be a lion is only fun for a very short time, or if one is younger, or if one's vanities are of a simpler nature. I got so utterly fed up with it that I cancelled a big press reception, refused all interviews, radio, etc., and shut myself completely off." The cancellation of the press conference was his riposte to a decision by Louis Aragon (whom Koestler had also criticized in "The French 'Flu"), the pro-Soviet chairman of the National Committee of Writers, to deny permission for the conference to be held at the committee's prestigious Maison de la Pensée Française. Aragon accused Koestler of "anti-Communist behavior" in Le Vernet before the war and expressed the view that Koestler should never have been issued a visa in the first place. In a fit of pique, Koestler canceled not only the press conference but all his scheduled public appearances and refused to go ahead with two radio programs. The only exception he made was for Maurice Nadeau of *Combat,* who found Koestler tense and strung out, making "precise nervous gestures" as he talked, and repeatedly brushing his hair back from his "mobile blue eyes."[9]

Koestler didn't carry his fame easily, and rejection by some former comrades in arms (some of whom were still Communists) hurt him more than he had anticipated. "My friends of the old 'scum' crowd," he wrote Mamaine, "are partly dead, and with those who are still here I can't recapture the old contact and warmth. I have so much looked forward to seeing Sperber, Németh and two or three others again—but it is all rather ghastly. They live in greater misery than ever and I have become an arriviste for them. That kills everything. I always comforted myself when feeling lonely that these people are there in the background to fall back upon, and now I feel more cut-off than ever."[10]

Koestler wasn't entirely blameless in this regard. Németh, penniless after surviving the war in Montauban, had had to borrow the fare to travel to Paris, but Koestler put off meeting him because he was "busy." Eventually they met at Koestler's hotel, which led to a "ghastly scene," the rich and fashionably dressed Koestler parrying his shabby and downtrodden friend's demands for a share of the royalties from *Twilight Bar,* of which he claimed to be co-author. If he didn't get some money, he said, he would have to return to Soviet-occupied Hungary. Koestler insisted the play in its latest form was almost all his own work and saw this as blackmail but arranged for Winkler to give Németh an advance against his next book, which Koestler would repay if Németh defaulted. The money was delivered to Németh's modest pension, and Koestler heard no more. Six months later, Németh returned to Hungary, leaving the book unfinished and Koestler to pay back the advance.[11]

With Sperber the power equation was reversed. Sperber was in a position of authority at the Ministry of Information and in charge of German translations for Calmann-Lévy. Graying, absentminded, and still charming, with a German accent in French to match Koestler's in English, Sperber was far more comfortable than Koestler with his Jewishness, his socialism, and himself. Koestler "poured out his soul" to Sperber about his problems with his friends, his depression, and his writer's block, hoping that the latter's training as a psychoanalyst would help him find a way out of his psychological impasse. But the "consultation" was a flop. Sperber didn't seem to understand what Koestler wanted from him, and Koestler was as furious as a jilted lover. He also turned his frustration on himself. He was a hopeless manic-depressive, he concluded, and his condition was incurable.[12]

Koestler also had two tense meetings with Dorothee, first alone and later with her partner, Hans Müller. Dorothee was grateful to Koestler for putting her in touch with Guy de Rothschild and helping her find a job, but she was pale and drawn from the aftereffects of a bout of food poisoning and was scared of being deported to Germany. They discussed their divorce. Dorothee's lack of French citizenship prevented her from pursuing it and also from taking up Koestler's offer to pay for a trip to England to see her mother and get medical treatment. Koestler gave her fifty thousand francs toward living expenses and promised to stay in touch.[13]

Fleeing Paris in 1940, Koestler had left behind an apartment, furniture, automobile, clothes, books, papers, and files (including the original manuscript of *Darkness at Noon*). Some of his papers and files had been confiscated by the French police and since then, unbeknownst to him, spirited to Berlin by the Gestapo and later to Moscow by the NKVD. They now nestled in, of all places, the NKVD archives in Moscow. Other files and manuscripts had been dropped off in suitcases in Limoges and Périgueux on his way south, and Koestler was hopeful of getting some of these back. Guy de Rothschild had tried with only limited success (even harboring Koestler's rusting convertible for a while), but at his old apartment in the rue Dombasle, Koestler was astonished to find some manuscripts still in his desk, including a small part of *Darkness at Noon* in German, and a bust of himself done by Gerda Grepp. He gave what furniture was left to the hard-up Sperbers and incorporated the fragments into the German translation of his novel.[14]

KOESTLER WAS REASONABLY SURE that most of his literary and political allies in France were to be found among that small group of writers known as existentialists. He considered Sartre's short story "The Wall" to be "the profoundest thing ever written" on the Spanish Civil War, and was aware that Sartre had coined the term *existentialism* to describe a philosophy of the cosmic loneliness and freedom of the individual that obligated him, in a cold and unfeeling world, to shoulder his ethical responsibilities and commit to some form of political activism. Sartre in turn had been influenced by Koestler's *Dialogue with Death;* and André Gide had noted of *Scum of the Earth* that it was "the best possible illustration of Sartrism—if not of existentialism proper." Sartre was its acknowledged prophet, and his recently published novel, *The Age of Reason,* one of existentialism's bibles. Another prophet was Albert Camus, whose "absurdist" works, *The Stranger* and *The Myth of Sisyphus,* were obligatory reading for French intellectuals of the period; and the third, decidedly junior, musketeer of existentialism was Sartre's lifelong partner, Simone de Beauvoir, nicknamed "Castor," or "the Beaver," whose novel *The Blood of Others,* along with her essays, had helped to popularize the new philosophy among the young.

After waiting in vain for their joint publisher, Charlot, to introduce them, Koestler met Camus by the simple expedient of walking into his office at Gallimard and introducing himself. "Humphrey Bogart young" was how one Left Bank journalist had described Camus, and Koestler compared him to "a young Apollo." Camus was "slim and sinewy, with a shock of light brown hair, an easy smile, and a dark complexion derived from his North African heritage," who "still looked like the athletic young soccer player of his youth." Friendship between the two men was instant. Actually, both were in the Bogart mold: short, compact, and muscular, affecting a cool manner to disguise a smoldering temper, with an eternal cigarette dangling from the lower lip. "With Camus," Koestler later wrote, "an easy camaraderie developed from our very first meeting. We tutoyed each other, and shared much the same tastes in wining, dining and running after women." Of all the Left Bank writers, Camus was the closest to Koestler in temperament and outlook. Koestler later described their relationship as "more intimate than deep;

we were, in fact, *copains*—chums rather than friends," but it seems to have gone further than that. Still, it wasn't long before the two men were drinking together at the Café de Flore and ogling the young flirts patrolling St.-Germain-des-Prés.[15]

Koestler met Sartre and Beauvoir in much the same way. The famous couple had recently transferred their literary headquarters from the Café de Flore to the basement of the Hôtel Pont-Royal, next to where Koestler was staying. Koestler went around the day after meeting Camus, walked up to Sartre, and said with boyish simplicity: "Hello, I'm Koestler." Sartre, even shorter than Koestler, with his stumpy limbs, long torso, and famously disconcerting squint, put Koestler in mind of "a malevolent goblin." But as with Camus, the rapport between the two men was instant, and Koestler approved the way the Beaver's close-fitting French dress hugged her figure, the thrust of her high, prominent cheekbones, and the long chestnut hair coiled in a bun on her head. The famous couple acknowledged in the author of *Darkness at Noon* a fellow thinker. Beauvoir had recently stayed up all night to read *Darkness at Noon* and had found it "enthralling."[16]

Mamaine arrived from England and found Koestler's hotel suite in "indescribable chaos," with "secretaries, publishers, producers" trooping in and out and people telephoning all the time. It seemed "impossible either to sleep or get dressed," but the chaos abated by the weekend, and on Sunday they went for drinks at the Café de Flore with an improbable assortment of friends: Sartre and Beauvoir; Sylvester Gates, the banker and diplomat, and his wife, Pauline Gates, from the British embassy; the American writer Harold ("Kappy") Kaplan; Teddy Kollek and his wife, in Paris to see David Ben-Gurion; and Leo Valiani, Koestler's old comrade from Le Vernet. Drinks were followed by lunch (which lasted until four thirty), and dinner was at six o'clock in the Sperbers' apartment, with "filthy food," according to Mamaine, no drink, and a polyglot conversation in French, German, and English that gave her indigestion.

At ten thirty that night they met Sartre and Beauvoir at Sartre's mother's apartment in the rue Bonaparte (Sartre still lived with his mother, despite his long-standing relationship with the Beaver). This time both the drink and the conversation flowed easily. Sartre, according to Mamaine, was "charming" and expounded at great length on his theory of existentialism, which she found difficult to understand. Early on in the conversation, according to Beauvoir, Koestler, "in a peremptory tone softened by an almost feminine smile," told Sartre, "You are a better novelist than I am, but not such a good philosopher," and launched into a summary of the ideas he was developing for a scientific book that would become *Insight and Outlook*. His goal, he said, was to "assure man a margin of freedom without departing from psychological materialism," and he explained to Sartre and Beauvoir that "systems governed by the cerebellum, the thalamus and the lower brain overlapped but did not rigidly control each other; between the lower and the upper parts there must be room for a 'bubble' of liberty."

Beauvoir felt that Koestler was "certainly a better novelist than he was a philosopher" and was highly amused by his pronunciation of "thalam*oo*se." Fluent in French, Koestler nonetheless spoke it with the same guttural accent that colored his English. As Camus said, "Koestler doesn't *speak* French, he massacres it." Beauvoir later claimed to be embarrassed by Koestler's "doctrinaire self-assurance" and "self-taught pedantry," saying that success had made him vain and gone to his head. But she had registered the approval of his deep blue eyes and showed no hostility at the time. On the contrary, she warmed to his passionate and voracious curiosity and found him a fascinating talker. Koestler came away feeling satisfied that he had made a dent in Sartre's arguments. Sartre "agrees that moral question the decisive one," he wrote in his diary, and is "prepared to drop *néant* [nothingness] side" (a reference to Sartre's celebrated treatise *Being and Nothingness*). "Seems to be moving away from USSR." The entry was another product of Koestler's wishful thinking.[17]

Koestler and Mamaine spent many hours arguing with their new French friends about literature and politics. On October 23 they missed a performance of Sartre's play *No Exit* after Willi Münzenberg's old secretary, Hans Schulz, turned up at Koestler's hotel and passed out blind drunk on the floor. Koestler "angelically coped" with his old comrade in arms until about ten o'clock, when they went next door to the Pont-Royal to scavenge something to eat. Mamaine returned to the hotel alone, leaving Koestler in the bar with Beauvoir, Sartre, and the playwright Jean Genet. Koestler, according to Mamaine, "got drunk" and didn't return "from Sartre's" until eight the next morning.

Soon after this Mamaine took to her bed in exhaustion, and Koestler brought Sartre and Beauvoir to her bedside for a dinner of lobster and ham salad and cheese, then embarked with them on a marathon pub crawl in Montparnasse. This was capped on October 31, the day before Koestler was due to leave Paris, by a spectacular bacchanal involving himself and Mamaine, Sartre and Beauvoir, and Camus and his wife, Francine. They started the evening at an Algerian bistro recommended by Camus, then moved to a small dance hall in the rue des Gravilliers, lit with pink and blue neon lights, where men with hats on danced with girls in short skirts. "Here for the first time in my life," wrote Mamaine to "Dearest Twinnie" in London, "I danced with K, and also saw the engaging spectacle of him lugging the Castor (who has I think hardly ever danced in her life) round the floor while Sartre (who ditto) lugged Mme Camus."

Koestler then issued an "imperious" (the word is Beauvoir's) invitation to the others to go with him to Schéhérazade, which after much protesting they agreed to do. The club was plunged into almost total darkness, with violinists wandering about playing soulful Russian music into the guests' ears. But the writers talked politics and literature as usual. "If only it were possible to tell the truth," exclaimed Camus at one point. Koestler grew gloomy as he listened to the sentimental Russian folk song "Dark Eyes," and accused Sartre and even Camus of wanting to compromise with the Soviet Union. "It's impossible to be friends if we differ about politics," he said. Camus contradicted him. "What we have in common, you and I, is that for us individuals come first, we place friendship above politics." Beauvoir agreed. "We are the proof of it at this very moment," she said, "since, despite all our dissensions, we are so happy to be together."

Sartre, according to Mamaine, "got very drunk almost at once, Beauvoir also got drunk and wept a great deal, and K got drunk too (we drank vodka and champagne, both in large quantities)." Francine Camus, who was "extremely beautiful and nice" according to Mamaine, also got tight, adding, "Camus and I did not get drunk, though we nearly did." Mamaine omitted to mention that she and Camus also danced cheek to cheek, and exchanged furtive kisses while the others remained behind at their table.

After prying Koestler from Schéhérazade at about four a.m., they repaired to Chez Victor in Les Halles for onion soup, oysters, and white wine. Sartre, according to Mamaine, was now roaring drunk and "kept pouring pepper and salt into paper napkins, folding them up small and stuffing them into his pocket." Koestler, resentful at having been made to leave the nightclub, threw a crust of bread across the table, hit Mamaine in the eye, and was filled with remorse as it turned bright blue and purple. Sartre kept giggling that he was due to give a UNESCO lecture at the Sorbonne that day on "The Responsibility of the Writer" and hadn't prepared a line. Camus said: "*Alors, tu parleras sans moi* [Well, you'll have to speak without me]." Sartre responded: "*Je voudrais bien pouvoir parler sans moi* [I wish I could speak without me too]" and subsided into giggles.

They broke up at dawn. Alone with Sartre, Beauvoir sobbed "over the tragedy of the human condition," then leaned on the parapet of a bridge over the Seine and said: "I don't see why we don't throw ourselves in the river." "All right," agreed Sartre, "let's throw ourselves in," and began to cry himself. In another part of the city, Koestler too burst into tears as he stared into the Seine. Then he disappeared into a *pissoir* and shouted to Mamaine, "Don't leave me, I love you, I'll always love you." They got home at about eight o'clock and slept all day, except for Sartre, who stuffed himself with pep pills and dragged himself off to the Sorbonne to give his lecture. It wasn't possible for even an existentialist to address the students *"sans moi."*[18]

BEAUVOIR AT THIS TIME found Koestler "vain and full of self-importance" but also "full of warmth, life and curiosity; the passion with which he argued was unflagging; he was always ready, at any hour of the day or night, to talk about any subject under the sun. He was generous with his time, with himself, and also with his money; he had no taste for ostentation, but when one went out with him he always wanted to pay for everything and never counted the cost." On the other hand, Koestler was also "touchy, tormented, greedy for human warmth, but cut off from others by his personal obsessions." Beauvoir quotes him as saying, "I have my furies," which made relations with him complicated and unpredictable. Later, after Beauvoir had fallen out with Koestler, she attacked him in the third volume of her autobiography, *Force of Circumstance,* and disparaged him in dismissive remarks to her American biographer, Deirdre Bair.[19]

She also expressed her hostility in her underrated roman à clef, *The Mandarins,* where she paints a portrait of Koestler that is undoubtedly colored by her later dislike but is also more nuanced than critics have allowed. Koestler appears in the novel as the Russian novelist Victor Scriassine (not a pleasant-sounding name to the French ear), who has a "triangular face," "prominent cheekbones," "hard fiery eyes," and a "thin, almost feminine mouth," belying his heavily masculine manner. He is bombastic and pedantic, morbidly self-absorbed, and gloomily pessimistic about the way he thinks the world is going ("there wasn't a place on earth where he felt really at home"), yet his passion is so all-devouring, his intelligence so blazing, that he is capable of sweeping others off their feet with the sheer intensity of his personality.

Beauvoir herself was certainly swept off hers, at least on the night Mamaine left Koestler in the Pont-Royal bar with Beauvoir, Sartre, and Genet. Mamaine thought that Koestler had returned the next morning "from Sartre's," but he was returning from a night with Beauvoir. Beauvoir told Deirdre Bair that Koestler had kept "pushing and pushing" her until she said yes to shut him up. "It wasn't any good. It didn't mean anything. He was too drunk, so was I. It never happened again. Only that night was real, the rest is how I loathed him. I really detested him, that arrogant fool."[20]

But in *The Mandarins* Beauvoir tells a different story, capturing both sides of Koestler-Scriassine: the sophisticated, world-weary seducer with a streak of cruelty in his makeup and the agonized adolescent dreamer morphing into the mischievous naughty boy. On the big night he kisses her hand and peppers her with questions. He tells her to stop talking about politics— "I hate talking politics with a woman"—but later concedes, "You're not so dumb. Generally I dislike intelligent women, maybe because they're not intelligent enough." Soon enough he propositions her, but without a hint of flattery. "I hate a lot of beating around the bush. Paying court to a woman is degrading for both oneself and for the woman." She accepts his suggestion, and they head back to her apartment.

Beauvoir's description of their night together reads like a documentary transcription from real life. In the bedroom scene, "Anne" wants to go slowly

Koestler Archive, MS2455/1/12

Henrik and Adele Koestler in a studio photograph taken in the early years after their marriage in 1900.

Phil Casoar

The facade of the Baroque apartment building at 16 Sviv Street, Budapest, where Arthur spent the first six years of his life, before moving next door to number 18 for another four years.

Koestler Archive, MS2455/1/13

Henrik in his prime as a successful textile importer. "He was a short man with quick movements charged with energy; his brown naïve eyes and his dark hair parted in the middle gave his face a kind of neat and tidy look that made people mistake him for an American."

Koestler Archive, MS2455/1/24

Laura Striker with her progressive kindergarten class in 1909. The three-year-old Arthur is kneeling on a chair with his back to the camera. Laura's daughter, Eva (later Eva Zeisel), is directly opposite Arthur, to her mother's left.

Arthur at age thirteen. "Henrik and Adele loved to dress him up in fancy items that Henrik obtained through his textile business and once sent him to school in an English Eton suit, an exceedingly rare outfit in Budapest."

Koestler Archive, MS2455/2/15

Koestler Archive, MS2455/1/30

Arthur, age seventeen, with classmates and teachers at his boarding school in Baden-bei-Wien. Arthur, at center in middle row, was teased for being the second shortest in his class.

Arthur at the age of twenty, in his last year as a student in Vienna and soon after finishing his term as president of the Zionist fraternity Unitas.

Koestler Archive, MS2455/2/27

Ullsteinbild/Granger Collection

Wolfgang von Weisl, Arthur's Zionist mentor and patron, in fur coat, with Ahmed Fath aboard the *Graf Zeppelin* airship on its flight to Palestine in 1929.

Koestler Archive, MS2456/1/119

Vladimir Jabotinsky, leader of the Zionist Revisionist party. Jabotinsky was the hero Arthur had been waiting for: poet, soldier, orator, statesman, a Jewish leader who didn't seem Jewish at all.

Hephzibah Archive

The dining hall at the Hephzibah settlement in Palestine in about 1926. "Arthur joined the *kvutsa* members at their trestle tables in the communal dining hall. Most were still under thirty, but they looked twice their age, exhausted by physical labor."

Koestler in Jerusalem in 1928, while working as a foreign correspondent for the Ullstein newspaper *Vossische Zeitung*.

Koestler Archive, MS2455/2/33

Eva Striker at about the time
she and Koestler became lovers
in Paris, in 1929.

Eva Zeisel Archive

Koestler aboard the
Graf Zeppelin on its historic flight to the North
Pole, 1931. His dis-
patches on the trip
made him a celebrity in
Germany for a while.

Ullsteinbild/ Granger Collection

Austrian Literary Archives of the Austrian National Library, Vienna, Photo Collection Manès Sperber, OLA 317/07

Manès Sperber, Jewish writer, communist, and close friend of Koestler's, shortly before they met in Berlin in 1931.

Koestler and Langston Hughes with unidentified man in Kazakhstan during Koestler's 1932 visit to Soviet Central Asia.

Beinecke Library, Yale University

Eva Zeisel Archive

Eva Striker and Alexander Weissberg in Kharkov in 1933, at the time Koestler stayed with them. Both were later arrested by the Soviet secret police, and some of Eva's experiences were incorporated into *Darkness at Noon*.

Koestler Archive, MS2456/1/120

Willi Münzenberg, former head of a communist media empire in Berlin and a leading antifascist, for whom Koestler worked in Paris on and off from 1933 to 1939.

Archives of the Préfecture de Police, Paris, Fund GA K4

Dorothee Ascher in the mid-1930s, about the time Koestler met and married her. "She was then a girl of twenty-five, with dark tousled hair and a pleasant oval face with a shy and earnest expression."

John Hillelson Agency

Koestler immediately after his capture by Franco's forces in Málaga, Spain, in February 1937. The photograph is by Joaquin Vazquez Torres, the officer who tied Koestler's wrists.

Koestler Archive, MS2455/2/49

Koestler arriving by steamer in Southampton, England, after an international campaign for his release from Seville prison in May 1937. He went on a lecture tour in Britain upon his return.

Koestler Archive, MS2455/1/85

"In the summer of 1939 he was powerfully attracted to a twenty-two-year-old English sculptor by the name of Daphne Hardy." Daphne became the translator of *Darkness at Noon* into English and was Koestler's companion from 1939 to 1944.

Koestler Archive, MS2455/2/93

Private Koestler in the uniform of the Aliens' Pioneer Corps soon after his enlistment in 1941.

Estate Gisèle Freund/IMEC-Images

Koestler in hiding in Adrienne Monnier's apartment in Paris in May 1940, on the eve of the German invasion and just before his flight south with the French Foreign Legion.

Mamaine Paget with Nellie, one of the Welsh collies that she and Koestler acquired when they moved in together at Bwlch Ocyn in 1945.

Ariane Bankes

Ariane Bankes

Celia Paget (later Goodman), Mamaine's twin sister and confidante, to whom George Orwell proposed in 1945.

Ariane Bankes

Koestler with his boxer, Sabby, in his jeep in Tel Aviv during Israel's 1948 war for independence.

Ariane Bankes

Koestler (at right) with Dick and Zita Crossman at Koestler's house, Verte Rive, on the Seine just south of Paris, 1949.

Süddeutsche Zeitung Photo

Koestler giving the keynote speech at the opening session of the Congress for Cultural Freedom in Berlin, June 1950. Sitting in front of him from right to left are Sidney Hook, Professor Weber, Jules Romain, Ernst Reuter (then mayor of Berlin) and Haakon Lie.

Dmitri Kessel, Time-Life Pictures

Koestler dictating a letter to Cynthia Jefferies, his South African–born secretary, who started to work for him in 1949.

Dmitri Kessel, Time-Life Pictures

Janine Graetz, wife of the film producer Paul Graetz. In 1955 Janine gave birth to Koestler's child, Cristina Isabel. This picture dates from 1963, when Janine married Fulke Greville, the seventh Earl of Warwick.

Erich Hartman, Magnum

Koestler in New York City, 1955.

Wolfgang Pfaundler

The Austrian painter Eva Auer, whom Koestler met in Alpbach in 1957. "Oh, Österreich, oh, Eva!" he wrote in his diary after their first meeting.

Koestler Archive, MS2456/2/26

Koestler's *Schreiberhäusl,* the house he had specially built for him in Alpbach in the Austrian Tyrol.

Koestler and Cynthia with guests on their canal barge, *Socrates*, entering a lock on the Thames. Cynthia is second from the right.

Koestler Archive, MS2455/4/62

Frank Herrman, Koestler Archive, MS2457/52/1

Koestler being interviewed by Cyril Connolly to celebrate Koestler's sixtieth birthday.

Koestler with
Babette Gross in
the late 1960s.

Peter Gross collection

Koestler Archive, MS2456/2/190

Cynthia in the early
1970s with her beloved
Newfoundland, Goliath,
whom she liked to take to
dog shows.

Peters, Fraser and Dunlop

Koestler's seventieth birthday celebration, 1975. From left to right: Charles Clark and Harold Harris (both of Hutchinson), Jill Craigie, Koestler, Cynthia, Michael Foot, and unknown man.

The British Library Board, Fay Godwin Collection

Two years before his death Koestler still played an aggressive game of chess, and afterward sat in the sunshine "with Mozart on the radio and a bottle of Moselle . . . looking rather like a wise squaw" (Julian Barnes).

The British Library Board, Fay Godwin Collection

Koestler, Cynthia, and their dog, David, in the sitting room at Montpelier Square, where they committed suicide a few months later.

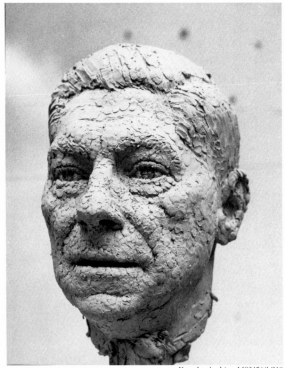

Koestler Archive, MS2456/1/219

Daphne Henrion's bust of Koestler in the National Portrait Gallery, London. Another copy is in the Psychology Department at Edinburgh University.

but finds a "discouraging hostility" in Scriassine's eyes. "You're not really cold," he says angrily. "You're resisting with your head. But I'll force you." His expression takes on a look of hate, he calls her a "stubborn mule" and strikes her "lightly on the chin." When she begins to weep, he is suddenly transformed. He kisses her eyes, and "a conquering tenderness," a "childlike tenderness," appears in his face. "I had pity as much for him as for myself. Both of us were equally lost, equally disillusioned." When she asks him, "Why do you hate me?" he replies regretfully, "It has to be, it just has to be," and when it is over and he wakes from a sudden sleep, he clutches at her in panic. "I was having a nightmare."[21]

In the novel Beauvoir also discusses their political differences, which came to a head with fine clarity at a meeting Koestler organized, with himself, Sperber, Sartre, Beauvoir, Camus, and a fourth writer of the French independent left, André Malraux, before leaving Paris. Malraux was one of Koestler's heroes, a figure in whom the writer, the political activist, and the man of action formed a seamless whole. He was the very embodiment of the independent, committed writer, with close ties to both the literary and political worlds. Malraux had told Koestler over a "long, explosive, intensive dinner" that he knew he was using his reputation as a man of the left to help the reactionaries around de Gaulle and that if his faith in the general turned out to be misplaced, he would put a bullet in his brain. Mamaine, recording these words, felt that Malraux was a man of "extraordinary honesty and courage (his vanity is quite extraordinary too)," and she was present again when they had dinner at Malraux's "enormous and flashy flat" in the suburb of Boulogne-sur-Seine. Mamaine thought Malraux "not in the least attractive" physically, with protruding eyes and a habit of talking nonstop "to the accompaniment of curious sounds at the back of his nose and throat," but Koestler was "rather in love" with Malraux, and Mamaine enjoyed the "fascinating spectacle" of the two of them together, "K unusually humble and hardly able to get a word in edgeways," Malraux eager to impress Koestler and show off his political insights.[22]

Four days later, Koestler "led a delegation" to Malraux's for a meeting to discuss his and Orwell's idea of a new League for Human Rights. Hoping to use his presence in Paris as a catalyst, Koestler proposed launching the new organization with an anthology of essays written by the authors present. He set out the "four fallacies" that usually got in the way of such initiatives: fear of ending up with the wrong allies, fear of playing into the hands of political opponents, putting ends before means, and having a false allegiance to the past. According to Camus, Koestler referred to an interview he had just given in which he was asked if he hated Russia. "I said that I hated the Stalinist regime as much as I had hated the Hitler regime, and for the same reasons. But something snapped inside when I said it." Koestler also spoke about his imprisonment in Spain and said that although he had lied for "them," he now felt like the man in the neighboring cell who had looked at him with his face covered in blood and said, "There's no hope left, no hope left."

Sperber read out a draft of the project. Malraux haughtily questioned Sperber's use of the word *proletariat*. "What is it?" he asked skeptically. "Can we say that it represents the highest historical value?" Sartre was openly hostile to the plan. The proletariat's best champion was the French Communist Party, he said, and the project was anti-Soviet. "It's true that the deportation of millions of people is worse than the lynching of a negro. But the lynching is the result of a situation that has lasted for over a hundred years, and in the last analysis represents the misery of as many millions of negroes over time as there are deported Circassians."

Camus, sitting "between Piero della Francesca and Dubuffet," took a humbler line. "Don't you think that we are all responsible for the absence of values? And that if all those of us who come out of Nietzscheanism, nihilism, or historical realism were to admit publicly that we were wrong, and that there is such a thing as moral values, and that despite our mistakes we will do all in our power to establish and illustrate them, don't you think that this would establish the beginning of hope?" He was in favor of the scheme, and Koestler warmed to him on that account, but without Malraux or Sartre there was no hope of getting it off the ground. Koestler felt that Malraux had "sabotaged the anthology" but had done it in a friendly way. Sartre's dialectics, on the other hand, were "talmudic" and deliberately obstructive. As writers, declared Koestler, they were betraying history if they didn't denounce what needed to be denounced. "The conspiracy of silence condemns us in the eyes of all who will come after us."[23]

The meeting was an excellent example of Koestler's theory of the writer's role in action and of the limitations of that theory. It was predicated almost wholly on the writer's capacity for collective political action and took little account either of a writer's individuality and unique vision or of the importance and value of a subjective view of the world, not to speak of a writer's relationship to language. Although an ethical imperative underlay Koestler's theory and actions, it seemed to matter little to him unless it issued in action, and he felt he had failed in France for the same reasons he had failed in Britain. But his interpretation of the reasons for that failure was melodramatic and grandiose, and Mamaine offered a useful corrective in a letter to Edmund Wilson. "K started a sort of marriage bureau for the 'atomised' *hommes de bonne volonté* [men of goodwill] of the left," she wrote, "but of course it's hopeless. For one thing, they haven't at all got over what the others did, or didn't do, during the last occupation; and for another, they are obsessed by whether they will be able to trust each other in the next occupation." By this Mamaine meant occupation by the Russians.[24]

CHAPTER TWENTY-SEVEN

FRENCH LESSONS

Political thought in France is either utopian or nostalgic.
— RAYMOND ARON

ON HIS RETURN TO BRITAIN, Koestler fired off an exasperated article to *The New York Times Magazine,* denouncing the French Communist Party as a Trojan horse that "openly confesses its loyalty and allegiance to a foreign power whose interests and traditions are alien to the interests and traditions of France." His alarmist scenario was reprinted by the Gaullist *Carrefour* in France, leading to more recriminations from Sperber and a frontal assault by the Communist-dominated press. "Judas Koestler's Intolerable Insults to France and Its Courageous People," ran one headline. Draping themselves in the colors of patriotism and nationalism, the Communists accused Koestler of being "in the pay of foreign secret services," and they were further incensed when *The Yogi and the Commissar* and *Scum of the Earth* appeared in France at the end of 1946. Koestler's jocular essay on "The French 'Flu" now took on the aspect of a deliberate slander—no matter that two of his literary targets in that essay, Gide and Vercors, were not in the least offended. Unfortunately the third, Aragon, had good reason to be, since Koestler had distorted his war record and misrepresented his role in the Resistance.[1]

Scum of the Earth, set during the "phony war" of 1940, seemed like an even greater insult, for it showed prewar France at its chaotic, collaborationist worst and reminded Communists that they had supported the Soviet pact with Hitler before war broke out. Its reception was further complicated by a botched translation, obliging Koestler to insist on an extensive errors slip being included—which reached all too few readers. Fortunately, the publication of the political essays in *Yogi* gave rise to a more sophisticated debate. In *Esprit*, Bertrand d'Astorg suggested that Koestler's real subject was the mentality of the revolutionary and the psychology of power. Koestler's "brilliant and stirring" arguments had a double goal: to reestablish the importance of the subjective factor in history, and to study what transmutations were responsible for bringing men of power to the point where their fundamental psychology was irrevocably changed. Koestler, he predicted, would win the Nobel Prize in about 1960. Thierry Maulnier, meanwhile, descried a philosophy of "Koestlerism," which accepted the basic goals of Marxism but rejected the terrible and implacable means by which Marxism sought to lead a militant proletariat to power. It represented the old philosophical debate between idealism and materialism transposed to the political plane: Should man be a subject and an end, or should he be an object and an instrument? For Koestler, the former obviously took priority.[2]

The weightiest riposte to Koestler appeared in Sartre's *Les Temps Modernes*. In a widely read article, "Le Yogi et le prolétaire" (The Yogi and the Proletarian), the Marxist philosopher Maurice Merleau-Ponty wrote that World War II had proven "beyond doubt" that the world could no longer live on the basis of capitalism. The future lay with economic collectivism, and when it came to the use of violence, there was little to choose between capitalism and communism. The important difference was that the goal of the Communists was to end the exploitation of man by man, whereas when the capitalists claimed they were defending "liberty and civilization," they meant liberty for some but not others.[3]

Merleau-Ponty published four further articles attacking Koestler, which were collected and published in book form as *Humanism and Terror*. "In the small universe of existentialist and Communist writers," wrote Simone de Beauvoir, "it unleashed a great tornado." To the democratic socialist Raymond Aron, however, Merleau-Ponty's arguments were "puerile" and immoral, while Camus sided with Koestler's: "The end justifies the means," he jotted in his notebook, "only if the relative order of importance is reasonable. I can send Saint-Exupéry on a fatal mission to save a regiment. But I cannot deport millions of persons and suppress all liberty . . . for three or four generations previously sacrificed." Camus wrote his own series of articles in *Combat* under the collective title of *Neither Victims nor Executioners,* in which he argued for a reformist leftism that was categorically hostile to all forms of Marxism, including the one practiced by Sartre and Merleau-Ponty. These and Merleau-Ponty's articles set the stage for an ideological confrontation that would split the existentialists down the middle.[4]

The symbolic expression of this split occurred not long after the appearance of Merleau-Ponty's first article, at a party thrown by the writer and jazz musician Boris Vian, where Sartre, Beauvoir, Jacques-Laurent Bost, and Merleau-Ponty were among the guests and to which Camus arrived late.

Camus, according to Beauvoir, violently attacked Merleau-Ponty for justifying the Moscow trials. "Merleau-Ponty defended himself, Sartre supported him; Camus, shattered, left, slamming the door behind him; Sartre and Bost rushed out and ran after him along the street, but he refused to come back." It was to be several weeks before Sartre and Camus spoke to each other again, but by that time Camus had decided he was through with "Left Bank revolutionaries," and the ideological rift between them was almost complete.[5]

ENTWINED WITH THESE POLITICAL and philosophical differences, as in the Bertrand Russell imbroglio in Wales, were some interesting personal dynamics. Sonia Brownell had come to Paris for an extended visit that summer and with her blonde good looks and vivacious manner had turned the heads of many of the existentialists clustered around *Les Temps Modernes,* none more than that of Merleau-Ponty. They began an affair, and Sonia told him of a brief wartime fling with Koestler that had resulted in an abortion. Koestler was "a sadist," she said, and Merleau-Ponty, who regarded Koestler as a pedantic boor with "no wit, no warmth, no grace, no sense of irony or humor," was pleased to have this further reason to damn his opponent.

Camus, too, had tangled reasons for taking Koestler's side. When he arrived at the Vian party, he was, according to Beauvoir, already "in a bad temper," having just got back from a trip to the Midi, where he had "spent a few days with a charming woman who has since died." Beauvoir, be it noted, had her own problems with Camus, having offered to sleep with him and been rejected. "Imagine what she would be saying on the pillow afterward," he joked to Koestler. "Such a chatterbox, a total bluestocking, unbearable." But on this occasion she was on the mark. The woman with whom Camus had just spent a few days was Mamaine. After an idyllic week he was totally infatuated—and depressed by their sudden separation.[6]

The affair had begun that memorable night at the Schéhérazade, when he and Mamaine had danced cheek to cheek and kissed while the others drank and argued. Camus told her he was strongly attracted to her but respected Koestler too much to act. Mamaine, equally attracted, was reluctant to hurt Camus's wife, Francine. But opportunity is the mother of transgression. Mamaine had arranged to stay on in Paris for a few days and take a vacation in the Basque country, and when she returned to her hotel from seeing Koestler off at the station, she found a rose and a note from Camus in her room. A few days later Camus told her he was unhappy in his marriage and was falling in love with her. Mamaine (in dark glasses because of her black eye) was immensely flattered. "For some reason he takes me seriously," she wrote to Celia in England. "I haven't a *very* violent physical longing for him, though I have fairly; but the fact is he *is* the one man apart from K that I think I could be in love with." She still held back, telling Camus she would kill herself if Koestler ever left her. At the same time she had an "intolerable feeling" that she was missing "a unique chance of the kind of which there are very few in one's whole life."[7]

Mamaine had cause to feel restless. She almost certainly didn't know about Koestler's night with Beauvoir but on arrival in Paris had found him in the midst of a torrid affair with a blonde Russian émigrée named Tania, the wife of the American journalist Harry Matthews. They had a violent row, and Koestler told Mamaine that he had slept with the "Russian spy," as he called her, "only twice" and was not in love with her. Mamaine accepted his explanation, but not before spending a sleepless night imagining him with his scarlet woman (he was in fact with Beauvoir) and feeling that his infidelity had cast a shadow over her entire visit.[8]

Camus pressed his suit with more roses and another letter. They took the Métro to the Bois de Boulogne for a stroll in the park. In the Métro Camus said, "I cannot leave you," and told Mamaine he was leaving for Provence. Mamaine agreed to meet him in Avignon. He arrived looking pale after a bout of tuberculosis, but they spent a romantic week together, exploring Romanesque churches, dancing the tango in a Spanish nightclub, wandering through olive groves to look for a house for Camus to buy. It was "more like a fairy tale than real life," Mamaine wrote to Celia afterward. Camus was "perfect"; she could find no fault with him. He in turn told her, "This week you have made me as happy and as unhappy as it is possible to make a man." Back in Paris they met in the Jardin du Luxembourg and Camus read to her from *The Plague*. Mamaine told Celia she was sure Camus was in love with her and thought of living with him in Provence, but she still held back. "However much one may long for real happiness I don't think one can let people down in the way I should if I left poor darling K. I haven't talked much to you about K's attitude to me, which is one of admiration and trust."[9]

Mamaine told Koestler about the affair as soon as she returned to Wales. Koestler was cut to the quick, but remarked wryly that the truth was bound to come out sooner or later. Camus was less philosophical. He "hated" her for her disclosure, but was reconciled to remaining friends: "The days I spent at your side were the happiest days of my life and I will never be able to forget them." This was possible. Camus had a habit of falling in love with foreign women. Mamaine wasn't the first and was far from the last, but she did make an indelible impression on him. For her the affair was truly exceptional. In January she confessed to Celia that she was still "terribly obsessed" with Camus: "I do seem to be rather in love with him, blast it."[10]

The affair had no visible effect on Koestler's friendship with Camus. In a brief postscript to a business letter Koestler jokingly referred to his rival as a *salaud*—a bastard—while indicating that he understood and forgave the affair with Mamaine. Misunderstanding the tone of Koestler's note, Camus was stung into writing a long reply in which he rejected the charge of "*salaud*" and accused Koestler of being "crazy" for pretending to condone his behavior. Camus had betrayed their friendship and had "no illusions" on that score. But he hoped their friendship would survive this trial: "It's not important whether you are unhappy or not, and in any case it's none of my business. What is important is that you shouldn't feel diminished. And not once during the whole time did I entertain a single thought that might have diminished you in my eyes."

Koestler replied that he had "condoned" the affair for a very simple reason: "I take great liberties in my private life and concede the same liberties, by mutual agreement. Naturally this leads sometimes to somewhat painful conclusions. On the other hand, it gives more basic stability to a relationship than things done on the sly." The incident was closed, and any residual embarrassment would be taken care of by the passage of time.[11]

As if to prove his point, Koestler did his best to find a British publisher for Camus's *Neither Victims nor Executioners,* but it was turned down by John Lehmann at Penguin's *New Writing* on the grounds that Camus hadn't gone far enough in his condemnation of Russia and support for America. Koestler defended Camus, saying that for an independent leftist in France it wasn't tactically feasible to go further (look what had happened to Malraux). The French Communists in fact feared Camus's "soft" analysis more than the harder line of Koestler and Malraux. But even Malraux wasn't prepared to go as far as Koestler and told him via Mamaine that Koestler had overestimated the influence of the French Communist Party and had underestimated "other elements" in France—by which Malraux meant himself and the supporters of de Gaulle.[12]

KOESTLER'S FRENCH EXPEDITION left him feeling restless and dissatisfied. Setting off for Paris, he had briefly entertained the thought that he might return there to live, a prospect that had filled Mamaine with enthusiasm. Now he was not so sure. Politically France seemed poised on a knife-edge between the Communists and de Gaulle. The former were by definition unacceptable, the latter looked as if he would introduce a dictatorship—milder than Franco's or Salazar's, perhaps, but a dictatorship nevertheless, and that, too, was unacceptable.

Ration-bound Britain, on the other hand, struck him as unbelievably dismal and dull. An unusually harsh winter was worsened by a rash of strikes and fuel shortages. The government was at loggerheads with the trade unions, and the Labour Party was floundering. In remote North Wales they were left without heating or hot water ("we haven't had a bath for 3 weeks and sometimes have a feeling that we may be beginning to stink," wrote Mamaine to Celia) and were forced to cook on a tiny kerosene stove. In March

1947, after a long freeze, Mamaine reported that they had endured "a 90-mile-an-hour gale." Then, "as we were frying our dinner on the sitting-room fire, there was a loud crash and half the big 17th-century west window fell in on us, followed by lashings of rain." Snow followed the rain, and not even the installation of their first telephone did much to relieve their isolation or to lift Koestler's spirits.[13]

For the first time in his life Koestler thought seriously of moving to the United States. He was deeply pessimistic about the future of Europe and felt that they should go as soon as their lease on the farmhouse expired. Mamaine hated the idea, reminding him of "the horrors of American capitalism," to which Koestler replied that they could always take a trip to Mexico when they were "sick of highballs and frigidaires." He said he needed to live in an English-language environment. His English had suffered even from his brief stay in France, and the only possible alternative to Britain seemed to be the United States.[14]

Koestler still couldn't bring himself to abandon Europe, however, for he remained convinced that France still held the key to Europe's future. Moreover, he was a celebrity and an intellectual force in France in a way he had never been—and it seemed never could be—in Britain. V. S. Pritchett had pointed to the brutal truth in his *Horizon* essay earlier that year. Koestler was "separated" from the British "by the education and politics of the continent, by the vast difference between the large, stable middle-class in England and the small, precarious middle class of Central Europe." He could "easily dazzle us because we have no cafe conversation and no cafe writers. We have no skill in playing poker with ideas. We are not trained to pretend that things which are entirely different may (for the pleasure of effect) be assumed to be opposites. We have no eternal students. We have no intelligentsia."[15]

Raymond Mortimer reinforced this British view in *The Atlantic*. To a French friend who had called Koestler the English novelist he liked best, Mortimer retorted, "He is wonderfully living, but he is not English; he is not a novelist; and how far is he, as a writer, even likable?" Koestler's work was stimulating because his thoughts and feelings had "all the fascination of unfamiliarity, exciting perpetual surprise" and because Koestler wrote "with an intensity of passion rare among Anglo-Saxons," which made his novels "impossible to put down." But Koestler's writing was "unlikable" because he accepted as normal "what I believe and hope is abnormal—because he treats ordinary peaceable enjoyment as trivial or even discreditable." "Mr. Koestler's writings" were dislikable because they neglected "the necessity or even the existence of gardening."[16]

For the French, these negatives were positive. "My English friends told me that the problems raised in [*Darkness at Noon*] were 'most interesting,'" wrote Bertrand d'Astorg, "and they talked about its 'curious psychology' and 'fine qualities.' Because for them, thanks to the bizarre pattern of their character, a novel is only a novel, whereas in France it is a question put to a political referendum." The French gloried in their café conversations, boasted of their intelligentsia, and were nowhere near as keen on gardening as the British. As a result, Koestler's name was rarely out of the news in France. *The Yogi and the Commissar* had recently appeared in volume form (newly dedicated to Malraux); *Thieves in the Night* had been serialized in *Combat;* and *Darkness at Noon* and the essays in *Yogi* continued to be the object of furious debate. *Arrival and Departure* was hailed as another ambitious novel of ideas by one of "the most glorious representatives of the left intelligentsia" and debate was just beginning about Koestler's Palestinian novel.[17]

The Communists, meanwhile, had moved from calling *Darkness at Noon* a Trotskyist caricature to calling it a conspiracy. "Koestler isn't studied, he is *propagated,"* wrote *Les Lettres Françaises.* Roger Garaudy, a member of the French CP's Central Committee, lampooned Koestler, Malraux, Mauriac, and, curiously, Sartre, as "gravediggers," part of a vast bourgeois conspiracy to distort the truth about the Soviet Union and dig communism's grave. The attack signaled a sharpening of the Communist line in the wake of Andrei Zhdanov's speech on ideological purity at the founding of the Cominform. According to the French CP's own ideological pit bull, Laurent Casanova, "Messrs. Koestler and Dos Passos are preparing ideological arguments abroad designed to nourish the numerous defeatists in countries weakened by war; and they are being offered prominent platforms in France. American films, carriers of a foreign ideology, are overrunning our screens, American books are flooding the windows of our bookstores, foreign movie producers and publishers are establishing companies aimed at degrading our national spirit inside France itself."[18]

The newly established Cominform represented the Soviet response to the Marshall Plan, and Zhdanov, with the brutal directness of Communist logic, had stressed the division of the world into two "irreconcilable" camps. The aim was to consolidate Russia's hold over the Soviet-occupied countries of Eastern and Central Europe while stirring up as much trouble as possible in Western Europe, especially in countries such as France and Italy, where the Communists were strong. In both places the CP had been forced out of government, and the burning question now was: Would they behave as loyal parliamentary oppositions, or would they foment unrest, and perhaps civil war, in a bid to take power? This was one of the questions in Koestler's mind when he made his second visit to France in the fall of 1947.

KOESTLER LOST NO TIME in looking up Sartre and Beauvoir at the Deux Magots. Beauvoir wrote to her new lover, Nelson Algren, in Chicago that she had gone to an exhibition of Impressionist painters with Koestler and his "charming and very pretty wife," Mamaine, and still liked him a lot. She told

Algren of the night she and Koestler had slept together. "We were very attracted to one another, though separated by political differences, he thinking me insufficiently anti-Communist," she wrote. "He became very aggressive, but I hate aggressiveness, especially when it's mixed with sex, so there was no second time."[19]

Malraux revealed to Koestler over a dinner of vodka, caviar, and Siberian soufflé that he had decided to risk his reputation as "a man of the left" by throwing in his lot entirely with de Gaulle. De Gaulle had come out of retirement in the hope of uniting the forces of the center and right to defeat the left, and Malraux wanted to mobilize the forces of anti-communism in much the same way Münzenberg had once mobilized anti-fascism—an analogy that had undeniable appeal for Koestler. "But what about the general's entourage?" asked the doubtful Koestler. "*L'entourage du général, c'est moi* [The general's entourage is me]," Malraux responded grandly, and Koestler wondered if Malraux was joking.

Koestler tried to describe a new psychology book he was working on to Malraux, but at the mention of the name of Henri Bergson, Malraux took over the conversation again, launching into a high-octane disquisition on the French philosopher's ideas. "I'm the greatest philosopher in the world," said Malraux in his notoriously shrill and strangulated voice. "Do you mean *you* are," asked Koestler, "or are you quoting Bergson?" "*Non, c'est moi qui parle* [No, it's me speaking]," replied Malraux enigmatically.[20]

About a week later, Koestler and Mamaine took Celia and the American writer Harold "Kappy" Kaplan to a potluck dinner at Camus's, where they were to meet Sartre and Beauvoir. Kaplan sat quietly as Koestler launched into an impassioned monologue about the "iron curtain" that separated French intellectuals from Anglo-Saxon culture, but after Kaplan left, the drunken Sartre attacked him as "a sexual swine" who was "anti-Semitic, anti-negro and anti-liberty." The charges were ludicrous. Kaplan was a Jew and famous for his fidelity to his wife. But he was a highly visible "American in Paris," working for the American Information Service and busy with the Marshall Plan. To Sartre and Beauvoir, this made him "a fanatical supporter of Truman's policies," a "crook and a sort of spy at the American embassy, whom we both detest." Koestler, as drunk as Sartre, haughtily asked how Sartre could possibly talk of liberty when he ran a magazine that was soft on communism and endorsed the deportation of millions of victims from the Baltic states. "This time we are enemies!" he exclaimed melodramatically and walked out.[21]

The next day Koestler sent Sartre a note of apology. He said he liked Sartre more than he did Kaplan, but Sartre's attack had left him no alternative. Sartre responded with a long, magnanimous letter in which he apologized for his outburst. He was fond of Koestler and hoped to remain friends, but there was a fundamental difference between them that guaranteed that they would continue to exasperate each other. "You have been molded by a *Party,* you have learned to consider personal relationships as *part* of a shared operation." Sartre asserted that he, on the other hand, "was brought up in that individualistic culture of French bourgeois society that considers personal relationships as primary, and thereby makes room for personal considerations." Sartre recalled their evening at Schéhérazade, "when I offered you my friendship (because of my psychological appreciation), and you deferred its acceptance (because I was not *a priori* committed to a shared operation that could provide the foundation of our friendship). I don't believe that my point of view is superior to yours, or yours to mine: I think that both are incomplete, and that is neither your fault nor mine."[22]

It was a pretty accurate summary of the main differences between them, but the paradox of the bourgeois individualist embracing Communist-style collectivism in his politics, while the trained party member stuck up for individualism in his own, seems to have been lost on both men. They could be friends because, despite his jesuitical justifications of Soviet policies, Sartre was not a Communist, he was just viscerally anti-American. He concurred with Merleau-Ponty that the Marshall Plan was "the generosity of an ogre," but he also rejected Stalinism and was determined to find a socialist "third way," even if it wasn't Koestler's way. Like Koestler, he was a "party of one," with his own views on everything. Koestler could see no virtue whatsoever in the Soviet Union, and Sartre could see none in the USA.

BEAUVOIR, HOWEVER, now turned violently against Koestler and put the case that Sperber had feared. "He hates the Communists so fanatically that he's able to team up with the worst reactionaries, write for conservative journals and approve right-wing policies while continuing to hobnob with the people at *Partisan Review.* This is exactly the attitude we denounce in *Les Temps Modernes.*" The last straw was when Koestler came to say goodbye and mischievously declared that he was now "a hundred percent for de Gaulle." It was pure provocation, a joke, but Beauvoir wasn't amused and concluded, "it was pointless to have wasted so much time with Koestler."[23]

Returning to Wales, Koestler dashed off a futuristic fantasy about a France taken over by the Communists. Its title, "Heroic Times," was a play on *Les Temps Modernes,* and some idea of its flavor can be gleaned from its opening: "Entering the House of Gallimardov, Zinaida Bovarovna had a slight palpitation of the heart. Twice, between the former Café de Flore and the bar of the Pont Prolétaire (formerly the Pont Royal), she had fallen into the cordons of the Liberty Police." The story appeared in *Occident,* an obscure Paris-based magazine that Celia worked for, but it had no real plot and the basic idea was never fully realized. There must have been something in the air, however, for Camus also embarked on a satirical story about Sartre and his entourage, "Philosophical Impromptu," which was not published until much later.[24]

A couple of months later, in January 1948, Koestler returned to a Paris polarized by the publication of Viktor Kravchenko's *I Chose Freedom,* which had exposed the truth about corruption and terror in the Soviet Union and the continuing existence of the labor camps. The book was denounced in *Les Lettres Françaises* and by the Communists as an American fabrication, but Sartre's new anti-American play, *Les Mains Sales* (Dirty Hands), didn't please the Communists either, earning him the ultimate insult of "Koestler's understudy."[25]

Koestler was still happy to see Sartre, Beauvoir, and, of course, Camus (the man in the middle), but the writing was on the wall, and a spectacular bender one night virtually ended their brief but explosive friendship. According to Mamaine's diary, it was a repeat of their earlier bacchanal: Russian nightclub, endless shots of vodka, sentimental Russian songs, dancing, only this time it was Sartre who propositioned Mamaine, causing Koestler to throw a glass at Sartre's head that missed and smashed against the wall. Camus took Mamaine out onto the dance floor and told her he was desperately unhappy, and later, outside in the street, he held on to her and said he'd cried all night when she left. "I said, 'I doubt whether you're capable of loving really, because you go with so many women and *ça pourrit les gens* [that spoils people] in a way, I think.' *'Tu viens de dire ma condamnation* [You are pronouncing my death sentence].' Only once before have I seen C in such a state and I was very moved too."[26]

Koestler returned to look for his wallet, then scrambled up the stairs on all fours, still determined to tackle Sartre over Mamaine. When Camus tried to intervene, Koestler lashed out, giving Camus a black eye. Camus leaped at Koestler and had to be clawed off by the others, and Koestler disappeared into the night. Camus drove Mamaine, Sartre, and Beauvoir home in his car. "He was suitably soused in vodka and champagne," wrote Beauvoir in her memoirs, "and his eyes began to fill with tears: 'He was my friend! And he hit me!' He kept collapsing onto the steering wheel and sending the car into the most terrifying swerves and we would try to haul him up, completely sobered by our fear."[27]

Camus was forced to walk around in dark glasses, and Koestler apologized but failed to see Camus before he left Paris for a quick trip to Italy. He did see Beauvoir but offended her again by introducing her to a drunken Gaullist friend as "Mme Sartre" and joking that Sartre probably harbored secret sympathies for de Gaulle. Beauvoir complained to Sartre, and Sartre told Koestler he was disloyal: he should have stuck up for Beauvoir the way he had defended Kaplan. Koestler explained to Sartre that the quarrel over Kaplan's alleged racist views and the joking with his Gaullist friend occupied completely different planes of seriousness. "I feel much closer to you than to

Kappy, but the flow of adrenaline is not a function of loyalty." Sartre, egged on by Beauvoir, seems to have seen the matter otherwise.[28]

Koestler's turbulent behavior in Paris was the product of several strands in his character. To a certain extent he felt "on holiday" from the gloom and austerity of socialist Britain, and enjoyed the fleshpots of gay Paree all the more for knowing that his furlough was temporary. The warmth and volatility of the Gallic character brought out his own vivaciousness and spontaneity, in contrast to the British phlegm he attempted to adopt (with limited success) as a protective camouflage at home. But his chronic insecurity and the temper tantrums of the spoiled brat were never far from the surface: moments of genuine sincerity and tenderness could morph with lightning and frightening speed into assertive arrogance, leading to offensive preening and prancing, and all too often to the fisticuffs that invariably got him into trouble (and often led to excessive feelings of guilt and remorse afterward).

He was better when not in direct competition with others, when he could be astonishingly generous to friends, colleagues, and even complete strangers, drawing, it seems, on sentiments of solidarity and mutual help forged during hard times before the war. One example was his treatment of Dorothee, whom he saw twice on this visit to Paris. Dorothee's health had mended, but she had recently endured an unbearable new tragedy. Hans had died at home in mysterious circumstances, and the police suspected an overdose of drugs. They had sealed Dorothee's apartment and carried off her homeopathic pills for analysis, suspecting that Dorothee was in some way to blame for Hans's death. She was obliged to move in with friends for a while, but charges were never brought, and she told everyone that Hans had died in a motorcycle accident. She had resumed her career in social work but was still desperately short of money, and still trying to finalize her citizenship.[29]

Koestler listened sympathetically and agreed to continue his financial help, and to expedite the divorce proceedings. He had been reluctant to divorce her earlier, according to Dorothee, because she provided him with an alibi for staying free and carrying on his affairs with other women. But Mamaine was still pressing him to marry her, and had changed her name by deed poll to Paget-Koestler, making it clear she regarded herself as his spouse. He agreed to send Dorothee a letter in which he admitted he had knowingly abandoned her and had no intention of returning. Meanwhile he regularly sent money to Leo Valiani in Italy and sought tirelessly to find publishers in England and America for him, as well as for Sperber and other former German colleagues down on their luck, such as Harald Landry and Gabriele Tergit. He helped Ruth Fischer find an English publisher for *Stalin and German Communism,* invited the Yugoslav ex-communist writer Anton Ciliga to spend a couple of days with him in Wales, and paid for Ciliga's book *In Soviet Siberia* to be translated into English. He also wrote prefaces for Ciliga and for Suzanne Labin's documentary study *In Stalin's Russia,* and found translators for T. S. Eliot at Faber to work on a book by Polish ex-prisoners of the Gulag, *The Dark Side of the Moon* (whose title came from one of Koestler's essays).[30]

Koestler's zeal for networking also spawned a plan for authors in different countries to translate one another's works. As a result of his own linguistic abilities, he was in the habit of working with the translators of his own work into French and German, but the disastrous French translation of *Scum of the Earth* persuaded him that more was needed, and in Camus and Sartre he seemed to find a sympathetic audience. They agreed that it was "tedious and repellent" to have to go over your own prose repeatedly in order to check a translation, which, in Sartre's inimitable phrase, was like being stared at by "your own cold vomit," and enthusiastically backed Koestler's plan that they should help one another. Back in England Koestler attempted to enlist Orwell in the scheme, but Orwell was sick and too busy with *1984* to take an interest, and the project came to grief the moment it was put to the test. Sartre's literary agent in New York asked Koestler to revise and adapt a rough translation of Sartre's play *Les Mains Sales* for an American audience. Koestler agreed, but Sartre vetoed the idea on the grounds that Koestler's reputation for anti-communism would damage the play's reception. The fact that the loudest critics of his play in France had been communists was outweighed by his horror of anti-communism.[31]

KOESTLER AND MAMAINE took a brief trip to Italy, visiting Florence, Perugia, Assisi, Rome, Bologna, and Milan before Koestler returned to Paris alone. In Florence they dined with the eighty-three-year-old Bernard Berenson at I Tatti, and Berenson jotted a brief description of Koestler in his diary: "He dark, nut-brown, jet-black hair, fine head, arresting eyes. Features not Jewish. Perhaps a touch of gypsy. His speech impeded by a successive word or phrase, leaping on the back of one he has not yet uttered. His English would be almost perfect but for his pronouncing W's as V's, and 'th' as Z." Koestler talked to Berenson at length about telepathy and ESP, and the great aesthete was reminded of "pre-Socratic man," not a bad description of someone for whom "mind and matter still seemed indivisible."[32]

In Rome they were greeted as celebrities. *Darkness at Noon* had been favorably reviewed by Benedetto Croce, while the Communists were calling Koestler a "fascist" and were rumored to have been stealing his books from the public libraries. Koestler and Mamaine spent much of their time with Valiani and other friends from the Italian Resistance, including Silone, who was again morose and provocative in Koestler's company, boasting of how during the war the socialists had refused to collaborate with either the Communists or the Americans. He had his own path, he said, and his overriding concern was to behave ethically wherever he was. Koestler agreed with the ethical imperative but told Silone it was a great mistake not to help the Americans.[33]

On the road back to Paris, Koestler got the news of a Communist coup in Czechoslovakia, signaling a betrayal of the Social Democrats in the coalition government and the complete Sovietization of Eastern and Central Europe. The coup fulfilled Koestler's direst predictions and worst fears: there was no room for a third force in Europe anymore—not, at least, in countries where the Communists were strong. In France, rife with rumors of a coup of its own and convulsed by increasingly violent strikes, he found a populace growing more jittery by the day. Malraux talked darkly of a plot to foment civil war and publicly threatened "a reorganization of the Resistance" to oppose communism. Charles "Chip" Bohlen, the new American ambassador, talked wildly about dropping an atom bomb on Baku, and newspapers were full of the threat of a new world conflict.[34]

Only Sartre and Beauvoir seemed unmoved by this latest turn of events. They made it clear that Czechoslovakia was no concern of theirs. The Soviet Union was on the side of history, and American imperialism was still the major problem. Beauvoir had come to regard Koestler as a "miserable traitor" and a hypocrite and had decided he was "still a Communist at heart," eager only to come out on the side of the victors. Unaware of how far things had gone, Koestler took out his calendar to arrange a further meeting. Beauvoir crossed her arms on her chest and said, "We are crossed like this about everything. As a philosopher you must realize that each of us when he looks at a lump of sugar sees an entirely different object. Our sugar lumps are now so different that there's no point in our meeting any longer."[35]

Returning to London, Koestler found symptoms of war hysteria almost as bad as in France. A leading Labour peer, Frank Pakenham, told him there was a 25 percent chance of war, and Dick Crossman was equally pessimistic. Koestler settled down to write two articles for *The Observer* on his visits to France and Italy. They were gloomy in tenor but not without hope. He pointed to France's symbolic importance as the bellwether of Western Europe. France was still struggling to come to grips with the conflicts of "the post-liberal era," in which disgust with party politics allied with a certain "anti-democratic nostalgia" among the masses had led to the formation of two extreme opposing blocs that were grinding "the softer mass between like millstones." One of those blocs, the Communist Party and its allies, presented France with the same dilemma with which the Nazis had presented Germany in 1930: "Should democratic privileges be extended to a party which aims at the destruction of democratic privileges?"

Koestler answered his question by pointing out that whereas the Nazis had openly expressed their intention to destroy democracy, the Communists posed as its defenders, and democracy would deny its principles if it tried to disenfranchise the Communists without circumstantial evidence. The French

crisis was a function of the world's crisis: not for the first time, France's struggles embodied those of Europe as a whole. "If France goes, Europe is gone,
and this the French know; on the other hand, France can only be saved as an
integral part of Western Europe—and this they have so far refused to accept."[36]

CHAPTER TWENTY-EIGHT

DISCOVERING AMERICA

America is so vast that almost everything said about it is likely to
be true, and the opposite is probably equally true.
— JAMES T. FARRELL

THE COUNTERWEIGHT TO SOVIET EXPANSION in Europe was the United States, and the more skeptical Koestler grew about Europe's future, the more he was drawn to investigating the country for himself. The huge sales of *Darkness at Noon* in America had been the bedrock of Koestler's financial independence. Since its success he had never wanted for money and never would. Americans had also hailed *Arrival and Departure* with far greater enthusiasm than European readers, and in a country with a large Jewish population, *Thieves in the Night* had attracted enormous attention for its depiction of the struggle over Palestine.

A sign of his growing reputation had been an invitation from the editors of *Partisan Review* to take over its "London Letter" from Orwell. "We need hardly tell you that there is a good deal of confusion and ignorance among American liberals on the question of Stalinism," wrote William Phillips. He didn't want the letters to be entirely political, but "I think you will agree that it is one of the central political and cultural issues today, and that the Left must not permit the struggle against Stalinism to be appropriated by the Right." Koestler did agree, and in 1947 responded with three London Letters, contrasting the "economic sanity and moral insanity" of France with the "reign of virtuous gloom" he saw as the hallmark of postwar Britain. In both countries the left was hamstrung by the false dilemma of seeming to have to choose "between East and West, capitalist democracy or state-capitalist totalitarianism, America and Russia." His left-wing friends in Britain wanted to avoid becoming "America's aircraft-carrier" and had "an almost mystical horror of American Big Business," but they couldn't seem to grasp that by turning their back on America they would be opening the way to Russian dominance.[1]

Koestler was ahead of most of his left-wing friends in realizing that the best American intellectuals and American statesmen had a firmer grasp of global politics and of the Soviet menace than did their European counter-parts. The Labour government's lukewarm socialism at home and timid re-luctance to assume the leadership of Western Europe in its foreign policy had disillusioned him with Britain, and he put little stock in the ability of France or Italy to withstand the blandishments of communism on their own. The United States was Europe's best hope—and, not coincidentally, the best hope of the Jews in Palestine. It was time to take a look at this new world power, see what it was like, and find out whether he might settle there after all. While doing so he would carry across the Atlantic his message that non-Communist leftists everywhere should stand firm against the Communist menace.

Of the many invitations he had received, Koestler chose to go with the New York–based International Rescue and Relief Committee (IRRC), suc-cessor to the Emergency Rescue Committee (ERC), which had done such sterling work in German-occupied Europe during World War II. The IRRC was blessedly noncommercial, but it was not as apolitical as Koestler later claimed, nor was it part of the non-Communist left. Despite its anti-fascist record during the war, it was conservative and right-wing, as its advance publicity demonstrated. Koestler's lecture tour was intended "to aid the cadres of freedom loving men and women who have thus far survived and are in the forefront of the fight for freedom." All the proceeds from the lec-tures, and from attendant fund-raising, would go to support that struggle—and *Life* magazine had offered a substantial sum for the right to print them.[2]

Life wasn't left-wing either, and the American political situation was more complicated than Koestler realized. Maintaining his reputation as a leftist would turn out to be more difficult than he had thought, and there was the further problem that his own rightward journey was being interpreted differently by different political forces. An early warning came when Koestler was informed, while still in France, that as a former member of the Communist Party, he was banned from entry to the United States. The FBI had investigated Koestler in 1944 and concluded that he was still an unrepen-tant Red, based on a "book report" on *Darkness at Noon* by a certain M. A. Jones. "The book is both dull and interesting," wrote Mr. Jones. "It is clogged with detailed descriptions of no particular value. It is filled with Communis-tic philosophy, but its value lies in showing clearly that regardless of your position in the Party, you must not deviate one iota from the Party line." Charles (Chip) Bohlen, the newly appointed American ambassador to

France, had to inform the myopic State Department that Koestler was now "actively opposed to Communism" and that his book *Darkness at Noon* had been "very effective in combatting the spread of communism" in France. Even so, the State Department felt obliged to consult J. Edgar Hoover before concluding that Koestler's entry to the USA was "highly desirable in the national interest." Attorney General Tom Clark's approval came a scant thirty-six hours before Koestler's departure, leading him to cancel, then reinstate, his original reservation.[3]

There were a couple of other hitches along the way. Koestler threatened to cancel if he was forced to attend all the cocktail and dinner parties the IRRC had planned as fund-raisers, and he also ran into the problem of America's blue laws. He had intended to take Mamaine with him but discovered that although he might travel with a woman who was not his wife, she wouldn't be permitted to share a room with him. In the end, the IRRC scratched most of the fund-raisers and Koestler agreed to go without Mamaine.

HE TRAVELED OVER on the *Queen Mary* in March 1948, finding congenial dinner companions in the Hungarian-American film director George Cukor and Edwin Knopf of Metro-Goldwyn-Mayer. Straight off the boat he was swept up into a round of press conferences, interviews, lunches, dinners, and cocktail parties that made it difficult for him to keep his balance. As A. D. Peters had warned a year earlier, he was much more famous and influential in America than he could possibly imagine. That day's "Celebrity Bulletin" for the New York press nominated him "Celebrity of the Day," ahead of Clark Gable, Admiral Byrd, Dizzy Gillespie, and Gracie Fields. His triumphal arrival was in many ways a replay of his earlier visits to Jerusalem and Paris. Within days of his installation at One Fifth Avenue, letters began pouring in from people he had known at every stage of his life, and former friends started turning up at his door. What had begun as a pleasant welcome turned into a "nightmare"of endless meetings and engagements. He foresaw that he would end up offending dozens of well-meaning people for sheer lack of time, and a number of old acquaintances did write bitter letters to complain of neglect.[4]

One bonus was seeing Eva Striker again, now a successful ceramicist and married to Hans Zeisel. At a dinner with numerous members of the Striker-Polanyi clan Koestler was introduced to Michael Polanyi's brother Karl, the eminent economist from New York, and got an early taste of the split on the American left. Karl Polanyi supported Henry Wallace's Progressive Party and was convinced that Wallace would make a far better president than Truman. Wallace was opposed to the Marshall Plan, had condoned and even supported the Communist takeover of Czechoslovakia, and was portraying Truman as an American imperialist bent on waging preventive war. It seemed a majority of the Strikers and Polanyis agreed with Karl and were none too happy with Koestler's anti-Soviet message.[5]

He got a very different reception from Philip Rahv and William Phillips at *Partisan Review*. Though Koestler had a somewhat exaggerated view of the importance of the magazine and like most Europeans tended to overestimate the importance of intellectuals in American life in general, *PR* was undoubtedly the closest thing Koestler possessed to a spiritual home in America. The magazine's leading lights were virtually all ex-Communists like himself, and most of them were Jews as well; they represented an anti-Stalinist left that in early 1948 was by no means as strong as it was to become in subsequent years. Phillips felt his encounter with Koestler was a "true meeting of minds." He found Koestler "very sophisticated" and "terrifically energetic," though perhaps a trifle glib in some of his pronouncements.

Phillips threw a small dinner party, to which he invited Delmore Schwartz, Mary McCarthy, Elizabeth Hardwick, William Barrett, James Burnham, and Sidney Hook, and Koestler held forth on the dangers of a Communist takeover in France and Italy. Mary McCarthy was "glowing" that evening, and Koestler made a big play for her. Phillips thought Koestler had "too many bridges to cross" with Mary, politically speaking, and that McCarthy would not go for Koestler's "brashness and intellectual aggression," but he was wrong. Koestler charmed her with his talk of eastern philosophies, passive resistance, and the importance of personal morality, and she drank up his words on the decadence of Europe. She was particularly impressed with Koestler's idea (which he had put forward in "The Fraternity of Pessimists") of forming oases of small libertarian groups that would try to change the world bit by bit. She was trying to do something similar with her "Europe-America" groups, helped by European exiles such as Nicola Chiaromonte and Nicolas Nabokov and was to borrow Koestler's term for *The Oasis,* her roman à clef about a utopian colony of New York intellectuals in Vermont.[6]

Hook was, however, offended by Koestler's attention to McCarthy, whom he regarded as a "politically irresponsible" lightweight, and loudly disagreed with Koestler about the problem of poverty in southern Italy. This short, Jewish, bespectacled ex-Trotskyite was every bit as pugnacious in argument as Koestler himself and was to become a staunch ally, but at this first meeting he upset Koestler with his badgering. "I didn't come three thousand miles to listen to that sort of remark," exclaimed Koestler angrily and stomped off, muttering about political dishonesty under his breath. The next day he wrote Hook a note of apology, and he caught up with McCarthy again a couple of days later at Rahv's but was disappointed to find her husband, the "fantastic, egg-shaped" Bowden Broadwater, in tow. Deep in discussion with Delmore Schwartz about the pacifism of the younger generation, he overheard Mc-

Carthy holding forth in another part of the room on "the tyranny of the or-gasm" and was dying to test her theory in person, but in vain.[7]

James Putnam, Koestler's editor at Macmillan, threw a party for Koestler to meet some more liberal heavyweights: James T. Farrell, John Hersey, Lionel Trilling, Hannah Arendt, A. L. Whyte, John Gunther, and Dorothy Thompson. Koestler sensed that Trilling and Arendt (who had criticized *The Yogi and the Commissar* but praised *Twilight Bar* in *Commentary*) were "offended" that he didn't pay more attention to them: he was engrossed in a long discussion with Hersey and Farrell about the differences between "gray" and black political situations and the need to distinguish between short-term and long-term goals. Later, at a *New Leader* party, he discussed politics with a galaxy of anti-Stalinist intellectuals that included Sol Levitas, the magazine's editor, Max Eastman (who said the term *socialism* should be abolished), Dwight Macdonald, Eugene Lyons, Alexander Dallin, and John Chamberlain. He also ran into Auden and Spender and before he left town was able to squeeze in dinner with Edmund Wilson and John Dos Passos. Dos Passos said that until recently, when he had killed his wife in a car acci-dent, he had never known what true suffering was. Wilson (presumably with thoughts of *The Wound and the Bow* in mind) was astounded. "Then how could you write?" Wilson cross-questioned Koestler about his work (thus turning the tables on his inquisitorial guest), leading Koestler to conclude re-sentfully that his rival for Mamaine's affections was "clever, insensitive and disagreeable" (he could have been speaking about himself).[8]

Koestler's encounters with the press were invariably testy. At the outset he ostentatiously declined to speak about politics, saying disingenuously that his purpose in coming to New York was "philanthropic" and that he preferred to speak about literature and his new psychology book, *Insight and Outlook*. Harvey Breit, of *The New York Times Book Review,* took Koestler at his word and found him "astonishingly free of nervous symptoms" and behaving "with wit and naturalness." Breit spoke of Koestler, Malraux, and Silone as "the most powerful triad of our time," but Koestler modestly declined the comparison, saying that he wasn't the equal of the other two artistically, al-though he might have a better political brain. Part of the reason for his un-popularity in Britain, he said, was that the political novel didn't appeal to the British temperament. He was more widely read in the United States and France than in Britain.[9]

BETWEEN LUNCHES, DINNERS, cocktail parties, and interviews Koestler tried to work on his speech with a stenographer provided by Jim Putnam, popping pills to keep himself awake. But the enterprise was hopeless. When March 26 came around, he still had no text to speak of and decided to speak impromptu. It was a bad mistake. Carnegie Hall was filled to capacity with more than three thousand people, and the air was electric with anticipation. As he stood fidgeting at center stage, the sound system failed and he was barely audible. He tried to make up for it by moving to the front of his table and perching on its edge, letting his legs dangle in the air. His aim was to establish a mood of informality, but the cavernous reaches of Carnegie Hall and the vastness of the audience defeated him. His tiny figure, pinned to the stage by floodlights, was dwarfed by his surroundings, and he could barely be heard in most parts of the auditorium.

What he said, had the audience been able to hear it, was an expanded version of his second *Partisan Review* article, and it made a strong impression on the few who sat at the front. He spoke of "the radical's dilemma" and the "seven deadly fallacies" that he felt were hindering the "Babbitts of the Left" from understanding the true nature of the Communist threat. One was the misconception that the Soviet Union was a socialist country, which it had long since ceased to be. Another was the theory that the United States had "dirty hands" because of its support of right-wing governments abroad and the presence of anti-Semitism and racism at home. Surely these things existed, but if that were the problem, how could America have fought against Hitler? Its hands had been just as "dirty" then as now. There was the fallacy of the false equation: Soviet totalitarianism was bad, American imperialism was bad, there was nothing to choose between them. Other fallacies included the sentimental fallacy (we fought with the Communists during the war, so how can we go against them now?), the fallacy of the perfect cause (only a cause without blemish could have any meaning), and, most important, the fallacy of "anti-anti-communism." "The power vacuum which two world wars have created in Central and Western Europe has inescapably linked your fate with that of the European continent," he told his American audience. "I feel the enormous burden which is falling on your shoulders. For there will either be a *Pax Americana* in the world or there will be no pax."[10]

Roger Baldwin, the director of the American Civil Liberties Union, thought that Koestler's excellent powers of analysis were undermined by his pessimism, but his message fell on fertile ground. It was just a few months since George Kennan had published his famous "X" article in *Foreign Affairs,* outlining the thesis of "containment" and predicting the Cold War. Shortly afterward, President Truman had established the Central Intelligence Agency and, on Kennan's advice, had authorized the agency to undertake "covert psychological activities" in support of American policies. Koestler was interested in *overt,* as opposed to covert, activities, and got a chance to explore the subject when Burnham took him to see General William "Wild Bill" Donovan, the former chief of the Office of Secret Services (OSS), the precursor of the CIA, and they discussed the desirability of organizing some sort of psychological warfare.[11]

Burnham was another formidably intelligent ex-Trotskyite, a cofounder of the American Workers Party who had moved steadily to the right since that time. He was in transition, like Koestler, and he was the author of two highly influential sociological treatises, *The Managerial Revolution* and *The Machiavellians*. In the first, Burnham had predicted a new form of society that would be neither socialist nor capitalist but run as a bureaucratic empire by a managerial elite. In the second, he had underlined the preeminence of realpolitik in world affairs and then, in an essay entitled "Lenin's Heir," had offered a brilliant analysis of Stalin's political achievements as the leader of the Communist world. Burnham's most recent work, *The Struggle for the World,* posited a mortal contest for world dominance between the two remaining great powers, the United States and the Soviet Union.

Burnham cut a vastly different figure from the bohemian and indifferently dressed Jewish intellectuals who made up the majority of the *PR* "family." In his dark suit, white collar, and narrow tie, with rimless glasses hugging the sides of his neatly trimmed head, Burnham looked more like one of the managers he had written about than an intellectual and had a low-key, courteous manner that was totally at odds with the rambunctious behavior of the literary set. Over drinks with Koestler he immediately got down to business, outlining what he called his "Atlantic Project," a scheme for the establishment of a non-Communist world federation that would consist of Britain and its dominions, the Continental nations not already under Soviet domination, and the United States as the federation's acknowledged leader.[12]

Burnham also briefed Koestler on the politically chaotic situation in Washington. The Cold War was already well under way, yet the CIA was still trying to define its role and decide on a program. Three days later, Koestler took the train to the capital to see for himself and repeat his New York experience: a press conference, meetings with old friends from Europe, a speech to a packed audience at the National Press Club. Koestler also got his first taste of political infighting among the crusaders at the State Department. One of his hosts was the barrel-chested Raymond Murphy, the State Department's leading expert on communism since the end of the war. Murphy had debriefed Grete Buber-Neumann, Münzenberg's sister-in-law, after her release from a Soviet jail, and had made a name for himself as the first and most important interrogator of the Communist defector Walter Krivitsky. He had also interrogated Whittaker Chambers, whose notorious appearance before HUAC was still a few months off. Murphy (like his political patron, Richard Nixon) turned out to be pathologically jealous of his colleagues and raved to Koestler about how important he was compared to Chip Bohlen in Paris. William Bullitt, a former ambassador to Paris himself, as well as to Moscow, informed Koestler that he, Bullitt, was the true author of the Marshall Plan.[13]

After listening to more political diatribes from the head of the Immigration and Naturalization Service and telling him that very few of the fellow travelers he feared would actually betray their country, Koestler felt he was beginning to understand Eva Zeisel's warnings about war hysteria in America. She repeated them in a letter commenting on his New York lecture. She was in no way soft on communism, she said, but Koestler should be careful of the company he was keeping. His audiences in America would consist not of sophisticated European intellectuals attuned to the nuances of psychological warfare but of blinkered conformists who were itching to start a preventive war. Walter Winchell (who had praised *Darkness at Noon* in one of his programs) was openly calling for war, and the Catholic Church was defending the concept of a "holy war" against godless communism. Eva implored Koestler to use his enormous influence to change the climate of intolerance instead of aiding it.

In a tender postscript Eva explained that she was trying to make up for her "sins of omission" in the past. Her alibi was that it had taken years for her to be able to sleep without being tormented by her memories of a Soviet prison, and even now she lived by the vows she had made "while thinking of my death." Koestler replied equally tenderly that he still felt closer to Eva than almost anyone on earth. With regard to her arguments, he was sure that "on the logical plane" he could prove her position to be one of honorable error, but on another plane he couldn't. He, too, had made vows in prison, one of which was never to meddle in politics again, but for him the sin of omission was too grievous to ignore. "As long as I still believe in the lesser evil, I have to carry on."[14]

KOESTLER'S IMPRESSIONS OF AMERICA at this stage of his journey were decidedly mixed. On the train to Washington he had been amazed by the amount of forest and uncultivated wilderness they passed through, and Washington, like New York, struck him as a place of "sprawling untidiness and improvisation," lacking the "streamlined, high pressure mechanization" and robotlike uniformity he had expected. "It is quite impossible to give you any impression," he wrote to Mamaine. "It is a kind of delectable nightmare. Five times a day I am telling myself that this is a country where I want to be forever, and five times a day that I would rather be dead than live here."[15]

From Washington, Koestler moved on to Los Angeles and encountered an atmosphere of political hysteria that surpassed even Washington's. The first hearing of the House Un-American Activities Committee on the movie industry had just been held in Hollywood, and one of its early victims was one of Koestler's Berlin comrades, the composer Hanns Eisler. Eisler had been denounced as "the Karl Marx of Communism in the musical field," a grotesque exaggeration that had forced him to flee the country. Hanns was paying for the sins of his brother, Gerhart, a bona fide Comintern agent and a much more sinister figure, who had been dubbed "the number one communist in the U.S." (the brothers had a way of attracting superlatives) and had made a well-publicized escape to East Berlin, where he now worked for the Propaganda Bureau of the East German government.

At subsequent hearings in Washington, the star witnesses against the "Hollywood Ten" had included Ronald Reagan, Gary Cooper, and Robert Montgomery, all of whom were among Koestler's hosts at the Los Angeles branch of the IRRC. Other committee members included Alma Mahler-Werfel and the movie union leader and prominent Red-baiter Roy Brewer, a leading spokesman for the right-wing Motion Picture Alliance for the Preservation of American Ideals (MPA). After listening to Brewer rant about Communists and subversion on the home front, Koestler realized that the HUAC hearings were the "focus, fulcrum and hub of the world" so far as Hollywood was concerned and that the people there weren't remotely interested in what was happening in Europe. He also understood better the import of Eva's warnings. American anti-communism came in two mutually hostile and very different varieties: the liberal anti-communism that reigned at *Partisan Review,* with which he fully identified, and the conservative, Red-baiting anti-communism that was obsessed with "subversion." It was this second variety that so upset Eva and that Koestler realized, to his dismay, was in charge of his tour.[16]

This was clear from the advertisment he now saw for his lecture in *Alert: The Confidential Weekly Report on Un-American Activities in California.* Koestler was "hated and feared by Communists," said the ad. "He knows what makes the madmen in the Kremlin tick," and his lecture would explain why. At the Philharmonic Hall he again had problems with the microphone (this time by standing too far away from it), and his heavy accent was again hard to decipher in most of the hall. But he was better prepared than in New York and Washington and emphasized even more strongly to his audience that if America wasn't ready to fill the present political vacuum in Europe, Russia undoubtedly would. For that reason, he added, trying to strike a balance between the American right and left (and in response to Eva, perhaps), he was an "anti-Wallacite," because the Wallace policy of appeasement of Russia would lead just as directly to war as "the hysterical irreponsibility of Walter Winchell."[17]

Koestler looked up his *Queen Mary* dining companion, Edwin Knopf of Metro-Goldwyn-Mayer, who introduced him to some of the stars active in the local Democratic Party—Danny Kaye, Olivia de Havilland, and Deborah Kerr—and arranged a meeting with the great Louis B. Mayer. During their meeting on the *Queen Mary,* Knopf had tried to talk Koestler into moving to Hollywood, referring to its residents Christopher Isherwood and Aldous Huxley as a commodity known as "talent." Koestler hated the cigar-chomping Mayer, however, seeing in him "a parahuman face modeled of shit" surrounded by executives who looked like "oxen from a Disney film posing as humans," complete with heavy jewelry, hand-painted ties, and solid gold cigarette cases.[18]

Though not in the least tempted to take up scriptwriting, Koestler was intensely interested in having some of his books turned into movies. *Darkness at Noon* was the most obvious candidate, and a small company called Pioneer Pictures had shown an interest, but Pioneer wanted to update the novel and set it in the postwar period and Koestler was dead set against the idea. Everett Freeman of Warner Brothers had decided the subject was too "delicate and difficult" to get past the front-office brass, notably Jack Warner himself. Leland Hayward, the theatrical agent, urged Koestler to turn it into a stage play first. The problem of play or film also dogged *Arrival and Departure.* Hayward had arranged for the *New Yorker* writer Victor Wolfson (whose track record included a successful adaptation of Silone's *Fontamara*) to dramatize the novel for the stage, but the project never came to fruition. Nor did similar proposals to stage or film *Thieves in the Night,* despite competing offers from Walter Wanger, Billy Wilder, and Ben Hecht.[19]

Thomas Mann had settled in Los Angeles, but when Koestler tried to see him, he was cold-shouldered by Erika Mann, who disapproved of the right-wing company Koestler was keeping. He did have lunch with an "amazingly young"-looking Aldous Huxley and the comparatively wizened Gerald Heard. Huxley and Koestler had an impassioned two-hour conversation about J. B. Rhine's ESP experiments, telepathy, and related subjects, and Koestler was much impressed with Huxley's pessimistic view (echoing his own) of civilization's discontents as seen from California. He also ran into Langston Hughes, whom he hadn't seen or heard of since Tashkent. Hughes, now living in San Francisco, told Koestler he had "a roaring sex-life in the north" and recommended that Koestler look up Ralph Ellison, "one of our best younger writers and critics," when he went back east.[20]

DISILLUSIONED WITH THE TURN his tour was taking, Koestler attempted to cut it short, and paid a brief visit to San Francisco before continuing on to Chicago. There he gave a speech that had been polished by repetition, and was rewarded with a trip to a nightclub featuring "the hottest striptease ever seen": a naked girl "performing mock coitus with the wall, dangling breasts and buttocks (like apples and melons) before the middle-aged clients' eyes ('Welcome Conventioneers')." At another club, the dancer wore sparkling lights on her breasts, her crotch, and her rear end and was encouraged with whoops by the customers. "The beastly thing about it all," he noted in his diary, "is that there are no prostis; the young men are heated up and then have to go home."[21]

His last lecture was in Boston, where he was given a tour of the Harvard laboratories and met the neurologist Molly Brazier, who was later to help him with his scientific books. His host was the young Arthur Schlesinger, Jr., another former OSS operative, whose almost-completed book, *The Vital Center,* was a kind of liberal riposte to Burnham's recent work. Though Schlesinger more or less agreed with Burnham's analysis of communism, he was much closer to the *Partisan Review* line. He distrusted Burnham's conservatism and advocated a radical form of liberalism as the best antidote, even going so far as to call for an American version of the welfare state. Koestler was closer to Schlesinger than Burnham, but Burnham was a far more forceful and abrasive figure, and it was he who, in the end, exercised the greater influence on Koestler.[22]

Back in New York, Koestler went out of his way to talk up Burnham's Atlantic Project over lunch with Henry and Clare Boothe Luce, and later the editors of the *New York Herald Tribune,* both times without success. Burnham and his wife drove Koestler to the Institute of Advanced Studies at Princeton, where he had an "exciting talk" with the eminent mathematician and fellow Hungarian John von Neumann, about levels of memory and related matters. Koestler also took to hanging out at the Oak Room in New York with Friedrich Torberg, an Austrian novelist he had known in Berlin before the war. Torberg was a staunch anti-Nazi and had served with the Czech Legion in France before escaping through Spain and Portugal to California. He had worked in the movies for a while and would later become a close ally in the Congress for Cultural Freedom.[23]

By the beginning of May, Koestler was enjoying an "end of holiday feeling" as he prepared to relax for the last week of his stay. He sent flowers to all the people who had hosted and entertained him and bought a precious wire recorder, a gadget that had not yet reached Europe, to help him with dictation. There was the inevitable farewell party with members of the IRRC, attended by Louis Fischer and Dwight Macdonald among others, and a last get-together with Eva Zeisel, whom he now tagged, because of her political reservations about his visit, as "neurotic and boring." There were also two unforgettable trips to Harlem, one to its nightclubs with Marlene Dietrich and Erich Maria Remarque, and another to visit its slums with Hannah Grünwald (who was doing the kind of social work she had done in Paris before the war). Koestler found the poverty-stricken, broken-down streets "as bad as Chicago, but with less glass around" and now understood why their driver of the night before had warned them not to go anywhere near 145th Street. But the race problem was beyond Koestler's range. Much as he sympathized with Grünwald and her clients, he pondered the futility of her struggle and found the whole thing "very depressing."[24]

One more dinner with Remarque and one last round of New York's nightclubs, accompanied by Dietrich and the Torbergs, left Koestler feeling exhausted and jaded. It was a typically alcoholic end to an action-packed month, but Koestler felt he had achieved what he set out to do despite the machinations of his conservative hosts. He had bolstered the anti-Stalinist intellectuals of the left, added his weight to those who were advocating a more active, anti-Communist U.S. foreign policy, and satisfied his curiosity about a country that was exercising a stronger and stronger pull on his imagination. Despite many reservations, his mind was almost made up. He was sure he would return to America soon, perhaps to stay.[25]

CHAPTER TWENTY-NINE

FAREWELL TO ZIONISM

I think a man is doing his reporting well only when people start to hate him.

— SAMUEL JOHNSON

RETURNING TO WALES in May 1948, Koestler was rocked by news of dramatic developments in the Middle East. Relations among the Jews, the Arabs, and the British had entered a downward spiral of violence and counterviolence that now seemed unstoppable. In August 1947, before Koestler's departure for the USA, the hanging of two British sergeants by the Irgun had led to anti-Jewish riots in Britain, culminating in an arson attack on a synagogue in Derby and the vandalizing of more than three hundred Jewish-owned properties in Liverpool. With his usual impetuosity, Koestler had jumped into the fray with a controversial article in the *New Statesman,* "Letter to a Parent of a British Soldier in Palestine," in which he tried to explain the rationale of the Jewish terrorists fighting for a homeland of their own. The solution, he declared, was to end the Mandate and introduce partition in Palestine.[1]

It was an extension of the argument he had made in *Thieves in the Night,* and, as with the novel, his article was read by many as an endorsement of violence, particularly since Koestler declared that had his life turned out differently, he might have ended up among the terrorists himself. But however much truth there was in the accusations against him, Koestler was far from advocating terror for its own sake. He realized better than most in Britain the dangers of a conflagration and was desperate to ward it off. Writing to Victor Gollancz to urge him to reissue the "Crossman-Foot pamphlet" (in reality written by Koestler) and follow it with another, "The Facts About

Palestine," he warned that if the government rejected the United Nations recommendations "we shall witness horrors compared to which everything so far is but a faint foretaste."[2]

The UN Commission of Inquiry's recommendations had been formally accepted by the UN in November 1947 (the chairman admitted he had been influenced by reading *Thieves in the Night*), and in May 1948, the British abruptly withdrew their forces, giving neither Jews nor Arabs much time to prepare. Israel declared its independence, and a day later, the surrounding Arab countries sent in their armies to crush the new state and drive its inhabitants into the sea. When the Jews fought back, more than thirty countries (including the United States and the Soviet Union) voted to recognize the new state, and the Security Council arranged a cease-fire, dispatching Count Folke Bernadotte of Sweden to negotiate a truce.[3]

Barely off the boat from New York, Koestler decided he needed to go as well. He had few illusions about Jewish Palestine. "It is already a Levantine, provincial and rather nasty little country," he wrote to a friend. "It will become even more Levantinized if and when partition comes about and the Sephardi Jews from the surrounding Arab countries flock in under pressure." But a "Jewish dwarf state" would probably change its character when "the Tarzans of the new generation" came to maturity. Meanwhile, he was prepared "to fight tooth and nail" for such a state and was eager to go there.[4]

Working through Paul Winkler in Paris, he acquired assignments to report on the war for *The Manchester Guardian, Le Figaro,* and the *New York Herald Tribune.* Mamaine declared her intention to go too. She was sick of Wales, sick of wrestling with the housekeeping, sick of having her asthma worsened by the damp climate, and sick of being left behind when Koestler went off on his travels. Parking the dogs on the reluctant Daphne, they packed up their movable goods, arranged to store or sell the rest (Koestler drew up a careful inventory with reserve prices next to some items), and left Bwlch Ocyn in a tearing hurry.

They picked up their visas in Paris (the new state had as yet no representation in London), getting numbers five and six issued by the Israeli Provisional Government, and flew out via Marseilles, Rome, Athens, and Cyprus to Haifa. The chartered aircraft took two days to make the journey, and the tense silence of the passengers reminded Koestler of flying into Spain during the civil war. The sight of Haifa Bay, which he had not seen for twenty years, and the prospect of war moved him more than he had expected. "The whole sunny landscape with its resemblance to the Gulf of Naples strikes at once the dominant chord of all journeys into war: it is so completely peaceful. This intense peace—the reflection of the sun on the ripples of the sea, the exhalation of the pine trees, the slow heartbeat of the surf—intermittent and superimposed upon the spectacles of war, is one of the archetypes of all war experience. The grass never smells sweeter than in a dugout during a bombardment, one's face buried in the earth."[5]

He went to work immediately, questioning wounded soldiers in the sanatorium on Mount Carmel and quizzing Abram Weinshall on Israeli losses during the first two weeks of fighting—three thousand out of a population of not much more than half a million—the equivalent of three quarters of a million in American terms. But the city of Haifa had fallen with surprising ease as a result of the Arabs' poor morale and the cowardice of their fleeing leaders. The same was true of Acre, Jaffa, Safed, Tiberias, and several other towns where fighting had erupted.

Driving down the coast to Tel Aviv, Koestler was also reminded of Spain. The road teemed with trucks and buses packed with singing soldiers. "In the open trucks they all stand upright holding on to each other, in the buses they sit on each other's knees with elbows sticking out of the windows and their fists banging the rhythm of the song on the tin plating." Recalling his hike down this empty coastal road twenty years earlier, he felt a surge of pride over the green, irrigated fields and "every acre of reclaimed desert."[6]

In Tel Aviv, he and Mamaine moved into the Hotel Gat Rimmon on the waterfront. The city was very much as Koestler remembered it: noisy, smelly, and ugly, a jumble of concrete and brick boxes lining down-at-heel streets that reeked (to him, at least) of a Central European ghetto. But the atmosphere in those streets was electrifying. Air raids, blackouts, and false alarms kept the newspaper correspondents pinned in the hotel, and information about the progress of the war was almost impossible to obtain. Israel's nascent army was led by Ben-Gurion's Haganah forces, but the Irgun still had a sizable number of its own troops in the field, and there were semi-independent militias too. Thwarted by the secrecy, Koestler tried to purchase an automobile to make field trips and wrote an irate letter to the English-language *Palestine Post,* pointing out that a war had to be fought on two planes—the military and the political—and that by neglecting the needs of foreign correspondents, Israel was provoking a backlash. It could end up winning the military campaign and losing the propaganda war (he was not alone in this opinion: the renowned Hungarian-American photographer Robert Capa told Koestler that nowhere from China to Russia to India to the USA had he encountered such abysmal public relations as in Israel).[7]

Koestler's letter was widely read and provoked great hostility among government supporters, for Koestler wasn't just another foreign correspondent but a world-famous author, identified with the Jewish struggle the way Hemingway had been identified with the Republicans in Spain. His arrival had again been news in the Israeli press. Every taxi driver in Tel Aviv had read *Thieves in the Night*—and was eager to argue with him about its conclusions—and every member of the Labor government had read it too. But there was the rub, for Joseph's conditional endorsement of terrorism was regarded as hostile to Labor and favoring the Irgun. Furthermore, Koestler had been meeting with his Revisionist friends, such as the Weinshalls and von Weisl, who insisted that it was the Irgun's forces, not Ben-Gurion's, that had driven the British out of Palestine.[8]

INDIFFERENT TO HIS UNPOPULARITY with the government, Koestler made friends with Alexis Ladas, a young Greek on the UN staff, and when Ladas leaked advance news of a truce between Arab and Jewish forces, Koestler put an excited call through to Moshe Shertok, now Israel's first foreign minister, eager to be the first to let him know. Koestler still had hopes of bringing the government and the Irgun together, but Shertok told him over dinner that he would never shake hands with Begin. "We belong to two different races," said Shertok. His government would assert its authority over Begin's allies "even if it means shooting them."[9]

The cause of Shertok's anger was a recently announced threat by the Stern Gang to assassinate some UN observers. Koestler was appalled and contacted an old friend named Amikam to say he would publicly turn against the Irgun unless the threat was withdrawn (it was). Koestler naively contrived a meeting between Amikam (a friend of the putative assassins) and Ladas (a putative victim), but it came to nothing. When attacked by a senior member of the government's political department for giving legitimacy to the Stern Gang, Koestler repeated that it was time to reconcile with the Irgun. "I told him that though I disliked many aspects of their activity, without terror the British would never have cleared out of Palestine, and that it was time for the government to make a generous gesture and to recognize publicly the nation's debt to the boys who got themselves hanged by the British while being called fascists and thugs by the official representatives of their own people."[10]

It was a mantra that Koestler would repeat in all his meetings with high government officials, in his dispatches, and in boisterous conversations with other correspondents at the Kaete Dan Hotel. The London *Times* correspondent Louis Heren noted that in addition to astonishing the other correspondents with his unerring knowledge of wine (he could identify most vintages blindfolded) during their noisy dinners, Koestler dominated them with his intricate knowledge of Jewish internal politics and consistently defended the Irgun's terrorism, with the exception of what amounted to a massacre at Deir Yassin village and the hanging of two British sergeants. In an extension of the message of *Thieves in the Night,* he argued that "ruthlessness was essential for human progress" and that the end could justify the means at decisive moments in history. He compared the Irgun to the IRA during the Easter Rising and saw it as a catalyst for human progress.[11]

Koestler couldn't help being a lightning rod for controversy. The *Jerusalem Post* reported that the London *Daily Worker* had accused Koestler of being part of an anti-Soviet conspiracy. He had cadged a ride with Ladas on a UN reconnaissance visit to Jerusalem over a dirt road (the "Burma

Road") that the Israelis had secretly constructed by night to relieve the besieged city. His presence in a UN vehicle was construed by the Communists
as "a provocation" and part of a plot to neutralize Soviet influence on the UN
mission.[12]

He escaped from Tel Aviv a second time in the car of a friendly businessman to visit Ein Hashofet (described as Gan Tamar in *Thieves in the Night*)
and Gal Ed, the protoype of Ezra's Tower. He had decided to write a book
combining a history of the Jews in Palestine with an account of their struggle
for independence and felt he needed to get out into the countryside to see
how it was faring. At Ein Hashofet he was met with icy hostility. One member of the secretariat refused to shake his hand, another said it was a pity he
hadn't announced his visit in advance (implying that he would have absented
himself), and Jonah Janai, his former host, who had publicly denounced
Thieves in the Night after its publication, argued with Koestler about the
novel's conclusions. At Gal Ed, Koestler did better. He was shown an album
commemorating the foundation of the kibbutz and heard only praise for his
description of its establishment and the early months of its existence.[13]

Koestler also toured Galilee to witness the results of the war at first hand,
stopping at places where there had been major battles between Jews and
Arabs: Degania; Ein Gev; Safed; Ramat Naphtali, on the Syrian border; and
Acre, north of Haifa on the Mediterranean coast. Everywhere he heard tales
of British perfidy, Arab cowardice, Jewish cunning, and the cynical manipu-
lations of Russia and America, leading him at one point to wonder if the
whole campaign didn't consist of smoke and mirrors. "No statement can be
taken at its face value; warlike bombast is a cloak for haggling for better conditions; humanitarian sob-attitudes serve electoral purposes. This lilliput
country has become a kind of ethical atom-bomb, which explodes the rotten-
ness of international morality and whose poisoned radiations reach from
Washington to Moscow."[14]

That thought was dissipated when he returned to Tel Aviv to find the
smoldering wreck of the *Altalena* cargo ship wallowing on the beach opposite
the balcony of his hotel. The Irgun had been using the ship to smuggle in a
thousand illegal immigrants, a large cache of armaments, and thousands of
dollars in cash to finance the war against the Arabs. They were breaking the
truce but thought they had tacit approval from the government until Ben-
Gurion apparently changed his mind and ordered his troops to open fire on
the ship, causing its crew and passengers to flee in small boats or simply swim
for the shore. Ben-Gurion also ordered all Irgun offices closed and arrested
up to two hundred of its leaders, including many of Koestler's friends.[15]

The idea of Jews firing on other Jews appalled Koestler, and he filed two
fiery dispatches blaming Ben-Gurion and the government for the debacle.
Better informed than other correspondents, he revealed the existence of a secret agreement between Begin and Ben-Gurion and insisted that Ben-

Gurion had reneged. It was a repeat of the blowing up of the King David Hotel, he wrote, when Ben-Gurion's Haganah had secretly agreed to the action but disclaimed all knowledge when it went wrong. But now the situation was worse, for an "unelected, self-appointed" government was displaying "fanaticism verging on hysteria" and "embryonic tendencies toward dictatorship." The only way to avoid further harm was to hold democratic elections, and the international community should insist on them as a condition of offering de facto recognition to the new state.[16]

The dispatches created a furor in Israel. The *Palestine Post* ran a two-column attack under the headline "Koestler Against Israel" and a few days later published an editorial denouncing his call for elections. In the progovernment Hebrew press he was accused of being either a British or an American agent—which was about the only thing all parties in Israel could agree upon. Koestler responded with an angry letter saying he had been misrepresented. His feelings for the young country were nourished by a "hard and bitter love" that didn't flinch from shortcomings, and he denounced the saccharine sentimentality about "Jewish stones" that passed for patriotism in Israel. In his diary he noted angrily, "A totalitarian Lilliput is no less totalitarian for the smallness of its people."[17]

GOVERNMENT SUPPORTERS SOON CHANGED their tune when Koestler attacked Count Bernadotte's proposals for a peace settlement awarding the whole of Jerusalem to the Arabs and imposing a two-year freeze on Jewish immigration, but his editor at *The Manchester Guardian,* A. P. Wadsworth, protested that Koestler's dispatches were alienating British public opinion from the Jewish cause. He was right, and Koestler knew it. Eager to start his book, he rented an apartment in Tel Aviv to escape the din at the hotel and at last succeeded in buying a jeep. Shlomo Avineri glimpsed him, dressed in fatigues and looking self-important, as he drove up and down the waterfront "like a maniac." Koestler was now in "surprisingly good form," according to Mamaine. They acquired a fawn boxer puppy, Sabir (Sabby for short), with a pedigree that went back to Austria and Hungary between the two world wars, and Koestler took the puppy for lessons with a Tel Aviv dog handler, who trained it to obey only its master's commands.[18]

Bernadotte's truce proposals were rejected by both sides, and fighting resumed in early July. During the next few weeks, Koestler filed dispatches highly favorable to Israel and critical of the UN and the Arabs, but in other articles on Israel's social structure, political parties, cultural life, and the rebirth of the Hebrew language (about which Koestler expressed his familiar doubts), he continued to write like a scolding mother dissatisfied with her offspring's shortcomings. Making few concessions to the young nation's inexperience, and still fewer to the fact that it was in a state of war, Koestler persistently measured Israel's performance against the highest European standards and found it (not surprisingly) wanting.

Koestler also interviewed the two main Jewish leaders, Begin and Ben-Gurion. Begin now struck him as an absentminded and unprepossessing figure, with "soft restless hands, thinning hair and wet lips," who peered shortsightedly through rimless glasses like a provincial schoolteacher from Eastern Europe. Ben-Gurion was just the opposite. Broad-shouldered, with tufts of white hair sticking out from either side of his large bald head, he looked every inch the patriarch and spoke with "great warmth, persuasive conviction and a paternally despotic authority."[19]

Koestler's relationship with the two leaders was a curious one. Though technically a foreign correspondent and an author looking for copy, he behaved like an insider, arguing with his interviewees over points of policy and freely offering his (largely unsought) advice. He lectured both Begin and Ben-Gurion about the need to latinize the Hebrew alphabet and endorse westernization. Begin said little, but Ben-Gurion argued back and told Koestler he "knew nothing of Jewish tradition" because he didn't know Hebrew and wasn't really a Jew. Koestler also revived his idea that Ben-Gurion should reach out to the Irgun by forming a grand coalition with it, but Ben-Gurion wasn't persuaded. He was well aware of Koestler's ties to the Irgun and particularly resented the fact that Koestler had visited some of the *Altalena* rebels in jail.[20]

Ever the romantic, Koestler still aspired to being something more than just a sympathetic foreign correspondent but didn't know what his role should be. According to Zifroni, Koestler hoped to be feted as *the* writer of the new Israel, its poet laureate, so to speak, and to be embraced by the new government. He also seems to have entertained the quixotic hope that he might become the missing minister of information. When Gershon Agronsky, the editor of the *Palestine Post* and a persistent critic of Koestler, was given the job instead, it must have dawned on Koestler at last that there was no place for him either as an official or as a figurehead in the new state. It should have been obvious. He was too large a figure to fit into the circumscribed position of a minister, too contentious and unpredictable to work with as a colleague, and too narcissistic and egotistical to respond to direction by a prime minister—any prime minister and not just Ben-Gurion. As for poet laureate, he couldn't even write in Hebrew, the new state's official language.[21]

Much of this became clear in the course of a tense meeting with Teddy Kollek, now a minor member of the government. After avoiding Koestler for a while, Kollek came to Koestler's apartment for a rushed dinner and sharply criticized Koestler's condescending dispatches to *The Manchester Guardian* and the *New York Herald Tribune*. "Either you feel that you belong to Israel or you don't" was the gist of Kollek's comments, and while Koestler admitted that much of the criticism was true, he was stung by its underlying hostility. Koestler felt that he had "come here to help" and was being rejected by the "same clique" that was making life hell for Kollek, too. Kollek had been glib, insincere, and pleasant, while he, Koestler, had been sincere but "cantankerous and bitter." It was a pretty good summary of many of his meetings at this time.[22]

THE MEETING WITH KOLLEK proved to be a kind of watershed for Koestler. In an exchange of letters, Kollek apologized for his rudeness and explained that his objection to Koestler's articles was not that they were untrue but that they told only half the truth, and it was the negative half. Koestler, meanwhile, had been listening to Begin on the radio and "marveling at the fool one had been the year before." He decided that he had been too extreme in his criticisms and that revisiting Palestine was a waste of time, but rationalized his behavior as necessary to "the asymptotic process of growing up." Jabotinsky, the Revisionists, and the Irgun were "an undigested lump in my stomach. When I touched upon these subjects, I descended from maturity to adolescent emotion. It remained a raw enclave in this hard and bitter strife for maturity. It was necessary to go through the tunnel to be able to emerge from it, to assimilate this last relic of unreasoning loyalty."[23]

Koestler's diagnosis of his problem was essentially true. He was an inveterate romantic, building castles in the air and complaining bitterly when they collapsed before his eyes. In his diary he now reexamined his whole attitude to the Jewish state and how he should write about it. Evocative language was often "demagogic and cheap," but where would Danton, Tom Paine, and Garibaldi have been without it? Likewise, propaganda was "evil," but "without this evil the world would have rested in the stage of its initial evil" (an argument that paralleled his defense of "controlled terrorism"). The problem was how to strike a balance between emotive language and a more objective discourse to achieve a synthesis. "*Thieves in the Night,* however little it helped, was necessary at the time," he concluded consolingly. Perhaps it was like scientific development: the cart of history had to be pushed "in blind enthusiasm and blind rage" until it had passed over a particular hump, and then it was possible to look around and "see in daylight."[24]

"Seen in Daylight" was the putative title of a sequel to *Thieves in the Night* that Koestler had just begun as an alternative to his "chronicle" (Koestler was hooked on sequels: he had started and abandoned sequels to both *Darkness at Noon* and *Arrival and Departure*). This sequel, covering the end of the British Mandate and the war for independence, turned out to be no different from his other sequels, and Koestler managed only one chapter before running out of steam.[25]

After nine days of fighting, a new truce between Israel and the Arabs was established and took hold, despite the assassination of Count Bernadotte on September 17, 1948. Ben-Gurion seized the opportunity to proclaim a new antiterrorist law and jailed three hundred leading Sternists, including Koestler's friends Amikam and Friedman-Yellin, whom Koestler visited in Jaffa Prison. There followed a strange interregnum of watching and waiting, which Koestler spent in gathering material. He had become "depressed and melancholic," according to Mamaine, but now turned resolutely against the Irgun and any form of terrorism.

Mamaine had wanted to help Koestler as much as she could when they first arrived. She took Hebrew lessons, gathered information, and ran errands for him. But there was only so much she could do, and as the torrid heat of summer took its toll, she grew tired and bored. As it happened, the "sweet and attractive" Ladas had a crush on her, and so, it seemed, did the American correspondent Cy Sulzberger, which provoked Koestler to increasingly rabid fits of jealousy. The tensions that had first welled up in Wales now returned with greater intensity, exacerbated by the strains of Israel. "I realize more than ever that I only feel free and happy when I'm not with K," Mamaine confided to Celia. "You can't think how browbeaten I am here." Their fighting culminated in a terrible row, in which Mamaine told Koestler she could no longer go on living with him.[26]

Koestler was philosophical about it and said he knew he was impossible to live with and always would be, and she should go back to Britain if she really wanted to. She settled for a holiday in Cyprus, returning at the beginning of September, and it was decided she should leave for Wales soon afterward and meet up with Koestler in Paris, where he planned to work on his book. Just before she left, someone tried to steal their jeep, and Mamaine sprang onto their balcony, yelling "Thieves in the night!" in Hebrew. The marauders fled, but a week later, Moshe Dayan's men stuck a Sten gun into Koestler's ribs and confiscated the jeep by force. Ordinarily Koestler would have applauded such derring-do, but not when the jeep was his, and not when the thieves were soldiers who had fired on the *Altalena*. An officer at the police station called him a "fascist," leading Koestler to punch him in the face. Yasha Weinshall was barely able to drag him away. The next day it emerged that Koestler had assaulted a high-ranking officer in the Israeli air force.[27]

Meanwhile, Paul Winkler had invited Koestler to write his book at his sixteenth-century Château du Pré at Chartrettes, just outside Paris, bought largely with the proceeds from Winkler's syndication of *Mickey Mouse, Popeye, Blondie, Jungle Jim, Flash Gordon,* and other comics (his press agency was dubbed "Disney's bridgehead in Europe"). The château was set in a huge wooded park across the Seine from the forest of Fontainebleau, with two lodges on the grounds, and Koestler, rejoined by Mamaine, took the smaller one. Winkler was the son of a Hungarian banker, a worldly Hungarian Jew with twinkling blue eyes, the girth of a Falstaff, and an expansive manner to match. He genuinely admired Koestler's talent, and Koestler admired

Winkler's entrepreneurial flair. When Winkler came out on weekends, they
would reminisce about prewar Budapest and compare their boyhood heroes
and experiences.[28]

Koestler had large ambitions for his book. He quoted Kant to Peters: "If
we could analyze all the events within a single grain of sand we would have
solved all the mysteries of the universe." Palestine was a grain of sand in
which the main "political, ethical and philosophical" problems of the time
were concentrated. But analyzing that grain of sand turned out to be trickier
than he had anticipated. The history of Palestine from 1917 to 1948 was relatively easy to write, but part two, "Close-up," on the war, was harder.
Koestler got around some of his problems by incorporating diary excerpts to
evoke his day-to-day experiences of the war but then found part three, "Perspective," harder still. This section was devoted to Koestler's reflections on Israeli politics and on Jewish language and culture and was driven by his
urgent emotional need to settle his relationship to his Jewishness and the
Jewish state once and for all.[29]

The narrative sections required the synthesis of an enormous amount of
information, and with Mamaine acting as Koestler's research assistant and
typist again, they worked eleven or twelve hours a day to master the material. James Putnam flew in from New York to help with the editing and found
Koestler in the midst of "a really serious crisis about his writing" and on the
brink of depression. With Putnam's help he recast parts two and three, and
the title went from "Seen in Daylight" to "Analysis of a Miracle" (the eventual French title) to its final version, *Promise and Fulfilment,* recapitulating a
phrase from Koestler's essay on Richard Hillary: "The last enemy was
promise and not fulfilment." Perhaps Koestler was thinking of himself when
he settled on that phrase.[30]

THE WORD "PROMISE" (with its echoes of the Promised Land) was a reference to the Balfour Declaration of 1917, described mordantly by Koestler
in his preface as "one of the most improbable political documents of all time,"
by which "one nation solemnly promised to a second nation the country of a
third." *Fulfilment,* a word not without irony in Koestler's lexicon, referred to
the foundation of the state of Israel. Koestler's goal was to go beyond mere reportage and to aim for the "subjective pursuit of objective truth." There was
no point in striving for a "cheap impartiality" that stood "outside the parties,
untouched by their emotions." The good judge, "like the playwright and historian, absorbs the subjective truth contained in each of the conflicting pleas
and his verdict is a synthesis of their part-truths, not their denial." Koestler
stressed the way that "irrational forces and emotive bias" affected not only
the historian but also history itself and felt that a "psychosomatic view" of

"one of the most curious episodes in modern history" would add to one's understanding of it.

As a work of contemporary history and reportage, *Promise and Fulfilment* was better researched and more comprehensive than anything Koestler had yet written, while informed by his trademark passion and subjectivity. Using his "psychosomatic" method, Koestler was able to illuminate the psychology behind British idealization of the Arabs and unconscious distaste for urbanized Jews, the embattled hostility of the Jewish settlers toward their British and Arab opponents, and, to a certain extent, the baffled resentment of the Arabs themselves. His personal chronicle and diary of his stay there remain one of the liveliest and freshest accounts of Israel's war for independence ever written, and his passionate defense of the role of the Revisionists in the creation of Israel, while overstated, served to redress the balance of public opinion between Ben-Gurion's Labor Party and Begin's Irgun.

The latter task carried Koestler back onto the perilously thin ice of again defending Jewish terrorism, which he knew contradicted his earlier views on the use of violence and needed a great deal of sophistry to explain. He had always held that the dilemma of ends and means was at the core of the human predicament, he wrote, and the problem admitted of no permanent solution. The end could justify the means only "within very narrow limits." The "arsenic of ruthlessness, injected in very small doses," was "a stimulant to the social body." In large quantities it was "a deadly poison."[31]

Much more controversial than his qualified defense of violence was his epilogue, in which he addressed the question of how Jews in the diaspora should respond to the founding of an independent Jewish state. The existence of Israel, he concluded, "puts every Jew outside Israel before a dilemma which will become increasingly acute. It is the choice between becoming a citizen of the Hebrew nation and renouncing any claim to separate nationhood." Jews should either move to Israel or abandon their Jewish identity. Citing Weizmann's comment that the Jews' very existence was the fundamental cause of anti-Semitism ("we seem to carry anti-Semitism in our knapsacks wherever we go"), Koestler declared that the only way to end it was for Jewry outside Israel to cease to exist.[32]

When published in the fall of 1949, *Promise and Fulfilment* divided Koestler's critics even more than usual. Leonard Woolf found Koestler's book "moving and brilliant" and "scrupulously fair." Another critic felt that Koestler had written "one of the best books that has yet appeared on Jewish Palestine," with an uncanny ability "to see, and to feel, both sides of any serious question." *The New York Times Book Review* singled out the war diary as "superb," but Leslie Fiedler, for one, thought the book a "political tract, enlivened by the crackle of aphorisms and brilliant observations which frequently cancel each other." It should be filed "under K for Koestler, not I for

Israel." Fiedler correctly saw *Promise and Fulfilment* as part two of a diptych, of which the first part was *Thieves in the Night,* and asserted that Koestler's flight from his own Jewishness shrank "the Covenant and the Exile, the struggle for the Land and Return" from "events in a dim history" to the context of "an autobiography and an apologia."[33]

Among Jews, the epilogue ignited such a heated controversy that it virtually eclipsed whatever service the book had done the Jewish and Israeli causes. Koestler received an avalanche of letters, many of them complimentary, some downright abusive. The London-based *Jewish Chronicle* expressed the view that Koestler was "willy-nilly" placing himself in "the evil company of anti-Semites" and sent Maurice Carr to Paris to interview him. Koestler expounded on his thesis at greater length, explaining that he was not advocating the conversion of Jews to other religions, simply that those who didn't go to Israel should melt into the populations where they lived or at the very least allow their children to do so. "To put it bluntly, I regard it as an outright crime for parents who neither believe in Jewish doctrine nor live up to its commandments, to impose the stigma of 'otherliness' on a defenseless child who has not asked for it."[34]

That "defenseless child" was of course a reference to Koestler's own childhood and the anti-Semitism he had resentfully endured. When asked how he regarded himself now in the light of his latest beliefs, Koestler declared that he considered it "a chance occurrence that my father happened to be of the Jewish faith," a repetition of his ealier half-truth and disingenuous by any standard, for it is the mother who determines whether the child is Jewish or not, and Koestler's mother was quintessentially Jewish. Koestler added that he regarded himself as first and foremost a European and second a naturalized Briton "of uncertain and mixed racial origin" who "accepts the ethical values and rejects the dogmas of our Helleno-Judeo-Christian tradition."[35]

Koestler seemed to think he might at last get free of his Zionism. There would be no need to visit Palestine again. He would melt invisibly into the crowd and slough off his Jewish skin. It was an illusion, of course, like the notion that he could slough off his Marxism without leaving major traces of it behind. He would never return to Israel, but he would continue to struggle with his Jewish heritage until the end of his life and never did find a "solution" to his dilemma.

CHAPTER THIRTY

A MARRIED MAN

Marriage indeed may qualify the fury of his passion, but it very rarely mends a man's manners.

— WILLIAM CONGREVE

DURING A PAUSE in the writing of *Promise and Fulfilment,* Koestler bought his first house. He was still hoping to move to the United States, but no invitation came, so he decided to invest his French earnings in some property and settle down to wait. It was in this casual fashion that, despite his reservations about French politics, he embarked on what would become a three-year sojourn in France.

The house in question was an unprepossessing stuccoed 1920s villa with an overhanging red-tiled roof that gave it a faintly Swiss air, not far from where he was staying in Winkler's château. Koestler fell in love with it because of its position on one bank of the Seine behind a row of fir and poplar trees. A small landing stage jutted into the river, firing his imagination with thoughts of boats and trips to the forest of Fontainebleau on the other side. The house had a suburban name, *Verte Rive* (Green Bank), which he never bothered to change, and a railroad track running along the other side of the road, which sometimes made conversation difficult, but Koestler was as indifferent to such details as he was to the sparse and ugly furniture that came with the house, the stinking septic tank, leaking water pipes, and the bare floors that echoed noisily under his footsteps. Koestler and Mamaine's own furniture was still in Wales, and camping out in a cold house in February was no joke, but Koestler speedily established his study in a room overlooking the river and carried on working as if nothing was amiss.[1]

Mamaine, having forgotten her earlier vow to leave Koestler, nevertheless found it hard to settle down. She had been felled by a cold soon after their arrival, followed by a bad bout of asthma, which had left her feeling drained and depressed. They started quarreling again. Koestler, as bourgeois in his domestic habits as he was bohemian in public, accused her of all manner of backsliding, which only made things worse. "Oh twin, what am I to do?" she wrote melodramatically to Celia soon after they bought the house. "However much I vow to myself to be efficient, hardworking, a good *Hausfrau,* not lose my biro, not forget to put a clean towel in the bathroom and all the other 101 things which drive K so wild, I never seem to get any better—or rather, I do, but it doesn't bring me up to the standard of the most idiotic secretary or any suburban housewife. What is there to do but put my head in a gas oven?"[2]

The threat came to seem like an omen when Mamaine almost died soon afterward. Responding to another asthma attack, the local doctor gave her a shot of novocaine that temporarily paralyzed her. This fresh setback coincided with the arrival of their furniture and books from Wales, which Koestler, in high dudgeon, was obliged to unpack and arrange himself. At the beginning of April, Mamaine had another relapse and was rushed to Levallois Hospital just outside Paris. She went into a coma, frightening Celia with biblical quotations that seemed to presage thoughts of death. A week later she was better and able to move back home again.[3]

Mamaine's asthma was a torment and its origins a mystery, for the illness was little understood at that time and treatment was rudimentary. It's now accepted that about half of all attacks are caused by allergies, though cold, damp air, infections, and emotional stress can also play a part. Mamaine might well have been allergic to Koestler's dogs, to his cigarette smoke, to some of the food they ate, or to the mold created by the dampness of the winter climate along the Seine, and she was certainly affected by the stress of living with an egotistical, mercurial, and unpredictable perfectionist like Koestler, whose demands knew no bounds.

But the hospital scare was a wake-up call, and once Koestler grasped the seriousness of Mamaine's illness, he went to great lengths to make sure she had the right doctors and medicines and to care for her as well as he could. After her return from the hospital, Mamaine found him "as angelic as ever" and told Celia that since her illness, "we have sometimes been able to talk to each other in a new, much deeper way, saying things one can't usually say to anybody at all and with a wonderful understanding between us." But she still didn't recover properly. Koestler flew with her to England and checked her into the Scottish Nursing Home in Hampstead, placing her in the care of a noted bronchial specialist, F. Croxon Deller. Mamaine's weight was now a catastrophic eighty-four pounds and she felt like "a gibbering maniac."

It was decided she should get plenty of bed rest and fatten up before being given a bronchoscopy, and her voluminous, virtually daily letters to Koestler show her alternating between manic elation and anxious depression. Deller, with the support of Eric Strauss, tried to persuade her to see a psychiatrist. Strauss was sure that her illness was psychosomatic and that an unhappy childhood was to blame for her depression. Mamaine dismissed the idea but agreed that she shouldn't return to France until she could deal with the "nervous strain" of handling life with Koestler again.[4]

A contributory factor to Mamaine's ailing condition, it turned out, was continuing anxiety about her unmarried state, leading Deller to cross-question Koestler on his impending divorce from Dorothee. Unfortunately that was still complicated. Koestler agreed to pay Dorothee five hundred pounds sterling, plus a further two hundred pounds for legal expenses, as part of a divorce settlement, but it turned out that Dorothee now wanted to become a British citizen and join her mother in London, where she planned to study for a diploma in social work at the London School of Economics. This meant further negotiations with both the French and the British citizenship departments, and involved a huge amount of red tape.[5]

MAMAINE'S STAY IN LONDON coincided with the appearance (between the writing and the publication of *Promise and Fulfilment*) of Koestler's first theoretical work, *Insight and Outlook,* a radical departure from anything he had written before. He had signaled his plan to explore new territory in the little-noticed concluding essay of *The Yogi and the Commissar,* in which he had discussed the conflict between free will and determinism in the context of the sciences. Its provisional title was "The Tragic and the Comic," and its subtitle, "Elements of a Theory of the Creative Mental Functions," indicated Koestler's desire to cover "art, humor, discovery and invention, the influence of emotion on thought, mysticism and ethics," with "detailed and popular chapters on the physiological aspect of mental processes." This ambitious new study was intended to be not a popularization but "the exposition of an original theory, introducing certain new concepts into psychology."[6]

The new work was heavily influenced by the appearance of a new *tudós* in his life, the brilliant Hungarian polymath Michael Polanyi, who had left his chair at the Kaiser Wilhelm Institute in Berlin after the Nazi takeover of the government for the chair of physical chemistry at Manchester University in England and had since published books on economics and social policy as well as chemistry. One of them, *The Contempt of Freedom,* contained an impassioned critique of repressive Soviet practices in politics, economics, and science, and it wasn't long after its appearance that Polanyi wrote to Koestler (still in the Pioneer Corps at the time) to praise *Darkness at Noon.* Koestler had sought Polanyi's advice while writing *Arrival and Departure,* and the two had corresponded on Polanyi's theories about freedom and creativity, leading Koestler to suggest that Polanyi collaborate on the new book, but Polanyi had declined.[7]

Koestler traced the book's genesis to that eureka moment in Budapest in 1935 when he had perceived David Rapaport's joke as "based on the discrepancy of two scales of values applied to the same event," a mental process he later termed "bisociation." Now he wanted to connect the idea of bisociation to the larger concept of creativity in general and to a line of inquiry that had run like a connecting thread through all his work so far, namely, an investigation of the Enlightenment claim that the true end of life was human happiness and the more questionable claim that the realization of that happiness was within man's grasp, if only he could find the right means to achieve it. In *Darkness at Noon,* Rubashov had achieved a sort of happiness by embracing an ethical code based on essentially nonrational foundations, and in *Arrival and Departure,* Slavek had returned to his country to fight fascism for reasons that lay "beyond the reach of cause and effect." Koestler wished to explore those reasons with the tools of biology and psychology rather than fiction and along lines suggested in Slavek's last letter to Odette at the end of *Arrival and Departure,* where he asserts that "the red tissue-paper of our scientific reasoning has obtained greater perfection than the blue of our intuition and ethical beliefs."[8]

Polanyi wasn't the only expert Koestler consulted about his new work. The entomologist Miriam Rothschild had arranged a dinner party with Isaiah Berlin and Sir John Foster, where they enjoyed "a hilarious evening telling Arthur funny stories, which he took down unsmilingly in longhand!" Koestler also consulted Eric Strauss, the head of the psychiatric department at St. Bartholomew's Hospital in London and the author of several works on psychology and neurology, including a wide-ranging, speculative book, *Psychotherapy, Religion and Science,* that had attracted Koestler's attention. Strauss in turn introduced Koestler to the neurobiologist Russell Brain, and both men helped Koestler extensively with the biological and physiological parts of his theory.

By the early summer of 1947 he had been working at top speed. With Mamaine's help a first draft was finished by early fall, and a final version, edited by Strauss, was handed to his publishers at the end of the year. Koestler also decided (much to Putnam's relief) to scale the book back from a threatened 300,000 words to about half that length—with the rest to come in a second volume—and settled on the title *Insight and Outlook,* with a new and only slightly more modest subtitle: "Inquiry into the Common Foundations of Science, Art and Social Ethics."[9]

He had been only half joking when he boasted to Sartre about his philosophical skills, for he truly hoped that this new book would establish him in a new field and help him reinvent himself as a writer. He had framed the work as an examination of the roots of human creativity, claiming that the accepted distinctions between the artistic and scientific imaginations were artificial and that all creative activities were based "on a common pattern." In this he was echoing Polanyi, who had argued that science depended heavily on intuition and, as one of the "higher arts," was rooted in a "spiritual reality" to which scientists voluntarily subordinated themselves. Adopting Polanyi's central idea, Koestler turned it around to suggest that the creative impulse itself could show the way to a system of ethics that was "neither utilitarian nor dogmatic" but derived from the same "integrative tendency in the evolutionary process" that controlled art and science. Polanyi felt that Koestler's conclusions were too sweeping to stand up to scholarly scrutiny but approved of the broad outline of his argument.[10]

At the core of Koestler's book were a theory of laughter as a "luxury reflex" found only in the human species and the concept of "bisociation" (Koestler invented the word) as the generator of the mechanism of laughter. Bisociation was a mental process "simultaneously associated with two habitually incompatible contexts," and Koestler went from there to an examination of what he called the self-assertive tendency in man (expressed through laughter) and the self-transcending tendency (expressed through tears)—in other words, the comic and the tragic. In biological terms, these took the form of differentiation and integration, and this brought Koestler back in due course to the polarity between "eastern" and "western" types of society: the yogi and the commissar. The yogi was too passive, and the commissar (the West in general) too self-assertive. What was needed for humanity was a "regenerative equilibrium" that would restore the balance.[11]

The book could be seen as either a tour de force of comparative synthesis or a hodgepodge of undigested ideas by an amateur who was neither a scientist nor a philosopher by training. Handing it in, Koestler was torn between feeling that he had made a total laughingstock of himself and wistfully hoping that he might at last have found the holy grail that could start a revolution in contemporary thought.[12]

Jim Putnam had prudently seen to it that Macmillan printed only five thousand copies, and his caution turned out to be fully justified. General reviewers were respectful of Koestler's reputation and enjoyed the jokes but expressed little enthusiasm for his "pre-Socratic" scientific theories. They were more sympathetic to his critique of western culture, which needed "more of the Yogi, less of the Commissar," in one critic's words, and Herbert Read coined the term *cosmic hedonism* (a neat twist on Orwell's comment) to describe Koestler's particular recipe for self-transcendence. A. J. Ayer spoke for many in concluding that Koestler had overworked his basic concepts, which came to "mean too little" because they were "made to do too much," and *Scientific American* cruelly described the book as smelling of Hegel, Spengler, and Freud, derived from "a Viennese philosophical system imbibed long ago at school and university and barely revised since."[13]

There was some truth to this gibe. Koestler's formal training *was* derived from the Vienna School, and the accusation that he had never transcended it would dog him till the end of his career. But he had also read and absorbed a great deal as a science editor in Berlin, and had read voraciously for the new book. Nevertheless, he remained an amateur in an increasingly professionalized world, and that was what undermined his authority. Fortunately, he had hedged his bets by indicating that *Insight and Outlook* was but volume one of a planned two-volume work and asserting that volume two would place his theory "on a more scholarly foundation." In fact, he had already drafted about three quarters of the second volume, but the scholarly reviews shook his confidence so badly that he decided to shelve the second volume indefinitely.[14]

NOVELS WERE STILL A PROBLEM, however. Koestler was painfully aware of the artistic deficiencies of *Arrival and Departure* and *Thieves in the Night* and sensed that the perfection of *Darkness at Noon* was no longer within his grasp. He had replaced the idea of a Zolaesque series of novels on Palestine with a similar series covering the years in Europe from 1918 to 1941. They, too, were never written, but some of the themes he planned for them began to find their way into his nonfiction, beginning with a short memoir for a volume of essays on the failure of communism. The idea for the volume had grown out of a heated argument with Richard Crossman about the blindness of British socialists to the evils of communism. "You hate our Cassandra cries and resent us as allies," Koestler had said, "but when all is said, we ex-Communists are the only people on your side who know what it's all about." This led to a plan for what would ultimately become *The God That Failed,* a title that subsequently caught the popular imagination.[15]

Contributors included Ignazio Silone, Stephen Spender, Franz Borkenau, Louis Fischer, Richard Wright, and, by proxy, André Gide, but Koestler's essay, "Memoirs of a Tightrope Walker," was by common consent the most memorable. Written in the late spring of 1949, it was his first piece of truly autobiographical writing since *Scum of the Earth,* and the story flowed from his pen with an ease and freedom he had not experienced for many years. Its starting point was again the contrast between faith and reason. "A faith is not acquired by reasoning," it began. "One does not fall in love with a woman, or enter the womb of a church, as a result of logical persuasion. Reason may defend an act of faith—but only after the act has been committed." Koestler gave a brief account of his childhood and youth, emphasizing his discontent with his life, and included a vivid account of his "conversion" in Berlin, his pilgrimage to the Soviet holy land, his efforts to remain on "the tightrope of self-deception," followed by first doubts and then final loss of faith after the Hitler-Stalin pact of 1939. Koestler diagnosed his years in thrall to communism as "an addiction," as difficult to cure as any other. "After the Lost Weekend in Utopia the temptation is strong to have one last drop, even if watered down and sold under a different label. And there is always a new label on the Cominform's black market in ideals."[16]

The God That Failed appeared a few short months after *Promise and Fulfilment,* and erased whatever negative feelings had been aroused by that book or by *Insight and Outlook.* Rebecca West called it "one of the most handsome presents that has ever been given to future historians of our time" and singled out Koestler's essay for its "three-dimensionality." Koestler was really three people, she pointed out astutely. He was "a believing poet who perpetually changes into an unbelieving critic savagely eager to tear up all evidence of his previous manifestations of faith but never able to complete the work of destruction before he changes back into the poet who is equally eager to fill the wastepaper basket with all evidences of the critic's skepticism; while another part of him, as tough and jaunty as a racetrack gambler, looks over the wall at this protean struggle quite unimpressed and comments on it with ribald wit. Here he recreates the most formative experience of his life, analyzes it, mocks it." The images of poet, critic, and racetrack gambler perfectly captured the elusive mixture of lyricism, analysis, and wisecracks that made Koestler's work unique and accounted not only for his sometimes doubtful taste but also for the power of his imagination and the sting of his incisive wit.[17]

The success of the memoir set Koestler thinking about the possibility of a full-scale autobiography, but a visiting Canadian editor gave him the idea for a new novel that suddenly revived his waning interest in fiction. What would happen, wondered the editor, if a Russian secret service agent fell in love with the daughter of an American diplomat in Paris? Romeo and Juliet meet the Cold War. Koestler decided to set the novel in the future—not as far ahead as in *Twilight Bar* but about five to ten years hence, when the Soviet Union (called the New Commonwealth in the novel) had devoured several more countries in Europe and the United States was thinking seriously about a preventive war. This was the germ of what would become *The Age of Longing.*[18]

Before he could get down to work, however, he had to overcome the many distractions that his new life in Paris had brought with it, not least the ownership of a new house and the need to establish a new routine. Outwardly, whether Mamaine was there or not, his routine varied little. He had an iron constitution and rarely suffered aftereffects from late nights or binge drinking. He still took a cold bath or shower every morning, and some Benzedrine if hungover, and was always ready for a full day's work, writing steadily until lunchtime, then taking a short siesta, and invariably returning to his desk until early evening. But he was a tremendously slow writer, perhaps because of the strain of writing in English—still a foreign language for him—and felt obliged to revise and rewrite as many as five or six times. Being fluent in French and German, he was still checking, revising, and sometimes changing the translations of his books in those languages too. In the summer of

1949, while Mamaine was mostly away, he worked intensively with Dominique Aury (the future author of *The Story of O*) on a French translation of *Promise and Fulfilment* and practically rewrote the book as he went along.

He acquired a Canadian sailing canoe and took to spending whole weekends on the Seine or in the forest of Fontainebleau. To the canoe were added a rowing boat for crossing to the forest and a sculler for exercise. When not rushing up to Paris to see friends, he would invite then down to Verte Rive, and the stream of visitors never seemed to cease: Aron, Sperber, Willert, Pierre Berthaux (head of the French Sureté Générale), Winkler, Calmann, and Guy de Rothschild, all from Paris (though Sartre, Beauvoir, and Malraux always seemed to find a pretext to stay away), and Dick and Zita Crossman, Michael Foot, and Jill Craigie from England, not to speak of other guests from Germany, Austria, Israel, and the United States.

On such occasions Koestler was a generous and solicitous host, but a controlling one. While guests were "free" during daytime hours, they were expected to present themselves for cocktails, dinner, and talk in the evenings and for meals, games, and sundry other forms of entertainment on weekends. "Talk" invariably meant politics, and these wide-ranging discussions and after-dinner verbal duels with Koestler were remembered by many as the high points of their visits. "Entertainment" meant Scrabble, chess, canasta, parlor games, canoeing or sailing on the Seine, and walks in the Fontainebleau forest or sightseeing trips to local beauty spots.

Koestler was still distressingly competitive in an adolescent sort of way, whether in board games, conversation, or dueling for the attentions of a pretty woman, and he hated to lose. When his new publisher, Hamish "Jamie" Hamilton, came to stay, Koestler challenged him to a sculling match and was soundly beaten, only to learn that Hamilton had won a silver medal for rowing in the 1928 Amsterdam Olympics. William Phillips, in Paris on a Rockefeller grant with his wife, Edna, enjoyed most of his visit but bitterly resented having to drink champagne with breakfast and play parlor games in the afternoon. Phillips also had a run-in with Koestler's "menacing boxer dog," Sabby, whose growl badly frightened him, and on their drive back to Paris overheard Koestler blatantly propositioning Edna to return alone with him to Verte Rive.[19]

AS LA VIE TRIVIALE increasingly overwhelmed *la vie tragique,* Koestler's depression returned with full force, and the more depressed he grew, the more he looked to women to revive his spirits. One dalliance was with Aury and another with the French Jewish journalist Danielle Hunebelle, who described him as looking much like the young boxer puppy that preceded him through the door when they met: muscled and expectant, as if waiting to pounce, and overflowing with nervous energy. "His blue eyes matched his suit. He had blond, cropped hair, flared nostrils, and a smile that was both smug and Machiavellian." Getting to know him better, Danielle thought that there was something of the hunted animal about him. He was always on his guard, and his "diabolical intelligence" worked overtime. Friendly yet tortured, passionate and completely in the moment, he seemed able to relax only when he was in company, for with heavy doses of wine, food, Hungarian music, gambling, and women, "all his complexes evaporated."[20]

The principal antidote to his distemper that summer was an attractive young secretary he had hired to do the work that Mamaine wouldn't and couldn't do. Cynthia May Jefferies was a pretty, chestnut-haired South African of twenty-two, with wide-set eyes, a winning smile, and a desire to please. Superficially without a care in the world, she secretly grieved for the father she had lost at the age of ten and had endured a lonely adolescence somewhat resembling Koestler's own. It seems she had been romantically involved with a couple of older men in Pretoria, one of whom, according to her sister, had treated her with violence, and she had moved to France to get away from him.[21]

Impressed by Cynthia's outstanding skills in dictation, shorthand, and typing and her eagerness to please, Koestler found that he enjoyed her company. He was lonely without Mamaine, while Cynthia was obedient, efficient, and in schoolgirlish awe of her famous boss and revealed a trim figure when she donned a bikini to join him in his sailing canoe. Evidently this is where the first seduction took place, though who was seducing whom remains a question. Koestler's skills in this department were formidable, but, judging from the chapters Cynthia later wrote for their memoir, *Stranger in the Square,* she had set her sights on a romance with Koestler almost from the start.[22]

Not long after Cynthia started work, Mamaine returned from England rested and refreshed. Camus had written to her in London to say he would always be faithful to her memory and was grateful for the happiness she had brought him. He added (possibly in response to a reproach from Mamaine) that he had never experienced anything other than respect and affection for Koestler. But it was one thing to respect someone, quite another to have to live with him, and he felt that Mamaine must have some grand motive for staying with Koestler. "On the other hand, I know he is a man of substance and one can rely on him. And I don't know many people of whom I could truthfully say the same."[23]

Whether it was grand or not, Mamaine had certainly regained her motive. "For all his faults he is the best of men," she told Celia. "I was struck, the last time I saw him, by his expression, at the same time serious, tender and resolute." At Verte Rive, she found him as full of vitality as ever, a living reproach to her own delicate health. He was visibly delighted to have her back again and insisted she get plenty of rest, sometimes going to absurd lengths to make sure she wasn't disturbed. But the house was still in the chaotic state in which she had left it, badly in need of redecoration and a woman's touch. Their housekeeper had given notice, and Sabby's visit to the kennels with a pedigree boxer bitch called Lucie had resulted in ten puppies, filling Koestler with inordinate paternal pride.[24]

Mamaine was buoyed by the thought that Koestler's divorce decree was imminent and they would be married by the end of the year, a prize that seems to have canceled the disturbing realization that she was losing weight again and that her lungs seemed to be suffering from the dampness of the river. It also compensated for the temporary loss of their sex life when Koestler started having treatment for a prostate problem. Even when Koestler lost his temper one day and struck her "a stunning blow on the head," she responded with stoicism. It was "only the third time" he had done this, she reported to Celia, which was "three times too many, of course," but "considering how berserk he goes, surprisingly few!" He apologized a half hour later for his bad behavior, and Mamaine quickly forgave him.[25]

In November she returned to London for her long-delayed bronchoscopy and found time to attend Orwell's wedding to Sonia Brownell. It was an extraordinary occasion. Orwell was confined to his bed in University College Hospital, where the ceremony was held. There were only a dozen people present, and Mamaine persuaded David Astor, the best man, to take Sonia and a few others out to lunch, "to avoid Sonia having to go home and eat bread and milk on her wedding day, which I knew she was rather dreading to have to do." Mamaine's operation went off more or less smoothly, though Celia later came to the conclusion that Dr. Deller was a quack. The bronchoscopy wasn't really necessary and made Mamaine "worse rather than better." Nevertheless, Mamaine and Celia were able to spend a delicious week together in Sussex as Mamaine convalesced, after which she collected Adele Koestler in London and traveled back to Paris with her.[26]

This visit to see her son was a rare treat for Adele and a rare ordeal for her grudging offspring. Adele was now living at a genteel residence for Jewish ladies, the Pension Sachs, in Hampstead, behind the Swiss Cottage tube station. Koestler paid the bills but rarely saw his mother, even when he was in London, and insisted on keeping her at arm's length. She made up for it by sending him a steady stream of letters in her copperplate Viennese hand, addressed to "my beloved," "my beloved son," "my precious son," and bombarding him with requests for money, favors, and visits, along with reproaches for his indifference, to which he replied with brief typed (and probably dictated) notes beginning "Dear Mother" and keeping anything personal to a minimum.[27]

Adele was immensely proud of her famous son's career but had been upset by his essay in *The God that Failed*. "Don't you have even a single nice memory of your childhood and youth?" she wrote from London. "Dear son, why do you keep thinking about awful experiences over and over again?" The essay had caused her a week's worth of sleepless nights, for "now the world, *my small world*" (she meant the pension in Hampstead), "knows that our dear *Papuli had frayed cuffs.*" She later apologized for her "snobbery and vanity," and Koestler was gentle in his reply, but her visit to Paris was not a happy one. Adele kept returning to the subject of Koestler's childhood and vehemently denied that it had been unhappy, though she did concede that she had kept him from mixing with "unsuitable" children for fear that he might catch some infection from them.[28]

Mamaine was amazed by Koestler's expression during this conversation. "K's face was worth seeing, but fortunately she didn't seem to notice—sparks of hatred flashed from his eyes, he grinned fiendishly." In bed afterward, he talked at great length about his childhood, convincing Mamaine that Adele was such a monster of selfishness that she felt a rush of pity for him. Before leaving for London, Adele handed Koestler a poem she had clipped, in which a mother tells her son he will realize how much he loves her only when she is dead.[29]

KOESTLER CONTINUED TO RELIEVE his tensions with liberal amounts of alcohol. After an unexpected reunion with the *News Chronicle*'s Willie Forrest at Troika 22, where they downed vast quantities of vodka and champagne, cried into their glasses over lost illusions, and swooned to the sound of balalaikas playing Russian Gypsy music, Koestler found it impossible to drive home and pulled off the road in Charenton to sleep it off. He woke in a filthy police cell with barred windows and a steel door. After pounding on the door with his shoe (as he had done in Málaga), he asked to be allowed to phone Mamaine and, when the superintendent refused, "socked him" (Mamaine's words) in the nose. Koestler was whisked off to the local courthouse, photographed full face and in profile (complete with two black eyes), and charged with assaulting a police officer. He was so hungover, he later told Mamaine, that for a moment he thought he was back in Málaga and on his way to be shot. It was Christmas Eve, and Mamaine was frantic over his failure to turn up for dinner. Luckily, one of their Christmas guests was a Gaullist official, Louis Vallon, who used his government contacts to find out where Koestler was and get him released.

Koestler swore to stop drinking, asking Mamaine mournfully if she believed he could reform, and loyally she said yes, but each suspected the other of lying. Koestler would indirectly answer the question later in *The Age of Longing,* in which a Russian writer wakes one morning with a hangover. His remorse is tempered by the fact that when drunk he experiences "an infinite well-being which abolished the future and the past, and made the present moment the sole reality, aglow with life and meaning." At such moments "the future had no reality—it had literally ceased to exist as if a whole department of his mind had been amputated with a knife." The "pounding of guilt in the chest, the torture of the contracted skull" would come only with the hangover, which it was impossible to take seriously the night before.[30]

When the news of the charges leaked out, the press had a great deal of fun at Koestler's expense. "Yogi Decks Commissar" was one headline. L'Humanité couldn't resist the opportunity to pillory "that Trotskyite Koestler," who "specialized in insulting the French people." Koestler was penitent. He told the court that he had nothing against the policemen, they were only doing their job, and he got off with the relatively light fine of 150,000 francs.[31]

Koestler's oath to go on the wagon was both relative (he had promised Mamaine to drink "not more than three cognacs" after dinner) and provisional, and gave way all too quickly when Sonia Orwell came for a visit. Koestler had been strongly affected by Orwell's death in January and had written an obituary for Astor's Observer in which he drew attention to Orwell's "ruthlessness towards himself." He was "the only writer of genius" among the social critics who had risen to prominence in Britain between the two world wars. Orwell had also been, though Koestler didn't say so, his best and closest literary ally in Britain, and his loss was more serious than Koestler cared to admit. Meanwhile, Sonia seemed to have forgiven Koestler their one-night stand and her abortion and wanted his advice about her plans for a new volume of Orwell's selected essays. She then rejected most of Koestler's suggestions, and they both ended up drunk and incoherent.[32]

Shortly after Sonia's visit, on April 15, 1950, Koestler and Mamaine were married at the British Embassy in Paris, with Paul and Betty Winkler as witnesses. The ceremony itself was perfunctory, and the aftermath, though not as sad as at Orwell and Sonia's wedding, was even more of an anticlimax. After a champagne lunch with the Winklers, Koestler went shopping while Mamaine took a nap. They were to meet up again that evening at the Café Flore, but by the time Mamaine arrived, Koestler was drunk again and very nervous, evidently because of the presence of "a horrible-looking Communist" (Mamaine's words) whom Koestler had recognized as an ex-comrade from his Berlin days and had called over to their table. They went for dinner at the Restaurant des Gourmets, accompanied by the Sperbers, Jim Putnam and his wife, Stephen Spender, a couple of Spender's friends, and Cynthia. Koestler grew increasingly rowdy and maudlin and offended Spender's friends so much they left in a huff, leading Koestler to bemoan "his inability to prevent people fighting with him" and to reproach himself for tactlessness. They went to a nightclub, but Koestler disliked the atmosphere and insisted they continue on to another club, the Lapin Agile, to which Mamaine agreed on condition that she drive. She gave her version of what followed in a letter to Celia.[33]

"K walked off. Stephen, Cynthia and I followed soon after and saw K sitting in his car. He said, I'm going home; are you coming? I said, yes if you let me drive; and at this, as foreseen, he drove off, so Cynthia and I spent the night with Stephen in a flat which had been lent to him. Sunday morning Cynthia went off early and I had breakfast in a cafe on the quais with Stephen and I went with him to see an exhibition of German primitives at the Orangerie. He said: I've always wanted to spend the night with you, it's too bad it was your wedding night. For some reason this was quite extraordinarily nice: Stephen is so easy to talk to, and one can talk to him about anything."[34]

Mamaine's coolness under fire and delayed return to Verte Rive left Koestler sitting at home on tenterhooks. She found him full of remorse and self-loathing. "He said if there was a nonreligious monastery he would go into it, because he has to lead a completely solitary life, however lonely, to achieve a real life of the spirit." In his diary he noted the need for "an uplift of virtue" and swore that henceforth he would drink only at "Saturday dinner and lunch and dinner on Sunday." Two weeks later he wrote "fortnight on waggon, seems much longer" but added with satisfaction that for the first time in years he could read after dinner, whereas before he hadn't been able to "remember a single word the next day."[35]

Being respectably married seems only to have made Koestler more difficult. "He loves me as much as he is capable of," Mamaine told Celia, "which isn't much. There is literally no one, man, woman or child, whom K really loves; he doesn't know the meaning of the word. He doesn't love himself either, in fact he simply projects his self-loathing onto other people." But Mamaine had no thought of leaving him. "I am awfully happy with K, simply because I do love him so much. Not a day goes by without my thinking what happiness it is for me to be with him. I take it for granted that people like us can't hope to find other people who can love us as much as we do, not that such people don't exist, but they seem rare among men. As a matter of fact, whatever happens to me from now on—and I have no reason to suppose that anything awful will—I shall consider my life has been well spent, since I have spent six years of it with K. For apart from anything else, I greatly believe in K as a writer, and I would do anything, even leave him, if it were necessary to help him fulfill what I believe to be his destiny. I should count myself and my life of little importance in such a case."[36]

CHAPTER THIRTY-ONE

TO THE BARRICADES

The last struggle will be between the Communists and the anti-Communists.

— IGNAZIO SILONE

WHILE KOESTLER WAS IN PALESTINE the Soviets had engineered their coup in Czechoslovakia and launched a blockade of West Berlin, to which the Allies had responded with a dramatic airlift and a vow to keep Berlin free. Tito's Yugoslavia was expelled from the Soviet-dominated Cominform and Tito himself vilified as a traitor. Mao's Communists proclaimed a people's republic in northern China, and Korea split into two mutually hostile ministates, one capitalist and one Communist. The still-unnamed "cold war" threatened to turn hot, and as Eastern Europe was absorbed completely into the Soviet bloc, there was talk in the West of following up the Marshall Plan with an Atlantic Pact to tie Western Europe more closely to the United States.

The tightening of the Soviet vise on the satellite countries was accompanied by show trials of dozens of political leaders there, including László Rajk, the foreign minister of Hungary, and Traicho Kostov, the deputy prime minister of Bulgaria, and a wave of arrests of lesser fry, including two of Koestler's Hungarian friends, Pál Ignotus and Endre Havas. Ignotus had foolishly agreed to become the London press attaché for the Hungarian Communist embassy in London and was arrested on a visit to Budapest to see his dying father. Under torture Ignotus confessed to all sorts of anti-Communist crimes and was sentenced to nine years' imprisonment. Havas, the Hungarian cultural attaché in Paris, refused to confess and was reduced to a gibbering wreck. He died in prison, insane, about three years later.

These arrests brought home to Koestler anew the true nature of the Soviet menace and increased his disgust with those French intellectuals who still seemed to reside in a cocoon of unreality, unsure which way to jump. Sartre, Camus, and Merleau-Ponty had made a last-ditch effort to establish a liberal third force in French politics between left and right, but its explicit anti-Americanism, and its much softer critique of the Soviet Union, had prompted Camus to leave and the new movement to fall apart. Koestler in any case regarded the idea of a third force as hypocritical and shortsighted. Sartre was widely read and admired in America as a philosopher and major author, whereas in Moscow his books were banned and he was characterized as an ideological enemy, yet Sartre perversely insisted that to oppose the Soviet Union was to go against the march of history, whereas to resist the United States was the ideological duty of everyone who was against imperialism and racism.[1]

Some notable defamation trials in Paris in 1949—distant echoes of the turbulence in Eastern Europe—allowed Koestler to play at least a small part in pushing back. Viktor Kravchenko, the author of a celebrated anti-Stalinist memoir, *I Chose Freedom,* sued *Les Lettres Françaises* for calling his book a pack of lies concocted by the American secret services. The star witness for Kravchenko was Grete Buber-Neumann, brought to Paris by Koestler. He had persuaded her to write a memoir about her experiences of Soviet and Nazi jails (it later appeared in English as *Under Two Dictators*) and had also found a French publisher for her. Petite and vivacious, Grete convinced even Simone de Beauvoir, who was in court, with her intelligence and shining honesty. Beauvoir, to be fair, had believed Kravchenko and had tried to persuade Sartre to publish an excerpt ("he tells the story of his own experience, which exactly matches Koestler's"), but in vain. The French court found in Kravchenko's favor, though by offering him only token damages it awarded a moral victory to the Communists.[2]

Grete was followed to Paris by Alexander Weissberg, who with Koestler's encouragement was also writing a memoir about his imprisonment in Russia and Germany. Tall and balding, with a Falstaffian girth, Alex towered over Koestler and Sperber and overpowered them both with his ebullient high spirits. When he laughed—usually at one of his own jokes—his entire frame shook and trembled, and his gold teeth reflected the light. Koestler edited and wrote a preface for Weissberg's memoir, "a rambling, spouting whale of a book," which with its endless asides, flashbacks, and digressions mimicked the headlong way that Alex spoke in person.[3]

Weissberg was the leading witness in another defamation case against *Les Lettres Françaises,* brought this time by David Rousset, the famous chronicler of Nazi abuses (in *L'Univers concentrationnaire*) and former ally of Sartre in trying to establish a third force. When Rousset had turned his attention to the Soviet camps, Sartre and Merleau-Ponty had admitted their existence but felt they were canceled out by detention camps in the French colonies and in Greece and Spain. The Russian proletariat could be relied upon to get rid of the camps when they were no longer needed, whereas the West's camps were systemic. "We have the same values as a Communist, and for that reason we can never support Rousset," they declared. When Weissberg was derided in court as an unreliable foreigner (and a German to boot), Rousset's lawyer read out the letters to Stalin on Alex's behalf that Koestler had procured before the war from Einstein and Joliot-Curie, and the defense was routed. Like Kravchenko, Rousset was awarded only token damages, another indication of French legal bias and the determination of the French intelligentsia to ignore the truth of Stalinism.[4]

Koestler responded to Sartre's sophistries in a review of Sperber's new novel, *Et Le Buisson Deviént Cindre* (The Burning Bush), in *Le Figaro Littéraire*. Sperber's novel had its weaknesses, wrote Koestler, "which I find all the more excusable since they are the same as mine: its ideas are more important than the characters, and its situations are more real than the people who participate in them." But Sperber's work had a lesson for the "little flirts of St. Germain des Prés." Just as a character in the novel was said to betray others "only out of loyalty," so did the French left betray humanity out of misplaced loyalty to ideals empty of moral content, to the "nausea of puberty" (a jab at Sartre)—translated into the class struggle—and to the artist's masochistic desire to prostrate himself before members of the so-called proletariat. This artist wasn't interested in "the real victims of social injustice" but in "a legendary and apocryphal figure, half Messiah, half Buffalo Bill."[5]

KOESTLER WAS ABSOLUTELY RIGHT, of course, and Sartre wrong, but this was by no means accepted at the time by most intellectuals on the left, not even in America, and by the spring of 1950 the political situation in Western Europe struck Koestler as worse than at any time since the summer of 1939. He even changed his mind about de Gaulle, irritably informing the astonished Sperber that de Gaulle was the only man in France who saw the Communists for what they were and was ready to take action against them. "Europe *fichu* [done for]," he noted in his diary. "Decided to get out to USA in good and earnest."[6]

His growing affinity for the USA was founded on his earlier conviction that only America could provide the necessary counterweight to the Soviet Union, yet it was obvious that in the sphere of propaganda, the Soviets had outsmarted the Americans with a cleverly conceived and conducted ideological offensive that was miles ahead of any western effort. In 1947 they had created the Cominform, designed to keep newly conquered Eastern Europe in line and support Soviet policies, and had followed that up with two highly effective peace conferences, both in the western heartland, one at the Waldorf-Astoria hotel in New York in March 1949 and the second in Paris a month later. Both were propaganda bonanzas, sponsored by amenable luminaries such as Charles Chaplin, Albert Einstein, and Paul Robeson, and both featured dozens of other prominent intellectuals among the participants. Each had culminated in a mass rally for peace, and the Paris conference had adopted Picasso's peace dove as a potent symbol of the Communist-dominated "world peace movement."

It wasn't hard for an old Münzenberg man such as Koestler to spot the hidden hand behind these manifestations, and he chafed over their success. Luckily, he wasn't alone. Sidney Hook, his quondam New York debating opponent, had revived the prewar American Committee for Cultural Freedom, with Mary McCarthy, Dwight Macdonald, Arthur Schlesinger, Jr., William Phillips, and a young émigré Russian composer by the name of Nicolas Nabokov (a cousin of the then little-known Vladimir) among its members. Hook had staged a counterrally in New York and attended a similar counterconference in Paris organized by Rousset and Georges Altman, editor of the independent socialist newspaper *Franc-Tireur*. This "International Day of Resistance to Dictatorship and War" had featured Silone and Franz Borkenau as speakers, and Sartre had attended solely in order to denounce American imperialism and announce his resignation.[7]

Koestler wasn't invited to the Paris counterconference but was encouraged in the fall of 1949 when Burnham sent news from the USA that "important changes" were taking place in Washington that had a potential bearing on "Chateau Conservation projects." Burnham's reference was to a branch of the newly created CIA that had begun to take an interest in the cultural field, namely, the Office of Policy Coordination (OPC), run by an old OSS hand, Frank Wisner, and Wisner's flamboyant assistant, Carmel Offie. Offie's dual responsibilities for labor and émigré affairs offered a perfect cover. He had funneled funds to protesters at the Waldorf-Astoria conference through David Dubinsky of the International Ladies' Garment Workers Union, and in Paris through the AFL labor leaders Jay Lovestone and Irving Brown, and was consulting Burnham and Schlesinger, among others, about what to do next.[8]

Soon after this news, a "delegation," consisting of Hook, Borkenau, Sperber, and a fiery young American journalist named Mel Lasky, came to see Koestler at Verte Rive to express their dissatisfaction with the Paris counterconference and talk about holding a better one in West Berlin. It seems that several people had thought of this project at more or less the same time. Ruth Fischer had discussed the idea with Koestler that summer, and both Lasky and Hook claimed to have had the idea independently of Fischer (Michael Josselson, who was just starting at the CIA, later claimed it as *his* idea, but he was a latecomer). The true intellectual progenitor of the conference was in fact Koestler. His speeches in America and his articles for *Life* and *The New York Times* had consistently and prominently advocated some sort of cultural offensive to oppose and offset Soviet propaganda, and he had actively furthered the cause with his essay for *The God That Failed,* not to speak of his energetic support for Buber-Neumann, Weissberg, Kravchenko, and Rousset.[9]

WEST BERLIN WAS an outstanding choice for a conference of this kind. Its political status was unique as a tiny outpost of western democracy in the surrounding sea of communism, and it was involved in a constant struggle to maintain its independence and viability. Stalin's physical blockade of the city had been answered by the western airlift, but beyond the purely military struggle there was a struggle of ideas, and the symbolism was irresistible. An international gathering of eminent and independent intellectuals would hold free discussions as far east as it was possible to go, thus boosting the West Berliners' morale and underlining the West's cultural vitality and freedom.

Lasky and Borkenau met with Ruth Fischer in Berlin to draft a program for "a gathering of ex-Communists, plus a representative group of anti-Stalinist American, English and European intellectuals" to "give the Politburo hell right at the gate of their own hell." A copy of the program made its way to OPC's office in Washington, and Josselson immediately grasped its importance. In January 1950 he wrote a report for Wisner in support of the proposal, and in April Wisner's OPC approved funding to the tune of fifty thousand dollars, a very large sum of money at the time.[10]

The CIA connection was kept a deep secret. Despite later recriminations, it seems that neither Fischer nor Lasky nor their immediate friends knew about it initially—perhaps because the CIA was so new and little known—though they were aware that some branch of the American government had agreed to write the checks. There is also the irony (missed by just about all later commentators, whether favorable or hostile) that the CIA was actually pleading for *less* overt anti-communism than its organizers seemed to desire. Wisner expressly warned Josselson to keep Lasky and Burnham under wraps for fear that their well-known anti-Communist views would compromise the conference. Wisner would probably have warned Josselson against Koestler, too, had he known of the latter's eventual role, but there is no record of him having done so.

Lasky had already appointed himself general secretary and mobilized the staff of the literary magazine *Der Monat* to do the work, and Josselson wisely decided to remain in the background. It's not clear who chose the conference name, but the title that appeared on Lasky's letterhead was "The Congress for Cultural Freedom," along with a planned date of June 25–30. Lasky lost no time in persuading the Social Democratic mayor of West Berlin, Ernst Reuter, to chair the host committee and was well advanced on putting together an international committee as well. Burnham, with his own connections to the CIA, was also able to bypass Wisner and with Hook became one of the organizers of the American delegation to the conference.[11]

Both Lasky and Burnham kept Koestler apprised of their plans, and Burnham traveled to Verte Rive to discuss who should be invited to Berlin and what themes needed to be addressed. Koestler was still struggling to finish *The Age of Longing* and finally did so at the end of May, after which he switched into high gear to prepare for Berlin. At Burnham's suggestion, he wrote a longish paper on the "Left-Right Dilemma" and the problem of neutrality, which was to be his main contribution to the congress and, at Lasky's request, a short keynote speech with which to close the opening day's proceedings. Lasky also asked Koestler to arrive a couple of days early, so that he could meet Ernst Reuter and take part in making the final arrangements for the program.[12]

Koestler was keyed up at the prospect of returning to Berlin. It was the scene of some of his greatest triumphs as a journalist, the city of his gilded youth, and the repository of tender memories. It was also the place where he had embraced communism, and he could hardly miss the irony of returning as an apostate, eager to undo his earlier errors and unmask the ideology he had once espoused. Finally he was eager to find out how his books had been received in Germany. His native language was German, and he had taken great care in checking and revising the translations to make sure they were as good as the originals.

His enemies claimed that *Darkness at Noon* had been subsidized and distributed by the Allies in Germany as an instrument of the Cold War, but from 1945 to 1947 the opposite was true: it had been banned by the British so as not to offend the Russians. In 1948 the American radio station RIAS had broadcast a dramatization of the novel, but it was not until 1949, a year before the conference, that German editions of the book were allowed to appear, along with some essays from *The Yogi and the Commissar* in pamphlet form. A fresh edition of *The Gladiators* (originally written in German but back-translated from English) was published by Axel Springer, and only then were the Germans able to catch up with the rest of his work. Babette Gross, now his literary agent in Germany, told him his writings were hugely successful and said the students at the Free University in Berlin had asked for Koestler to come and lecture to them. "You have no idea what a strong attraction the Berlin air has for East Berlin and the satellite countries," she wrote, "and your name there has a magic resonance."[13]

Boarding the night train to Frankfurt at the Gare de l'Est in mid-June 1950, Koestler and Mamaine discovered that Police Commissioner Bertaux had provided them with a bodyguard as far as the frontier and that the next sleeper contained none other than Jean-Paul Sartre. It had been eighteen months since Sartre bid Koestler a frosty farewell, but he accepted Koestler's invitation to share some boxed food and wine. Sartre was friendly and cheerful but said that he had sworn off alcohol and rarely went out in the evenings anymore, since so few people agreed with his politics.[14]

In Berlin, Burnham and Lasky were at loggerheads over the program, and Koestler spent much of the weekend bullying them into forming an unofficial steering committee, with himself, Hook, and Brown as additional members. Over dinner the first evening, Koestler and Silone renewed their argument over the desirability of the left cooperating with the right on certain issues. The Italian political scene wasn't that different from the French, and Silone, like the French leftists, adamantly opposed the idea that the right could be right about anything, even communism. Koestler argued that a situation that threatened war changed the equation and got Silone to admit grudgingly that he was not entirely against the Atlantic Pact. The differences between the two men were never ironed out, however, and would assume great significance in the days to come, for Silone and Koestler represented the two poles of the chief ideological division at the congress over how best to conduct the struggle with communism. Silone and his supporters from Britain, France, and Italy emphasized the need for social and economic reforms in Europe and a policy that emphasized the West's achievements in order to steal the Communists' thunder, whereas Koestler, with the support of the Americans, advocated taking the battle to the enemy and challenging Communist expansion and imperialism in every way possible. In the long run, the CIA would embrace Silone's strategy, but in Berlin it was Koestler's militancy that carried the day.

ON JUNE 25, 1950, more than a hundred writers, scholars, and scientists gathered in the Titania Palace theater in the U.S. zone of Berlin, two blocks from the Brandenburg Gate, to attend the congress's opening ceremonies. The large American delegation included Tennessee Williams and Carson McCullers, along with the usual suspects, while the British contingent was more modest and low-key, comprising A. J. Ayer, Hugh Trevor-Roper, Herbert Read, and a brace of Conservative MPs (Crossman was supposed to be there but canceled at the last minute). From France came Jules Romain, Claude Mauriac, Rousset, and Altman (Malraux cried off for health reasons, and it was never clear whether his illness was genuine or diplomatic); from Italy, Silone and Carlo Levi; from Germany, Golo Mann and Richard Löwenthal; from Norway, Haakon Lie; and from Switzerland, Denis de Rougemont. There was one delegate from Latin America, one from Asia, and none from Africa. Messages of support were read out from, among others, Eleanor Roosevelt, André Gide, Julian Huxley, Louis de Broglie, and George Grosz.[15]

Opening day was dominated by the sensational news that the North Korean army had crossed the thirty-eighth parallel and was invading the South. "We are on the eve of a global conflict," Hook said to Schlesinger when they met at the airport. The drama of that invasion lent an urgency to the opening ceremonies that was enhanced by the strains of Beethoven's *Egmont* overture and by Mayor Ernst Reuter asking the delegates and the four thousand people in the audience to stand for a minute of silence.

Silone was the first to speak. He stated soberly that the writers and artists gathered in Berlin were far from unanimous in their views and that liberty needed to be defended everywhere. They were there as a duty and in order to express their solidarity, not to abandon democratic freedoms and put on the uniform of totalitarianism (which was taken by some as a swipe at Koestler's militancy). Silone was followed by Romain, Hook, and a number of other speakers, and Koestler was left to wind up the session. He had spent all morning rewriting his speech and translating it into German, and from his very first words, "Friends, comrades in suffering and comrades in arms!," it was clear he intended to strike a high, oratorical note. His words were not overtly addressed to Silone but continued their argument and were haunted by the invisible presence of the man on the train to Frankfurt.[16]

Two forms of political action were possible, said Koestler. One was to refuse the world of black-and-white choices, strive cleverly for synthesis and compromise, and search for a third way forward, which might be called the "neither-nor" approach. This (though he didn't say so) was the attitude of Sartre and his followers and to a certain extent of Silone. The alternative lay in the biblical injunction "Let your communication be, Yea yea, Nay, nay; for whatsoever is more than these comes from evil." Both responses were appropriate and necessary at different times, but at a moment of vital emergency like the present, it was idiotic to preach "neutrality towards the bubonic plague." He softened his words by saying that many who cherished freedom had failed to realize that the time had come for "Yea and Nay." "Destiny's challenge to man is always couched in simple and direct language, without relative clauses, and requires an answer in equally simple terms."[17]

Koestler endeared himself to his listeners in the auditorium by speaking in fluent German and delivering his speech with an eloquence and sincerity that impressed all who heard him, regardless of whether they agreed or not. In one swoop he also raised the temperature of the meeting and set a tone of urgency that was to dominate the proceedings for the rest of the week. The words "Yea, yea, nay, nay" became a catchphrase among delegates and in the press—much to the discomfiture of some of the waverers present, especially Ayer and Trevor-Roper, who went out of their way to distance the British delegation from Koestler. It was a phrase worthy of the great Münzenberg himself, but that was also a problem. Koestler's talent for phrasemaking and his histrionic impulses led to oversimplification. The invocation of "evil" had an apocalyptic ring to it that seemed to preclude compromise, and his sloganeering alienated some of the more moderate and thoughtful people present.

He made up for it midweek when it was his turn to speak again. It was a hot day. He peeled off his jacket, rolled up his sleeves, loosened his tie, and launched into an impassioned speech that became the focal point of the congress. Appealing to a host of historical analogies as he went along, he proposed that the "old antinomies" of socialism versus capitalism, and of left versus right, were out of date and meaningless. The term *left* in particular had become a "noxious anachronism," implying a continuous spectrum between "liberal progressives and worshippers of tyranny." The sense of neighborly solidarity implicit in it was "an emotional trap" that paralyzed the well-meaning progressive's defenses and made him incapable of attack. Koestler traced the way Soviet manipulation of the word *socialism,* along with other left-wing buzzwords, such as *peace, brotherhood,* and *democracy,* had emptied them of meaning. Non-socialist America was far more internationalist than Soviet Russia, and socialist Russia was infinitely more tyrannical than even the worst forms of capitalism in America. The decisive conflict was no longer between socialism and capitalism but between "total tyranny and relative freedom."[18]

> We have no panacea to offer to the manifold problems that beset the civilization we are defending. We do not wish to embark on a crusade. We have learnt the tragic lesson of our times: we are conscious of the fact that most crusades in history have ended in disaster and brought only misery and disillusionment in their wake. Democracy, by its very nature, can create no conspiratorial instrument comparable to the Cominform, nor produce a counter-phantom to the communist creed. The weapons in our fight can only be truth, sincerity, courage; an acute sense of reality and our appreciation of the basic values of our complex civilization. Without the return of moral and intellectual sanity no economic or military aid can save us. We count on your support.[19]

The speech was a "dialectical tour de force," as even his British critics admitted; it seems unexceptional in retrospect, but it caused a furor among the other panelists. Abusing his authority as chair, Ernst Reuter heatedly exclaimed that if Koestler were to live in Social Democratic Berlin for a while, he would quickly change his mind. Several delegates accused Koestler and other ex-Communists (employing an argument that would become a mantra in coming years) of being typical converts who rush from one extreme to another, provoking the ex-Communist Borkenau to spring to Koestler's defense and say he was glad the Americans had sent their troops to Korea. Rousset protested, and there were more cries of "Hear, hear" from Ayer and Trevor-Roper. Hook later commented that Koestler "could recite the truths of the multiplication table" in such a way as to madden people and that he didn't help matters by "grinning like a Cheshire cat" as the others lashed out at him.[20]

IT WAS CLEARLY KOESTLER'S DAY, and there was more to come. Koestler had arrived at the congress with the draft of a "Freedom Manifesto" (composed with Sperber's help) and throughout the congress pressed the steering committee to edit and refine it for adoption at the closing session on Thursday. Each evening Koestler would announce: "Mel, it's six o'clock. Ze bar is open, time for a 'night cup,'" at which the entire committee would retire to the bar to confer. On the Tuesday night, at Lasky's home in Zehlendorf, Koestler insisted on working until four in the morning on what was meant to be the final draft. Three hours later he was up again to redraft it and to supervise the translations into French and German, and on Thursday morning he presided over an editorial meeting to approve the text.[21]

The only serious criticism of Koestler's draft came from Ayer and Trevor-Roper, who wanted to drop a clause stating, "totalitarians have no right to membership in the republic of free spirits," and to add language calling for "new freedoms" and "new and constructive answers to the problems of our time." Koestler demurred at first but, at a plenary session in the afternoon, amicably agreed to the amendments, much to the surprise of those present at the meeting.

The congress concluded with a public rally at the Funkturm (Radio Tower) Gardens attended by about fifteen thousand people sitting in the open air. There were routine speeches by Silone, Rousset, Brown, and others, and then Koestler stepped up to the microphone to read the fourteen points of the Freedom Manifesto. Point one, "We hold it to be self-evident that intellectual freedom is one of the inalienable rights of man," carried clear echoes of the American Declaration of Independence and set a lofty tone for the document that followed, which had Koestler's fingerprints all over it. After reciting all fourteen points with mounting excitement, Koestler paused dramatically, then shouted into the microphone, in German, "Friends, freedom has seized the initiative!" The startled audience roared with delight.[22]

All agreed that, like it or not, Koestler was the star of the congress and, in public at least, completely overshadowed the taciturn Silone (a poor public speaker at the best of times). Behind the scenes it was a different story. Silone held his ground and obviously had many supporters, and though the two men remained outwardly friendly, their mutual incomprehension (if not hostility) surfaced at a celebration dinner at Lasky's. The drunken Koestler complained across the table to Silone that although he had great fraternal feelings for the other man, the Italian failed to reciprocate, behaving as if he, Silone, were some sort of "broad-bottomed Abruzzi peasant" and Koestler "some kind of cosmopolitan gigolo." The befuddled Silone tried to humor Koestler but, after the latter had left, was heard to say wonderingly, "He seems to think I think he's a gigolo."[23]

Hook, never on close terms with Koestler, conceded that in Berlin Koestler had been in his element, "masterful in expression, keen in give and take, and unwontedly eloquent." Hook barely recognized "the tempestuous, irrational literary lion" of New York in the "sober, disciplined people's tribune" who kept biting his words back, "even when he was baited by garrulous fools and spitefully clever Englishmen. More than any of us, Koestler was prepared to compromise on every issue, except one of principle, to preserve harmony."[24]

Before the program even began, Koestler had toured the city with Mamaine in search of old haunts. Not many of them had survived the bombing, but the tour gave him the opporunity to speak with Berliners from all walks of life, and he reveled in their expressions of feisty independence. He went twice to meet members of a human rights group that tracked arrests and trials in the eastern zone, and he lectured at the Free University to an enraptured audience of students. He also made several impromptu broadcasts in German, speaking freely about his Communist past and accusing Eastern Bloc writers such as Brecht, Georg Lukács, and Anna Seghers of being deluded. He taunted Brecht for his cowardice, pointing out that when Brecht's first wife had disappeared, Brecht had never mentioned it nor referred to her ever again.[25]

The Communist-controlled eastern sector of Berlin couldn't help but respond to the congress and to Koestler's taunts. Gerhart Eisler, his former comrade in arms and now East Germany's propaganda chief, contemptuously referred to the congress as "an imperialist intellectual six-day bicycle race" attended by "literary monkeys and American police spies." In one of his radio broadcasts Koestler struck back, reminding Eisler of their days "carrying latrine buckets to the outhouse" in Le Vernet. Another former comrade, Johannes Becher, invited Koestler to a public discussion in the eastern sector of the city, for "only there can physical and intellectual liberty be guaranteed." Koestler refused the invitation on the grounds that exactly the opposite was true (though he did send Becher a friendly note) and declined a meeting with Brecht for similar reasons.[26]

Back in Paris, Koestler thought of Berlin as "a frontier town" whose inhabitants thrived, intellectually and morally, on the stimulus provided by their exposed environment. Constant contact with the eastern zone and with Soviet ways of doing things meant that *freedom* and *democracy* were not just words but everyday, concrete reality. He felt that the mentality of the Germans had undergone a decisive change since he last had been there. Their gods were no longer Hegel and Kant but Hume and Locke, and the intensity of their experience had forged a new empiricism. Koestler tempered his reflections with a note of pessimism: "If Berlin survives, of which there is little chance, a new European spirit might be born there." But he felt cheered that Berlin and Germany seemed to have much more to offer the free world now than did Paris or France.[27]

CHAPTER THIRTY-TWO

THE CONGRESS FOR CULTURAL FREEDOM

All faults may be forgiven him who has perfect candor.
— WALT WHITMAN

THE CONFERENCE HAD VOTED to open two permanent offices, one in Berlin to work on Eastern Europe and one in Paris to work on the West. The goal was a worldwide movement for the defense of human rights and for the free exchange of ideas across national borders. A second conference was scheduled for 1951, and a twenty-five-member international commission established to oversee it. In the interim a five-man executive committee was delegated to take up the reins, consisting of Koestler, Silone, Rousset, Brown, and either Carlo Schmid or Eugen Kogon from Germany.

"I have a feeling that we have started something which is going to turn out bigger than any of us realized at the time," Koestler wrote to Burnham in the United States. He felt more cheerful than he had for months. At last people were beginning to listen to his message, and he was determined not to lose the momentum generated in Berlin. He confided to Mamaine that he was thinking of taking six months off from his writing to devote himself to the new movement. Mamaine felt he was bound to be frustrated but refrained from comment, and Koestler launched himself into organizational matters.

Within days of his return he had drafted a memo setting out "immediate tasks for the transition period." These included publication of a pamphlet summarizing the main congress speeches and resolutions, an international publicity campaign, the inauguration of a political campaign to "break the influence of the Joliot-Curies and cultural neutralists like *Temps Modernes*," and publication of a newsletter for supporters. To help Eastern Europe, a first step would be for authors to make up to two hundred copies of their books in German available gratis for smuggling into East Germany; second, all authors who had signed the Freedom Manifesto should contribute 1 percent of their worldwide royalties to the costs of running the new organization; third, there should be a series of "dialogues across the iron curtain," in which a western author or scholar addressed a counterpart in the East by radio. These broadcasts should be brief, "non-demagogic," and couched in tones of commiseration rather than bitterness. The best could be edited by a western writer ("I suggest Silone or Kogon—the Christian touch") and published as a collection.[1]

Koestler's vision was generous, concrete, and far-reaching and envisaged rapid action even before the next executive committee meeting in September, with a Paris conference foreseen for "not later than Christmas." Lasky, whose *Monat* offices had effectively become the eastern bureau in Berlin, had equally far-reaching plans, and was busily working out an organizational chart, a constitution, and a set of ambitious goals that ranged from documentary movies to a research institute to a new university (complete with four-year curriculum), as well as pressure groups and national bureaus that would eventually blanket the world. Lasky was concerned lest the two wings of the congress split and advocated peaceful coexistence between "the uncompromising resisters against the East" (Koestler, Burnham, and Co.) and "the optimistic builders of the West" (Silone, Rousset, and Co.). In mid-July he came to Paris to meet Koestler, Irving Brown, and Burnham, and Verte Rive became the site of a series of intense conclaves between this core group and Aron, Rousset, Altman, Jean-Jacques Servan-Schreiber, and other French intellectuals.[2]

Koestler's involvement immediately became a topic of discussion in the French press. The radical socialist *L'Observateur* headlined its feature article on the Berlin meeting, "K.K.K.K. 'Koestler's Congress' in Berlin," and began with an imagined interview fragment: " 'So, Mr. Koestler, was this the KKK Congress? *Kultur* [Culture]? *Kampf* [Struggle]? *Koestler?*' 'And Korea,' riposted Koestler, thus plainly stating his 'cultural' position." This transparent allusion to the Ku Klux Klan was backed by charges that the congress was nothing more than an American-organized propaganda exercise in the Cold War and that Koestler, "in the name of democracy and liberty," was attacking "the fundamental principles of intellectual freedom," namely tolerance and respect for the views of others. Koestler was "a marvelous speaker, a consummate comedian, full of dodges and tricks," but he was also a "crafty demagogue" and a "devil," "diabolically" attacking his friends as virtual traitors.[3]

This caricature was reinforced by André Stil in the Communist daily *L'Humanité,* who maintained that Koestler was a traitor, a "bard of treason" at a congress that gathered the "entire cream" of "Marshallizing" and "Atlanticpactisizing" intellectuals in one place. Such polysyllabic epithets were fashionable in France at the time. A book of Koestler's was described as "Kravchenkist," and *Esprit* added *ne koestlérisons pas* (let us not Koestlerize) to its vocabulary, offering a backhanded compliment to its intended target. Stil rested his case on a recently published and widely distributed booklet by the Communist novelist Jean Kanapa, *Le Traître et le prolétaire* (The Traitor and the Proletarian), which advanced the thesis that Koestler had been "turned" by Franco's police agents while in prison in Seville and was now working for British intelligence. The Communist weekly *L'Action,* having learned of Koestler's congress meetings at his home, accused him of planning some sort of terrorist action and published a map of Fontaine-le-Port with a large arrow pointing to Koestler's villa, Verte Rive. "This is the headquarters of the Cold War," ran the caption. "This is where Chip Bohlen, the American ambassador, trains his para-military, fascist militia."[4]

Such charges were fantastic and said more about the paranoia of the left than the paranoia of the right. Others took a subtler line, describing the split between the "two wings" of the congress as one between the "extremists or 'totalitarians' led by Koestler and the Americans" and the "left-wing moderate federalists led by Silone, Italy, and France." The "Koestler Congress" was in reality "a struggle for influence between those who, in order to combat totalitarianism, employ the same weapons as the totalitarians, and the 'good European democrats,' squeezed between the two big blocs, East and West."[5]

This theory was a travesty but greatly appealed to some British leftists too. Upset by Koestler's dismissal of the left-right paradigm and his slashing attack on the Labour Party's isolationism, Trevor-Roper repaid Koestler's flexibility over the wording of the final resolution with a scathing denunciation in *The Manchester Guardian,* and followed it with a letter to *The Economist* in which he echoed the French in portraying Koestler, Burnham, Hook, and Borkenau as a bunch of hard-faced ex-Communists determined to take over the congress and bend it to their will. These conspirators were not just anti-Communist but anti-socialist and anti-Russian, and the "hysterical German applause" that greeted the manifesto contained "echoes from Hitler's Nuremberg."

Coming from a noted specialist on Hitler, Trevor-Roper's irresponsible words carried considerable weight, and in his view, it was the plucky British delegates (that is, himself and Ayer), rather than the French and Italians, who had ridden to the rescue of the congress by "killing" a manifesto clause "advocating intellectual intolerance." A long article in the *New Statesman* echoed Trevor-Roper's patriotic tone, while neatly eliding, with Trevor-Roper, the uncomfortable fact that the infamous "intolerance" clause had been removed by Koestler amicably and without argument.[6]

*   *   *

IT WAS TRUE, of course, that the Berlin congress was financed by the Americans (though nobody besides Burnham, Brown, and Josselson knew of the CIA connection at the time) and that ex-Communists played a major role in organizing it, but that was because the ex-Communists understood the dangers of the Soviet advance far better than most of their untainted colleagues and were not at all obeying American orders. The proof lay in the famous "split" and the less obvious fact that the Americans (in the form of the cautious bureaucrats at the CIA) were closer to Trevor-Roper's position than to that of Koestler and the ex-Communists.

The most grievous canard, and one that would dog Koestler for much of his life, was that he favored using "totalitarian methods" to oppose totalitarianism and that this represented an attack on intellectual freedom in the West. "Totalitarian methods" at the time included spying, lying, censorship, blackmail, infiltrating double agents into democratic institutions, and rigidly controlling one's own population, not to speak of terror and murder. What Koestler advocated was international debates, the open exchange of ideas across borders, the publication of newsletters, magazines, and books, the defense of human rights, and a robust resistance to the efficient propaganda machine being operated by the Soviet Union and its satellites. The closest his proposals came to the operations of the other side were his insistence on establishing an information stream explicitly directed to rebutting Soviet propaganda and the risky project of smuggling books (not guns) into Communist countries. These were light-years from the "terrorist" and "fascist" accusations flung at him by his enemies—and no one could have been less anti the Russian people and Russian culture than Koestler himself.

The nationalistic responses of the French and British left at the time were driven in part by an automatic anti-Americanism and showed how right Koestler was to identify the isolationist impulses of left-wing intellectuals once proud of their socialist internationalism. The Britons' attitudes were further complicated by the uncomfortable fact that on the five-man executive committee, Koestler was their representative. As it happened, he was now a naturalized citizen, representing what he ironically labeled the "rootless cosmopolitan element" in Britain, a jibe at Trevor-Roper's characterization of him and Burnham as rootless intellectuals, but no one could mistake him for a member of the club.

But despite his outward defiance, Koestler was wounded by so much hostility. The *Action* map and accompanying article were a direct incitement to violence, and though he publicly dismissed the idea that his life was in danger and resisted the suggestion that he carry a weapon, he became convinced that local party members were snooping on his mail and spying on his movements. He had long concealed his address from all but personal friends, having Cynthia mail his letters from Paris, for example. Now he wrote to ask the American embassy in Paris if it would handle his congress mail. "All this seems extremely silly, but we hope that the Congress will grow into a world movement to counter the communist peace campaign and it would not be prudent to take chances."[7]

Fighting back against his critics, Koestler insisted to a gathering of British and American correspondents in Paris in July that all differences between right and left in Berlin had "vanished into the background." The Freedom Manifesto had "explicitly" rejected neutrality and indifference in the face of the totalitarian challenge and for the first time established a united front of right and left. It was wishful thinking on Koestler's part, but he was serious about trying to make it happen and exhorted his CCF colleagues to be more businesslike and get down to practical work. He personally drafted a prospectus and a recruiting letter for the new organization, even designing accounting and card-filing systems for the new office. Drawing on his wartime experiences with the BBC, he expanded his earlier idea for broadcasts to the East into a detailed proposal for a West European Radio Network, which he nicknamed the "Deminform." The latter could never match the Cominform in size or resources, but would maintain "a high intellectual level" and act as a counterbalance to the propaganda pouring out of the Soviet bloc.[8]

Koestler also proposed the formation of a mass movement called Les Amis de la Liberté (Friends of Freedom) and with Sperber composed a pamphlet, "Que veulent les Amis de la Liberté?" (What Do the Friends of Freedom Want?), in which they set out the CCF's policies in question-and-answer form and tried to deal with some of the objections raised by Trevor-Roper and others about the rationale for a new movement. Koestler and Sperber proposed local committees in all the big provincial towns of France to collect signatures, organize demonstrations, put up anti-Communist posters, circulate anti-Communist pamphlets, and organize mass meetings on such subjects as the Korean War or the position of Yugoslavia, preferably in conjunction with the Gaullist movement.[9]

The inspiration this time was Münzenberg, and these were indeed Communist methods, albeit methods that were exclusively legal and peaceful. Koestler and Sperber also advocated the establishment of a new journal to compete with Sartre's Les Temps Modernes and other left-leaning magazines. For the editor's position Koestler pressed the claims of an attractive young French journalist, Suzanne Labin (with whom he had a brief affair while she helped him with the French text of "Amis de la Liberté"), and he foresaw an ambitious cultural and political monthly along the lines of New York's Partisan Review, with an international cast of contributors. Sperber even started commissioning articles for the new magazine, until he realized that he and Koestler were more or less alone.[10]

Their proposals were in fact running into opposition from a number of sources, notably a talented and multilingual young Swiss journalist named François Bondy and Silone. At a meeting to discuss the pamphlet, few present had bothered to read it, and Silone's only proposal was to add a phrase saying "we are opposed to *Reader's Digest* and Coca Cola." The Deminform idea was shelved for lack of funds, and Bondy (supported by Aron and Altman) rejected Koestler's proposal for a full-fledged journal for the same reason (having preempted the idea by starting a modest CCF newsletter instead).[11]

Koestler took out his frustrations on Irving Brown. Bondy was a "political nitwit," he told Brown, obsessed, like the French leftists, with opposing the Gaullists at all costs, and his objections to Koestler's program were false, naive, and counterproductive. The normally effervescent Brown was quiet and evasive on the subject and, when personally confronted by Koestler, told him he was too preoccupied with "formal" questions and should wait for things to develop. Koestler concluded, correctly as it turned out, that Brown was hiding something from him.[12]

Mamaine, who had been kept up till one thirty one morning listening to Koestler's "ravings," noted in her diary that Koestler had been "in a great state about the Congress ever since Berlin," that is, for about six weeks. "He hardly sleeps at night over questions like the Bondy question, and thinks about the work all the time. It is an obsession with him. For one thing he feels that he alone is really capable of running it; but of course nobody believes K's willingness to work at it is not dictated by some ulterior motive. After Irving and Altman had gone he was in despair, said: 'In the Comintern days there were dozens of good men at hand with whom one could work, and now one has to run a world movement with people like Altman (a despicable coward), Aron (also a coward), Rousset (a cynical politician with absolutely no sincerity or integrity), Burnham (a dangerous lunatic), Silone (a political catastrophe . . .), Malraux (mad and hopelessly inefficient . . .), and Lasky (who goes to the Musée de l'Homme when he's come to Paris to do some work).'"[13]

Koestler's rant was exaggerated but shows how thoroughly he was out of step with his colleagues at the time, although in the long term he was vindicated. The Deminform idea was eventually embodied in the establishment of Radio Free Europe (and later Radio Liberty) to broadcast to the Eastern Bloc. The "Amis de la Liberté" pamphlet turned out to be one of the most popular publications and recruiting tools of the French committee and was translated into English for American readers. In France the establishment of the Amis as a membership organization led to the creation of a string of Maisons de la Liberté (Freedom Houses) in cities such as Grenoble, Lyons, Saint-Étienne,

Nice, and Bordeaux, and Bondy's newsletter, *Preuves,* in due course became a distinguished literary monthly of exactly the type Koestler had envisaged.[14]

But Koestler's clashes with Brown, Bondy, and others were leading to complications that had less to do with differences over programs and personalities than with the logic of the paymasters. Brown was ultimately answerable to his bosses in the CIA, and the unpredictable Koestler was proving too headstrong and too independent for their taste. Getting involved with a bunch of left-wing, mainly socialist intellectuals was already a big gamble for CIA bureaucrats in a country where Joseph McCarthy was on the rampage, and there were limits to how far the CIA could go. Even the swashbuckling Wisner and the easygoing Brown found Koestler's push for a mass movement and an active confrontation with communism fraught with risk, whereas the more cautious and passive line personified by Silone (and embraced by Bondy and his supporters) had the allure of being both safer and more predictable. Koestler's problem was that he was *too* militant, too much in a hurry, and too difficult to control, and the organization men in Washington were beginning to wonder if there was any place at all in their enterprise for the star orator of Berlin.

STILL UNAWARE OF THE CIA CONNECTION, Koestler thought of the CCF as an offshoot of the State Department or the Marshall Fund and still regarded it as fundamentally poor, hence his proposal for writers to donate a part of their royalties. His growing frustration with Brown and Washington's inexplicable inertia raised his suspicions, however, and came to a head in the middle of August 1950, when his attitude to the CCF sharply changed for reasons that have never been explained.[15]

The best witness to what happened, as usual, is Mamaine. On August 15, 1950, Koestler drove from Verte Rive to Paris for a meeting of the CCF and a conference with the American playwright Sidney Kingsley, who had agreed to dramatize *Darkness at Noon* for the American stage. The next morning he phoned Mamaine to say he had a burst tire and later the same day called to say that, owing to the summer holidays, it had taken him a full day to find another one, and he would stay in Paris another night. The next time the phone rang, it was Raymond Aron to say that he'd found Koestler lying outside his apartment in a state of nervous collapse and had put him to bed. "Do you mean he's got an awful hangover?" asked Mamaine. "Well no, 'e says it's not exactly that," replied Aron (the transcription is Mamaine's). A bit later Koestler rang to say he was spending the night at Aron's, but at eleven he and Aron unexpectedly turned up at Verte Rive. Koestler had "pinpoint eyes" and looked "somewhat disheveled."

Mamaine thought Koestler was suffering from "a mild attack of the DTs" and persecution mania, while he thought he might perhaps be going mad and complained of hallucinations. Earlier in the day (though he could no longer remember it) he had taken A. D. Peters's daughter, Catherine, to lunch and made a drunken pass at her in his car, causing her to jump out and run off. He had then smashed the car before making his way to Aron's apartment on foot. Astonishingly, this seems to have been Koestler's first experience of the DTs, and he was badly shaken. He vowed (for the *n*th time) to "give up drink completely for a trial period of three months," to resign from the executive committee of the Congress for Cultural Freedom on health grounds, and to go away for a vacation before moving back to England.[16]

The swiftness of this turnabout was unprecedented, even for one as mercurial and unpredictable as Koestler, and raises the question of what Koestler might have learned in Paris during those two days to provoke his meltdown. Did Brown take him into his confidence about the CIA funding sources that August afternoon? Did Rousset, Altman, or Bondy get wind of Washington's doubts about him and let word of them slip to Koestler? Kingsley said that Koestler had arrived for their meeting in "a highly nervous state," after having had "a fight with a member of his committee," and was too agitated to go through the script of the play as planned. All that can be said for certain is that Koestler at once wrote to Brown, Bondy, Burnham, and Lasky to say he was resigning from the executive committee because of "a nervous crack up," and would no longer participate in their deliberations. He also wrote to Kingsley to say that he now planned to donate his share of the income from the play of *Darkness at Noon* to the IRRC, or some similar organization, to help refugee intellectuals from Eastern Europe.[17]

In his diary Koestler expressed relief that he was "emerging from one of the major periodic shocks that determine my life. Novel finished; Berlin triumph and resignation; Kingsley dramatization of D. at Noon a major disappointment; summer of 1939 feeling." He informed Mamaine that he regarded the incident as a mysterious warning from fate, like his earlier drunk-driving adventure in Charenton, and it was his "pattern" to be saved by episodes of this nature from plunging into outright disaster. "K is full of faith in a kind of guardian angel who looks after him and points out the right path, which he is then particularly good at taking. His pattern when drunk is one of self-annihilation: he has fantasies about hanging himself, and tends to do suicidal things like hitting police *commissaires* or having a car accident."[18]

Whatever her doubts about the strength of his good intentions, Mamaine was ecstatic when Koestler added that he had changed his mind about England and wrote to Celia that they would be spending the winter there. She hoped to look for a house in the country but feared that Koestler wouldn't approve, since he hated country life in England and was dead set against the idea of getting a house to live in "for the rest of his days." They decided to take a holiday in the Midi, but the trip was poisoned by Koestler's intense disillusionment with everything around him and newfound hatred of the

French. Everywhere they went he saw only profiteering innkeepers, greedy garage owners, and grasping restaurant proprietors, all out to cheat him. France reeked of the same "corruption and decay" that he had experienced so vividly in 1940. Within days of their return to Verte Rive, Mamaine left for England and Koestler promised to follow soon, after arranging to rent the house on the Seine and arrange for their mail to be forwarded. Almost in parenthesis, he mentioned that he also had to make a quick visit to the United States to confer with his publisher and work on the proofs of *The Age of Longing*.[19]

CHAPTER THIRTY-THREE

BACK TO THE USA

. . . perpetually in search of a country.

— ANDRÉ MALRAUX

KOESTLER WAS DISINGENUOUS in telling Mamaine he planned a short visit to America. He hadn't given up on the congress, only its European branch. If he wanted to influence events on a global scale, he concluded, the place to do it from was not London or Paris but New York and Washington. He had already applied for a resident's visa, but because the McCarran Act banned former Communists from immigrating, he needed a congressional resolution for a long-term stay.

Arriving in New York in the fall of 1950, he saw all the main movers and shakers of the anti-Stalinist left, and a party was thrown in his honor by *Partisan Review.* Foy Kohler, the newly appointed chief of Voice of America, told Koestler of plans to start Radio Free Europe, just as Koestler had recommended in his Paris memorandum. Burnham came up from Washington and told Koestler that his impulsive resignation from the executive committee of the CCF was tantamount to "the symbolic liquidation of the Congress" and "must not stand," for Koestler was its heart and soul. Burnham explained that the main reason for the slow progress on the CCF was bureaucratic inertia. It was difficult to find the right people and even more difficult to find the money. "There is no doubt plenty of money somewhere, but those who have control of the monies are always tough cookies to convince."[1]

Burnham didn't say who the tough cookies were, but in the wake of America's fumblings in Korea and China, President Truman had ordered General Walter Bedell Smith to cleanse and reorganize the CIA, and one of

Smith's first decisions was to tame the OPC, which seemed to be out of control. Burnham wanted Koestler to go to Washington to meet "some serious persons who have specific interests that intersect our own—and I am not referring to the editors of the *Partisan Review*." Koestler wasn't so sure. "My 7-year rash of world-saving is beginning to wear thin," he wrote in his diary. "Am beginning to hate intellectuals with their frivolity, disorganization, vanity. But, *après tout,* the Jacobin Club was the same, even worse."[2]

With nothing moving on the CCF front, Koestler turned his attention to starting a fund for refugee writers. The idea had come to him after his breakdown in France. He had decided that since the CCF wouldn't lift a hand to help individual refugee intellectuals from Eastern Europe, he would do so himself by donating his royalties from the play of *Darkness at Noon.* He had made a start by enlisting Graham Greene's support for the scheme, telling Greene that making a financial sacrifice was a way to hurt himself and appease his conscience. Greene commented drily that he had other ways of hurting himself and that Koestler could hardly expect other writers' neuroses to match his own but agreed to let his name be used and to donate 10 percent of his Continental royalties once the fund was established.[3]

In New York, Dorothy Norman threw a party for Koestler to announce his plans, and he paced the floor as he spoke "rapidly and impatiently" about them. "I don't want to form a committee or an organization," he said, evidently with his CCF experiences in mind. "I want what is to be done to be done spontaneously, voluntarily, without anyone having to urge anyone to do anything." There would be no staff, no overhead. The important thing was to make a sacrifice. "There should be a sense of voluntary identification with those who have been trapped and have refused to be trapped. I feel we all must help. What do you think?"[4]

As usual, Koestler out in front of his confrères. Funds and organizations to help Eastern Bloc writers would proliferate some ten to fifteen years hence, but in 1950 they were unheard of. In the next few weeks he garnered moral support from James G. Farrell, Aldous Huxley, and John Dos Passos and drafted an appeal to Hemingway, John Hersey, and other prominent writers. "The intellectual elite of the bigger half of Europe is being wiped out," he wrote, while the few who escaped "are being reduced to a degrading and sterile existence of disguised beggary." The letter generated disappointingly few replies, but Koestler wasn't deterred. In late October he incorporated his scheme as the Fund for Intellectual Freedom (FIF) and in December formally signed over his play royalties, while making a million francs (about three thousand dollars) available to a branch fund in Paris and earmarking part of that sum for use in Germany.[5]

Koestler persuaded Agnes Knickerbocker, the widow of H. R. Knickerbocker, to serve as the fund's unpaid secretary in New York and Louis Fischer's Russian former wife, Markoosha, to funnel money to an émigré

Russian literary magazine, *Literaturny Sovremennik* (Literary Contemporary), in Munich, that went on to achieve real distinction. Louis Fischer wrote to describe its first editorial meeting in an unheated room, where the editorial staff huddled in their overcoats and scarves. "They looked hungry, but their eyes were full of fire. Their enthusiasm was contagious. You will be happy some day (maybe you already are) to be responsible for this development."[6]

KOESTLER WAS STILL TRYING to find his feet in America, and his reputation was complicated by an article he had written earlier in the year on the subject of Alger Hiss and Whittaker Chambers. Hiss's conviction for perjury and the vindication of Chambers had stunned American liberals and signaled a political victory for Hoover's Red-obsessed FBI, not to speak of the Red-baiting House Un-American Activities Committee and a relatively obscure congressman called Richard Nixon. Because of the political stakes involved, many, if not most, liberals were convinced that Chambers was a liar—and Hiss innocent—in the teeth of all available evidence.[7]

Koestler had stumbled onto this holy ground largely innocent of the American context. To him the idea that Chambers was lying was complete nonsense: he knew enough of the Communist underground to grasp intuitively that Chambers was telling the truth, and he identified with Chambers as both a social outsider and the man who cries wolf (hadn't Koestler done something similar in 1938—though without a victim?). Examining the trial as a piece of political theater, a "deathly duel" between two individuals, Koestler noted that Hiss and Chambers were miscast. Hiss appeared to be "the prototype of the decent, modest, hard-working, well-spoken, idealistic American liberal," who would act only from the highest principles, whereas his accuser was an admitted perjurer who had "traveled with false passports, lived with mistresses under a false name, and was described as a psychopath." Chambers should have got the part of Hiss and Hiss, the part of Chambers.[8]

When the essay was published in the Sunday *New York Times,* the paper was inundated with letters denouncing his thesis, and Koestler reproached the editor, Lester Markel, with bias in his printed selection. Markel denied it, but Koestler was closer to the truth than he knew, for Markel had fabricated one of the denunciations and published it as a letter from a reader. Making no mention of this subterfuge, Markel pointed to a dimension of the trial that Koestler understood but had little sympathy with, namely that Chambers had allowed himself to be used for the support of causes "in which Chambers himself did not believe." The right wing of the Republican Party had adopted the slogan of "a generation on trial" and was exploiting the Hiss conviction to mount a comprehensive attack on "Roosevelt, Truman and the New Deal itself."

Markel's scenario was a replay of Sperber's reproaches to Koestler three or four years earlier in France, when Sperber had accused him of giving succor to their political enemies. Koestler had ignored Sperber's objections for the same reasons he now rejected Markel's arguments. The greater evil was the Soviet threat, together with western gullibility about the Soviet Union's methods and goals. He would follow his convictions on that score wherever they led, regardless of local conditions and alliances. In the long term he was undoubtedly right, and his verdict on Hiss and Chambers has been vindicated by posterity, but in the short term his insistence on the ethics of the case and his intransigence about the outcome worked to his disadvantage. As he told his first biographer, "I cut my throat in America with that article"—an exaggeration, perhaps, but an acknowledgment that in the eyes of many liberals he seemed to be moving into the enemy camp.[9]

Liberal misgivings were strengthened by two further essays reflecting Koestler's despair over what he saw as the impending political collapse of Europe. Western Europe was "a patient in an iron lung," kept alive by the oxygen of American economic and military aid, and its sickness resulted from the fact that it had lost faith in itself. As an antidote, Koestler proposed the formation of a European army, a "Legion of Liberty." Volunteers from eleven European nations should form a common army that would galvanize the European spirit and pave the way for a future European Union.

In "Appalling Alternatives," written for the *Saturday Review of Literature*, he suggested provocatively that socialism in Europe was outmoded, if not dead, and was holding the continent back. But it was inconceivable that the world could remain divided along the present "insane frontier," which cut Europe and the streets of Vienna and Berlin into halves. Europe, he wrote, had become a power vacuum between the two major powers and would have to choose between appalling alternatives. "In our century, the seat of the Holy Roman Empire has shifted to Washington, D.C." The inescapable conclusion was that Europeans should accept American hegemony and the Americans should accept their responsibility, in order to bolster the European spirit. As it happens, Koestler was far from the only observer thinking along those lines (the European army idea was picked up—and then dropped—by none other than General Dwight D. Eisenhower), but the approval he garnered in right-wing circles, combined with the boldness of his attack on European socialism, suggested to some that lurking behind Koestler's speculations was the ghost of a preventive war, and this drove another nail into his coffin among American liberals.[10]

Between the publication of the two essays Koestler got to meet the man who had started his downward slide. On a visit to Washington, he spent some time with Ray Murphy, who was still basking in his triumph of getting Chambers to testify before the House Un-American Activities Committee. Murphy took Koestler to see Chambers on Chambers's Maryland farm, and the two reminisced about their days in the party. Koestler was impressed by Chambers's work ethic: five hours of farming and five hours of writing his book every day. Chambers shocked Koestler by saying how much he admired Murphy's boss, Senator McCarthy. Koestler was taken aback. Though he suffered from guilt by association, he wasn't prepared to go anywhere near the right wing of the Republican Party. He ruefully concluded that the man he had risked his reputation for was "sincere, but fanatical."[11]

THE FACT IS THAT KOESTLER fit none of the usual molds, and the impression created by his aggressive articles was soon complicated by the appearance—only weeks apart—of two major literary works: the play of *Darkness at Noon* on Broadway, reflecting his earlier period, and his latest novel, *The Age of Longing,* composed some ten years after *Darkness.*

The play had been adapted by Sidney Kingsley, an experienced playwright well known for gritty, realistic problem plays such as *Dead End, Men in White,* and *Detective Story* (the last two turned into successful movies, with Clark Gable and Kirk Douglas as their respective stars). Kingsley had contacted Koestler about dramatizing the novel in the summer of 1949, and after they signed a contract dividing the credits and royalties equally between them, Kingsley had set to work on the play at once. That August Kingsley and his wife, the actress Madge Evans, had visited Koestler in Verte Rive to discuss the first drafts, and Koestler had liked the first act, except for the closing dialogue between Rubashov and his first interrogator, Ivanov. "Wherever you have, so to speak, raped my novel," Koestler told Kingsley, "I like it. In this particular scene, where you followed the novel too closely, I don't like it." Koestler worried that the American wasn't capturing the nuances of the way communists talked to one another, especially in scenes featuring Arlova and Little Loewy, and in the scene of the Marseilles dock strike, and his anxiety on those and other points seems to have contributed to his breakdown that month, for it was during their last meeting that Kingsley found him to be in a "highly nervous state," and immediately afterward that he made his decision to donate all royalties from the play to refugee writers. It was a way, he told Mamaine, to "free himself of responsibility" for the Kingsley version.[12]

Unfortunately, the two men had parted with different understandings of how the work was to proceed. Kingsley left Paris under the impression that Koestler would send on his suggestions on the drafts Kingsley had left with him. But Koestler either forgot or changed his mind, saying that he would make his comments only when he got to New York in the fall. When he arrived, they had an acrimonious lunch. Kingsley was furious over Koestler's decision about the royalties, complaining that it would turn the play into a political demonstration (this alone showed how far he was from understanding the work he was dramatizing). The completed script was delivered just as rehearsals were beginning, which Koestler learned about through the newspapers. Kingsley explained that he had scheduled the play for Broadway early in the new year and needed to hurry, and he urged Koestler to send him his comments on the play, but Koestler used this alleged breach of etiquette as an excuse to plead lack of time. He eventually wrote to Kingsley to say he wanted "no share in the artistic responsibility of this play. Whether it is good or bad, it must be your burden."[13]

He later regretted this rash decision, which came back to haunt him when it got in the way of later productions in Europe, while copyright considerations ensured that no alternative version could appear in his lifetime. Luckily for Kingsley (though it was a bittersweet moment for Koestler), the Broadway production was highly successful. Claude Rains took the starring role of Rubashov, and Kim Hunter, Walter Palance, and Philip Coolidge featured in a strong supporting cast. Reviews described the play as "gripping and provocative, a fiercely lucid arraignment of communism and an affirmation by implication of the democratic way of life"; Kingsley's adaptation was acclaimed as a "tour-de-force." He had fashioned a drama that ranked with Shaw's *Saint Joan* in the pitilessness of its logic and the tragedy of its conclusions, and Claude Rains, never offstage for a single moment, was "superb" in the intensity of his performance. Only Brooks Atkinson in the *Times* seemed to share Koestler's reservations. Kingsley was "less a writer than a showman" and had reduced Koestler's "haunting terror" to "a pungent spectacular melodrama on a political theme," lacking "the wild, evil music that made Mr. Koestler's novel so piercing and so memorable."[14]

Koestler ostentatiously stayed away from opening night, writing to Calmann-Lévy that it had attracted "a gathering of all the New York celebrities, including the Duke and Duchess of Windsor and excluding myself." The play went on to win the New York Drama Critics' Circle Award and ran for fourteen months. Koestler petulantly waited a year to see it and was in no mood to be generous. It was a "competent propaganda-melodrama" that preached only to the converted. The prison was a cross between a boys' boarding school and a "movie loony bin" and Rains wholly unconvincing as a former revolutionary leader.[15]

Hard on the heels of the stage play came *The Age of Longing*. The novel accurately reflected Koestler's growing disillusionment with France and Europe and was intended to sound the alarm over Communist advances and the threat of war. His Romeo, Fedya Nikitin, was a Russian working-class orphan who represented "a new, successful breed of Soviet official" and was working as a diplomat in Paris. His Juliet was Hydie Anderson, the daughter of the American ambassador, and a lapsed Catholic from the upper classes, "symbolizing the West's loss of a universal faith." There was a gallery of "types" representative of left-wing intellectual circles in France, including writers, professors, publishers, Eastern European émigrés, and members of the Soviet élite, and Koestler constructed the novel around a series of set pieces, starting with a Bastille Day celebration in Paris, continuing with a peace rally, a Left Bank party, and a publisher's soirée, and ending with a high-society funeral.[16]

Hydie seems to have been modeled on Sonia Orwell, who had once told him of her unhappy Catholic girlhood. There were parodies of Sartre, Beauvoir, Merleau-Ponty, Malraux, Ilya Ehrenburg, J. B. S. Haldane, Richard Wright, and Paul Winkler, among others, and many scenes were based on Koestler's own experiences in France. The book was conceived "as a warning, not a prophecy," he said when he finished it in May 1950, and into it Koestler poured all his disillusionment with the sophistries of the French intelligentsia, contrasting their weak vacillations to the "iron certainties" of the new conquerors from the East. Through Hydie and her father, he also expressed his doubts about the resolve of the Americans in the face of the Communist threat and about the West's ability to stand up to the Russians.

Advance publicity for the novel was good. Macmillan had printed 100,000 copies, and individual chapters had appeared in *Harper's Magazine* and *Partisan Review*, but Koestler rightly had serious misgivings about the novel and had originally equipped it with a defensive preface, describing it as modeled on the work of one A. Koestler, whose style, "lacking in ornament and distinction, is easy to imitate." Reflecting how low his confidence had sunk, Koestler described himself as "a much afflicted scribe of his time, greedy for pleasure, haunted by guilt, who enjoyed a short vogue and was then forgotten, like the rest of them." He also included an epilogue explaining that after the dropping of an atomic bomb on Europe, the world had been saved by a new religious sect, and he equipped the novel with fictitious footnotes.

Jim Putnam persuaded Koestler to drop the preface and the notes and allow the novel to stand on its own feet, but Koestler's premonitions were more or less justified. Critics in America acknowledged Koestler's "acute and searching intelligence," his unerring ear for "cant and deception," his commitment to the service of "decency and dignity," and admired the novel as a talkfest, a series of monologues and dialogues that often crackled with "intricate ironies, witty hypotheses, ingenious theories." The names of Dostoyevsky, Oscar Wilde, and Aldous Huxley were invoked to give a sense of Koestler's themes and dialogue, and Orwell's *1984* was frequently mentioned as a precursor, but *The Age of Longing* was "not a novel," for its characters possessed little flesh and blood of their own.[17]

One curiosity noted by Anthony West (among others) was that the two most successful characters in the novel were the Soviet Russians, Fedya Nikitin and Leo Leontiev, and Nikitin was described as "the only sexually adequate man" Hydie had ever met. Koestler's other characters, West felt, were also "thinly disguised Slavs, trapped in Slav dilemmas and racked by

Slav longings." Koestler was variously compared (to his disadvantage) to T. S. Eliot, Curzio Malaparte, and Louis-Ferdinand Céline, but the writer to whom he was most often unfavorably compared was Koestler: the Koestler of *Darkness at Noon, Scum of the Earth,* and *The Yogi and the Commissar.* Far from moving forward from his masterpiece, he was thought to have moved backward (in his fiction, at least), and one reviewer claimed to find it hard to believe that the two books had been written by the same man.

In Britain the novel's reception was a little better, but not much. Richard Crossman ingeniously characterized *The Age of Longing* as an "antistrophe" to *Darkness at Noon,* "a conversation between Mr Koestler and the Devil, in which Mr Koestler gives the Devil a superb brief, but still seems surprised and resentful when the Devil proceeds to win the argument." Crossman felt that Koestler should take a holiday from the politics of the intelligentsia and study the human condition instead.[18]

THOUGH BITTERLY DISAPPOINTED by the American reviews, Koestler had already made up his mind to settle in the United States, as Mamaine learned to her consternation shortly before the book's appearance. "We are the proprietors of a steel bridge of 250 feet in length with an island attached to it and accommodation for 2,800 chicks. Also 112 acres of woodland, *kuku-rucz* [corn] fields and pasture. Also a rather lovely 1824 Pennsylvania farmhouse at present inhabited by Aunt Maria and a 14-year-old nymphomaniac. The whole as per attached prospectus." He had by chance attended an auction in Bucks County, Pennsylvania, where "a Beautiful, Convenient, Self-sustaining Island Kingdom All Your Own" was being sold to the highest bidder. When he arrived, about twenty people were standing in a semicircle on the lawn, making bids that struck Koestler as ridiculously low (the usual high bidders had gone to the Princeton-Army football game). Koestler impishly joined in, and before he realized it, the property was his for a song. "When the auctioneer said 'sold' I didn't know it was to me!"[19]

Koestler paid $41,000 for a property he had never seen, but for once it matched the auctioneer's glowing description. Island Farm was set in the middle of the Delaware River, separated from the "mainland" by a narrow suspension bridge. The Pennsylvania Dutch house was more mansion than farmhouse, with broad porches overlooking the river, an airy solarium, eight bedrooms, a huge dining room with exposed beams, and a walk-in fireplace. There were seven acres of gardens, an avenue of fruit trees running from bridge to house, lofty oaks and maples for shade, broad lawns, flower gardens, a rose bower, a large barn, poultry sheds, and a hundred acres of mostly farmland.

Koestler's Walter Mitty imagination didn't stretch to who would clean the rooms, farm the land, tend the seven acres of lawn and gardens, or care for the acres of woodland that surrounded the property. "I don't want to do anything about Treasure Island until you come over," he told Mamaine, "but my idea is to cut down the corn, plow it all up and convert it into pasture and lawns, put a couple of hundred sheep on it—not to mention bees, ducks, dogs and tortoises, and have one couple looking after the whole thing whether we are present or absent. It doesn't tie us down in the least as no maintenance is required."[20]

Famous last words. More to the point, Koestler had blithely ridden roughshod over the doubts and fears Mamaine had been expressing about America since her move to London in August. She had also just written to Edmund Wilson to tell him how happy she was in London. It was wonderful to be back among friends, close to her twin sister, Celia, and best of all, taking piano lessons again. She was "in the most terrific form, mentally and physically," she told Koestler, feeling better than she ever had at Fontaine-le-Port, and she was in no hurry to join him. "God knows when I will see you, my Sweetie, because I don't want to come over for at least another two months, and after that it will be arctic in New York."

She had already nerved herself to tell him that she couldn't return to Verte Rive outside the summer months because of the damp climate, but Koestler ignored the subtext of her letters and pressed his advantage. There was "no fog" on the island, and the climate was quite unlike the Seine Valley. There was lots of room for a piano in the new house, and his proposal was to live "the six winter months on Treasure Island, the six summer months in Verte Rive."[21]

The whole thing seemed decidedly unrealistic and still depended on Koestler's application for a residence visa and the requisite act of Congress. In the meantime he was obliged to marshal persuasive evidence (persuasive to uncomprehending senators and congressmen, that is) that he was indeed the anti-Communist he said he was, and he cheerfully asked Mamaine to go to Verte Rive and gather up the "cartloads" of newspaper clippings, articles, reviews, and documents on the Berlin Congress and the CCF that were needed to prove his reliability and bring them to America with her, preferably before the end of January. She should also check up on their Verte Rive tenants—and could she bring Sabby with her? The congressional bill would take at least until the end of March, if not longer.[22]

Mamaine meekly caved in and spent a week in Paris gathering the papers before flying out to join him after Christmas. On the last day of the year, they motored from New York to Island Farm in the used black Cadillac convertible Koestler had picked up, also "for a song." The island was in a bend of the river, just north of the country town of New Hope in Pennsylvania, and Mamaine was relieved to find it better than she could possibly have imagined. The house was "heavenly" and the surrounding countryside "absolutely lovely too." The local people were friendly, and there were the novelty of a

nearby supermarket (then unknown in Britain), where "you just wheel a barrow round and pay as you go out," and the wonder of electric central heating
and refrigeration. It was really "one's dream place," she wrote Celia—if only
they weren't so far from Europe and plagued by "the insuperable problem of
servants."[23]

IT WAS THE THIRD TIME in five years they had moved house and started
life in a new country, a procedure that didn't bother the irrepressible Koestler
but imposed a terrible strain on Mamaine. She had been unable to bring
Sabby with her, so they acquired a Saint Bernard puppy named Nellie, who
grew to an enormous size, and a small Labrador named Rubashov. Carrying
out renovations and buying furniture and equipment in the unfamiliar
United States was fraught with more than the usual number of misunderstandings, delayed deliveries, and upsets, and Koestler raged at the "mechanized and stereotypical culture patterns" of the Americans, which reminded
him, he wrote in his diary (unconsciously echoing the criticisms of his political opponents in Europe), of the slavish suppression of individuality in Soviet
Russia. Ever the European, he professed himself stunned when a thunder-
storm knocked out all those comforts (heat, water, lights, and refrigeration—
all dependent on electricity) that had so delighted Mamaine and was personally
affronted that the power windows of his Cadillac wouldn't open unless he
turned on the ignition.[24]

Mamaine had more intimate frustrations to deal with. Koestler was
"much fatter" than she remembered him (that American food), and it was a
strain to live with him again "after these months of freedom." He was cold
and distant and rarely talked to her, so she got "bored and fed up." They
managed to find a cleaner, who drove over from Stockton, New Jersey, in her
mink coat three days a week, but if the roads were icy or covered in snow
(which happened all the time in winter), she didn't come at all, and even with
help, Mamaine was overwhelmed with cleaning, cooking, washing, mending, ironing, and shopping, not to speak of typing Koestler's letters for him
and assisting with the French translation of The Age of Longing.

Over dinner in the kitchen one night, Koestler worked himself into a fury
over Mamaine's supposed imperfections and the poor state of the house,
overturned the table, stomped on the food-spattered plates and glasses, and
charged out with a bleeding foot. For a whole week he barely spoke to Mamaine, who predictably came down with a bout of asthma (she called it bronchitis) and took to her bed for three days, leaving him to get his own meals
and fend for himself. The following weekend he launched into another diatribe, prompting a chalk-faced Mamaine to stalk out and go to her room. She
described these domestic crises in long dispatches to Celia, in which, with ex-

traordinary detachment, she dissected Koestler's "compulsion neurosis" and manipulative personality.[25]

"I hate the thought of ever becoming indifferent to K, at the same time I often hope I will do so quickly and thoroughly. I already am rather indifferent in some ways, because I no longer admire him at all, but on the contrary, really despise him; I certainly think him in many ways inferior to myself, and this deprives him of the power to make me feel guilty."[26]

In the midst of the crisis, Koestler hit upon the idea of bringing Cynthia over to work with him again. Cynthia was the best secretary he had ever had. She was now in London, listlessly working for the media mogul Sidney Bernstein and, as Koestler probably guessed, pining for him. Within three weeks she was in Bucks County and ready to roll up her sleeves, a boon to Koestler and even to Mamaine, who had succumbed to bronchitis and flu again. Cynthia was like one of the family, an assistant wife, ready to type letters and manuscripts, cook, clean, weed the garden—and do all the other duties expected of a wife. It seemed like the perfect way out.[27]

CHAPTER THIRTY-FOUR

POLITICALLY UNRELIABLE

*If you ask me what I came to do in this world, I, an artist, will
answer you: "I am here to live out loud."*

—ÉMILE ZOLA

KOESTLER'S MAIN REASONS for moving to the United States were the formation of the Congress for Cultural Freedom and his desire to build bridges
between America and Europe. But the CCF had held its second international
meeting in Brussels in November without him (the McCarran Act made it
too risky to leave the country), and Nicolas Nabokov had been preferred as
general secretary to Koestler's choice, Louis Fischer, which was understood
by all concerned as a defeat for the "Koestler line" and victory for the "Silone
line."

The delegates also discussed Koestler's Paris memo and adopted his proposal to form Les Amis de la Liberté, but there was to be no mass movement,
no information war, no direct confrontation with the Soviets. The CCF
wouldn't *koestlerize*. Instead there would be more congresses—in Asia, Latin
America, and Paris. The Paris congress, in Nabokov's hands, would become
not a political event but a gigantic arts festival, "Masterpieces of the Twentieth Century," designed to showcase the cultural strength of the West. "It will
be a huge international affair," Nabokov wrote to Arthur Schlesinger, Jr.,
"which I believe will have much more *retentissement* than a hundred speeches
by Arthur Koestler, Sidney Hook and James Burnham about the neurosis of
our century."[1]

The Brussels delegates chose Bondy's friend and ally Denis de Rougemont
to chair the executive committee, which proposed inviting Sartre, Beauvoir,
and Thomas Mann to the Paris congress. Koestler again threatened to resign

and asked Jay Lovestone to call for the resignation of the "whole secretariat" in Paris if the invitation were not withdrawn. In a postscript he ironically drew attention to "a disarming phrase" in the CCF's latest financial report: "The budget of the Congress for the next six months has been submitted to Mr Irving Brown and approved by him." Koestler had no objection to the content of this statement, but "to hand arguments to one's enemies on a silver platter in this way betrays a political naiveté which must make the prospect of any effective political fight appear hopeless." To Burnham he wrote, "You know I am a great admirer of your books. I believe that you are an important political thinker in our time, but a rotten judge of people. Bondy and Denis de Rougemont were so to speak your inventions. The latter two have apparently succeeded in undoing all we have tried to do. Unless they immediately retrace their steps I am out of this."[2]

Lovestone wasn't impressed by Koestler's threat to resign—he was beginning to hear it too many times—but he was alarmed by Koestler's obvious insight into the sources of CCF funding. He told Brown that Koestler had asked him "the crudest and most embarrassing questions" and that it had taken all his strength to maintain "a formal, chilly and firm politeness." He didn't care for Koestler's attitude, he wrote, even though Koestler admitted that literary people like himself were "neurotic." Burnham replied to Koestler that although the congress was "certainly having its troubles," it also had some real accomplishments to its credit and urged Koestler to come to Washington again to meet some of the influential people he had mentioned earlier.[3]

Koestler went down with Mamaine in April 1951 and attended a dinner party at Frank Wisner's with bureaucrats from the OPC and the CIA. He realized that Wisner's goal was to look him over, but the canny lawyer steadfastly refused Koestler's overtures to talk about the congress and remained discreetly noncommittal when Koestler broached the subject. Bob Joyce, the consummate insider, was less discreet, and Koestler's suspicions about funding were confirmed when he learned how deeply Joyce and Wisner (and therefore the CIA) were involved in the workings of the congress. He wasn't in the least surprised or upset, only contemptuous that its officials were so bad at keeping a secret.

He went to see the "bitter, explosive" Ray Murphy again, and Bob Morris, who now worked for McCarran and was shepherding Koestler's bill through Congress. At Morris's suggestion Koestler had sent tickets for the play of *Darkness at Noon* to Owen Brewster, his Senate sponsor, and to Richard Nixon, his sponsor in the House. Morris arranged for drinks with Senator McCarthy, and they discussed "Europe versus Asia." McCarthy told Koestler that "some people" (meaning Dean Acheson and the Democrats) had already betrayed Asia and would do the same to Europe if they could. There was some irony in this, since Koestler's misgivings about McCarthy arose precisely from a belief that McCarthy's antics were alienating the European allies. Koestler had said as much to Brewster over dinner in New York. Brewster, a stiff New Englander and strict teetotaler, had little interest in foreign policy and only a vague idea who Koestler was (the only member of his household who had heard of Koestler was his gardener).

Brewster listened politely as Koestler recommended an amnesty for contrite ex-Communists as an antidote to the witch hunts and he offered to take McCarthy to Koestler's farm if Koestler wished to discuss it with him. It is amusing to think what Koestler might have said to McCarthy there, but he declined unless he could gather some other European intellectuals to join in the discussion, and it never happened.[4]

Mamaine realized that, like Malraux in France, Koestler was increasingly caught in a trap of his own making. Having turned against the "woolyminded liberals of the Left," he still entertained illusions about "liberalizing the Right," just as Malraux talked of "strengthening the left wing of the Gaullists." But to "humanize" all these right-wing senators as Koestler hoped was a thankless undertaking. McCarthy was "a hairy-pawed thug," and his allies in Washington weren't much better. Koestler saw Wisner one more time at Bob Joyce's house, where the visitors included Senator Henry Cabot Lodge, the author of a bill to enlist Eastern European émigrés into the U.S. Army. Koestler tried to interest Lodge in his Legion of Liberty proposal, but the "smoothe [sic], smug" Lodge brushed him off. Wisner was again inscrutable, and Koestler left Washington little the wiser about his standing with Wisner or about his possible future with the CCF.[5]

IT TURNED OUT that Koestler had penetrated deeper into the CIA's secrets than was good for him, deep enough to sound alarm bells not only with Lovestone but also with his former friend and sponsor James Burnham, who now turned against him. A month after Koestler's Washington visit, Burnham sent the CIA an extraordinary memo on the subject of Koestler's security clearance. "There can be little doubt that Arthur Koestler's personality is neurotic in the strict pathological sense," wrote Burnham. "Observation over a number of months shows a manic depressive cycle. There is also an aggressive compensatory defense mechanism, and at least one specific obsession. This obsession might be described as a fixation on 'conspiracy.'" Koestler was intent, wrote Burnham, on ferreting out the secrets of "American networks and clandestine activities."

Furthermore, according to Burnham, Koestler's slashing criticisms of everything to do with the CCF, his fierce independence, his repeated threats to resign, and his insistence on understanding its finances made him more of a liability than an asset. Koestler was "intelligent, persevering, and unscrupulous," and it would be "unwise to underestimate what he can accomplish if he sets his mind to it." He was also politically unreliable, thanks to a split between "his reason and his feeling." Koestler was politically and philosophically of the right but hadn't succeeded in breaking from his leftist past. In Koestler's writings (and here Burnham obviously had *The Age of Longing* freshly in mind), "Bolsheviks are rationally condemned, but imaginatively displayed as firm, purposeful and sexually dynamic. Non-communists are usually weak, confused, and sexually impotent." Moreover, "the implicit audience" of all Koestler's writings was still "the Left."

Burnham certainly had a point. Koestler's sympathies *were* still on the left, and that was a big problem both for Burnham and for the CIA. Burnham insisted that because of his unreliability, Koestler should be refused a security clearance and his participation in "organizational matters" (underlined) concerning the CCF should be kept to a bare minimum. But since Koestler's intellectual abilities were of such a high order, and his writings and public personality of "major and worldwide significance in the anti-communist movement," literary collaboration with him should continue to be encouraged.[6]

Mamaine had seen it too: Koestler was caught between two stools, irremediably stuck between left and right. The left in both Europe and America ignored his claims to still be a socialist and accused him of selling out to the right. The right, in the shape of Burnham and the CIA, refused to accept him as one of their own because they *did* accept his claims to be a socialist. The liberals were wrong and the conservatives were right about his fundamental beliefs. Koestler was undoubtedly a man of the left, but, given the vehemence and strength of his anti-communism, he had ended up in a sort of no-man's-land with very few sympathizers for company.

He was joined there by friend Manès Sperber, who had come around to Koestler's way of thinking. In a long, pessimistic letter about developments in Europe, Sperber praised Koestler for withdrawing from the CCF in good time. "I did not withdraw," Koestler wrote in reply. "I was made to withdraw in a very gentle and effective way. But that is a story for a long winter evening." It's a story Koestler never told, and it's not clear whether the messenger was Burnham or an official with the CIA. Koestler continued to work with the American committee in New York, which under Hook's guidance was much closer to the Koestler line than CCF headquarters in Washington and Europe. In March he participated in an American Congress for Cultural Freedom conference with Mary McCarthy and others called "In Defense of Free Culture," and in May he spoke alongside Schlesinger, Hook, and Diana Trilling at Freedom House on "Totalitarian Myth Compulsions and Stalinism." The text of his "Amis" pamphlet, translated into English as "We Put Freedom First," was published in the *New Leader*, then broadcast over the

Voice of America, and finally read into the *Congressional Record* by Senator Hubert Humphrey. In July 1951, Koestler formally resigned from the CCF's executive committee, citing pressure of work as the reason.[7]

Koestler wouldn't be the only victim of the CCF's change of direction. Hook and eventually Burnham himself were soon to be eased out of the inner circle as too militant for the softly-softly line pioneered by Josselson, Bondy, and Nabokov (who sneered at Koestler as "uncultured" behind his back). Despite the sinister reputation it was to acquire in later years, and despite its right-wing leanings, the CIA, or at least that branch of it represented by the OPC, was tentative and timid in its approach to the Soviet Union and determined to eschew confrontation at all costs. Koestler remained in touch, made speeches on the CCF's behalf, and contributed articles to its publications (thus fulfilling, unawares, Burnham's prescriptions for him), but his fleeting illusion of becoming a new Münzenberg and leading a new crusade turned out to be a total mirage.

IN OCTOBER 1951 Koestler published a sensational piece of futuristic science fiction, "The Shadow of a Tree," in a special issue of *Collier's* magazine captioned "Russia's Defeat and Occupation 1952–60, Preview of the War We Do Not Want," prepared by a team of consultants that included Stuart Chase, Edward R. Murrow, J. B. Priestley, Walter Reuther, Walter Winchell, and several officials in Washington, with Cornelius Ryan as editor in chief. The magazine opened with an editorial stating, "We do not think that war is inevitable. We are emphatically opposed to any suggestion of a 'preventive' war," heading off the critics who held that merely to imagine a war of liberation was tantamount to advocating one.[8]

The project resembled a kind of sequel to *The Age of Longing,* and Koestler was as happy as a schoolboy when Ryan and his wife came to stay at Island Farm for a week, and he and Koestler prepared maps and diagrams to illustrate the articles. The editors were perhaps disingenuous in their disclaimers, for the magazine envisioned a three-and-a-half-year war, with 32 million casualties, and when Koestler reprinted his piece in *The Trail of the Dinosaur* some four years later, he pointed out that the article had been written before the invention of the hydrogen bomb, as if to suggest that war *was* acceptable after the atom bomb, if not after the hydrogen bomb. This was absurd, of course, but it seems he had moved closer to the "mad" Burnham on war, as he revealed in a letter to Sidney Hook. He disapproved of appeasement, he wrote, because "appeasement leads to war" and only a "firm, principled, non-opportunist policy can prevent war." But he left open the question of what might happen if a firm policy seemed to be failing.[9]

Koestler's contribution imagined a newly liberated Soviet Union in the year 1961, still anarchic but trying to establish a semblance of democracy with the help of United Nations task forces. It seemed totally fantastic at the time but, viewed from the far side of the Soviet Union's collapse in 1989, turns out to have been quite insightful. Among the events Koestler foresaw were severe food shortages, the breakdown of social services, and elections featuring a plethora of parties, ranging from the "Unified Monarchists" through Agrarians and Liberal Democrats to Syndicalists and even an "American Party." He described a journey to "The Convicts' Republic" in Kolyma, Siberia, where an uprising had just taken place in the labor camps—anticipating reality by only two years: an uprising did take place in Kengir in 1954, following the death of Stalin. In Koestler's version, the revolt was successful; in reality, it was brutally crushed, as the world learned only in 1973, with the publication of Solzhenitsyn's *The Gulag Archipelago.*

Ousted from active involvement in the CCF, Koestler redoubled his efforts on behalf of his Fund for Intellectual Freedom. In addition to the Russian-language *Literaturny Sovremennik,* he was now helping the Polish magazine *Kultura* and journals in Hungarian and Romanian, as well as continuing to send money to individual writers. With the help of Agnes Knickerbocker, he kept up a busy correspondence, wrote reports on progress achieved, supervised the accounts, and arranged for money to be sent to recipients in Paris and Munich. Given the strict American tax laws and international exchange control regulations of the time, he had to resort to all sorts of semilegal convolutions to move money from one country to another. At one point he asked Winkler to loan him a million francs against future royalties to fund refugee writers in France, while taking an equivalent sum in dollars from the fund in America; at another he loaned Sperber some money through the IRRC office in Europe and reimbursed the IRRC from his royalties in the USA.[10]

In every case his motives were honorable, but his machinations weren't acceptable to the American tax authorities, and Koestler's dream of keeping the fund informal and unbureaucratic began to evaporate. Stephen Spender and Richard Rovere joined the list of contributors, adding to the number of people who had to be kept informed, while Graham Greene lowered his offer to encompass only the Continental rights to his new novel, *The End of the Affair.*[11]

Koestler was reluctantly persuaded by David Martin of the IRRC to hold a fund-raiser in New York, leading Dos Passos to exclaim in mock horror, "Something most disagreeable happens to people when they band together to do good. The relations of dope peddlers *et al* in the writings of Genet seem charming by comparison." Dos Passos voted for a dinner (planned for when Aldous Huxley came to town for the opening of his new play) in preference to a cocktail party. "Wouldn't most writers rather be stared at by gapers at X dollars a plate than drink warm martinis with other writers with reputations which they probably feel are highly inflated?"[12]

Reinhold Niebuhr signed invitations to about five hundred intellectuals and five hundred professional authors, but the dinner at Delmonico's restaurant in May 1951 was a flop. Koestler gave a speech pointing out that the goal of the fund was to save not just writers but "exiled national cultures" that were being suppressed under Communist rule. He again advocated a form of "self-taxation" by writers in the West and pointed out that there was no overhead. "This is an organization that hates to be an organization." But only two of the invited authors came, and the amount raised was a paltry thousand dollars, a pittance compared with what Koestler alone was contributing. The next month's financial statement showed Koestler's contribution at just over $22,000. The next largest were Huxley's at $500, and Budd Schulberg's at $200, and the rest were pitifully small.[13]

A year later the total income had grown to $34,000, of which $31,000 had come from Koestler, though by now about half that sum was tied up in escrow to satisfy the tax authorities. The fund donated a thousand dollars to the eighty-year-old Nobel Prize–winning Russian author Ivan Bunin for an operation, paid for a printing press and the first three issues of the Russian-language *Literaturny Sovremennik*, and helped a dozen other writers to survive, including the Russian surrealist Alexei Remizov and an unknown young Romanian playwright by the name of Eugène Ionesco. The fund also helped writers from Ukraine, Poland, Czechoslovakia, and Hungary, and interceded with the U.S. government on behalf of a promising young Polish defector by the name of Czesław Miłosz.[14]

KOESTLER'S PRINCIPAL ALLY in promoting the fund was his Bucks County neighbor Budd Schulberg, to whom he had been introduced by the publisher Michael Bessie. Schulberg was well known for his screenplays and his satirical novel *What Makes Sammy Run?* and was enjoying a huge success with his new novel, *The Disenchanted,* about F. Scott Fitzgerald. Like Koestler, Schulberg was a confirmed anti-fascist and former member of the Communist Party, now thoroughly disenchanted with his former comrades, and he had made himself hugely unpopular in liberal circles by testifying to HUAC on Hollywood's Communists. Schulberg had a fifty-five-acre farm not far from Koestler's and was by far the fund's most energetic American supporter, tithing 10 percent of his royalties and writing letters on behalf of Bunin and others. He also tried to interest Norman Mailer and Irwin Shaw in the fund, but without success.

Schulberg was a head taller than Koestler, solidly built, with a shock of brown hair and a severe stammer that he overcame by sheer force of personality. He told Koestler that he was happy to work against the Communists, "but I don't like to attack the left." Koestler told him to get over it: "They're not left, they're east." The relationship between the two writers alternated

between cordial and stormy, for Schulberg was just as opinionated and stubborn as Koestler. One night over dinner, he questioned the primacy given
to Russian writers and wondered aloud about the wisdom of funding a
magazine. Who was in charge and making the decisions? And weren't they
promoting a form of nationalism when internationalism was needed? Seemingly incapable of arguing without a fight, Koestler lost his temper and
started yelling that Schulberg was too negative.

The next day Koestler wrote a six-page letter denying Schulberg's implication that he was "totalitarian" in the way he ran the fund, saying that most
of the decisions about whom to help were being made by Markoosha Fischer
in Munich. He believed in the magazine scheme because he felt that money
given as charity was "humiliating and demoralizing," whereas payment for
work done preserved the writers' pride, and he cited his own experience in
exile in the thirties. "If you had lived under those conditions you would have
a more practical appreciation of what it means to have a market, an audience,
a platform from which you can speak in your own language, and you would
be impatient with people who say it is nationalistic or narrow-minded to
maintain these vital enterprises."

Schulberg replied with a soothing letter saying that he had no doubts
about Koestler's sincerity and had not meant to be as negative as Koestler
made him sound. They resumed their collaboration but clashed again in the
fall over McCarthyism. Despite his willingness to testify before HUAC,
Schulberg was one of those clear-eyed liberals who detested the Communists
and McCarthy in equal measure, and he was offended when Koestler dismissed hostility to McCarthyism as frivolous and exaggerated. This time it
was Koestler who apologized. Schulberg wrote that he could understand
Koestler's impatience with Americans but couldn't help wishing that
Koestler would explore the American mind further before swallowing "the
weird and unprecedented concoctions being whipped up for us by wild-
mouthed senators. I think it is our fear of these people, and our right to express this fear, that is our hope and strength."[15]

It was a reprise of the liberal dismay over Koestler's Hiss-Chambers article six months earlier, and Schulberg was making essentially the same point.
Koestler's vaunted ability to parachute into a country, take its pulse, and
write cogently about it may have served him well in Europe, it but didn't
work so well in America. His new editor at Macmillan, Al Hart, offered a
crasser version of Schulberg's thought when he suggested that Koestler write
a book on an American theme that would reveal his attitude to "this country
and its problems" and placate some of his American critics. Koestler replied
that he could never pander. He was a social critic, and any criticism of America he might make was more likely to alienate his audience than please it.

In truth, he understood the country too little to offer much constructive
criticism, as he showed when he remarked to Mamaine that the only thing

that interested American writers was success (as evidenced by the best-seller list) and that American writers were not inclined to criticize their country. He was wrong on both counts and insufficiently informed to weigh the complexities of a nation in which self-criticism was as much a condition of success as of its opposite.[16]

BUCKS COUNTY, located in the so-called genius belt of America, had been a magnet for writers, painters, and theater people since the Depression. It was also, as Al Hart's wife, Nancy, remarked disdainfully one day, "full of Jews," but that didn't help Koestler at all, since many were radical socialists close to the Hiss circle, who automatically shunned Koestler as a turncoat, while the many local show-business luminaries such as George S. Kaufman, Oscar Hammerstein, Moss Hart, S. J. Perelman, and Dorothy Parker were uninterested in politics and (with the signal exception of Schulberg) largely ignored him.[17]

The choice of a farm to live on was also unfortunate. Several writers of Koestler's acquaintance (Chambers, Schulberg, Dos Passos, Remarque) lived on farms, and he probably thought it would be fun. At times it was. When the yard ran riot in early May, he purchased a tractor-mower and had a glorious time mowing the meadow at top speed. Mamaine tried out some electric shears, Cynthia raked the grass into piles, and they all played at gardening. But Koestler had hopelessly underestimated the constant work involved. Whittaker Chambers spent half of each day working on his farm, and the other writers hired laborers to do the work. Koestler couldn't afford laborers. He could barely manage an ancient Italian-American gardener and a cleaning lady, so that the vast old house, rambling and dusty (and drafty and smoky in winter), with primitive appliances and dilapidated barns around it, became an albatross. Mel Lasky, the city slicker from Berlin, was appalled when Koestler insisted he climb fences and tramp through muck to look at all the sheds and stalls surrounding the house. "These," said Koestler grandly, "I will clean and fix up for the refugees." "What refugees?" asked Mel innocently. Koestler said he meant refugees from Eastern Europe in the event of a war, which he still feared to be around the corner.[18]

Koestler's preferred bolt-hole became Princeton, to the south. He and Mamaine went down to have lunch with Edmund Wilson and his wife and attended a John Berryman "Brush-Up-Your-Hebrew" cocktail party (as one guest put it), where Koestler, Wilson, Saul Bellow, and Irving Howe got into a passionate discussion about the Hebrew language and the Dead Sea Scrolls. Koestler also looked up the brilliant, Hungarian-born polymath John von Neumann at the Institute for Advanced Studies at Princeton, and the von Neumanns became regular visitors to Island Farm.

Von Neumann was a true genius, one of the few people for whom

Koestler entertained not only respect but reverence, and he shared Koestler's Central European addiction to abstruse philosophical discussions, political debate, and dirty jokes. The two of them derived considerable pleasure from discussing the state of American civilization (was it in crisis or simply at the stage of adolescence?), the likely future of Europe (would there be war?), free will versus determinism, and the definition of pregnancy ("the uterus taking seriously what was pointed at it in fun"). Von Neumann denied the existence of a crisis in America, asserted that the only alternative to a preventive war in Europe was Russian occupation (whispering to Koestler in Hungarian that he preferred war to occupation), and said that the "feeling of freedom" was important, even if it couldn't be proved. Koestler said he couldn't bear the thought of determinism, because it would deprive him of responsibility for his actions, and he had to assume "the intervention of a hidden variable." Koestler's belief in freedom was not so much based on reason as "quasi-mystical."[19]

Koestler's most fruitful discussion with von Neumann occurred when he was invited to a party with von Neumann's scientific colleagues at Princeton, where the talk moved to the subject of scientists' motives. Von Neumann maintained that their motives were "primarily esthetic" and suggested that although Archimedes had been almost as advanced as Kepler or Galileo in his thinking, no progress was made between their eras because humanity's taste had switched from science to religion. One strong spiritual force weakened the other, and when there was a resurgence of science in modern times, it was religion's turn to be eclipsed. This idea became a central plank of Koestler's astronomy book, *The Sleepwalkers,* published eight years later, in which he traced the interrelationship of religion and science, and it surfaced again in *The Act of Creation,* in which Koestler elevated the aesthetic principle to first place. Whether Koestler was directly influenced by von Neumann is unclear—Michael Polanyi had already expressed similar thoughts to Koestler in England—but von Neumann's support for the notion certainly reinforced Koestler's interest in the subject.[20]

But these Princeton excursions didn't save Koestler from his demons. His heavy drinking escalated still further (characteristic was the night he passed out in the car on the way back from von Neumann's), his skirt chasing grew more shameless, and his arrogance knew no bounds. Diana Trilling noted that at the ACCF panel where they both spoke, Koestler delayed the start by arriving late, appeared at the door just as she was in the middle of her opening remarks, and strode ostentatiously down the center aisle in a way that attracted the audience's attention toward him and away from her. Afterward in the bar, he had eyes only for a young girl he had picked up, and rudely ignored Schlesinger, Hook, and the other distinguished members of the panel. Edmund Wilson and his wife, Elena, endured an evening with the Koestlers at "21" in New York, during which a drunken Koestler, enraged by the proprietor's babble about hunting, had picked up their table and thrown it into the middle of the room. And Marietta Torberg, whose Viennese-born novelist husband, Friedrich, had introduced Koestler to Remarque, describes a dinner at a restaurant with Remarque and Nicolas Nabokov during which Koestler made a little cannon out of toothpicks and flicked bread pellets at the others. On the one hand, she reported, "there was nothing mean or petty about Koestler" when it came to serious issues, and he had done more to help her husband than ever Remarque did. But he could be distressingly infantile and childish when things weren't going his way and become unrecognizable. "I wouldn't have wanted to spend even half an hour with him alone."[21]

Koestler himself was rarely alone. When not working, he couldn't bear to be without company even for a moment. Weekend after weekend he filled Island Farm with guests from New York, Washington, Princeton, France, England, Germany, and, when all else failed, from surrounding Bucks County. Details of this fevered social life are sparse, but from accounts given by Ruth Goetz, Michael Bessie, and others, it seems he cut a particularly wide swath among his neighbors' wives, "leaving a trail of enraged husbands" behind him (Goetz) and making him "the most widely hated man in Bucks County" (Bessie). Judging from a cryptic comment in Koestler's diary that summer, he must also have started sleeping with Cynthia again. He grew painfully paranoid (perhaps with good reason, where the husbands were concerned), and couldn't go into a restaurant or bar without concluding that people were staring at him. Burnham was right. Koestler now looked over his shoulder before starting to speak, imagining enemies everywhere, which made him more unpredictable than ever to be with.[22]

Even by Koestler's standards, his demented conduct in the spring and summer of 1951 was excessive. The alcohol certainly had something to do with it, but it appears he was clinically sick, with a bad case of manic depression. Kay Redfield Jamison could almost have had Koestler in mind when, forty years later, she formulated her famous definition of manic-depressive artists as identifiable by "an inflated self-esteem, as well as a certainty of conviction about the correctness and importance of their ideas." Poor judgment leads to "chaotic patterns of personal and professional relationships," and other features of the disease include "spending excessive amounts of money, impulsive involvements in questionable endeavors, reckless driving, extreme impatience, intense impulsive romantic or sexual relations, and volatility." In its chronic form, according to Jamison, this kind of mania is characterized by "violent agitation, bizarre behavior, delusional thinking, and visual and auditory hallucinations." Last, there are heavy alcohol use and a tendency to suicide—case closed.[23]

In Koestler's case, his volatility was increased by his ouster from the Congress for Cultural Freedom, which had pulled the rug from under his plans to become an intermediary between America and Europe. In addition, the largely negative critical responses to *The Age of Longing* had deeply depressed him, while the wrangling with Kingsley had poisoned even the success of the play of *Darkness at Noon* in New York. At the age of forty-six, he sensed he was at a crossroads. He hadn't written an artistically successful novel in ten years, and he began to consider turning the panoramic autobiographical novel he had planned in Paris into straight autobiography. He explained to Mamaine that characters like Willi Münzenberg would lack conviction in a novel and that if he stuck to fiction, it would inevitably turn into a coming-of-age novel, which he wanted to avoid. Mamaine added that Koestler himself as a character would also lack conviction, "unless he split himself into ten characters."

Koestler agreed. He was beginning to realize that autobiography, with its mixture of introspection and documentary reportage, actually suited his talents better than fiction, which required a depth of psychological insight into other characters that he found hard to achieve. Autobiography also centered on the person he knew and loved best—himself. The more he thought about it, the more enticing it seemed, and the choice would prove to be inspired, eventually unlocking the door to his finest writing since *Darkness at Noon*.[24]

CHAPTER THIRTY-FIVE

THE LANGUAGE OF DESTINY

He would have been admirable, except that he was an absolute
egomaniac, a Beast—no recognition existed of the existence of
anything beyond the range of his reach.
— NORMAN MAILER

LIFE IN BUCKS COUNTY for Mamaine was increasingly hellish. It wasn't so much Koestler's infidelities that got her down as his drunkenness and selfish and manipulative ways. After she had intervened in one of his drunken quarrels with Schulberg, they had "a really major row." They decided to separate, then changed their minds, then left the matter open after Mamaine weakly admitted she couldn't face living alone.

"I had started to feel that perhaps I really should have the courage to leave K now, and not postpone the inevitable," she wrote to Celia. "It was a dark night, pouring with rain, and a strong gale blowing. However, I put on a lot of clothes and wandered off down the island and back, but was too worn out to think clearly. Ever since then things seem to have gone all right and K has been affectionate and cheerful. But God, how many more of these scenes will I have to go through, and how will the whole thing end? Aren't I fighting a losing battle against dehumanization, I sometimes wonder?"[1]

A continuing irritant was Mamaine's fragile health and inability to do physical work for long periods of time, a condition for which there were both physical and psychological reasons. It didn't help that the big, dust-laden house, with its mildew and smoky fires, was again located by a damp river— in fact in the middle of it—causing Mamaine to suffer from colds, bronchitis, and flu, even after spring brought warmer weather. On good days Koestler was solicitous, insisting that she go to Johns Hopkins Hospital for exhaustive tests (they found little wrong with her except a supposed allergy to dogs, a fine thing to suffer from given Koestler's preference for dogs over humans). On bad days he would bitterly criticize her weaknesses, provoking a tension that played on her nerves and made her physical condition worse.[2]

One consequence was a debate about where to live. Both were missing Europe, and they decided that their best plan would be to spend half the year in America and half in Europe—but where? Verte Rive was deadly for Mamaine's asthma, and Koestler was disillusioned with France, so it was preferable to sell it. They agreed that Mamaine would leave for England at the end of June 1951 and Koestler would follow when his bill came up in Congress. It was eventually passed by the Senate on June 11 and by the House of Representatives a month later—at a time when he was almost ready to leave.[3]

The move to Europe brought no visible improvement in their relations. After a tense week in England, they flew to Paris "barely on speaking terms." At Verte Rive Mamaine complained of "constant nagging, eternal reproaches, tantrums about trifles," all magnified by Adele's arrival for nine days and the hovering presence of Cynthia. Mamaine went out for a dinner date with Camus in the Halle aux Vins. Camus sweet-talked her in an attempt to explain away his affair (now over) with the actress María Casares, and for a moment, when "C was looking at me with his tender, serious, smiling eyes," Mamaine was tempted. Camus was almost as much a philanderer as Koestler, but his soft, dreamy manner was a welcome respite from Koestler's bluster and made her think wistfully of what might have been.[4]

She returned to London in mid-July, taking Adele with her, while Koestler stayed on in Paris. They had changed their minds about selling Verte Rive but planned to take Maxime and Anna back to Island Farm with them as caretakers. If all went well, they would leave at the end of September on the *Île de France*. Koestler resumed work on what had now become the first volume of a full-scale autobiography, corrected a poor German translation of *The Age of Longing* (eventually published under the dreadful title of *Gottes Thron steht lehr* [God's Throne Is Empty]), and dealt with the fallout from the novel's recent publication in France (under the rather better title *Les Hommes ont soif* [Men Are Thirsty]).

Koestler had freely caricatured Sartre, Beauvoir, and Merleau-Ponty in his novel and didn't mind the consequences, but he was dismayed when both Sperber, who oversaw the French translation for Calmann-Lévy, and Malraux took exception to the characters based on them. He had to scramble to soothe their feelings. Sperber had gone through the book with a fine-toothed comb, severely trimming comments about the grossness of French eating habits and removing or changing some of the more insulting epithets in the text, but Koestler's portrait of France was still so negative that the critics predictably hated it. The only people who would be pleased by the novel, wrote one, twisting the knife in the wound, were Koestler's enemies, for he had turned himself into "the Ilya Ehrenburg of anti-communism." Koestler was further stung when the published edition of Kingsley's play of *Darkness at Noon* reached him in Paris, showing Kingsley's name on the cover in large type, with Koestler's much smaller below, which gave him several sleepless nights before he got over it.[5]

BACK IN LONDON, Mamaine picked up the threads of her life of the year before, spending as much time as she could with Celia, starting piano lessons again, and resuming old friendships. Koestler had asked a Hungarian doctor friend, Tibor Csato, to take charge of Mamaine's medical care, and after a battery of tests Csato informed her that her liver and gallbladder were barely functioning, her cholesterol was sky high, and she was suffering from latent jaundice, which explained her recurrent bouts of nausea and inability to put on weight. Though this would intensify her asthma, he recommended a protein-heavy diet and no alcohol for a year before tackling the asthma proper. Away from Koestler, Mamaine's mood improved by leaps and bounds, but she was still beset by agonizing indecision over what to do next. She told Celia she "quaked" at the mere mention of Koestler's name, yet the thought of leaving him was "awful too," though it increasingly seemed like the only solution.[6]

She returned to Paris on Bastille Day. The subdued Koestler met her train and took her for a gloomy dinner in Fontaine-le-Port. The following day Koestler was intensely irritable, as if spoiling for a fight, yelling for the most trivial reasons, and it wasn't until eleven p.m. that Mamaine screwed up her courage to tell him of her decision to leave. He was surprised but also re-lieved, noting in his diary that he had been "terribly careful, holding my breath, [so as] not to make the wrong choice. Whether I could have talked her out of it is a moot question. I knew much less about her than I did about other women [sic]. But did I want to talk her out of it? And did she want me to?"[7]

They settled on a compromise. They would live for eight months of the year on Island Farm and during the remaining four months take separate vacations. Koestler would fire Cynthia. Mamaine would return to London until it was time to leave for the United States, and he would remain in Paris. After packing, she asked him to do her one last favor and drive her to the spot in Fontainebleau forest where he had once told her he loved her. Ma-maine then asked to get out of the car and walk a bit, but Koestler insisted they had to hurry to catch the train and refused to stop. They had a terrible row, completely undoing the compromise arrived at earlier, and missed the train anyway. Later, over drinks with the Winklers at the Café de la Paix, Koestler infuriated Mamaine by announcing with mock solemnity that since the Winklers had been witnesses at his and Mamaine's wedding, it was fitting that they should be present at their last drink.[8]

Though nothing had been formally stated, their marriage was in effect over, and Koestler admitted as much to his diary. Marriage was not his style, he concluded, and he was glad to be done with it. But Koestler's thirst for rationalization was unquenchable, and a few days later, he returned to his diary to find an explanation for what had happened. For weeks now he had been working on his autobiography and had just completed the chapter describing himself at the age of twenty-five, where he confessed to his chronic sense of insecurity, his pathological promiscuity, and his frantic search for oblivion in the arms of his latest "Helena." It wasn't at all difficult to fit Mamaine into the old pattern, which had reasserted itself "fatally and inexorably." He thought of it in strictly Freudian terms: "incest barrier" resulting from frustrated mother love, "guilt, aggression, inferiority complex, an irrational thirst for freedom," but "no amount of knowing the mechanism of the machine could stop its pistons." Mamaine had faults of her own, he decided, but no woman he had ever met could replace her. "If I was to settle down, it was to be [with] her." He had said virtually the same of Daphne when leaving her for Mamaine, but it is doubtful he remembered that part of the pattern.[9]

He concluded that the breakup with Mamaine was part of a larger spiritual crisis that had been building for some time and that he needed to bring it to a head for his own purposes. But was he ready "to shoulder the burden of ultimate loneliness; to settle for good on the tragic plane; to obey the apparent unreason of what I feel to be my destiny?" The answer was a conditional no. It was still too early for a complete retreat from the outside world. On the other hand, in four years he would be fifty, and perhaps then, despite the persistent "itch in the flesh," he would be able to pull it off. Either way, a "radical shedding of ballast" was in order: two houses, three dogs, two cars, a wife, a secretary, and two "retainers" (Anna and Maxime) were too much. They externalized him, diffused his energies, and left him with none for his essential work, his "dialogue with destiny." Such was his pattern, however, that he could shed the past only through a "radical smash-up."[10]

NEWS ARRIVED FROM NEW YORK that his bill to become a permanent resident of the United States had been signed into law. He was more relieved than he had expected, leading him to conclude that he still didn't know himself and to contemplate for a moment the depths of his own selfishness. Perhaps the root cause of the crisis had been his insecurity sharpened by archetypal "visa-anxiety" all along? If so, Mamaine, "cruel as it sounds," was still only secondary, just as, when he had thought his mother had been deported in 1944, the real cause of his suffering was the separation from Mamaine. The relief, in any case, revivified him. He decided not to take Maxime and Anna to America after all but to build them a small house in Fontaine-le-Port (since they were relying on him to look after them in old age) and to rent Verte Rive to a couple of American army officers who were interested.

He would leave Cynthia behind as well, though whether this was a belated gesture to Mamaine's feelings or a response to American puritanism (she would be alone in the house with him) is not clear. Either way, Cynthia would be obliged to return to London and look for secretarial work once more. Feeling better about himself, Koestler decided he should eschew both "masochism" and "opportunistic compromise" in his response to this latest crisis. He would return to Island Farm for at least a few months, then rent it out for several years and take a small furnished apartment in London. On a pad in his study he wrote in capital letters: "Don't betray or whittle down resolution this time—the warning was clear—it may be the last chance."[11]

What's so astonishing about these musings, apart from their stark honesty, is their illustration of the apparent ease with which Koestler accommodated himself to the rupture with Mamaine and the sense of relief with which he greeted it. There's little doubt that he loved her as much as he was capable of loving anyone and that, as he later realized, she was the one true love of his life, but his egocentrism was such that he was able to brush it off as of little consequence. There would be little "masochism" in his response, at least in the short term, and plenty of "opportunistic compromise," as his immediate actions showed.

The last Paris engagement that he and Mamaine had fulfilled as a couple was dinner with the German movie producer Paul Graetz and his wife, Janine, and it was to Janine's that Koestler returned for a drink after seeing Mamaine off on the boat train to London. Koestler had been having an off-and-on affair with her for several months, and they now spent "four lovely days" in the Loire Valley. Paul, best known for his famous study in sexual obsession, Le Diable au corps (Devil in the Flesh), had broached to Koestler the idea of making a film on psychoanalysis, and Koestler had dashed off a synopsis about a young woman made frigid by the memory of seeing her father seduce their maid when she was a child. Graetz's scriptwriter, Jean Aurenche, had rejected the idea as "too literary," and when Graetz suggested filming Arrival and Departure instead, Aurenche said it would be difficult to make a film from the book that was "neither pro-Communist nor anti-Communist."

That particular evening had been significant not so much for the conversation about movies as for the current of attraction passing between Koestler and Janine. The daughter of a Belgian newspaper magnate, Georges Détry de Marès, and flamboyantly stylish in a Dior dress and expensive perfume, Janine had ostentatiously flirted with Koestler the whole evening. Cynthia had been "consumed by the blackest jealousy," while Mamaine observed the scene disdainfully from the other end of the table. After dinner, Janine persuaded Koestler to take her for a midnight row on the Seine. Koestler cautiously asked Mamaine if she wanted to go too, but Mamaine declined and Koestler and Janine went on their own.[12]

There had been more dinners after that. Koestler was fascinated to learn that Janine's maternal grandmother was Russian and that she had studied law in Cambridge, England. She spoke several languages and according to one person who knew her well was a "vital force," outspoken in her likes and dislikes and very headstrong, rather like Koestler himself. Janine was also contradictory, able to be "very generous and yet very mean, iconoclastic and ferociously traditional, a stickler for good form, but also extremely rude." She was "manipulative, impulsive, unscrupulous, amoral, and an inveterate romantic who would stop at nothing to get her man." And she was clearly a match for Koestler, although he didn't know it then.

He had sealed their relationship with the gift of his favorite boxer puppy, named (alas) Romeo, and they had started an on-and-off affair that had lasted for several months. They now spent "four lovely days" in the Loire Valley together before Koestler returned to Paris to consider his options.[13]

AFTER THIS INTERLUDE, Koestler traveled to London to see the small house Mamaine planned to buy in Chelsea with the help of an interest-free loan from him. Their relationship was much easier now. They still referred to each other as "darling" and signed letters with "love" and were able to discuss divorce proceedings with equanimity. A lawyer advised Mamaine that their situation was complicated, because Koestler was domiciled in France but planned to live in the USA. In France the only grounds for divorce were desertion and adultery, whereas in the United States one could go to Reno and cite "cruelty," which would be much speedier. Both were recognized in Britain, and it was up to Mamaine to decide. Koestler told her there was absolutely no hurry from his point of view and she should take her time.[14]

Returning to Island Farm in late September, he found himself truly alone for the first time in years, "a little man in a big house," with only Nellie and Rubashov for company. The Ryans had mowed the lawn, but the gardens and grounds were a jungle. Koestler spent a hectic couple of weeks mowing grass, clipping hedges, cutting brush, burning rubbish, clearing out the garbage, and cleaning up the property. He contracted a painful kidney stone, which he convinced himself was psychosomatic in origin, taking megadoses of morphine until he was able to pass it after an agonizing ten days. When he finally resumed work on his autobiography, his lingering depression was magically dispersed. All fall and winter he worked away at it, completing a first draft in mid-November and the revision by the end of February. It was laborious work, since he now wrote in longhand and typed many passages himself, before handing the whole thing over to a professional typist.[15]

As he wrote he returned to the meaning of the end of his second marriage and its implications for the future. He identified a schizophrenic split in himself between his longing for deprivation and a desire to live on the "tragic plane," implanted, he thought, by his prison experiences, and a hedonistic greed that drove him to enjoy to the full the "frivolous life" that he intellectually despised. His urge to be away from Mamaine arose from contradictory impulses: on the one hand to live on the tragic plane, on the other to indulge his thirst for erotic adventures. Morbid masochism and self-mortification could be justified only if they brought "peace through faith." But his faith was brittle and unsteady.

> I can't believe in a historic God. I can't, on the other hand, believe in the tale told by an idiot, in *tant de bruit pour une omelette* [all that noise to make an omelette]. I believe in something beyond the human brain, beyond the range of frequencies visible to the ear; a message written in invisible ink, of which fragments become visible when [one is] listening to music, standing on a mountain, praying, reading poetry, being in love, contemplating a beautiful math solution. Fragments of the message have been copied in mutilated versions in the scriptures, the Vedas, etc. But those copies are as inadequate as ignorant monks' copies of antique texts.[16]

Privately he admitted to himself that he had no idea when he would be ready for a life lived only on the tragic plane—perhaps in four years, when he was fifty? Perhaps in ten? He wasn't fit for a life alone in the country or on his island. He needed the town, perhaps London, which he had found so enjoyable on his last visit. But could he endure the "terrible snobbery, insularity, and allergy to political books" that had driven him from England in the first place? That had to be set beside the "spiritual and physical unhealthiness" of the USA, its "mechanized fruit and veg," its "psychoanalytical supermarket." No, "if Europe must perish, perish with it."

Not for the first time he felt his interest in politics waning. He had "done his duty" with regard to anti-communism, and (an odd thought, this) his active religious phase had passed too, with the failure of the sequel to *Arrival and Departure*. All he knew was that the "invisible writing" existed and his job was to obey its admonitions wherever it led him. Here, too, he identified a "schizophrenic split" in himself between the didactic crusader and the contemplative historian and found an excuse for the hostility he had provoked with his actions and writings. "I have fought my battles and been misunderstood and slandered because my temperament is a rare mixture of the two." It was time to "swing the pendulum toward detachment" and not to accuse himself of being a traitor.

In January 1952, after a particularly bad hangover, he "capitulated" to his demons and tried therapy again, this time consulting a New York hypnotherapist named Wollberg. After Wollberg had helped him recall certain incidents from his past, Koestler conceived the idea of using Wollberg's skills for autobiographical purposes, taking the "truth drug" Pentothal to make the therapy more effective. He was so elated by the initial success of the treatment that he contemplated writing a joint book with the therapist to realize his "Seville vow"—to outdo both Rousseau and Cellini with the frankness of his autobiography. He admonished himself not to be "too humble" in his attitude to Wollberg or to regard him as "a shaman," for he had it in him to write a book "to last a hundred years." All he had to do was submit to a procedure that was "not distasteful," face up to what was coming, and not distrust the therapy simply because he enjoyed it.

The plan came to nothing. In working on his autobiography he had already found a way to wrap passages of "ruthless sincerity" in a membrane of speculation and explanation that kept self-immolation safely at bay. He wasn't ready to dig deeper into his psyche after all. After two months of diminishing results he returned the Pentothal to Wollberg and abandoned the therapy on the pretext that his depression was too deep to respond to treatment.[17]

THROUGHOUT THESE MONTHS ALONE on the island Koestler tried to maintain some sort of social life. After struggling in the kitchen for some time, he prevailed on Agnes to spend several weekends there to help him cook and entertain his visitors. These included Janine, who came for a short visit in January, the Burnhams (despite Burnham's treacherous memo to the CIA), the Schulbergs (until Koestler broke off with Budd on the pretext that he "couldn't stand" Budd's wife, Vicki), and a number of friends from Europe. He also began to spend more time with near neighbors, Rube and Gretel Barkin and Jack and Christine Newsom. Newsom, a freelance writer and former director of the Federal Writers' Project, gladly responded to Koestler's request to help him edit and polish the first volume of his autobiography. Astonishingly, Koestler still didn't trust his English enough.[18]

He was temporarily distracted by the long-awaited court case on Kingsley's dramatization of *Darkness at Noon*. About a year earlier, Koestler had learned of plans to broadcast and perform the play in French and other languages and started worrying about its political naiveté. American audiences were one thing, European another, and Sperber confirmed his fears that a French audience would shoot the play full of holes. Koestler had asked Kingsley to make several changes and, when Kingsley objected, had sued him for breach of contract, claiming that the latter had refused to consult him properly or give "reasonable consideration" to his criticisms and suggestions. Kingsley countersued for damages, and Koestler presented an amended claim, alleging that his "proprietory rights" would be damaged if the play were produced abroad.[19]

The case came before a New York Arbitration Tribunal in February 1952. Burnham, Schlesinger, Edgar Mowrer, and others testified on Koestler's behalf, and Sperber (with Mamaine's help) procured letters of support from Camus, Aron, Altman, Rousset, and Malraux. The tribunal faulted Koestler for manifesting a "strange apathy" toward the play in its formative stage by refusing to comment on the text when Kingsley was working on it and for waiting too long to voice the exact nature of his objections. This was partly a side effect of Koestler's breakdown after his rupture with the CCF in Paris and partly a result of his impulsive decision to wash his hands of the New York production, but these reasons didn't stand up in court, and Koestler's case was juridically weak.[20]

Koestler also managed to antagonize the three tribunal members by threatening to take a negative verdict "before the court of public opinion," but Kingsley, too, emerged as devious and calculating, both in his insistence on retaining artistic control of the play and in his unwillingness to concede that he had underestimated the novel's ideological complexity, just as he underplayed the importance of ideology in the politically charged atmosphere of Continental Europe. Koestler lost on purely legal grounds and was obliged to sign off on contracts for European productions of the play that he had been holding up with his litigation. As it turned out, there weren't many, and the play was never produced in the countries that Koestler truly cared about—France, Italy, and Germany. Most of his huffing and puffing (and the personal misery it generated) were for nothing.[21]

Koestler returned to his farm and listened for the "language of destiny," which he had just defined in the closing pages of his autobiography.

> I have always held a perhaps superstitious, but deep belief in the significance of events which come in series. When major and minor calamities crowd together in a short span of time, they seem to express a symbolic warning, as if some mute power were tugging at your sleeve. It is then up to you to decipher the meaning of the inchoate message. If you ignore it, nothing at all will probably happen; but you may have missed your chance to remake your life, have passed a potential turning point without noticing it. It is not an altogether naive superstition if one concedes that such series are often produced by unconscious arrangement; that the warning may have been issued by that "he in me who is more me than myself."[22]

Soon afterward he ran into Whittaker Chambers at the Berkshire Hotel in New York. Koestler had sent Chambers a congratulatory cable on reading the first installment of Chambers's autobiography, *Witness,* and the two men arranged to have dinner that night, but Chambers decamped to his farm, sending Koestler a strange, apologetic letter in which he attributed his odd public behavior not to fear but to horror—horror at what he had seen and experienced in his life: "I am a man ill of horror." This was the language if not of destiny, then of paranoia, a language that Koestler also recognized, and it renewed his sympathy for Chambers.[23]

It wasn't long before Koestler found a New Jersey builder with five children who was willing to sign a three-year lease on Island Farm, starting in March, and decided to move to Europe. As he was packing, the language of destiny rapped out a few more messages. Janine came to stay for three days, and they had dinner with the von Neumanns. Driving home afterward, Koestler almost killed everyone in the car by cutting too quickly in front of a truck. The next day he backed into Janine's car, and that same afternoon Janine was detained by the police for two hours for speeding. In a snowstorm the following day, Koestler collided with yet another car, and a few days later, on his way for a week at Yale, he stopped on the highway, causing a multicar pileup behind him. Given Koestler's erratic driving skills and reckless habits, the message was obvious: he was a lousy driver. But Koestler thought he sensed a more mystical message. "What does it all mean?" he asked his diary. The language of destiny didn't answer.[24]

Working on the proofs of his autobiography on the twenty-fifth floor of the St. Moritz Hotel in New York and "loathing the book, as usual at this stage," he replaced his original title, "Memoirs of a Tightrope Walker," with a shorter and better one, *Arrow in the Blue,* a reference to his childhood fascination with the idea of infinity and a potent metaphor for his preoccupation with utopia. He attended a PEN reception in honor of Langston Hughes, and Hughes said he would refuse to sign anything anti-Russian even if Koestler asked him. "If they had put me into a labor camp I would also be against them, but to me they were very nice."[25]

Koestler went back to Island Farm to finish packing and say goodbye to friends. Agnes Knickerbocker and Jack Newsom helped him marshal his belongings and place them in storage, and Jack agreed to keep an eye on them until Koestler could send for them from Europe. Nellie was left in the capable hands of the Barkins. In early April Koestler crossed the bridge leading from the island for the last time and "without regrets," bringing to an end his brief and unhappy love affair with America. He flew to Paris, where Janine was waiting for him, and they spent a happy week checking up on Verte Rive, dining with Calmann-Lévy, the Winklers, and other old friends and carrying on like a well-settled couple, after which Koestler crossed the channel to London.[26]

CHAPTER THIRTY-SIX

THE PHANTOM CHASE

Seeking always and again the moment of conquest when he might escape his history, himself, and soar unburdened for a stolen hour.

— CLAIRE MESSUD

KOESTLER'S FIRST FEW WEEKS in England were as hectic as any in his overcrowded life. Uncomfortably aware of his responsibility for houses in France and the United States, he had every intention of renting an apartment now. But he decided to go house hunting anyway and, chancing upon an empty Georgian terrace house in a Knightsbridge square, he felt the irresistible, greedy urge to possess it. The house was a tall, narrow eighteenth-century "gentleman's residence" on four floors on a corner of Montpelier Square, tucked behind Brompton Road and Harrods. This part of London was densely populated by the rich and powerful and filled with upper-class mandarins among whom Koestler increasingly felt at ease. Although the house was technically for rent, Koestler pressed to be allowed to buy it and as a result of his importunate bargaining skills (Henrik would have been proud of him) was allowed to start negotiations.

It was an excellent start to his "second honeymoon" with England, "the last solid country in the world." But the problem of being accepted by the English was a serious one. England, "the nearest approximation of home to me," was also the place where he was least respected as a writer and where he was "permanently snubbed as a foreigner." He felt, entirely illogically, that his naturalization should count for something. It was like "legal marriage"—it shouldn't have mattered, but it did—and he came to the startling decision to go to a phoneticist to work on his music-hall German accent. He was tired of being made the butt of English jokes and—surprisingly for him—agreed with the subliminal message that it was a foreigner's duty to fit in.[1]

In quick succession he saw the Hamish Hamiltons, Paul Willert, Sylvester and Pauline Gates, Humphrey and Moira Slater, his Hungarian doctor friends—Plesch and Csato—and Zita Crossman (but not Dick, with whom he was still not on speaking terms). There were cocktail parties in his honor and a lunch at the House of Commons with several of his Labour Party buddies. The only dark spots were lunches with his mother, who berated him for abandoning Mamaine (he had waited months to tell Adele in the first place), and several meetings with Mamaine herself, whom he found in a "precarious state" and "sadder than ever." She had moved into her small Chelsea house and was working as an editor with the small publishing firm of Derek Verschoyle. Koestler was just in time for her housewarming party and felt mellow enough to renew relations with Stephen Spender ("wetter than ever, fatter and losing that Shelleyan look") and mend fences with Freddy Ayer.

He also visited Cyril Connolly, who had left Lys and married the predatory Barbara Skelton, with whom he was now living near Ashford in Kent. The fastidious Koestler found their rustic retreat of Oak Cottage "sunk in the usual Cyrilian filth" and was appalled by the state of the bathtub but was pleased to see his old friend again. Their teasing relationship barely camouflaged a fierce sense of competition, and Connolly soon switched the subject from Koestler's life in America to the sales of Koestler's books, accusing Koestler "like an envious fishwife" of being unfairly rich and famous. Koestler got his own back by flirting outrageously with "lissom, green-eyed" Barbara, who clearly remembered their wartime romance and seemed ready to resume where they had left off.[2]

IN THAT EARLY CHAPTER of his soon-to-be-completed autobiography where Koestler had referred to the chronic promiscuity of his youth, he had called it a "phantom chase" for "victory over loneliness through the perfect physical and spiritual union," a chase he likened, by implication, to his chase after causes and utopias. Only in his forties, he wrote, had he come to recognize this pattern, thus seeming to consign it to the distant past, but it was as valid now as ever. The pattern hadn't faded, nor had the behavior changed, and even if the phantom chase had slowed for a while, it had never stopped, as his diary entries over the next few years showed with painful clarity.

Thus Koestler had little need of Barbara's attentions in London. He was still deeply involved with Janine, who despite being married came over from Paris regularly to see him. The ever faithful Cynthia had jumped at the chance to take dictation from him in the evenings (after her day job was done), and Koestler had also started affairs with Moira Slater and Pauline

Gates. Nevertheless, a few days after his Kent visit, the eager Barbara started coming to London for torrid afternoons at his furnished apartment in Athenaeum Court (when Connolly got wind of the affair, he broke off all relations with Koestler), and other conquests included a young Russian-born woman named Christine and a married woman named Felicity. The delighted Koestler recorded all these adventures in his diary with adolescent glee: "The last fortnight in London one of the gayest ever spent. Regarding phantom-hunt, 5 new Helenas during 5 week stay. Childishly pleased—and no hangover, no anxiety neurosis. Indian summer? Maybe. But how rejuvenating!"[3]

It must have been this sense of amorous invincibility that led him into an unfortunate encounter with Jill Craigie, Michael Foot's wife, soon after his arrival in London. Koestler's hunt for a place to live had taken him to Hampstead Heath, where Craigie and Foot occupied a large house. Foot was away for the weekend, and Craigie agreed to give Koestler a tour of the neighborhood. Craigie, a documentary film director, was thirty-six and knew Koestler only slightly from the time she and Foot had stayed with him for a weekend at Verte Rive. In the course of their drive around the heath, they stopped at numerous pubs, where Koestler imbibed heavily, and when they returned to Craigie's place, he asked her to make him an omelette. After lunch, according to Craigie, he helped her wash the dishes and then made a sudden pass at her. She resisted, and he grabbed her and pulled her down to the floor. She struggled free and went outside to gather her thoughts, but when she went back inside again, Koestler allegedly pulled her hair and placed his hands around her throat, until "I was overborne."[4]

When Craigie told David Cesarani about it in 1998, Cesarani's account in his biography of Koestler caused a furor in the British press, provoking a stream of righteous abuse of Koestler that continues to the present day. It also led to such newsworthy events as the removal of Koestler's bust (sculpted by Daphne Henrion) from the foyer of the psychology department at Edinburgh University after a feminist organization, Scottish Women's Aid, mobilized female students to protest that its display "glorified" Koestler's behavior and made them "uneasy."[5]

There are many ambiguities surrounding Cesarani's (and Craigie's) account of the incident. First of all, Craigie waited so long (nearly fifty years) to make her accusation public that Koestler was no longer alive to defend himself or give his own version of this meeting. His diary entry for that day reads only, "Jill Foot—Sunday pubcrawl on Heath." Given that Koestler was gloatingly totting up the nature and number of his conquests in his diary at that very time, it's surprising that he made no mention of having had sex with Craigie, unless he was so drunk he completely forgot about it.[6]

There is also the unanswered question of whether the incident was as violent as Craigie described it half a century later. Apparently she told the film director Ronald Neame about it the very next day, but when contacted by Craigie's biographer, Carl Rollyson, after all the publicity, Neame remembered the details differently and couldn't recall any mention of violence. Other oddities are that Craigie joined Foot and Koestler for lunch at the House of Commons just one week later, and some twenty years after that, in 1975, she and Foot were guests of honor at Koestler's seventieth-birthday party.[7]

Twenty years passed after the birthday party before Craigie made her accusation, and it came about accidentally. At a dinner party for Salman Rushdie in 1994 or 1995, the name of Koestler came up, and the eighty-four-year-old Craigie blurted out her story to her guests. The television anchor Jonathan Snow, who was present at the dinner, felt that she hadn't intended to tell it but couldn't help herself, and never expected it to go beyond that room. Foot, apparently, sat in frozen silence, leading Rushdie to wonder whether Foot was hearing this story for the first time. This seems unlikely, but it was Foot who soon afterward went public in a book review published in April 1995, saying that Koestler had *tried* to rape Craigie many years before. Craigie was angry with him for doing so, but three years later, when David Cesarani contacted her, she gave him the detailed story that appeared in his book.[8]

So what really happened? Given Craigie's prominence as the wife of the former leader of the Labour opposition in Parliament and the fact that she had nothing to gain from her confession, the inference has to be that Koestler did behave extremely badly on that occasion, but it is worth trying to set this painful issue in context. The exercise of male strength to gain sexual satisfaction wasn't exactly uncommon at that time. According to popular belief, it was a man's prerogative to press his claims by all possible means and a woman's duty to put up a show of resistance even if she was willing, so the line between consensual and forced sex was often blurred. Koestler had demonstrated similar behavior on his first night with Mamaine (to whom he later apologized and for which she forgave him) and with Simone de Beauvoir, who later described him as rough but never as a rapist, even after she had come to hate him.

He was almost certainly drunk, and he almost certainly behaved like thousands of other men of his generation (and since); he may also have regarded Craigie, who was thrice married and known to have had several affairs, as fair game and likely to welcome his overtures. She obviously didn't but, like most women of her generation, seems to have responded by pushing the incident to the back of her mind and accommodating herself to it. In later life as an ardent feminist, she evidently came to see the episode differently, as an object lesson in women's vulnerability. She described it as such to at least two younger women well before the dinner party, but the emphasis on extreme physical violence seems to have come later, and it's possible to doubt whether it was as bad as she later recalled it. According to Foot's biographer Mervyn Jones, Craigie had become extremely emotional and hypercritical by the time she reached her eighties, and Craigie's own biographer, Rollyson, records his difficulties when weighing Craigie's version of events concerning her daughter and the latter's very different memories of the same events.[9]

Cesarani chose to complicate the situation by dressing up the episode as the action of a "serial rapist," citing Crossman's casual remark that Koestler was "a hell of a rapist" as an indication that Zita Crossman was just one of several other victims. That the allegation is absurd can be seen from Zita's note to Koestler written just two months after the Craigie episode. "Darling Arthur, Welcome home! I hear that you are in splendid form and one and all are delighted you are back, especially Zita." Zita's sudden death in July prompted a sympathetic cable from Koestler to Crossman and an emotional letter back, describing the circumstances of Zita's early death. No one else has come forward to confirm Cesarani's claim.

The full truth about Koestler's actions on that day is ultimately unknowable. The fact that he isn't known to have raped anyone else doesn't prove that he didn't rape Jill Craigie, just as the fact that he raped her (if he did) wouldn't prove that he had raped anyone else. The likeliest explanation is that behavior that wasn't at the time seen as rape has since come to be regarded as such, and that it is necessary to keep both of the standards in mind when contemplating what happened. Unfortunately, Craigie's story and Cesarani's embellishment of it have left a stain on Koestler's reputation far larger than he deserves and need to be kept in proportion. There is evidence that Craigie herself didn't intend such an outcome. She thought of the incident as an aberration, not a defining moment in Koestler's life and career, and keenly regretted the way it was sensationalized.[10]

AFTER HIS SIX-WEEK SPREE in London, Koestler went back to Verte Rive. He had handed in the manuscript of *Arrow in the Blue* and needed to get down to some serious work on volume two of his autobiography, *The Invisible Writing*. Janine was a continuing distraction, but she had a new rival, a tall, dark-eyed beauty he had met at the Gates's country house in Wiltshire—Priscilla Bibesco. Priscilla, newly divorced and between husbands, lived mostly on the Île Saint-Louis. Well-to-do and much traveled, she looked French but had the no-nonsense forthrightness of an upper-class Englishwoman. Koestler was "too short for me," she said later. "He had an appalling German accent and wasn't at all attractive physically. But like all small men he was relentless with women, and I was fascinated by his cleverness and his conversation. I wasn't in love with him, but I was ready to have an affair."[11]

Koestler now alternated weekends at Verte Rive with Janine and Priscilla and got caught up in a series of farcical incidents that reawakened his paranoia. Priscilla got some anonymous telephone calls, warning her to "stop sleeping with that fascist" or the two of them would be killed. Janine's husband, Paul, set some private detectives on his wife and confronted Janine with compromising photographs of her and Koestler together. Fearing that it was part of a Communist plot to assassinate or blackmail him, Koestler got the French police to place Verte Rive under observation, but nothing more happened. According to Janine, "the whole of Paris" had been talking about them, from Marlene Dietrich on down, and Paul had learned about the affair from this gossip. Janine managed to pacify her husband and the watch over Koestler's home was discontinued, but he was disturbed to discover how strong his "anxiety neurosis" remained and how little it took to reawaken his persecution mania.[12]

He had arrived in France in time to witness the end of Nicolas Nabokov's giant arts festival, "Masterpieces of the Twentieth Century," the Congress for Cultural Freedom's first big international event since the Berlin conference two years before. It was an immensely splashy affair, spread over two months, featuring performances, exhibitions, and discussions by world-class musicians, artists, and writers chosen to illustrate the theme that Europe and America shared a common culture. It had attracted huge publicity (both good and bad), but Koestler sourly dismissed it as a "useless pageant" and a waste of money, distracting the CCF from its intended aims. "I and others created [it] as a potential Deminform, which became a ladder for climbers like Nicholas, Rougemont and little Bondy. Yet the labor was not wasted. Les Amis are better than nothing, and for me it is worth knowing that politics is an all or nothing game, and a Deminform an intrinsic impossibility."[13]

An unexpected buyer turned up for Verte Rive, and in his usual headlong fashion, he rushed through the paperwork, packed up his books and belongings, and decamped to Paris, assisted by the indispensable Janine. There was a tearful farewell from Anna and Maxime, on whom Koestler had spent, according to his calculations, over half a million francs for their house and various repairs. "Nobody else would have done it, but Monsieur," said Maxime, to which Koestler responded in his diary, "That, I guess, is true."[14]

THAT FALL SAW THE PUBLICATION of the first volume of Koestler's autobiography, *Arrow in the Blue*. It was quite unusual and a considerable risk in those days for a writer under forty-five to launch a two-volume memoir, especially when he had already written about his life in *Dialogue with Death*, *Scum of the Earth*, and *The God That Failed*. In some ways, in fact, it was an act of literary desperation, for the failure of *The Age of Longing* had seriously shaken Koestler's faith in his powers as a novelist, and he was beginning to wonder where his future lay. By seeking safety in autobiography he was able to put the question off and to return to a genre that had worked well for him in the past, and the gamble paid off, for the two new works represented a major advance on his earlier memoirs. Whereas those had been episodic, relying on vivid, up-to-date reporting to carry the reader from page to page, *Arrow in the Blue* and *The Invisible Writing* featured a carefully organized narrative designed to illustrate the author's progression from innocence to experience. In this the autobiography reflected its origins as a planned bildungsroman, and Koestler's artistic success depended on the way he exercised the novelist's freedoms in foreshortening some time periods, expanding others, inserting dialogue and personal commentary, and resorting to quick sketches, bordering on caricature, to capture family members and friends.

Arrow in the Blue spanned the first twenty-five years of his life, from his childhood in Budapest to his decision to join the Communist Party in Berlin in 1931. In between he portrayed his student adventures in the dueling fraternity in Vienna, his conversion to Zionism, his wanderings in Palestine as a would-be settler and budding writer, and his success as a journalist in Paris and Berlin, ending with the set piece of his trip to the North Pole on board the *Graf Zeppelin*. All this was set within a framework designed to elicit a larger meaning from his experiences and to point up, if not a moral, then a kind of message about human nature and the nature of the world (which to Koestler essentially meant Europe, with Jewish Palestine as an extension of Europe) in the twentieth century.

The controlling device was the establishment of his nuclear family as a comical bunch of unsuccessful bourgeois upstarts and of his younger self as a sort of hapless innocent, buffeted and bounced from Budapest to Vienna to Palestine to Berlin like a modern Candide. Koestler portrayed himself by turns as a naive and passive child of fortune, a reckless leaper into the unknown, a wandering vagabond, and an adventurer, who miraculously succeeds time and again in landing on his feet.

There was enough truth in this exaggeration to make it psychologically persuasive, and it enabled Koestler to elide or make fun of such personal problems as his inferiority complex, his egocentricity, his frustrated ambition, and his promiscuity. He also underplayed the role of Jewishness and anti-Semitism in shaping his childhood and youth (until he reached his conversion to Zionism) and left the dynamics of his relationship with his parents frustratingly obscure. While personal weaknesses were admitted and condemned, they were also rationalized, so that Koestler's evident self-hatred had a narcissistic flavor. As Nietzsche put it, "He who despises himself, esteems himself thereby."[15]

It was in the key third chapter of *Arrow in the Blue* that Koestler cast his "secular horoscope," mused on his intentions in writing his book, and introduced his chronicler/behold-the-man binary, citing Defoe (in his *Journal of the Plague Year*) as an exemplar of the first kind of autobiographer, and Rousseau (in his *Confessions*) as an exemplar of the second. The implication was that Koestler wanted to situate himself midway between the two, and the critic Richard Freadman has pointed out the probable influence of John Stuart Mill, whose *Autobiography* Koestler also read in Seville. Like Mill, Koestler sets his life in the context of the larger world, weighs "mechanistic accounts of reality against more spiritual ones," and uses autobiography both for political and philosophical reflections and as "a means of morally assessing and of intervening in the world that he experiences and describes." It needs to be added that in organizing his material, Koestler also relied on a number of binary ideas that he had evolved in his earlier work. One was the opposition between the self-assertive and self-transcending tendencies he had described in *Insight and Outlook*. Another was a parallel distinction between the two planes of the tragic and the trivial, and a third was the concept of the "language of destiny." "Astrology," writes Koestler, "is founded on the belief that man is formed by his cosmic environment; Marx held that he is the product of his social environment. I believe both propositions to be true."[16]

Another tutelary god hovering over the autobiography was Sigmund Freud. Koestler had been steeped in Freud's theories as a young man, and though he had since ceased to be a true believer, it was through the eyes of Freud that Koestler saw many key moments in his life, starting with his relationship with his parents. Koestler interpreted his promiscuity, for example, in Freudian terms, ascribing it to his inability to separate from his mother and his frantic desire to be loved as a result of the "incest taboo." He must also have been aware of Freud's statement that "all politics is reducible to the primal conflict between father and son." Substitute "mother" for "father" and it fitted Koestler's situation to a tee. Koestler's self-confessed "moral cowardice" in refusing to write about himself as "a clinical case history" was both a denial of Freudianism and an acceptance of it (via Koestler's remark that he thought of his case as "clinical").

Arrow in the Blue was thus not a memoir of self-revelation in the sense the form came to be understood in the late twentieth century, yet the frankness of Koestler's self-analysis and the honesty of some of his self-descriptions were exemplary, as in his diagnosis of "absolutitis."

> The thirst for the absolute is a stigma which marks those unable to find satisfaction in the relative world of the now and here. My obsession with the arrow was merely the first phase of the quest. When it proved sterile, the Infinite as a target was replaced by Utopias of one kind and another. It was the same quest, the same all-or-nothing mentality, which drove me to the Promised Land and into the Communist Party. In other ages aspirations of this kind found their natural fulfilment in God.[17]

What came through equally powerfully was the commissar-yogi split in Koestler's personality. As a child and adolescent he seemed to have been the dreamy yogi, reading voraciously, writing poetry, contemplating infinity, but his encounter with the militant Jewish fraternities had transformed him into a young commissar, pushing art into the background. Only with his impetuous rush to Palestine did the two come together in a potent cocktail of heady idealism and practical Zionist zeal.

Koestler awaited the reviews with his usual pessimism and wasn't entirely misguided. His old nemesis, Peter Quennell, slammed the book in the popular right-wing *Daily Mail* under the mocking headline "Three Koestlers: Clown, Careerist, Philosopher," provoking Koestler to wonder if this amounted to libel. Anthony West panned the book in *The New Yorker* (despite the fact that *The New Yorker* had serialized a chapter in an earlier issue), and Koestler confessed to his diary that he was "shaken" by the charge that he was "just a journalist" pretending to rise above his station.

But the consensus in both Britain and America was that Koestler had handsomely redeemed himself. The book had a stylishness and fluency that easily outdid his recent novels and showcased his strengths as narrator, reporter, and social critic. The portraits of the real-life characters he had encountered during his youth were more vivid and more engaging than almost any of the invented people in his novels, and his description of his parents alone was fit, thought some, to stand beside Dickens's Micawbers. Pritchett and Spender both gave the book rave reviews, the former welcoming the autobiography as a "mellower and far wiser book than any he has yet written," and the latter praising Koestler's "capacity for entering into what I can only call the conscience of contemporary events. That this is a shifting conscience, which tells him at one time to be on one side or at one place and another at a quite different one, is disconcerting and bitter to his political allies, but it is what really makes for his significance as a man and a writer."[18]

The reviewers were right. *Arrow in the Blue* was by far Koestler's best book since *Darkness at Noon* and showed him writing at the top of his form. Among other things it highlighted his phenomenal instinct for somehow seeming to be around at so many turning points in modern history—the end of World War I in Hungary, Vienna in its decline, the Jewish settlement of Palestine, Berlin during the rise of Hitler, the spread of the Communist Party into Western Europe—and illustrated both his fascination with history and the extraordinary passion he brought to the causes he embraced, be they Zionism, communism, or the "mission" of modern science. All this was conveyed in a supple first-person voice that was delightfully varied, vivid, full of humor, and imbued with an ethical urgency that was Koestler's most appealing quality and carried total conviction.

Never one to wallow in his successes, Koestler allowed his satisfaction with the reviews to be marred by continuing worries about his English. He had long since come to think in English, he told a Norwegian journalist, and was glad he no longer wrote in German, but he feared that German icebergs still sometimes floated in his English prose. Jack and Chris Newsom had essentially cleaned up *Arrow in the Blue* before he left Island Farm, and Koestler asked the critic Bonamy Dobrée if he would do the same for volume two. Dobrée declined. "Your English is excellent," he replied, "and if here and there one might detect a slight flavor of something that is not quite English that is all to the good. It adds just that little piquancy of the unexpected, the slightly unfamiliar, which gives individuality. After all, you are you, just as Conrad is Conrad, in whom these minor divergencies from common usage are more marked than in yourself." This was high praise, and Koestler was pleased to hear from Bertrand Russell that his accent was "not as strong as Conrad's" either. It was high time he put his inferiority complex to rest, but as *Arrow in the Blue* had shown, that was no longer possible.[19]

THE WINTER OF 1952 saw the staging of a huge show trial in Prague, at which Rudolf Slansky, Arthur London, and twelve others were charged with "conspiring against the state." It was one more step in the purging of the Eastern European Communist parties that had begun with the Rajk trial in Hungary and seemed to parody the earlier trial in the extravagance and absurdity of its charges. For Koestler it was further confirmation of the truth of *Darkness at Noon*'s thesis that the Russian Revolution was doomed to devour its own children through show trials. He sat by the radio "convulsed" for two days as his former comrade in arms Otto Katz gave his rehearsed testimony.

Otto confessed to being "a triple agent of the British, U.S. and French intelligence services" (the French bit was true, but not the others), but the most disturbing aspect of the trial was Otto's final plea, in which he asked for the gallows. "The only service I can still render is to warn all who, by origin or character, are in danger of following the same path to hell. The sterner the punishment . . ." At this Otto's voice fell too low to be intelligible. Koestler recognized it as a virtual paraphrase of Rubashov's last plea and wondered if Otto had departed from the script to send him and other former comrades a message in code. He felt sick to his stomach and wept for his old friend—and for himself.[20]

It was easy to identify with Otto just then, for Koestler was writing about his own party days in the thirties and was disconcerted by the way the past kept coming back to haunt him. Whittaker Chambers had recently sent him a copy of *Witness,* in which he described Paul Willert (without hostility and under a pseudonym) as a "former member" of the CP, privy to the party's hunt for Chambers after his defection but not a part of it. Koestler would soon be writing about Willert in Paris, and he cornered him one day to quiz him about Chambers. Willert denied the charge of party membership and called Chambers a "mythomaniac"—a description that fit Willert as much as Chambers.

Koestler in fact thought differently. After reading *Witness* from cover to cover he wrote to Chambers that it was "a great book in the old, simple sense of greatness. There are books which, if they had remained unwritten, would leave a hole in the world." Hearing that Chambers had suffered a heart attack, Koestler persuaded Malraux to write a letter of encouragement to Chambers, "one of the most outstanding, most maligned, and most sincere characters whom I have ever met," the victim of "a bizarre and symbolic twentieth century martyrdom."[21]

Katz was far from being the only former comrade of Koestler's in trouble behind the Iron Curtain. The brothers Hanns and Gerhart Eisler were being assailed by the party in East Germany, and Koestler wondered if they would be the next to go on trial. His own status as a renegade was confirmed by a German election poster featuring cartoons of two book burnings, one by Goebbels in 1933, with Hitler looking on, and another by the East German leader Wilhelm Pieck in 1952, with Stalin looking on. Among the books being burned, one in each pile is clearly marked "Köstler." The cartoon embraced an anachronism—*Spanish Testament* didn't appear until 1937, and Koestler's name had meant little at the time—but it was a compliment nevertheless. Soon after came the news that "Uncle Joe" Stalin had died. "My feeling," wrote Koestler optimistically to a friend, "is that unless they start a war within the next twelve months as a solution for their internal difficulties, their regime will begin to disintegrate—slowly at first, and then with sudden cracks and shocks." It wasn't a bad forecast, but when Lavrenty Beria was arrested a few months later, he was more cautious: "Bad for them," he noted, "but how good is it for us?"[22]

Work on the autobiography brought Koestler back into touch with another piece of the past, his friendships with Hungarian authors. After seeing an article on Hungarian poetry in the *Times Literary Supplement,* he contacted its author, the Hungarian-born humorist George Mikes, for help with translating some Attila József poems into English. Mikes, the author of the wildly funny and successful *How to Be an Alien*—on British snobbery and disdain for foreigners—was an ironist like Koestler, but with a lightness and wit that were at the opposite pole from Koestler's mordant pessimism. The two men spoke English together at first but later switched to Hungarian. Koestler's Hungarian, according to Mikes, was rusty and a bit halting, but his accent was faultless. The two men did some translations and Koestler showed them to Auden, who was polite but firm: They were no good, he said, and Koestler unhesitatingly scrapped them.[23]

KOESTLER SPENT MUCH of 1952 and 1953 renovating his new house in Montpelier Square. The basement became a separate apartment for rent

(Koestler was ever the good businessman), and on the first floor he installed a large "American" kitchen and a spacious dining room, overlooking the square. The second floor housed a spacious L-shaped drawing room, which eventually acquired a Courbet painting over the fireplace. On the third was Koestler's master bedroom, with a king-size bed in the middle and a painting on the wall by André Civet, showing a nude with her legs spread-eagled in the midst of washing herself (Joan Lee Thompson, to whom Koestler willed it after his death, described it as "a woman washing her pussy"). The top floor was turned into a large paneled study, filled with books and papers, with its own fireplace—the coziest and most comfortable room in the house.[24]

Koestler was helped by Priscilla (and to a lesser extent Cynthia) in choosing wallpapers and furniture, but it was Janine who assumed most of the responsibility for fitting out the house, flying in regularly from France and spending days poring over catalogues, selecting materials, arranging furniture, and attempting to add a woman's touch to Koestler's severely masculine arrangements. She did her best, but the house was always to have a slightly forbidding and unlived-in atmosphere. One notable feature was its security system. Koestler was still afraid of some Communist provocation and was one of the first people in London to install a buzzer and an intercom.[25]

The regular but alternating presences of the three women who helped him proved to be a further distraction from his work but perfectly fitted the sexual merry-go-round he had resumed on returning to London. In October he made an inventory of his mistresses. "Christine—since married, decided to go straight; Felicity—Bovary complexes; Pris (hopeless croup); Moira—in Lescun; Janine—*demain;* Cynthia—*toujours là;* Barbara. . . ." Not long afterward he noted that for weeks he had read and written nothing and was living "as perhaps never before" in the present. "When I broke up with Mamaine, I felt I was destined to live on the tragic plane, all alone; now [have] swung to opposite extreme. For how long?"[26]

The answer was to be several years, and the next two years were particularly crazy. It wasn't long before Barbara followed Christine off the list, to be replaced by the Swedish-born literary agent Lena Wickman. Lena was seduced by Koestler's "beautifully deep voice—I hardly noticed his accent. He loved women so much that it was easy to fall for him." She too was amused by the way Koestler stood on tiptoe at cocktail parties to make himself look taller, less so by his rigid insistence on cocktails precisely at seven thirty, and not at all by his demand that she take a cold bath in the morning. Over the Christmas holidays, he felt "lonely as a dog" and got involved in a frantic affair with a publicity girl named Phyllis, investing far more energy and emotion in the relationship than it warranted. On his way to see her after a dinner with Alec Guinness and Alan Herbert, among others, he ran over a traffic island and crashed his Citroën, which led to a nasty run-in with the police and a summons for drunk driving. He ended up seeking refuge with Priscilla for the night.[27]

This, his second car crash of the season, was hardly surprising. After a dinner at Ian Fleming's one evening, Koestler offered the critic John Russell a lift home. Once in his Citroën, he turned to Russell and said, "Let's do it the continental way, shall we?" and proceeded to run all the red lights. Not long after that, he ran off the road rounding Hyde Park Corner at what he regarded as a safe five miles per hour. "But officer," protested Koestler, "I was driving slowly so as not to hurt other people." "Yes," said the policeman, "but that doesn't mean that *we* can't hurt *you*." Koestler was fined and this time lost his license for a year.[28]

In the midst of these shenanigans, Cynthia began to tire of being *toujours là*. She had changed jobs since the summer and was now working for Koestler in the afternoons, which made her more available but also a nuisance, since the afternoon was his favorite time to take other women (especially the married ones) to bed. Increasingly despondent and jealous, Cynthia couldn't stand the glamorous Janine, whose clinging French perfume drove her to distraction. The deeper Janine dug herself into Koestler's affections, the darker Cynthia's mood grew, especially after she overheard Koestler call Janine "angel," a pet name formerly reserved for her.

Janine was now helping her husband with an Anglo-French coproduction, *Monsieur Ripois* (*Lovers, Happy Lovers* was its English title), and planned to be in and out of London for several months. Cynthia dropped off Koestler's list altogether and by her later account contemplated suicide. She had an unfortunate romance with a socialite called Villiers A'Court "Bill" Bergne, who, according to someone who knew him well, was "a complete fake from his name on down" and little better than a gigolo. Tall, ramrod straight, and fashionably dressed, Bergne had accumulated five wives (to Koestler's three) and, according to rumor, several hundred mistresses. Bergne evidently had a streak of sadism, and according to her sister, Pamela, Cynthia began returning to her shared lodgings with deep welts on her back. Pamela was aware that Cynthia had been abused by a young Pretoria lawyer when still a teenager, and that she "craved a dominant man" and "needed someone who would kick her around," but she didn't suspect the truth of what was going on with Bergne. It seems that Bergne also bullied Cynthia into not using birth control, and she became pregnant. She refused to have an abortion until Koestler took her to Regents Park zoo one afternoon and talked her into it.[29]

Cynthia then took up with Mark Paterson, a personable young editor who was visiting London from Cambridge University Press in New York. Mark was also tall, but with a self-deprecating bashful manner at the opposite pole from Bergne's. He fell instantly in love with Cynthia: "She was the most beautiful woman I had ever seen in my life. I was determined to marry her," and he proposed on his next visit to London. Cynthia insisted on taking him to meet Koestler. "It was like going to see a father for approval. I was overawed at meeting him in the flesh, but stunned by how short he was." Koestler affably gave his consent, and they married secretly at a London registry office. Six months later, Koestler saw her off to New York with a huge bunch of flowers and an expensive, monogrammed toilet set from Fortnum & Mason.

He discovered he was "unexpectedly depressed" at losing her. She was "exceptionally sweet, cheerful, naive, pretty, devoted," and seeing her go meant "breaking off another bit of my life." Cynthia was even more depressed and burst into tears as she left. When Mark met her off the boat in New York, she "couldn't stop talking about Koestler," and Mark soon realized he was "a poor substitute" for her volcanic employer. Worse still, he was a virgin, unable to consummate the marriage, and Cynthia wrote long letters to Koestler to consult him about "Mark's problem" and Mark's lack of self-confidence. "The result is that I boss him about and don't get any pleasure from it," wrote Cynthia, "as he never retaliates. How I long to be bullied mercilessly!"[30]

MEANWHILE, KOESTLER HAD started seeing his mother again once a month, usually taking Mamaine or Margaret "Stevie" Stephens along to dilute the intimacy of the visit. Adele was still spry and youthful for her age (she was then in her eighties), with piercing blue eyes and virtually no gray in her light brown hair. Despite her five feet three inches, she had a commanding manner that brooked no contradiction and was clearly a queen bee at her pension in Adamson Road, where she bragged shamelessly about her famous son.

Adele had seen a copy of *Arrow in the Blue* and was even less happy with it than with *The God That Failed*. She berated Koestler for making fun of his parents, for exaggerating their poverty during the Depression, and for making her out to be such an ogre. He should never have revealed her family's disdain for "Dr. Freund," and by the way, what on earth was he thinking when he separated from that lovely girl, Mamaine? It was all his fault, and he should take her back again. Stephens was amazed to see how Koestler writhed and squirmed under his mother's tongue-lashing, like a guilty schoolboy caught with his hand in the cookie jar. He concluded gloomily that Adele was getting senile, but that was far from the case. Soon afterward, she gave a perfectly lucid account of her Freud consultation to Kurt Eissler, the secretary of the Freud Archives in New York.[31]

Koestler also managed to restore links with Daphne, now with two children and working hard at her sculpture, and saw Mamaine from time to time. He had a tense meeting with Dorothee, now a psychiatric social worker in London, congratulating himself on having seen the "three Mrs K's" within twenty-four hours. His reason for seeing her was to discuss the second volume of his autobiography and to assure her he wouldn't reveal any embarrassing secrets about their marriage (he kept his word: there is so little about his first marriage that Dorothee barely emerges as a character at all). Dorothee was still in shock after the recent death of her mother. She resented Koestler's neglect of her and told him so, and Koestler found her "depressing, helpless, neurotic, unchanged."[32]

Mamaine informed Koestler that she planned to marry the movie and television mogul Sidney Bernstein (Cynthia's former employer), and Koestler agreed to hasten his and Mamaine's divorce and pay the costs. The only grounds accepted under English law at the time were desertion and adultery, and Koestler made a deposition admitting that he had "frequently committed adultery with a woman whose name and identity are at present unknown to the Petitioner" and was cohabiting with her. This could only have been Janine (whose identity was most certainly known to Mamaine), but the law demanded such a fiction, and Mamaine's petition went through unopposed the following year.[33]

CHAPTER THIRTY-SEVEN

I KILLED HER

Life isn't fun, life isn't a burden; life is a task.
— Johann Wolfgang von Goethe

WHEN MANÈS SPERBER went to London for Christmas in 1952, he was surprised to discover how anglicized Koestler had become. In fact, it struck him that Koestler was turning into a regular British snob. Koestler sought to justify himself on the grounds that the British upper classes were "endearing, naive, relatively decent and uncorrupt," compared with their French counterparts, and that all British intellectuals and writers were from the upper middle class or the aristocracy anyway. British snobbery differed from the awful American variety, because "climbing into a different stratum" was impossible—if nothing else, the school system prevented "vertical displacements."[1]

Koestler still retained some of his populist instincts, but after seeing Maxime and Anna on a visit to France, he concluded that "no friendship was possible with the working-class." He now hobnobbed with more than a few titled individuals, not to speak of the queen's secretary, a couple of newspaper proprietors, politicians, civil servants, publishers, lawyers, professors, and journalists. His literary friends were upper class to a man. His new drinking crony, Henry Yorke (the novelist Henry Green), was a blue-blooded aristocrat with a family fortune and an engineering plant in the Midlands.[2]

The British class system easily tolerated foreigners if they were well off, clever, or amusing in their own right—and Koestler was all three. But he still suffered from "the torture of my accent," which frustrated his desire to "grow roots." He knew that enemies and friends alike still made fun of him behind his back and gloomily confided to his diary that he would always be "the stranger on the square."[3]

He compensated by adding more women to his lengthening list of lovers—a "nice debutante" named Joan Redgrave, and June Osborn (wife of the well-known but chronically sick concert pianist Franz Osborn), with whom he had recently started a "dangerous" liaison. "Am living again w. harem of 5, considering 50 more," he wrote boastfully in his diary that summer, and in a later entry, "But my harem is wearing me out." Not coincidentally, he began signing letters to his girlfriends "Uncle Arthur," a kinky salute he had used initially with Mamaine and now extended to each new conquest in ironic acknowledgment of the age difference between him and most of his paramours—and in a bid, perhaps, for familial intimacy and control.[4]

With so many extracurricular activities under way, he began to find Janine's visits "oppressive" and to regard her with increasing "boredom and pity." He had been suffering from prostate problems but found they disappeared with Janine's departure, leading him to conclude smugly that it had been "the protest of the prostate against coition as a duty," since he was now "three times more potent" than before. Janine was in Cannes for the opening of *Monsieur Ripois,* oblivious of Koestler's growing disenchantment, and invited him to join her for a holiday in Ischia the coming summer, baiting the hook with news of a thirty-five-foot sailboat she had bought in London and shipped to Naples. The *Anemone* was ready for them to go cruising in as soon as he could get away.[5]

In September 1953, exhausted by the effort to finish a first draft of *The Invisible Writing,* he accepted Janine's offer and traveled out to the island of Ischia. It was a primitive place, eighteen square miles of volcanic rock off Naples inhabited mainly by Italian peasants and goatherds but now beset by increasing numbers of literary sunseekers looking for a cheap place to relax and work. Auden and Chester Kallman were summer fixtures, renting a spacious house in the main village of Forio. Truman Capote and Tennessee Williams had cavorted there not too long before, and the vacation crowd was slowly growing in number. Koestler loved it and, after several weeks of swimming, sailing, and rock climbing, decided "on the spur of the moment" to buy yet another property—a small peasant cottage that would serve as a holiday home. It was in the next village from Forio, and he and Janine agreed to split the expense equally. "Casa Acquedutto," Koestler wrote to Jack Newsom, "stands on a steep slope, surrounded by vineyards and fig trees with the loveliest view over the sea. We got it, together with 3,000 square meters of vineyard, dirt cheap, and during the winter months will have a bath, WC, and kitchen put in. By the end of March it should be habitable. Life in Ischia is ridiculously cheap." Knowing that Jack and his wife dreamed of moving to Europe, Koestler invited them to come to Ischia anytime they could make it.[6]

Back in London, Koestler found himself mired in a "stupid and harrowing predicament" with Joan Redgrave, but felt that it had taught him a lesson. "Al Capone too was caught on his income tax." A depressed Mamaine informed him that her marriage plans were off, and from New York came a letter from Cynthia saying that her own marriage, to Paterson, had been annulled on the ground of nonconsummation. She was taking a job as secretary to the bridge champion Ely Culbertson and hoped that things would work out for her. Koestler mused in his diary that there seemed to be "no accidents, only gaps and blanks in the text of the invisible writing. But are there erasures and corrections? Can the past be erased and redeemed, or is time, unlike space, really irreversible?"[7]

THAT WINTER KOESTLER developed an obsession with Janetta Jackson, a young woman he had first met in the *Horizon* offices during the war years. Slim, tomboyish, and seemingly waiflike but with considerable self-possession and dignity, Janetta was irresistibly attractive to men (Connolly had had a crush on her for years). Her third husband, the millionaire Oxford professor of spectroscopy Derek Jackson, had left her for her younger sister soon after Janetta had given birth to their baby. She was in poor shape when Koestler met her at a party given by the literary agent Barley Alison, and they talked long into the night. Not long afterward, Janetta moved with her three children into a house on the other side of Montpelier Square, making her a virtual neighbor.[8]

Like Priscilla, Janetta was not particularly attracted to Koestler physically and she still remembered him from the war years as "a very sad and beaten down little man in a Pioneer Corps uniform that was much too big for him," standing in a corner of the room at one of Connolly's parties. But now he was rich and well dressed, and she found herself fascinated by the intensity of his personality and the brilliance of his conversation. As a new mother abandoned by her husband, she was more vulnerable than usual, and soon they were sleeping together. They had plenty to talk about. Janetta had spent part of her childhood in Spain and during the civil war had escaped from Málaga around the time Koestler had arrived there. She and her mother had then lived in France, and like Koestler had left to escape the German occupation. But Janetta was by no means the "sweet and fading" flower of Koestler's imagination, and his new obsession led to "a month of hell and heaven." It began with "ten wonderful days in Cornwall," during which she inspired him to perform "on average twice a day" and he was able to discard his reading glasses—which he attributed to her aphrodisiac powers. But she was hard to pin down, and back at home in Montpelier Square, he found it impossible to work with her sitting only a hundred yards away, "not because I love her so much, but because her casualness continues to hurt me."[9]

He talked her into taking a trip to Paris, Vienna, and Salzburg with him. Vienna was unrecognizable, and he failed to find a single acquaintance from his old life. The Jews were almost all gone, and the old literary and journalistic establishment had been decimated. He was drunk when they boarded the train to Salzburg, and when they passed through the Soviet-occupied zone of control, some Russian guards dozed in the next compartment. Suddenly Koestler grew violent, cursing the Russians and threatening to go next door and beat them up. Janette tussled with him in the corridor and finally prevailed on him to return to their compartment and quiet down, but she was "frightened by such rage and madness, by someone who was suddenly and totally out of reach of reason," and sensed the depth of his loathing.[10]

After their return home, Koestler worked himself into a terrific lather over Janetta's aloofness and indifference, filling page after page of his diary with a detailed account of her comings and goings, and speculation about whether she loved him. Over a drink, Janetta told him, "I can't, I won't, I don't want to" get involved, and they quarreled so violently that Koestler slapped her as she left the house, phoning afterward to apologize.

He sat up all night writing her an anguished seven-page letter that he didn't send. In its place he sent a short note asking her to marry him: if the answer was yes, she should ring before noon. Janetta was amazed and horrified. She had no intention of marrying Koestler, and she didn't ring. They made up, and she eventually spent the night at his home "for the first time ever," but when she refused to go to France with him again, he suddenly lost interest, telling himself he "hardly cared" anymore. He later put it down to "a shattering change-of-age crisis." "Had I not decided to leave London I would at least have had a nervous breakdown, if not a car accident or a similar self-destructive manifestation. For the first time in [my] life I felt it would be worthwhile to hang or do 20 years in jail for killing a woman."[11]

Janetta knew nothing of these murderous impulses. Years later she said that Koestler's attitude to her had been "an odd mixture of consideration, thoughtfulness, and extraordinary brutality." "He was not the sort of man who was systematically violent to women or got pleasure out of it. It was just that he sometimes lost his temper and slapped you. But then," she added philosophically, "you always finish by hitting one another in the end, don't you?" She recalled an incident when she had offered him a cigarette. "Oh no," said Koestler, "I never accept a cigarette from a woman, it's so disgusting. It always smells of scent and lipstick." Janetta reminded him that she wore neither, but Koestler insisted: "Oh no, I have a very strong sense of smell." Janetta concluded he was a woman hater at heart. He feared and was disgusted by women but loved their company too—so long as he thought he could manipulate and control them.[12]

THAT SUMMER, Koestler returned to Ischia, driving out to Naples in his Citroën sedan. Casa Acquedutto wasn't ready, and he blamed Janine for letting him down. Within days came news that Jack Newsom had died of a heart attack on board the SS *Roma* en route to Italy. Koestler and Janine met the distraught widow and son on the dockside in Naples and helped them get Jack's body to Rome for cremation (the Catholic Church in Naples wouldn't allow it).[13]

Koestler returned to Ischia to try to write. His trip to Vienna had given him the idea for a new autobiographical novel, provisionally called "Closing Time" (a reference to Connolly's famous phrase about it being "closing time in the playgrounds of the west"), but the upheavals of the past few weeks had destroyed his concentration, and less than a month later Newsom's death came to seem like an omen when he received another devastating cable. "Mamaine died today. Please do not return unless you specially want to." Celia informed him that Mamaine had died on the night of June 1, 1954, in University College Hospital (where Orwell had died some eight years earlier) from an asthma attack, after seeming to recover from an earlier one. "The funeral will be private," she wrote in a follow-up letter, "and probably in Suffolk if I can manage it."[14]

Koestler might have had some premonition of the way things were going from his last meetings with Mamaine in London, when he had found her increasingly sickly and depressed. He also knew from her long, chatty letters that she had been in and out of the hospital with asthma three times. After the last attack, she had been found unconscious and later wrote to Koestler that "the shock just about finished off my frayed nerves." She was permanently exhausted and, when out of the hospital, often "longed to be back" inside. One result of the third attack was that she missed Celia's wedding to Arthur Goodman (they were obliged to cancel their honeymoon so that Celia could stay with Mamaine), which made her even more miserable than before.[15]

Mamaine's last letter to Koestler was quite upbeat and cheerful and ended, "Love, darling sweetie, and *alles Gute von Deine immer getreuen Mamaine* [all the best from your ever-faithful Mamaine]." To Sperber she was more honest. "I've been most awfully ill since I last wrote to you, and have been down to the bottom of the sea. I do wish you had been here for Easter as you originally planned, because that was my lowest moment, or one of them, and I would have given anything to have you with me—Arthur being abroad, and my chief doctor too, and I longed for a strong man to hold my hand." She also made a curious comment about her asthma. "I must say, Munjo, there is of course a lot in what you say about asthma, but it is a great oversimplification—after all, *all* illnesses are useful as a means of putting off decisions and for other purposes, and I've had a surprisingly large number of other violent illnesses in my life, and very little *bad* asthma. Besides you are wrong in saying it is useless. Only other people achieve the same ends in less painful ways."[16]

Was Mamaine implying that her asthma (and other forms of illness) was a way of coping with reality, or rather, of *not* coping with reality? And was this her own thought, or had it been suggested by Sperber or by the hospital doctor who was treating her for psychosomatic symptoms? John Russell visited her in the hospital and formed the distinct impression that Mamaine had lost the will to live, that it wasn't so much her physical condition that ended her life as a sense of profound hopelessness, because "she couldn't see any point in going on." Dr. Csato explained to Koestler that the official cause of death was "exhaustion" and that it was due to a "simultaneous failure of the vital functions," leading to a fourth ventricle failure while she was comatose. In such a condition death would have been relatively painless. Passing this on to Sperber, Koestler lamented that neither he nor Celia had been warned that Mamaine's life was in danger. "Whether it would have made any difference to the length of her life is unknowable, but at least we would have been *there*."[17]

Ignoring Celia's suggestion that he needn't return, Koestler flew immediately to England for the funeral, which Arthur Goodman managed to delay a day until Koestler could get there (it was held in Hoxne, Suffolk, in East Anglia), and Koestler spent part of the night beside Mamaine's open coffin. "As the hours pass," he wrote to Camus a day or two later, "the horror subsides, and one gets reconciled with this new face—so beautiful and smiling, reduced to essentials—which supplants the memory of the deceased person when she was alive." The funeral was a grim affair. Celia was absent. She and Mamaine had made a pact that neither would go to the other's funeral, and Koestler was ostracized by the Paget family. He stood off to one side at the graveyard, and one aunt was heard to say very loudly, "If it wasn't for *him* she'd still be alive," a thought that was to occur to many others (including Koestler) in the months and years to come.[18]

In his letter to Camus, acknowledging Camus's special place in Mamaine's affections (Mamaine had kept up a tender correspondence with Camus ever since their meeting in Paris in 1951—he addressed her as *Chère Twinkie* and signed himself *Tinkie* and at the time of her death was urging her to come and convalesce at his place in the Midi), Koestler said that Mamaine had died peacefully in her sleep, without pain or anguish. "All the same the death of a bird, old friend, is very hard on the rest of us." But he was more honest with Sperber, whom he knew better, and to whom he gave a different version. "Her face was stern and calm," he wrote, "but not at peace, not reconciled to death." "The senselessness of it all" was appalling, leaving him "condemned to an ongoing feeling of guilt that sometimes scorches me and sometimes only gnaws and drills—and that too is senseless."[19]

Sperber reassured Koestler that Mamaine's friendly feelings toward her ex-husband were "unconditional, boundless, and rational" and expressed the view that decisive for Mamaine's state of mind had been Celia's decision to marry and start a new life, leaving Mamaine to fend for herself and make a life on her own. This was a new thought for Koestler and seemed to soften the blow a bit. Perhaps he wasn't solely responsible after all? Sperber's view was shared by Mamaine's psychologist, but her medical doctor felt that the decree absolute in her divorce from Koestler (which had taken effect in March) had also played a significant role. Poor Celia's honeymoon could now go ahead, though under the most horrible cloud. Koestler offered to pay for her and Arthur Goodman to have a vacation in the Dolomites. He also gave them a Graham Sutherland lithograph as a wedding present and loaned them various items of furniture from Montpelier Square for their cottage in Lincolnshire. Celia was grateful for the lithograph and the furniture but declined the vacation for lack of time.[20]

KOESTLER MOVED IN with Janine at Casa Acquedutto, but there was little pleasure in it for him. The house had few comforts, and he characteristically blamed Janine for her constant comings and goings, which left her little time to attend to the details of the house. "Mamaine dead and J[anine] back. Moved into new house—the joyless Paradiso." He continued to be haunted by the memory of Mamaine's face in the coffin, the "softness of her hair over the parched, still suffering face. The wrinkle in one eyelid, the light sinus-swelling on the other side, the stern schoolmadam look that had finally conquered the sweet turnip." It was not that she was "constantly in my mind, but lurking under it." He felt guilty to be looking at landscapes that she would have enjoyed so much more but could no longer see.[21]

After a month of "constant depression and exasperation," Koestler told Janine that he had had enough of the island, their cottage, their relationship: It was time to call it a day. He admitted he was to blame. He had been seduced by the luxury and comfort with which she had surrounded him and had taken the path of least resistance. To his diary he confessed brutally that he had "never had such a long affair with somebody of so little value, for all her sweetness. 'The chink in K's armor' was this time gaping wide."[22]

Koestler picked up his car on the mainland and drove to Canazei in the Dolomites. Janine had agreed to put Casa Acquedutto up for sale, and while in Canazei he learned that a buyer had been found for Island Farm. His life was being simplified again, but neither this nor hiking in the mountains brought much relief. He recalled Janine's last words to him: "You are kind and even self-sacrificing to people who are indifferent to you, but if you agree to live with somebody, you become inhuman to them and yourself, and torture them the way you torture yourself." It was a fitting valedictory, a truth he couldn't deny, and he was fleetingly reminded of being trapped in France in 1940 and thinking of suicide. Memories of Mamaine came flooding back, and he thought of her lying in a public ward in University College Hospital, waiting for visitors. At four a.m. one sleepless night he confided to his diary: "I killed her through blindness of the heart."[23]

CHAPTER THIRTY-EIGHT

CASSANDRA GROWS HOARSE

*Brilliant and indefatigable, [he] refuses to distinguish between
setback and catastrophe, worships accomplishment above all else
and makes himself unbearable to others because he genuinely
believes he can root out and reform every incidence of human
fecklessness and mediocrity.*

— MICHAEL CUNNINGHAM

VOLUME TWO OF KOESTLER'S AUTOBIOGRAPHY had proved harder to
write than he expected. First of all, he had to find a structure that convinc-
ingly resembled the framework of the first volume while doing justice to the
turbulent events of the 1930s, and secondly he needed to find new ways of
saying things he had already written about in *Dialogue with Death, Scum of
the Earth,* and *The God That Failed.* It had also turned out to be emotionally
draining to relive his life of the thirties, especially when it came to his resignation from the party, his Seville prison experiences, and his refugee years in
France. Then there was the problem of accuracy. His story involved dozens
of living people who would hold him to account if he got the facts wrong. He
hired a research assistant, became a frequent visitor to the British Museum's
newspaper archives in Colindale, corresponded with such of his old comrades as were neither dead nor behind the Iron Curtain, and even tried using
Pentothal again, with the help of two psychiatrists (one of whom was German-
speaking).

The experiment backfired and Koestler had ended it rather quickly. "My
purpose was a technical and limited one," he wrote to the primary physician,
Dr. Jonathan Gould, "to try through hypnosis or Pentothal to re-live certain
episodes in connection with volume two of the memoirs that I am writing.
But apparently this cannot be done without going too much further back into
the past and without entering into some kind of therapeutical situation. This
I did not wish to do, for reasons which I have explained to you. I suppose it

was a rather amateurish idea on my part." It had been a repeat of Koestler's unsuccessful experiment with hypnosis. There were parts of his psyche that he dreaded exploring and places he didn't wish to go; and he still feared an emasculation of his talent through therapy. Gould had readily understood. "Sometimes the thread of emotionally determined associations is so strong that one end of the thread cannot be pulled without pulling the whole thread from its moorings," he replied diplomatically, adding that "radical analysis" was not to be undertaken lightly.[1]

Koestler persevered with the help of only Benzedrine and alcohol, and *The Invisible Writing* appeared in the summer of 1954, not long after Mamaine's death, while Koestler was still in Switzerland. Volume one had ended with a cliff-hanger: What was to become of the young idealist who had resigned his job and plunged into the Communist underworld in search of utopia? Would the fascists catch up with him, or would he escape? Where would his adventures take him next, and what would he bring back from his experiences? Koestler didn't disappoint. Though covering a mere nine years in his life, from 1931 to 1940, the book was a hundred pages longer than *Arrow in the Blue* and packed with incident, covering his travels in the Soviet Union, his years with the anti-fascist movement in Paris, his adventures in the Spanish Civil War, and his experience of prisons in three different countries. It offered a picaresque narrative fit to stand beside any novel, with numerous reversals of fortune: triumph and success in Russia, hunger and failure in Paris, civil war and a death sentence in Spain, flight in time of war to Casablanca, and ultimate salvation through escape to Lisbon and England.

Because of Koestler's earlier autobiographical works, this account of his evolution from neophyte believer to disillusioned apostate was in some respect a "twice-told tale," with its attendant dangers of repetition and boredom, but the success of the book rested not on a simplified story of journeying from darkness into the light but on a nuanced portrayal of perplexity and impotence, of wandering in the desert toward an unknown destination.

The opening sentence sounded the book's major theme: "I went to Communism as one goes to a spring of fresh water, and I left Communism as one clambers out of a poisoned river strewn with the wreckage of flooded cities and the corpses of the drowned," a parody of Picasso's famous declaration that he had gone to communism "as one goes to a spring of fresh water." And the book concluded equally ironically. "At this point ends the typical case-history of a central-European member of the educated middle classes, born in the first years of our century," a reference to Koestler's description of the second part of his life as a kind of political pilgrim's progress, intended as an object lesson to others.[2]

One critic found "this cocky little man, over-impressed with his own virtues and his own vices," guilty of "immense pomposity" for daring to present himself as typical, and a British reviewer asserted that Koestler's claim to typicality would arouse doubts in Britain, since a tale of "spiritual convolutions, narrow escapes, gaols and the pursuit of Utopia is regarded as exceptional, not to say eccentric." Most critics, however, agreed that *The Invisible Writing* was an even better book than *Arrow in the Blue* and that of all the ex-Communists who had written novels or memoirs about their experiences, Koestler possessed a "greater freshness of feeling and ideas" and greater originality than any of them. This "unusually brilliant and hypersensitive individual, ranging the decline and fall of European civilization," had brought back untold riches. His insights into "the neuroses that underlie the surrender to extremism" were subtle and revealing, buttressed as they were by an "unflinching scrutiny of his own conscious and unconscious motives" and a "high charge of moral drama." In a penetrating insider's review, Stephen Spender noted a new facet of Koestler's "double mission" in the book. Depicting himself as the "typical representative" of his generation, he had also succeeded in asserting the value of his individuality. The subject of the book might be the story of an individual struggling to free himself of typicality.

Readers recognized the chapters about Koestler's arrest in Málaga and imprisonment in Seville as the high point and moral fulcrum of the book, and Spender singled out Koestler's prayer not to play the martyr or the saint and not to assume the virtues of his suffering, but to retain the vices and faults that made him human, as particularly admirable. ("It may well be a major misfortune of our time that the good Lord granted his prayer so completely.") *The Invisible Writing* was by common consent a warmer and more generous book than *Arrow in the Blue* and showed a gentler, mellower Koestler writing about former friends with affection and compassion (even his portraits of women were said to be better). *The Invisible Writing* was "the record of Koestler's search for his own soul," and Reinhold Niebuhr suggested that Koestler was at bottom "a religious man in search of penitence, homesick for a communion of saints."[3]

Niebuhr was closer to the truth than he perhaps knew. Koestler's thinking had undoubtedly acquired a religious dimension of late, and the metaphor of the invisible writing itself pointed in that direction. "If the conceptual world was mistaken for ultimate reality," Koestler had written, echoing Dostoyevsky, "the world became an equally absurd tale, told by an idiot or by idiot-electrons which caused little children to be run over by motor cars, and little Andalusian peasants to be shot through the heart, mouth and eyes, without rhyme or reason." Ultimate reality was "a text written in invisible ink; and though one could not read it, the knowledge that it existed was sufficient to alter the texture of one's existence, and make one's actions conform to the text." The concept of a guiding intelligence in the world was new for Koestler, and he would spend the rest of his life trying to define and refine it, especially in his later scientific works.[4]

Still, to "creep back into the warm, protective womb of faith" was cowardly in Koestler's view, though he was certainly tempted. "Oh, Jesus Christ, if I could only believe in Thee," he had exclaimed to his diary in the fall of 1952, adding characteristically, "But am not going to capitulate out of mixture of hysteria and failure of nerve." He had renewed a friendship with Lord Pakenham, a prominent Anglo-Catholic, and Pakenham had introduced Koestler to the "charming and insidious" Catholic priest Father D'Arcy. Koestler's discussions with Pakenham and D'Arcy, and his invitation of D'Arcy to a private dinner for two, led to rumors that he was contemplating conversion. Koestler told a stunned Janetta it was true he was "thinking of turning Catholic," but he eventually judged Father D'Arcy a "fraud" and a "snob," with no interest in the ethical or spiritual dimensions of Christianity and a distrust of mysticism. D'Arcy's real interest, he concluded, like that of so many churchmen, was in power, not faith.[5]

A few months later Koestler confessed to his diary that he "was, of course, attracted to Roman Catholicism," but the Roman Catholics had "cured" him. After a conversation about religion with Auden (a Protestant), in which Koestler said that an "absolute commitment" to a faith was out of the question for him, he sought temporary consolation in the secular mysticism of parapsychology. A favorable comment about J. B. Rhine's ESP experiments in *Insight and Outlook* had brought some grateful letters from Rhine and an exchange of letters with Gerald Heard. Koestler felt he had had at least one genuinely telepathic experience in Seville (his reading of *Buddenbrooks* and its consequences), but he tried to be hardheaded about it. "I am convinced that telepathy and clairvoyance are empirically established facts," he told Vita Sackville-West, but also added that more than 90 percent of the reported cases were "based on self-delusion," owing to its "astonishing power." Still, in the winter of 1953 he took out his first subscription to the *Journal of the Society for Psychical Research* and offered to write about Seville for it (the offer was declined). Misi Polanyi wrote to say that although scientists were doubtful about Rhine's experiments, the British mathematician S. G. Soal had achieved better results. Excitedly, Koestler began to plan experiments of his own, but had to postpone them for lack of time.[6]

THE INVISIBLE WRITING had brought Koestler a flood of fan mail—more than for any other book he had written to date—and he was genuinely surprised by his success with the critics. But while truly new for him in form and composition, in subject matter the autobiographies were essentially retrospective. He had been thinking and writing about utopian ideology and politics and their effects on the individual for fifteen years now and felt that he had said almost everything he had to say on that subject. He concluded he was marking time and feared he might have come to an intellectual and creative dead end. The search for a new faith was a reflection of his search for new subjects and a new inspiration.

While still on Ischia he had contemplated the success of Hemingway, whom he had ridiculed in *The Invisible Writing* but secretly envied and admired. He reflected that the American writer seemed to have spent his whole life trying to make up for the fact that he had been humiliated and called a coward as a child. "If such a hurt produces such an artist," he concluded, "let it happen any time." (Koestler also had a theory about Hemingway having "a small prick," but it's not clear if he attributed Hemingway's achievements to that too, or identified with the American in that regard.) Reading Sperber's latest novel (which Mamaine had planned to publish in English), Koestler came to the conclusion that Sperber's characters were not credible, and reminded himself that without characters the reader can identify with, "there is no art." Clearly he also had himself in mind.[7]

He admonished himself to "bisociate" his pattern of life and break out of his old rut. "Have at last the courage to be yourself. They all write the same type of stuff all their lives. . . . Nobody writes your type of stuff—Silone and Malraux have stopped, Orwell and Serge are dead. The continentals who have had my experiences can't write. Take pains over your style, but don't get obsessed with it." He had decided to put himself to the test with writing "Closing Time," the novel he had conceived in Vienna. He would reverse his recent practice and write "autobiography in the form of a novel," but although he started the work three times, he was unable to find an adequate approach and point of view. The narrative voice he settled on mimicked the casual tone and affected manner of the upper-class Englishmen he was surrounded with in London, and the prose was hopelessly at odds with Koestler's explosive and temperamental personality. He was also stung when Auden, whom he saw from time to time on Ischia, told him that he should forget fiction and stick to autobiography. The remark induced a "paralyzing depression" that became entwined with guilt over his neglect of Janine and remorse over the death of Mamaine.

"Work is impossible, letters a torture," he told Sperber. "The novel's a bust: I can't visualize the characters, and my chronic doubts about whether the novel is my métier are turning into a certainty. Auden, who is my neighbor here, and no sadist, has contributed significantly to that feeling." Koestler wondered if it was time to give up writing altogether. He would complete the revision for a new edition of *Scum of the Earth,* due out shortly, write a third volume of *Insight and Outlook* (a planned second volume was only half sketched out so far) *"et puis, Schluss"* (and then finish).[8]

It was an extraordinary place to be so soon after his triumph with *The Invisible Writing,* and he certainly had plenty of material for more autobiography, including his wartime experiences in the British army and at the BBC, his visits to Palestine, his intellectual battles in France, his triumph at the Berlin congress, his dalliance with the CCF, and his two years in America. These subjects could take him into new autobiographical territory that was rich with possibility, but for some reason Koestler was unwilling. Mercurial as ever, he had already lost interest in the genre and wanted to explore new pastures. The way forward was pointed by another of his eureka moments, when the invisible writing seemed to manifest itself with renewed clarity. A book arrived in the mail on the subject of bisociation, a word and concept Koestler had invented (or reinvented) and discussed in *Insight and Outlook*. He interpreted it as a sign that his metaphysical and scientific interests weren't a waste after all and might be melded into a fresh way of writing. He resolved to renew his explorations of the "tragic plane" of existence in a different form. "All the hell" of the summer's turmoil was worthwhile, he decided, if it had taught him this simple lesson: "Concentrate on what you still have to say. If you now fail, then you have failed."[9]

HE MADE A START by handing the responsibility for the Fund for Intellectual Freedom to International PEN in London and establishing a modus vivendi with the Congress for Cultural Freedom. Norris Chipman, on a visit to London, confirmed Koestler's suspicions that the congress was being funded by the CIA, but the congress had finally gotten around to establishing a stable of literary magazines along the lines Koestler had envisaged three years before—*Encounter* in London, *Preuves* in Paris, and *Der Monat* in Berlin (a continuation of Lasky's magazine)—and Koestler approved. The congress still didn't approve of Koestler, however. Irving Kristol, the CIA's choice as co-editor of *Encounter* (the other co-editor was Stephen Spender), egged on by Nicolas Nabokov, had deliberately kept Koestler out of the first issue, telling Herbert Luthy that Koestler's writings were now "history." Not long afterward, Kristol and his colleagues changed their minds, and Koestler's "A Guide to Political Neuroses" appeared in all three magazines simultaneously.[10]

Koestler's decision to start life anew was supposed to extend to his love life, too. Ruminating on the crisis that had gripped him after the death of Mamaine, he concluded, "I can neither live alone, nor with somebody. It is true, I always picked one type: from Helga and Eva to Daphne and Mamaine and J[anine] and J[anetta]: beautiful cinderellas, infantile and inhibited, prone to be subdued by bullying, but this realization doesn't solve the problem." Koestler was too hard on his women (and on himself). Eva, Daphne, Mamaine, Priscilla, Janetta, and Janine were far from infantile Cinderellas, but it was true he had met many of them at vulnerable moments in their lives and had harassed and bullied them all into submission. He could never be satisfied, it seemed, with a romantic relationship until he had gained the upper hand—after which, sooner or later, he lost interest.[11]

The mechanism emerges with perfect clarity from the hundreds of love letters and notes that he saved in his files, with the same few themes running through them like threads in a carpet: "thank you for loving me; I hope you're not angry; forgive me for what I said (or did); I know I'm being unreasonable, but. . . ." Koestler was almost always in control—and went crazy when he wasn't, as in the case of Janetta. And it's true that most of the women he courted were pathetically anxious to please, while he himself blew hot and cold, making it clear he could never fully commit himself. He had a knack for concentrating totally on the woman of his choice, smothering her with flowers, treating her to expensive food and wine, and flattering her with complimentary remarks, and he could open himself up to women, confide in them, even seem to throw himself on their mercy in a way that was extraordinarily endearing—and then brutally abandon them once his goal was achieved. In many cases his coldness seemed only to increase his allure, but it made him incapable of true intimacy. If, at bottom, there was an element of calculation and manipulation in his dealings with women, he was also helpless to change it, and incapable of mastering the emotions that held him in their grip.

Thus all his resolutions to behave himself went straight out the window the moment he returned to London. He quickly slipped back into his old ways, exploiting the lusts of literary groupies, picking up an air hostess in Europe, arranging a rendezvous with a young Italian woman in Paris, and sleeping with Janetta and Priscilla whenever they were available and in the mood. He restarted his affair with June Osborn and hired a naive girl called Gillian Richardson as his secretary, with whom he also started an affair, marveling at her lower-middle-class manners and ignorance of the ways of the rich. She reminded him of Cynthia, especially in bed, but he soon grew bored and relegated her to taking dictation again.

On meeting Priscilla, Koestler had joked, "I only like upper-class girls," and there was much truth to the jest. He was truly fascinated by the upper reaches of the British class system, but could never quite get the hang of it and was constantly being frustrated by failed attempts to fit in. The contretemps he endured were both comical and painful, and arose in part from the sheer difficulty for a foreigner of mastering the intricacies of the British social scene, but they were also a consequence of Koestler's chronic inferiority complex and his desperate urge to belong. The irony is that they didn't matter. As a distinguished and successful foreigner, Koestler simply needed to be himself, but he could never quite grasp that fact, so his attempts, especially later in life, to act like an English country gentleman (on one occasion he casually informed Priscilla and her husband that he had brought them "a brace of partridges," which they hadn't the slightest notion how to pluck and cook), or to dress like one in tweeds and brogues, frequently misfired. His response of trying to be always in control of the situation or losing his temper when he wasn't also led to complications, for his emotional outbursts and tyrannical ways tended to drive away people of talent and discernment (his equals, in effect), leaving mostly those content to occupy more subservient roles to take their places.

This outcome was at the root of his complaint about "infantile cinderellas," and its consequences were on full display when Janine came to London in October 1954 to discuss the sale of the Ischia house and casually dropped the news that she was pregnant and intended to have the baby. The child was Koestler's, she said, but her husband, Paul, had accepted it as his, and there was nothing standing in her way. It is not clear why she took this course of action. Was she desperate to have a child, perhaps with a genius? Did she hope that Koestler would come around when presented with a fait accompli? Or was there perhaps an element of revenge for his abandonment of her and this was her way of fighting back? Koestler's verbal response to the news is not recorded, but they had a huge fight, which ended when Janine picked up all the pots and pans and cans she could find in the kitchen and threw them through the window into the street. Koestler informed Janine that he would have nothing to do with the child. Only that summer he had noted in his diary that not only was an "absolute commitment" to a faith out of the question for him, but so was having children as "a biological absolute-commitment-ersatz," for they didn't represent commitment in the true sense of the term.[12]

Janine returned to Paris to work on her husband's movie and over the next few months bombarded Koestler with increasingly gushing letters about the state of her health, the special dress that Dior had made to conceal her pregnancy, her plans to spend six weeks in Gstaad before entering an exclusive clinic in Lausanne, for all the world as if he were a doting father-to-be and she the devoted wife and mother. The doting father-to-be was preoccupied with other matters (and with other women), but he did write politely to congratulate Janine when a baby girl was born to her on April 15, 1955. Janine christened the child Cristina Isabel and took her back to Paris, placing her in the care of a nanny while she resumed her career.[13]

WITH ALL HIS PHILANDERING, Koestler was still looking for a stable relationship, and he thought he had found it when he got to know the novelist Elizabeth Jane Howard, whose thick auburn hair, high cheekbones, sea green eyes, and hourglass figure put her in a class for looks with Mamaine. They met at a cocktail party, where Jane was surprised by a short, stocky stranger offering to refill her glass. "He was no taller than I, with a bullet-shaped head and thick brindled hair brushed straight back from his forehead with a parting so low on one side that at first it was hardly visible." He had high cheekbones, she noted, and flirtatious eyes brimming with curiosity.[14]

They exchanged pleasantries, and Koestler invited her to dinner. As they were leaving, she asked him if he was perhaps a writer. "Dar*leeng,* don't you know who I am?" "No," she replied. "I am Koestler. Arthur Koestler." Jane looked blank, and Koestler burst out laughing. "She doesn't know who I am!" he shouted across the room, and swept out with Jane at his elbow.

Over dinner he took an almost childish pleasure in his fame, yet he was neither pompous nor arrogant about it. That night he took her back to Montpelier Square but insisted on hustling her out in the morning so as not to shock the cleaner. "We were speeding across Hyde Park in his open two-seater by eight forty-five." Two days later, on Valentine's Day (though it's highly doubtful Koestler took the date into account), he proposed to her. It was hard to take him seriously after such a whirlwind courtship and Jane said no, but she did agree to move in for three months "to see how we both feel." Koestler was on the cusp of fifty, and Jane was thirty-two.

Jane's first impression of Koestler was of an old-fashioned schoolboy, with a "terrific, continuous, crackling, almost irritable energy," which made other people seem anemic by comparison. She dubbed him "Arturo," and he called her "Janie." Their experimental ménage lasted for about four months and was predictably stormy. Jane was fascinated by his volcanic temperament— so different from that of any Englishman she had met—and it was clear to her that he needed the company of women even more than he needed sex. But she was staggered by his contradictions. He was full of idealism one moment and heartlessly cynical the next, arrogantly self-confident one day and extravagantly humble on the morrow, and "a noble little goblin, full of glee and childish jokes" when in a playful mood.

Koestler liked cozy little rituals—*cozy* was one of his favorite words—like the day Jane sat in one of his armchairs looking at a book and he sat on the arm beside her. "Janee! *Zis* is what I really like. So cozy—domestic bliss. *Vy* don't we have it every day?" Jane quickly realized that there was "nothing that Arthur wanted every day," that he feared and hated true domesticity. He was endlessly changeable—"irascible, obsessive, infinitely courageous, a manic-depressive and an idealist." Still fearing the possibility of assassination, he insisted on answering the intercom himself and mentioned that he kept a gun in his bedroom. But Jane noticed that Koestler was invariably generous and kind to ex-prisoners who came to see him and ask for help, abandoning his strict work schedule without complaint, talking to them for hours at a time, and giving them money or advice (or both) if they asked for it. When she asked how he knew if they were genuine or not, he told her that ex-prisoners always used the pronoun *thou* (in French, German, or Hungarian) when speaking to one another.

Soon enough, Koestler began to bully her. This had its positive side, as when he locked her into a freezing room on weekends and forced her to work on her new novel, *The Long View,* before taking her to the pub for drinks and lunch with Henry Yorke and his wife, Mary, known to all as Dig. Jane had won a literary award for her first novel, *The Beautiful Visit,* and was now trying to finish her second while working as an editor for Chatto & Windus. Koestler read her work carefully and told her when it was time to stop writing, for which she was extremely grateful. But he would also demand that after a full day at the office she prepare a three-course dinner and dress up for guests, and his "obsession with perfection" dogged her at every turn, just as it had dogged Mamaine. Jane noted—and resented—Koestler's reverence for Mamaine. He kept her portrait on his study wall, and Jane was made to feel she could never live up to her predecessor. Only much later did she realize that Koestler had a fatal urge to smash things up, like a small boy smashing his toys. His demand for perfection was a way of ensuring failure in advance.

The cause of their final breakup was drearily predictable. Jane got pregnant and to her surprise felt a rush of love for Koestler and a desire to have his baby. He hated the idea and immediately called a Harley Street specialist to arrange for her to be "treated." Knowing nothing of Koestler's views on children, Jane resisted for about a month before capitulating. "But I wasn't going to have him arrange it. I put my foot down and said, it's my body and my choice, and I'll arrange my own abortion." It wasn't Jane's first, but she was embittered by the way Koestler started avoiding her, and though he did go to see her once after the abortion, he reported "a ghastly scene" in his diary, followed by the words "Exit Jane."[15]

But it wasn't the end of Jane. In a letter to Koestler after the abortion, she explained that her intentions toward him had never been aggressive, and that she had no wish to add to the load of guilt he carried around with him. The fact was that she loved him. She had "never wanted anyone who hasn't wanted me. More important, I've never loved anyone before whom I've objectively thought was good." She alluded to the affair in her next novel, *After Julius,* which Koestler hotly claimed "got all the facts wrong." Later, true to form, he made up with her and they remained friends till the end of his life. Writing about it all some thirty years later, she expressed no bitterness. "He had several virtues that were pure, so to speak—uncontested by any disparate parts of his nature. He was entirely brave; had courage on every level, physical, moral and spiritual, and he was also the most honorable man—with many enduring loyalties. His capacity for indignation—that invaluable ingredient for making things happen—remained with him always."[16]

ANOTHER SEEMING CANDIDATE for marriage was Joan Lee Thompson, a tall, slender young woman with a square, startlingly pale face framed by thick brown hair. As Joan Henry, while still young, she had published three moderately successful novels and had bet her royalties on the horses, running up such huge debts that she had landed in prison. Her experiences spawned a memoir, *Who Lie in Gaol,* that caused a minor sensation with its frank discussion of lesbianism and how women were treated in British jails, and later a novel, *Yield to the Night,* about a woman condemned to death, which became a best seller. The American director J. Lee Thompson made a successful movie of the same title out of it, with Diana Dors in the leading role, and both book and film contributed powerfully to a growing sense of unease in Britain about capital punishment and its shortcomings.

Victor Gollancz, a leading opponent of capital punishment and the book's publisher, had sent a copy to Koestler on Ischia. Koestler read the book and was astonished by its compassion and by how much it reminded him of his experiences in Seville, and on his return, he had asked Yorke (Joan's cousin by marriage) to introduce him. Extravagantly kissing her hand in Viennese fashion, Koestler told her that when he read her novel, "I wanted to send you a cable asking you to marry me." Joan was not deceived but appreciated the flattery and began joining Koestler and Yorke for drinks and dropping in on Koestler to discuss her prison experiences. Koestler opposed the death penalty and wanted to hear her views on the subject.[17]

Known to one and all by her childhood nickname of Gogi, Joan quickly grew accustomed to fending off Koestler's advances and thought the idea of going to bed with him ridiculous. She was in her late forties, newly married to J. Lee Thompson and not in the least interested in stepping out on him. But her marriage soon ran into stormy waters and she relented, only to discover that, despite the buildup, Koestler wasn't much of a lover. "He was always in a terrific hurry. Barely gave you time to get your clothes off." He was also surprisingly conventional. "He wouldn't tolerate any changes of position, or, God forbid, let the woman go on top. I said to him once: 'I want a change, I'm getting tired of being pinned down like a butterfly.' 'Ah,' he said, 'but that's what I like, pinning you down like a butterfly.'"

According to Gogi, Koestler was not at all affectionate or interested in cuddling. He also had a couple of fetishes. He was turned on by French women, he told her, because they didn't shave under their armpits, and he was also aroused by large vaccination marks. Much the most astonishing thing about him was his repeated urgings to Gogi to examine a long scar on his testicles. He told her that when he was in the French Foreign Legion, he had slashed his balls in despair—without doing any permanent damage. He seemed proud of his feat, but Gogi declined the offer. He used to fall into a deep "comalike" sleep after making love, which Gogi attributed to denial. On one occasion Gogi feared he had had a heart attack and tried to pummel him awake, without success. This gave her an idea for a play about a society woman who thinks her clandestine lover has died in her bed, leading to all sorts of farcical complications. It was broadcast on BBC television as *Person to Person*. Gogi watched it with Koestler, but he never suspected (and she never told him) that he was the inspiration for it.

Koestler was fascinated by Gogi. She was a twin and a former debutante, like Mamaine, and she openly made fun of him—his height, his accent, his driving. In the summer of 1955, he asked her to marry him. "Oh, Arthur, don't be silly," she said. "You're no more in love with me than I am with you. Besides, I wasn't brought up to be a slave girl. Why don't you marry Cynthia?" "Cynthia's too immature and too dependent," he said. "That's what you need. You turned Mamaine into a slave, and you would do the same to any other woman." Koestler claimed to be scandalized by her frankness, but secretly admired her for it. She was one of the few women he knew who stood up to him, and she soon morphed from lover to friend.[18]

A small postscript to these marital overtures was provided by Janine's visit to London at the end of July. She arrived at virtually the same time as Cynthia from America, and an apprehensive Koestler insisted she stay at the Dorchester. He also arranged for Cynthia to be present when Janine came to see him at Montpelier Square, and for other friends to accompany them to dinner. Janine had already sent pictures of their baby to Koestler, and her mission now was to persuade him to go to Paris to see Cristina Isabel in the park when the nanny took the baby for a daily walk. Koestler adamantly refused, but was shaken by Janine's visit. "She looked so lovely and sad," he wrote in his diary. "Unable to understand why I insisted on her staying at the Dorchester. Isabelle-Christine looks really a darling. Am I missing my last chance here?" He had characteristically misremembered his daughter's name but was genuinely wistful about the lost opportunity of children and a family. He was running around London proposing marriage to a variety of women, yet to the women who loved him and wanted a child with him, he was cold and hostile.[19]

AFTER FINISHING *The Invisible Writing* Koestler had started work on a new volume of selected essays, *The Trail of the Dinosaur*. It would be his first since *The Yogi and the Commissar*, and included the speeches he had given in Berlin for the CCF; the political essays he had written for *Partisan Review*, *The New York Times*, and *Collier's* between 1947 and 1951; a sprinkling of articles on literary subjects; and four new essays, written specially for the new book, among them "A Guide to Political Neuroses," on the role of subjectivity and emotion in politics, and "An Anatomy of Snobbery," summing up Koestler's views on a topic that had preoccupied him since his conversation with Sperber. The collection was perhaps not quite as strong as *The Yogi and the Commissar*, but the political essays were up to Koestler's highest standards, and the title essay broke new ground for him.

When the book appeared in the winter of 1955, however, it was another essay, "Judah at the Crossroads" (which Irving Kristol, "a good Jew," in Koestler's words, had refused to publish in *Encounter*), that attracted the most attention. The essay was in answer to an Isaiah Berlin article in *The Jewish Chronicle* criticizing Koestler's earlier call for Jews either to emigrate to Israel or assimilate. Berlin wrote that he sympathized with Koestler's stress on the evils of anti-Semitism and the sufferings Jews had endured as a result of their "difference." Jews were like hunchbacks: some gloried in their humps, some sought to disguise them, while still others pretended they had no hump at all. Berlin couldn't endorse the third course, because he believed that total assimilation was impossible. Berlin evidently saw Koestler's arguments as a challenge to his own position as an assimilated Jew par excellence who was also a practicing Zionist. He expressed the view that Koestler's either/or challenge was a form of intellectual bullying, which Koestler was prone to because he was "too much under the influence of totalitarian systems of thought" and "too inclined to deny society the openness that was essential to freedom." Citing his favorite philosophical aphorism, Kant's "out of the crooked timber of humanity no straight thing was ever made," Berlin maintained that Koestler was acting like an intellectual bully and that Jews had the absolute right to freedom of choice in the matter.[20]

The two men had already discussed their differences by letter and over dinner in Montpelier Square, but without resolving anything, and they clearly regarded each other as intellectual rivals. Now, in "Judah at the Crossroads," Koestler attempted to have the last word. Acknowledging the force of Berlin's arguments and the aptness of his metaphors, Koestler restated his position that "ethnic assimilation" was impossible if one clung to the Mosaic faith and the Mosaic faith was incompatible with ethnic assimilation. He agreed with Berlin that it was "unreasonable" to expect people to behave reasonably but wrote that appealing to human irrationality and emotion opened the door to unspeakable dangers, as shown by recent history. "If my saying that we can't eat our cake and have it are figments of a totalitarian mind, then I must confess to a totalitarian mind. If 'out of the crooked timber of humanity no straight thing was ever made,' I still think it more honorable to try to straighten the timber than to make it more crooked for sweet crookedness' sake."[21]

The exchanges led to a certain amount of personal rancor. Berlin came to feel that Koestler was "a racist" where Jews were concerned. "It was clear from his novels that Koestler loved the fact that there were fair-skinned, blue-eyed Jews in Israel, and he made a great fuss about it because he hated the racial stereotype of the Jew as dark and curly-haired, with a hooked nose, and so on," said Berlin later. "I pointed out to him once that the scene in *Thieves in the Night* where the Englishwoman is shocked to find the hero circumcised wasn't plausible, because there was a long tradition of the royal family and the aristocracy in England being circumcised. He was very upset, because he was a great snob and thought he knew all there was to know about English society." Berlin, no mean monologuist himself, said that while Koestler was usually interesting one on one, in company he was "a brilliant, witty, monomaniacal bore." He would take over the room and "talk at you endlessly in a machine-like, totally humorless manner."

Koestler's private opinion of Berlin remained that he was "frivolous and super-donnish." Some months after their dinner, a drunken Koestler detached the young American writer Nora Sayre from a cocktail party conversation with Berlin, muttering that she could see "that little Baltic Jew" some other time. Some have interpreted this remark as proof that Koestler was anti-Semitic. It's true that Koestler (like Herzl, Weininger, and Kraus before him) hated anything that showed the Jews in a bad light or that suggested they were in any way inferior to Aryans. He also loved to be provocative and to make shocking remarks about Jews in a way that only a Jew could get away with. Gogi reports him saying angrily one day, "What were those six million Jews doing walking into the gas ovens?" She, a non-Jew, was shocked but later realized that what Koestler hated was the idea that Jewish weakness and passivity might have contributed to the tragedy of the Holocaust. As one of the first people in Britain to write about the Nazi slaughter of the Jews, he could hardly be called anti-Semitic in any conventional sense or indifferent to the fate of the Jews and felt he could permit himself such impieties in private without being misinterpreted.

Manès Sperber understood this too. Himself thoroughly Jewish, he passionately disagreed with Koestler's views in "Judah" and told him so. "You have been an active, even a militant Zionist, but for you, Jewishness is just an accident of birth." It was easy for Koestler to abandon Judaism, Sperber felt, because he had never known the Jewish faith. But Sperber took a kinder view of of Koestler's motives, realizing that his friend's main targets were hypocrisy and untruth, wherever he found them, and Sperber agreed that the Jews were not immune to these vices. "I have absolute confidence in Koestler. He believes absolutely in what he writes, and if I don't agree with him— which happens all the time—I find it most honorable that he completely commits himself to what he believes. That's much more important to me than what he thinks about Judaism."[22]

IN THE EVENT, Berlin had the best of the argument, and in intellectual terms rightly so. Koestler had pushed his personal obsession too far, and his conclusions were too sweeping. Eventually the two men composed their differences and in later years established amicable relations, but it's worth noting that in accusing Koestler of "totalitarian" leanings, Berlin was falling back on a false stereotype of Koestler that had taken root among leftists and liberals as far back as the Congress for Cultural Freedom in Berlin in 1950. It was after that meeting that Trevor-Roper and Ayer had returned to Britain with accusations that Koestler was a dogmatic hard-liner with anti-democratic tendencies, unduly influenced by his years in the Communist Party, and fellow travelers in both Britain and France had gone out of their way to pour fuel on the fire. In America, a timid CIA had accepted that argument, and liberals had raised a similar cry after Koestler's outspoken support for Whittaker Chambers and his refusal to place McCarthy's Red-baiting on the same level of seriousness as the Soviet show trials, the Gulag, and the subjugation of Eastern Europe.[23]

Koestler was partly to blame for the stereotype because of his take-no-prisoners style of argument and proneness to exaggeration in his polemics, but these were more a product of his personal character and temperament than of brainwashing by any sort of ideology or party. It was his deep-rooted instincts that had made ideologies and parties so attractive to him in the first place, but he had also been among the first to see through them and turn against them, and there was something ineffably ridiculous in the idea of Communists and their allies clothing themselves in nationalism and accusing Koestler of being anti-patriotic and anti-democratic. Conservatives might have had a better right to do so, but they faced a different dilemma: While they embraced Koestler's anti-communism, they couldn't stomach his socialist leanings in domestic affairs.

Berlin wasn't engaging in the pro- versus anti-Communist debate, of course, but he had fallen back on that same stereotype to bolster his argument, and it was a symptom of Koestler's increasing intellectual isolation that Berlin's allegation wasn't seriously challenged by any other commentators. Koestler was isolated, a party of one, and he was well aware of his isolation. It was a factor, along with his fear of repeating himself, in his decision to abandon politics and seek new pastures.

The public signal of this change came in the new book of essays. Most of the essays, apart from "Judah," were retrospective, but the most significant were the last two pieces in the book, "A Guide to Political Neuroses" and "The Trail of the Dinosaur." In "Guide," Koestler offered a tongue-in-cheek psychological analysis of contemporary politics that emphasized the irrational forces at odds with rational attempts at change, and suggested that politicians should study psychology in addition to history and economics. Then they might gain a better understanding of "the strange mental forces which compel people to act with such stubborn determination against their own interests."

The subtext was Koestler's weariness and growing estrangement from his former subject matter, and in "The Trail of the Dinosaur" he expanded on his dillusionment and issued a stirring farewell to arms. Elaborating on von Neumann's idea about the competition between religion and science,

Koestler wrote that the dinosaur of his title was western civilization, which had achieved prodigious material power through science yet was spiritually bankrupt, a massive body with no brains. The crisis of the West, according to Koestler, dated to the seventeenth century, when the discoveries of Copernicus, Galileo, and Kepler had displaced the earth from the center of the universe and God from his throne, causing man to begin to lose his religious belief. Dismissing the doctrines of the Anglican and Roman Catholic churches as contrary to common sense, Koestler expressed the hope that a new kind of faith might bring spirit and reason into some sort of equilibrium. "We shall either destroy ourselves or take off to the stars. Perhaps the conquest of interplanetary space will cause a Copernican revolution in reverse, the emergence of a new type of cosmic consciousness."

It was another way of announcing Koestler's disillusionment with the ideology of the Enlightenment, which had been his guiding star until now, and his decision to look for new paths to human happiness, though it was characteristic of his unorthodoxy—and his confusion—that he planned to search for them through science, the archetypal expression of the Enlightenment if ever there was one. But paradoxes were meat and drink to Koestler, and in the meantime he was eager to make it clear that he had said all he had to say on political subjects and now planned to alter the whole direction of his work. "The errors are atoned for, the bitter passion has burnt itself out; Cassandra has gone hoarse, and is due for a vocational change."[24]

CHAPTER THIRTY-NINE

MATTERS OF LIFE AND DEATH

Any man's death diminishes me.

— JOHN DONNE

KOESTLER BROKE HIS CASSANDRA PROMISE almost as soon as he had made it, though the cause was not international politics but the abolition of capital punishment in Britain. The renewal of his opposition to the death penalty had occurred when he was reliving his Seville experiences while at work on *The Invisible Writing,* and the seed had been watered when Gollancz sent him *Yield to the Night.* Since then his long conversations with Gogi and others had convinced him it was a barbaric practice that needed to be ended—at least in civilized Britain.

Gollancz, of course, was hoping for such an outcome when he sent him the novel. Gollancz's own opposition to the death penalty was of long standing, and in the mid-fifties was beginning to be shared by many others in Britain after some notorious miscarriages of justice. In 1953 a mentally retarded youth called Derek Bentley was executed for a murder in which he had been a barely witting accomplice. In 1955 Timothy Evans was wrongfully hanged on the evidence of a neighbor who turned out to be the multiple murderer being sought. Most controversial of all was the death sentence imposed on Ruth Ellis, a young mother who had shot her abusive and unfaithful lover in a fit of jealousy. Because the movie of *Yield to the Night* appeared shortly after Ellis's execution, many thought it had been inspired by the Ellis case, but it was not so. Gogi had anticipated the incident, rather than exploiting it, but her novel and the movie undoubtedly contributed to the growing swell of unease about to the death penalty.[1]

After an article on the Ellis case by Raymond Chandler and a follow-up letter by Gollancz appeared in London's *Evening Standard* in July 1955, Koestler impulsively rang Gollancz to propose a national campaign. Gollancz enlisted Canon John Collins, then the head of Christian Action, and in August the freshly minted National Campaign for the Abolition of Capital Punishment (NCACP) held its first committee meeting. Koestler offered to write a book making the case for abolition, and he struck a remarkable deal with the crusading editor of the London *Observer,* David Astor. Astor agreed to put several members of his staff at Koestler's disposal to carry out the research, and Koestler agreed to let his book be serialized by *The Observer* in weekly installments.[2]

Cynthia had just arrived in England to spend a vacation with her family, and Koestler shamelessly asked if she would work for him instead. Cynthia, who had been addressing her letters to Koestler from America as "your loving ex-slavey," didn't hesitate. After four and a half days with her mother and sister at the seaside, she was back in London and ready to begin.

To judge from her lyrical account of that summer, it was a fateful decision. Koestler was possessed by his subject with a fierce passion he hadn't experienced for years, and Cynthia entered into his mania so completely that they bonded in a wholly new way. Koestler began to refer to their project as a folie à deux and to Cynthia as his "junior partner." Cynthia was enthralled. "I sat in his study, curled up in the armchair beside the fireplace. Every bit of space was covered with books, lying open or piled up, bristling with bookmarks in the form of brightly colored tapers which he bought at Woolworth's for lighting the fire. We were living in a world of gallows and gibbets 'creaking and groaning with the bodies of criminals.' He had warned me that parts of the book would be stomach-turning. Sometimes he turned pale when dealing with the physiological facts about hanging and looked to see whether I could bear it."[3]

Koestler worked frantically through the month of August and into September 1955. Whenever they broke for lunch at the pub or went for a drink, Koestler would engage the publican and his customers in a discussion about capital punishment. The publicans were die-hard hangers to a man (as were most of their customers), and Koestler honed his dialectical skills by debating with them before returning home at night to dictate ever new arguments to Cynthia. On some nights, according to Cynthia, he would continue dictating even in his sleep. There was a heat wave that summer—a rare luxury in England—but they worked straight through it, and Cynthia postponed her return to the United States for ten days to help Koestler finish.

For Cynthia it was a "magical" summer. She left for the United States feeling "strangely elated" and wrote from New York to say she would love to come back and work for him again whenever possible. Continuing without her, Koestler finished his book, *Reflections on Hanging,* in October and dis-

patched it to Gollancz. Gerald Gardiner, a leading lawyer and fellow cam-
paigner, wrote Koestler, "I thought that I knew pretty well everything that
there was to be known on the subject, but I find that I have learned a lot from
it." But as Gollancz's legal adviser, he worried that Koestler's swinging attacks on, among others, Her Majesty's senior judges, were too libelous to
print and pointed to numerous passages that needed to be toned down.

IN NOVEMBER 1955 the NCACP held its first mass rally in Central Hall,
Westminster. Koestler was on the platform but did not speak. "A foreign accent and a foreign name would be an added liability in a campaign basically
directed at irrational, emotional prejudice," he wrote to his colleagues on the
committee. Gollancz publicly acknowledged him as the principal initiator of
the campaign, which made him "very proud," and other speakers included
J. B. Priestley, Lord Pakenham, and Gardiner. After Christmas, Koestler's
Reflections on Hanging was serialized in five lengthy installments in *The Observer,* scoring a huge success with readers and not incidentally raising the
sales of *The Observer* by a considerable amount (Astor's gamble had paid off).[4]

Koestler refused to soften his comments on Britain's hallowed judges, as
Gardiner had recommended. He argued that Britain was barbarous and out
of step with of the rest of the world in clinging to capital punishment, and
that the death penalty was immoral, ineffective, and bad law. He also set
out to arouse readers' emotions against it by painting a vivid picture of its in-
justices and the sufferings of its victims. The tone was set in a preface in
which Koestler recalled his memories of prisoners being executed in Seville.
"These three months left me with a vested interest in capital punishment—
rather like 'half-hanged Smith,' who was cut down after fifteen minutes and
lived on. Each time a man's or a woman's neck is broken in this peaceful country, memory starts to fester like a badly healed wound. I shall never achieve
real peace of mind until hanging is abolished." Capital punishment was not
just a problem of statistics and expediency but of "morality and feeling."[5]

Koestler had many more arguments against capital punishment up his
sleeve, but two that have an undeniably contemporary ring were the difference in treatment for rich and poor and the prevalence of error in identifying
the criminals. Money governed a great deal in capital cases, wrote Koestler,
ranging from the type of legal advice the accused could get to the testimony
of expert witnesses to the quality of the defense lawyers. As for error, there
were far too many cases where the wrong person had gone to the gallows,
and each fresh execution of an innocent victim was an additional stain on the
conscience of society.

The serialization of Koestler's book made a stirring impression on British
public opinion, but its very success led to a seriocomic rift with Gollancz.
He and Koestler were much alike—energetic, egotistical, ambitious, and

domineering—and Gollancz was mortified when he returned from a business trip to America to find Koestler the toast of the town and top dog in the NCACP committee. "Don't people realize that I'm *much* more famous than Arthur Koestler?" he said to Peggy Duff, the committee's secretary and treasurer. When the House of Commons finally held its long-awaited debate on capital punishment, it voted 293–262 in favor of abolition, and Koestler, Gollancz, Gardiner, and Duff were present in the visitors' gallery. The jubilant Gollancz announced victory and an end to the NCACP's meetings, but Koestler opposed him on the grounds that the Commons had voted for abolition before and never done anything about it. Once more he was prescient. Prime Minister Anthony Eden decided to leave the issue of abolition to a private member's bill, which was not necessarily a kiss of death but severely weakened its prospects of passing. Gollancz and Koestler both offered to resign from the NCACP committee, and Koestler finally did so, saying he would continue to "write and work for abolition" but not attend meetings. True to his promise, Koestler persuaded Astor to let him write an occasional column for *The Observer* under the name of "Vigil," and his last column, published as a pamphlet entitled *Patterns of Murder,* was sent to every member of Parliament.[6]

Koestler's frontal assault on the judges, and especially on Lord Chief Justice Goddard, hadn't escaped notice in the House of Lords, where the judges sat as members. Lord Mancroft, undersecretary of state for home affairs, accused Koestler of misquoting a confidential Home Office instruction to prison governors, and Lord Hailsham said that Koestler and *The Observer* should be investigated by the Press Council. Koestler did some research and found that the phrases he was alleged to have omitted had never been published—until, that is, Lord Mancroft revealed them in the Lords. He demanded, and got, an apology from the two peers, but it was so grudging that Koestler himself referred the matter to the Press Council, which censured the noble lords instead.

Koestler gave up his royalties on the hardcover version of the book, and *Reflections on Hanging* appeared to considerable fanfare in Britain in April 1956 (and a year later in the USA), earning praise on both sides of the Atlantic. In Britain he was compared to Jeremy Bentham, though some felt that his explicit descriptions of the grisly physiological aspects of hanging were unfair to doubters, while others thought that logical argument was beside the point, since capital punishment was an atavistic ritual that appealed to man's most primitive instincts anyway. The consensus was that Koestler had placed his considerable rhetorical gifts in the service of a noble cause and had clearly bested his opponents, even if his dramatic excesses had occasionally led him to distort or exaggerate the facts.[7]

An excerpt from *Reflections* was published in *Demain* (Tomorrow) in

France and went a long way toward restoring Koestler's reputation in that country as well. Camus agreed to join him in producing a French version of the book and wrote an essay on the guillotine that powerfully reinforced Koestler's argument against hanging. The book came out under the joint names of Koestler and Camus as *Réflexions sur la peine capitale* (Reflections on Capital Punishment) and was later adapted for publication in Germany. To get the German edition issued as a cheap mass-market paperback, Koestler again renounced his royalties and persuaded Camus to do the same.[8]

In the summer of 1956 the conservative House of Lords (egged on by the judges in its midst) threw out the private member's bill to abolish capital punishment, and it took another ten years to get the death penalty suspended in Britain. Outright abolition came only in 1970, but it was generally agreed that Koestler's book, and the campaign he started, were hugely influential in altering the climate of opinion and making it possible. When the initial campaign was over, David Astor wrote to Koestler, "I don't want to sound sententious, but want to say all the same that I believe your 'hanging' journalism has contributed something of real value to this country and this newspaper. It is the episode that most deserves to be recorded in the history of this paper since I've been here. I'm very proud of being associated with what you've done."

Koestler also felt pleased with himself. "People say: 'He used to want to save humanity. Now a dozen souls are enough,'" he told a French interviewer sometime later. "It's true. To snatch even a single man from the gallows is very gratifying. It's the whole point of my life's path. I don't believe that the end justifies the means. I don't believe that an individual is the result of a crowd of a million divided by a million. I don't believe any more in humanity. I believe in the individual."[9]

THE SERENE, WORLDLY-WISE narrator of the autobiographies and the self-confident tribune of *Reflections on Hanging* had little in common with the walking bundle of raw nerve endings that constituted Koestler in his daily life. Frustrated and discouraged by his inability to conduct a permanent relationship with a woman of his choice, he wrote a psychological "self-analysis" for himself and started treatment with the Jungian psychiatrist Alan McGlashan, who told him that the amount of alcohol Koestler had consumed might have caused brain damage and that his psychological state was precarious. "Discovered that never grew up: from infantilism straight to senility; summer of manhood missed" was Koestler's pithy, self-pitying summary of the meeting. The second session went better, "soothing and cheering—unloaded quite a lot." By the middle of the month he was talking to McGlashan about his current life, his relationship with Cynthia, and other topical matters. But his interior chaos was if anything worse. Even as the analysis continued, he got involved in adolescent shenanigans with two young women less than half his age and conducted a desultory affair with Griselda Kentner, the wife of the Hungarian pianist Louis Kentner, until she dumped him.[10]

He hastily arranged some extra sessions with McGlashan in the hope of explaining and recovering from his "breakdown week." He also chose that moment—with who knows what subconscious motives—to invite Cynthia to return to London to work on a new book with him. "Dear old Cynthia" was thrilled. Ditching her new boyfriend, she packed up her New York apartment at top speed and rushed to London, arriving just in time for Koestler's fiftieth birthday. Koestler read the flood of telegrams alone in his study and burned them before going downstairs. "Alas, only once," he noted sadly in his diary. "Very depressed, despite spectacular lunch at Overtons."[11]

McGlashan strongly disapproved of the invitation to Cynthia, and this seems to have become the pretext for Koestler to abandon the therapy, for there is no record of any sessions after the first week of November. Koestler celebrated by rushing off to Paris for more assignations with young women, aware even as he did so of how sordid and puerile his behavior had become.[12]

Though alcohol abuse undoubtedly had a lot to do with Koestler's troubles, it's doubtful that he was clinically an alcoholic. Gogi described him as recklessly tossing off tumblers of whiskey or brandy whenever he felt like it, but Jane Howard said he fought a constant battle to keep his consumption down and never drank before evening on the days when he was working. But he had several of the personality traits associated with alcoholism: self-hatred, depressive tendencies, an inferiority complex. He was dependent on alcohol in the sense that he couldn't do without it for any long period of time. On the other hand, he was able to control the times at which he drank until the very end of his life. Drinking rarely interfered with his work, and he remained healthy into his late seventies. All the evidence points to him being psychologically dependent on alcohol but not physiologically. It was close to being an addiction but was not a disease.[13]

Knowing nothing of McGlashan's reservations, "Good old Cynthia" was more than happy to take up once more the role of both amanuensis and companion. She accompanied Koestler on a canoeing vacation to France, moved with him for the summer to a cottage in Wiltshire called The Lacket (where Lytton Strachey had stayed while writing *Eminent Victorians*), and helped him find at a London dogs' home a black Labrador that he christened Attila (whether in honor of the Hun or the poet—or both—is not clear). She also had another abortion, but Koestler kept her status deliberately ambiguous, saying simply, "This is Cynthia," to visitors and leaving it to them to decipher where she stood. In the meantime she acquired ever wider responsibilities, sliding imperceptibly into the role formerly occupied by Mamaine but with far greater deference to Koestler's moods and feelings than Mamaine and less consideration for her own.[14]

Hoping to slow, if not end, his frantic social life, Koestler decided to rent out the Montpelier Square house and find a cheaper place in the country. "Since I have decided to write no more novels or political journalism, only scholarly books which nobody wants to buy," he told Sperber, "I have to cut down drastically my standard of living in general." After an extended search he found what he was looking for, Long Barn, a storied house that was, like The Lacket, haunted by the ghosts of Bloomsbury: It had been home for many years to Harold Nicolson and Vita Sackville-West, and much visited by Leonard and Virginia Woolf and other Bloomsbury notables. The house was situated in the rural Weald of Kent, about twenty-six miles southeast of London, and Koestler moved down in the fall of 1956.[15]

KOESTLER HAD BARELY MOVED IN when he was distracted by an explosion that seemed expressly designed to tempt him out of his retirement from politics: a revolt against Soviet rule in Hungary. Koestler had followed the progress of de-Stalinization in the Soviet Union with a combination of dark satisfaction and guarded optimism. Khrushchev's "Secret Speech" to the Twentieth Party Congress in February had ratified and reenergized the grudging liberalization set off in the Eastern Bloc by Stalin's death, and it had also sent shock waves through the satellite countries of Eastern and Central Europe. First Poland, then Hungary erupted in revolt. The Poles were brought back into the fold by far-reaching concessions from the Soviets, but the Hungarians were refusing to make a deal and had elected a popular reformist politician, Imre Nagy, as their leader. The Soviets sent tanks into downtown Budapest, and fierce street fighting went on for two weeks before the back of the rebellion was broken.

The first Koestler heard of the Soviet strike was when he returned to Montpelier Square late on the night of October 24, 1956, to continue the process of moving his belongings to Long Barn. At the house he found a hastily scribbled note from Zoltán Szabó, the husband of Count Károlyi's daughter, Judith, and a commentator for Radio Free Europe. Koestler rushed around to Szabó's place, improbably carrying a basket with two bottles of wine, some salt pork, and some green peppers in it. It was two o'clock in the morning. "It's impossible to sleep," he told Szabó, "I can't bear this helplessness. If only we could go to Hungary and do something." Then he thought of the Hungarian Embassy. "We've just had some work done in our garage. There are some bricks left over. What if we went and broke some windows?"

Legend has it that Koestler actually tossed bricks through the embassy windows. He was quite capable of doing so, but it never happened. Before doing anything he called Irving Kristol at *Encounter* and gave him detailed instructions on how the CCF should respond to the invasion and what sort of publicity was needed. At three o'clock in the morning he called George Mikes. "Come to the embassy with us," he said insistently. Still half asleep, Mikes was less than thrilled with the idea. "Okay, but will you tell me what this is in aid of?" "It's clear enough, I think," said Koestler. "We want to draw attention to events in Hungary." Mikes replied that the newspapers and TV were full of news about Hungary. Did they want to draw attention to Hungary or to themselves? Koestler was indignant. Was Mikes suggesting they go to sleep in their comfortable beds while people were fighting and dying in the streets of Budapest? Mikes was unmoved and suggested they get together the next day to discuss the situation. "Damn your moderation!" yelled Koestler, and slammed the receiver down.

Koestler and Szabó did drive over to the Hungarian Embassy, not with bricks but with a couple of empty soda bottles in the car just in case. It was past five in the morning. The embassy was ablaze with lights, and the police were much in evidence. They slowed their car but were told to keep moving and had no chance to throw even bottles through the windows.[16]

The next afternoon Koestler, Mikes, Szabó, and Judith met at Koestler's house to make a plan (Andrew Révai, Count Károlyi's former secretary and a Hungarian analyst at the British Foreign Office, was an unofficial fifth member of the ad hoc committee). Mikes booked Denison Hall near Victoria Station for a public meeting on Sunday, and Koestler was put in charge of finding some big names to sit on the platform. Bertrand Russell declined. Eliot, Auden, and Spender were out of the country. Koestler ended up with J. B. Priestley, Rose Macaulay, Veronica Wedgewood, Henry Green, Sir Jacob Epstein, and Mikes and himself—not a bad roster for a hastily organized protest meeting. Judith was delegated to chair the gathering, and a message of support for Hungarian Writers and Intellectuals was received from the Congress for Cultural Freedom.[17]

When they arrived on the Sunday morning, they could hardly make their way into the hall. Vast crowds thronged the streets, and there were hundreds of policemen—some of them mounted—trying to maintain order. The atmosphere was electric. After several people had spoken, the crowd started yelling for Koestler. He reluctantly came to the microphone and explained somewhat lamely that since he had just published his farewell to politics, he didn't feel he should speak, and he sat down again, feeling sheepish and inadequate. The crowd was dumbstruck, but Koestler was adamant. He declined to make or sign any public protests and insisted throughout the crisis on keeping a low profile.[18]

* * *

KOESTLER'S PUBLIC SILENCE was interpreted in some quarters as a sign of indifference or lack of patriotism, and it's true that raising his voice at such an exceptional time would hardly have violated his vow to cease writing about politics. As it was, his quixotic decision deprived the Hungarians of a matchlessly powerful advocate to make their case. It was a rare tactical mistake on his part and an unfortunate line to take, though behind the scenes his behavior was vastly different, and he did more to help the Hungarian cause than has generally been realized.

During the following week, as Soviet troops first withdrew from Budapest and then moved back, Koestler was in a "dreadful state" of anxiety and anticipation, according to Szabó, who was making daily broadcasts into Hungary with news of the latest developments. During a lull in the fighting, the Hungarian Writers' Federation sent a desperate SOS to writers. "You know the facts. Help Hungary. Help the Hungarian people. Help Hungarian writers, scientists, workers, peasants, and our intelligentsia. Help. Help. Help." The CCF asked Koestler how it should respond, and Koestler signed a telegram to eighty British writers urging them to apply for visas so they might go to Hungary to "investigate the facts behind the deeply disturbing reports" at first hand. Koestler didn't expect the visas to be issued but hoped the requests alone would exert moral pressure on the Soviet Union to show restraint.[19]

Throughout those two weeks there were widespread demonstrations in Britain and other European countries. A Hungarian Committee for Freedom was hastily formed, with vague plans to raise an Anglo-French brigade of volunteers to fight the Soviets in the streets. A few intrepid souls even crossed the border to join the rebels, but as the Soviet and Hungarian armies gained the upper hand, there was a much bigger exodus in the opposite direction, and hundreds of thousands of Hungarians fled westward. But they were doubly unlucky. Western support was fatally weakened when Egypt's President, Nasser Gamal Abdel, nationalized the Suez Canal, triggering an invasion by Israel and an even larger invasion by Britain and France. The United States forced the Europeans to withdraw, leading to the most serious split between the western allies since World War II, and in Britain, Hungary was forgotten in a surge of national controversy. It was only natural, given the echoes of empire evoked by Suez, but Koestler was dejected to see how thoroughly Suez eclipsed Hungary in the national consciousness. Philip Toynbee said he wanted to organize a "*mea-culpa* youth pilgrimage simultaneously to Budapest and Cairo," which Koestler regarded as "the fallacy of the false equation." He congratulated himself on the correctness of his decision to quit politics and remain silent.[20]

*   *   *

HE DID, HOWEVER, help on a more modest scale when Hungarian refugees started arriving in England at the end of the year and sixty or more ended up in the region of Sevenoaks. Koestler did some interpreting for them and contemplated starting a Hungarian-language newsletter. He took the family of a Professor Nagy from Budapest into his home at Long Barn, but entertaining refugees at such close quarters wasn't Koestler's style, and after some difficult scenes he nimbly dumped them on another good Samaritan.[21]

Among the thousands who had escaped Hungary during the brief uprising were Pál and Florence Ignotus. Pál was now stooped from his years in prison, with a deathly pallor and thinning hair, but he remained his old charming self and spent several weekends at Long Barn. Two other escapees from Hungarian jails, Paul Kövesdy, a leading member of the Hungarian Social Democratic Party, and the poet George Faludy, also came down from London, and one upshot of these gatherings was the formation of a committee to fight for the release of two jailed writers (and Koestler's friends), Tibor Déry and Julius Hay.[22]

Soon afterward, when Koestler heard that Déry ("a bad writer, but a decent chap") was ill in prison and that Hugh Gaitskell, the leader of the Labour Party, was about to leave for Moscow, he finagled Gaitskell's private number out of one of his Labour friends and called him late one night. Faludy and Kövesdy were listening in on an extension and heard a voice respond that Gaitskell was asleep. "Please wake him up and tell him it's a matter of life and death," said Koestler. There was a longish pause, and Gaitskell came to the telephone. Koestler told him what a great writer Déry was and asked Gaitskell to intervene with Khrushchev. "I will," said Gaitskell, "but you know what he will say, that he can't interfere in the internal affairs of Hungary." "That's good," said Koestler. "That's exactly what you need to hear from him. Tell him you know that, but you also know that he is good friends with Kádár, and ask if he can just whisper a word in his friend's ear about the plight of the poor writer Déry. Forgive me for putting words into your mouth, but I know Hungarian conditions better than you do."[23]

Gaitskell kept his word, but it brought no change in Déry's prison conditions, and Koestler appealed to Gaitskell and the Labour Party twice more the following year, especially after the execution of Imre Nagy in the summer of 1958. He also asked Camus to start a publicity campaign in Paris and began sending ten pounds a month to Julius Hay's wife, Eva, who was destitute in Budapest. Cassandra may have grown hoarse, but he continued to whisper when the cause was urgent.[24]

IN THE MIDST OF these Hungarian events Koestler struggled to make his new home comfortable. Long Barn was a quintessentially English country house, and Koestler probably thought that by purchasing it, he was purchasing some Englishness for himself. Part Tudor and part Elizabethan, with half-timbered brick walls and a steeply pitched, red-tiled roof, the house had been modernized by Sir Edward Lutyens at the beginning of the twentieth century and gained a beautiful long gallery imported from Italy. Vita Sackville-West had laid out the terraced gardens, complete with neatly clipped yew hedges, aubretia-covered walls, a manicured croquet lawn, and a rustic fishpond. The gardens were glorious, with lovely views over the surrounding fields and woods, but the interior of the house was typically English: cold, drafty, and uncomfortable, with smoky fireplaces, no central heating, and ancient, inefficient appliances.

Koestler prided himself on his ability to work with his hands (setting him off, he thought, from the majority of his intellectual friends) and settled down to rewire parts of the house, to panel the room he had chosen for a study, and to mend and patch the barns (he would later find himself stripping and repainting the garden furniture, digging up clogged and overflowing drains, and again mowing like mad). "I love buying houses, doing them up, furnishing them, and running round to antique shops and auctions," he confided to a French interviewer, and he meant it. After several weeks of strenuous physical labor he felt exhilarated and refreshed. "Siesta abolished since here," he noted in his diary. "No aspirin or methedrine for a month."[25]

Koestler was now to be seen in tweeds and brogues, rather than the city suits and sport jackets he had favored earlier. He and Cynthia purchased a goat, Petronella, for fresh milk, and a couple of hundred chicks to be raised for eggs, which they housed in one of the barns. They hired an Italian couple as cook and handyman, and Koestler acquired a Labrador bitch, Heidi, as a companion to Attila, proudly announcing to a diplomat friend of Priscilla's that he was breeding Labradors. "How many have you got?" asked the friend innocently, imagining a kennel and a pack of dogs. "Two, of course!" exclaimed Koestler irritably, giving him a wrathful look.[26]

It was a new and more successful version of Island Farm. Koestler continued to entertain extravagantly, bringing his friends to the country rather than traveling to London. Cynthia's position was still ambiguous, more that of cook and "crew," as Elizabeth Young put it in her diary, than of partner or spouse, but she was much more efficient than Mamaine. Koestler's face was now "creased with deep lines," but he still looked young for his age. "His hair is thick and black," reported the French interviewer, "his skin coarse and weatherbeaten, and the gray-blue eyes looking out from beneath his bushy brows are a real surprise: lively, mobile, changeable, sometimes commanding, sometimes narrowed and piercing, and sometimes misty, dreamy, and languid."

Elizabeth Young found him "completely alive—public face, private face, inner face," full of knowledge, enthusiasm, and understanding, and Celia, who had drawn closer to Koestler since the death of Mamaine, wrote to a friend about the "human sympathy and understanding, the suffering and compassion" that shone from Koestler's "extraordinary, emotional, complicated face. Parts of that may surprise you, but I assure you that it's so. The whole two hours I spent with him we were talking about things we really cared about." It appeared that Koestler had truly settled down at last and found a suitable niche for himself in the tranquillity of the English countryside. That is how it struck his friends, at least, but appearances were deceptive.[27]

PART FOUR:

ASTRIDE THE
TWO CULTURES

The Author as Polymath
(1959–1983)

CHAPTER FORTY

COSMIC REPORTER

I had had enough of politicians. Suddenly I was enveloped by a feeling that only science is lasting.
— THEODOR VON KÁRMÁN

KOESTLER WAS DEEPLY SERIOUS about the decision he had announced in *The Trail of the Dinosaur* to abandon politics and turn to scientific subjects. Since he now considered the scientific revolution to be to blame for the current spiritual crisis of the West, he had decided that the best way to approach the subject was through the life and work of one of his boyhood heroes, the German astronomer Johannes Kepler. In the spring of 1955 he had visited Kepler's birthplace in Weil-der-Stadt and stumbled across a treasure trove of Kepleriana in German that opened his eyes to a whole new way of approaching the subject. This material wasn't available in English, and with the support of Dr. Franz Hammer, one of the editors of Kepler's collected works, Koestler conceived the idea of taking a new look at Kepler's discoveries and introducing him more thoroughly to the English-speaking world.

Between his various distractions Koestler had then spent most of 1955 and 1956 working on Kepler, but the more he investigated the great astronomer's life and work, the more convinced he had become that he must also write about Copernicus and Galileo, and the more he wrote about them, the more he realized he needed to go all the way back to the ancient Greeks and what *they* knew about astronomy. So part one became an exposition of classical astronomy. Part Two, "Dark Interlude," was devoted to the early Middle Ages, and by the time he got back to Copernicus and his successors he had hit upon a title for the new book, *The Sleepwalkers,* expressing his view that the great astronomers had made their discoveries as much by fumbling their way through imagination and intuition as by experiments in the laboratory. This theory recapitulated one of the theses Koestler had put forward in *Insight and Outlook*, and he was greatly excited by its intellectual potential.[1]

The work ground on into 1957, and Koestler put the final touches on *The Sleepwalkers* in the spring of 1958. In a letter to a friend dated "March 18, 1958, 6.15 P.M." he wrote, "Exactly an hour ago I *really* finished the book. When I was in Vienna I had already handed in the *text,* but the *notes* were only half done; now the notes alone have blossomed into an appendix of 100 pages! There's been nothing like it since Mommsen. So what next? All my heroes, from Pythagoras to Galileo, are dead, buried, memorialized and gone, and I am left here, widowed."[2]

The book was slated for publication at the start of the following year by Hutchinson (with whom Koestler had signed a new contract after increasing dissatisfaction with Hamish Hamilton and Collins) in Britain and by Macmillan in the United States six months later. Koestler was terrified of what the critics might do to it, especially those from the scientific establishment, and had managed to secure a brief introduction by the English historian Herbert Butterfield, who had famously written that the Scientific Revolution "outshines everything since the rise of Christianity and reduces the Renaissance and Reformation to the rank of mere episodes."[3]

Koestler deeply admired Butterfield's work and hoped that Butterfield's imprimatur would secure for him "a label of academic respectability," something he desperately craved after being described as a novelist "trespassing into scholarly preserves." In fact Koestler was better qualified than most readers realized. He had related in his autobiography how, as a child, his heroes had been "Darwin and Spencer, Kepler, Newton and Mach; Edison, Herz and Marconi—the Buffalo Bills of the frontiers of discovery." He had elected to study math and engineering at the Vienna Polytechnic in preference to the liberal arts at the university. The very title of the first volume of his autobiography, *Arrow in the Blue,* derived from his adolescent musings on the power of gravity, and it was not by chance he had consoled himself in a Spanish jail by scratching mathematical formulas and equations on his cell wall.

Koestler still had one foot firmly planted in the German culture of his childhood. "In Goethe's day," he wrote in his autobiography, "it would have been as shocking for an educated person to say that he took no interest in science as to declare that he was bored with art." Koestler had grown up during the closing years of the old era, "before science became so formalized and abstract that it was removed from the layman's grasp. Atoms still moved in three-dimensional space and could be represented to the senses by models—little glass spheres revolving around a nucleus like planets around the sun. Space was still non-curved, the world infinite, the mind a rational clockwork. There was no fourth dimension, and there was no subconscious id—

that fourth dimension of the mind which transforms straight lines into crooked lines, and the deductions of reason into a web of self-delusions."[4]

This passage itself bespeaks the depth of Koestler's fascination with the aesthetic properties of science, as well as with the ideas that drove them. He responded to scientific theories the way most of his fellow writers responded to a sonnet or a painting, and the scientific metaphors and similes in his writing that so discomfited Pritchett, Mortimer, and others were organic, coming as easily to his pen as the literary references that were more familiar to them. Astronomy held a special place in his affections, and the names of Kepler and Galileo crop up repeatedly in the autobiographies and in *Insight and Outlook*.[5]

But the leopard hadn't completely changed his spots. Koestler's polemical zeal was too deep-rooted to be cast away with his change of subject matter, even if he liked to pretend to academic objectivity. In his preface he deplored what he dramatically called the "state of cold war" that existed between the sciences and the humanities and the "academic and social barriers" that had been erected to keep them apart (this was just a few months before C. P. Snow defined the existence of the "two cultures" as a blot on British intellectual life). What was needed were creative trespassers who could bridge the divide and bring new perspectives to the history of science. In his own case he hoped to make a contribution to the history of cosmology through a "personal and speculative account of a controversial subject." But his approach to science would also be profoundly political.

KOESTLER HAD A THESIS that he wanted to test. If it was true that religion had become irrevocably separated from science and that "new determinants of man's fate" had begun to take over—"mechanical laws, atoms, glands, genes"—which provided "no guidance whatsoever for his conscience," the essential question was why? Surely such a separation was neither inevitable nor necessarily permanent? He had a hunch that it was time for the pendulum of history to swing back again, and he would help it along by persuading people to shed habits of thought conditioned by post-Copernican (and especially post-Galilean) developments and reimagine the whole process from the beginning.[6]

Koestler divided his book into five parts and an epilogue. Part one, "The Heroic Age," covered the discoveries of the ancient Greeks, notably Pythagoras and Aristarchus. Part two, "Dark Interlude," dealt summarily with the fifteen centuries from the birth of Christ till the start of the scientific revolution, with a brief mention of the "scientific" ideas of St. Augustine and Thomas Aquinas. Part three, "The Timid Canon," was about Copernicus and his discoveries. Part four, "The Watershed," contained a detailed account of the life and work of Kepler, with chapters on Tycho Brahe and

Galileo. And part five, "The Parting of the Ways," was mainly on Galileo, but with a concluding chapter on the work of Isaac Newton.

Koestler made little secret of where his sympathies lay. Pythagoras and the Pythagorean golden age represented his lost paradise, when faith and reason were one, and the "unitary source of inspiration" for prophet, poet, and philosopher were still taken for granted. This "heroic age" of science was ended, according to Koestler, by a failure of nerve and a flight into mysticism, after Plato had laid "a curse on astronomy whose effects were to last till the beginning of the seventeenth century."

At the heart of his imaginative effort lay Koestler's conviction that the psychology of scientific investigation was as irrational and unpredictable as the processes of artistic discovery and the wellsprings of religious inspiration. He had attempted to describe and explain the process (with limited success) in *Insight and Outlook,* where he had advanced his theory of bisociation and the "eureka" process in science, and now he wanted to try again through a detailed study of the creative processes of a single (and singular) scientific genius, Johannes Kepler. Kepler stood at the very fulcrum of the original scientific revolution, and Koestler felt he had a special affinity with him. "K=K," he had jotted in one of his notebooks, convinced that he had many things in common with the great man, including an unhappy childhood. Kepler's life embodied

> the timeless case history of the neurotic child from a problem family . . . who feels that whatever he does is a pain to others and a disgrace to himself. How familiar it all is: the bragging, defiant, aggressive pose to hide one's terrible vulnerability; the lack of self-assurance, the dependence on others, the desperate need for approval, leading to an embarrassing mixture of servility and arrogance; the pathetic eagerness for play, which he carries with him like a portable cage . . . the exaggerated standards applied to one's own moral conduct which turn life into a long series of Falls into the ninefold inferno of guilt.[7]

Kepler possessed an argumentative nature, an urge to synthesize, and a habit of questioning everything around him that also recalled Koestler's character. Koestler's most original contribution, however, was the idea that Kepler was barely aware of the importance of his discoveries at first, for he had "sleepwalked" his way into them. "The roads by which men arrive at their insights into celestial matters," Kepler had written, "seem to me almost as worthy of wonder as these matters in themselves."[8]

Between a third and a half of the main text was devoted to Kepler, making it the longest and most thrilling section of the book. For Koestler, Kepler was the first astronomer since antiquity to attempt to describe the motions of the heavenly bodies in terms of their geometry, and to assign those motions a physical cause. "We have arrived at the point where astronomy and physics meet again, after a divorce which last two thousand years. This reunion of the two halves of the split mind produced explosive results. It led to Kepler's three Laws, the pillars on which Newton built the modern universe." Kepler had discovered that God was a mathematician and that the harmony of the spheres was a mathematical harmony. But the point for Koestler was that Kepler was barely aware of the importance of his discovery at first. He had "sleepwalked" his way into it, and to illustrate his point, Koestler cited a pregnant remark by Kepler himself: "The roads by which men arrive at their insights into celestial matters seem to me almost as worthy of wonder as these matters in themselves."

Owing to the voluminousness of Kepler's writings, Koestler was able to follow Kepler's thought processes "as in a slow motion film," and his account of how Kepler arrived at his breakthrough was a tour de force of psychological penetration, explicatory analysis, and descriptive writing. It showed more mastery of character and psychology than anything he had written since *Darkness at Noon,* and through carefully chosen quotations he was also able to demonstrate what a remarkable writer Kepler was: baroque in his arabesques and rhetorical flourishes, yet very much to the point when it came to questions of scientific theory and rational argument.

In his next section, Koestler introduced the renowned figure of Galileo, whose life had overlapped with Kepler's and who had taken up and developed some of Kepler's discoveries. But Koestler's treatment of Galileo, by contrast, was close to blasphemous. Acknowledging Galileo's mythic celebrity and scientific brilliance, he set out to demythologize him as a cold, sarcastic, querulous individual whose "vanity, jealousy and self-righteousness drove him to the brink of self-destruction." Galileo was a self-centered zealot, "wholly and frighteningly modern"—ethically neutral in his personal behavior and a pioneer in divorcing moral from intellectual values.

Just as Koestler had indentified a part of his younger self with Kepler, so was there an element of settling accounts with another part of his younger self in his harsh treatment of Galileo, who was the idol of progressives everywhere (including the younger Koestler) and had been sanctified in Brecht's play *Galileo*. The author of the standard work on Galileo's trial, Giorgio de Santillana, had actually drawn a comparison between Galileo and Rubashov, and Koestler himself had compared the OGPU with the Inquisition. But Koestler no longer felt much sympathy for the Rubashovs of this world and found himself arguing (astonishingly for one with his reputation) that the Inquisition was not nearly as bad as it was painted—at least in Galileo's case. "One of the points that I have labored in this book is the unitary source of the mystical and scientific modes of experience, and the disastrous results of their separation. It is my conviction that the conflict between the church and

Galileo (or Copernicus) was not inevitable; that it was not in the nature of a fatal collision between opposite philosophies of existence . . . but rather a clash of individual temperaments aggravated by unlucky coincidences."

That clash, according to Koestler, did have dire consequences, however. Since Galileo's time, science, unfettered by faith, had "carried the species to the brink of physical self-destruction" and simultaneously into an "unprecedented spiritual impasse." Why had the word *purpose* been banished from the vocabulary of science? It didn't necessarily have to be connected to an anthropomorphic deity.[9]

It's unlikely *The Sleepwalkers* would have attracted anywhere near as much attention if its author hadn't been a famous novelist, and it fared much better with readers than Koestler had dared to hope, even making it onto the best-seller lists for a while. The book's popularity was helped by the fact that Koestler's narrative method hadn't really changed. It was still novelistic: informal, chatty, laced with homely metaphors and similes and quotations from Shakespeare, Milton, and Goethe sprinkled among the scientific sources. It was also highly iconoclastic, showing no great reverence for the giants of antiquity, and weighing their virtues and vices as if they were from the family next door or down the street. This approach, more commonplace now, was daringly new in 1959, and highly controversial.

Sample views were that in "this whale of a book," Koestler had produced "a searching inquiry that puts an old story into a vivid new perspective." It was "a brilliant and beautifully written re-creation of the psychological process of discovery," with explanations of astronomical theory that were "so ingenious that even the most lunkheaded layman can follow him about the heavens with no more than reasonable effort." His biographies of individual astronomers were "vivid, exciting, largely convincing and based on a great deal of hard work." Koestler had absorbed as much information about his four central characters "as any man living," and even some specialist critics expressed sympathy for Koestler's goal of dramatizing and demystifying scientific discovery, noting that Koestler was the first major author to bring literary methods of character analysis to the task of understanding the creative process of scientists.

Specialists, however, charged Koestler with disrespect. They felt that his trenchant and provocative style and taste for "bold speculation" had caused him to overreach, especially in the case of Copernicus and Galileo, and they generally rejected his theory that scientists had displayed hubris in divorcing science from faith. Unfortunately, the bitterest attack on *The Sleepwalkers* came from Santillana and Stillman Drake, the world's two foremost experts on Galileo, who accused Koestler of calling the founding fathers of the scientific revolution "moral dwarfs, antisocial schemers, cowards, liars, hypocrites, irresponsible cranks or contemptuous snobs" and concluded that Koestler's thesis was "utterly repugnant to everything we have written, and in contradiction with all that we have learned in the course of years devoted to these studies."

There's little doubt that this broadside by two noted specialists had a decidedly negative effect on Koestler's reputation among scientists. It was later demonstrated that they had misquoted Koestler (especially on the "moral dwarfs" question) and had made many errors of their own. More recently, Koestler's analysis of Galileo has found support in at least two scholarly studies of the subject and has come to seem much less outlandish than before, and it has been acknowledged, not least by Thomas Kuhn, that Koestler's ideas on the nature and manner of scientific discovery prefigured in many ways the central argument of Kuhn's celebrated book *The Structure of Scientific Revolutions,* published three years later, on the centrality of paradigm shifts in scientific progress. Meanwhile Koestler's scintillating chapters on Kepler were later excerpted and issued as a separate book, *The Watershed,* which took on a life of its own, and although Koestler's thesis was regarded as exaggerated at the time, his basic point that the processes of discovery in science are different from those of testing and confirmation was later upheld. The problem, as with so much of what Koestler wrote, was the polemical zeal with which he expressed his ideas. If, as Hook had said, he could recite the two times table in such a way as to antagonize his audience, his rehearsal of the history of cosmology and the relationship between science and faith was bound to infuriate the experts, even when he had right on his side.[10]

KOESTLER HAD TAKEN PAINS to be away when the first reviews of *The Sleepwalkers* came out—a couple of thousand miles away, in fact, on a lecture tour of India and Japan sponsored by the Congress for Cultural Freedom. The CCF hoped that Koestler's worldwide reputation as an anti-Communist would strengthen its cause in a region where liberal democratic ideas seemed to be faring badly, and although Koestler had been extremely reluctant to begin with, he changed his mind after the CCF agreed that he could conduct some research of his own as well. In view of his increased interest in the connections between science and religion, he was eager to learn more about the spiritual practices of the East. In this he was also ahead of the curve. Though Alan Watts's pioneering book *The Way of Zen* had come out just before his departure, the Beats and the Beatles had yet to descend on the ashrams of India, and there were still very few yoga studios in Haight-Ashbury or Greenwich Village. With his journalist's nose for the zeitgeist, Koestler sniffed a trend, and his reporter's heart quickened. Having abandoned all interest in the commissar, he was eager to learn more about the yogi.[11]

Arriving in India on almost the last day of 1958, he had been rocked on his heels (like so many others) by the heat and squalor of Bombay. The sewers had been opened for the tide to wash the sewage away, and the almost lifeless heaps of rags and bones on the sidewalks reminded him of the "emaciated corpses dug out of the mass graves of Auschwitz." Once settled he spent most of his time giving lectures and talking to local authors and journalists, but also found time to inspect yoga institutes and interview psychiatrists, who he seemed to think held the key to the Indian character. He would doggedly rise at four or five in the morning, spend long days in meetings, and work on his notes often until midnight; but his main goal, which was to visit a variety of holy men and women and form an understanding of Indian religion, he never lost sight of, and as soon as he could he flew to Madras to interview a holy man named Sri Sankaracharya of Kanchi Kamakoti Peetam at his temple.[12]

"Last night I spent two hours with a true saint," he wrote afterward to Cynthia. Sri Sankaracharya had "a gentle, saintly personality, lovable and loving, peaceful and peace-giving," and an exquisite, childlike smile "that made one want to weep." He was well informed about the contemporary world, including Aldous Huxley's writing on mystical experiences, but wrapped himself in traditional Hindu theology and answered Koestler's questions with riddles. When Sri Sankaracharya asked Koestler what he was looking for, Koestler told him, "the survival of spiritual values in a rapidly changing world." Sankaracharya asked him if he had come to India to "guide" the people, and Koestler said no, his own influence was negligible.[13]

Sankaracharya had a point, however. Koestler naively thought he could travel about the country as an anonymous pilgrim without drawing too much attention to himself, but as in Israel and New York, he himself was news, and his visit was covered at considerable length in the Indian press. He seemed genuinely surprised to find himself a celebrity. "Amazingly," he wrote to Cynthia incredulously, "everybody has read my books." His fame backfired when he visited Trivandrum, the capital of Communist-ruled Kerala, to interview another holy man, Swami Krishna Menon Atmananda. Koestler experienced a distinct frisson flying into "communist terrority," and again when he discovered a Soviet trade delegation sitting in the hotel dining room, but this gave way to outrage when he was evicted from his room and made to sleep on a cot in the lounge, where he felt "like a rare animal in the zoo." His hosts had failed to book him a room in advance, and there was only one decent hotel in the city. Unable to sleep or read, he was pestered by a stream of unwanted visitors, including a local journalist who tried to get him to make a political statement. Koestler refused but cut short his visit, prompting a headline in the local opposition paper announcing that Koestler had been "run out of town" by the Communists to spare the Soviet trade delegation undue embarrassment.[14]

Koestler was assiduous in carrying out his personal program. After meeting with one "female saint," Anandamayee Ma, at her "filthy" ashram in Calcutta, he made a quick expedition to Delhi to meet Radhakrishna, paid a flying visit to the Yogic Research Center in Poona, and undertook a bone-shaking cross-country drive to Dohad and Dungarpur in Rajasthan to spend a couple of days with Sri Vinoba Bhave, Gandhi's spiritual heir. India was "more exciting than I had ever dreamt," he told Cynthia, but, as usual, he was disenchanted with its official religion. Hinduism had degenerated "from a philosophy to depressing idolatry and crass superstition." Still, "the non-orthodox have a spiritual vision and depth unknown in Europe. It is, alas, not exportable."[15]

Squatting on an uncomfortable cushion to listen to Bhave address his followers, Koestler concluded that Bhave was the real thing. He had "that curious gift of radiating peace which is physically felt like a laying on of hands, of making people feel enriched by his mere presence." Gurus had died out in Europe, but in India the tradition was still alive. "It was the secret of India's greatness," he later wrote, the emotional yeast by which its great gurus, from Buddha to Gandhi, had kept the race in spiritual fermentation. Koestler spent several days with Bhave and his disciple, Jayaprakesh Narayan, whose homegrown socialism, based on empowering village communes, appealed to Koestler as strongly as Bhave's spiritual message. The politics of India, it turned out, interested him more than its religions.[16]

Eventually the rigors of traveling in India and of smiling and shaking hands day after day began to wear thin, especially as his research goals and the goals of his CCF hosts began to diverge more and more. After several weeks of worsening relations with the officials delegated to look after him and with the local press, he abruptly refused to give any more interviews, sending his hosts into a spin. At their insistence he agreed to give a talk on "Literature and Ideology" in Calcutta, and then, after a week's rest at the Assam home of Verrier Elwin, a gentle ex-Anglican clergyman and Gandhian with an Indian wife, he set off for Bangkok, Hong Kong, and Tokyo.

IN TOKYO, he spent his first few days "in a colorful haze of euphoria." Strolling along the Ginza, festooned with balloons and streamers and thronged with eager shoppers and shiny cars, was like "being taken to a toyshop in one's childhood." He was particularly impressed with Japanese refinement, the ceremonial meals, the kneeling waitresses in their brightly colored kimonos in "an atmosphere with an erotic flicker like the crisp sparks from a comb drawn through a woman's hair." Soon enough, he passed through his usual cycle from euphoria to disillusionment, concluding that geisha girls were disappointingly "pseudo-erotic" and that the robotic demeanor of Japanese tour guides and tourists suggested a sinister underside to Japanese politeness and self-discipline. The crazy wrestling matches in the Tokyo subway, the nightmare vision of a citizenry hustling back and forth in smog masks worn on days of high humidity, and the cacophony of a million transistor radios grated on his nerves even more than the crowding and poverty of India.[17]

Unlike in India, the language barrier prevented him from penetrating much beneath the public surface. Herbert Passin, an American anthropologist, arranged for Koestler to be accompanied by an attractive young interpreter, Yoshie Nakajima, who noted Koestler's "streak of melancholy" and surprising air of defenselessness. The British writer Quentin Crewe took him to a Buddhist temple just outside Kyoto, but the ensuing discussion about the tenets and practices of Zen Buddhism proved to be an exercise in frustration. Koestler had hoped to draw comparisons with Indian and western religious beliefs, but the monks answered his questions (rather as Sri Sankaracharya had done in India) with koans and riddles. "Is there a metaphysic in Zen?" "No." "Is there a judgment between good and evil?" "None." "Why then is Zen not immoral?" "By Zen you cross into a world where good, evil, and beauty do not exist, and having seen this, you are free to come back to this world and see that they do not exist here either."

Koestler attempted to play the monks at their own game, coming up with parables of his own to match theirs, but just as they had "answered logic with parables," they now "answered parables with logic," and when it came to direct questions about their means of support, the chief priest simply lied: "We live by mendicancy—two or three of us go out into the street, but we don't beg, we just happen to have a bowl in our hands into which people happen to put money." Having delivered himself of this whopper, the priest announced that the visitors' logical questions "embarrass us" and cut the interview short.[18]

Koestler was determined not to repeat the political problems he had experienced in India, but the vexed subject of Japanese attitudes to communism betrayed him into a Kerala-type scandal again. Shortly before Koestler was scheduled to address a meeting of the Japanese PEN Club, Boris Pasternak was awarded the Nobel Prize for Literature and was forced to renounce it by the Soviet government. International PEN and numerous centers sent protests, but the Japanese PEN Center's diplomatic statement was so opaque it provoked a protest from three foreign members (Ivan Morris, Father Josef Roggendorf, and Edward Seidensticker), and Koestler wrote an open letter to Japanese PEN canceling his planned appearance there.[19]

The letter was splashed on all the front pages of Japan's leading newspapers and created a furor. Japanese PEN replied that the foreigners' interpretation was a mistake, based on their misunderstanding of the Japanese language, but this subterfuge fooled no one. Typically, Koestler's gesture managed to infuriate his CCF hosts as well. "The SOB has given us a black eye," Mike Josselson complained to Lasky, and concluded that it had been a mistake to send Koestler in the first place. But he was wrong, for Koestler's presence acted as a kind of litmus test. As the controversy rumbled on, the

CCF discovered that its own ranks were replete with fellow travelers, and it took Passin months to sort out the CCF's operation in East Asia.[20]

ON HIS RETURN TO ENGLAND, Koestler wrote three articles for *The Observer* on the problems of poverty in India and the progressive policies of the Bhoodan Movement, led by Bhave and Narayan. The articles led to the formation of a Friends of Bhoodan Committee, organized and funded by the ever generous David Astor, and Koestler invited Narayan, "a prince among Indians," to come to London for three weeks at Koestler's expense. He hoped that an urban version of the Bhoodan Movement might help the homeless in teeming cities such as Bombay and Calcutta and arranged for Narayan to lead a seminar, organized and paid for by the CCF, with Polanyi, E. F. "Fritz" Schumacher, Salvador de Madariaga, and Koestler himself among the participants. The Bhoodan Committee soon faded into oblivion, but Fritz Schumacher was inspired to travel to India and later wrote his groundbreaking best seller, *Small Is Beautiful*. Koestler's part in that development was small but honorable.[21]

Narayan's visit gave Koestler an excuse to postpone the book he had promised to write about his journey, but the real reason for his delay was a reluctance to grapple with the complexities of India and Japan and a sense that he had failed in his mission to understand their religions. He asked Quentin Crewe to write it with him, but Crewe was planning a book of his own and there was no one else available. Popping "happy pills" three or four times a week, Koestler spent ten to eleven hours a day on the book and managed to complete it in four months, delivering the final manuscript exactly on time in May 1960. He called it *The Lotus and the Robot*.

When it appeared that fall, readers didn't know what to make of it. There was far less reportage than a travel book promised, with far less description of people and places, and much more analysis and commentary. It was shaped as a quest for enlightenment, and it was clear that Koestler liked the Indians but disliked India, and disliked the Japanese but liked Japan. In the Indian section Koestler did justice to the four "Hindu saints" he had met during his travels, and to Narayan and Bhave, but the focus was on India's unique religious practice (which just happened to be the object of most western interest and envy) of Hatha yoga. Based on his research, Koestler concluded that the yoga so widely admired and studied in the west was a radically bowdlerized version of the real thing, and in a chapter called "Yoga Unexpurgated," he offered an unsparing account of physiological exercises that seemed to reflect an obsession with bowel movements and seminal fluids. At their most extreme, yoga disciples were supposed to be able to suck liquids up into their anuses and retract semen from uteruses back into the penis from which it had been discharged.

Japan's Zen Buddhism got more or less similar treatment. Though Koestler felt more at home in Japan's modern, materialistic culture than in chaotic, spiritual India, he met virtually no individuals who impressed him as much as the holy men in India, and his narrative was correspondingly less rich. The more he tried to place Zen under a microscope, the more it baffled him. "Zen knows no god, no afterlife, no good and no evil," he wrote, paraphrasing his conversation with the Kyoto abbots. "It has no doctrine or holy writ, its teaching is transmitted mainly in the form of parables." Zen was "an existentialist hoax, a web of solemn absurdities, a form of psychotherapy for a self-conscious, shame-ridden society." It worked beautifully for the Japanese but had nothing vital to offer the West.

He concluded provocatively that India and Japan were "spiritually sicker" and "more estranged from a living faith" than the West. "Our cherished habit of contrasting the contemplative and spiritual East with the crude materialism of the West is based on a fallacy. The contrast is not between spirituality and materialism, but between two basically different philosophies." The East was less interested in factual knowledge and the workings of the outer world than the West. It had experienced no equivalent of the Renaissance and no scientific revolution and preferred "intuition to reason, symbols to concepts, self-realization through the annihilation of the ego to self-realization through the unfolding of individuality."[22]

Such sweeping generalizations would be hard to make in that form now, but they had sufficient truth in them to make readers sit up and take notice (and some recent studies have confirmed Koestler's thesis). Two long chapters, "Yoga Unexpurgated" and "The Stink of Zen," appeared as separate essays in *Encounter* and with their uncompromising assertions and physiological detail stirred a fierce controversy even before the book's publication. Ann Fleming, the wife of Ian Fleming, the creator of James Bond, urged Evelyn Waugh to be sure to read Koestler's piece. "If you are sufficiently versed in that art, you never when mating leave the stuff in the woman, it is too valuable, you take it back into yourself and it strengthens your body and your mind. Thunderbird [Ian Fleming] is very excited about it."[23]

It was the controversial nature of the subject matter that distracted attention from the book's literary values, packed as it was with analogies, images, and aphorisms that were vintage Koestler. "There is more peace to be had in Manhattan than in any Indian town or village, temple or shrine." Indian villages were "sunk in protoplasmic apathy." A middle-aged professor "naked to the navel is an unusual sight." "The Hindu pantheon knows no Eros; his place is occupied by Kama, the prime force of desire." "Life in Japan may be compared to a scented bath which gives you electric shocks at unexpected moments" (this was the phrase singled out by Sidney Hook as more instructive than a whole guidebook). A row of trees in a Tokyo park looked "like a procession of invalids walking on crutches." Satori was "a wonderfully rubbery concept," and Zen was "at best an existentialist hoax, at worst a web of solemn absurdities."

It would be absurd, of course, to suppose that after six weeks in each country, Koestler could return with definitive answers to the questions he raised about ethics and religion in either India or Japan, or that after mere months of investigation he might plumb the depths of yoga or Zen. The book was an example of impressionistic reportage, with the strengths and weaknesses of the genre. Koestler's particular strength as a commentator was that he laid his cards on the table and didn't pretend to be anything other than he was. He wasn't an orientalist, nor an initiate into the occult, nor a believer in eastern religions, but neither was he hostile or unwilling to listen and learn. Even those critics who distrusted his generalizations appreciated his respect for facts and his fidelity to the evidence of his eyes and ears. As the science writer Reginald Kapp wrote to Koestler, the true value of *The Lotus and the Robot* was that it confronted the cleavage between eastern and western modes of thought with total frankness, and warned against easy solutions.

Critics of the book disliked this idea and accused Koestler of neocolonialism. William Empson called him an "ugly European," first cousin to the "ugly American" of evil renown, but Koestler wasn't inclined to praise the West either. "I feel the same resentment of [Coca-colonization] as the Asian traditionalist," he wrote, even in Europe. "I loathe processed bread in cellophane, processed towns of cement and glass, and the bible processed as a comic strip; I loathe neon and subtopia, the Organization Man and *Reader's Digest*. But who coerced us into buying all this? The United States does not rule Europe as the British ruled India; it waged no opium war against us to force the revolting "coke" down our throats. Europe bought the whole package because it wanted it. The Americans did not americanize us—they were merely one step ahead on the road towards a global civilization with a standardized style of living, which, whether we like it or not, is beginning to emerge all over the world. For we live in a state of cultural osmosis where influences percolate across the porous frontiers, native traditions wane, and the movement towards a uniform, mechanized, stereotyped culture-pattern has become irresistible."

Cyril Connolly praised the book, which led to a reconciliatory lunch at Janetta's house shortly afterward. D. J. Enright, a longtime British resident of the Far East, found it refreshing that, unlike most recent travelers to Asia, Koestler had conspicuously failed to return with easy answers to hard questions. C. G. Jung praised the book as "a meritorious as well as a needful act of debunking," and James Burnham was moved to write to Koestler that he was "just about the world's best journalist," a term, he said, that had "an entirely positive meaning in my lexicon."[24]

CHAPTER FORTY-ONE

THE SQUIRE OF ALPBACH

*[He] is not ashamed of inconsistency. It is one of the many things
I like him for.*

—E. M. FORSTER

KOESTLER'S RESEARCHES into Copernicus and Kepler had reawakened
memories of his childhood and drawn him back to the German-speaking
part of Europe. Austria had been freed of partial Russian occupation in the
fall of 1955, and when the Austrian publisher Otto Molden invited him to
take part in the 1957 European Forum, organized by the Austrian College in
Alpbach, Koestler was eager to see the country for himself.

The college was made to measure for someone with Koestler's views. It
had been started by a group of Austrian intellectuals from the resistance,
whose goal was to promote an anti-Communist and pro-American united
Europe. Molden was allied with Torberg, now editing the CCF journal
Forum in Vienna, and was married to the daughter of the CIA chief, Allen
Dulles. He was aided by his brother Fritz, Otto's partner in their family publishing firm. One further advantage of the European Forum was that, despite the college's political mission, its forums were usually about one or
another aspect of science and were often organized by Misi Polanyi, the hy-
peractive chair of the CCF's Committee on Science and Freedom.[1]

Koestler and Polanyi traveled to Alpbach together, and Koestler was en-
chanted by what he found. Perched high in the Tyrolean Alps, Alpbach reminded him of the picture-perfect villages he had hiked to as a schoolboy in
Baden. He stayed at the Böglerhof, a rambling, rustically styled hotel in the
central square, where forum participants gathered to drink and talk in the
bar at night, and Koestler quickly made friends with the rambunctious pho-

tographer and filmmaker Wolfgang Pfaundler, a short, stocky man with an explosive ego to match Koestler's and an equally high tolerance for alcohol.

Best of all, Koestler fell in love again—following an incident that would have sounded contrived in one of his novels. As he was leaving the Böglerhof by the revolving door, he locked eyes with a self-confident young woman marching in from the opposite direction. Continuing around until he was back inside, Koestler followed her to her table, introduced himself, and sat down. After a short conversation he said theatrically, "I will buy a house here because you are here." It was a corny line, easily recognized as a come-on, but she chose to be flattered and tentatively agreed to help him look for something suitable.

The attractive young woman with cropped hair and high cheekbones was Eva Auer, a painter from Vienna. Her husband, Alexander "Atti" Auer, was the general secretary of Molden's European Foundation and in charge of organizing the Alpbach conferences. Eva spent every summer in Alpbach and knew it intimately. The next day she took Koestler on a tour of the village, and he was like a moonstruck schoolboy. Nothing like this had happened since his infatuation with Janetta. Eva even resembled Janetta in some ways. Rich, self-possessed, and cosmopolitan, with the independent manner of someone who completely knew her own mind, Eva was no cinderella. She was a natural, spontaneous, and outspoken person without a trace of shyness or pretension.

The fact that she was married and had two little girls aged five and three seemed to make little difference to either of them. Atti was a civil servant, depressed by health problems and away in Vienna most of the time, and his marriage to Eva had become largely one of convenience. Since the children spent their days in kindergarten or with a nanny, Eva had plenty of time on her hands and took full advantage of it. "For me it was like a crash. I fell instantly in love with him, and the next ten days were like a whirlwind," she said later. For the rest of the week they were inseparable, and by the time Koestler left they were probably lovers.[2]

"WAIT FOR ME TO CALL YOU," Eva had said when they parted, and Koestler returned to England in "a bittersweet daze, homesick for Alpbach, for Austria, and lost youth." Eva was "not at all my type," yet it was a "friendly torture" to think of her. "Oh, Österreich, oh, Eva!" he exclaimed to his diary. Under the spell of his infatuation he was even pleased to see Cynthia, but his benevolence evaporated when he learned that she was pregnant yet again. Her coil had failed to work. Koestler got McGlashan to persuade Cynthia that she and Koestler should spend more time apart, and Cynthia meekly agreed.[3]

Koestler now started to wonder if he should sell Long Barn. He had been in the house less than a year and had spent a small fortune on repairs, but the place was big and expensive and trapped him alone in the country with Cynthia. He decided to buy a place in Alpbach, spending his winters at Montpelier Square and his summers in Austria. He arranged a rendezvous with Eva in Paris and took her for a wild night out at some of his favorite Russian nightspots. Eva was an ardent admirer of all things Russian (Koestler suspected her of being soft on the Soviets), and he regaled her with stories about his travels in the Soviet Union. He asked her to marry him—the fourth time he had proposed to a woman in four years. Eva said no. She was a Catholic and wouldn't dream of leaving her husband and children. Besides, divorce was terribly "low class."[4]

From then on their cozy interlude started to go downhill. Eva suffered severe guilt pangs and insisted on going to church. Koestler read that Camus had been awarded the Nobel Prize for Literature and felt an irresistible stab of jealousy but "got over it." Still, he drank too much at a party thrown by George Weidenfeld and "slept alone" before returning to London with "death in my heart." Sensing his misery, Cynthia was sweetness incarnate, but that only increased his unhappiness. "Where do she and I go from here?" he wrote in his diary, referring to Cynthia. He had cut himself off from many friends because Cynthia wasn't *"sortable"* (presentable). She was too shy, too limited in education and intellect, and too plain for him to want to show her off, but now he was stuck with her. Cynthia felt the change keenly. He was disloyal, distant, and unfeeling, she said, which he conceded was "partly true," but he felt he couldn't help himself, and his diary for the period is punctuated with references to "depression re Cynthia," "heart to heart talk with Cynthia," "row with Cynthia." By the end of the year he felt they had landed in "a cul-de-sac," from which not even McGlashan could rescue them.[5]

Koestler went back to Vienna to see Eva again and revisited some of the haunts of his youth, but he met only two people he knew from former times and realized that nostalgia was pointless and there was no way to pick up the old threads again. He also got news of his relatives in Hungary. The Somló family had escaped during the Hungarian Revolution and were now living in Vienna. They sent their daughter Eva to Koestler's hotel to beg for some money, but he was so put off by her greed and fake protestations of closeness that he refused. Another cousin was luckier. Agnes Aczel was the granddaughter of his aunt Zsanett, who had sheltered Adele during the war. She told him hair-raising stories about life in Communist Hungary and her escape across the heavily mined border when pregnant. Koestler hugged her and slipped some money into her overcoat pocket, which she found only when she got back to her lodgings. A few months later, she and her husband emigrated to Venezuela.[6]

Koestler was now fixated on getting a house in Alpbach. "A foothold on the continent is as important to me as air and water, otherwise I'm only half alive." Austria represented his childhood, he told Eva, and it seemed "right and proper to return to my roots, even when my old friends are gone. Anyway, after fifty you have to make new friends so as not to ossify." The Böglerhof, where he had stayed during his first visit, was owned by Alpbach's energetic and autocratic mayor, Alfons Moser, and Moser found him a plot at the highest and westernmost point of the village, on a steep slope looking out over Alpine meadows and pine woods to the snowcapped crags of the Schatzberg and Grosse Galtenberg mountains. It had the same wild and lonely feel as Wales, only with more grandeur, and Koestler accepted it on the spot.

The land belonged to Otmar Radinger, a short, blocky farmer with a powerful handshake and piercing blue eyes. Under Moser's paternal gaze, Radinger was ready to sell at a fair price. Koestler took out a pocket compass and staked out the foundations so that the four sides of the house would face north, south, east, and west. Pfaundler found him a builder, and Eva recommended an architect. Koestler wanted to use hardwoods and expensive imported tiles for the house, but Moser insisted that all new construction in the village had to be in the vernacular Tyrolean style, and Koestler reluctantly complied.

Throughout the spring and early summer of 1958, with a great deal of assistance from Eva and Pfaundler, Koestler concentrated on getting the house started, and in midsummer he and Cynthia returned so he could supervise the process himself. The Alpbach Foundation had put up a spanking new Congress House for the college in glass and steel, with modern accommodations at the back, and though Koestler privately regarded it as a monstrosity, he preferred its anonymity to the Böglerhof. Free of all writing for a while, he was able to revel in the mountain air, the gorgeous scenery, and the Alpine vistas and to relish the prospect of owning a house in this Tyrolean paradise. Pfaundler lived in nearby Innsbruck and had a profound knowledge of the art, architecture, customs, and folklore of the Tyrolean region. He spent hours explaining the psychology and the folkways of the Tyrolean peasants to Koestler and teaching him the local customs and dialect. Koestler was warned that Pfaundler was also a nationalist who had blown up pylons in the South Tyrol (awarded to Italy after World War II) and had almost gone to jail for it. But this endeared him to Koestler all the more. Indifferent to the politics of it, Koestler secretly admired Pfaundler's spunk, much as he had admired the spunk of the Irgun and the Stern Gang.

Another kind of pleasure was to be derived from hobnobbing with the distinguished scholars and public figures who came to Alpbach for the conferences. One day he ran into an old flame from Palestine, Annemarie "Anny" Bertel, now married to the eminent German biochemist and Nobel Prize winner Erwin Schrödinger. Schrödinger also had a summer house in Alpbach and Koestler was dying to meet him (he had interviewed Schrödinger for Ullstein long ago in Berlin), but Schrödinger was famously irascible, so Koestler asked Eva to go with him when invited. Eva was then presented with the unusual sight of Koestler acting like a bashful schoolboy and seeming lost for words, with an imploring look on his face that begged her to help him out. But Schrödinger was gracious and the two men hit it off. Learning that Schrödinger was terrified of wasps, Koestler purchased a fly-swatter in Innsbruck and the following year presented it to Schrödinger and demonstrated how to use it—a demonstration caught by Pfaundler for an album of photographs about Alpbach.

Koestler's affair with Eva became the talk of the village. Atti, still commuting back and forth from Vienna, seemed to tolerate it easily enough. Eva was used to leading a bohemian life and somehow managed to combine devout Catholicism with considerable sexual freedom, which put her on equal terms with Koestler. But Cynthia found the situation intolerable. With scant knowledge of Austria and no knowledge of the German language, she was a complete outsider in Alpbach, relegated more firmly than ever to her role as Koestler's secretary and excluded almost completely from his intimate and emotional life. When Eva Zeisel turned up from New York and Marietta Torberg from Vienna, both powerful and attractive women with strong personalities and opinions, Cynthia faded even more completely into the background.[7]

In the summer of 1959, Koestler sold Long Barn to the London real estate developer Max Rayne and returned to Alpbach with Cynthia to supervise the finishing of the house himself. It was surrounded by a sea of mud when they arrived but just about habitable, and he spent the rest of the summer consulting with contractors and craftsmen to construct the perfect Tyrolean chalet. The result was a picturesque Alpine house with a gently pitched tiled roof and wide eaves overhanging balconies edged with flower boxes that looked as if they had been there forever. The windows faced south and west, with glorious views of the village and the mountains in the distance. In the months to come, Koestler equipped the huge, open-plan living room with an antique tiled stove and an open fireplace and furnished it with a mixture of painted peasant furniture and Italian antiques. On the floor above he arranged for the construction of a wood-paneled study with an antique English desk and built-in bookcases, and hung a huge portrait of Mamaine on the wall. The master bedroom contained a tiled stove, a huge Austrian peasant bed, and a horsehair mattress given to him by Eva.[8]

Koestler also made a new arrangement with Cynthia. In London he moved her from his "bachelor's fortress" in Montpelier Square into a rented apartment in nearby Thurloe Place. Henceforth she would still be his secretary, housekeeper, cook, and consort of choice in England but would defer to Eva when in Alpbach. For her there was a small unheated bedroom in the attic.[9]

THIS STATE OF AFFAIRS suited Koestler perfectly but took little account of Cynthia's feelings and led to a succession of "depressing rows" with Cynthia in Alpbach that cast almost the only shadow on his new paradise, until, sitting with Eva one evening at the Böglerhof, he was subjected to another disagreeable surprise. They were at their favorite table in the lounge when Koestler suddenly exclaimed, "Oh, my God!" and stared out the window. Eva followed his gaze and saw a tall, skinny blonde teetering up the hill in a frilly dress and high heels, looking "like a stranded pink flamingo." It was Janine. "You've got to help me," said Koestler. "You can't leave me alone with that woman. Promise you'll stay and have dinner with us."

Janine offered that she just happened to be passing that way and had dropped in to see him, but her real reason for coming was to tell Koestler she was separating from Paul Graetz and wanted Koestler to take a greater interest in Cristina. Koestler wouldn't budge. Janine was "sweet but trying" and as always too much for him to handle, and all he could do was stonewall her. Janine and her husband eventually decided against a legal separation to "shield" Cristina from the consequences, and Janine informed Koestler in excruciating detail about Cristina's behavior, character, and education, to which Koestler responded with a stony silence.[10]

But that was a mere blot on his delightful new life, and the compensations that summer included a long-promised visit from Whittaker Chambers and his wife, Esther. In Alpbach on the night of Chambers's arrival, they had a "glorious dinner and drinks till 3 a.m.," switching between English and German and reminiscing about their party days. *"Wir sind einfach paganische Dichter,"* Chambers told Koestler, *"und das ist alles* [We are simply pagan poets, and that's all]*."* Koestler told Chambers the story of his escape from France, the dose of morphine he had shared with Walter Benjamin, and Benjamin's death in Spain the night before he was due to be "allowed to escape." In the light of episodes like these, said Koestler, it was hard to take the protestations of the Beat generation seriously. "What do they know of such things?"[11]

For Chambers, according to his biographer, Sam Tanenhaus, this was "a culminating moment," for Koestler was "the contemporary he esteemed above all others." Koestler summoned Grete Buber-Neumann from Frankfurt to tell Chambers about her grisly experiences in Ravensbrück and about her book on Milena Jesenská, Kafka's last love. Grete had met Milena in the camp. Koestler suggested she write the memoir and secured publication by writing an introduction. But Chambers was unwell and left Alpbach suffering from an attack of paranoia, and though he promised to return one day, he died before he could do so. In a memorial tribute published in the *National Review,* Koestler called Chambers "the most misunderstood person of our time. When he testified he knowingly committed moral suicide to atone for the guilt of our generation. The witness is gone, the testimony will stand."[12]

Back in London, Koestler got a less pleasant reminder of his party days when Alfred Kantorowicz came to see him. "Kanto" had moved to East Germany after World War II and had loudly and publicly denounced Koestler as a "highly paid expert in anti-communist ideology." After defecting to the West, he published a groveling apology and Koestler sent him a magnanimous telegram of welcome. In London Kanto refused to discuss his experiences in East Germany and launched into a diatribe against the crypto-fascists he said were blocking his employment in West Germany. Koestler meanwhile did his best to be a good host for old times' sake, but was bored by Kantorowicz's tirades and frustrated by the latter's refusal to discuss communism at all. A couple of years later Kantorowicz published a vitriolic portrait of Koestler as an arrogant fat cat, surrounded by British aristocrats and enjoying the capitalist spoils of his ill-gotten fame. He wasn't entirely off the mark, but in the light of Kantorowicz's earlier somersaults Koestler undoubtedly held the moral high ground. He replied to Kantorowicz's lampoon in notably moderate terms, which reflected his lingering attachment to his old party comrades even as he rejected them intellectually. He never heard from Kantorowicz again.[13]

IN THE SUMMER of 1960 Adele died at the ripe age of ninety. Koestler's strained relations with her had barely changed over the years, except that during the last year of her life, as a result of his Asian journey and his repeated visits to Alpbach, he had seen her hardly at all. She had continued to write with expressions of love and pride over her son's achievements and to reproach him for his neglect. "I feel abandoned, forgotten, unpopular and unloved," she exclaimed on one of her postcards, but Koestler continued to treat "my fucking mother," as he referred to her in the company of friends, as a thorn in his side. When the faithful Stevie informed him that Adele had been taken to New End Hospital in Hampstead and was probably dying, he rushed over from Alpbach, downed a couple of stiff brandies, and set off with Stevie to visit her. Adele died a couple of days later, but her demise induced no softening in the son. The following day he turned up at Lena Wickman's apartment, dead drunk and brimming with self-pity, and lashed out at his mother for this "last act of selfishness. She kept me there holding her hand till she died."[14]

Koestler asked Stevie to accompany him to the cremation in Golders Green. To Stevie's surprise, she and Koestler were the only two people present, and she wondered if he had avoided informing anyone else on purpose. Maybe Adele had outlived her friends in Adamson Road. The only other person there was Rabbi Jakob Kokotek, who had a brief conversation with Koestler before conducting the simple ceremony. It was clear that Koestler remained pitiless toward his mother to the end. Not even when she was beyond the grave could he forgive her his unhappy childhood, and he went to his own grave holding Adele responsible for all the humiliations and injuries he felt she had inflicted on him.[15]

Such private cruelty was painfully at odds with Koestler's public benevolence. A few months before Adele's death Koestler had contacted C. H. Rolph, the *New Statesman*'s legal correspondent, about a scheme Rolph was developing for the rehabilitation of discharged prisoners. Koestler's experiences with the antihanging campaign had given him the idea of establishing an annual prize (or prizes) for the best artistic work produced by prisoners who were still incarcerated. He was willing to set aside four hundred pounds a year from his royalties for the purpose, with the hope (despite his setbacks with the Fund for Free Expression) that others would support the venture as time went on.

Rolph asked him why he was doing it. "I *v*ill put it like *z*is," Rolph quotes Koestler as replying. "Zat is becoze I *v*ish a leetle cheap immortality." Koestler's cynicism was an inoculation against sentimentality. "Being in prison leaves its imprint on you for the rest of your life," he had written earlier. "This trauma can turn you into a neurotic, but it can also act as a stimulant with positive effects. The prisoner's worst enemy is boredom, depression, the slow death of thought." Koestler's goal was to make the prisoner's life more bearable, to help him acquire something that would aid him in making a new start when he left the prison behind, and perhaps to "discover hidden talents within himself."[16]

It was a novel form of rehabilitation, and Koestler hoped it might act as a spur to other types of prison reform. At the same time he insisted his name not be used for the cause ("coze") in any way. He was convinced that after the antihanging campaign his participation would infuriate the Home Office, but Rolph took Koestler to meet the assistant prison commissioner in charge of education, Charles Cape, who turned out to be an amateur poet and a fan of Koestler's writing. Cape did such a thorough job describing the bureaucratic hurdles facing them that Koestler came away convinced the scheme was a flop, but Rolph assured him he was wrong, and two years later the plan was approved.

Koestler promised to contribute a thousand pounds a year for the first ten years of the scheme and persuaded David Astor to give a lunch at the Waldorf-Astoria hotel in Aldwych to form a steering committee. Despite Koestler's protests, his name was considered indispensable by the others to attract money and attention, and the Koestler Awards, as they were called, came into existence in 1962. "I do not profess to have understood him," Rolph later wrote, "but I know that at the center of his unchangeably distorted nature was a hatred of authority, a distrust of the officials who represented it, and a certainty that all the authorities hated him. He thought the very sound of the Koestler Award must impinge upon the ears of officialdom as if it were the Lenin Award."[17]

CHAPTER FORTY-TWO

RETREAT FROM RATIONALISM?

One of the strongest motives that leads men to art and science is escape from everyday life, with its painful crudity and hopeless dreariness, and from the fetters of one's own ever-shifting desires.
— ALBERT EINSTEIN

THE LAY CRITICAL RESPONSE to *The Sleepwalkers* hadn't been at all bad, and Koestler persuaded himself that, despite the carping of the specialists, it hadn't been a mistake to start writing about science after all. He was still brimming with ideas about creativity, which he now felt needed a separate book of their own, and when invited to participate in a symposium entitled "Control of the Mind" at the University of California Medical Center in San Francisco, he jumped at the idea. He chose to regard it as a blessing on his scientific labors (though in reality he was invited as a creative writer, along with Aldous Huxley and the ubiquitous Father D'Arcy) and decided it was the perfect place to present his new theories. To help him prepare, Michael Polanyi arranged for Koestler to give three lectures on creativity at the University of Manchester, which he then compressed into a single paper for San Francisco, hoping both to test his ideas and to show his academic mettle.[1]

Paradoxically for an author who in one book had mourned the passing of the age of reason and in another eviscerated Zen with rational arguments, Koestler's concept of creativity embraced not only orthodox science but also some of the less orthodox ideas emanating from the burgeoning American counterculture of the sixties. About a year before the invitation to San Francisco, Timothy Leary had interviewed him in London and had offered to draw up his "psychic horoscope" based on psychological tests. Koestler declined, but was intrigued by Leary's offbeat ideas and stayed in touch with him. Now, on the eve of his departure for San Francisco, he received an ebullient letter from Leary informing him that "the big, new, hot issue in America is *drugs*" and inquiring if Koestler was "tuned in" to the noise.

"I stumbled on the scene in the most holy manner," wrote Leary. "Spent last summer in Mexico. Anthropologist friend arrived one weekend with a bag of mushrooms bought from a witch. Magic mushrooms. I had never heard of them, but being a good host joined the crowd who ate them. Wow! Learned more in six hours than in past sixteen years." Leary spoke of visual, intuitive, and emotional transformations and a complete reordering of his "mental and perceptual machinery." He was working with Aldous Huxley, Alan Watts, and Allen Ginsberg to explore the use of peyote and mushrooms (and their psychoactive derivatives, mescaline and psilocybin) to "expand consciousness." His "soul-wrenching mystical experience" in Mexico had reminded him of Koestler's description of a similar experience in the Seville prison, and he offered to send Koestler some mushrooms to try for himself. Hoping to keep the drugs "free and uncontrolled," Leary and Ginsberg were inviting distinguished artists, writers, and scholars to experiment with them and write about their experiences.[2]

Leary's descriptions reminded Koestler of some of the dubious mystical experiences he had heard about in India, but their chemical trappings disarmed and intrigued him, and they certainly seemed linked to creativity. He didn't need the mushrooms in London, he told Leary, but would visit him at Harvard and pursue the subject there. He planned also to visit J. B. Rhine, the head of the Parapsychology Laboratory at Duke University and the world's leading authority on ESP, to see if ESP could be incorporated into his theory of creativity, and to stop off at the University of Michigan to see James V. McConnell, an unorthodox young scientist working on a study of flatworms. The relevance of flatworms was their status as the lowest creatures on the evolutionary ladder to possess a brain and a central nervous system, and the attraction of McConnell's experiments was that they seemed to challenge neo-Darwinian views on heredity and natural selection.[3]

ARRIVING IN SAN FRANCISCO at the end of January, Koestler was delighted to find himself rubbing shoulders with distinguished psychologists, neurologists, and pharmacologists, as well as Huxley, D'Arcy, and the humorist Leo Rosten. His own paper, "Some Aspects of the Creative Process," began with his theory of humor and the concept of bisociation, and went on to show how creativity in both the arts and sciences depended on the association of formerly dissociated ideas. Fifteen hundred members of the public attended the televised final session and Koestler felt that he had acquitted himself quite well. "There was time for the others to realize gradually—and some reluctantly—that I know, more or less, what I am talking about," he wrote to Cynthia afterward. He had "learnt a lot, made new professional friendships (*and* didn't drink too much)."[4]

From San Francisco, Koestler went to Ann Arbor to learn more about McConnell's flatworms. McConnell was an enthusiastic iconoclast of a type Koestler invariably found appealing, not least because of his quirky sense of humor (Polanyi had described him in a letter to Koestler as "a bit mad" and "a man of genius"). He was the founder and sole editor of *The Worm-Runner's Digest,* "an informal journal of Comparative Psychology," which he filled with jokes, parodies, and cartoons, as well as with serious articles on scholarly subjects. His worms, according to McConnell, possessed a memory and were capable of a primitive form of learning, which, if true, undermined Darwin's theory of random mutation and natural selection and suggested that Jean-Baptiste Lamarck's views on the inheritance of acquired characteristics might have some merit after all. Koestler had a soft spot for the unorthodoxy of Lamarck and was delighted by McConnell's findings.[5]

One of McConnell's colleagues at Michigan was an unassuming young Englishman called John Pollard, who was conducting his own experiments with hallucinogens and offered to let Koestler take some under his supervision. Koestler was given eighteen milligrams of psilocybin in the form of little pink pills and installed on a couch in one of the psychology department's consulting rooms equipped with a tape recorder. Nothing happened for the first hour. Then Koestler began to see "luminous moving patterns of great beauty," followed by opulent visions resembling the "explosive paintings of schizophrenics." "If I had allowed myself I could have shared the vision of the prophet Elijah as he was swept up to heaven. But I felt this was buying one's visions on the cheap, so I forced my eyes open. No easy paths for me. I congratulated myself on my sober self-control. Mine was a rational mind, not to be fooled by little pills."

After a while, however, he lost control of his vision. The room assumed fantastic shapes and colors, and every sense seemed intensified. A standard lamp developed a bird's claws, and when Dr. Pollard entered, he underwent an incredible transformation. "His face was a sickly yellow. It was split in two like a cell dividing. A small scar on the doctor's neck was gaping wide, trying to swallow the flesh of his bulbous chin. One ear had shrunk. The other had grown several inches. He looked like a smirking, vicious devil."

For the rest of the three to four hours the experiment lasted, Koestler was still in control of his limbs, still able to get up from the couch and converse with his companions, but his perceptions went haywire, and he fell in thrall to delusions and hallucinations. "Now at last the Gestapo have got me" was one of his thoughts, or was it the KGB? He got up to touch the claws on the lamp, certain they were a mirage, but they refused to go away. It was not only a visual but also a tactile hallucination. "I suppose I took the mushrooms in the wrong state of mind," he said later. "They awakened memories of past experiences as a political prisoner, memories of torture, brainwashing, and extorted confessions." Afterward he was given a sedative and by dinnertime seemed more or less normal again, but he was still suffering from mild hallucinations and looking "terrible" when Leary met him at Logan Airport the following week.[6]

Leary took Koestler to lunch with the noted behaviorist B. F. Skinner, who said, apropos of *The Lotus and the Robot,* that Hindus should be "conditioned like animals" to give up their superstitions. The encounter seems to have been polite enough, but in years to come Skinner and behaviorism would become a prime target of Koestler's polemics. Koestler also met the cognitive psychologists Jerome and Blanche Bruner and Frank and Nancy Barron. After dinner they gathered at Leary's house, where the plan was for the others to take psilocybin pills and Koestler to observe, since he was still suffering from his bad trip in Michigan. Charles Olson was there, with one of Leary's graduate students, and Leary carefully took out an oriental box inlaid with tropical woods and counted out the pills for each person present. "I'll go along too," said Koestler impulsively and washed down ten pills with a highball.

They put Bach on the stereo and settled down to see what would happen. "This is perfection," Koestler murmured, according to Leary, and closed his eyes, assuming "a Cheshire cat smile." Again he experienced hallucinations and delusions that made the room expand and contract and assume fantastic colors, but this time the faces of his companions seemed beautiful, not distorted, and the music sounded like the music of the spheres. Olson declaimed verses about cosmic awareness, expanding consciousness, and Zen enlightenment, for all the world as if Koestler were back in the mysterious East. Koestler went to bed "giggling" and "radiating pleasure" but the following day decided that alcohol was better than mushrooms. "Alcohol is a social stimulant. It warms you up; brings you closer to people. Mushrooms are nonsocial. They whirl you inside. Bring you closer to yourself. I solved the secret of the universe last night, but this morning I forgot what it was. There's no quick and easy path to wisdom. Give me alcohol any day."[7]

Koestler spent the rest of the week reading poems and essays written by Ginsberg, Kerouac, and others under the influence of psilocybin and was unimpressed. They were "artistically worthless" and far below the level of their normal work. He also read Huxley's *The Doors of Perception* and *Heaven and Hell* and argued with Leary about Huxley's conclusions. Koestler felt that Leary and Huxley were misguided to advocate "the chemical opening of doors into Other Worlds" (Huxley's words) and were looking for a shortcut to enlightenment and grace that was illegitimate and self-defeating. This "instant mysticism" was ersatz. Puritanically, Koestler insisted that sweat and toil were the price of knowledge. There was a huge difference between those who climbed a mountain on foot—as he had done as a schoolboy—and those who went up by motorcar. "The view is the same," but "their vision is different," because of the experience of hiking up the hard way. "This pressure-cooker mysticism is the ultimate profanation."[8]

It's not clear why Koestler reacted with such skepticism to the psilocybin. He was no stranger to chemical stimulants of one kind or another and certainly had no ethical objections. The most likely explanation is that he couldn't bear the loss of self-control. Though he habitually lost control of his physical and mental faculties when drunk, the loss was gradual and incomplete, leaving him still conscious and with the illusion of control, whereas the mushroom derivative seemed to take over his mental faculties altogether. He was probably frightened by the effect, just as he had been frightened by psychoanalysis and hypnosis. Though the "oceanic feeling" still beckoned to him as the ideal mystic experience, he felt it shouldn't be self-induced, nor should it be anything more than temporary and fleeting.

Parapsychology, by contrast, though equally unorthodox, seemed much more manageable, and Koestler had a highly satisfying visit to Duke to observe experiments in ESP, telepathy, clairvoyance, and related subjects conducted by J. B. and Louisa Rhine. Koestler had been interested in Rhine's work since the early fifties and took "an immediate liking" to Rhine and his wife. "Rhine's burly figure, his broad open face, his obvious sincerity, made me think of a woodcutter" (Koestler must have forgotten his identical description of Willi Münzenberg) "yet during my whole stay I had a feeling that these admirable people were living under a cloud, have become accustomed to its shadow, and accept it as unavoidable." Koestler admired their stubbornness and courage and was sure they were right, feeling that his own experiences demonstrated the existence of telepathy, even if it couldn't be scientifically proven.[9]

From Britain, Koestler wrote to Leary that though the mushrooms wouldn't work for him, he had grown "obsessed" with the idea that they might be combined with ESP and urged him to contact Rhine as soon as possible. He had a hunch that the physiological changes wrought by Leary's mushrooms might open the door to enhanced clairvoyance, while Rhine would bring greater academic discipline to Leary's freewheeling experiments. It was Koestler's old zeal for networking in operation again, and Leary and Rhine did visit each other. Rhine sampled Leary's mushrooms at Duke, and Leary entertained Rhine at Harvard, providing large audiences for Rhine's talks on ESP. But the stiff and formal Rhine proved too stodgy for the ebullient Leary, and Leary was too erratic for any lasting collaboration to be possible.[10]

Koestler published four provocative articles on his American trip, one on his experiences with psilocybin and three on what Koestler referred to as "the poverty of psychology." In the psilocybin article, he rejected the use of psychedelic drugs for enlightenment as promoted by Huxley, Leary, and Ginsberg and described their use as uncomfortably akin to behaviorism. In "Pavlov in Retreat," he elaborated on his hostility to the behavioral sciences and expressed his belief that they represented the intrusion of Marxism into science. Behavioral techniques were a form of "brainwashing," and behaviorists were hidebound exponents of "psychiatry in the age of the juke box." In "Behold the Lowly Worm," Koestler exaggerated the success of McConnell's experiments with flatworms to assert that they provided clear evidence of the "transmission of acquired experience" and that current interpretations of Darwinism might be wrong. And in his last article, Koestler mounted a comprehensive defense of Rhine and his methods on the grounds that, although ESP seemed "contrary to modern scientific logic," it merited serious investigation.[11]

Koestler's articles were good journalism but not particularly good science and did nothing to further his academic reputation. "The idea is growing in this country that the opinions of any novelist or playwright on any cultural subject are worth hearing, and nothing ridiculous is seen in this," commented one critic acidly. Koestler retorted that of course artists had the right to talk about culture, and that when it came to science, he knew a great deal more than his critics realized. It would become his favorite refrain from then on, but no amount of repetition could change the fact that in science he was essentially an amateur among professionals and would remain so until the end of his life. The question was: Could an amateur see things that the scientist couldn't?[12]

Koestler's dogged support for ESP was particularly perverse and hurt him most of all, for the problem with ESP wasn't that it was impossible—or even improbable—but that it couldn't meet the standard of proof. Koestler's openness to ESP, it seems, was a corollary of his deep skepticism about scientific orthodoxy in general and what he regarded as the unthinking acceptance of the limits of the human mind. He approached the subject from the opposite end: Since no one had been able to *disprove* ESP, he was unwilling to deny its existence simply to conform to the conventional view.[13]

The furthest limit of his fascination with this subject was the revival of his eccentric preoccupation with levitation. Not since his experiment with Orwell and the Strausses in 1943 had he given much thought to it, but his visit to India had persuaded him to investigate the subject again, and again he had failed to turn up a shred of evidence in its favor. Now, after reading about the possibilities of losing weight through hypnotism-induced psychokinesis, he decided to purchase a large weighing machine and test this hypothesis too—though he was too embarrassed to keep it at Montpelier Square and persuaded Cynthia to have it at her apartment. He asked Rosalind Heywood, the author of *The Sixth Sense: An Inquiry into Extra-Sensory Perception* and a stalwart of the Society for Psychical Research, to help him with the experiments but to keep the whole thing secret. "It was decided to try it out a bit ourselves," according to Cynthia, and "to have a master of ceremonies to give a ritualistic and serious atmosphere to the whole undertaking."

The first session was held on December 1, 1961. The master of ceremonies was the SPR's research officer, John Cullen, an "insignificant looking little man" whose eyes became "enormous, liquid and hypnotic" as the experiment progressed. Cynthia sat in a chair on the weighing machine. Koestler put Brahms on the stereo, plied Cynthia with drink, and tried to provoke mood changes, while the unidentified hypnotist tried to exert his own influence and Heywood watched from the sidelines. "I seemed to have become lighter or heavier, according to mood," noted the suggestible Cynthia, "but then we discovered the weighing mechanism was faulty." At a second session ten days later, Heywood "went into a swoon on the chair, listening to a Mozart Violin Concerto," but "the needle did not budge" and the "jealous and over-emotional Heywood" flew into a tantrum. The scene was pure farce, but fortunately for Koestler, his plea for secrecy was observed, and the levitation experiments were allowed to lapse until he resuscitated them once more toward the end of his life.[14]

CYNTHIA'S OBSERVATIONS of these proceedings come from a diary Koestler had persuaded her to start in the spring of 1961, seemingly with McGlashan's encouragement. Whether Koestler envisaged her as Boswell to his Johnson or simply wanted to give her something to do to occupy her time is not clear, but Cynthia complied with her usual docility, doggedly chronicling Koestler's daily moods and snippets of conversation, his multifarious writing projects and related activities, the comings and goings of their numerous visitors. Cynthia found it hard work, stopped after a year, started again in response to Koestler's nagging, and kept at it, despite occasional lapses ("Bloody diary! Have written nothing since June 30" was a typical entry), for the next thirteen years. Much of the resulting journal is either mind-numbingly boring or maddeningly vague, with titillating notations like "Holger told us Karl's secret," "Arthur explained why he couldn't go to Israel," or "Arthur and Celia had their first serious conversation in years," with no indication of the content of these exchanges.

The diary is similarly devoid of self-awareness or self-analysis, demonstrating how willingly and totally Cynthia subordinated herself to Koestler. The impression she gives is of a blank slate on which Koestler wrote at will, or of an echo chamber playing back his words, giving them an eerie feel of ventriloquy—which may have been what Koestler wanted. Cynthia seems to have been aware of her deficiencies, consulting McGlashan for advice on what to put in. "Just write the kinds of things you put in your letters," he replied; she would put "Pepys, Boswell and Madame de Montesquieu permanently in the shade. Above all remember it's useless unless it's wildly indiscreet."[15]

The reputations of Pepys and Boswell remain safe, for wild indiscretion was beyond Cynthia's powers. She plodded faithfully on, recording Koestler's everyday life in Alpbach and London. It was a lot of work for such a small return but not entirely without its rewards, for Cynthia did eventually smuggle in some reflections of her own, and for certain events in Koestler's life it remains the only source.

KOESTLER CONTINUED TO labor away at his creativity opus, which somewhere along the way acquired its final title, *The Act of Creation,* but his restless mind craved other outlets too, and his reformer's instincts never slept for long. Having rejected a proposed BBC television interview about his recent work owing to his "abominable accent—I do not *vant* my readers to hear what they read overlaid by that foreigner's voice"—he began to wonder about his position in Britain in general and about spending his winters in Paris instead of London. One reason for the latter idea was his inability to take his beloved dogs to Alpbach with him. The British loved their dogs with a passion that Koestler fully shared. What he didn't share was the chauvinistic conviction that their tight little island was a uniquely disease-free canine paradise, whose only protection against the lethal sicknesses that raged "abroad" were draconian quarantine regulations. This meant that every time Koestler went to Alpbach for the summer he was obliged to leave his beloved Attila in a kennel.[16]

He decided that if he set his mind to it, he could get the government to do away with the regulations altogether. He persuaded Peregrine Worsthorne to float the idea in one of his columns for the *Sunday Telegraph* and followed it up with a long letter to the editor, quoting the World Health Organization's statistics on rabies and pointing out that the number of human deaths from dog rabies in Europe and America had been reduced to zero. The column and letter provoked a flood of replies, ranging from incendiary allegations of treason to passionate cries of support, the latter reinforced by moving testimonies to the sufferings of heartbroken dog owners (and their dogs) on being forced to part company at the frontier.

Remembering his earlier campaign against capital punishment, Koestler asked David Astor, "*Vat* is our next crusade?" and answered his own question with "dogs and *kv*arantine." Astor was not sure. Quarantining dogs was not in the same league as capital punishment. The Englishman's fear of rabies, like the Englishman's love of fox hunting, was one of those instinctive folk beliefs with deep roots in the national psyche that defied rational logic. Astor nevertheless offered Koestler a prominent page in his Sunday edition, and Koestler published an impassioned (and entirely rational) denunciation of quarantine, complete with medical background, statistical tables, and a plea for the rights of dog owners. *The Observer*'s letters columns were filled with replies, most of them expressing outrage: how dare this foreigner, who spends half his time in Austria, place all our lovely English dogs at risk?

But the Canine Defence League came out in favor of Koestler's idea of a national petition. A committee was set up with the help of Lady Beckett and Lord Arran, and eminent signatories included Sir Julian Huxley and Peter Scott, with assorted ambassadors and generals—those with a direct interest in being able to take their pets on prolonged sojourns abroad. But the government refused to budge. The House of Lords voted against the idea; the Royal Veterinary College, the Lister Institute, and the Royal Society for the Prevention of Cruely to Animals all opposed it. Koestler tried again to persuade Astor to embark on a full-blooded crusade, but Astor demurred. He published an editorial calling for an independent government inquiry and allowed Koestler space to reply to his critics but warned him to try to use "a bit of British understatement and not get too heated on such a minor subject," for it would ruin his reputation for seriousness about more important matters.[17]

The anti-quarantine campaign fizzled, but a year later Koestler got his revenge in a magnificently angry essay, "When the Daydream Has to Stop," which he contributed to Astor's "What's Left for Patriotism?" series in *The Observer*. For some time now he had begun to think of the British as "a tired-out race" and since his return from the United States had kept a file called "suicide of a nation," into which he put clippings about wildcat strikes, demarcation disputes, class conflict, and industrial decline. Now he drew on them to show that, compared with the rest of Europe, Britain was an economic basket case. Once "the world's workshop," this proud nation was now an international byword for shoddy goods and late delivery and still seemed determined to turn its back on Europe. Koestler put the blame on the private schools, the class system, and British complacency. At the very least the private schools should be abolished and the class system reformed.[18]

The article had little to do with patriotism per se—it was a cry of outraged patriotism—and *The Observer* was reputedly unhappy with it, but Astor printed the piece and it had an unexpected sequel. Shortly after its appearance, Koestler announced over lunch with Mel Lasky, "Mel, I've got a bombshell for you." Mel turned a shade paler, according to Cynthia, but "never moved a muscle." Koestler proposed a special issue of *Encounter* under the general title "Suicide of a Nation." It would develop the themes of the *Observer* series (or rather, Koestler's contribution to it) at greater length and examine the current state of Britain. Lasky was enthusiastic about the idea, though less so about the title, which Koestler insisted should be "The Lion and the Ostrich" (taking Orwell's *The Lion and the Unicorn* as his inspiration).[19]

The special issue appeared in July 1963 (and six months later as a book), with essays by a variety of contributors, including Cyril Connolly, Goronwy

Rees, Malcolm Muggeridge, Henry Fairlie, the academics Marcus Cunliffe and John Vaizey, and the MPs John Grigg and Aidan Crawley. Two thirds of the articles were devoted to negative manifestations such as the class war and Britain's difficult relations with Continental Europe, while the last third appeared under the hopeful heading "Towards a New Society?," which cautiously attempted to look for a silver lining among the clouds, though without a great deal of conviction.

It was a characteristic exercise in British self-flagellation, and in his introduction, Koestler drove his message home. The average Briton was a cross between the lion and the ostrich. "In times of emergency he rises magnificently to the occasion. In between emergencies he buries his head in the sand." Contemporary Britain was fixated on past glories and handcuffed by class war, the rule of the "mediocracy," the cult of the amateur, and inveterate isolationism. In his postscript, he tried to sound a more hopeful note. Nationalism in Western Europe was dead. A liberal and modestly progressive society was coming into being, and there was hope for the future in the "silent generation" of younger people, but he didn't sound very convinced—or convincing.[20]

KOESTLER CLEARLY COULDN'T KEEP his promise not to write about politics at all, and recent events had given his views on communism a fresh topicality. In October 1961, Khrushchev had given his sensational speech denouncing the crimes of Stalin and admitting that torture had been used to extract the confessions of party leaders at their show trials in the thirties. This prompted the Polish émigré journalist Kot Jeleński to accuse Koestler of conferring on the confessions (in *Darkness at Noon*) "a sinister dignity which they did not altogether possess." Stalin's methods were entirely old-fashioned—"torture and the bait of peaceful dachas"—and psychology had very little to do with it.

Koestler responded in a radio interview with George Urban that he had never claimed that *everybody* had confessed for psychological and ideological reasons, only the hard core of the Bolshevik old guard. They were "great men" in their way, who had succumbed neither to bribery nor to torture. They had died because of their sense that human reason had "run amok," while unable to escape the logic of their faith. Koestler cited the evidence of friends such as Eva Zeisel and Alex Weissberg (without naming them) and of General Krivitsky, the former head of the Fourth Bureau of the Red Army, who had described almost identical scenes of interrogation to those Koestler had depicted in *Darkness at Noon,* without even knowing about the book.

A different critique of *Darkness at Noon* came from Koestler's old friend John Strachey. Discussing the work of Koestler, Orwell, Whittaker Chambers, and Pasternak, Strachey suggested that the "literature of disenchantment" produced by these authors wasn't only, and "not even principally," a reaction against communism but a reaction against "five hundred years of rationalism and empiricism," in other words, against the Enlightenment. Unlike Jeleński, Strachey had no doubt that Koestler's book told the truth about the show trials: Khrushchev's revelations had confirmed rather than contradicted it. But Koestler's was the first book "to begin to reveal the far-reaching consequences upon the mind and spirit of the west of the rejection of communism," for communism couldn't be rejected without "calling in question the whole rationalist tradition." *Darkness at Noon* was "the starting-point of the literature of reaction," of "the retreat from rationalism."

Koestler replied that Strachey had identified rationalism and reason with "the materialistic and mechanistic philosophies of the last century," which were now "as dead as mutton." What the "literature of disenchantment" rejected was not the Enlightenment but "the arrogant and shallow optimism of the nineteenth century" and particularly its "utilitarian ethics." "Our 'strangled' cry was uttered against the idea that the ends justify the means."[21]

Koestler was right about himself and his own generation, but Strachey was prophetic in thinking that the intensity of the revulsion experienced by Koestler and others against communism might lead to a larger retreat from reason. The forty years since he wrote those words have seen a headlong retreat in the West not only from communism and socialism but from many forms of liberalism as well, and the message of the Enlightenment has been called into question more seriously than at any time since its inception. Strachey was equally farsighted in spotting the direction in which Koestler's own writing was moving, for, as George Urban pointed out in his interview, Koestler had supported an essentially irrational type of philosophy in *The Sleepwalkers* and promoted a "religious type of perception" over the scientific kind. Koestler was forced to agree, citing Freud's "oceanic feeling" as his point of reference but also arguing for the importance of the role of prerational thought and intuition in scientific discoveries. It was a mistake to insist on the duality of the rational and the intuitive, and "perverse" to "indentify the religious need solely with intuition and emotion, science solely with the logical and the rational."[22]

Koestler, as usual, wanted to have his cake and eat it. Confronted with what he regarded as the irrationality and intuitive spirituality of the East, he had recoiled from its practices and debunked its claims to a special form of understanding of nature, just as he had turned against its manifestations in the counterculture of Leary and his associates. Faced with the confident claims of western science to have decoded nature and to be able to control it, however, he had recoiled again. Not for the first time he was looking for a synthesis, and he hoped to approach one in his magnum opus on creativity, which, after four years of work, he felt almost ready to publish.

CHAPTER FORTY-THREE

A NAIVE AND SKEPTICAL DISPOSITION

Reason is a gift of God and we should believe in its ability to comprehend the world.

— CZESŁAW MIŁOSZ

KOESTLER'S CLAIM TO RECOGNITION as a serious scholar was reinforced when he was awarded Germany's Kepler Medal for 1962 and published an article on Kepler in a *Festschrift* honoring Michael Polanyi (he later expanded it for the *Encyclopedia of Philosophy*). Koestler also traveled to Galileo's native village of Arcetri, near Venice, to take part in a German television documentary to mark the four hundredth anniversary of Galileo's birth and to write about the subject for *The Observer*. He ended his article on a note that seemed to signal his worries about the reception of *The Act of Creation*. The "Galileo scandal" he wrote, "marked a turning point—a hardening of the fronts, the polarization of rigid orthodoxies," but the blame was not all on one side. The "hubris of an unbalanced genius" was matched by the presumption of theologians and "the vindictiveness of a benighted academic coterie." Though attitudes had since changed, it could not be said that "behind the polite façades, academic orthodoxy has become much more tolerant."[1]

Koestler didn't go so far as to consider himself an "unbalanced genius" of Galilean proportions, but he was still fearful of the academic establishment, and for good reason. While knowledgeable amateurs like Plesch, McGlashan, and Wayland Young had expressed enthusiasm over his various drafts of *The Act of Creation,* professional friends were more cautious. Russell Brain and Donald Hebb were "noncommittal." Dennis Gabor was taken aback by Koestler's "bold generalizations," and even the faithful Misi Polanyi confessed his doubts. "The miraculous agility of your mind endows you with excessive powers of breaking intellectual barriers," wrote Polanyi, "so you do not sufficiently distinguish between those to be demolished and those to be discovered, built higher and respected." If only Koestler would attach his speculations to a human being, as he had done with Kepler, he would find "a principle of restraint," and his abstract universe would be "subdued and made to bear live fruit."[2]

Among Koestler's supporters was the English psychologist Sir Cyril Burt, who wrote a lengthy foreword for the book. It seemed like an excellent move at the time, for Burt (the "father of the eleven-plus" examination in British schools) was world famous for his psychological studies of twins and for his strenuous advocacy of IQ tests as the best means to measure intelligence. After his death in 1971, unfortunately, Burt was unmasked as a scientific fraud who had faked his data and as a political reactionary with a soft spot for the pernicious doctrine of eugenics—the polar opposite of Koestler politically. Koestler couldn't possibly have known this and silently removed Burt's foreword from later editions of the book without explanation, but it was a sign of poor judgment, and Burt wasn't the last of the questionable gurus Koestler would seek out to support his scientific endeavors.[3]

KOESTLER HANDED THE BOOK to his publishers in the fall of 1963. It represented nearly five years of sustained labor and was truly monumental, running to more than seven hundred pages, with two appendices, numerous scholarly footnotes, an extensive bibliography, and a thorough index. Koestler pictured himself imitating Darwin by bringing a "naive and skeptical disposition" to the subject of creativity and asking questions no one had thought to ask before. In an author's preface he explained that he had divided the work into two parts. Part one proposed a theory of the act of creation, and part two attempted to show the basic principles of creativity operating throughout the "whole organic hierarchy—from the fertilized egg to the fertile brain of the creative individual." Koestler conceded his enterprise was "presumptuous," adding modestly that he had "no illusions" about the prospects of his theory, for it was bound to be proven wrong "in many or most details" by advances in psychology and neurology. "What I am hoping for is that it will be found to contain a shadowy pattern of truth, and that it may stimulate those who search for unity in the diverse manifestations of human thought and emotion."[4]

The Act of Creation was indeed an act of hubris. Koestler had brought off the difficult feat (in which he had—and has—few peers) of writing many hundreds of pages on abstract and abstruse topics in clear, vivid, and picturesque language, proceeding by way of the dialectical method that seems to have been inscribed in his DNA (to use a scientific metaphor still unknown to Koestler). It was also an act of folly, for its very ambitiousness illustrated

the degree to which Koestler was captive to an older, Central European concept of science as natural philosophy and had failed to grasp the degree to
which the scientific disciplines had bifurcated into a multitude of subdisci-
plines that no one person could hope to encompass anymore. What he also
failed to consider was the degree to which modern science depended on experiment and verification for its success or failure and the correspondingly
smaller role that inspiration and "eureka moments" played in propelling scientific progress forward.

    This would have mattered less if Koestler had approached his subject with
the humility he claimed for himself in his preface, but by dressing up his theory of bisociation and creativity in the language of the exact sciences, especially in his second part, he gave too many hostages to fortune. Worse still,
Koestler's polemical instincts had led him to mount a frontal attack on the
fashionable school of behaviorist psychology, whose mechanistic notions and
determinist philosophy he regarded as an offshoot of Marxism. He certainly
had a point, but it just wasn't done to express oneself so vehemently about scientific matters in print (nor, for that matter, to speak about those matters in
such an irrepressibly lively and witty manner). Moreover, Koestler's version
of behaviorism turned out to be a gross oversimplification, and his eruption
into the cozy world of professional scientists was regarded as at best an inap-
propriate intrusion, at worst an unpardonable insult.

    When the book was published in May 1964, most of the scientists who re-
viewed it hit back hard. In a widely read article for the *New Statesman,* the
eminent British biologist Peter Medawar eviscerated the book for its "ama-
teurishness," made fun of its "overstretched metaphors" and "fatuous epi-
grams," and remarked that Koestler's psychological insights were "in the
style of the nineteenth century." Medawar said his admiration for *Darkness at
Noon* remained undimmed, but Koestler clearly didn't understand either the
procedures or the sociology of science, and his scientific manners were deplorable. The article was a tour de force of wit and condescension in the best
mandarin manner and, beneath its polished surface, extremely insulting.
Koestler wrote a bad-tempered reply, which Medawar answered in kind,
and it was widely felt that Medawar had gotten the better of the exchange.[5]

    Koestler, in fact, did have something new to say on bisociation, humor,
and the mechanisms of intellectual discovery, even if his terminology was a
bit old-fashioned. He had significantly refined and clarified many of the
ideas first advanced in *Insight and Outlook* and was still a pioneer in analyzing creativity as it was manifested in both art and science. The problem lay
with the indigestible terminology and clotted arguments of part two, and in
later editions he dropped that part entirely, coming to agree with his critics
that it was presumptuous and unnecessary, a distraction from his central
ideas. In its shorter form the book was to prove more durable and popular
than either he or his critics had anticipated, especially with members of the

younger generation and the counterculture (despite his reservations about psychedelic drugs). The secret was in seeing the book not as scientific history but as metaphysics. As Henry David Aiken wrote in *The New York Review of Books,* what Koestler had produced was "not a thesis but a vision, not a theory, but a unifying picture which, in an age of specialization, of bifurcations—and walls—is a refreshment of the soul. One touch of genius may indeed make the whole world kin. Let us see."[6]

Support for Aiken's view came two years later, when the quarterly *Review of Metaphysics* published a long and detailed analysis of *The Act of Creation* by Carl R. Hausman that was the most thorough, scholarly, and objective account of the book to appear anywhere, and some later responses have supported Aiken's point of view rather than Medawar's. *The Act of Creation* proved particularly popular in California (making it very quickly, for example, into *The Whole Earth Catalog*) and has remained continuously in print. After *Darkness at Noon,* it is by far the most widely quoted of Koestler's books (most recently in Stephen Pinker's *How the Mind Works*), and Koestler's theories about the essential unity of creative thought in the arts and sciences, the role of the emotions in creativity, and the importance of aesthetics in scientific discovery have become commonplace, as seen in the work of such diverse scientists as the astronomer John D. Barrow, the physicist Brian Greene, the neurologist António Damásio, and the philosopher Paul Feyerabend. It would be foolish to credit Koestler with directly inspiring these notable scientists, for his book receives only sparing mention in the later literature, but there can be little doubt that its path-breaking explorations helped pave the way for later investigations of the subject.[7]

READING THE CRITICAL RESPONSES to *The Act of Creation* through rose-tinted glasses, Koestler persuaded himself to think of the book as a qualified success and hoped it might get him back to the United States again—not as a visiting novelist or celebrity speaker this time but as a specialist, ready to discuss scientific theory with colleagues and do the grunt work of original research. He thought the Center for Advanced Study in the Behavioral Sciences at Stanford would be the ideal place for a maverick like himself and, after pulling some strings, was appointed a visiting scholar in 1965.[8]

Since the invitation was for a whole academic year, it posed the question of with whom he should go, for it seemed out of the question to go alone. All his proposals to get married had come to naught. Janine, the one woman who did want to marry him, had been spurned, and the only other candidate was Cynthia, who presented a different sort of problem. She was still living in her separate apartment in Thurloe Place and, since Koestler had acquired a tape recorder, was no longer needed to take dictation. For a brief period in 1961, he had told her to stay away completely, thinking he might end the relationship altogether.

As a result, Cynthia had fallen into a depression and with Koestler's encouragement had adopted his habit of popping "happy pills"—Benzedrine or Seconal—to maintain her equilibrium. She was still seeing McGlashan for analysis, and McGlashan told her that her resentment of Koestler stemmed from her inability to understand "what Koestler was about." McGlashan told her that her emotional growth had been arrested owing to a lack of love in her life, especially after the death of her beloved father, making her afraid to connect with other people. McGlashan asked her to write down her dreams for him, and over the next few years she filled several notebooks as painstakingly as she was keeping her diary. The treatment was intermittent, ceasing for up to six months at a time when she went away to Alpbach or elsewhere, but it fulfilled its purpose, which was to reconcile her to the conditions of her relationship with Koestler. Koestler read the books of dreams as well, and participated in her analysis on almost equal terms with McGlashan, which would appear to be a violation of psychoanalytical ethics but seems to have been taken for granted by all three of them.

Cynthia was still indispensable in other ways. She handled Koestler's voluminous correspondence, typed his manuscripts, and managed his household. She organized his travel, made his appointments, paid his bills, dealt with the cooks and cleaners, poured his drinks, and still obligingly slept with him when he felt like it. She filled almost to perfection the multiple roles Koestler had demanded of Mamaine and that Mamaine had despairingly enumerated to Celia shortly before her separation from Koestler. In the fall of 1961, at Koestler's urging, Cynthia had agreed to take Le Cordon Bleu courses in cooking (Koestler's dinner parties from then on were accompanied by a neatly typed menu, recording the food and wine to be served that day, with a list of guests and the date at the top), and a couple of months later she got her reward: a legal change of her last name to Koestler.[9]

Whenever the stress got to be too much for Cynthia, as when she needed another abortion in November 1962 or rebelled against Koestler's bullying the following summer in Alpbach, McGlashan was on hand to sign the forms or explain to her that an eruption of temper in front of others was a good sign, an example of "the well known phenomenon of 'the Confrontation with the Shadow.'" The decision to bring out her "dark side" and show it to herself and everybody else was "the real thing" and would enable her to gain her psychological bearings and reorient herself.[10]

McGlashan occasionally addressed himself to Koestler's behavior too. After a wild night of violent outbursts in Alpbach, which Koestler blamed on his drinking and regretted afterward, McGlashan wrote to Koestler that his periodic explosions were a serious cause for concern. They seemed to result

from a "mounting state of tension, originating in a damming up of your creative powers by some perhaps quite trivial irritation," which induced a feeling
that everything was "conspiring to thwart and frustrate you." Koestler probably drank to blunt this feeling. "But even if you did not drink at all, once this
chain reaction has started I think it would reach its flash-point just the same,
though maybe a bit later."

McGlashan speculated that Koestler "needed these storms at intervals to
clear [his] inner tensions" but recommended that he try to head them off by
taking "what you call 'happy pills.'" Since Koestler couldn't be the best judge
of when to do so, McGlashan wondered if Koestler could bring himself to
let Cynthia decide. "The point is that these explosions of affect constitute a
phenomenon to be considered, not a leit-motif for guilt." His words fell on
deaf ears. Koestler's relationship with Cynthia was essentially sadomasochistic in character, which required him to dominate her at all times, not to let
her gain control over him. On occasion he would take a fiendish pleasure
in flirting with other women in Cynthia's presence or leaving her behind
while he went out with his latest conquest. At one point Cynthia refused to
accompany him to social events in London at all and begged Gogi to go in her
place.

Yet Cynthia endured her humiliations with fortitude, and almost came to
expect them. According to her sister, Pamela, she needed Koestler just as
much as he needed her. Jane Howard also noted how Koestler regularly reduced Cynthia to tears, yet nothing could make Cynthia leave him, and Gogi
compared her to a dogged Shetland pony that "plodded on, drooping under
its heavy burden, but always kept going." All these women liked and sympathized with Cynthia and could only shake their heads over her self-imposed
servitude.[11]

AS THE MENUS INDICATED, Koestler needed Cynthia to entertain his ever
growing circle of friends—writers, scientists, politicians, social reformers,
and CCF stalwarts, not to mention former girlfriends and their spouses.
Koestler still found it virtually impossible to spend an evening alone, was still
addicted to disputation and argument in all their forms, and if he wasn't entertaining visitors in Montpelier Square he was out in other people's dining
rooms being entertained himself.

One of his firmest friendships now was with Henry Yorke. They were the
literary odd couple: Henry Yorke, the startlingly experimental, understated
modernist, and Arthur Koestler, the polemical social realist who liked to dot
every i and cross every t. They were an odd match in other ways too: Yorke,
the upper-class son of a wealthy landowner and manufacturer, married to a
blue-blooded wife, and Koestler, the Jewish parvenu, self-made and living in
sin with his South African secretary. What bound them together in the first

place was propinquity: the Yorkes' house in Trevor Place was just around the corner from Koestler's and literally across the street from both men's favorite pub, the Trevor Arms. They shared a fondness for women and alcohol, an intolerance of fools, and an admiration for each other's very different novels.

When Yorke lapsed into an acute form of alcoholism in the early sixties and stopped writing, Koestler was the first to step forward to help him. He urged Yorke to tackle a second volume of memoirs (the first, *Pack My Bag,* had appeared in 1940) and read and commented on the chapters as Yorke wrote them. He asked Spender at *Encounter* and John Lehmann at *The London Magazine* to publish excerpts, tried to find a publisher for them, and invited Henry and Dig to Alpbach ("thank you a thousand times," wrote Dig, who didn't always approve of Koestler's influence on her husband, "I shall never forget it, lots and lots of love"). When Yorke stayed in bed for days on end, "with several days' growth of beard and a glass of gin in his hand," Koestler helped Yorke's son, Sebastian, check his father into a clinic for treatment, though Yorke returned from the clinic more gloomy and misanthropic than ever.

Unfortunately the friendship ended badly. Yorke had often teased Koestler about his Jewishness, leading Koestler to terminate one of his letters with the ironic salutation "yours rabbinically," but at their annual Christmas Day dinner in 1962, Henry, "who didn't shave or change," according to Cynthia, "made a bloody remark about not having a drop of Jewish blood" in his veins. "I'll never be able to see Henry again," Koestler announced melodramatically to Gogi. "I never realized he was truly anti-Semitic. He said something so awful I can't repeat it." But according to Gogi, who was present, the whole thing was a drunken misunderstanding. Yorke had drawled casually in his upper-class way, "Arthur, I don't care how Jewish you are, but I do wish you wouldn't write those bloody books and those articles about dogs," which Gogi assured Koestler had nothing at all to do with anti-Semitism. Gogi did everything she could to bring about a reconciliation, assuring Koestler that Yorke was "too sick" to be responsible for his words. "He *does* love you, and I think you would be unhappy if he died suddenly and you hadn't shown him your affection for him isn't based on his capriciousness." However, Koestler saw Yorke only grudgingly and intermittently until the latter's death in 1973. Even then Gogi had to drag him to Yorke's memorial service.[12]

Gogi herself had reason to be grateful to Koestler. He had shepherded her through a disastrous and highly publicized divorce when Lee Thompson ran off to Hollywood with a young actress. "I have known enough clever people to know that they may seem 'arrogant' on the surface," wrote Gogi, "but they are seldom sure of themselves. If they were they would be satisfied with their achievements, as less intelligent people often are. That is, partly, why I am so fond of you, and why you are such a lovable person. You have a 'sweetness'

that outweighs your 'difficult' character." Celia experienced Koestler's sweetness when her husband, Arthur Goodman, died in a hunting accident, leaving Celia with two young children to support. Koestler offered all sorts of
help, saw her and invited her to dinner parties even more than before, and
even took to kissing her hand when they met—a curious throwback to his
Austro-Hungarian upbringing. David Astor found Koestler "lovable because of his sensitivity to people, and because of the sense of excitement he
brought to everything he did. He could certainly be harsh when he felt in any
way offended, but he also was somebody with whom one had a strong sense
of intimacy."[13]

There were also warm and tempestuous evenings with his Hungarian
friends Polanyi, Gabor, Mikes, Ignotus, Faludy, and Schöpflin, for whom
Koestler regularly organized a "Hungarian stag party" or an "Austro-Hungarian dinner" at Montpelier Square, or a gathering at Czardas in the West
End. The news about his friends in Hungary itself wasn't good. Déry and
Hay had been released from jail but banned from publishing and had smuggled out a letter asking for publicity in the West. On one of his stays in Alpbach, Koestler paid a sentimental visit to Burgenland to look at the
Austro-Hungarian frontier, marked by a tall barrier painted in red and
white stripes and a mined strip fenced off with barbed wire and overlooked
by a watchtower. A middle-aged Hungarian standing there told him he had
escaped from Hungary in 1956 and came every year for his two-week vacation to "look at the acacia trees on the other side."[14]

Still, as a result of Khrushchev's "thaw," Hungary was at last opening up
a little. Koestler was agreeably surprised to receive a letter from his cousin
Jenő Somló, informing him that on a visit to the Jewish Cemetery, Jenő had
found the grave of "our benefactor, Uncle Henrik" in a dreadful state of disrepair. Koestler agreed to pay seventy pounds for a new headstone and approved the design. Learning of this largesse, another cousin wrote to remind
Koestler of the favors her family had shown Henrik and Adele when they
were down on their luck and asked him to "return the money," since she and
her husband were retired and sick. Koestler regarded this as an other opportunistic attempt to exploit him (Jenő had asked for nothing for himself) but
sent her a small sum anyway.[15]

That the times were changing was confirmed when Koestler's name appeared in print in Hungary for the first time since the end of World War II,
in an article on Németh and his circle. Mikes had recently been back to Hungary for the first time to explore the possibility of being published there, and
Koestler asked Mikes to find out if he himself might go as a tourist. To his astonishment, the Hungarian foreign minister approved, but when Koestler
went to the Hungarian consulate in Vienna to apply for a visa, he was told the
Hungarians had set two conditions: first, that Koestler not speak in public

while in Hungary, and second, that he not write anything on his return. Koestler felt the first condition was easy to satisfy, but not the second, and decided not to go.[16]

KOESTLER CONCLUDED THAT ALPBACH was as close to Central Europe as he was likely to get. He had established a strange double existence there, reflecting the double life of the village itself. For three quarters of the year Alpbach was a remote Alpine farming community with parochial concerns and an ingrained suspicion of strangers; in the summer, it was home to a cosmopolitan university campus with eminent visitors from all over the world. Though Koestler was there mainly during the summers (and for an occasional Christmas vacation), he was determined to straddle both worlds. What visitors saw was the cosmopolitan Koestler in the academic setting of the college, but among the villagers Koestler played the role of a sort of Central European country farmer (without the farm), not quite "the squire of Alpbach" of Martin Esslin's description, but an eccentric, slightly comical version of that figure.

At the center of Koestler's small Alpbach universe was the incomparable Eva. Eva never wore makeup, always cut her own hair, designed her own clothes and shoes (which were made to measure by the best bespoke houses in Vienna), and passionately avoided being pigeonholed. She detested the role of wife and mother, hated being photographed, and thought of herself as an independent, inner-directed artist with a vision of her own. Deeply Catholic, she had a huge circle of artists and priests for friends (many derived from her days in the Resistance) and, according to one of her daughters, had been proposed to by many prominent men in Vienna—giving them the same dusty answer she had given Koestler.

Eva overflowed with animal spirits, and possessed of the same sort of self-absorbed childishness as Koestler. She was invulnerable to his aggression, because she couldn't be browbeaten or seduced. She relied on intuition and instinct, and when she started her affair with him, it was strictly on her own terms, as she explained after his death. "I was always in love with someone else at the same time, and Arthur knew this. He saw that I was independent, and I never asked him for any help. I was grateful for the relationship and used to adore spending the night with him, but I was also grateful not to have to see him the next morning. He used to be overcome with waves of guilt and get very stormy. He seemed to need his guilt and even long for it. I didn't feel guilty myself and did everything I could to help him overcome it. Guilt made him appear pathetic and small, and I couldn't possibly love a pathetic person, so it was in my own interest to stop him."

Eva had two secret weapons, one physical, the other spiritual. She was taller than Koestler, and she noticed that whenever he was with her he wore thick-soled shoes and walked on tiptoe. She got an insight into how absurdly self-conscious he was when he showed her an invitation to a reunion at his old boarding school in Baden and asked her to go with him. But he later changed his mind, telling her that in the school newsletter he had read that two of his classmates had been killed in the war. "One of them was shorter than me, so that if I went now I'd be the shortest one there."

Eva's other secret weapon was her Catholicism, "the religion of thieves and criminals," as she put it. She had a strong mystical bent and seemed able to float through life untouched by remorse or shame. "I knew I was guilty, but I didn't *feel* guilty," she said. Koestler couldn't fathom her invulnerability. He questioned her over long evenings in the Böglerhof about her belief in the powers of confession and resisted her attempts to get him to try it. "You know I can't convert to Catholicism," he told her, "because a man can't convert twice in a lifetime." What the first conversion had been he didn't say.

Eva was generally impervious to his sudden changes of mood and alarming lapses into aggression, because she felt she knew what lay behind them. She understood that when Koestler got depressed between books or when checking translations it was out of artistic frustration and that he was often powerless to stop himself from getting carried away. She also knew that afterward he felt worse than the people he quarreled with, because he knew he was to blame. That was the main reason she resolved not to get into fights with him herself.[17]

Eva's elder daughter, Alexandra, recalls the sight of Koestler at their house, "one hand holding a glass of whisky, the other gesticulating vehemently or thrust deep into his trouser pocket, marching up and down with lowered head, passionately holding forth, and every now and then snorting in a very distinct way through his nose—the more excited he got, the more he snorted." Eva was a sympathetic listener but refused to be browbeaten and would insist on changing the subject when he got too technical or boring. She also teased him about Cynthia and said it was time for him to marry her.[18]

Koestler would rather have married Eva than Cynthia. In 1964 he discussed the pros and cons of adding a guest room to the Schreiberhäusl and even toyed with the idea of inviting Cristina for the summer vacations. "We'll have children the same age and we can all live together." He let Eva see the pictures Janine had sent him every Christmas, showing Cristina in a variety of formal outfits, and told her about the phonograph records of Cristina reading English poems in a heavy French accent. Eva realized it was just another pipe dream on Koestler's part but said nothing.[19]

As a kind of substitute for family he went out of his way to be kind to Alexandra and her sister, Margarita. Alexandra had heart disease (this was one reason Eva had built a small house in Alpbach), and her father, Atti, traveled a lot and didn't take much interest in her, so Koestler became a sort of surrogate parent for a while, especially during Alexandra's teenage years. (Margarita had alienated him as a small child by skipping after him in the village main street and chanting, "Koestler, Koestler, schnapps, schnapps!") According to Alexandra, Koestler was "the only person in the world who spoke to me seriously and didn't only tell me what to do, but listened carefully and asked me what I was interested in." Koestler used to take the girls for rides in his big convertible and invariably drove too fast. After a spectacular crash on the bend just below his house, it was christened the "Koestler curve." Eva was with him at the time. Koestler threw open the door, said, "You know the locals better than I do," and walked away, leaving her to deal with the apoplectic driver of the other car and call the garage.

Koestler talked to Alexandra about books, communism, the death penalty, quarantine for dogs, parapsychology, Jung's synchronicity, and the newest developments in behavioral psychology. "He played me records of Dukas's *Sorcerer's Apprentice* and Beethoven's Ninth Symphony and explained them to me. He patiently questioned me about my impressions and associations. I felt as if I were learning to fly." Koestler similarly encouraged Moser's daughter, Karin Duftner, who was only a couple of years older than Alexandra, sitting up till two a.m. to discuss politics and astronomy with her. Karin was fascinated by his face, which changed expression from minute to minute like no other person's she knew. "When he was angry, his eyes changed color, paling to a steely gray."[20]

CYNTHIA HOVERED ON THE PERIPHERY of this cozy world. She still knew virtually no German and rarely ventured out of the house without Koestler. The Catholic villagers disapproved of the fact that they weren't married—and blamed her, of course, not Koestler. Hanna Molden noticed that Cynthia's excruciating shyness and nervous tics made her eyes "twitch and flutter," and she would "tremble all over" when Koestler roared "Angel" at her. At other times her jaw set tight and she "gritted her teeth as if in pain." According to Alexandra, Cynthia followed Koestler about like a shadow, "sitting with an agonized, abstracted look on her face whenever they had visitors or went to visit someone, trying to make herself thinner and smaller, and saying hardly a word. When asked about something she would let out a little laugh, as if excusing herself, or look imploringly at Arthur, fearful of saying anything to annoy him. We felt incredibly sorry for her, but her passivity also inspired in us a faint dread."[21]

In the summer of 1964, in a rare accession of guilt, Eva decided to make a pilgrimage to Lourdes to cleanse herself. Her reason for going was that not long after meeting Koestler, she had stolen away for a day to meet him in Kitzbühel, leaving her two children with their nanny. Alexandra had stumbled into a wasps' nest and been so badly stung that she needed several injections to quell the inflammation, and Eva was convinced that this was the cause of Alexandra's heart problem (Alexandra later denied that she had ever had a heart problem, and felt that the doctors had made a mistake). Koestler had fiercely opposed Eva's decision, accusing her of superstition, but had agreed to join Marietta Torberg in keeping an eye on the children while Eva was away.

As soon as she returned, Eva arranged to meet Koestler at the Böglerhof, but he hustled her away, saying he needed to talk to her in private. He shepherded her down to the river, where they ended up on a rock in the middle of the stream near a sewage pipe, which stank to high heaven but guaranteed privacy. Koestler agitatedly informed Eva that the long-awaited invitation to spend several months at the Center for Advanced Study in Stanford had come through. He was desperate to go but was in a blue funk about how to reply. If he went, he would have to take Cynthia with him, for Cynthia was such a depressive and so dependent on him he was afraid to leave her behind, but the United States was such a puritanical country that if he took her, he would have to marry her. What should he do? Behind the spoken question lurked two unspoken ones: Why couldn't Eva go with him, and why couldn't he marry Eva instead? If Eva recognized the unstated questions, she chose to ignore them and said at once that he should marry Cynthia.

Koestler recoiled from the idea and plunged into one of his depressions. Two days later he returned to the Schreiberhäusl at one in the morning, woke Cynthia, and told her he intended to take their entire stock of Seconal and end it all. Cynthia was taking daily "happy pills" herself by this time and responded to his threat by saying that if he insisted on killing himself, she would kill herself too. She went up to her attic room and waited. When she looked in on Koestler a couple of hours later to see if he had carried out his threat, he was "peacefully asleep."[22]

Cynthia's position as companion and cohabitant now seemed secure, though still not without a certain ambiguity. After the crisis with Eva, Koestler talked to Cynthia about moving to America with her, and they agreed that if it didn't work out, Cynthia would return to London alone. In November 1964 he made a preliminary trip to the United States and spoke at a symposium entitled "Brain Functions and Learning" at the University of California in Los Angeles (his paper was received in silence) and lectured at UC Santa Barbara. After that he traveled to Palo Alto and rented a house with "citrus trees, fig trees, black bamboo and other exotica" that he thought would keep Cynthia busy and happy during their stay.[23]

Koestler returned to London for a while, and then he and Cynthia left for New York on January 4, 1965. By this time the ambiguity in their arrangement seems to have been resolved, for on January 8 they were married at New York's City Hall, with the Burnhams as witnesses and sole guests.

Koestler hoped to keep the wedding secret, but the next day the news was in *The New York Times* and flashed to Europe, prompting letters of congratulation and telegrams from dozens of friends on both sides of the Atlantic. Koestler had bowed to the inevitable and was launched on his third marriage. With silence and cunning, Cynthia had captured her man.[24]

CHAPTER FORTY-FOUR

SEEKING A CURE

His limitless ambition as a writer was not simply a matter of ego, but of his commitment to the writer's vocation to make sense of things for himself and the rest of us.

— JASON EPSTEIN

CALIFORNIA'S PERPETUAL SUMMER was a welcome change from foggy London and exercised its own peculiar influence on Koestler's lifestyle. Soon he and Cynthia were playing badminton and volleyball to keep fit and enjoying the open air in a used blue Oldsmobile convertible with a white top. Cynthia grappled with the exotic flora of her tropical garden, and they adopted a tan and white mutt from the Lost Dogs Home, Tycho (after Brahe) but had to give him away when he started chewing the landlord's furniture. In the evenings they socialized with Stanford faculty members, and Koestler found a ready-made corps of admirers at the Hoover Institution for the Study of Communism. He and Cynthia also made regular trips to San Francisco and toured Monterey, Carmel, and Big Sur in their new car.[1]

The center had forty-nine fellows in residence that year: forty-eight academics and Koestler. He had set off for Stanford filled with "childish expectations" of an intellectual adventure, and embarked on his duties as scholar and teacher with his usual optimism and verve. He was to conduct two interdisciplinary graduate seminars, one called "Habit and Originality" and the other, "Self-Regulating Hierarchic Organization" (which he jocularly referred to as a "Colloquium on Half-Baked Ideas"). The first proved unpopular with graduate students, but it didn't matter because Koestler was much more interested in the second, in which he explored his idea that human psychology and physiology could best be explained in terms of interlocking hierarchies. The codirector of the seminar was the neurophysiologist Karl

Pribram, whose work Koestler had copiously quoted in *The Act of Creation,* and Koestler invited several other scholars as guest speakers.[2]

It seems that he alienated some graduate students by strictly limiting their numbers for his seminar and by his gladiatorial approach to discussion, but the seminar was still popular, not least because of Koestler's talent for incorporating diverse subject matter. One week he described to students his experience of taking psilocybin with Timothy Leary and discussed the highly topical subject of the role of drugs in creativity, saying that though skeptical himself, he had been persuaded by the Stanford psychologist Willis Harman to maintain an open mind. He launched into a lengthy disquisition on the uses of LSD, mescaline, and other drugs and made a highly convincing case in their favor. The discussant that day was the noted psychologist Erik Erikson, who embarked on an equally lengthy rebuttal, asserting that for scientists, hallucinogens were no good at all. The aim of creativity was to transcend scientific disciplines, not to evade them. There was a long and pregnant silence, broken only when Koestler let out a long sigh and said, "Actually, I agree with you."[3]

Other discussants at the seminar included Frank Barron, Paul Weiss, Roman Jakobson, and Ernest Gellner, but most members of the Stanford faculty kept their distance. Koestler greatly admired Ernest Hilgard, for example, a staunch and indefatigable opponent of behaviorism, and was hoping he would take part, but though outwardly friendly, Hilgard proved elusive. Pribram was more forthcoming, and Koestler proposed they write a book together on hierarchic systems. It turned out they disagreed on how the emotions worked, and Koestler decided to start the book on his own. It would be "a revision and a correction" of *The Act of Creation,* he thought, for he was no longer fully satisfied with the term *bisociation* and felt that creativity arose from collision, combination, and confrontation. Despite the seeming clunkiness of these terms, his new book, he told Cynthia, would be "as light as a soufflé."[4]

Koestler gave some public lectures at Stanford and Berkeley and was dismayed that so few faculty members showed up. He feared that "hardnosed" experimental scientists disdained "softnosed" theorists like himself and was particularly disappointed when Barron declined to join him in some "ESP experiments with mushrooms." Barron did interview Koestler on creativity as part of a series that included William Carlos Williams, Truman Capote, W. H. Auden, and others, but that was not a scientific collaboration—and unfortunately no transcript seems to have survived.

Koestler's dissatisfaction stemmed in large part from his unfamiliarity with modern campus life. He seems to have had a vision of the Center for Advanced Study as a kind of cozy think tank, in which the scholars rubbed shoulders and exchanged ideas in Socratic dialogues, and attended one another's lectures out of intellectual curiosity. The idea was strangely old-

fashioned, as was a humorous skit he composed for the commencement celebrations in June. Modeled after Aristophanes' *The Birds,* it was set on a mythical campus called Nephelokokkuxia, or Cloudcuckoocamp, and satirized
such features of campus life as academic jargon, the competition for comfortable research facilities, the conference merry-go-round, and the doctrine of
publish or perish. Koestler made jabs at all the main psychological schools
represented at Stanford, singling out the behaviorists for special treatment,
and parodied himself in the guise of a slothful theorist who "bisociates all
day" and draws inspiration from his unconscious while asleep.[5]

It was more like a fraternity spoof than a commencement event, and
Koestler's sharply satirical tone aroused considerable opposition. A special
committee was formed and after endless deliberations decided to go ahead
with the performance, but the experience was either the last straw for
Koestler or a convenient pretext to end his scholarly career. He concluded
that there was little more to gain from the academy and, after a last-minute
rapprochement with Pribram, left the prospect of a return to Stanford open:
each would work on separate chapters of their joint book (which was on
again) before comparing notes and planning the shape of the final volume,
and perhaps Koestler would see him again in the fall.[6]

IT WAS WITH A SENSE of relief that Koestler and Cynthia left for Paris and
Alpbach. Koestler had just reviewed a memoir by the painter Françoise
Gilot, about her tumultuous life with Picasso, and Robert Calmann-Lévy,
their joint publisher, threw a dinner party at a fashionable art nouveau
restaurant famous for its wine cellar. Koestler competed with Sperber for
Gilot's attention and won hands down by monopolizing the conversation and
sending back two bottles of expensive Bordeaux, causing Calmann-Lévy to
turn pale. After they had barhopped until three in the morning, Cynthia collapsed on a bench. "Arthur ordered sausages and some rough red wine," according to Gilot, "and insisted on playing the pinball machine. I beat him
hollow, of course, which laid the basis for our future friendship."[7]

Koestler spent much of the summer working on some lectures for the
General Science section of the British Association Meeting in Cambridge in
the fall and the Bicentennial Celebration of the birth of James Smithson at
the Smithsonian two weeks later. In Washington he challenged Darwinism,
defended Lamarck, and made out a case for intelligent design (though the
term hadn't been invented yet). He also floated some of the ideas that he had
developed at Stanford on hierarchies and scientific discovery. "If you take a
kind of grandstand view of the history of any branch of science, you will find
a rhythmic alternation between long periods of relatively peaceful evolution
and shorter bursts of revolutionary change," he said. Koestler acknowledged

that this schema resembled Thomas Kuhn's "paradigm shifts" but added truthfully that he had arrived at similar conclusions in *The Sleepwalkers* well before Kuhn's book had appeared.[8]

Between the two lectures, Koestler celebrated his sixtieth birthday in London. Cards, telegrams, and letters poured in from all over the globe, but integral to Koestler's personality was a perverse determination not to do the accepted thing, so there was to be no party or celebration. Cynthia laconically captured the homely substitute in her diary: "September 5. A's birthday. Row last night. Depressed. Lance and Eve [Whyte] came to tea, the McGlashans to drinks (Alan looked tired; was soon aggressive to A; did not seem to like Lance.) Goronwy [Rees] came and we had sausages in the dining room. Played the Schubert trio. Just the right kind of evening for A's 60th birthday."[9]

There were other celebrations on the way. The Danube Edition of Koestler's collected works (twenty volumes) had been promised by Hutchinson as a sixtieth-birthday present, and, after much chivvying by Koestler, it was finally started. It was an odd and old-fashioned idea for a living author to be so treated, but Koestler regarded a collected edition as both an affirmation of his importance and, more mundanely, a way to make more money, for his flight to science had cost him a large part of his readership, and even his earlier books were selling many fewer copies than before.[10]

The London *Sunday Times* marked the occasion by asking Cyril Connolly to interview Koestler at Montpelier Square. Amid a great deal of banter, Connolly quizzed Koestler on his early life and his feelings about being British. "I think of myself as a European of Hungarian background, Austro-French formation, and a naturalized British subject," replied Koestler (making no mention of his Jewishness), "but a European first of all." He said he was fed up with the British class system, puzzled by the hostility of the working class to the rest of society, perplexed by the hostility of the whole society to Europe, and bemused by British complacency and inefficiency. His books were less popular in Britain than in any other major country, and he was still considered as something of an alien. But to live in France would be worse, Germany was unacceptable, Austria parochial, and the United States (though objectively "a force for good") unthinkable.

Connolly cited Gide's comment that Koestler was a better journalist than a novelist. "You know, Cyril, this business about journalist or novelist, I've had that up to my neck, just as H. G. Wells had it up to his neck. I have heard that at a writers' congress one day Wells suddenly burst out: 'I am a journalist, I know nothing about art,' put on his bowler hat and walked out." Koestler said that ten years after publicly renouncing politics and turning to science, he was still invariably referred to in the media as Arthur "Darkness at Noon" Koestler. When Connolly suggested that Koestler was wasting his time writing popular science, Koestler claimed that he wasn't writing popular science but making a serious contribution to scientific thought and cited the invitation to Stanford as confirmation of that point.[11]

As if to reassure himself, Koestler hammered out some chapters on the concept of hierarchy in psychology and biology, ostensibly for his collaboration with Karl Pribram, but it soon became clear that, separated by a distance of six thousand miles, they were not going to bring the project to fruition. Meanwhile, his omnivorous quest for material had led him to other scientists whose work he now preferred. One was Paul MacLean in Washington, D.C., who had developed a model of the human brain as "three brains" coexisting in the human skull. At MacLean's invitation, Koestler traveled to Washington in May 1966 to lecture on evolution and afterward went to see Paul Weiss at Rockefeller University in New York, whose work on embryology he planned to quote in his new book. Another scientist whose work influenced him was Sir Alister Hardy, a professor of zoology at Oxford, who argued that evolutionary progress was due not only to random mutations produced by natural selection, as orthodox neo-Darwinists insisted, but also to the initiative of the living organism; and a fourth was Ludwig von Bertalanffy, a pioneer of general systems theory, whose skepticism about neo-Darwinism paralleled that of Hardy, Whyte, and Koestler himself.[12]

With the sense that at least some significant scientists were swimming in the same direction, Koestler spent the whole of 1966 working feverishly on his new work. His shorthand name for the book was "Janus," the Roman god facing both ways, whose double nature was an apt symbol of Koestler's own bifurcated character, not to speak of his dialectical way of thinking, his love of binaries, and his ability to straddle the two cultures. In this case he employed it as an analogy for the Janus-like nature of individual cells, or "holons," as he called them, using a term of his own invention, and their behavior within the open-ended hierarchy of evolution: facing downward or outward they were wholes, facing upward or inward they were only parts.

By the time he reached Alpbach in the summer of 1966, Koestler had completed the first two sections of his book on evolution and was able to start part three, tentatively labeled "The Predicament of Man." Koestler hadn't yet worked out the details, but he already had a pretty good idea of what that predicament was and also what the cure might be. As early as 1959 he had drafted the outline of a book, "The Madness of Man," for the scientific publisher Wolfgang Foges, describing man's quest for immortality, "mystical and secular systems of salvation," the "madness of sex," the "madness of science," and the "madness of art" and correcting what he regarded as a "quite misleading picture of human evolution" that emphasized the successes and ignored the failures. The last chapter was to look toward "a new humanist synthesis of transcendental ethics and empirical science."[13]

Nothing came of that proposal. What survived was a sense that man's "predicament" stemmed from an inveterate paranoia and lust for aggression. Koestler was finding it hard to formulate what he meant until he read Konrad Lorenz's *On Aggression* in Alpbach that year. Lorenz studied animal behavior, but in his new book contended that the evil in man stemmed from an evolutionary shortcoming, the absence of any inhibition about killing fellow humans. The idea dovetailed neatly with MacLean's theory of the three brains: one of which, according to MacLean, was a primitive remnant left over from man's days of hunting for food. Koestler was equally impressed by Lorenz's view that "the holocausts of human history" were the result of militant enthusiasm in the service of a cause and told Cynthia that Lorenz had helped him achieve a breakthrough.[14]

Lorenz's insights fed an idea that Koestler had been nursing for some years now. Struck by the Christian emphasis on original sin, Koestler wondered if the human race had been formed with a biological defect in the brain. He speculated about the possibility of performing a small operation at birth, "as in circumcision," that would cut the offending connection in the brain and remove the defect. This idea gave way to the notion of "tranquilizers in the drinking water," which Koestler tried out on Paul Weiss (with negative results), and he ultimately arrived at another solution, inspired in part by Hydén's work in biochemistry. Would it not be possible, he wondered, to find a drug that would alter the brain's chemistry to produce the desired effect instead?[15]

WHILE KOESTLER WORKED FURIOUSLY on the last part of his book in Alpbach, his relationship with Eva changed. Sensitive to Cynthia's new status as Koestler's wife, Eva was reluctant to continue their affair as before and fell out with Koestler over her decision to visit the Soviet Union. "Promise me that you won't talk to me about the Soviet Union," Koestler had written from California, "and I won't talk to you about America." He became convinced that Eva was having an affair with an Alpbach neighbor of theirs and quarreled with her over the religious education she insisted on giving her children. Surely she had lost her own faith long ago, he said aggressively.

Their last argument was followed by a curious little scene in which Koestler got up to leave and gave her a parting kiss. "That was a Gertrud-like kiss," said Eva. "I'll give you a dry one." She kissed him chastely and stroked his cheek, leading Cynthia to wonder what it was all about. The implication was that Eva forgave him for what he had said about her religion but also that they could not continue as before.[16]

This wasn't the end of their relationship. The following summer Eva was hospitalized in Innsbruck with a detached retina. Atti was stuck in Vienna, so Koestler rushed to the hospital and sat in the waiting room while she was operated on. Eva had to stay for another three weeks with her eyes bandaged, leaving the two girls with their nanny in Alpbach. Koestler visited her almost every other day, sitting and talking with her or reading to her aloud. On his first visit he brought a big bunch of flowers. "I don't know the names of many flowers," he said, "so I went to the shop and asked for flowers that you can touch. Here, touch them and see if you can recognize them. They are blue." Eva touched them and realized they were monkshood, poisonous to eat though not to the touch. Back in Alpbach, Koestler and Cynthia did their best to entertain and distract the girls, and Koestler drove them to Innsbruck to see their mother. Though he and Eva were no longer lovers, she still meant more to him than almost any other woman in his life, possibly including Cynthia.[17]

The seismic shift in his relationship with Eva overlapped with a sudden cooling of relations with McGlashan, whom Koestler now suspected of exerting an undue influence on Cynthia. In the fall of 1966, McGlashan published *Savage and Beautiful Country: The Secret Life of the Mind,* a Jungian plea for the liberation of the psyche and a polemic against all "will-driven, over-masculinized betrayers of life." Koestler took it personally, declining to review the book when asked, and McGlashan excused himself from a dinner planned by Koestler and Cynthia in his honor, leading to all kinds of misunderstandings. The final insult was when McGlashan referred to Koestler slightingly as a "materialist."[18]

In a post-birthday letter to Eva that fall, Koestler complained that since his return from Stanford he was losing his friends. The McGlashan episode seemed to confirm his complaint, and it was true that his move into science had alienated many of his literary admirers. Though Cynthia's diary lists a social round that would exhaust most people, it was definitely less hectic than before, and there was always the factor of Koestler's difficult personality. Françoise Gilot had recently moved to London and was startled by his possessiveness. He would go to her studio and snub her other friends who were there. "He had a star mentality. He had to be number one, and everybody else was supposed to defer to him." Françoise was very fond of Koestler but dared not show it, "because he would abuse and exploit it. You had to keep him at arm's length, treat him with strictness. He was completely undisciplined and unpredictable. If you showed your affection for him, he would become demanding and exploitative." She felt that the "depth of his angst and anxiety placed the whole of reality in question." He "couldn't find any solid ground under his feet," which dictated his "existential doubt" and the intensity of his search for a way out.[19]

AFTER FINISHING HIS BOOK in March 1967, Koestler celebrated by drinking too much at the home of Sir Martyn and Lady "Pinkie" Beckett and getting arrested for drunk driving again, news of which provoked an animated correspondence in the London *Times* (most letter writers were against him) and was followed by a one-year suspension of his license. The arrival of the galley proofs sparked serious doubts about the new book's worth. Would it ensure he was remembered "at least fifty years after his death," he wondered, or would he and all his works disappear into oblivion?[20]

While waiting for the new book to appear, Koestler was entertained by a tempestuous debate over the early history of the Congress for Cultural Freedom. In April 1966 *The New York Times* had revealed the CIA's links with the Congress for Cultural Freedom and subsidy of *Encounter* and other magazines. The roll call of prominent intellectuals who lined up to deny they had known anything about the subsidies was impressive and lengthened further after *Ramparts* magazine ran a long article of its own on the subject. Thomas Braden, a former CIA operative, wrote a controversial article for *The Saturday Evening Post*, "I'm Glad the CIA Is 'Immoral,'" in which he described the CIA's cultural offensive on a worldwide scale, boasting that it had placed "one agent" in the CCF and "another at *Encounter.*"[21]

The left was split down the middle again between the anti-Communists and the anti-anti-Communists, and between the old and the new left, while the right comfortably gloated. Lasky (presumably the *Encounter* agent referred to by Braden) admitted that he had been "less than frank" with his colleagues, and Spender resigned from *Encounter* in a blaze of publicity, insisting he had been duped. There was a cry for the head of the CIA's other agent, Michael Josselson, who was working out of the congress's headquarters in Paris. Koestler, unaware of Josselson's earlier role in ousting him from the CCF, stuck up for him and urged him to stand firm, but Josselson (unlike Lasky) was forced out.[22]

Koestler wasn't in the least shocked by Braden's revelations and doubtless nodded with approval at his reference to Willi Münzenberg as a propaganda model. He thoroughly agreed with the notion of fighting fire with fire: hadn't he said as much in Berlin? "I knew from the beginning that there was American government money behind the Congress," he said later, and "had no objection as long as there were no strings attached." His contributions to *Encounter* had been written out of conviction, and if they also "served the American power structure," this was highly preferable to serving the alternative.[23]

History plucked him by the sleeve once more when the Six-Day War erupted in the Middle East. Koestler was tempted to dash off to Israel, but the conflict was over almost as soon as it began. Israel launched its lightning strike and captured the Sinai Peninsula, the Gaza Strip, the West Bank, and East Jerusalem in less than a week. Glued to his radio in Alpbach, Koestler said nothing publicly, prompting Abram Weinshall to write in anguish, "Many friends are asking: Where is Koestler? Why is he silent? Why does he not raise his voice? Have you any suggestions to make as to what should be

done in this moment to find a solution?" He was of course extremely concerned about the fate of Israel but had "kept his mouth shut," like other
prominent Zionists, so as not to injure the Jewish cause. Public opinion in
Britain and America was "fervently and unanimously pro-Israel, as united as
it had never been since the Hungarian Revolution of 1956," and there was no
need to stir it up any more. The reference to the Hungarian revolution is significant, because then, too, Koestler had received urgent appeals to raise his
voice and had similarly declined. He was deadly serious in saying that the
leopard had changed his spots, but it's hard to believe that speaking out
would have hurt him in any way.[24]

The irrepressible Janine had also reminded him of her existence again,
sending "affectionate best wishes" for his birthday and informing him that
Paul Graetz had died the year before. Cristina was staying with her in Rome,
but they would go to Gstaad for the winter, to be near Cristina's school.
Cristina was "dark, blue-eyed, with a lot of charm," and spoke fluent French,
English, and Italian. Janine slyly informed Koestler that she was married
again, this time to an Englishman, and had "become very English," adding in
a postscript, "My name, if you ever wish to know that I still exist: the Countess of Warwick."[25]

KOESTLER HAD DECIDED to call his new book *The Ghost in the Machine,* a
play on a phrase coined by the Oxford philosopher Gilbert Ryle, who had
dismissed all claims that mental and emotional events might be independent
of physical causes and referred to the idea of mind as the "ghost" in the
(human) machine—a phrase he later amended to "the horse in the locomotive." Koestler's concept of original sin as rooted in a biological defect was not
all that far from Ryle's idea, but Koestler wasn't prepared to reject the concept of mind altogether and was opposed to Ryle's materialism. In time-
honored fashion, he turned Ryle's label on its head (using "The Horse in the
Locomotive" as the title for the French translation of his book), and it was
Koestler, rather than Ryle, who turned "the ghost in the machine" into a popular catchphrase.[26]

The Ghost in the Machine appeared in Britain in October 1967 and in the
United States in January 1968. It was a hybrid work in the tradition of *The
Sleepwalkers* and *The Act of Creation:* part scientific treatise, part literary
essay, part philosophical speculation, and part polemic. Like the two earlier
books (though considerably shorter), it was another quixotic attempt by
Koestler to straddle the two cultures with a variety of ends in view: to enrich
science with new insights, to search for a general theory embracing nature
and mankind, and to extract from science a secular solution to the rampant
unhappiness and suffering that Koestler perceived as afflicting an increasingly dangerous world.

The book's literary virtues were considerable. It was marvelously elo-quent, and Koestler showed himself equally adept at conjuring both the glo-rious variety and the elegant structure of the great chain of being. He found beauty and poetry in chromosomes and genetic codes, mystery and meaning in flatworms and flying squirrels, and to the plodding cadences of scien-tific explication he brought the winged instruments of analogy, metaphor, parable, and story. Innumerable citations attested to Koestler's encyclopedic reading and fantastically retentive memory and ensured that for most of its length the book was, if not "as light as a soufflé," entertaining and highly readable.

The book included a witty critique of behaviorist psychology and a theory of interlocking hierarchies, accompanied by an explanation of Koestler's Janus-faced holons. "No man is an island, he is a holon. A Janus-faced entity who, looking inward, sees himself as a self-contained unique whole, looking outward as a dependent part. His *self-assertive tendency* is the dynamic mani-festation of his unique *wholeness,* his autonomy and independence as a holon. Its equally universal antagonist, the *integrative tendency,* expresses his depen-dence on the larger whole to which he belongs: his *part-ness.*"[27]

Koestler couldn't resist flirting again with Lamarck's theory that acquired characteristics could be inherited, as an alternative to Darwin's random mu-tations. It was the randomness of Darwinism that stuck in Koestler's throat. Lamarck had failed to prove his theory, but the failure of Lamarckism in its primitive form didn't mean that "the monkey at the typewriter" was the only alternative to choose. All this, apart from the vehemence of Koestler's attack on behaviorism and his Lamarckian deviation, was well within the parame-ters of normal scientific discourse, but in the last part of his book, Koestler went off on a tangent to discuss the nature of consciousness (the ghost in the machine) and the problem of free will. The cruelty and chaos observable in human history derived not from man's self-assertive tendencies, he wrote, as Koestler had once supposed, but from his self-integrative drives, that is, his persistent attempts to merge with a larger group. "Aberrations of the human mind" were the result of "an obsessional pursuit of some part-truth, treated as if it were a whole truth—a holon masquerading as a whole"—leading to religious, political, and philosophical extremism.[28]

Koestler had a point. The world was (and still is) full of individuals and groups insisting that their grasp of a partial truth is equivalent to under-standing the whole truth, and in some ways the book was a lengthy elabora-tion and restatement of Koestler's original insight in *Darkness at Noon*—that groupthink conformity and crowd psychology have been responsible for many of the worst excesses in history. But Koestler now sought the cause not in politics or psychology but in physiology. The fundamental "delusional streak in man's mental nature" stemmed from the fact that he was probably "a biological freak, the result of some remarkable mistake in the evolutionary process," because his "old" brain (here Koestler relied on MacLean's theories), responsible for man's emotions, was permanently at war with his "new" brain, responsible for his cognitive or rational faculties, and too often got the upper hand.[29]

Koestler detected a "paranoid streak running through human history"— which had the ring of personal projection to it—and Koestler's proposed solution also made better sense if one knew his personal habits. Since the problem was physiological in origin, the cure might be chemical. Modern chemists possessed an array of new chemical compounds capable of controlling the human mind—tranquilizers, barbiturates, stimulants, and so on— and if antidepressants were merely a first step toward "a more sophisticated range of aids to promote a coordinated, harmonious state of mind," why not take this trend a step further? "Nature has let us down, God seems to have left the receiver off the hook, and time is running out. To hope for salvation to be synthetized in the laboratory may seem materialistic, crankish, or naive, but when man decides to take his fate into his own hands, that possibility will be within reach." There would be no one in control, because just as pep pills and tranquilizers had spread around the world with little official encouragement, so would a "mental stabilizer." Its use would spread spontaneously, like chlorine in drinking water, vaccination, and contraception, "not by coercion but by enlightened self-interest."[30]

IT WAS AN EXTRAORDINARY CONCLUSION from the author of *Darkness at Noon* and friend of the author of *1984,* and just as extraordinary coming from the man who, five years earlier, had denounced Huxley's *Doors of Perception* for its advocacy of "the chemical opening of doors into Other Worlds" as "instant mysticism" and "a shortcut to enlightenment and grace." Koestler attempted to neutralize the problem by asserting that he himself had a "healthy aversion" to the "excesses of social engineering, various forms of brainwashing, and other threatening aspects of the air-conditioned nightmare surrounding us," and that in *Brave New World* Huxley had imagined the inverse of perceptual nirvana, namely an enire population living in a kind of passive stupor induced by "soma" pills fed to them by their leaders.

The distinction wasn't really very clear, and inevitably it was the "pill" that attracted all the initial publicity, provoking incredulity in certain quarters, derision in others. The headlines told the story: "Towards the Freudian Pill," "A Pill That Elides Evolution," "A Biochemical Treatment for Original Sin." Macmillan, in America, had gone out of their way to play up Koestler's proposal with a letter to reviewers suggesting that "Koestler's peace pill" could do for genocide what the birth control pill had done for overpopulation. Glued to the bottom of the letter was a little red heart-

shaped pellet next to the question "If there were such a pill—a 'peace' pill—
would you take it?" Some reviewers found the stunt playful, some thought it
silly, others were offended, but whichever way they took it, the letter was
counterproductive in the way it undermined the seriousness of Koestler's intentions.[31]

As a result, the last ten pages of a three-hundred-page book became, in effect, the center of discussion and offered a tempting target to Koestler's numerous critics. The very idea was "science-fiction in orbit" and had "the aura
of instant Miracle Whip." Leslie Fiedler compared Koestler to Timothy
Leary, R. D. Laing, Norman O. Brown, Aldous Huxley, Teilhard de Chardin,
and other "pop-gurus" whom Koestler affected to despise. Koestler's pill proposal was pronounced ludicrous, anticlimactic, even malignant, and it was
felt that this "profoundly thoughtful, civilized man and a rare companion"
might have become as "balmy as a crumpet."[32]

Koestler was criticized by specialists for his "unfair and unscholarly" attacks on behaviorism and his overpolemical treatment of neo-Darwinism,
and for failing to understand that scientific discourse wasn't a battle between
reactionaries and progressives but a "multifarious process," with diverse
groups and competing theories. Again, he struck some of them as intellectually stuck in the late nineteenth century—or at the latest the early twentieth—in both his polemical attitudes and in his knowledge of some branches
of science. Part of the problem was that *Ghost* encompassed two different
books (as Koestler had feared all along), one on hierarchical systems and the
other on the fall of man and what to do about it. Even his critics found much
to praise in sections one and two of the book, and felt that for perhaps two
thirds of its length *Ghost* was "persuasively argued." It could also be read, as
David Krech put it in *Science*, as a set of "lucidly written and compelling critical speculative essays on the many-faceted life sciences," which the scientist
could read not only with profit, but "above all—and that is so rare—with
pleasure."

It was the "second" book that caused the difficulties. Rycroft guessed that
Koestler was a neo-vitalist, like George Bernard Shaw and Henri Bergson.
Stephen Toulmin added Leibniz and Goethe (both opponents of the "new
mechanical philosophy" of Descartes and Newton) to the list of influences,
and pointed out that though many of Koestler's "truths" were true enough,
they didn't support the larger "Truth" proposed in part three of his
book. Koestler shared with Teilhard de Chardin "an all-embracing cosmic
vision borrowed ultimately from Lamarck," but whereas Teilhard preached
a bland optimism, Koestler was insisting that the final outcome of evolution
might be the damnation of the species. His book was more theology than science.[33]

The playwright Dennis Potter also saw Koestler's writing as theological.

Koestler was "a terrible raven, clothing the polychromatic brilliance of his intellect with dark plumes of anxiety and foreboding." Koestler's theory of human destructiveness and human deficiency aspired to shift "the ancient mark of Cain back into the even more ancient depths of our skulls." Koestler was writing in the vein of Genesis, replacing the religious concept of Original Sin with "the unholy concept of Biological Error." The biblical parallels were important, for Koestler's book worked on the imagination in the same fearful and feverish manner as the ancient prophets. "Metaphor and fact become almost as inseparable as dancer and dance; vivid analogies proliferate until they can scarcely be shaken back into their more humdrum compartments, and the dream-like totality of the argument (or the image, or the dread) is so overpowering that one instinctively genuflects before daring to attempt the blasphemy of atomizing the evidence or questioning the conclusions." Potter ultimately judged the whole enterprise "eccentric," but deeply admired the writing it had brought forth.[34]

Koestler himself did and didn't acknowledge the religious analogy. On the one hand *The Ghost in the Machine* was written, he said, to try to fill the "vacancy in every living soul" and slake the "deep thirst in all of us," but on the other he described these things as "the legacies of the enlightenment." The book was also the fruit of his view, expressed to Polanyi some twenty-five years earlier, that the scientist had "a mission of social usefulness to fulfil," not in the vulgar Marxist sense of economic utility but in the sense that every activity that tended to "establish the maximum of harmony between society and nature, and within society itself" was socially useful. In the present case, he lived up to the latter prescription with his ideas on hierarchies and his invention of the Janus-faced holon, which has entered the language and proved to be a useful concept in systems theory, and he demonstrated that he had lost none of his *Fingerspitzengefühl,* his talent for keeping his finger on the cosmic pulse, for his identification of aggression as a prime psychological, social, and political problem for modern man foreshadowed a large literature on the subject that continues to grow.[35]

As for his infamous "cure," less than a month after *Ghost*'s American publication an experimental psychologist reported to a UNESCO conference on brain research that "both man and animals possessed 'circuits' in the brain, which, when stimulated, produced 'well organized' aggressive behavior." It was well known that aggressive capacities could be removed by surgery or neutralized by the implantation of electrodes, but "anti-hostility" drugs were being administered to violent criminals with considerable success, and it was "not inconceivable" that "specific anti-hostility agents" could be "placed in the water supply to make a peaceful population." Thirty years later, geneticists were discussing the pros and cons of implanting genes for "emotional stability," and five years after that, pharmacologists testified that it was "quick, easy, cheap and safe to block many unwanted emotions." These have been the proposals of hard-nosed experimental scientists, not some soft-nosed novelist, and are considered unremarkable in the age of Prozac. Except for the sweeping breadth of his conclusions, Koestler wasn't so far out after all.[36]

CHAPTER FORTY-FIVE

WUNDERKIND

In science nothing seems easier than what was discovered yester-
day; nothing more difficult than to say what will be discovered
tomorrow.

— JEAN-BAPTISTE BIOT

IN THE SPRING of 1968, the University of Copenhagen awarded Koestler the Sonning Prize for work "advancing European civilization" and for his contribution to literature and European culture (former recipients included Winston Churchill, Bertrand Russell, and Laurence Olivier). The citation was for his novels and essays as much as for his scientific works, but when accepting the prize in Copenhagen, Koestler chose to emphasize the latter.[1]

Holger Hydén, his Swedish scientist friend, vowed to propose Koestler for the Nobel Prize for Literature. Koestler told Cynthia it "didn't mean a thing" but was flattered nonetheless. He had been nominated before and had made the short list of six on at least three occasions, but had never been chosen. One theory held that the Swedes were too attached to their proclaimed role as a bridge between East and West to offer the prize to the author of *Darkness at Noon,* but there was also the problem of how to classify Koestler in his middle and later years, especially after his switch to science.[2]

After speaking at several symposia in Europe and America, Koestler conceived the idea of staging a conference of his own, hoping to create the kind of intellectual forum he had failed to find at Stanford. What he wanted was "a *real* interdisciplinary seminar," which meant "about ten people sitting for five days, tape-recorded proceedings carefully re-edited and published as a book." Such was the continuing attraction of his name that he convinced Hutchinson, Macmillan, and Molden (with Calmann-Lévy on the fence) to pony up advances that would pay for the participants' travel and hotel expenses and a modest honorarium, and he extracted a further thousand dollars from the International Association for Cultural Freedom (the CCF's new name after the CIA revelations). With these resources he was able to pull off something unique: a private academic conference of his own—in Alpbach, of course—to which he could invite anyone he liked, with no interference from a foundation, university, or committee of colleagues.

Koestler uncompromisingly called his conference "Beyond Reductionism," and an impressive array of scientists took part, including several whom he regarded as allies in his opposition to behaviorism and neo-Darwinism: Bertalanffy, Weiss, MacLean, Smythies, Blanche Bruner, Hydén, Hayek, and one of the world's leading experts on evolution, C. H. Waddington, who Koestler thought was wavering in his commitment to Darwinism. W. H. Thorpe, the distinguished Cambridge ethologist, took the chair.

The group met in Alpbach on June 5, 1968, for five days of formal papers and discussions, punctuated by meals at the Böglerhof and drinks at the Schreiberhäusl. There were the usual conference distractions. Weiss grandstanded, Bertalanffy mumbled, and Cynthia caught Hydén giving Blanche Bruner "a passionate kiss" when his wife wasn't looking. Weiss and Bertalanffy both cautiously shared Koestler's skepticism about neo-Darwinism, but Koestler's own paper, "Beyond Atomism and Holism—the Concept of the Holon," fared badly in discussion. The Harvard psychiatrist Seymour Kety commented that Koestler's description of the nervous system was both "intriguing and satisfying," but it was also "a model of mechanism." The "leap" that Koestler made into free will and consciousness didn't fit the system as described. It was similar to the problem that had bedeviled his book: the conclusions didn't fully fit the diagnosis. Koestler protested that he had devoted fifty pages of *Ghost* to free will and the mind-body problem and that there wasn't time in a short paper to go into it, but the consensus was that Koestler had characteristically overstretched his theory of hierarchies and overdone his analogies by pushing a basically sound theory too far.[3]

It had been foolhardy of Koestler to surround himself with so many topflight scientists, and he suffered in consequence. Both Hayek and Weiss opposed him in the informal discussions between papers, and Waddington thoroughly disconcerted him with his unexpectedly forthright defense of neo-Darwinism. At the end the bruised Koestler professed himself "disappointed" with the outcome and referred to himself jokingly as "an accidental catalyst," which was true except for the "accidental" part. The published volume of the proceedings, *Beyond Reductionism: New Perspectives in the Life Sciences,* edited by Koestler and Smythies, offered a quick survey of the key issues in the life sciences in the 1960s and was prescient about the directions in which research was moving but was much less polemical than Koestler had wished. It also, despite the best efforts of friends such as Lance Whyte and George Steiner, attracted very little attention in the serious press.[4]

*   *   *

KOESTLER HAD CONCEIVED *The Ghost in the Machine* as the third and final part of a trilogy on science, and he wasn't sure what to do next. Should he go on with his science writing or return to the mainstream, perhaps even write fiction again? He told Cynthia he was determined to write another novel, "even if it was bad" (violating, he said, Connolly's principle that he wouldn't write a novel if he knew it was going to be no good). Koestler preferred Thomas Mann's dictum: Vanity is justified, but vanity should stand *behind* the work and not in front of it. He asked Cynthia if he could go through her diaries for material about their life in Alpbach, citing a number of episodes he remembered, but Cynthia was startled. "I don't think I have any of this," she confided to that same diary, "it will be disappointing."[5]

In November 1967 he flew to Kingston, Ontario, to take part in yet another symposium ("The University and the Ethics of Change"), at Queen's University, and to accept an honorary doctorate. It was his first university degree of any kind, and he was delighted. "I think it is high time I was called Herr Doktor," he wrote to Misi Polanyi. His paper "Rebellion in a Vacuum," repackaged some of the ideas expressed in *The Ghost in the Machine,* updated to take account of the student demonstrations of 1968. He blamed the near-universal belief in "the ethical neutrality of science" for the student unrest. Science promoted the idea that we were at the mercy of impersonal forces and that randomness was an immutable fact of life. This outlook had infected all branches of learning and the arts, leading to disillusionment and rebellion and a sense of futility on the part of the young.[6]

At pharmacology conferences in Puerto Rico and Zurich, and in several interviews during the next few months, Koestler continued to explain and defend his views on drugs. A medical drug to counteract aggression would be good ("the individual G.I. has no hatred of Ho Chi Minh, whose name he had never heard of before; but he is prepared not only to kill, but also to die out of loyalty to his government"), but LSD and other hallucinogenic drugs were bad, representing a "commercialized, mechanized mysticism" called forth in protest against a "commercialized, mechanized society" (a trip was "a confidence trick played on one's own nervous system"). When a Norwegian woman wrote to ask if he had ever taken cannabis and whether he would agree to take part in some experiments with the drug if he ever came to Copenhagen, Koestler replied that he had tried LSD twice and opium ages before "but never cannabis." He had no plans to visit Copenhagen, but if he did, "I shall be delighted to get high in the name of science."[7]

In between conferences Koestler paid a disastrous visit to Australia. He was curious to see the place and had agreed to appear in a television talk show, *Encounter,* hosted by the well-known broadcaster Barry Jones, in order to support Jones's campaign for the abolition of the death penalty. Jones also expressed the hope that Koestler would speak out for "other good causes" as well. After a week's vacation in Iran and two sleepless nights en route, Koestler arrived in Melbourne in November feeling tired and irritable, only to ignite the sort of firestorm that seemed de rigueur for any visit he made to a foreign country. The local branch of Amnesty International had advertised a lecture by Koestler on the theme of "Europe in Conflict" and sold eight hundred tickets on the strength of his name. This was news to Koestler, who had expected to speak to a small group of Amnesty members on his Prison Awards scheme and capital punishment, not to give a public lecture on an explicitly political subject.[8]

He insisted that the topic be prison reform, and Jones hastily scrambled together a six-man panel that included Koestler, Jones, and Sir John Barry, chief justice of the Appeals Court of Victoria. On the night of the discussion there was chaos. The hall was full to overflowing. One microphone had been provided for the six speakers on stage, and it hummed and whistled so badly that the voices of the panelists were inaudible. The audience's microphone didn't work either, and dozens of people walked out, guaranteeing negative headlines in the next day's newspapers and setting the tone for what was to become another uneasy expedition.[9]

In the first of three scheduled television programs, the aggrieved Jones adopted an aggressive, inquisitorial tone in his interview that seemed to want to portray Koestler as a political turncoat and ideological zealot. Koestler insisted that a second program on religion and a third on science take the form of round-table discussions, and they went off much better. Before he left, Koestler gave *The Age* newspaper a new short story, "The Misunderstanding," which purported to relate Christ's thoughts immediately before his crucifixion, causing a new uproar.[10]

The point of the story was to suggest that Christ had died in order to draw God's attention to the parlous state of the world, a theme that had become an obsession with Koestler. The story is clearly blasphemous. Koestler's Messiah is emphatically flesh and blood, fears that he might lose control of his bladder or bowels when they hoist him onto the cross, and excoriates God for His seeming indifference. "Speak, damn you, speak to me as you did on that night on the mountain." Christ believes in God yet doubts his existence. God is "a parable," he concludes, and the crucifixion another parable. Men will "remember it and twist its meaning. They will torture and kill in the name of a parable. And thus will your will be done, not mine."[11]

It was a restatement of Koestler's desolate view of a world gone mad, clothed in the language of Christian doctrine, and it appeared (with the title "Episode") in the December issue of the London *Encounter* without incident. When *The Age* published it on Christmas Eve in Melbourne, however, with a suggestive new title blazoned across the page—"A Christmas Story of Christ's Thoughts on the Cross"—it provoked a blizzard of readers' letters and righteous outrage. "Philosophical pornography" was the way one angry reader described it. Koestler had his defenders, but he had a knack for stirring up scandal wherever he went (which was part of the attraction for his hosts, of course), and provocation was second nature to him.[12]

THE SHORT STORY reflected Koestler's reawakened interest in fiction, and he thought again of writing an autobiographical novel based on his life since 1940, which would be about "the madness of man." He gave a lecture on this subject to the Nobel Symposium in Stockholm in the fall of 1969 but continued to grope for a new nonfictional subject in case his plan for a novel didn't work out. The obvious solution was a third volume of autobiography, and he drew up a list of possible chapters: "Quarrels, Crusades, Do-Goodings, Alcohol, Women I Thought I Knew, Dogs, Author and Critics, Vanities, Honesties, Quixotries, Guilt, Taste, Call-Girls, *Littérateurs,* The Snob in Us, Jews and Hebrews, Houses, Essences." He also jotted down some aphorisms about himself: "Koestler A and Koestler B: until 7 [he] works like a slave, after 7 gets tight as a lord. Trouble is Koestler only visible to people after 7"; "K has always been an introvert posing as an extravert"; "I am going into my second childhood without ever having grown out of the first"; "to swim against the current is meritorious, but oh, how tired one's arms become"; "paranoia is the price *homo sapiens* pays for creativity"; "the last illusion is the belief that one has lost all illusions."[13]

He reread Orwell's 1944 essay on him and brooded over it yet again. "He can't really have liked me. Twice he mentions 'hedonism' (plus the chink passage elsewhere). A bitter man, a tortured mind—but not a twisted one." Orwell's essay suggested a chapter on "the art of being disliked." Recalling his youthful achievements, Koestler commented sourly, "Once a Wunderkind always a Wunderkind, at present performing at academic symposia as an academic call-girl." He remembered Thomas Mann's remark that it wasn't only the quality of a writer's work that mattered, it was also the bulk. Over time it sank in, instead of floating on the surface. His own ambition, "starting at 30," had been to produce a book a year for thirty years, but now he was no longer sure. He worried instead about "the pointlessness of adding yet another book to the exploding libraries of the world."[14]

Thoughts of death came and went. Not long ago he had written in his notebook that *la comédie humaine* no longer stimulated him. "It's time to depart. I apologize for causing grief to my wife and a few others who may miss me for a while. But curiosity is getting the upper hand over loyalty. If curiosity is to be disappointed, *tant pis* [so much the worse]. But I still believe in Schopenhauer's intuition expressed in *Leben und Tod und seine Beziehung zum Willen an sich* [Life and Death and Its Relationship to Pure Will]." He felt he was experiencing an "irrepressible *joie de vivre* (Orwell's 'chink')," he noted, but it was "contaminated (or purified) by a growing expectation of the *joie de mourir.*"[15]

Unable to make headway with the autobiography, Koestler filled the gap with a lecture to the World Psychiatric Association symposium in London on the uses and abuses of psychiatry ("Can Psychiatrists Be Trusted?"—Koestler's answer was no), and a polemical article, "Mahatma Gandhi—Yogi and Commissar, a Re-evaluation," to commemorate the hundredth anniversary of Gandhi's birth, which recapitulated at greater length Koestler's view that the merits of Gandhi's nonviolent campaigns were outweighed by his appeals to irrational mysticism and his ethical hypocrisy. Koestler's conclusion ("blasphemous though it may sound") that "the Mahatma was the greatest living anachronism of the twentieth century" and that India would probably be "better off today and healthier in mind without the Gandhian heritage" provoked sheaves of letters from enraged readers of *The Sunday Times,* causing the paper to be banned in India, like Koestler's earlier essay on Gandhi and his book *The Lotus and the Robot.*[16]

In November 1969, he gave the keynote speech at the Cheltenham Festival of Literature, "Literature and the Law of Diminishing Returns," in which he examined the question of whether there could ever be such a thing as "progress" in literature and the other arts. Comparing the evolution of art to the evolution of science, Koestler suggested that both moved forward "not along a steady curve, but in a jagged, jerky, zigzag line." The life cycle of a new movement began with "passionate rebellion" against an existing orthodoxy, continued with explorations of newly discovered territory in "a climate of optimism and euphoria," and ended with saturation and decline, leading to new dissatisfactions and a new rebellion. The chief enemy of the artist and writer was the "progressive habituation" of creator and audience to the methods and styles in use at any given time, even methods that had been considered revolutionary when first employed.

"The writer's best friend," he said, was his pair of scissors, or, as Hemingway had put it, "The more bloody good stuff you cut out, the more bloody good your novel will be." "The reader should never be given something for nothing," added Koestler, "he must be made to pay in emotional currency by exerting his imagination," just as the writer paid in terms of his craft and hard work.

"It is a joy to listen to the march of your memories, particularly after reading professional literature on this subject," wrote Michael Polanyi after reading the essay in *Encounter,* recalling that their own "partnership as outsiders in philosophy" had lasted for twenty-one years. Clearly Koestler's literary instincts were still in the right place, but he was finding it increasingly difficult to follow them. Alex Comfort had put his finger on the problem in a review when he noted that Koestler had become overly obsessed with analyzing "Man," and insufficiently interested in analyzing himself.[17]

A further distraction from writing came with the revival of the antihanging campaign after the Labour government proposed a new criminal justice bill. Koestler loyally attended meetings of the Anti–Capital Punishment Campaign and was asked to write a new pamphlet for distribution to members of Parliament. He completed a first draft but when faced with the statistics for executions went into a tailspin. All the old painful memories of Spain resurfaced, and he told Cynthia he couldn't go through another campaign like the last one, but he held on through the fall and was astonished when first the House of Commons and then the Lords voted for abolition. When Koestler got news of the Lords decision, Cynthia noted, he "came downstairs looking exceptionally cheerful and gay—have rarely seen him so happy." And with good reason. Koestler had done as much as any person alive to secure this vital reform for his adoptive country.[18]

Koestler told Cynthia heretically that he was looking forward to the time when he could give up writing altogether, move to France, and open a kennel for breeding dogs. Shortly afterward, he was chagrined to read that Samuel Beckett had been awarded the Nobel Prize for that year, and was "more disappointed this year than last." Looking up a list of former prizewinners, he was consoled by the fact that H. G. Wells had never won it either and by Holger Hydén's assurance that he was on a "permanent shortlist of five," although Hydén himself had been kicked off the chemistry list for not doing "the right kind" of experiments.[19]

STILL BAFFLED BY how to tackle his novel, Koestler began to think about nonfiction again. After discarding Mesmer and Semmelweiss as possible subjects, he settled on another misunderstood scientist, Paul Kammerer, the Lamarckian biologist who had committed suicide in Vienna in 1926 at the comparatively young age of forty-six. Koestler reread Kammerer's *The Law of the Series,* a treatise on coincidences that he had admired when a student in Vienna, and asked an Austrian graduate student to do some research for him. She came back with a trove of articles that sparked a small explosion in his head: He had found the subject for his next book.[20]

Kammerer was an extraordinary individual who possessed an amazing knowledge of the natural sciences and leaned heavily on intuition in making his discoveries. He was a gifted musician, amateur composer, versatile linguist, inspiring lecturer, eloquent writer, notorious Casanova, committed socialist, and champion of the underdog. His left-wing politics were thought to be the chief reason he had been refused tenure by the University of Vienna, and Kammerer retaliated by persuading the Soviet government to build him an institute in Moscow. He was due to leave for Russia when he blew his brains out on a footpath in the Austrian mountains.[21]

Kammerer's greatest claim to fame was that at an early age he had seemingly proved the possibility of acquired characteristics being passed from generation to generation. His experiments had been carried out with salamanders, sea squirts, and, most controversially, with a small, ungainly, landbound creature called the midwife toad, which allegedly developed pads on its hands when bred to live in water. Only one experimental specimen had survived the devastation of Kammerer's laboratory during World War I, and that specimen (on which his case for inheritable characteristics rested) was in extremely poor condition.

The point was that if Kammerer was proved right, Lamarck could well have been right as well, and the prevailing neo-Darwinist theory of evolution would need to be seriously reconsidered. But an American zoologist, Gladwyn Noble, traveled to Vienna to inspect Kammerer's single specimen and demonstrated that it had been injected with India ink and was almost certainly a fake. Kammerer's suicide was thought to result from this exposure, but it turned out he was also facing financial ruin at the time and, though married, was deeply in love with a married ballet dancer who had refused to accompany him to Moscow.

The story had everything Koestler could have wished for: controversial science, tangled politics, academic intrigue, illicit love, and a hero he could identify with, a new "K=K." The events had unfolded in a post–World War I Vienna that he remembered clearly from his youth, and Kammerer's financial plight reminded him vividly of his father's experiences at the time. A further piquant detail was that soon after Kammerer's suicide, the Soviet commissar for education, Anatoly Lunacharsky, had written the script for a movie about Kammerer, *Salamandra,* starring Lunacharsky's wife, and Koestler had seen it in the Soviet Union in the early thirties. The movie attacked the western scientific establishment as reactionary and vengeful and suggested that Kammerer had been right about acquired characteristics— which conveniently fit Pavlov's theories about the overriding influence of the environment. The irony of Koestler siding with the Soviet establishment didn't bother him. The important thing was that the treatment of Kammerer showed the scientific establishment in a bad light, and Kammerer's experiments left a small crack open for the rehabilitation of Lamarckism.

Koestler worked on the book through most of 1970 and into the early months of 1971. He located Kammerer's daughter, Lacerta (named for a genus of lizards Kammerer had studied), in Australia, and was able to interview the two daughters of Kammerer's laboratory chief and a leading player in the controversy over the midwife toad, Hans Przibram. Bertalanffy had known Kammerer personally and irritated Koestler and Cynthia by sitting in their Alpbach living room with his feet up on the butler's tray ("like a midwife toad," said Koestler), smoking up a storm and saying he doubted that Kammerer's experiments had proved anything. Paul Weiss, who had been an assistant in Kammerer's lab when Noble inspected the toad, agreed with

Bertalanffy, and the only visitor to take Koestler's side was Hydén, who offered to inject some frog specimens with India ink himself to see if he could throw light on the doctoring allegations.[22]

Disturbed by his friends' doubts, Koestler framed the book as a detective story, an investigation into whether Kammerer's experiments were genuine or faked, whether his claim to have validated Lamarckism was true or false, and whether his suicide was the result of exposure or an unhappy love affair. The result was a highly entertaining guided tour of the intricacies of evolutionary theory and the psychology of individual scientists. As in *The Sleepwalkers,* Koestler emphasized the human weaknesses and fierce prejudices of scientists, who operated as much through instinct and intuition as through rational inquiry and ranged themselves into parties and schools as readily as politicians. His account of a visit Kammerer made to England in 1923 (where doubts about his toad were first raised) was a first-rate piece of psychological analysis and forensic argument, while Noble's trip to Vienna to settle the matter of the toad's nuptial pad was presented as a true cliff-hanger: Had the toad been faked (and by whom), or were there truly modifications inherited after pressure from the environment?

In a brief epilogue Koestler stated that his principal goal in writing the book was not to prove the neo-Darwinists wrong and Lamarck right but simply to suggest that Lamarck might not have been "completely and entirely wrong." What he hoped was that someone else would try to duplicate Kammerer's experiments and show once and for all whether there was anything in them, for only then could the controversy be finally laid to rest. But it was obvious that his heart, if not his head, sided with Kammerer, and in his conclusion Koestler quoted some poetic words by Kammerer that summed up his own philosophy. Evolution, according to Kammerer, was simply "truth—sober, delightful reality. It is not merciless selection that shapes and perfects the machinery of life; it is not the desperate struggle for survival alone which governs the world, but rather out of its own strength everything that has been created strives upward toward the light and the joy of life, burying only that which is useless in the graveyard of selection."[23]

THE CASE OF THE MIDWIFE TOAD was launched in September 1971 in Britain on a tide of publicity. *The Sunday Times* of London did a four-page feature in its magazine, and BBC television showed a documentary that set out the controversy over the nuptial pads and played some songs composed by Kammerer. Six months later, to less fanfare, the book came out in the United States. Koestler had kept his book blessedly short (133 pages of main text), but it was replete with human drama, intellectual challenge, and an unsolved mystery and had a satisfyingly tragic ending. It also didn't hurt that, in contrast to his usual hostility to the scientific establishment, Koestler displayed a rare compassion and understanding toward Kammerer himself.[24]

The book was hailed by literary critics as a return to top form by Koestler. George Steiner called it "enthralling" and a "superb intellectual thriller," and the British biographer Richard Holmes dubbed it "a brilliant book," comparable to Crick and Watson's *The Double Helix*. Koestler's "great gift" was to be able to emerge from "the jungle of over-specialization" with a major intellectual issue "fraught with every conceivable kind of scientific, social, political and even religious implication." Koestler "appropriates and deploys the scientific and human evidence of the Kammerer case with the thoroughness of a barrister and the elegance of a chess master."

Most generalist reviewers felt that Koestler had made his case against an unfeeling biological establishment and for a reexamination of Lamarckism, and Michael Polanyi wrote from Oxford to say that he too found the book "a masterpiece which no one else could have written." Other scientists were less generous. Stephen Jay Gould, a presumptive ally, acknowledged Koestler's "richness of style and intelligence" while deciding that scientifically the book was a failure and he was joined in this opinion by several other specialists. There was an element of circling the wagons in the scientists' responses to Koestler, made explicit by Gould, who felt that Koestler's "confusion" about evolution was shared by "most critics in the humanities" and was symptomatic of the great gulf "between the two cultures." Gould, however, exaggerated Koestler's failings and made many mistakes himself in his summary of evolutionary theory, and some of Koestler's ideas were later supported by the work of the Australian immunologist E. J. Steele.[25]

Perhaps the most interesting debate about *Midwife Toad* occurred in France. Again there was a divide between the literary critics, who hailed it as "an astonishing masterpiece" that was "passionate, harrowing, astonishing," and the specialists, who disparaged it. What emerged from the ensuing debate was a fruitful comparison of Koestler's vision with that of "vitalists," such as Bergson and Polanyi, and "animists," such as Spencer, Marx, and Teilhard de Chardin, all of whom, like Koestler, sought to explain the universe as somehow possessing meaning or direction. The French biologist Pierre Debray-Ritzen picked up this question when interviewing Koestler for *Le Figaro Littéraire* and pressed Koestler on his position. Was he an "animist" in the sense that he discerned intention in Nature? "Well, yes, I suppose I am just a bit," replied Koestler. "But I want to explain myself. What I suspect in nature is not a 'project' in the human sense of the word, but a system of forms and structures that functions hierarchically from the electron all the way up to the human spirit. I don't want to be trapped in a rigid antithesis between the part and the whole. I insist on intermediate levels for a hierarchical approach to natural phenomena."[26]

The key concept for Koestler was still free will. Without it man was a machine, and a machine was deprived of all meaning. He admitted that perhaps Lamarckism wasn't the answer to the riddle of evolution, and he wasn't insisting that it was. But there had to be a moving force somewhere that negated Sartre's pronouncement that for man there was "no exit." Whether one called this belief vitalism, animism, or holism was a matter of indifference to him. The main thing was not to close the door to a search for that exit.

CHAPTER FORTY-SIX

CHANCE GOVERNS ALL

I don't much care for coincidences. There's something spooky about them: you sense momentarily what it must be like in an ordered, God-run universe, with Himself looking over your shoulder and helpfully dropping coarse hints about a cosmic plan.

—JULIAN BARNES

KOESTLER'S FASCINATION WITH KAMMERER extended to Kammerer's treatise on coincidences, *The Law of the Series*, but in *The Case of the Midwife Toad* he had relegated the subject to an appendix for fear that an extended discussion of synchronicity theory (a lofty term for coincidences) would undermine his hard-won scientific credentials—just as it had undermined Kammerer's in his time. But Koestler's fascination with the subject was too strong for him to let it go, and he decided to expand the appendix into a full-length essay, where he could explore the subject of coincidences with proper seriousness and in greater depth.[1]

For months, starting in the summer of 1970, while working in Alpbach on *Midwife Toad*, he and Cynthia had collected examples of coincidences (the "puns of destiny," as Koestler called them) from friends, newspaper articles, and books. Cynthia's diary was filled with stories of every possible description, ranging from seemingly impossible instances of long-range communication to trivial examples of people turning up in unexpected places at unexpected times. Back in England that winter, Rosalind Heywood joined in the game, bombarding Koestler by letter, by phone, and in person with endless stories of "synchronicity" of her own, along with communications from "the other side." Heywood introduced Koestler to a second expert on the far side, Renée Haynes, author of *The Hidden Springs* and currently editor of the *SPR Journal*. Haynes, a Roman Catholic, insisted to Koestler that it was perfectly possible for a departed soul to make its presence felt in a room, and assured him that this was not at all uncommon. Haynes introduced Koestler to the honorary secretary of the Society for Psychical Research (SPR), John Cullen, and shortly afterward Koestler was persuaded to join the SPR Council and take part in its meetings.[2]

In March 1971, after an enjoyable vacation in Morocco with the Becketts (Koestler smoked *kif* and wrote a benevolent article about Marrakech—without the *kif*—for the *Sunday Telegraph*), he started an essay that quickly grew into a short book. The ease of the writing surprised him, and tempted him to go perhaps further than he had intended. For months he had agonized over the dive in his reputation after the publication of *The Ghost in the Machine*. His antiaggression pill had been treated in some quarters as a bad joke, and his apparent embrace of Lamarckism in *The Case of the Midwife Toad* had done further damage to his scientific credentials. Could he possibly afford to come out publicly in favor of ESP? He professed himself "horrified" at the prospect, yet seemed drawn on almost against his will, fearing and relishing the risk, and feeling that after having come so far, it would be cowardice not to follow his instincts.[3]

Koestler dug up an early title he had considered for *Midwife Toad, The Roots of Coincidence;* added a modest subtitle, "An Excursion into Parapsychology"; and prefaced it with a mock-modest quote from Max Beerbohm: since the topic he was about to discuss was "rather an exciting one," he would approach it "in a gentle, timid, roundabout way." *Gentle* and *timid* were not the adjectives usually associated with Koestler, but he did manage to keep his voice down for at least the first three quarters of the new work.

Its surprising centerpiece was a chapter on quantum physics. In his best pedagogical manner, Koestler conducted readers on a mind-bending tour of the new physics, wittily introducing them to the paradoxes of wave mechanics and the indeterminacy principle, elementary particles and invisible neutrinos, psi fields, negative mass, black holes, and "time flowing forward and backward." Every previously sacrosanct law of nature known to man had been broken by the intrepid explorers of this surreal and fantastic world, Einstein, Heisenberg, Rutherford, and so on, so that parapsychology appeared "much less preposterous in the light of the truly fantastic concepts of modern physics." There was a "negative" rapprochement between quantum physics and ESP, even if a "positive" connection was harder to establish, perhaps because physics and ESP were operating in different dimensions.[4]

It was a highly ingenious way of softening up his readers, which Koestler preceded with "The ABC of ESP," a summary of parapsychology through the ages, and followed with an account of Kammerer's "law of seriality." Koestler compared the latter to Jung's theory of "synchronicity" as the "simultaneous occurrence of two meaningfully but not causally connected events." Provocatively, he cited parallels between Lamarckism and ESP and later invoked the names of Schopenhauer, Pythagoras, and Plato to suggest that synchronicity and seriality might be seen as modern derivatives of the concept of the "harmony of the spheres" and the "fundamental unity of all things" (an image he had first evoked in *The Sleepwalkers*). ESP, telepathy, clairvoyance, psychokinesis, and serial or synchronistic coincidences might thus represent "the highest manifestation of the integrative potential of living matter," accompanied, in humans at least, by "a self-transcending type of emotion." It was a hugely speculative step, but Koestler was unrepentant. "The limitations of our biological equipment may condemn us to the role of Peeping Toms at the keyhole of eternity. But at least let us take the stuffing out of the keyhole, which blocks even our limited view."[5]

The Roots of Coincidence was Koestler's slenderest book to date, but it provoked a prodigious amount of criticism, most of it from scientists (one review was headlined "Psi in the Sky"). Koestler must have been comforted when old friends such as Connolly, Foot, and Philip Toynbee stepped forward to defend him, but Toynbee was one of several who wondered why Koestler seemed to prefer "an ersatz or parody religion" to the real thing. Koestler replied (in an interview for *The New York Times*) that he had "no patience" with religious dogma but did believe there were "other levels of reality" than those seen by the common man or the scientist. "If that's mysticism, I'm all for it." He believed, he told an interviewer, in a "grand design" but not in a "grand designer." Strict determinism, said Koestler hopefully, was dead, and many great physicists now accepted the dualism between mind and body. Brain research was "on the verge of a breakthrough comparable to that of atomic physics in the nineteen-thirties," and he went out of his way to refute the theory that a humanistic ethic could be built on an acceptance of the Darwinists' conception of the universe as a chance occurrence.[6]

THE PUBLICATION of *The Roots of Coincidence* represented a kind of swan song for Koestler's involvement with Austria, for the spell the country had exercised over his imagination for the last ten years had at last been broken. The old Vienna was no more ("the vacuum no longer hurts, the tooth no longer aches, I killed the nerve years ago"), and his beloved Alpine village had become a noisy tourist trap, overrun by camera-wielding Germans and made unbearable by local youths driving their Vespas with manic glee past the Schreiberhäusl and revving their engines as they roared up the hill. The college was up for sale. Eva had drifted away. Her daughters had grown until they towered over him, and even the mountains had lost their charm. "Alpbach is slowly dying on me," he noted in his diary. "The panorama no longer moves me. A landscape can die on one, like a love affair."[7]

He thought of turning the Schreiberhäusl into a writers' residence for exiles from the Iron Curtain countries, or even from Spain, but after failing to interest anyone in the project, sold it to his Austrian publisher, Fritz Molden, for exactly the price he had paid for it. "You know, it doesn't have to be a writer who buys it," he told Fritz, "but it really shouldn't go to a butcher" (nor, he added later to Cynthia, to a "Kraut businessman"). Koestler meticulously listed every item in the house, from nails and screws to pots and pans to major fittings and pieces of furniture. "Hanna," he said to Fritz's wife when they were done, "of course you will change the house and I don't mind, but please don't wound it if you can possibly help it."[8]

BUT KOESTLER WASN'T QUITE DONE with Austria yet. He had decided to return to his novel on "the madness of man," which had coalesced with another idea for a novel about the "call-girl circuit," his term for the academic symposia and conferences that he had been attending for the past few years. This novel was to be set in the Magic Mountain atmosphere of a place like Alpbach and would take the form of a letter from one of the female participants to her lover (presumably stand-ins for Cynthia and Koestler—or Eva and Koestler), offering a satirical behind-the-scenes look at the antics of the academic participants. Koestler worked on it throughout 1971 and into 1972 but found it fiendishly difficult to write, even with the copious help of happy pills. He couldn't define the character of the hero (in the case of Rubashov, he told Cynthia, he had started out with the theme and plot, and had worked backward to find the hero's character by deduction), and the worldly irony he sought to inject into the book, in the manner of Voltaire or Flaubert, completely escaped him.[9]

The result was a flat little novel about a weeklong scientific-cum-political conference in the Alpine village of "Schneedorf." The characters were mostly based on the members of his Alpbach conference, and Koestler mildly satirized himself in the form of the host and chief organizer, Nikolai Borisovitch Solovief, a world-weary "melancholy hedonist," to whom he awarded a Russian background and a Nobel Prize in physics. Cynthia appeared in the guise of Solovief's much younger wife, Claire—with Eva's sharpness and independence of character in place of Cynthia's deferential manner.

The best that could be said about it was that as the ventriloquist behind the speechifiers, Koestler got an opportunity to display his wide knowledge of a variety of scientific disciplines and to restate his diagnosis of man's ills in a more accessible form than in The Ghost in the Machine. Although the book was all talk, some of the talk was quite entertaining, leading one reviewer to praise Koestler for his "wonderful wit, intelligence and memory" and others to compare him with Thomas Love Peacock or Aldous Huxley. But The Call-Girls represented a sad decline from even the weakest of Koestler's earlier novels and was quickly forgotten.[10]

Koestler was forced to acknowledge that his career had reached its lowest ebb ever. *The Call-Girls* had fared worse with readers than *The Roots of Co-incidence,* which had done worse than *The Case of the Midwife Toad,* which had done worse than *The Ghost in the Machine.* The graph was running steadily downward, and Koestler seemed helpless to reverse it.[11]

AFTER GIVING UP ALPBACH and considering the Riviera as an alternative, Koestler decided to look for a country house closer to home and found a seventeenth-century farmhouse in the village of Denston, some twenty miles from Cambridge. Its stuccoed, apricot-colored walls, small leaded windows, and peg-tiled roof proclaimed it another attractive piece of English history, much as Long Barn had been, though much less grand. The large farm kitchen and low-beamed parlor were reminiscent of Bwlch Ocyn, and it had splendid views over meadows and cornfields. This English country cottage symbolized a sort of homecoming for Koestler (though he had never given up the Montpelier Square house), and he hoped the presence of an ancient university nearby would guarantee some intellectual company.[12]

This embrace of Britain seemed to be reciprocated when a letter arrived from Buckingham Palace asking him if he would accept a CBE in the Queen's New Year's Honours List. Not quite a knighthood yet better than an OBE or MBE (reserved for civil servants and other worthies), a CBE, Commander of the British Empire, reflected with British precision the exact degree of regard in which Koestler was held in his adopted country: with respect, certainly, and a modicum of admiration, but not too much, and not much affection either. Unsure of the subtleties of the British honors system, Koestler rang Pinkie Beckett to ask what he should do and what would happen if he declined. After all, the royal family was a ridiculous anachronism, and though secretly flattered, he was disappointed that the honor wasn't bigger. Pinkie consulted her aristocratic friends and replied that "the crown would be offended" if he didn't accept, though she agreed he should have gotten something better. Pinkie and Martyn accompanied Koestler and Cynthia to the palace for the ceremony, and for all his protestations, Koestler was touchingly proud of his medal.[13]

Not long after this, in the fall of 1972 the Countess of Warwick (aka Janine) got in touch with him about Cristina again. Two years before, she had announced her arrival in London with a hand-delivered, scented letter, in which she asked him to meet her for a drink and inspect their daughter. Commenting that Janine had said nothing about "the £500 she owes me," Koestler was nonetheless tempted, and was all set to call Janine's number when he noticed that her husband, Lord Warwick, was included in the party. This was not at all to his taste. He sent Janine a letter saying he didn't think "a family reunion" a good idea. "Cristina might intuitively guess something"; it would be "an embarrassing situation all around."

Janine now wrote from Rome, ostensibly to congratulate him on his sixty-seventh birthday but really to let him know that she had informed Cristina who her father was. "She's brilliant and loves reading. She read your books with great curiosity and interest, and asked so many questions about you—she knows that you know—and her requests were so natural and serious that I let myself go on talking about you, and she instinctively pushed me to the limit, and when she had cut your photos out of *Arrow in the Blue* and told me she had your forehead and your eyes, I lost my balance completely and told her everything." Janine took Cristina to Ischia and showed her the villa where she had been conceived. The house was still intact, "closed up and asleep among its vines." She enclosed some photographs of Cristina, a handsome girl in her last year of high school, strikingly possessed of her father's broad face, high forehead, and strong chin. According to Janine, Cristina was gifted in music and languages and mature for her age. It was time for Koestler to meet her, in London, Paris, or Rome. "It's up to you. Think about it at your leisure and write me back."

Koestler felt that Janine was blackmailing him. The temporary urge to see his daughter passed, and he wrote to Cristina to explain why he thought it a bad idea. "You are seventeen and I am sixty-seven. We are not one, but almost two generations apart—total strangers, and I have never believed in the significance of biological bonds, except for the intimacy which family life creates—but that is a consequence not of heredity but of environmental influences. If, as Janine says, you have read some of my books, you might have a flattering image of me, which I would not like to spoil. The suggested reunion would either be Victorian melodrama or an exchange of banalities, both embarrassing and disappointing. As a writer I can vividly imagine the situation, and if you make an effort you will see it in the same way and get the giggles. Cowardice may have its occasional merits. You might think I am a monster, or you might agree with me and heave a sigh of relief. In both cases—*amitiés* [best regards]."[14]

This turned out to be Koestler's last contact with Janine and his first and last contact with Cristina. Janine died in Geneva in 2005, outliving Koestler by over twenty years, and Cristina lives in France. She no longer believes that Koestler was her father.[15]

KOESTLER WAS UNDOUBTEDLY beginning to feel his age. *Vieillir c'est les autres* (only other people get old), he had once noted in his diary, but now he was turning into "a cantankerous old man" and needed to cultivate a stiff upper lip to conceal his moodiness. He decided to decorate that lip with a mustache in a vain attempt to conceal the vertical furrows running from his nose to the corners of his mouth (in the one photo that shows him with the mustache, he looks like a Balkan warlord) but quickly shaved it off again, convinced that it made him look even older. His body was breaking down and "becoming a stranger" to him while he watched from outside, "unable to accept that it is 'me.'" He felt he had inexplicably progressed "from late middle age to lower old age" with unexpected suddenness. His eyesight was failing, and after a lifetime of rising early, no matter what the debaucheries of the night before, he surprised Cynthia by starting to sleep late and taking his time to get to his desk.[16]

They had finished modernizing and furnishing the Denston farmhouse, adding guest quarters in the barn, and were now spending a good part of their summers there. Cynthia planted the flowers in their big garden, and they acquired some "children" of their own—a lolloping Newfoundland puppy called Goliath, and a tiny Lhasa apso called David. "As you know," Koestler wrote to Eva Zeisel, "I have always preferred dogs to bambinos." Cynthia was thrilled by the arrival of her beloved puppies and used it as a pretext to abandon her diary for six months, having neither the "time" nor the "inclination" to keep it going.[17]

This small act of rebellion was symptomatic of a slowly growing sense of independence on Cynthia's part. It had not come easily to her, nor without a struggle. The catalyst had been a routine quarrel with Koestler over a lost letter and his accusation that she was constantly in denial about her mistakes. Soon afterward, Cynthia went to see her mother (who had just moved to London) and for the first time heard the true story of her father's death. After a lifetime of heroin use, Dr. Jefferies had committed suicide by slitting his wrist and injecting himself with morphine while lying in his bath, so that when help arrived it was too late. "Now at last I knew the truth. My mother said that the police came and there was an inquest. The newspaper report said that he died of 'an overdose of drugs.' She tore it up."[18]

Cynthia wondered why she had remembered every detail about the day of her father's death so vividly, including the houseboy's cry, "the master's in the bath and there's blood all over the place," but not the circumstance that it was a suicide. "Through the years I had recapitulated that scene and the days that followed hundreds of times. How could it be that with all the facts staring me in the face I had not realized the truth?" She decided that the bloodbath scene had so shocked and numbed her she had suppressed the desire to draw conclusions from it and that the three days that had elapsed between her father's death and her mother's decision to inform the children had buried the knowledge seemingly forever, until this latest revelation. Her denial had to be the cause, she decided, of her chronic evasiveness and inability to face up to reality.

After a visit to the British Newspaper Library in North London to read the story in the *Pretoria News,* she sat down at Koestler's bidding and wrote out the whole story as she remembered it from childhood on, up to and including her visit to Colindale. "After all these years of seeing this episode through the eyes of a child, I at last see it as an adult," she concluded. "The row is over. Let there never, never be another—it's up to me."[19]

On the face of it Koestler had won again. His bullying had forced apologies for the lost letter and submission from Cynthia, just as he had intended. But Cynthia's catharsis had unforeseen results. Though still superficially compliant, she began to assert herself. The next time they quarreled (over getting lost in Monte Carlo one night and taking the wrong turn), she insisted she was right, and recorded the incident in great detail in her diary, adding that she had never written out a quarrel in this detail before. "If his mood changes so abruptly from good to bad humor, why shouldn't it change back again, with an effort? And why can he never forgive? What about compassion of the heart?" She took "three Mogadon" that night, which "semi-worked," and the next morning read him the diary, to let him know what she was thinking. There was another row in London when Cynthia objected to him referring to her as "hysterical," and another in Suffolk after a difficult visit to her gynecologist to get yet another abortion. She insisted on discussing these explosions "to clear the air," and to judge by her diary, they gradually had their effect. The tables were slowly turning in Cynthia's favor, and Koestler was powerless to stop the process.[20]

KOESTLER WAS STILL VERY MUCH in the public eye. At the end of 1971 he had delivered a variant of his "man's predicament" lecture to a packed audience at the Institute for Contemporary Arts in London, impressing, among others, the young Salman Rushdie with his remarks on the role of language in promoting conflict. In 1972 *The Sunday Times* commissioned him to write about the world championship chess match between Bobby Fischer and Boris Spassky in Reykjavik. Billed as "the match of the century," it was seen by all concerned as a symbol of the Cold War, a contest between free-enterprise America and state-controlled Soviet Russia. Koestler was by far the most famous commentator to arrive in Reykjavik for the contest. "He sniffs the air with animal cleverness," noted David Pryce-Jones, who accompanied him. "He makes me think of an otter, trim, the coat in tip-top condition."

As a celebrity Koestler was at once drawn into the circle of grandmasters sent by the world's newspapers to analyze the match as it progressed. Out of modesty—or self-protection—he declined to join their improvised, move-a-minute games while they waited for the action to begin and wrote one of the most entertaining essays of his late period, "Reflections of an Addict," in which he offered a rare glimpse into the reasons for his own passion for the game. Chess was "a symbol or a paradigm of the working of the human mind, a battle of ideas," he wrote, but it was also a violent game (literally so in ancient times), and all chess players intuitively knew that each piece "embodies a dynamic threat, as if it were alive and animated by the desire to inflict the maximum damage on the opponent's men. When a chess player looks at the board, he does not see a static mosaic, a still-life, but a magnetic field of forces charged with energy." There was also a "strong element of animism and magic" in chess, but whereas in other competitive games, such as bridge, poker, or Scrabble, there was an element of chance, in chess there was none. The player's mind was on the line, and he alone was responsible for success or failure: "To be called clumsy is an acceptable insult, to be called stupid is unpardonable."

Koestler illuminated his reflections with tidbits from the rich history and literature of the game, and a comic account of the political shenanigans in Reykjavik, Fischer's quixotic postponement of his arrival, and Spassky's calculated maneuverings. By the time the match started, ten days late, Koestler had returned to England and to write a second article was obliged to follow it on television and in the newspapers, until "young Siegfried, the kosher hero from Brooklyn," ritually slaughtered the Russian dragon and Spassky's "slow, protracted agony" ended forty years of Russian chess supremacy.[21]

Oddly enough, Koestler's interest in parapsychology hadn't slackened after the pasting he took for The Roots of Coincidence. If anything it was perversely strengthened. John Beloff, a professor of psychology at Edinburgh University with a keen interest in paranormal phenomena, had invited him to join the international Parapsychological Association some time before, eager to add a "big name" to the organization. Beloff now persuaded Koestler to attend a Parapsychology Foundation symposium in Amsterdam in the summer of 1972 and to give the banquet address at the annual convention of the Parapsychological Association in Edinburgh in the fall. Koestler's delivery in his heavy Hungarian accent was a disaster, but the lecture itself, a compressed paraphrase of The Roots of Coincidence, was notable for its brevity and wit (anyone wanting to know the essence of The Roots of Coincidence should read the essay instead).[22]

Ever since the publication of The Ghost in the Machine, Koestler had kept up a cordial correspondence with the marine biologist Sir Alister Hardy, who had loved The Case of the Midwife Toad and saw in Kammerer's law of the series and Jung's synchronicity some reinforcement for some of his own ideas. In 1967 Hardy had conducted a series of public experiments at Caxton Hall in London that seemed to suggest at least the possibility of a mathematical proof for telepathy, and had invited Koestler to view the evidence. "We really seem to be moving along convergent lines," Koestler responded. "I do share your feeling that we are faced here with a more paranormal aspect of reality than the classic forms of ESP." They agreed to do a book together. Hardy would write up a detailed description of his experiments, and his research assistant, Robert Harvie, would do a statistical analysis. Koestler would write parts three and four, consisting of a "natural history of coincidences" and some speculations on "problems beyond our present understanding."[23]

The beauty of the project from Koestler's point of view was that part three offered him a chance to publish some of the anecdotal evidence he had accumulated and not used in writing *The Roots of Coincidence* and the opportunity to collaborate with a prominent scientist in propagating the case for ESP. His hoard of stories had grown considerably after the publication of *Roots*. Dozens of readers (including J. B. Priestley, Jacquetta Hawkes, Rebecca West, and Michael Meyer) had written to him about coincidences they had experienced, and after the Edinburgh lecture he expanded his store by placing an announcement in *New Scientist* requesting more. The accounts that came in were by definition from scientists or readers with a scientific bent, and thus, on the face of it, more trustworthy than those of the average person.

The resulting book, *The Challenge of Chance,* edited by Hutchinson's Harold Harris (also a believer in ESP), came out in Britain at the end of 1973 and in the United States a few months later. ("Is it not a happy chance," wrote Hardy to Koestler, "that our work is being published in America by *Random House?*") Hardy contributed a detailed description of his experiments and offered page after page of the participants' drawings, comparing them with the original images they were trying to divine through ESP, while Harvie applied probability theory to the results. Hardy stated that he was skeptical about "other forms of psi," such as clairvoyance and precognition, and conceded that his experiments, while revealing some indications of correlation, didn't prove the existence of telepathy either. Harvie's battery of statistical tables also failed to show that the experiments went beyond the bounds of chance—in fact they seemed to show even fewer coincidences than probability theory suggested. But *any* deviation from the norm was welcome, he said, as proof that at least something was happening, and supported the case for ESP.[24]

This hardly added up to a resounding endorsement and left Koestler in a vulnerable position. What was he to say in the face of such anemic results? He put the best face he could on it by providing eighty pages of anecdotal cases, with a detailed commentary, and a chapter of speculations based largely on his Edinburgh lecture. Koestler justified the anecdotal material on the grounds that almost all the people engaged in parapsychological research, no matter how dry and scientific their methods, were motivated by spontaneous experiences that were more convincing (to them, at least) than even the "best-designed laboratory experiment"—a point more or less conceded by Hardy in his introduction. Koestler also emphasized the element of subjectivity. Whether a person believed that highly improbable coincidences were manifestations of an unknown principle "operating beyond physical causality" or were produced by the immortal monkey at the typewriter was a question of temperament, for "no amount of scientific knowledge can help a person to decide which of their alternative beliefs is more reasonable or nearer to the truth."

Koestler did his best to boost the book with an interview in the London *Sunday Times Magazine,* and it got respectful notices from old friends again, but the feebleness of its conclusions only contributed to the impression that Koestler had gone off his head, while the parapsychological journals were of two minds. One (in Britain) found the evidence for ESP "impressive, both in quality and amount," while the other (in America) expressed doubt about the entire validity of the experiments.[25]

Koestler had now moved to the outer fringes of scientific inquiry—and felt comfortable there. When Frank Barron wrote from Santa Cruz to tell him about the plight of Timothy Leary, who had been sentenced to two years for the possession of marijuana and had broken out of jail and fled to Afghanistan before being captured by U.S. narcotics agents, Koestler was highly sympathetic. He sent Leary copies of his last three books and a friendly note saying that although he had not been in touch for many years, "I have followed your adventures with fascination, and I very much hope that your appeal will be successful."[26]

Koestler's imagination now fastened on the Israeli "mentalist" Uri Geller, who had shot to world fame with his apparent ability to bend spoons and forks, stop and start watches, and guess the contents of sealed envelopes without touching them. He had convinced Wernher von Braun, Margaret Mead, some researchers at the Max Planck Institute in Germany, and some physicists at Stanford, and when he came to Britain, Koestler observed as Geller was tested by two physicists at Birkbeck College in London. When the physicists turned out to be cautiously uncommitted in their conclusions, Koestler was indignant. Geller, he asserted, was "at least partly genuine," probably more than partly. It was mealy-mouthed and cowardly of the two scientists not to have the courage of their convictions.[27]

As Gellermania reached its apogee in Britain, Koestler traveled to Bishop Auckland in the north of England to observe two young working-class children said to be capable of bending forks. Only one of the children, an eleven-year-old girl, succeeded in his presence, but that was enough for Koestler. We "witnessed several spoon-bendings (one spoon was wrapped in transparent plastic) under conditions which excluded the possibility of cheating. As far as I am concerned, psychokinesis, and with it the power of mind over matter, is no longer in doubt." Koestler arranged for the children to be secretly tested in London, anxious to avoid the media circus that had enveloped Geller, but they failed to perform there. The reason, Koestler told Celia, was that the presence of an investigator interfered with their powers—the same reason Uri Geller gave for failing on the Johnny Carson show and at other "unsuitable" venues.[28]

Koestler didn't give up on parapsychology. He pursued the grail of proving extrasensory perception to the end of his life, regardless of what the majority of his contemporaries (and his public) thought. The very qualities that had made him such a penetrating and incisive critic of political ideologies and scientific orthodoxies—his courage in challenging commonly held beliefs, and his willingness to pursue ideas to their natural conclusion—now worked against him, pushing him to the fringes of the intellectual community and turning him, in the eyes of many, into a figure of fun.

CHAPTER FORTY-SEVEN

THE KOESTLER PROBLEM

He is a man whose faults, though many, add to rather than sub-tract from the sum of his natural achievements.

— GORE VIDAL

AS KOESTLER APPROACHED his seventieth birthday, Secker and Warburg suggested commissioning a biography to mark the event. Early candidates for the job included Julian Symons and Goronwy Rees, but in 1973 Koestler was introduced to Iain Hamilton, a journalist, critic, occasional poet, and former editor at Hutchinson who was currently editing *The Spectator.* Hamilton was flattered by the proposition, and Koestler said he would make "thousands of documents" available to Hamilton, together with a collection of Mamaine's letters to her sister, Celia, that Celia had lent him. Some of these offered such an unvarnished picture of his treatment of Mamaine that Cynthia was moved to protest and wanted to censor them, but Koestler was firm. "Write about me as if I were dead," he told Hamilton and gave him a completely free hand. Harold Harris, his loyal editor at Hutchinson, set about orchestrating a *Festschrift* in Koestler's honor, and in France, Pierre Debray-Ritzen, a doctor, essayist, and novelist, began a comprehensive review of Koestler's life and work for L'Herne's series of miscellanies on contemporary authors. Scholars, too, were beginning to write papers and dissertations on Koestler's work, and he was perilously close to becoming a sort of monument.[1]

These plans had an autumnal air to them. The lightning storms that had swirled for so long around Koestler's head seemed to be subsiding at last, and celebration seemed in order. Old adversaries such as Hugh Trevor-Roper and Isaiah Berlin wrote friendly letters indicating a readiness to forget and forgive. Berlin said he planned to be at the British Academy for a forthcoming lecture by Koestler and hoped they could meet. Koestler replied that he was dreading the lecture, to which Berlin responded, "Dear Arthur, do not dread the Academy: everything you say stirs and stimulates and possesses life-enhancing qualities, as our old friend used to say, far beyond even the most distinguished potential members of your audience." Another sign of respectability was an invitation from the Royal Society of Literature to become a Companion, one of only ten, joining Rebecca West, John Betjeman, and Angus Wilson among the Augustans.[2]

But there were losses, too. In February 1973, A. D. Peters died after a short illness. Koestler had dedicated *The Case of the Midwife Toad* to Peters "in friendship and gratitude," and Peters had written back, "What can I say except that I owe you far more gratitude than you do me and that my affection is equal to yours? I am also very proud that my name should appear in a book by one of the best writers and certainly the cleverest man I have ever met." Koestler wrote a moving obituary for the London *Sunday Times* about the man who was a fellow refugee and had been a father figure and a literary catalyst for him.[3]

Other significant losses came with the deaths of Wolfgang von Weisl in Israel at the age of eighty-four and Cyril Connolly at the age of seventy-one. Koestler learned from Sonia Orwell that Cyril had left a heavy load of debt and sent a small donation to the Cyril Connolly Fund for his widow and children. Equally disturbing was the news that Michael Polanyi was suffering from Alzheimer's disease. Polanyi was moved to a nursing home, and Koestler did his best to ensure that he was comfortable until his death in March at the age of eighty-five. Polanyi's illness led to a renewed and tender correspondence with Eva Zeisel, who sent Koestler a recording of the poems she had composed in German while in a Soviet jail. "Moved and shaken by them," Koestler said he would try to get them translated and suggested Sperber might publish them in Germany. Sperber had recently won several literary prizes and was "very much in the swim."[4]

POLITICS (WHATEVER KOESTLER said to the contrary) was never far from his mind, and in 1973, after Britain had at last decided to tiptoe into the European Common Market, Koestler celebrated with two excellent essays, "A Sentimental Pilgrimage" and "The Lion and the Ostrich" (a pun on Orwell's 1941 book on the English character, *The Lion and the Unicorn*). "A Sentimental Pilgrimage" retraced his hectic flight to the south of France when fleeing the Nazis in 1940. To refresh his memory he drove with Cynthia through snowbound central France in February, with Cynthia now in the driver's seat, for Koestler had developed a cataract in one eye and was no longer able to drive. The French provinces oozed prosperity, in sharp contrast to the still-pinched look of economically backward Britain, and the locals treated English tourists "with the condescending courtesy due to poor relatives who have seen better days."[5]

The paradox was striking against the background of 1940, when France had been slipping into chaos and Britain represented a beacon of light, but few signs were left from that tumultuous time. At Le Vernet, still "a desolate part of the world," they failed to find any traces of the camp at all until Dmitri Kasterine, the photographer who traveled with them, unearthed some of the squat stone pillars on which the barrack huts had rested. They found the small railroad station where Koestler and his fellow prisoners had disembarked and a tiny cemetery with a rough inscription on a slab of stone: "In memory of 147 people who died far from their countries"—a polite euphemism for the executions that had been carried out at Le Vernet. "Discretion," commented Koestler, "could not have been carried further." A posy of purple plastic flowers on one of the graves showed that someone still remembered and cared.[6]

In Biarritz they visited the spot where Koestler had parted from Daphne, and in Bayonne the huge Châteauneuf fortress where he had been quartered when he first caught sight of the invading German army. They then followed the route of his French Foreign Legion company through the small towns and villages of the Basses Pyrénées. Koestler resented the villas, chalets, and weekend bungalows that had begun to spread over the previously empty countryside; the roar of traffic along the Rhône Valley, which he said looked "more and more like the Ruhr"; and the factories belching smoke over vineyards "originally planted by the Ninth Roman Legion," but he envied French prosperity and hoped that Britain's entry into the Common Market would create "a psychological channel tunnel," via which the French might acquire some of the "stoic virtues" of the British and the British some of the French genius for adaptation and *débrouillage* (improvisation).

"The Lion and the Ostrich" again contrasted the courageous lion of wartime Britain with the myopic ostrich that had superseded that noble beast, and revisited the themes of the *Encounter* special number he had edited ten years earlier. It was based on the lecture Isaiah Berlin had attended at the British Academy and was still pessimistic about the obstructionism of the British trade unions, Britain's reluctance to join Europe, and the enduring persistence of class snobbery. It was true there had been greater social mobility since the war and even a cultural revolution (symbolized by the Beatles, miniskirts, and the slogan "Swinging London"), but he felt these social changes were superficial and the cultural innovations ephemeral, leaving Britain, as before, "the sick man of Europe." Still, there was something about British innocence and phlegm, the force of tradition and resistance to change, that gave him hope. Even when the odds against them had looked overwhelming, Britons had never doubted for a moment that they would win

World War II—and at such moments you could say that the ostrich became "an indispensable partner of the lion." As an adopted Briton, he had started out admiring the lion and ended up growing "rather fond of that preposterous ostrich" too.[7]

Shortly after his French tour Koestler delivered a paper in Bellagio, Italy, on free will, the subject that had fascinated and tormented him since Spain. Now it was in the context of the "mind-body problem," delivered to a symposium of neo-Darwinists that included Waddington, Dobzhansky, and Thorpe. "They are all over seventy and mostly deaf," he wrote to Debray-Ritzen in Paris, "so they gave my paper a friendly reception." Koestler wasn't deaf yet, but he was in danger of going blind in one eye, and that summer he was operated on at Moorfields Eye Hospital in London. The operation was a success, but the glasses prescribed by his surgeon caused such dizziness and nausea that he threw them away and wore a black patch over his left eye for six months. It was in this condition that he set out with Cynthia to spend winter with the Becketts on the Riviera, depressed by his inability to see well or to drive and wondering if he would lose the use of his second eye too. In Nice, however, he found an ophthalmologist who fitted him with a contact lens, and he felt reborn: he was able to read again without discomfort and to lead a semblance of a normal life.[8]

By the time Debray-Ritzen turned up in Nice with the almost completed manuscript of his miscellany, Koestler was in top form. Debray-Ritzen had brought along a friend. "Ah, you've come to meet the author," said Koestler. "It doesn't always work out, you know. It's a bit like having a wonderful meal of goose liver and then meeting the goose."[9]

IN 1975 KOESTLER CELEBRATED his seventieth birthday, which was marked by a very small party with some old friends present, including Jill Craigie and Michael Foot. Koestler hated getting old and liked to quote Oliver Wendell Holmes: "Ah, to be sixty-nine again!" Eighty-year-old Rebecca West wrote, "I am so glad you have gone on so long and always pledged yourself to your opinion and shown such courage and wisdom. You are the most precious of human beings, and I love you dearly—and may you live *much* longer, only stopping when you weary—which I think will be never." A celebratory article appeared in the London *Times,* but *Time* magazine marked the occasion by reminding readers that Koestler had once "taken orders from Moscow" and, as a Communist, "falsified atrocities." An indignant reader from New Zealand wanted to know if Koestler intended to respond. Koestler said no. "When I was a correspondent in the Spanish Civil War I did indeed follow the instructions of the Communist propaganda apparatus," and he referred the reader to the relevant pages in his autobiography.[10]

Biography and memory were much on Koestler's mind of late, and he was fearless in contemplating what others might make of his past—hence his permission for Hamilton to use Mamaine's often anguished letters about his treatment of her. So when Rebecca West followed her warm praise of Koestler with a litany of the troubles she was having with her son, Anthony, in the wake of Gordon Ray's book on her romance with Anthony's father, H. G. Wells (which West had vetted and approved), Koestler wrote to reassure her that time would straighten the record. "Your contemporary readers and admirers will intuitively distinguish between fact and fiction, and look at you with undiminished respect and affection. Including myself."[11]

But Koestler's faith in the verdict of readers and posterity was beginning to wobble as he encountered the risks and difficulties of the biographical enterprise. Hamilton's biography had been planned to appear in time for Koestler's seventieth birthday, but after interviewing Koestler a few times at the start of 1974, Hamilton had found himself in a predicament painfully familiar to the biographers of living subjects: he was in serious disagreement with his subject on how to interpret his career. Like most of Koestler's admirers, Hamilton was in thrall to *Darkness at Noon* and Koestler's political role in opposing communism but completely indifferent to the scientific works of Koestler's later years and frankly appalled by Koestler's interest in parapsychology.

This didn't suit Koestler at all, for he now saw his career exactly in reverse. "These last twenty years, since I stopped writing about politics and turned to natural philosophy, are for me the most important," he wrote Hamilton. "The books and lectures of this period form a coherent whole, which asks for a coherent treatment. I think I told you in our first conversation that what I resent most is being labelled forever as the author of *Darkness at Noon* and other political books at the expense of the second half of my work. To put the main emphasis on the former to the detriment of the latter would give just that distorted picture which I was anxious to avoid. As a token of my confidence, I made accessible to you private correspondence of an intimate nature which certainly does not make me appear in a favourable light. About that I don't care a damn; but about a balanced representation of my work I do care."[12]

The biographical gap was filled temporarily by Harold Harris's *Festschrift, Astride the Two Cultures*. Heavyweights such as W. H. Thorpe, Paul MacLean, Mark Graubard, and Frank Barron wrote essays praising Koestler's scientific ideas, John Beloff and Renée Haynes wrote about parapsychology, Hamilton contributed an excerpt from his biography on Koestler as a novelist, and Goronwy Rees wrote an exceptionally eloquent essay on *Darkness at Noon*, deftly identifying thematic and philosophical links between Koestler's celebrated novel and his scientific works and linking the two halves of his career in a stimulatingly creative way. Nevertheless, when the book was published, readers sided heavily with Hamilton in much preferring Koestler's literary and political achievements to his scientific work, and the same was true in France when Debray-Ritzen's miscellany appeared. In Britain, Koestler was described as "the freakiest of our sages," in France as "the Rimbaud of the Carpathians," and widespread affection replaced much of the hostility his more inflammatory works had provoked. Retrospect lent admiration for Koestler's "rage to leave a trace in the folds of time," whatever genre he was working in.[13]

Interest in Koestler was also beginning to show up behind the increasingly porous Iron Curtain. In 1974, the year Solzhenitsyn was expelled from the Soviet Union (Koestler sent a telegram welcoming his release and presciently looking forward to the time when Solzhenitsyn could return home), a young dissident named Andrei Kistyakovsky read *Darkness at Noon* for the first time and was galvanized into translating it for samizdat. Russia was still in pretty bad shape, wrote Kistyakovsky in his introduction. Russians desperately needed this book in order to understand their own past, and they could now read the novel "without risking their lives."[14]

Koestler's work still didn't make it back to his native Hungary, however, even in samizdat. When George Mikes went to Budapest in 1979 and gave a copy of *The Sleepwalkers* to the director of the Europa publishing house, the latter had no idea who Koestler was, still less that he was a Hungarian and had written *Darkness at Noon*. The first samizdat translation of *Darkness at Noon* into Hungarian didn't appear until 1982, a year before Koestler's death, and the book wasn't officially published in Hungary until just before the Berlin Wall came down in 1989.[15]

SINCE BEFORE HIS BIRTHDAY Koestler had been facing the problem of what to write next. In 1974 he was invited to contribute an article, "Humour and Wit," to the fifteenth edition of the *Encyclopaedia Britannica,* and he delivered a paper, "Quantum Physics and ESP," to the Parapsychology Foundation Conference in Geneva, but these were mere bagatelles for which he regurgitated some old material. A less driven author might have been content to hang up his pen or lock up his typewriter ("You are a living monument," said an interviewer for the French journal *Réalités*—to which Koestler retorted, "Monuments are for birds to drop their droppings on"), but it never occurred to him to stop working. He had thought again about writing a third volume of his autobiography and had jotted some more aphorisms on the subject: "Memory is the paradise from which we cannot be expelled; memory is the hell from which we cannot escape." "If I were six feet tall it would be much easier to be modest." "When you blow your own trumpet, what a lovely sound it makes."

Unfortunately, he decided against it. "Since I settled in England in 1940, my life has been uninteresting," he told the French journalist Olivier Todd, disingenuously. "It's all in what I write, or at least I hope it is. I detest these autobiographies that end up as nothing more than collections of manicurists' gossip. They are incredibly boring. I haven't the slightest desire to emulate Richard Crossman or Harold Nicolson [both of whom had recently written memoirs]—in less than ten years their books will be lying on library shelves covered with inches of dust."[16]

He made yet another attempt at an autobiographical novel, "Confessional," set partly in Israel. He may have been influenced by a letter from Menachem Begin asking him to write a book about a dead hero of the independence struggle, Arye Ben Eliezer. The idea reawakened his longstanding intention to write a sequel to *Thieves in the Night*, and since he had been closely following the progress of the Yom Kippur War on TV and radio, unable to work from worry, the moment seemed ripe for it, especially when the death of von Weisl provoked a flood of memories. He even contemplated returning for a visit to refresh his memories, but decided it was too late to go back, either metaphorically or physically.[17]

His solution was to write neither an autobiography nor a novel but a book about "our people, the Jews" (which was not at all the kind of thing to please Begin). It would take the form of a history of the Khazars, a mysterious people from the north Caucasus who had converted to Judaism—the only nation to do so—before disappearing from history at the start of the second millennium. According to one school of thought, a portion of the Khazars had merged with the Magyars to form modern Hungary; according to another, the Khazars had formed the nucleus of the Jewish population in Eastern Europe, and it was this idea that caught Koestler's interest. The book would be yet another new departure for Koestler, a work of historical inquiry, though behind it lay a very old obsession, the origins and character of the Jewish people, and Koestler's conclusions would be as shocking and scandalous as anything he had written so far.[18] Koestler had first heard about the Khazars as a schoolboy in Budapest, for all the history books linked them with the early Magyars, and it had been fashionable among Jews of his father's generation to think of themselves as Khazars too—which may have been the origin of Koestler's interest in the subject. Koestler may also have come across the subject in the mid-twenties when Jabotinsky's newspaper, *Rassviet*, dismissed the theory that Polish Jews were descended from Khazars on the grounds that the Khazars had Mongolian facial features (Polish Jews were held to be of the "Alpine" type). But on this subject Koestler thought differently. He had once described himself as having "Mongolian eyes" and gave Joseph in *Thieves in the Night* the nickname of "monkeyface." The rabbi in *Schweik in the Second World War* is described as being descended from the Khazars, and his racial makeup leads to a farcical dissection by Schweik of the absurdity of the Nazi racial laws, some of which Koestler recapitulated in his wartime script on Nazi racial theories for British radio.[19]

Koestler was also intrigued by the argument of a French Orientalist he had met at Stanford who told him that Jewish historians had deliberately played down the Khazar connection because of their contention that modern Jews were directly descended from the twelve tribes of Israel. This was the basis of the Jews' claim to be the "Chosen Race" and of a "right of return" to their ancestral lands in Palestine (which had led ultimately to the establishment of Israel). If they were wrong, it could have far-reaching consequences for the Jews and the Jewish state.[20]

Koestler was aware that some extreme anti-Semites and some Arab politicians favored the Khazar theory as a pretext for expelling or excluding Jews from the Middle East. He told Debray-Ritzen that the book was bound to damage his reputation still further, but he thought the risk worth taking. Israel was a political reality, its legitimacy rested on the UN resolutions of 1948, and its future was not in doubt. What excited him were the implications he saw for the diaspora. He was convinced that if he could prove that the bulk of Eastern European Jews (the ancestors of today's Ashkenazim) were descended from the Khazars, the racial basis for anti-Semitism would be removed and anti-Semitism itself could disappear.

The case for identifying the Khazars as the principal ancestors of the Eastern European Jews rested on the argument that after the Khazar ruling classes converted to Judaism somewhere around the eighth century, they had not simply disappeared from the Caucasus as formerly thought but had fled west to what was now Eastern Europe, and it was they, rather than the western Jews from Germany, who formed the bulk of the modern Jewish population there. The theory was almost entirely hypothetical and based on the slenderest of circumstantial evidence, but swept away by its iconoclastic and subversive potential, and influenced by the work of the Russian-born Israeli historian Abraham Poliak, Koestler transformed possibility into probability, arguing that the Khazar contribution to the genetic makeup of modern Jews was "substantial, and in all likelihood dominant."

The significance for Koestler became apparent in his last chapter on "race and myth," where he underlined the fact that Jews were extremely diverse in their physical characteristics and surprisingly similar to the populations among which they lived. The notion of a chosen race directly descended from Hebrew tribes was demonstrably false, a form of anti-Semitism devoid of all meaning. This didn't matter to Israelis or affect Israel's right to exist, he said, and it was the moral obligation of all civilized people, whether Gentile or Jew, to defend that right, but it did matter to the Jews of the diaspora. "Every prayer and ritual observance proclaims membership of an ancient race, which automatically separates the Jew from the racial and historic past of the people in whose midst he lives. It sets the Jew apart and invites his being set apart. It automatically creates physical and cultural ghettoes." Diaspora Jews were a "pseudo-nation," with none of the attributes and privileges of true nationhood, held together by "a system of traditional beliefs based on racial and historical premises which turn out to be illusory."[21]

Koestler had come full circle, revisiting the emotions and theories that had powered his youthful Zionism, but now emphasizing the second part of the equation, that Jews ought to emigrate or assimilate. He compounded his heresy with a long essay, "The Vital Choice," in which he resumed his argument with the only opponent who mattered to him, Isaiah Berlin. Citing Berlin's views from as long ago as 1950 and recapitulating Berlin's riposte to "Judah," Koestler claimed that they were essentially in agreement, except for Berlin's suggestion that Koestler's attempt to bring a sort of order through assimilation smacked of "petty tyranny" and was a reflection of the "totalitarian systems" that Koestler had so long opposed. "If my saying that we must decide whether we belong to the chosen race or to the nation whose citizens we are, and if the revolutionary discovery that we can't eat our cake and have it are figments of a totalitarian mind, then I must confess to a totalitarian mind."[22]

The Thirteenth Tribe went straight onto the American best-seller list and stayed there for several weeks, primarily for its scandal value, and was predictably shredded by Jewish critics. Equally predictably, the neo-Nazi organ *The Thunderbolt* praised the book as "the political bombshell of the century," and the Saudi Arabian delegate to the United Nations was heard to argue that the Khazar theory negated Israel's right to exist. This led an Israeli ambassador to make the absurd charge that Koestler's book had been secretly subsidized by the Palestinians, and a number of Jewish libraries refused to stock the book at all. Koestler was obviously not a neo-Nazi nor an Arab nationalist, but it was the racial undertone of the book that caused offense. The very term *chosen race* reflected the language not of the Bible but of anti-Semitism. The words in the Old Testament were "the chosen people." The Jews were a people chosen to receive the law, not chosen in any other way, and the mere fact that there could be converts to Judaism proved that there was nothing racial or exclusive about the faith.[23]

Koestler, according to the Jewish journalist Hyam Maccoby, was nothing but "a typical, old-fashioned, self-hating assimilationist, in love with Gentile culture, and hoping to become absorbed in a blue-eyed and fair-haired paradise, where 'the Jews' will be only a bad memory of a people who insisted on bringing trouble on themselves." Another critic pointed out that Koestler's "extreme proposal" was certainly one kind of solution—if not a "final" solution—to Koestler's imagined dilemma. If the Khazar theory were accepted, then Jews would lose their last excuse to be Jews, "most of the world would be Jew-free at last, and Koestler could relax."[24]

These were extreme responses to what was widely regarded as an extreme thesis, but even to hostile critics, Koestler remained a member of the club. Leon Wieseltier, of *The New Republic,* allowed that Koestler was "of course free to go his own way, but not because his grandfathers roamed the steppes. He is no Khazar. The evidence for his Jewishness rests not in the ratio of his blood cells, nor in his Hungarian birth, but in the much less controvertible fact that only a Jew would have taken so much trouble to come up with an alibi for his own self-effacement." Maccoby also softened his verdict later. Koestler was "a Jew to his finger-tips, not only in physical appearance, but in his whole habit of thought." He was in the "great tradition of Enlightenment Jews from Solomon, Maimon and Heine to Freud." Besides, if Koestler's hopes for the disappearance of a distinctive Jewish culture were ever to be fulfilled, "where should we get another Koestler?"[25]

THE THIRTEENTH TRIBE was to be Koestler's last original book. His health was beginning to falter, and his body was increasingly unable to keep up with his brain, which itself, on the evidence of *The Thirteenth Tribe,* was starting to fail him too. In his last letter to Koestler, Peters had written that it was time for Koestler to produce a synthesis of all he had learned and felt—"your *Faust,* your *War and Peace,* your *À la recherche du temps perdu.*" Koestler was no longer up to such an arduous undertaking, but the idea of a synthesis was appealing, and he decided to put together an apologia not *pro vita sua* but in defense of the theories about science, creativity, evolution, and human psychology that he had advanced in the second half of his career.[26]

The result, after two years of intensive labor, was *Janus: A Summing Up. Janus* was not intended to be original. It essentially recycled and restated the main arguments of Koestler's earlier works, notably *The Act of Creation, The Ghost in the Machine,* and *Beyond Reductionism,* with nods to his other books. Koestler attempted to endow the work with a sense of urgency by framing it with a prologue embodying his now familiar apocalyptic view of human history on the downward path but weakened it by presenting his excursions into parapsychology as the logical outgrowth of his scientific theories. The book perplexed and divided the critics as surely as his earlier works had but was best understood as yet another return to some early obsessions.

This was noted by Stephen Toulmin, a veteran Koestler watcher, in a long, respectful essay in *Encounter.* Koestler's earlier scientific books had been marked by an elusive quality stemming from the multiple messages they carried on many different levels. While they had always contained a complex body of well-digested material, the reader was aware of "an undertow: a rhetorical animus directed against some supposed purblind cabal of hardline embattled scientists." *Janus* now made the nature of the "Koestler Problem" clear. Science was still secondary to philosophy in Koestler's worldview, and the break with his earlier political ideas was less radical than it had appeared.

His pharmacological solution to man's ills, for example, revealed that Koestler hadn't lost the innocence of his youthful socialism at all. Supposing that such a drug existed, its administration was far from being the trivial practical matter that Koestler had imagined, for it led straight back into the world of politics and problems of political choice. Psychopharmacology held out no more hope of ending conflict than scientific Marxism, though it might help if the right political institutions were in place.[27]

Toulmin was very close to the mark. Science was indeed secondary to philosophy in Koestler's worldview, but Toulmin was wrong to conflate philosophy with politics. It was science that paired with politics in Koestler's mind. He had started out with politics in his youthful rush to Zionism, then communism, then democratic socialism, and had repeatedly run up against a problem that he was only dimly aware of at first, namely that politics couldn't seem to answer the existential question of "how to live." This was the implied or underlying question in all Koestler's work, from his earliest (when he had been barely aware of it) to his latest, and though he later substituted science for politics, he had still failed to find satisfactory answers.

The alternatives to politics and science were philosophy and religion, and curiously enough, religious yearnings had been apparent in his work from the start. Already in *Darkness at Noon* Koestler had expressed a yearning for a new party, whose members would "wear monks' cowls and preach that only purity of means can justify the end." The monks' cowls image had turned up again in *Scum of the Earth*, in which, sometime in the future, "preachers would probably wear monks' cowls and walk barefoot on the roads of a Europe in ruin." *Arrival and Departure,* especially in its closing pages, had been saturated with biblical imagery, and in *The Age of Longing,* he had posited a "new spiritual ferment," which would be "as spontaneous and irresistible as early Christianity."

These religious themes had appeared in his work almost as contraband, for his political principles decreed that he should be militantly opposed to all organized religion, and so the two poles of his thought were reimagined as the yogi and the commissar (representing, in his psychological terminology, the "self-transcending" and "self-assertive" aspects of human nature). And as the commissar gave way to the behaviorist, the reductionist, the determinist, and the neo-Darwinist in his scientific works, the yogi was replaced by the Enlightenment philosopher, who appealed to reason in trying to solve the practical and moral problems posed by life. Yet reason too was not quite enough, and that was how Koestler ended up baffling his readers with an appeal to a kind of natural law, whose tenets came not from within society but from "out there." It was on that law that "free will" depended, and its spiritual manifestation was to be found in visitations of the "oceanic feeling."

Not all of this was spelled out in *Janus*. It was a kind of subtext, which Koestler alluded to in his interview with Olivier Todd. He said he was resigned to his readers not being able to classify him and explicitly appealed to the eighteenth-century concept of natural philosophy as an explanation for his interests and procedures. "If there were no opposition, no debate, what would be the point of writing?" he added. Besides, he enjoyed provoking his readers. "Everyone pays a tax on what he produces. In my case the tax is to be attacked and denigrated." The only way to convince your detractors of anything was to wait until you were dead.

Pressed to describe his virtues as a writer, Koestler supposed that he had a flair for making complex scientific ideas easy to understand, a clarity that he hoped wasn't superficial, a taste for metaphors that expressed abstract concepts in visual terms, and a certain concision and fluency that his critics derided as journalistic but was the result of hard work and many drafts. When asked about his vices, he said he was repetitive, obscure, and addicted to difficult subjects. It had been ever so. As a novelist he had known how to bring abstractions alive through action, dialogue, and character, but his besetting sin, as his many critics had underlined, was his preference for ideas over character.[28]

The interview had a retrospective cast to it, as did a similar interview given to John Heilpern in London. Heilpern asked Koestler if he felt any closer to understanding the meaning of "the Absolute" than when he was younger. "In my twenties I regarded the universe as an open book full of mathematical formulae," said Koestler. "And now I regard it as a piece of invisible writing in which we can now and then decipher a letter or a word—and then it's gone again." In that case, was he afraid of death? "I've always been afraid of the *process* of death," said Koestler. "I fear the pain and humiliation." But death itself didn't bother him. "Why should it? I don't envisage a hell or purgatory. I think it's conceivable that I will become a grain of salt in the ocean. I find that a pleasant prospect."[29]

CHAPTER FORTY-EIGHT

AN EASY WAY OF DYING

*If one could only use as much imagination planning one's death
as one used planning one's life.*
— KOESTLER DIARY ENTRY

AS KOESTLER APPROACHED his seventy-fifth year, he seemed finally to accept the consequences of old age. Perhaps he had in mind Eva Zeisel's advice in a recent letter from America. "Oh, Arthur—one doesn't always have to write books or be between books—one must also wander about aimlessly and look up into the trees." Buying the farmhouse in Denston for the summers instead of traveling abroad was a symbol of this new realism. So was his increasing dependency on Cynthia. Margaret Stephens noted that Cynthia grew increasingly motherly toward Koestler after they bought the Denston house, though she would still look startled or anxious when he barked an order at her. Cynthia preferred her garden and dogs to any other kind of diversion, and appreciated the tranquillity of their Suffolk village even more than Koestler did. But working for such a harsh taskmaster had aged her too, as had the large amounts of alcohol she had imbibed as the price of intimacy. Her face had grown red and puffy and though she was still visibly Koestler's junior by many years, the age gap between them seemed to have shrunk both physically and psychologically.[1]

Koestler had hoped when buying a house near Cambridge that he would somehow get drawn into the life of the university and be able to rub shoulders with some of the brilliant scientists and thinkers who were there, but the Cambridge dons took their academic rank seriously, and Koestler's books on parapsychology and the Khazars had put him beyond the pale. Thorpe, the zoologist, was a rare exception to the rule, but there were precious few others. Koestler's chief intellectual sustenance (apart from visitors) came from George Steiner, another "difficult" foreigner, who had also been kept at arm's length by the Cambridge hierarchy and had ended up as Extraordinary Fellow of Churchill College—a title that suited him in more ways than one.

Steiner was almost as un-English, prickly, and intense in argument as Koestler himself, and in an odd sort of way, the two men neutralized each other. Polymaths both, with an Austro-German education, they understood each other better than those who surrounded them, and Steiner had proved to be one of Koestler's most perceptive and sympathetic critics. But Koestler was grudging in his appreciation of Steiner's talents and often foiled their conversation from becoming too serious by drinking too much. "An acquaintance, an exchange of views, a frequent round of mutual visits could not ripen into unguarded closeness," wrote Steiner later, because Koestler quickly descended into inebriation, while Steiner drank only sparingly.

Their chief social bond was chess. Steiner had also reported on the Fischer-Spassky match and like Koestler was passionate about the game. "Koestler played rapidly and sharply," according to Steiner, "but rather than lose to someone patently his inferior in intelligence, in talent, in knowledge of life, he would break off the game or refuse to play." Steiner's mock modesty makes it clear he thought he was winning. Julian Barnes played chess with Koestler one day and asked him about Steiner's game. "He played like a *schoolboy*," said Koestler. "Did you ever win?" asked Barnes. "Yes," said Koestler. "Al*ν*ays."

For Steiner their testy disagreements were "an undeclared cloud on our reciprocal trust, on the simple ease of being together." Koestler's spasms of irritation and of exasperated sarcasm, "which could chill and humiliate those nearest to him," were a sore trial to bear. Yet on good days Koestler "radiated a rare passion for life, a deep merriment in the face of the unknown." According to Steiner, Koestler exemplified Nietzsche's comment that an even stronger motivation in men and women than love or hate was "being interested," and Koestler was supremely interested in life, in knowledge, and in "tomorrow's newspaper."[2]

Koestler also saw a great deal of Daphne Henrion and Celia Goodman during these last years of his life, both of whom lived in Cambridge. Daphne had divorced Henri and lived alone at Poke Mill, some ten miles from Denston, while working full time as a sculptor. She had become "rather gruff and masculine," in Celia's delicate description, and was one of the few individuals around Koestler to treat him as an equal. She had a habit of contradicting Koestler as if they were still living together and on one occasion infuriated him by deriding his beloved Montpelier Square house as dark and gloomy. Another day they were arguing furiously about their past and Koestler said pompously, "But *I* was the one who was sentenced to death." "Oh, anyone can be sentenced to death," said Daphne, barely pausing in midsentence before going on with her thought.[3]

Koestler had dedicated *Janus* to Daphne, but Daphne was unimpressed. "That's all very nice," she said, "but frankly, it would mean more to me if the old bugger would just sit still long enough for me to do his head." After endless procrastination, Koestler finally agreed to sit for her. The finished work was exhibited at the Royal Academy and then bought by the National Portrait Gallery. After Koestler's death a copy was donated to the psychology department at Edinburgh University and placed on a pedestal in acknowledgment of Koestler's endowment of a chair in parapsychology.[4]

Celia was dear to Koestler as a permanent reminder of Mamaine, whose picture now hung on his study wall in Denston and whom he still regarded as the love of his life. Celia was the epitome of loyalty and tact, and would never cross Koestler. She admired him profoundly and loved to play Scrabble with him, listen to music together, or just chat over a glass of wine. She recorded the details of his career, his daily life, his sayings, and his illnesses in her diaries and letters, convinced that he was one of the greatest writers she had ever known—and she had known many, including Orwell, Connolly, Spender, Toynbee, and most of the other literary lions of her day.

Celia was grateful to Koestler for the unexpected way he took her fatherless daughter, Ariane, under his wing. Ariane was fourteen—about the same age as Alexandra Auer when Koestler had "adopted" her in Alpbach—and her first memory of a change in their relationship is of a ceremonial dinner at which he insisted she try everything on the menu (including wine), and talked to her as if he had just noticed her existence and was admitting her into the world of grown-ups. On her later visits to Denston, Koestler questioned her on her schooling and offered suggestions for reading. He was very natural and "incapable of being boring," and never asked personal questions. "There was a kind of greatness about him," she remembered, "a lack of triviality, an inner light that radiated outward from him. It was as if all vanity had fallen away." He was "very, very lovable."[5]

KOESTLER AND CYNTHIA'S LIFE in Denston during the summer months soon came to resemble their summers in Alpbach. They continued to entertain a stream of visitors from London and abroad, but they didn't mix much with the local villagers. Koestler gave money to the local church but wouldn't dream of attending, and there wasn't much social life outside the church. The hushed jollity of their favorite pub, the Cherry Tree, a couple of miles away, was no match for the boisterous gaiety of the Tyroleans at the Böglerhof. Their only real friends in the village were the screenwriter Donald Wayne, who dramatized *Arrival and Departure* for television (the film was never made), and his wife, Helena.

John Batt, the village doctor, remembered an occasion when Cynthia was pruning roses at the bottom of the garden and he was attending to Koestler in the house, and Koestler asked him if he'd like a snack. Batt said yes. Koestler went to the back door, clapped his hands, and called out, "Cynthia! Emergency!" Cynthia dropped her flower basket and came running to the house with a worried look on her face, wondering what the doctor had to say. "Darling, the doctor would like some sherry and a biscuit." Julian Barnes noticed during his brief stay at Denston that whenever the phone rang, Koestler would go to the back door and yodel, "Oo-oo, telephone, angel," and Cynthia would sprint up the garden to answer it as if her very life depended on it.[6]

This unfeeling tyranny, combined with true dependency, reached its apogee when Cynthia fell ill with acute appendicitis. Batt and a distinguished surgeon of his acquaintance had the greatest difficulty convincing Koestler to let Cynthia go to the hospital. "He cross-examined me thoroughly, questioned the need for surgery, and wanted to know my qualifications and experience in removing appendixes," said the surgeon. "Some of his questions were more searching than I had been subjected to when taking my Final Fellowship Examination at the Royal College of Surgeons." The surgeon prevailed and operated on Cynthia that night. The next day, on his rounds, he found Koestler in Cynthia's room. Cynthia was holding a pencil in her right hand, with an intravenous drip attached to her arm, taking dictation from Koestler.[7]

When not working as Koestler's secretary, cook, and companion or tending her flower beds, Cynthia spent her time exercising and grooming her beloved dogs. Golly had grown into a full-size Newfoundland, standing over three feet tall and weighing in at well over a hundred pounds, while tiny, long-haired David could be picked up with one hand. Both were thoroughbreds, and whenever she could, Cynthia would sneak off to exhibit them at dog shows, winning several prizes with Golly. One day in 1979, however, Golly went berserk and savaged Cynthia's arm so badly she had to be rushed to Bury St. Edmunds again for treatment. Much to Cynthia's dismay, Golly had to be put down, leaving her to grieve with only Davy for company.

KOESTLER WAS STILL PREOCCUPIED with thoughts about how to prove the existence of ESP and telepathy. He toyed with the idea of seances, got distracted for a while by the subject of "unidentified flying objects (UFOs)," renewed his interest in psychokinesis, and agreed to join the author and broadcaster Brian Inglis and a London banker named Instone Bloomfield in starting the KIB (for Koestler, Inglis, Bloomfield) Foundation, for research into "unconventional science and alternative therapies."

Still fascinated by the subject of levitation, he wondered aloud to Heywood whether it might be practical to construct some sort of "weight-measuring bed" that children could play on without knowing why they were doing it. Heywood liked the idea but feared the consequences. "I wish I could at once produce a platoon of levitating children for Arthur," she wrote Cynthia, "without the danger of parents and publicity." Koestler designed a weighing machine that would supposedly register tiny changes of weight and record them automatically, while providing feedback to the subject. The machine was built to his instructions and installed in the basement apartment at Montpelier Square. A friend, Ruth West, was persuaded to move in as curator and chief research officer and to record the results.[8]

In 1980 "Project Daedalus" started experimenting with children, psychics, practitioners of transcendental meditation, and other volunteers. Koestler suggested that the experimenters should look for "mood-induced fluctuations in body weight" rather than levitations per se, but volunteers were hard to find. Bloomfield and Koestler tried to persuade *The Times* to run a full-page advertisement inviting readers to write in about their psychic experiences and to volunteer for experiments, but the proposal was squashed by John Maddox, editor of the scientific journal *Nature,* who was still smarting over a clumsy attempt by Koestler to get a regular column in his journal to advance his ideas.[9]

Koestler got news at about this time of a young Australian immunologist named E. J. "Ted" Steele, who had been inspired by Koestler's *Janus* to test Lamarck's theories in his laboratory and had demonstrated that mice were able to transfer acquired immunity against certain diseases from one generation to another. Steele's short book, *Somatic Selection and Adaptive Evolution,* with the provocative subtitle "On the Inheritance of Acquired Characters," had an approving quote from Koestler on the back and caused a considerable stir in scientific circles. No less an authority than Medawar wrote that if the results were confirmed, they would represent "one of the landmarks in the history of modern biology."

Steele came to London and proved to be smart, contentious, and irreverent, rather like Koestler himself. Koestler persuaded his colleagues in the KIB Foundation to support Steele's work, which Steele conducted in Medawar's section of the Clinical Research Centre before returning to Australia. He ran into problems replicating his experiments (much like Lamarck before him), and though he continued to maintain his position on the inheritance of acquired characteristics, he failed to persuade the scientific establishment that he was right. His grant also put such a strain on Koestler's relations with Bloomfield that the KIB Foundation was closed down.[10]

Frustrated but undaunted, Koestler fleetingly entertained the idea of putting the study of parapsychology on a sounder footing by bequeathing his estate for that purpose. The seed had been planted by John Cullen some ten years earlier, when he had written to Koestler about the SPR's scheme to fund one graduate student per year to study parapsychology. "I don't think the Society will ever be in a position to do serious research," wrote Cullen, "but at least we are trying to raise the status of parapsychology. It is for others to make the breakthroughs." John Beloff, the Edinburgh psychologist who had recently published *New Directions in Parapsychology,* with an afterword by Koestler, offered to provide a home for Cutten's graduate students at his own university and even to approve a doctorate, so long as mainstream psychology was included in their studies.[11]

MEANWHILE, KOESTLER WATCHED with fascination and disgust as the Labour Party fought desperately in 1979 to ride out its "winter of discontent." The trade unions had brought the country virtually to its knees with a series of wildcat strikes. Hospitals closed, the trains stopped running, garbage piled up in the streets, and in Liverpool even the dead went unburied owing to a strike by municipal gravediggers. *The Times* ceased publication for the first time in its history, and the whole country seemed on the verge of chaos. Koestler, who still regarded himself as a leftist at heart, had voted Tory at the last election for the first time in his life, and told Olivier Todd that socialism in its various forms had brought nothing but disillusionment. "We live under a sort of benevolent dictatorship of the trade unions that has nothing to do with socialism or capitalism."

Koestler was still infuriated by the British left's continuing reluctance to cooperate with the European Common Market, which he vehemently supported and Labour opposed. Koestler was in favor of a "United States of Europe" that would be as powerful as the USA and the USSR. "Why should we remain the poor relation at the mercy of the United States?" he exclaimed to Todd. "I would like to hear a European anthem as stirring as the Marseillaise, to see a European flag fluttering in the breeze, to have a European currency and a European government." Again he was far ahead of both the Labour and Conservative parties in Britain, and as usual out of step with both. But his views attracted the attention of the astute new leader of the Tory opposition, Margaret Thatcher, who was aware of Koestler's disenchantment with the left and sought a meeting with him in Montpelier Square.[12]

"How did you open the conversation?" asked Celia when she heard about the visit afterward. "I said: 'Would your bodyguard like to come into the house or remain outside?'" said Koestler. He was charmed by Mrs. Thatcher, who was not yet the iron lady of legend. "She is very feminine and she uses it." They drank white wine and discussed the power of the unions, and Koestler advised her to set up an inquiry into how the unions in other countries worked. She asked him if she could seek his advice on a regular basis, but Koestler declined. The former Labour leader Harold Wilson had recruited two Hungarian economists, Thomas Balogh and Nicholas Kaldor, as economic advisers, but Koestler was averse to following in their footsteps. "I will not be your Hungarian guru," he said. A couple of months later Mrs. Thatcher trounced Labour in the general election and invited Koestler to a reception at 10 Downing Street. He declined. A couple of years later she invited him to a private supper and he wanted to go, but he was too ill to appear in public and was forced to decline again.[13]

Illness also kept him from being the guest of honor at a glittering party thrown at the Royal Academy in July 1981 to celebrate the twentieth anniversary of the Koestler Awards. Since their establishment, the awards had become a huge success, rewarding more than four thousand inmates of prisons and special hospitals with prizes for painting, sculpture, poetry, playwriting, musical composition, and the applied arts, and had enlisted a whole arsenal of rotating juries (including many famous names) to judge the entries each year. Sir Hugh Casson, president of the Royal Academy, was chairman, and the party was attended by a large number of the great and the good: a couple of former prime ministers, some cabinet members, judges, businessmen, publishers, editors, writers, and artists. There was a certain irony in this display, for as David Astor, one of the scheme's founders, pointed out, the Koestler Awards were directed toward the most humiliated and least respected members of society. Astor found it touching that a man as self-centered as Koestler could have found such satisfaction in relieving the mental strain of others. It was a shame Koestler couldn't be there to bask in his achievement.[14]

KOESTLER HIMSELF was under considerable stress at the time as a result of an ongoing wrangle with Iain Hamilton. Hamilton had missed Koestler's seventieth birthday and was well on his way to missing the seventy-fifth, and a draft showed that he had relied almost exclusively on long excerpts from Mamaine's letters and Koestler's published works for his material, without conducting a single interview of his own. He had also cited Mamaine's often harsh comments about Koestler without seeking Koestler's side of the matter and had disregarded Koestler's plea to write about his scientific works on the grounds of ignorance.

Koestler had no desire to censor Hamilton. When Celia suggested publishing Mamaine's letters as a separate volume and promised to cut out the bits about their domestic rows, Koestler was vehemently opposed. "Oh no, leave rows [pronounced "rose," according to Celia] in!" What he objected to was a partial or tendentious presentation of the correspondence, not its publication per se. But the silence on his scientific work led him to threaten an injunction against Hamilton, and Harold Harris was forced to broker a compromise. The book could come out when finished but without Koestler's authorization.[15]

The Hamilton fiasco impelled Koestler to embark on what would prove to be his last book, a bulky omnibus anthology called *From Bricks to Babel*. The title referred to the story of the building of the Tower of Babel in Genesis, which Koestler offered as a parable of his career: "Thus we continue to carry bricks to Babel, although we know the tower will never be completed, and that even its existing parts might be smitten with lightning and destroyed at any time." Like *Janus,* the book was a compilation with commentary, but the arrangement was autobiographical rather than theoretical, and the book was considerably larger, including excerpts from the novels, autobiographies, and early essays, as well as from his later scientific works (though the latter predominated in terms of the number of pages devoted to them). The advantage of this arrangement was that it allowed him to showcase his best writing from a wide variety of works and genres and demonstrate his versatility. It also showed how well Koestler's work lent itself to being anthologized, and revealed more successfully than *Janus* the underlying unity beneath the diversity of his vast oeuvre. The disadvantage was that since he had written so much (by now he had published more than thirty books for a total of over nine thousand pages) the new book was overstuffed and unwieldy, yet still tantalizing because of the brevity of the excerpts. Compiling it, however, enabled him to rebut and preempt Hamilton's version of his career.

The book appeared at the end of 1980, and unaware of the conflict with Hamilton, some critics interpreted Koestler's book as a defensive reaction to the fear of being forgotten, while others thought it immodest and self-congratulatory to anthologize one's own writings and comment on them. "Arthur Koestler is passé," began the review in *Maclean's*. "The prodigious mind from Hungary is falling into disrepute." Koestler's writings radiated "immense intelligence, insight and integrity," but the "diminishing echoes of the voice of reason" were doomed to "vanish unheard inside the hollow tower." But the *New Scientist's* reviewer felt that "this furiously reasonable man" was "a genuine sage," and *From Bricks to Babel* "a formidable compilation." It demonstrated, among other things, the "peculiar power of an intellectual stance which, however passionately it attacks Communism, opposes hanging, or ridicules reductionism, never even approaches cynicism." Another critic, noting that Koestler's work, early and late, had a unity that was not at first apparent to most readers, and that the animating principles of his life had been both a quest for truth and what he immodestly termed "a thirst for the absolute," termed the book "a strangely moving monument to the vain efforts of one man to transcend the uncertainties of a chaotic, bloody century."[16]

A year passed before Bernard Crick, fresh from writing his biography of George Orwell, tumbled to the fact that *From Bricks to Babel* could also be read as a "substitute autobiography" and regretted that Koestler hadn't written a proper account of his life since 1940. Was it because Koestler was uncertain about where his real achievement lay and saw "a contradiction between his ideal image and his actual best work?" Koestler's themes were great themes, wrote to Crick, but was he a great writer? Crick thought not but allowed that a final assessment of Koestler's "particular genius" was difficult, if only because few had read all the books and essays and articles he had written over a long and productive life. At the very least he was "a prince of journalists, a cosmic reporter," and his reputation had been "earned and not easily achieved."[17]

When the book was published in France, Koestler's reputation underwent a major revision in the opposite direction. He was compared with Malraux and Sartre but now judged much deeper than either, an eternal heretic, filled with energy and the courage of his convictions. He was "an irreplaceable witness to our times, one of the most lucid warriors in the battle for human rights and against totalitarianism," and it was likely that *La Quête de l'absolu* (The Quest for the Absolute), the book's title in French, would become a classic. Even *Le Canard Enchaîné* praised the book as "a veritable library in itself," which few readers could hope to encompass in its totality. It was like having a mirror held up to the twentieth century, along with the thoughts of the person holding the mirror, the "most intelligent and erudite of guides." This soon-to-be-octogenarian, "so admired by some, so detested by others," was one of the greatest minds of the twentieth century.[18]

HARD ON THE HEELS of Koestler's book came Hamilton's biography. Hamilton made it explicit in his introduction that his book was "in no sense an 'official' or 'approved' biography" and that he was mainly concerned with Koestler's "middle years," not the later period. Indeed, in the published version, just sixty pages were devoted to the thirty-five years of Koestler's life up to 1940, and forty-two pages to his last twenty years, leaving upward of two hundred pages for the "middle years." Reviewers got around this by consulting Koestler's autobiographies, but the book was pronounced pedestrian and superficial and was a pale shadow of the testament that Harris had planned. Bernard Crick opined that Hamilton's book would also make it harder, rather than easier, to write "a genuine life" of Koestler in the future.[19]

Hamilton's book seems to have prompted the composition of a sort of joint autobiography by Koestler and Cynthia that was published posthumously as *Stranger on the Square*. The origins of the project are obscure. Koestler first spoke of it to Harold Harris at the end of 1982 and swore Harris to secrecy, but when Harris examined the manuscript after their deaths, it was clear that Cynthia had started writing her part of the book much earlier, perhaps after the success of her contribution to the Koestler Festschrift, *Astride the Two Cultures*. Koestler's contribution was much shorter than Cynthia's, and seemed to consist of some excerpts from the third volume of autobiography that he had attempted earlier and then abandoned. An additional impetus for the book may have been Cynthia's wish to have her own memorial to living with Koestler to set beside the book of Mamaine's letters that Celia was preparing as a riposte to Hamilton.[20]

Koestler's efforts in this direction were increasingly hampered by growing ill health. For some time now he had been experiencing a trembling in his arms and legs, and one day he noticed that his handwriting had grown cramped and small. He was almost imperceptibly dragging one leg and shuffling instead of walking. The doctor diagnosed Parkinson's disease and put him on a daily dose of Sinemet tablets to keep it under control, but his condition continued to deteriorate, and some days, according to his charwoman, Ann Cutts, he would "shake like a leaf." When Koestler saw her staring at him, he would laugh and say, "This is one of my good days." But from time to time he lost control of his voice and had difficulty getting out of his armchair or out of bed. He also suffered occasional dizzy spells and by 1980, the year of his seventy-fifth birthday, was finding it hard to work more than two or three hours a day.[21]

He was philosophical about these privations and for a while told nobody but Celia and the Becketts. When Julian Barnes stayed briefly in Denston in 1981, he was surprised to find Koestler's willpower still strong. Koestler played an aggressive game of chess despite the slowness of his movements and afterward sat in the sunshine "with Mozart on the radio and a bottle of Moselle in a wine cooler before him, looking rather like a wise squaw." Koestler was able to get about with the aid of a stick and used to walk twice around the house to clear his head when he felt dizziness coming on. "Zis Parkinson's, it knocks me sideways," he said repeatedly to Barnes and frequently referred to it when apologizing to guests for his tiredness. But he forced himself to grind out five hundred words a day and do the *Times* crossword puzzle, telling Barnes his brain needed exercise just like any other muscle.[22]

Koestler remained stoic even after he learned that he had contracted chronic lymphatic leukemia. He needed regular blood transfusions and was put on steroids, and guests got used to hearing an alarm clock go off at ninety-minute intervals to remind him to take his medicine. Like Parkinson's, the leukemia could be controlled by drugs, but also like Parkinson's, it was incurable, and Koestler knew that the two together were fatal.

He was no stranger to the idea of death and had strong ideas about how it should be handled. As long ago as 1969 he had joined the British Euthanasia Society and supported a bill in Parliament to legalize assisted suicide. For a while he had contemplated writing a pamphlet on the subject but never got around to it and instead wrote a preface for the society's *Guide to Self-Deliverance*. In it he repeated the distinction he had made in an interview be-

tween the fear of being dead and fear of the process of dying. Mystics and be-
lievers had their faith, and if agnostics could be assured of "an easy way of
dying," they too would be much less afraid of being dead.

If access to the "unknown country" of death was through a torture chamber, it would be frightening, but "the prospect of falling blissfully asleep"
could make it positively desirable to "quit this pain-racked mortal frame and
become unborn again." It was the transition, the "getting unborn," that
turned people into cowards. Euthanasia was more than the administration of
a lethal analgesic, it was a means of reconciling individuals with their destiny.[23]

There was an echo in this argument of Koestler's case for a corrective pill
in *The Ghost in the Machine*. The pill would reconcile individuals to life; euthanasia could reconcile them to death. But what did "getting unborn"
mean? In one of his last essays Koestler expressed a view of mind and matter
that was closer to eastern thought than to classical western ideas, and he said
to Celia one day, "If you were to ask me whether I was a mystic, I would say
yes; if you were to ask me whether I believe in the all in one and the one in all
I would also say yes."[24]

THOUGH KOESTLER WAS INCREASINGLY reconciled to thoughts of his
own impending death, he was troubled about what would happen to Cynthia. A scary car accident in 1979 (they hit a patch of ice and flew off the road
into a twenty-foot ditch) prompted him to confide to Celia that he was increasingly worried about what would happen to Cynthia when he died. Celia
offered to have Cynthia come to live with her, and told her cousin Peg that
the prospect of Cynthia living alone was "almost too awful to contemplate,
simply because he has been the centre of it for *so* long and she has hardly any
friends of her own." Koestler passed the news of Celia's offer to Cynthia, and
Cynthia told Celia she would love to live with her, but Celia remained doubtful. "She still seems to be toying with the idea of staying on in the Suffolk
house, which I really think would be intolerably lonely. Anyway, it made me
realise I must look for a house big enough for her when I move."[25]

The situation was complicated by the fact that Cynthia's relationship with
Koestler had continued to change with the onset of Koestler's illnesses.
George Mikes was astonished one day to hear Cynthia laugh almost hysteri-
cally over one of Koestler's mispronunciations of an English word. She
would never have laughed that loudly before, he felt, let alone in front of others, and he realized that as Koestler had grown more dependent on Cynthia,
her self-confidence had steadily increased. She had "achieved her childhood
dream." She was not just the secretary of a writer, she was his wife and
keeper. She was now obliged to drive him everywhere. He couldn't go out
without her, and was in effect her prisoner. "Cynthia was an understanding,

gentle and sweet jailer. But Arthur—given to depressions at the happiest times of his life—did feel a prisoner. He did not rebel: he accepted his fate and became resigned to it. There was no bitterness in Arthur: they grew closer and closer to each other." But what did this mean for Cynthia's future?[26]

Finally, in June 1982, Koestler sat down to write a careful suicide note. He made it clear that the decision to kill himself was his own, that he had legally collected and stored the necessary drugs over a period of time, and that he would take the drugs "without the knowledge or aid of any other person," a phrase intended to spare Cynthia any unpleasant legal consequences. He knew it was a gamble whose outcome would be known to the gambler "only if it fails," adding that if it did fail, he didn't wish to be kept alive by artificial means nor removed to a hospital ("my wife, or physician, or any friend present, should invoke *habeas corpus*"). He said he wished his friends to know that he was leaving their company "in a peaceful frame of mind, with some timid hopes for a depersonalized after-life beyond the confines of space, time, and matter, and beyond the limits of our comprehension. This 'oceanic feeling' has often sustained me at difficult moments, and does so now, while I am writing this."

The most difficult part about making his decision, he wrote, was knowing the pain it was bound to inflict on his "few surviving friends" and "above all my wife Cynthia. It is to her that I owe the relative peace and happiness that I enjoyed in the last period of my life—and never before."[27]

In September 1982, as Koestler prepared to celebrate his seventy-seventh birthday, Celia wrote her cousin Peg: "I've been over to the Koestlers several times, but now often feel terribly depressed when I go because of poor Arthur's plight. He never complains, being tremendously stoic . . . but sometimes lately I feel like Pollyanna trying to inject a bit of gaiety into such grim circumstances." Pinkie Beckett came down from Yorkshire, Mary Benson came up from London, and the day turned out jollier than Celia had anticipated. The London *Times* sent the photographer Sam Haskins to take a portrait, and Haskins photographed Koestler peering steadily out of his study window, with giant sunflowers to one side.[28]

Koestler and Cynthia moved back to Montpelier Square later that fall and continued to have close friends over for the occasional dinner or drinks and Scrabble, but Cynthia had to bathe and dress Koestler every day, and it was increasingly hard for him to get through an entire evening. Mary Benson discussed with him his plans to commit suicide, because she wanted advice for herself, and returned from his house one December night convinced he was on the verge. His mind wandered and his hands shook, and Cynthia had to help him walk. "I was terribly upset. I thought of writing and sort of begging him to hang on because he was so important to so many of us—and I didn't, because I thought it was a sort of presumption."

Not long after this, Cynthia told Mary about her father's suicide. There was no hint that Cynthia might do the same, but appearances were deceptive. Cynthia had recently typed two new paragraphs at the bottom of Koestler's handwritten suicide note. The first read, "Since the above was written in June, 1982, my wife decided that after thirty-four years of working together she could not face life after my death" and was signed with the initials A.K. (in handwriting much shakier than in the body of the note itself). The second paragraph read, "I fear both death and the act of dying that lies ahead of us. However, I cannot live without Arthur, despite certain inner resources. Double suicide has never appealed to me; but now Arthur's incurable diseases have reached a stage where there is nothing else to do." It was signed with Cynthia's full name.[29]

Koestler briefly rallied in the first weeks of 1983, but it was only a temporary reprieve, and after falling down a number of times he began to spend most of the day in bed, with a nurse to look after him. He still insisted on getting up in the evenings, but the final blow was a glandular swelling in his left groin, for which Dr. J. Q. Creightmore advised a biopsy at the local hospital. Koestler told Mikes he wouldn't go and that he preferred to die in his own house. On February 27, Cynthia rang Mikes and Pinkie Beckett to cancel their planned Scrabble games and Pat Kavanagh to cancel dinner at a Hungarian restaurant. On Monday the 28th she canceled the newspapers, and on Tuesday morning took her beloved Davy to be put down. She lied to the cleaner, Amelia, that she had taken him to stay with friends. Amelia left without seeing Koestler that day, and Cynthia arranged for her to return two days later, on Thursday, March 3.[30]

That evening, with Cynthia's help, Koestler got fully dressed, put on a jacket and tie, and dictated two letters for Cynthia to type, one to his doctor and the other to his lawyer. To his doctor he wrote, "Dear John, Disappointing news. I have decided not to go along with the biopsy, because whatever it reveals would be malignant and require treatment which would make work impossible. At that price I don't want to live, and Cynthia who witnessed my physical and mental deterioration has come around to the same opinion." Then he and Cynthia took their places opposite each other in the sitting room, sipped their whiskey and wine, and steadily chewed on the Tuinal tablets until they slipped into a coma and passed away.

THANKS TO THE ARRANGEMENT with Amelia, the bodies remained undiscovered in the sitting room for another whole day and a night. When Amelia arrived on Thursday morning, she found a note on the stairs warning her not to go up and to call the police. She tried the number in the note without success—Cynthia had uncharacteristically gotten it wrong—and in a state of rising panic asked the tenant of the basement flat to help her. The tenant, a young French student named Jean Larsignarde, noted the unread newspapers (they had been delivered after all) and the letters from Koestler to his doctor and solicitor, and went upstairs to spare Amelia the shock of seeing her dead employers. At that moment Pinkie Beckett rang to inquire how Koestler was doing. Amelia told her in broken English about the note and her inability to contact the police, and Pinkie rang the police herself. Inspector David Thomas arrived at the house at 12:30 p.m., and Dr. Creightmore was called to identify the bodies before they were removed by ambulance to the morgue.

Koestler had meticulously planned the suicide down to the last detail. In his desk was an "Exit booklet" with details of how to kill oneself, with Koestler's own summary of the steps required, and he had done his homework well. The barbiturates in the Tuinal were quick-acting and their effect was sped up by the alcohol, since both were depressants that acted on the central nervous system. Koestler and Cynthia must have been dead within hours of sitting down. Koestler had chosen a method that was painless and would leave the bodies (as he had told Mikes one day) looking "dead but not disgusting." There was "only one prospect worse than being chained to an intolerable existence," he thought, and that was "the nightmare of a botched attempt to end it." But one detail spoiled the final picture. When the police found the bodies, Koestler was still sitting upright in his armchair, his hand clutching a whiskey glass, his face wizened and pale. Cynthia, however, had fallen forward on her face, which was suffused with blood and had turned the color of liver, suggesting that her end may have been less peaceful than Koestler's.

A postmortem three days after the deaths confirmed that both had been technically fit at the time of their deaths and had died from an overdose of barbiturates. Dr. Creightmore testified that Koestler's illnesses had induced a "chronic depression—mild with occasional short troughs of greater severity," and that Koestler had originally agreed to a biopsy of the swelling in his groin before changing his mind. He confirmed that Koestler had "no fear of death, but only of living as a complete invalid. His wife was, so far as I could tell, utterly devoted to him and nursed and tended him with great care and concern." Creightmore added that he had never prescribed Tuinal for either Koestler or Cynthia, and the Westminster Coroner's Court brought in a verdict of suicide.[31]

The funeral service was held at Mortlake Crematorium in South London on March 11, 1983. Between twenty and thirty people attended, mainly friends and professional colleagues. Koestler had no near relatives, except for the unacknowledged Cristina. Cynthia had just one, her sister, Pamela Merewether. It was a simple ceremony. Two plain coffins with handwritten labels were brought out and placed side by side in the mortuary chapel. There was no religious service, just a reading by the undertaker of five passages from Koestler's *From Bricks to Babel,* selected by Harold Harris. Julian

Barnes was surprised by the undertaker's eloquence (the man was an amateur actor) and watched as he solemnly placed the book atop Koestler's coffin. The small congregation filed out, and there was a moment of silence before the coffins slid through the curtains to the oven. A few days later the ashes were taken to Denston and scattered around a garden bench where Koestler and Cynthia had used to sit together.[32]

In the course of his long and turbulent life, Koestler had often thought about death. While not in the least drawn to the idea of a personal god, he did seem to allow for some form of immortality, however impersonal. He was attracted to Schopenhauer's idea of death as a shedding of the self and a merging with the All-One, the end of self-assertion and the beginning of self-transcendence. It was this image that had come to him unbidden in his Seville jail cell, along with that "oceanic feeling" of oneness with humanity that had changed him forever. "I was floating on my back in a river of peace, under bridges of silence. It came from nowhere and flowed nowhere. There was no river and no I. The I had ceased to exist."[33]

EPILOGUE

Every writer is forgotten after his death.
— KOESTLER DIARY ENTRY

IN THE IMMEDIATE AFTERMATH of his death Koestler was widely recognized as "one of the most versatile and protean writers of the twentieth century." His brilliant mind, exceptional inventiveness, intellectual rigor, and campaigning verve went with "a love of honesty and liberty that was exemplary." His thinking about communism had influenced an entire generation, and his scientific works had given him a huge following, especially among young people. Koestler was "one of the last survivors of the Renaissance men who had emerged from the diverse pre-war culture of Middle Europe," the "brilliant, brooding, introspective archetype of the Central European intellectual" who was consistently ahead of his times. Walter Goodman called *Darkness at Noon* "the greatest novel of ideas of the twentieth century," placing Koestler alongside Orwell, Silone, Camus, Malraux, Sartre, and others of his generation.[1]

Koestler's achievements and private virtues were recapitulated in a memorial service at the Anglican church of St. Nicholas in Denston in mid-March and at a requiem mass for the Koestlers (arranged by Eva Auer) at the Roman Catholic church in Alpbach on Easter Monday, to which friends came from as far away as Munich and Vienna. In April a memorial meeting was held at the Royal Academy in London, chaired by Sir Hugh Casson and attended by upward of a hundred and fifty prominent intellectuals, politicians, writers, and personal friends, including David Astor, Mary Benson, John Grigg, Maurice Cranston, Rosamond Lehmann, Lord Kennet, George

Mikes, Mel Lasky, and George Steiner. A veteran prison officer testified from the floor to the tremendous amount of "pleasure and happiness" Koestler had given prisoners with his art awards, and among the flowers was a huge bouquet from the inmates of Maidstone jail.[2]

All this was to be expected so soon after Koestler's death, but Koestler's disregard for conventional sentiment and disdain for received opinion had unleashed resentments that were not so easily purged. As Philip Toynbee presciently noted, Koestler had made as many "virulent enemies" as he had "admiring and deeply affectionate friends." After setting Communists' hearts aboil against the treachery of his apostasy, he had antagonized Jews with his unorthodox sentiments on assimilation, offended scientists with his attacks on neo-Darwinism and determinism, and alienated the liberal writers and rationalists who were his natural supporters with his excursions into parapsychology. He had become an intellectual outlaw, and almost before the sound of the eulogies had died away, he began to suffer the steady erosion of his reputation that he had forecast so many years before.

THE FIRST PROBLEM was Koestler's provocative bequest of £400,000 (virtually his entire estate) for the establishment of a university chair in parapsychology. No university in Britain had accepted parapsychology as an academic discipline at that time, but Koestler slyly sought to breach the walls of academe by enticing its defenders with generous research funds if they would provide the subject with a modicum of respectability. Oxford and Cambridge refused the bait. Prince Charles, as chancellor of the University of Wales, expressed an interest, but in the end John Beloff was able to persuade his own university of Edinburgh, where parapsychology had been a subdiscipline for twenty years, to offer a degree and take the money, along with a trove of Koestler's diaries, correspondence, personal papers, manuscripts, newspaper clippings, and photographs, itself worth many thousands of pounds. It was a posthumous coup for Koestler but one that prompted his his fellow Hungarian novelist Stephen Vizinczey to complain that Koestler had "committed suicide twice." No one would now suspect that "this loony Arthur Koestler" had written "some of the most lucid and rational books of our time."[3]

Two books hastily published as a riposte to the Hamilton biography and intended to burnish Koestler's reputation also backfired. The first, the unfinished memoir by Koestler and Cynthia, *Stranger on the Square,* which Harold Harris assembled from a set of drafts found on Koestler's desk, was not the sequel to *Arrow in the Blue* and *The Invisible Writing* that Harris had hoped to find. The book dealt with roughly ten years in Koestler's life, from 1949 to 1959, and only three chapters were by Koestler. The remaining nine, by Cynthia, lifted the curtain on Koestler's chaotic private life, revealing the foibles of an incorrigibly volatile, egocentric, irascible, and promiscuous tyrant. A year later, Celia Goodman published a lightly edited version of Mamaine's letters and diaries, *Living with Koestler,* which covered their turbulent seven years together and was a sort of prequel to *Stranger on the Square.* Mamaine was a much better writer than Cynthia, more observant and more articulate, and her book had many good things to say about her former husband, but its domestic passages reinforced Cynthia's portrait of Koestler as a kind of Jekyll and Hyde at home.[4]

Hovering over the discussion of both books was the vexed question of Cynthia's suicide at the relatively young age of fifty-five and the matter of Koestler's responsibility. Had she been an unwilling victim of his overbearing personality, and could he have stopped her if he had wanted to? The waters were muddied when George Mikes, after publishing a slim book on his friendship with Koestler, caused a mild sensation when he claimed to have learned from a family doctor of the Koestlers that Cynthia had been suffering from cancer. He was proved wrong, but the headline over Mikes's article in the London *Observer*—"Who Killed Cynthia Koestler?"—floated free to haunt Koestler's reputation far into the future. Seven years later, in an article called "The Dangers of Devotion" in *The New Yorker,* Bernard Avishai posed the question "Does the story of Koestler's marriage make a mockery of his work?" Avishai declined to answer his question, nor the linked question of who was responsible for Cynthia's death.[5]

In *Arthur Koestler: The Homeless Mind,* published in 1998, David Cesarani had no doubts at all that in "consenting" to Cynthia's suicide, Koestler had signed her "death warrant" and added, "this negation of another human being casts a pall over the life, work, and reputation of Arthur Koestler." Cesarani ingeniously linked his charges to Koestler's ideological and political "crimes" (thus realizing Toynbee's fears), devoting a large proportion of his 573 pages to the proposition that Koestler's alienation as a de-Judaized Jew accounted not only for his treachery and apostasy as a "renegade" from communism but also for his "eccentric and extreme behavior" in his private life. Cesarani drew amply from Cynthia's and Mamaine's pictures of Koestler as "an opinionated and quarrelsome bully" and quarried Koestler's diaries and notebooks in the Edinburgh archive for incriminating material, adding "intemperate, obsessive, egomaniacal, petty, selfish, arrogant, lecherous, duplicitous and self-deluding" to the list of Koestler's vices. But his trump card was Jill Craigie's accusation of rape, which he embellished with lurid allegations of serial rape based on nothing but his fevered imagination.[6]

In countries such as France, Germany, and the United States, Cesarani's more extreme charges against Koestler were dismissed as overheated, but in the cozy world of the British literary establishment, where Craigie had many friends and everyone knew everyone, his allegations were taken far too seriously. The novelist Anthony Burgess, a longtime expatriate, had identified one possible reason when he noted, soon after Koestler's death, that although

Koestler had "bestowed a gift on English literature" when he became a British citizen, and had loved his adopted country, "he never quite understood the British or the British working man," like, say, Orwell, who in other spheres owed a considerable debt to Koestler. Nor, wrote Burgess, did Koestler understand the British preference for "unthinking instinct" over theory. George Steiner finished the thought when he added that the British didn't really understand Koestler either, for to be "a quintessential European universalist, a polyglot, and a writer who literally breathed ideas, in postwar Britain," was to be a misfit and out of step.[7]

Cynthia, had she lived, might have prevented this precipitate fall from grace by acting as keeper of the flame and tending to Koestler's literary heritage, much as Sonia had done after Orwell died. Koestler had clearly expected as much until the moment Cynthia signed the suicide letter, and so had just about everyone else who knew her. She had their unfinished memoir to complete, her beloved dog and garden to care for, and a wide circle of friends to support her, even if most of them came courtesy of Koestler.

That she decided otherwise is a mystery the bystander cannot penetrate, but it became clear soon afterward that she knew what she was doing. Pinkie Beckett remembered Cynthia telling her shortly before her death, "there's going to be a big change in your life soon," but Pinkie had failed to grasp its significance. Pat Kavanagh recalled asking Cynthia about her garden and being astonished when Cynthia refused to talk about it, saying she wasn't interested since "Arthur won't be around to see the flowers." Pamela Merewether had called Cynthia two nights before the suicide to tell her about a forthcoming trip to South Africa to visit friends and relatives, and Cynthia had been completely uninterested and "incredibly depressed." "I had never ever known her as low as that," Pamela said later, "and told my husband I thought Arthur must be dying, but I never thought of Cynthia." Perhaps the most conclusive proof of her calm and certainty is Amelia's comment that during the last week of her life, Cynthia had dressed up in her best clothes every single day, and had put on all her best rings and jewelry, some of which she hadn't worn for years.[8]

Koestler was in any case too feeble and too far gone physically and mentally to have any further control over Cynthia: he depended on her totally to get him out of bed, bathe and clothe him, prepare the drinks and pills, and possibly administer them as well. Moreover, he would have hated the idea of a double suicide as "foolish, vulgar and anachronistic," according to Pat Kavanagh and Julian Barnes, and would have resented it for interfering with the message he wished to give the world on the virtues of euthanasia. In this sense Cynthia, with her new sense of self-confidence and control of the situation, had disobeyed Koestler and muddied the impression he wanted to leave behind. The closest anyone in their immediate circle came to blaming Koestler for Cynthia's death was Pamela, who suggested that Cynthia would never have done it if Koestler had allowed her to have children. "You have to have something that grows," Cynthia had once said to Pamela, explaining her passion for gardening, "and you have your children."[9]

But not even Pamela held Koestler accountable for Cynthia's death. She was all too familiar with her sister's underlying toughness and stubbornness, her determination to get her own way. "The point about Cynthia," as Elizabeth Jane Howard said, was that "she couldn't be broken." She was totally flexible and totally accommodating toward Koestler, accepting his bullying, his seductions of other women, and everything he could throw at her, but "she never broke. And in the end he became dependent on her, and it was she who got the upper hand."[10]

WHATEVER THE TRUE REASONS for Cynthia's decision, it proved disastrous, in combination with Cesarani's tendentious book, for Koestler's later reputation. The centenary of Koestler's birth in 2005 was virtually ignored in Britain and the United States. The few articles that appeared in the press were short and apologetic, and two small conferences held to discuss his work took place not in Britain, the United States, France, or Germany, where his influence and fame had been at their greatest, but in tiny Hungary, the country he had been forced to flee when fourteen and where his work had been banned until the collapse of communism only sixteen years before.[11]

Maybe it would have been better for Koestler if he had died in his forties, like his friends Orwell (later canonized as "St. George" in the eyes of millions of admirers) and Camus, and acquired an aura of martyrdom, instead of sullying his career with speculations about astronomy, evolution, parapsychology, and Jewish racial theories. He would still have been a man without a widow or a country to claim as his own, but perhaps the one where he lived at the time would have been prouder of his achievements and its citizens would have taken him under their wing and basked in the reflected glory of his fame.

Luckily the passions he stirred when alive and that still seethed after his death have gradually begun to fade. His major works, such as *Darkness at Noon* and the autobiographies, have withstood the test of time, and the moment seems ripe to recognize Koestler's achievements for what they really were. Koestler was (in Isaiah Berlin's famous formulation) a fox, rather than a hedgehog: He knew a great many different things, rather than one big thing. But he was a peculiarly swift and preternaturally clairvoyant sort of fox, with a phenomenal sense of smell, which led him very early to the centrality of "the Jewish problem" in twentieth-century European history, to the dangers of fascism and the false promises of Soviet communism, to the crucial importance of political freedom and ethical clarity, to the glories and dangers of hegemonic, materialist science, and to the spiritual void of a twentieth-century culture lacking in faith. This was a huge amount of territory to cover, and Koestler covered it, as Bernard Crick said, as a kind of "cosmic reporter," using his formidable assimilative intelligence and genius for synthesis to try to pry open the secrets of the universe.

In so doing, Koestler undoubtedly transcended the limits of "mere" journalism to produce works of literature that are fit to stand beside those of his literary peers: *Darkness at Noon, Arrow in the Blue, The Invisible Writing, Dialogue with Death, Scum of the Earth,* and the essays in *The Yogi and the Commissar, The God That Failed,* and other books. At his best, Koestler achieved a fusion of autobiography, psychological penetration, and dialectical analysis that constitutes his unique contribution to twentieth-century prose, accompanied by a vivacity and immediacy of expression, wit, and polemical brilliance, and an infatuation with ideas and the ethics of political choice that are as thrilling and compelling today as when they were written.

ACKNOWLEDGMENTS

Most biographies are just novels with indexes.
— JOHN UPDIKE

I MET ARTHUR KOESTLER and his third wife, Cynthia, just once, in 1980, not long before they died. It was at the home of the late David Astor, formerly editor of *The Observer* in London, who had invited Koestler to learn about a magazine I was editing at the time (and David was backing), called *Index on Censorship*. There was nothing particularly memorable about the meeting, except that Koestler preferred to stand rather than sit and had a habit of pacing back and forth when he spoke. I also learned that he had a long history of supporting "causes" and that he was interested in my work, but his health was already beginning to fail and there was no further contact. Needless to say, I had no inkling at the time that I would one day write his biography.

The suggestion that I do so came some eight years later from the late Harold Harris, Koestler's long-standing editor at Hutchinson and his literary executor. Harris had written to me after reading my biography of Aleksandr Solzhenitsyn, and I eagerly accepted the opportunity to explore the life and writings of this extraordinarily gifted and charismatic individual and to combine it with my interest in the impact of ideology on twentieth-century literature and history. I couldn't start right away, because I had just taken a full-time position at Cornell University and was in the midst of writing another book (which never came to fruition). I eventually made a start in 1989, by which time Harris had shared his memories of Koestler with me, made his personal papers available, promised exclusive access to the papers in the

Koestler Archive for the purposes of writing a biography, and recommended me to a large number of Koestler's personal friends and professional colleagues with the request that they cooperate and answer my questions.

Among the latter I should single out David Astor himself, who was a constant support and submitted to being interviewed several times; also, and especially, the late Celia Goodman (née Paget), the twin sister of Koestler's second wife, Mamaine Paget, and a close friend of Koestler's until the end of his life. With her wide network of friends among the leading writers and publishers of her day, Celia proved a wise and tactful guide to the intricacies of the English literary scene, as well as an invaluable witness to the ambiguity and complexity of Koestler's character. Celia also made available to me those parts of Mamaine's letters and diaries that had not been published in her book, *Living with Koestler,* and offered valuable comments on various parts of my manuscript. I deeply miss her and regret she is no longer alive to read the book to which she contributed so much.

Celia was one of many extraordinary women I met in the course of my research. Others who were unstinting in providing me with information and sharing memories of an often intimate character include, in alphabetical order, the painter Eva Auer, of Vienna and Alpbach; the late Daphne Henrion, sculptor, translator of *Darkness at Noon,* and Koestler's companion of many years; the late Joan Lee Thompson, an author of novels and screenplays who wrote under the name of Joan Henry; Janetta Parladé, now living in Spain; and Eva Zeisel, ceramicist extraordinaire, of Budapest, Paris, Berlin, and finally New York. I should also like to thank the late Dorothee Koestler, Koestler's first wife, for overcoming her reluctance to speak about her marriage and granting me two interviews before she died; and Pamela Merewether (née Jeffries), Cynthia Koestler's sister, who consented to be interviewed and corresponded with me about Cynthia's childhood and early years.

Koestler was nothing if not a rolling stone, and in the course of tracking his movements over a long career, I followed him to fourteen countries on three continents, meeting and interviewing a host of interesting people whom I cannot thank enough for their interest and support. Among those who gave freely and generously of their time are Phil Casoar of Paris, an ardent admirer and critic of Koestler's work and an indefatigable support in ferreting out sources and connecting me with others; the late Mme. Jenka Sperber, also of Paris, who shared her memories of Koestler with me and gave me access to the private correspondence between her husband, Manès Sperber, and Koestler; the late Erzsebet Vezer of Budapest, a pioneering specialist on Koestler's early life at a time when it was politically inexpedient to reveal such an interest; József Hruby, also of Budapest, who helped me with contacts in Hungary and translated many documents for me; Leona Toker, of Jerusalem, who opened many avenues for me; and my old friend Hermann Hendrich of Vienna, who helped me track down many sources, accompanied me on research trips, and read parts of my manuscript as it was taking shape.

For granting me interviews and in many cases corresponding with me on aspects of Koestler's life and work I would like to thank, in alphabetical order, Tania Alexander, Mme. Aron, Shlomo Avineri, Ariane Bankes, Julian Barnes, Istvan Bart, Heidi Beck, Sir Martyn Beckett, Lady Priscilla Beckett, John Beloff, Mary Benson, Isaiah Berlin, Michael Bessie, Otto Bihalj-Merin, Menahem Brinker, Jerome Bruner, William F. Buckley, Jr., Sir Hugh Casson, Stanley Cohen, Susan Colt, Diana Cooke, Maurice Cranston, Harold Crooks, Imre Cserepfalvi, Anne Cutts, Pierre DeBray-Ritzen, Miranda DeKay, Émile Delavenay, Andre Deutsch, Karin Duftner, Moshe Erell, George Faludy, François Fejtö, Moshe Felsenstein, Louisa Eisler Fischer, Dora Fisher, Jean Flack, Michael Foot, Richard Freadman, Françoise Gilot, Georg Glaser, Ruth Goetz, Igor Golomstock, Pierre Grémion, John Grigg, Anne Hartmann, Diana Henderson, Sir Nicholas Henderson, Priscilla Hodgson, Hedvige Horpacky, Elizabeth Jane Howard, John Hunt, Charlotte Ignotus, Yoram Kaniuk, Elisabeth Kashey, György Kassai, Pat Kavanagh, Janos Kenedi, Lord Kennet, Marina Kistyakovsky, Stephen Koch, Leszek Kolakowski, Teddy Kollek, Hillel Kook (a.k.a. Peter Bergson), Paul Kövesdy, Irving Kristol, Walter Laqueur, Melvin Lasky, Patrick Leigh-Fermor, Herbert Lottman, John Maddox, Madeleine Malraux, John Midgeley, Tania Midgeley, Fritz Molden, Hanna Molden, Otto Molden, Robert Morris, Leni Moser, Istvan Nogradi (formerly Neubauer), Kate Nott, Pierre Pachet, Janetta Parladé, Mark Paterson, Eleanor Perenyi, William Phillips, Jeffrey W. Pollard, Otmar Radinger, Pál Rézs, Robert Ringel, Anne Robinson, József Román, Charles Ronsac, Guy de Rothschild, Michael Rubinstein, John Russell, Arthur Schlesinger, Jr., Julian and Kotolin Schöpflin, Michael Sissons, Natasha Spender, Stephen Spender, Margaret Stephens, Catherine Storr (née Peters), Bonita Strauss, Lord George Strauss, Jenny Stringer, Suzanne Szabó, Sam Tanenhaus, Alexandra Terzic-Auer, Devina and James Thackera, Marietta Torberg, Diana Trilling, Istvan Vas, Michael Ward, Donald Wayne, Daniel von Weisl, Mrs. H. Weiss, Victor Weisskopf, Lena Wickman, Paul Willert, Betty Winkler, Elizabeth Young, and Gavriel Zifroni.

For correspondence (in addition to the above) and for other kinds of moral support I would like to thank Joseph Abeles, David Andersson, Bernard Avishai, Eszter Balazs, Shoshana Barzilai, Brian Bayly, Roy Behrens, Arnold Beichman, Michael Benedikt, François Bondy, Josephine Boss, Thompson Bradley, Dr. Manfred Briegel, Kevin Brook, Dr. David Bryson, Christian Buckard, James B. Burnham, Len Bushkoff, Catherine Camus, Dr. J. Q. Creightmore, Bernard Crick, András Csejdy, Istvan Deak, Colin Deane, John Patrick Diggins, Shale Dworan, Clive Fisher, Katherine Forsyth, Lady

576 ACKNOWLEDGMENTS

Antonia Fraser, Emery George, John Gheeraert, Sandra Goldstein, Arpad Göncz, Louis Gordon, Peter Gross, Hans Haider, Tibor Hajdu, Leo Hamalian, Miklós Haraszti, Anne Hartmann, Béla Hidegkuti, Hildegard Hnatek, Diana Holman-Hunt, Michael Holroyd, Dr. Eva Irblich, Douglas Johnson, Barry Jones, Ethan Klingsberg, Nicolaus Kogon, Marion Kreith, Judith Liberman, Henry MacAdam, Dr. Henriette Mandl, David Martin, Kati Marton, Thomas Massa, Sean McMeekin, Larry McMurtry, Reed Merrill, Jeffrey Meyers, Sarah Miller, Paul Mishkin, Dr. Joseph Nossiff, Susan Pedersen, Lawrence Pitkethly, Roger Poirier, Martine Poulain, Martin Prokopp, Ursula Prutsch, Julius Purcell, Anson Rabinbach, Sandra Reina, Jehuda Reinharz, Gisela Riff, Will Rivinus, Paul Roazen, Christopher E. Robins, Ronald Roizen, Steven Rose, Miriam Rothschild, Salman Rushdie, Bryan Ryder, Dorothy Salmon, Dominique Schnapper, Eugene Schulman, Harald Seewann, E. J. Steele, Dr. C. Tepperberg, Alexandra Terzic-Auer, Claire Tomalin, Dr. György Trerdota, Andrea Tyndall, Tamas Ungvari, Robert Walker, Theodore Weinshall, and E. Thomas Wood.

I would also like to offer sincere thanks to Polly Gannon, Marianne Kerekes, Elisabeth Kis, Barbara Neumann, Carol Rounds, Peter J. Schwartz, and Andrea Toth for translating texts for me from Hungarian, Hebrew, Dutch, and Old German, and to Marie Arne, Annie Choi, Olivia Gomolinski, Harvest Henderson, John O'Connor, Daniel Oppenheimer, Jamie Pietras, Marcia Romano, Scott Smith, Andrea Toth, Eszter Toth, and Felicia Francisci, who acted as research assistants at different times during the writing of this book, and especially to Aura Davies for her invaluable help with photographs.

Even with sabbatical leaves and vacations from my teaching jobs I would not have been able to secure sufficient time to complete this book, or to travel to so many destinations, without fellowships and financial support from the Guggenheim Foundation; the Historical Research Foundation; the Joint Committee of the Hungarian Academy of Sciences and the Soros Foundation, Hungary; the Marie Syrkin Fellowship in Letters; and the Jerusalem Foundation. I am also indebted to the Publications Committee of the Harriman Institute, Columbia University, for a grant to help defray the cost of obtaining photographs of Koestler and his circle.

Much of the subject matter of this book derives from materials excavated from the vast Koestler Archive, housed in the Special Collections division of the Edinburgh University Library, where I spent many weeks over several years, and I am deeply indebted to the staff for their generous assistance, notably Brenda Moon, formerly university librarian, John V. Howard, formerly librarian of the Special Collections, and his successors, Murray Simpson and Richard Ovenden; also the extraordinary Jean Archibald (who came to my assistance again after she had retired), along with Sandra Goldstein and

Sheila Noble, who quarried the vaults for me. I would also like to thank the staff of the Olin Library, Cornell University; Mary Cargill and the staff of the Butler Library, Columbia University; and Claudia Morner and the staff of the Dimond Library, University of New Hampshire, for assisting me with my research.

I owe a further debt to the following individuals and institutions for access to, and in some cases permission to quote from, their collections: Archiv der Technischen Hochschule, Vienna (Dr. Lechner); Archives de la Préfecture de Police, Paris; Beinecke Rare Book and Manuscript Library, Yale University, New Haven; Bibliothèque du Centre Historique des Archives Nationales (CHAN), Paris; Bibliothèque de Documentation Internationale Contemporaine (BDIC), Nanterre; Center for the Preservation of Historic Document Collections (CPHDC), Moscow; Central Zionist Archives, Jerusalem (Yoram Mayorek); Ford Foundation Archives, New York; Hoover Institution Archives, Stanford University; Houghton Library, Harvard University; Institut Mémoires de l'Édition Contemporaine (IMEC), Paris; Department of Sound Records, Imperial War Museum, London; Institute for Research in the History of Zionism, Tel Aviv; Internationaal Instituut voor Sociale Geschiedenis, Amsterdam; International Association for Cultural Freedom (IACF) Records, University of Chicago; Israelitische Kultusgemeinde, Vienna (Mrs. Weiss); Jabotinsky Institute, Israel, Tel Aviv; Sidney Jones Library, Special Collections, University of Liverpool; John F. Kennedy Presidential Library, Boston; George Meany Memorial Archives, Washington, D.C.; Modern Records Centre, University of Warwick Library, Coventry; National Archives, UK, Public Records Office, Kew; National Archives of the United States, Washington, D.C.; National Library, Budapest; George Orwell Archive, University College, London; Österreichische Nationalbibliothek, Vienna (Dr. Eva Irblich); Party Institute Library, Budapest; Pedagogical Library, Ministry of Culture, Budapest; Petőfi Irodalmi Múzeum, Budapest; Harry Ransom Humanities Research Center, University of Texas, Austin; Russian Center for the Preservation and Study of Documents of Modern History (RCPSDMH), Moscow; Weizmann Archives, Rehovot, Israel.

In the long list of people I need to acknowledge I should not forget my three editors at Random House: the late and legendary Joe Fox, Koestler's last American editor, who took on this book but didn't live to read it; Jonathan Karp, his successor, who read and commented on a partial first draft; and Will Murphy, to whom fell the task of reading and commenting on the entire manuscript and seeing the book through the press. I should also like to thank my first editor at Faber & Faber, Robert McCrum, and his successor, Julian Loose, who oversaw publication in Britain. And I owe gratitude for help and guidance to my New York agent, Amanda Urban, at ICM, to my British agent, Derek Johns, at A. P. Watt, and to Derek's predecessor, Hilary Rubenstein.

No superlatives can overstate the debt I owe to my first and last reader and chief support, Rosemary Nossiff, whose invisible hand shows on more of these pages than she can possibly know.

SELECT BIBLIOGRAPHY

BOOKS BY ARTHUR KOESTLER

Koestler wrote and published (excluding translations) in two languages, German and English, but with a few exceptions I have restricted myself to works in English. I have also listed some books of which he was a co-author, notably some early detective stories, written with Andor Németh, and the sex guides published by Koestler's cousin Francis Aldor. It is not known which parts of the sex guides were written by Koestler and which by others. The books were in any case cut up, shuffled, and republished under a variety of titles, so the few listed here are mainly for information's sake.

The titles are listed in the chronological order in which they were written, with an indication of the genre. The editions cited are the ones used in the composition of this book.

Wie ein Mangobaumwunder (The Mango Tree Miracle). Stories, with Andor Németh; edited and with an afterword by Phil Casoar. Berlin: Verlag Das Neue Berlin, 1995. In French: *Au chat qui louche* (At the One-Eyed Cat). Stories, with Andor Németh; translated by Chantal Philippe. Paris: Calmann-Lévy, 1996.

Von weissen Nächten und roten Tagen (White Nights and Red Days). Nonfiction. Kharkov: Ukrainian State Publishing House for National Minorities, 1934.

The Encyclopaedia of Sexual Knowledge. By A. Costler, M.D., A. Willy, M.D., and others, under the general editorship of Norman Haire, Ch.M., M.B. London: Francis Aldor, 1934.

The Practice of Sex. By A. Willy, A. Coester, R. Fisher, and others. London: Francis Aldor, 1944.

Spanish Testament. Essay and memoir, no translator (in fact translated by Trevor and Phyllis Blewitt). London: Gollancz, Left Book Club Edition, 1937.

The Gladiators. Novel, translated by Edith Simon. London: Cape, 1939.

Darkness at Noon. Novel, translated by Daphne Hardy. London: Cape, 1940.

Scum of the Earth. Memoir. London: Cape, 1941.

Dialogue with Death. Memoir. London: Cape, 1942 (an edited and rewritten version of the second half of *Spanish Testament*).

Arrival and Departure. Novel. London: Cape, 1943.

Twilight Bar. Play. London: Macmillan, 1945.

The Yogi and the Commissar. Essays. London: Cape, 1945.

Thieves in the Night. Novel. London: Macmillan, 1946.

Promise and Fulfilment. Nonfiction. London: Macmillan, 1949.

The God That Failed: Six Studies in Communism. Memoir, with others. Ed. Richard Crossman. London: Hamish Hamilton, 1950.

Insight and Outlook. Science. London: Macmillan, 1949.

The Age of Longing. Novel. London: Collins, 1951.

Darkness at Noon: A Play Based on the Novel by Arthur Koestler. Dramatized by Sidney Kingsley. New York: Random House, 1951.

Arrow in the Blue. Autobiography. London: Collins, with Hamish Hamilton, 1952.

The Invisible Writing. Autobiography. London: Collins, with Hamish Hamilton, 1954.

The Trail of the Dinosaur. Essays. New York: Macmillan, 1955.

Reflections on Hanging. Nonfiction. London: Gollancz, 1956.

The Sleepwalkers: A History of Man's Changing Vision of the Universe. Science. New York: Macmillan, 1959.

The Lotus and the Robot. Nonfiction. New York: Macmillan, 1961.

Suicide of a Nation? Nonfiction. London: Hutchinson, 1963.

The Act of Creation. Science. New York: Macmillan, 1964.

The Ghost in the Machine. Science. London: Hutchinson, 1967.

Drinkers of Infinity: Essays, 1958–1967. London: Hutchinson, 1968.

Beyond Reductionism: The Alpbach Symposium, New Perspectives in the Life Sciences. Ed. with J. R. Smythies. London: Hutchinson, 1969.

The Case of the Midwife Toad. Science. London: Hutchinson, 1971.

The Roots of Coincidence. Parapsychology. London: Hutchinson, 1972.

The Call-Girls. Novel. London: Hutchinson, 1972.

The Challenge of Chance. Parapsychology, with Alister Hardy and Robert Harvie. London: Hutchinson, 1973.

The Heel of Achilles: Essays, 1968–73. London: Hutchinson, 1974.

Life After Death. Essays, with Arnold Toynbee et al. New York: McGraw-Hill, 1976.

The Thirteenth Tribe: The Khazar Empire and Its Heritage. History. New York: Random House, 1976.

Janus: A Summing Up. Selections from earlier works. London: Hutchinson, 1979.

From Bricks to Babel. Selections from earlier works. London: Hutchinson, 1980.

Kaleidoscope. Essays and stories. London: Hutchinson, 1981.

Stranger on the Square. Memoir, with Cynthia Koestler. Ed. Harold Harris. London: Hutchinson, 1984.

BOOKS ABOUT ARTHUR KOESTLER

Atkins, John. *Arthur Koestler.* London: N. Spearman, 1956. Humdrum monograph on Koestler's novels and early essays.

Buckard, Christian. *Arthur Koestler: ein extremes Leben* (Arthur Koestler: An Extreme

Life). Munich: C. H. Beck Verlag, 2004. Thin as a biography but excellent on Koestler's Zionism and attitude to his Jewish origins.

Calder, Jenni. *Chronicles of Conscience: A Study of George Orwell and Arthur Koestler.* Pittsburgh: University of Pittsburgh Press, 1968. Good study of Koestler's novels.

Cesarani, David. *Arthur Koestler—The Homeless Mind.* London: Heinemann, 1998. Opinionated, thinly researched, and heavily slanted biography, masquerading as a study of Koestler's Jewishness.

Day, Frank. *Arthur Koestler: A Guide to Research.* New York: Garland, 1987. The second major bibliography of works by and about Koestler, with summaries of each of his books and principal essays. Good (with a few omissions) on British and American sources up until its publication date.

Debray-Ritzen, Pierre, ed. *Arthur Koestler.* Paris: L'Herne, 1975. In French. A miscellany and a very mixed bag.

Debray-Ritzen, Pierre. *Arthur Koestler: un croisé sans croix* (Arthur Koestler: Crusader Without a Cross). Paris: L'Herne, 1987. Popular biography.

Freadman, Richard. *Threads of Life: Autobiography and the Will.* Chicago: University of Chicago Press, 2001. Has an excellent chapter on Koestler's autobiographies.

Goodman, Celia, ed. *Living with Koestler: Mamaine Koestler's Letters, 1945–51.* London: Weidenfeld and Nicolson, 1985. Contains both letters and diary extracts—searing insights into Koestler's domestic life and particularly good on his years in France.

Hamilton, Iain. *Koestler: A Biography.* London: Secker and Warburg, 1982. Superficial and ill-researched.

Harris, Harold, ed. *Astride the Two Cultures.* London: Hutchinson, 1975. A broad array of critics and scholars commenting intelligently on Koestler's literary and scientific works.

Laval, Michel. *L'Homme sans concessions: Arthur Koestler et son siècle* (The Man Who Wouldn't Compromise). Paris: Calmann-Lévy, 2005. A scissors-and-paste biography of Koestler for a French audience.

Levene, Mark. *Arthur Koestler.* New York: Frederick Ungar, 1984. A brief but good introduction to Koestler's fiction.

Merrill, Reed, and Thomas Frazier. *Arthur Koestler: An International Bibliography.* Ann Arbor: Ardis, 1979. This first comprehensive bibliography of works by and about Koestler is international in scope and good on Koestler's publishing history up until 1979.

Mikes, George. *Arthur Koestler: The Story of a Friendship.* London: Deutsch, 1983. An article blown up to book length.

Pearson, Sidney A., Jr. *Arthur Koestler.* Boston: Twayne, 1978. A brief overview of Koestler's works published before 1978 and an explication of his ideas.

Quilliot, R. *Arthur Koestler: de la désillusion tragique au rêve d'une nouvelle synthèse* (Arthur Koestler: From Tragic Disillusionment to the Dream of a New Synthesis). Paris: Librairie Philosophique VRIN, 1990. A rigorous scholarly examination of Koestler's political and philosophical ideas.

Sperber, Murray A. *Arthur Koestler: A Collection of Critical Essays.* Englewood Cliffs, N.J.: Prentice-Hall, 1977. A first-rate selection of previously published essays on a wide variety of Koestler's works.

GENERAL

Abusch, Alexander. *Literatur im Zeitalter des Sozialismus* (Literature in the Age of Socialism). Berlin and Weimar: Aufbau, 1967.

Agassi, Joseph. *Science and Society*. Dordrecht and Boston: D. Reidel, 1981.

Aron, Raymond. *Mémoires*. Paris: Julliard, 1983.

———. *Memoirs: Fifty Years of Political Reflection*. Translated by George Holoch (abridged). New York: Holmes and Meier, 1990.

Aronson, Raymond. *Camus and Sartre: The Story of a Friendship and the Quarrel That Ended It*. Chicago: University of Chicago Press, 2004.

Badia, Gilbert, et al. *Les Barbelés de l'exil* (The Barbed Wire of Exile). Grenoble: Presses Universitaires, 1979.

———. *Les Bannis d'Hitler* (Banned by Hitler). Paris: Presses Universitaires de Vincennes, 1984.

Bair, Deirdre. *Simone de Beauvoir*. New York: Summit Books, 1990.

Beauvoir, Simone de. *Force of Circumstance*. Translated by Richard Howard. New York: Putnam, 1964.

———. *The Mandarins*. Translated by Leonard Friedman. New York: Norton, 1991.

———. *A Transatlantic Love Affair: Letters to Nelson Algren*. Compiled and annotated by Sylvie Le Bon de Beauvoir, translated by Ellen Gordon Reeves. New York: New Press, 1998.

Beevor, Antony, and Artemis Cooper. *Paris After the Liberation 1944–1949*. London: Hamish Hamilton, 1994.

Begin, Menachem. *The Revolt*. New York: Nash Publishing, 1977.

Beloff, John, ed. *New Directions in Parapsychology*. Metuchen, N.J.: Scarecrow Press, 1975

Bergonzi, Bernard. *Wartime and Aftermath: English Literature and Its Background, 1939–60*. Oxford: Oxford University Press, 1993.

Berkley, George E. *Vienna and Its Jews: The Tragedy of Success, 1880s–1980s*. Cambridge, Mass.: Abt Books, 1988.

Brook, Kevin. *The Jews of Khazaria*. Northvale, N.J., and Jerusalem: Jason Aronson, 1999.

Bullock, Malcolm. *Austria 1918–1938: A Study in Failure*. London: Macmillan, 1939.

Butterfield, Herbert. *The Origins of Modern Science*. London: Bell, 1949.

Camus, Albert. *Carnets, Janvier 1942–Mars 1951* (Notebooks, January 1942–March 1951). Paris: Gallimard, 1964.

Caute, David. *Communism and the French Intellectuals, 1914–1960*. London: Andre Deutsch, 1964.

———. *The Fellow-Travellers*. New York: Macmillan, 1973.

Chambers, Whittaker. *Witness*. New York: Random House, 1952.

Clarke, Thurston. *By Blood and Fire: The Attack on the King David Hotel*. New York: Putnam, 1981.

Cohen, I. Bernard. *Revolution in Science*. Cambridge, Mass., and London: Belknap Press, 1985.

Coleman, Peter. *The Liberal Conspiracy*. New York: Free Press, 1989.

Congdon, Lee. *Seeing Red: Hungarian Intellectuals in Exile and the Challenge of Communism*. DeKalb, Ill.: Northern Illinois University Press, 2001.

Conquest, Robert. *The Great Terror*. London: Macmillan, 1968.

Crick, Bernard. *George Orwell, a Life*. London: Secker and Warburg, 1980.

Dugrand, Alain, and Frédéric Laurent. *Willi Münzenberg, artiste en révolution (1889–1940)*. Paris: Fayard, 2008.

Edwards, Ruth Dudley. *Victor Gollancz, a Biography*. London: Gollancz, 1987.

Farber, Seymour M., and Roger H. L. Wilson, eds. *Man and Civilization: Control of the Mind, a Symposium*. New York: McGraw-Hill, 1961.

Fejtö, François. *Mémoires, de Budapest à Paris* (Memoirs, from Budapest to Paris). Paris: Calmann-Lévy, 1986.

Fisher, Clive. *Cyril Connolly*. London: Macmillan, 1995.

Frei, Bruno. *Die Männer von Vernet* (The Men of Le Vernet). Berlin: Deutscher Militärverlag, 1961.

Fry, Varian. *Surrender on Demand*. New York: Random House, 1945.

Gill, Anton. *A Dance Between the Flames: Berlin Between the Wars*. London: John Murray, 1993.

Gilman, Sander L. *Jewish Self-Hatred: Anti-Semitism and the Hidden Language of the Jews*. Baltimore: Johns Hopkins University Press, 1986.

Grémion, Pierre. *Intelligence de l'anticommunisme: le Congrès pour la Liberté de la Culture à Paris (1950–1975)*. Paris: Fayard, 1995.

Gross, Babette. *Willi Münzenberg: A Political Biography*. East Lansing: Michigan State University Press, 1974.

Hansel, C.E.M. *ESP: A Scientific Evaluation*. London: McGibbon and Kee, 1966.

Hayman, Ronald. *Sartre: A Biography*. New York: Simon and Schuster, 1987.

Hewison, Robert. *In Anger: Culture in the Cold War, 1945–1960*. London: Weidenfeld and Nicolson, 1981.

———. *Under Siege: Literary Life in London, 1939–1945*. London: Weidenfeld and Nicolson, 1977.

Hook, Sidney. *Out of Step*. New York: Harper and Row, 1987.

Howard, Elizabeth Jane. *Slipstream*. London: Macmillan, 2002.

Hughes, Langston. *I Wonder as I Wander: An Autobiographical Journey*. New York: Rinehart, 1956.

Jeiteles, Israel. *Die Kultusgemeinde der Israeliten in Wien* (Jewish Religious Communities in Vienna). Vienna: Verlag von L. Rosner, 1873.

Judt, Tony. *Past Imperfect: French Intellectuals, 1944–56*. Berkeley: University of California Press, 1993.

———. *Reappraisals: Reflections on the Forgotten Twentieth Century*. New York: Penguin, 2008.

Kantorowicz, Alfred. *Deutsche Schicksale: Intellektuelle unter Hitler und Stalin* (German Destinies: Intellectuals under Hitler and Stalin). Vienna: Europa Verlag, 1964.

———, *Die Geächteten der Republik* (Outlaws from the Republic). Berlin: Europäische Ideen, 1977.

Katz, Shmuel. *Lone Wolf: A Biography of Vladimir (Ze'ev) Jabotinsky*. Vol. 2. New York: Barricade Books, 1996.

Koch, Stephen. *Double Lives*. New York: Enigma Books, 2004.

Laqueur, Walter. *A History of Zionism*. New York: Schocken Books, 1989.

Leary, Timothy. *Flashbacks: A Personal and Cultural History of an Era*. New York: Putnam, 1983.

———. *High Priest*. New York: New American Library, 1968.

Lewis, Jeremy. *Cyril Connolly: A Life*. London: Cape, 1997.

Lewis, Peter. *George Orwell: The Road to 1984.* New York and London: Harcourt Brace Jovanovich, 1981.

Lottman, Herbert. *The Left Bank.* Boston: Houghton Mifflin, 1982.

Lukacs, John. *Budapest 1900.* New York: Weidenfeld and Nicolson, 1988.

Malraux, André. *Man's Hope.* New York: Random House, 1938.

Marx, George. *The Voice of the Martians.* Budapest: Akadémiai Kiadó, 1994.

Merleau-Ponty, Maurice. *Humanisme et terreur* (Humanism and Terror). Paris: Gallimard, 1947.

Mitchell, Sir Peter Chalmers. *My House in Málaga.* London: Faber and Faber, 1938.

Morgan, Ted. *A Covert Life: Jay Lovestone, Communist, Anti-Communist, and Spymaster.* New York: Random House, 1999.

Münzenberg, Willi. *The Brown Book of the Reichstag Fire and the Hitler Terror.* New York: Knopf, 1933.

———. *The Reichstag Fire Trial: The Second Brown Book of the Hitler Terror.* London: Bodley Head, 1934.

Navasky, Victor. *Naming Names.* New York: Viking, 1980.

O'Neill, William L. *A Better World: The Great Schism—Stalinism and the American Intellectuals.* New York: Simon and Schuster, 1982.

Orwell, George. *Homage to Catalonia.* London: Penguin, 1975.

Palmier, Jean-Michel. *Weimar en exil* (Weimar in Exile). Paris: Payot, 1988.

Phillips, William. *A Partisan View.* New York: Stein and Day, 1983.

Polanyi, Michael. *Personal Knowledge.* New York: Harper Torchbooks, 1962.

———. *Science, Faith and Society.* Oxford, UK: Oxford University Press, 1946.

Rees, Goronwy. *A Chapter of Accidents.* New York: Library Press, 1972.

Regler, Gustav. *The Owl of Minerva.* New York: Farrar, Straus and Cudahy, 1959.

Rolph, C. H. *Further Particulars: Consequences of an Edwardian Boyhood.* Oxford, UK: Oxford University Press, 1987.

Saunders, Frances Stonor. *The Cultural Cold War: The CIA and the World of Arts and Letters.* New York: New Press, 1999.

Sayre, Nora. *On the Wing.* Washington, D.C.: Counterpoint, 2001.

Schechtman, Joseph B., and Yehuda Benari. *History of the Revisionist Movement,* vol. 1 (1925–1930). Tel Aviv: Hadar, 1970.

Shelden, Michael. *Friends of Promise: Cyril Connolly and the World of* Horizon. London: Hamish Hamilton, 1989.

———. *Orwell: The Authorized Biography.* New York: HarperCollins, 1991.

Sissons, M., and P. French, eds. *Age of Austerity (1945–1951).* London: Hodder and Stoughton, 1963.

Spender, Stephen. *World Within World.* New York: Harcourt Brace, 1948.

Sperber, Manès. *Till My Eyes Are Closed with Shards.* Translated by Harry Zohn. New York: Holmes and Meier, 1977.

———. *The Unheeded Warning.* Translated by Harry Zohn. New York: Holmes and Meier, 1975.

Stancic, Mirjana. *Manès Sperber: Leben und Werk* (Manès Sperber: Life and Works). Frankfurt am Main: Stroemfeld, 2003.

Strachey, John. *The Strangled Cry.* London: Bodley Head, 1962.

Tanenhaus, Sam. *Whittaker Chambers: A Biography.* New York: Random House, 1997.

Todd, Olivier. *Albert Camus: A Life*. Translated by Benjamin Ivry (abridged). New York: Alfred A. Knopf, 1997.

———. *Albert Camus, une vie,* Paris: Gallimard, 1996.

Ullstein, Herman. *The Rise and Fall of the House of Ullstein*. London: Nicholson and Watson, 1943.

Wasserstein, Bernard. *Britain and the Jews of Europe, 1939–1945*. Oxford, UK: Oxford University Press, 1979.

———. *The British in Palestine*. Oxford, UK: Blackwell, 1991.

Weininger, Otto. *Sex and Character*. London: Heinemann, 1906.

Weinstein, Allen. *Perjury: The Hiss-Chambers Case*. New York: Knopf, 1978.

Weissberg, Alexander. *The Accused*. New York: Simon and Schuster, 1951.

Wilford, Hugh. *The CIA, the British Left and the Cold War: Calling the Tune?* London: Frank Cass, 2003.

Wilson, Edmund. *Europe Without Baedeker*. New York: Noonday Press, 1966.

———. *The Fifties*. New York: Farrar, Straus and Giroux, 1986.

Wood, E. Thomas, and Stanislaw M. Jankowski. *Karski: How One Man Tried to Stop the Holocaust*. New York: John Wiley and Sons, 1994.

NOTES AND SOURCES

This, the first authorized biography of Arthur Koestler, is also the first to make full use of the extensive archive housed at Edinburgh University. I would like to say that "full" means complete and that I have looked inside every one of the more than 160 capacious boxes of material there, but that would not be true. There are boxes of business and financial papers, of academic correspondence on subjects such as astronomy, evolution, neurobiology, and parapsychology, and of clippings and articles by other authors that I either skimmed or did not investigate at all, and even the inspection of the 130 or so boxes I did look at was complicated by the chaotic organization of the papers themselves and by the lack of any accurate search aids. The finding aid that does exist, a booklet drawn up a few years after the papers arrived in Edinburgh, misidentifies (or completely fails to identify) many of the correspondents and is often misleading or wrong about documents pertaining to Koestler's early years, probably because many of these documents are written in Hungarian or German. It cannot be ruled out, therefore, that there are hidden treasures still waiting to be discovered and that another researcher will unearth valuable new information.

My book is further based on upward of two hundred interviews with relatives, friends, and professional colleagues of Koestler, supplemented by extensive correspondence with them and others, as detailed in the acknowledgments. The citations from those interviews and letters are almost all verbatim, but in a few places I have eliminated connecting words without providing ellipses, while taking care not to alter the sense of the original. The same is true of certain passages quoted from books and other printed sources. I should add that, with very few exceptions owing to the passage of time, all interviews are dated.

Since I dislike an excess of acronyms and abbreviations in notes, I have tried to keep them to a minimum. All the files in the Koestler Archive are identified by the initials MS. In the few cases where there are question marks, this is because the individual pages were not stamped or numbered at the time I inspected or photocopied them, and some had wandered far from their original order. "AK" stands for Arthur Koestler, and in the case of his works, I have generally used a single word as an identifier after the first appearance of a title, for example, *Darkness* for *Darkness at Noon, Ghost* for *The Ghost in the Machine,* and so on. A full list of the archives and collections I consulted can be found in the Acknowledgments.

The notes mainly refer to sources, often multiple in number, and in the interest of minimizing distractions I have restricted note numbers to the ends of paragraphs, hoping that the reader can connect each reference to its correct source. There are occasional amplifications and comments in the notes for readers interested in knowing more, while the truly curious should go to my website, **www.michaelscammell.com**, for more extensive outtakes from this already lengthy narrative and information of a more technically political or historical nature.

1. BEGINNINGS

1   AK, *Arrow in the Blue,* 17-18.

2   AK, *The Invisible Writing,* 423.

3   *Arrow,* 25.

4   Author's interviews with Daphne Henrion, 3/6/89, and Margaret Stephens, 1/14/90.

5   *Arrow,* 36. Shortly before his death AK told Celia Goodman that Henrik had doted on him but that his own feelings toward his father had been "up and down" because Henrik was "schizophrenic." CG's diary (with permission), 9/10/81.

6   Koestler may have been misled by the fact that in 1952, when he was writing his autobiography, the eastern Hungarian town of Miskolc (where his grandfather surfaced in 1860) lay only 60 miles from the Russian border, whereas a hundred years earlier the border had run 250 miles farther east and Miskolc was part of the Austrian province of Galicia, home to the overwhelming majority of the *Ostjuden* (Eastern Jews) who emigrated westward after the revolutions of 1848.

7   According to Dr. Tepperberg of the Archive of Military History in Vienna, the 15th and 42nd infantry regiments were stationed in Comorn at the time of Leopold's discharge (Dr. C. Tepperberg to author, 9/15/93). Details of the wedding are taken from the marriage register of the Orthodox Jewish Registry district of Miskolc for 1861. The Hungarian word for a government official or civil servant is *közszolga.*

8   See Budapesti Czim-És Lakjegyzék (Budapest Address and Apartment Index), 1882–1911, where Leopold is listed after his retirement as a *maganzo,* that is, person of independent means; see also Henrik's marriage certificate in MS2302/1. Henrik and Adele's situation in the class hierarchy may be judged from the following passage in John Lukacs's book *Budapest 1900,* 55: "Many middle class apartments consisted of not more than one living room, one bedroom and kitchen. . . . The existence of a separate children's room often marked the difference between the upper and lower middle classes." Another sign of prosperity was "the existence of

at least one live-in maid." The Koestlers had both a children's room and a live-in maid.

9 Koestler's implied reason for concealing the family name was to protect relatives from possible reprisals in the light of his anti-Communist reputation at the time he was writing (at the height of the Cold War). However, few, if any, Jeiteles family members were living under the Communists at the time, and Koestler's main motive appears to have been to conceal his privileged background on his mother's side. His success may be judged by the fact that two early biographers, Hamilton and Debray-Ritzen, simply accepted Koestler's invented name of "Hitzig"; Cesarani mistook *J* in the German Gothic script of Koestler's birth certificate for a *Z* and was copied by Buckard (who surely would have known better had he inspected the papers for himself) and Laval. Information about the history of the Jeiteles family is taken from *The Encyclopedia Judaica* (Jerusalem: Keter Publishing House, 1971), vol. 9, 1331–34; *The Universal Jewish Encyclopedia* (New York, 1942), vol. 6, 55–56; and *The Jewish Encyclopedia* (New York: Funk and Wagnalls, 1904), vol. 7, 90–91. Israel Jeiteles became head of the chief pastoral organization for Jews in Vienna and in 1873 published a brief history, *Die Kultusgemeinde der Israeliten in Wien* (Jewish Religious Communities in Vienna), with statistical tables and a detailed analysis of the actvities of the Jewish community in the city. One table shows that the Jeiteles family was "tolerated" in Vienna from 1848 onward.

10 Koestler writes in his autobiography that the reason for the visit was persistent headaches; see *Arrow,* 26. However, when Adele was interviewed about her visit to Freud by Kurt Eissler in 1953, she told Eissler that she had been suffering from a nervous tic, which caused her head to shake. Adele Koestler interview with Kurt Eissler, Edinburgh, MS2302/3, 1–2, 9, and 14.

11 The exact New York addresses were 142 West 53rd Street, 432 East 71st Street, and 214 West 120th Street. The first address appears in the U.S. census returns for 1900 in National Archives of the United States, Microfilm 1934, Reel 1062-344; other listings come from *Trow's General Directory of the Boroughs of Manhattan and Bronx, City of New York,* vols. 115 and 123 (New York: Trow Printing and Bookbinding Company, 1902 and 1910). The photographs are in MS2302/3.

12 *Arrow,* 27; see also 33, where Koestler characteristically refers to Aldor's son as "a distant cousin." He was in fact Koestler's first cousin and a good friend during Koestler's childhood. There is another mystery here. On 159–60 of *Arrow,* Koestler writes that Otto married a woman called "Henne" and changed his surname to "Devrient." However, Adele's address book for 1945 lists the wife's name as "Agnes Jeiteles," and by Koestler's own admission, it was Adele who corresponded with her. It seems likely that "Henne" was Agnes's nickname.

13 Adele is described as *maganzo* ("of independent means") in the Budapest Address and Apartment Index (see note 8) for the years after her arrival. For the name change and wedding, see Henrik and Adele's certificate of marriage (in Hungarian), MS2302/3.

14 See letter to AK (in Hungarian) from P. Frank Partos, 8/20/53, MS2378/4. The photographs are in MS2455-57.

15 The birth certificate is in MS 2302/1. The family name was originally spelled Kösztler, but Henrik Germanized it to Köstler, and Arthur spelled it that way in school, at university, and until his arrival in Palestine. His name lost the umlaut, acquired an *e,* and became *Koestler* when he began working as a journalist in Palestine in the 1920s and was obliged to use an English typewriter.

16 *Arrow*, 28.

17 One of Koestler's former governesses, a Miss Lediski, contacted him in London in 1941 after reading about him in the *Evening News*. AK to Miss Lediski, 9/17/41, MS2372/1; *Arrow*, 34 and 44–45; Celia Goodman, ed., *Living with Koestler*, 118.

18 *Arrow*, 19.

19 *Arrow*, 19.

20 Author's interview with Istvan Nogradi (formerly Neubauer), 6/3/91. In 1955 a second cousin of Koestler's wrote to him to describe a family Passover meal she had just attended and added, "After supper we reminisced about the seders that Uncle Jónas, Uncle Markusz, and grandfather used to give, and talked about Aunt Adele and Uncle Henrik and you. How wonderful those days were, and how long ago it seems now!" Lenke Singer to AK (in Hungarian), 4/13/55, MS2380; for the frieze see AK, *The Sleepwalkers*, 19; AK, unpublished interview with Iain Hamilton, 3/14/74, MS2436/5; *Arrow*, 19.

21 *Arrow*, 34 and 37.

22 Michel Tournier, *The Wind Spirit* (Boston: Beacon Press, 1988), 7.

2. A BUDAPEST CHILDHOOD

1 Parents were obliged to sign an undertaking to support the aims of her "Common Private Tutoring," as Laura Polanyi called it, with "financial, sanitary, and pedagogical contributions." See declaration form signed by Henrik and Adele Köstler in 1910, MS2302/3. See also *Arrow*, 56–57, and Eva Zeisel, "Memories of Arthur Koestler" (unpublished typescript). Author's interview with Eva Zeisel, 4/27/94.

2 Suzannah Lessard, "The Present Moment, a Profile of Eva Zeisel," *The New Yorker*, 4/13/87, 37; William O. McCagg, *Jewish Nobles and Geniuses in Modern Hungary* (Boulder, Colo.: East European Quarterly; distributed by Columbia University Press, New York, 1972), 72-74; Lukacs, 201.

3 Arthur Koestler, "Die Ergründung des Schöpferischen" (Exploring Creativity), interview with Sven Hasselblatt, Hamburg Television, 1/4/72, transcript, 3, MS2340/1. Copies of some childish notes by Koestler are in MS2302/3. See also *Arrow*, 49.

4 AK, "Viszontlátás" (Seeing Her Again), unpublished short story in Hungarian, typescript, 1, MS2342/5.

5 AK, "Lectures de jeunesse" (Childhood Reading), in Pierre Debray-Ritzen, ed., *Arthur Koestler*, 47; AK, "Micromemoirs," *Encounter* special issue, June 1983, 57–59.

6 Ibid., and *Arrow*, 50.

7 Lukacs, 187. See also the autobiographies of near contemporaries of Koestler such as Leo Szilard, Georg Lukacs, Edward Teller, and Eugene Wigner.

8 *Arrow*, 59.

9 Ibid., 39.

10 The detail of having seen something unmentionable is in a letter from AK to Eva Auer, 11/25/58, MS2383/1.

11 *Arrow*, 40–41. In his autobiography Koestler dubbed the contending forces of terror and courage in his psyche "Ahor" (for "archaic horror") and "Babo" (for "baron in the bog"). I have avoided these cute expressions, because if Koestler thought at all about these emotions at the time, it would have been in Hungarian or German, not the English of his later writing.

12 See *A Budapesti Hatodik Kerületi Állami Főreáliskola 26-ik Évi Értesitője, 1915–1916*

(Twenty-sixth Annual Report of the Budapest Sixth District State Realschule, 1915–1916), Budapest, 1918, 58–59, and ditto, *1916–17,* Budapest, 1920, 12. Also William Lanouette with Bela Silard, *Genius in the Shadows: A Biography of Leo Szilard* (New York: Scribner's, 1992), 31 and 37. Undated letter from AK to Adele Koestler (in German), MS2302/3.

13 *Arrow,* 28; AK, "Méta," in *Múlt és Jövő* (The Past as Future), October 1927, 339–40; Leo Valiani, "Koestler the Militant," *Encounter,* July–August 1983; letter to AK from Lewis Herman, 12/10/43, MS2372/3. Eugene Wigner remembered that there were groups in his school who regularly started fights with the Jewish students; see Wigner, *The Recollections of Eugene P. Wigner* (New York: Plenum, 1992), 37–38. AK to Adele, op. cit.

14 AK letters to Adele (in German), undated and 7/30/18, MS 2302/3.

15 *Arrow,* 50–53. Koestler was far from alone in these aspirations in Budapest at this time. Several commentators have noted the extraordinary number of outstandingly talented scientists, social scientists, thinkers, and writers born in Hungary during the last two decades of the nineteenth century and the first decade of the twentieth, many of them imbued with a combination of optimism and ambition that carried them to brilliant careers either in Hungary or in the diaspora (for example, Thomas Balogh, Nicholas Kaldor, Georg Lukacs, Karl Mannheim, Karl Polanyi, Michael Polanyi, Karl Popper, Leo Szilard, Edward Teller, and Eugene Wigner, to name just a few); see Richard Rhodes, *The Making of the Atomic Bomb* (New York: Simon and Schuster, 1986), 106, for the importance of Hungary's scientists; see also Lukacs, chapter 5, and McCagg, 208–22.

16 A young cousin of Arthur's, Hedvige Horpacky (one of Zsanett's many children), later remembered the high quality of the toys that were handed on to her after her rich cousin had outgrown them, and also his fashionable clothes, including a pair of patent leather pumps that she cherished as an unheard-of luxury. Author's interview with Hedvige Horpacky, 6/4/91.

17 *A Budapesti Hatodik, 1916–1917,* 6–8.

18 *Arrow,* 59–60; Paul Ignotus, *Hungary* (New York and Washington, D.C.: Praeger, 1972), 143.

19 Adele to AK, 5/1/51. MS2302/3.

20 Péter Nagy, *Szabó Dezső* (Budapest: Akadémai Kiadó, 1979), 187–89. Evidently Szabó was a poor teacher, beating the students and provoking a strike by setting them too much homework. He called his fellow teachers stupid and incompetent, and they retaliated by petitioning for his removal. See also National Library, Budapest, Document OLK 500 1918/28/135243; *Arrow,* 63; *A Budapesti Hatodik, 1918–1919, 1919–1920,* 3–4.

21 *Arrow,* 60–63; Julius Hay, *Born 1900* (London: Hutchinson, 1974), 71.

22 *A Budapesti Hatodik, 1918–1919, 1919–1920,* 4.

23 Ignotus, op. cit., 149–51; Lukacs, 212.

24 Leo Lania, *Today We Are Brothers* (Boston: Houghton Mifflin, 1942), 164; *Arrow,* 68.

3. RISE, JEW, RISE

1 *Arrow,* 112.

2 Ibid, 70–72.

3 *Alfred Ehrmann von Falkenau (1865–1938)—feinsinniger Dichter und Musikliterat*

(Alfred Ehrmann von Falkenau [1865–1938]—Sensitive Poet and Music Critic), *Badener Zeitung,* 10/15/87 and 10/22/87; letter to AK from Edith Hummel, 7/6/41, MS2371/1; AK to Adele Köstler (in German), 6/8/21, MS2302/3; *Arrow,* 70–74.

4 AK to Adele Köstler (in German), 5/26/21, MS2302/3.

5 AK to his parents (in German), 7/4/21, MS2302/3. Osip Dimov was the pen name of Joseph Perlman (born 1878), who emigrated to the United States in 1913 and continued actively writing plays (mostly in Russian) until his death in 1959. *Shma Yisroel* was written in Russian and later translated into Yiddish; see Nahma Sandrow, *Vagabond Stars: A World History of Yiddish Theater* (New York: Harper and Row, 1977), 193. "Hear, O Israel" are the first words of a prayer uttered by someone about to die.

6 *Arrow,* 102. See also Luba Kadison and Joseph Buloff, *On Stage, Off Stage: Memories of a Lifetime in the Yiddish Theatre* (Cambridge, Mass.: Harvard University Library, 1992), 42–43.

7 AK to Adele Köstler (in German), 6/25/21, MS2302/3.

8 Adele Köstler's notebook (in German) for 1917, MS2302/4.

9 AK, "Viszontlátás," 2. Author's interviews with Sir Nicholas Henderson, 6/1/00, and Istvan Nogradi, op. cit.; AK to Adele Köstler (in German), 8/22/21, MS2302/3.

10 *Invisible Writing,* 168–71.

11 *Arrow,* 74–75.

12 AK to his parents (in German), undated, MS2302/3.

13 George E. Berkley, *Vienna and Its Jews,* 147; Malcolm Bullock, *Austria 1918–1938,* 106.

14 By law the universities were unable to refuse entry to applicants, since every student who matriculated had a right to a higher education. The usual recourse was to declare courses filled. See Edmund Schechter, *Viennese Vignettes* (New York: Vantage Press, 1983), 19.

15 *Hauptkatalog der Technischen Hochschule in Wien* (Main Catalogue of the Vienna Technical University), 1922–23, Matriculation no. 649, Köstler, in Archiv der Technischen Hochschule (Archive of the Vienna Technical University), Vienna.

16 Ibid.

17 *Arrow,* 111; AK interview with Sven Hasselblatt, 5.

18 Manès Sperber, "Arthur Koestler and Zionism," 5/31/73, unpublished typescript, 4; with the permission of Jenka Sperber. Sperber's papers are now in the Austrian National Library, reference *Österreichisches Literaturarchiv des Österreichischesn National Bibliothek* (ÖLA), 2/88.

19 The German *Kneipe* means literally "tavern" or "pub" but was taken over by the fraternities to describe their drinking ceremonies as well. The verse is in my translation from the German cited in Harald Seewann, *Zirkel und Zionsstern* (Circles and the Star of David) (Graz: private publication, 1990), 219–20. The anthem continues:

Freedom is the noble prize
That the Jew must attain.
Jewish hearts beat with ardent fire
And also know sacrifice.
Reach for the sky, noble falcon,

Your breast so strong, your eye so clear.
War's night gives way to victory's light,
Enthralling, wonderful, and glorious!

20 *Arrow*, 89. The Balfour Declaration, named for Lord Balfour, the British foreign secretary at the time, sanctioned "the establishment in Palestine of a National Home for the Jews." The British exercised a mandate over the territory after the defeat of the Ottoman Empire in World War I.

21 Adapted from Koestler's translation of the German; see *Arrow*, 94. The original words were by Victor von Scheffel.

22 AK, untitled typescript, MS2302/3. The German term for "frock-coat brigade" was *Frack-Uniten*. See *Zirkel und Zionsstern*, 134 and 147, note 3.

23 Benjamin Akzin, "Meine Begegmissen mit Arthur Koestler" (My Encounters with Arthur Koestler) in *Be-Ayin Bochenet* (With a Critical Eye), (Haifa, 1975), 63–65; see also Harald Seewann, "Der Kampf der jüdisch-nationalen Studentenschaft an österreichischen Hochschulen am Beispiel Wien" (The Struggle of the Jewish National Student Organizations in Austria's Colleges as Exemplified in Vienna), in *Zirkel und Zionsstern*, 105–7. A special educational commission set up by the authorities concluded that there had been an "alarming invasion" of the universities by "racially and temperamentally alien elements" and in a phrase that achieved wide currency in Austria called for a reversal of the "continuing Levanticization of Vienna."

24 See *Zirkel und Zionsstern*, *Begleitband* (Supplement), vol. 2 164; *Arrow*, 94. Seewann, in *Zirkel und Zionsstern*, vol. 2, 164, reproduces an official report of the duel from the archives of the Marchia fraternity. The duel took place on January 29, 1925. Koestler was also nominated as a second to Paul Diamant when Diamant challenged a Weizmann supporter to a saber duel, but it's not clear if the duel actually took place; see Hamilton, 369. See also Alex Ott, "Arthur Koestler," in *Yedi'ot Acharonot*, 7/2/48, cited in Christian Buckard, *Arthur Koestler*, 40–41, and transcript of the report of a hearing held by the rectorate of Vienna University, 5/26/25, in Archiv der Technischen Hochschule, Z 2220. For more on the *Bummel*, see Schechter, 57.

4. ZIONIST

1 AK, "Lectures de jeunesse," op. cit. 48–49.

2 AK, "Viszontlátás," 7.

3 Ibid.

4 Walter Moore, in *Schrödinger, Life and Thought*, 27, mentions that in autobiographies of this period "the sexual initiation of the hero is provided by the family maid, usually portrayed as a fresh country girl whose upbringing on the farm had left her innocent of bourgeois morality and susceptible to the sophisticated urban student." See also *Arrow*, 91; Dr. Rudolf Paschkis to AK, 3/24/48, MS 2376/1.

5 Otto Weininger, *Sex and Character*, 88, 92, 146, 149, 194–95, 307, and chapter 13, "Judaism." See also Sander L. Gilman, *Jewish Self-Hatred*, 244–45.

6 AK, "Spuk im Alltag" (Phantom of the Daily Round), undated typescript.

7 "Spuk im Alltag," op. cit.

8 *Arrow*, 102.

9　See Robert S. Wistrich, *The Jews of Vienna in the Age of Franz-Joseph* (New York: Oxford University Press, 1989), 501–2; and Carl Schorske, "Revolt in Vienna," *The New York Review of Books*, 5/29/86, 25.

10　Manès Sperber, interview with Olivier Bourdet-Pléville, in Debray-Ritzen, 72. Sperber was himself an East European Jew who had studied in Vienna but in contrast to Koestler was totally at ease with his origins. As a student he had been a member of the nondueling, left-wing Jewish defense organization Hashomer Hatzair.

11　Lucy Adler-Weinor to Koestler, 1946(?), MS2374/3; *Arrow*, 105. Something else that greatly appealed to Koestler was a madcap scheme of von Weisl's to round up all the unemployed Jewish ex-soldiers in Vienna after the war, equip them with rifles, machine guns, and light artillery, and ship them off to defend the Jewish settlements in Palestine. The scheme came to nought, but von Weisl had still managed to sell Jabotinsky twenty-one heavy machine guns and use the profit to finance his fund for a year. See Wolfgang von Weisl, "Skizze zu einer Autobiographie" (Sketch for an Autobiography) in his *Die Juden in der Armee Österreich-Ungarns* (Jews in the Austro-Hungarian Army) (Tel Aviv, 1971), 35–38.

12　Wolfgang von Weisl, "Un pionnier de grand coeur" (A Great-Hearted Pioneer), in Debray-Ritzen, 131.

13　See Walter Laqueur, *A History of Zionism*, 198 and 346–48.

14　Schechter, 65; Norbert Hoffmann to AK, 10/28/65, MS2385/2.

15　*Arrow*, 108.

16　Ibid., 55.

17　Laqueur, op. cit.

18　*Arrow*, 97–99.

19　*Arrow*, 108–10. See also Iain Hamilton, *Koestler*, 369. Betar was an acronym for Brit Trumpeldor, the Covenant of Trumpeldor, named for a Haganah commander, Joseph Trumpeldor, who had been killed during an Arab raid in 1920. Koestler's attraction to Betar was a function of the similarity of the movement's ideology to that of Unitas. One of Betar's central tenets was adherence to the principle of "Hadar," an educational ideal implying outward beauty, respect, self-esteem, politeness, loyalty, cleanliness, tact, and quietness of speech, which was supposed to accompany such military qualities as leadership, discipline, and self-denial. See Laqueur, 360.

20　AK, letter to Henrik (in German), undated, MS2302/3; Schechter, 37–38; Joseph B. Schechtman and Yehuda Benari, *History of the Revisionist Movement*, 35; *Rassviet* (Dawn), no. 37, 1925, 7; *Wiener Morgenzeitung* (Vienna Morning Daily), 8/18/25.

21　Akzin, 34, and Hamilton, *Koestler*, 369. Koestler and Joseph Herrlinger were named as seconds.

22　Akzin, 35–36.

23　AK, typescripts (in German) dated 5/10/24 and 5/19/24, MS2343/2, and *Arrow*, 98–99. See also *Wiener Morgenzeitung*, 4/26/25. It's not clear if Koestler wrote any more articles. The Austrian publisher Fritz Molden once recalled Koestler saying he had earned extra money for himself by writing for the newspapers as a student, but there is no evidence of further publication. Author's interview with Fritz Molden, 9/9/93.

24　AK, notebook, undated, MS2343/2. I have based my account on Buckard, 54. For Jabotinsky and the Fourteenth Congress, see Cesarani, 44.

25　For a contemporary Jewish source on Jewish currency speculators, see Grunwald,

463, and for a non-Jewish source, Malcolm Bullock, op. cit., 45; for Henrik, see *Arrow*, 112–14. It has to be said that the story of Henrik's bankruptcy bears a suspicious similarity to the story of the alleged swindling of Koestler's maternal grandfather, which suggests that Koestler was drawing on family folklore rather more than he admitted.

26 Buckard, 57; *Hauptkatalog der Technischen Hochschule* (Central Register of the Technical University), Vienna, 1925, entry for Köstler, Arthur.

27 *Arrow*, 116–117.

28 AK, notebook, undated, MS2343/2, cited in Buckard, 56 and 59.

29 Buckard, 57. Buckard (60–61) points out that although almost no Revisionists had applied for certificates before Koestler, joining collective farms and tilling the land did not in any way contradict Jabotinsky's prescriptions for settling Palestine.

30 Buckard, 59.

31 Ibid., 119–20. See also letter to AK from from Ellen Delp, 12/21/47, MS2375/1. In his own account of this episode, Koestler refers to Ellen Delp as "Anny Mewes." This would appear to result from his having forgotten the actress's name and having looked up Rilke's published correspondence when writing his autobiography. Rilke did correspond with *Anni* Mewes, but also with Ellen Delp; see *Letters of Rainer Maria Rilke, Volume Two, 1910–1926* (New York: Norton, 1947). Delp wrote to Koestler after coming across one of his novels.

32 *Arrow*, 121; Dr. S. Orochow to Koestler, 4/8/45 (see note 23 above), MS2373/3.

5. A RUNAWAY AND A FUGITIVE

1 Mount Gilboa, a site sacred to the settlers, was the place where Saul had killed himself and where his son Jonathan had been slain by the Philistines. It was celebrated in one of King David's finest and best-known laments, "How are the mighty fallen!" The name Hephzibah came not from Arabic, as Koestler believed, but from the prophet Isaiah, who had foretold the restoration of Jerusalem and of Zion. See *Palestine, a Study of Jewish, Arab, and British Policies* (New Haven: Yale University Press, 1947), 290–91.

2 *Arrow*, 126–27.

3 *Arrow*, 128–29. Author's interview with Moshe Felsenstein, archivist and librarian of Hephzibah, 5/6/93.

4 Itzhak Meridor, "Koestler Was Charming, but Failed in Fruit-Picking and Refused to Learn Hebrew," *Davar*, 3/8/83.

5 AK to Weinshall, 9/9/64. He names 5/1/26 as the date of his arrival by boat in Haifa, and his first article after returning to Haifa appeared in *Ha-Tzafon* on 5/15/26, MS2385/1. According to one source, some fraternity members did hold his abrupt departure from the *kvutsa* against him; see Fritz Roubicek, *Von Basel bis Czernowitz: Die jüdisch-akademischen Studentenverbindungen in Europa (Beitrage zur österreichischen Studentengeschichte—Band 12)* (From Basle to Czernowitz: The Jewish Fraternities in Europe [Contributions to the History of Austrian Students, vol. 12]), Vienna, 1986. On the other hand, Koestler was briefly back in Vienna the following year and met some Unitas friends for "a two-day binge at the *Kneipe*," after which they gave him more money to make his way back to Palestine, so by no means everyone felt that way; see *Arrow*, 164.

6 *Arrow*, 135; Buckard, 65.

7 See Adolf Böhm, "Revisionistische Geistesverfassung" (The Revisionist Mentality), *Jüdische Rundschau,* no. 46, 6/15/26, 336–37. Arthur Köster (*sic*), "Der Revisionismus antwortet. Die Dogmatik des Weges" (Revisionism Replies. The Dogmatism of the Means), *Jüdische Rundschau,* no. 57, 7/23/26, 418. The article was cogently argued and drew blood. Böhm felt obliged to respond to "Comrade Köster" in the next issue, objecting to the article's sharpness of tone and pointing out that the polemical zeal of its author was an illustration of that very "Revisionist mentality" to which he objected. "Köster" was a misprint that the *Jüdische Rundschau* corrected at the foot of Böhm's reply to Koestler; see Adolf Böhm, "Revisionistische Geistesverlassung, ein Schlusswort" (The Revisionist Mentality, a Last Word), *Jüdische Rundschau,* no. 58–59, 7/30/26, 426. Böhm's qualifier was *Gesinnungsgenosse,* literally "partisan," which I have rendered as "comrade" to convey its rhetorical flavor, without its usual left-wing political coloration. See also AK, "Träumer und Zweifler" (Dreamers and Skeptics), *Morgenrot* (Dawn), May 1926; also in *Ha-Tzafon* (in Hebrew), 6/18/26.

8 For Doeg, see Buckard, 74; Theodora Fischer, "The Darkness of Arthur Koestler," *I.R.P. Review,* vol. 16, 1987, 45–46.

9 *Arrow,* 144.

10 AK, *Thieves in the Night,* 240.

11 AK, "Der Besen und der Samowar" (The Broom and the Samovar), unpublished typescript, MS2339/6. Owing to his faulty Hebrew, Koestler translated *kettle* as "samovar." AK, "Europe and Us" (in Hebrew), *Ha-Tzafon,* 12/31/26.

12 AK, "Avigdor Hameiri, Versuch einer Synthese" (Avigdor Hameiri, an Attempt at a Synthesis), *Jüdische Rundschau,* 5/25/27, 300.

13 *Arrow,* 153; for "Méta," see chap. 2, note 13; Arthur Köstler, "Märchen für unsere Kinder" (Fairy Tales for our Children): "Das Märchen vom Krokodil, der schönen Rachel und den fünfzig Kätzlein" (The Tale of the Crocodile, the Fair Rachel, and the Fifty Kittens); "Das traurige Märchen vom König der immerfort lachen musste" (The Sad Tale of the King Who Couldn't Stop Laughing), *Jüdischer Almanach* (Jewish Almanac), Prague, 1928–29, 231–40.

14 AK, "Will Jabotinsky Give a Speech on Mount Scopus?" (in Hebrew), *Ha-Tzafon,* 9/8/26; AK, "Jabotinsky and the Fourteenth Congress" (in Hebrew), *Ha-Tzafon,* 10/3/26. AK to Joseph Schechtman, 3/6/56, MS2380/3. Both the newspaper articles were inspired by a meeting Arthur had with Jabotinsky in Tel Aviv, when the Revisionist leader addressed an open-air gathering of forty thousand people. In the first article, Arthur attacked the Hebrew University for refusing to allow Jabotinsky to speak there during his whirlwind tour of Palestine. Jabotinsky's speech in Tel Aviv was called "In Catilinam," after Cicero's *In Catilinam* ("Oration Against Catiline," also known as "The Catilinarians"), which begins *"Quo usque tandem,"* meaning "How much longer [will you abuse all patience]?"

15 Author's interview with Gavriel Zifroni, 4/28/93.

16 See von Weisl, *Skizze,* 46; Paul Ignotus, *Hungary* (New York and Washington, D.C.: Praeger, 1972), 131; Robert Blumstock, "Arthur Koestler: Hungarian Writer?," *Hungarian Studies Review,* vol. 14, no. 1 (Spring 1987), 43 and 47, note 26; Dr. T. M. Kinory to AK, 2/6/45, MS2373/3.

17 Jabotinsky to Schechtman (in Russian), 6/29/27, Jabotinsky Archive, Tel Aviv, 17/2/11C.

18 *Arrow,* 158.
19 Ibid., 163.

6. FIRST STEPS IN JOURNALISM

1. The Street of the Prophets has since been widened and much of the area around it cleared for new development by the Israeli administration of Jerusalem. Number 29, though badly neglected and in a state of disrepair, is still standing (there is a picture in Buckard).
2   *Arrow,* 171 and 178; A. Köstler, "Tragödie im Zwischendeck" (Tragedy in Steerage), *Vossische Zeitung (VZ),* 1/18/28; Arthur Koestler, "Besuch beim 'Messias'" (Visit to the "Messiah"), *Neue Freie Presse (NFP),* 1/29/28; Artur Köstler, "Weihnachtsfeiern in Bethlehem" (Christmas Festivities in Bethlehem), *NFP,* 12/18/27; a slightly shorter version appeared as Arthur Koestler, "Jesu Geburtstag" (Jesus's Birthday), *VZ,* 12/25/27.
3   Arthur Koestler, "Die sich das Sterben überlegt haben . . ." (Those Who Have Pondered Death . . .), *VZ,* 5/26/28; Arthur Koestler, "Das Strafkloster in der Wüste Juda" (The Penal Monastery in the Judean Desert), *NFP,* 7/25/28; Arthur Köstler, "Besuch bei Adam und Eva" (A Visit to Adam and Eve), *NFP,* 8/5/28.
4   Arthur Koestler, "Das Café zu tausendundeiner Nacht" (The Café of a Thousand and One Nights), *NFP,* 10/2/28; Arthur Köstler, "Die Laster von Libanon" (The Trollops of Lebanon), *NFP,* 5/18/28.
5   Arthur Koestler, "Wie Aegyptens Nationalregierung stürzte" (How Egypt's National Government Fell), *VZ,* 7/5/28, and *NFP,* 7/8/28; Arthur Koestler, "Oelkonflikt am Mittelmeer" (Oil Conflict in the Mediterranean), *VZ,* 11/25/28; A. Koestler, "Das Geheimnis um Haifa" (Haifa's Secret), *VZ,* 1/31/29; Arthur Koestler, "Zwischen London, Moskau und Mekka" (Between London, Moscow and Mecca), *VZ,* 11/20/27; Arthur Koestler, "Kleinkrieg in Arabien" (Guerrilla Warfare in Arabia), *VZ,* 3/6/28; also as "Wetterleuchten in Arabien" (Summer Lightning in Arabia), *NFP,* 3/8/28.
6   Arthur Koestler, "Ibn Saud ante portas . . ." (Ibn Saud at the Gates . . .), *VZ,* 6/7/28; Arthur Koestler, "Ibn Sauds Kriegsdrohung" (Ibn Saud's War Threat), *VZ,* 2/1/29.
7   AK, "Kleinkrieg in Arabien," op. cit.
8   Artur Koestler, "Die Wirtschaftskrise in Palästina" (The Economic Crisis in Palestine), *NFP,* 9/9/27; Arthur Koestler, "Stillstand in Palästina" (Stagnation in Palestine), *VZ,* 12/28/27. For the economic background, see Buckard, p. 63.
9   Arthur Koestler, "Polizeiskandal in Palästina" (Police Scandal in Palestine), *NFP,* 8/29/28. See also Bernard Wasserstein, *The British in Palestine,* 157–65 and 220–38.
10 Buckard, 90.
11 *Arrow,* 180–82.
12 Arthur Koestler, "Der Zwischenfall an der Klagemauer" (Incident at the Wailing Wall), *NFP,* 9/4/28; Arthur Koestler, "Das siebente Dominion" (The Seventh Dominion), *VZ,* 11/17/28, and *NFP,* 12/2/28. See also Schechtman and Benari, *History of the Revisionist Movement,* 180–81. The Revisionists took a close interest in the Wailing Wall. It was von Weisl who had forced the original compromise over allowing the chairs by threatening to denounce British and Arab obstruction in the *Chicago Tribune* and to stir up public opinion in America. After the riots, the Revisionists

pressed for the complete transfer of the Wailing Wall to Jewish control; see Schecht-man and Benari, 183.

13 *Arrow,* 182–83; and *Doar Hayom,* 12/7/28. Koestler had some fun with the form of the crossword puzzles. The second time the puzzle appeared, the black squares were in the shape of a menorah to celebrate Hanukkah. Later the entire puzzle metamorphosed into the shape of a cross, a comic touch, given that the word *cross* had had to be eliminated from the game's name because of its Christian connotations. "Crossword puzzle" was rendered as "brain acrobatics" in Hebrew. See *Doar Hayom,* 12/14/28.

14 *Arrow,* 178–80; Artur Köstler, "Die Stadt der dreizehn Parteien" (City of Thirteen Parties), *NFP,* 1/23/29; and "Stadtverordnetenwahl in Tel Aviv" (City Council Elections in Tel Aviv), *VZ,* 1/27/29; Artur Koestler, "Flucht von der Heiligkeit" (Flight from Holiness), typescript (publication details are not known), MS 2339/6.

15 Von Weisl, *Skizze,* 48; Arthur Köstler, " 'Zeppelin'-Fieber in Palästina" (Zeppelin Fever in Palestine), *NFP,* 3/29/29. See also Fred F. Blau, "The L.Z. 127 'Graf Zeppelin' over Palestine," typescript, MS2389/4; Buckard, 93.

16 Arthur Koestler, "Die Locken Absalons, der neue Regisseur der 'Habimah' " (Absalom's Curls, the New Director of Habimah), *VZ,* 4/4/29; Arthur Koestler, "Die Krone Davids" (David's Crown), *VZ,* 6/9/29; Arthur Koestler, "Jerusalem Letter: Art as Propaganda," *The New Palestine,* 9/26/28, 311–12; and "Habimah in the Motherland" (in Hebrew), *Doar Hayom,* 12/14/28.

17 Koestler was naturalized on March 6 and received his passport a day later; see letter to Professor Norman Bentwich from the Office of the Commissioner, Migration and Statistics, Jerusalem, 3/20/43, MS2372/2(?).

18 Arthur Koestler, "Scheintote Jahrtausende" (Seemingly Dead Centuries), *VZ,* 4/14/29. The excavations were carried out by E. L. Sukenik, the archeologist and father of Yigael Yadin, who later became famous for his excavations of the fortress at Masada.

19 As many commentators have pointed out, Koestler's views were distorted by his lack of background in Hebrew culture. He was unaware of the continuity of Hebrew literature as practiced in medieval Spain and in various parts of Europe during later centuries, not to speak of the contributions of the Jewish Enlightenment (to which one of his own ancestors had belonged). Nor did he take account of the achievements of the Hebrew Revival and of the Odessa school, whose outstanding writer (later to be dubbed the Hebrew "national poet"), Bialik, had revolutionized modern Hebrew and was now living in Palestine. Bialik was a fellow contributor to *Doar Hayom* and a friend of that other native of Odessa, Jabotinsky, who wrote poetry and prose in fluent Hebrew, in addition to mastering European languages.

20 *Arrow,* 183–84.

21 Fifty years later, in 1978, Lisa Luria wrote to Koestler from Jerusalem, informing him that she had spent forty-eight years in the Soviet Union before returning to Israel in 1975. She was working on a book about Ilya Ehrenburg and wanted Koestler's opinion of Ehrenburg as a "Jewish writer." Lisa Luria-Klebanova to AK, MS2391/3.

22 Arthur Koestler, "Zwischen Paris und Budapest" (Between Paris and Budapest), *VZ,* 7/20/29; AK, *Promise and Fulfilment,* 70; von Weisl, *Skizze,* 47.

7. HELLO TO BERLIN

1 My account of Koestler's early weeks in Paris is based on *Arrow,* 187–96.

2 Eva Zeisel, "Memories," 3–5; Suzannah Lessard, "The Present Moment," profile of Eva Zeisel, *The New Yorker,* 4/13/87, 39–40.

3 Author's interview with Eva Zeisel, 4/26/94; AK, "Die Heimkehr des letzten Mohikaners" (Homecoming of the Last Mohicans), unpublished typescript, MS2339/6; Buckard, 105-6.

4 *Arrow,* 211; "Das Mysterium des Lichts" (The Mystery of Light), *VZ,* 11/19/29.

5 Countess Waldeck to AK, 4/1/48. MS2413/3.

6 *Arrow,* 211–12; and Herman Ullstein, *The Rise and Fall of the House of Ullstein,* 185–87.

7 Peter de Mendelssohn, *Zeitungsstadt Berlin, Menschen und Mächte in der Geschichte der deutschen Presse* (Berlin: Ullstein, 1969), 262; AK et al., *The God That Failed,* 31.

8 See Peter Gay, *Weimar Culture: The Outsider as Insider* (New York: Harper & Row, 1968), 135; Anton Gill, *A Dance Between the Flames* (London: John Murray, 1993), 193; Thomas Friedrich, "Die Berliner Zeitungslandschaft am Ende der Weimarer Republik" (The World of Berlin Newspapers at the End of the Weimar Republic), in Diethart Kerbs and Henrick Stahr, eds., *Berlin 1932: Das letzte Jahr der ersten deutschen Republik—Politik, Symbole, Medien* (Berlin 1932: The Last Year of the First German Republic—Politics, Symbols, Media) (Berlin: Hentrich, 1992), 56–67.

9 AK, "Licht aus dem Okean" (Light from the Ocean), *VZ,* 10/10/30.

10 AK, "Millionen wohnen in den Atomen" (Millions Live in Atoms), *VZ,* 10/22/30. Koestler cites a more poetic version of this passage in *Arrow,* 267. It's not clear if this came from a similar article published in one of Ullstein's sister papers or is a later embellishment by Koestler.

11 AK, "Der Kampf um das Naturgesetz" (Struggle over the Laws of Nature), *VZ,* 10/12/30.

12 *Arrow,* 265–67 and 269–70; AK, "Unwälzung in Dynamobau?" (Revolution in Dynamo Construction?), *VZ,* 4/21/31; "Sturm um eine Dynamomaschine" (Tempest over a Dynamo), *VZ,* 5/17/31; letter to AK from Dr. Hans Schweitzer, 12/14/30, and letter to the editor of the *Vossische Zeitung* from an unknown correspondent, 5/29/31 (the last page of the letter, with the signature, is missing), MS2302/3(?); author's interview (by telephone) with Victor Weisskopf, 3/22/93.

13 AK, "Wo hält die Forschung: Im Labyrinth der Vererbungslehre" (The Frontiers of Research: In the Labyrinth of Heredity Theory), *VZ,* 12/14/30; "Wo hält die Forschung: Der sezierte Intellekt" (The Frontiers of Research: the Dissected Intellect), *VZ,* 12/20/30; "Wo hält die Forschung: Erbgut und Schicksal" (The Frontiers of Research: Heredity and Fate), *VZ,* 12/28/30; "Wo hält die Forschung: Lebensstrahlen, Todesstrahlen, utopischer Ausblick" (The Frontiers of Research: Life Rays, Death Rays, a Utopian Prospect), *VZ,* 2/22/31.

14 Hearst's original scheme had started with the backing of a submarine voyage to the North Pole by the British explorer Sir Hubert Wilkins, and Hearst had added an extra twist by suggesting that Wilkins's submarine, the *Nautilus* (named in homage to Jules Verne), rendezvous there with the *Graf Zeppelin,* which would be flown to the pole specially for the occasion. Hearst had offered big money, and the *Nautilus* had set out from North America for Spitzbergen as planned, but in the mid-Atlantic its engines broke down and Hearst withdrew his offer. See *Arrow,* 275–78. Koestler

gives a much more detailed and slightly different version of the assignment in part one of his book on the Soviet Union, *Von weissen Nächten und roten Tagen* (White Nights and Red Days), 7–72, but I have mainly followed the autobiography.

15 AK (unsigned), "Zeppelin in Berlin," *VZ,* 7/25/31; *Arrow,* 285–86.

16 *Arrow,* 291; AK, "Feststimmung in Leningrad" (Festivities in Leningrad), *VZ,* 7/27/31.

17 Koestler had remarked by way of local color that the Soviet professor had arrived late for takeoff after being delayed by shaving. The German popular press made a joke out of this incident, which was considered demeaning by the prim standards of Soviet manners. In *Von weissen Nächten und roten Tagen,* written for a pro-Soviet audience, Koestler blamed an anti-Soviet Ullstein editor for blowing up the story in its *Tempo* version and for causing him difficulties with Samoilovich. See "Zeppelin in Berlin," op. cit.; *Arrow,* 286–87 and 298–99; *Von weissen Nächten,* 32.

18 *Arrow,* 300.

19 Poster and handbill, AK archive, MS2302/3(?). One of Koestler's listeners in Nuremberg was the anti-Semitic editor of *Der Stürmer* (The Storm Trooper), Julius Streicher, who ostentatiously sat alone in the back row to avoid having to share a bench with any Jews who might be present (he didn't realize he was listening to a Jew); see letter to AK from Moshe Gelernter, 1/30/45, MS2373/3.

20 *Arrow,* 301.

21 Manès Sperber, *Till My Eyes Are Closed with Shards,* 47–48; Manès Sperber, "Koestler, croyant sans foi joue sa vie sur la corde raide" (Koestler, Believer Without a Faith, Stakes his Life on a Tightrope), *Arts,* Paris, 6/12/53, 3–4.

22 Alfred Kantorowicz, "Abschied von Arthur Koestler" (Farewell to Arthur Koestler), in *Deutsche Schicksale: Intellektuelle unter Hitler und Stalin* (German Destinies: Intellectuals under Hitler and Stalin) (Vienna: Europa, 1964; 234–35), *Arrow,* 213.

23 Manès Sperber, *The Unheeded Warning,* 136–37.

24 Anton Gill, *A Dance Between the Flames,* 120-121 and 127; Weisskopf, 52; Sperber, *Warning,* 147-148; Ruth Ludwig, *Pistolen im Zucker* (Pistols in the Sugar) (Berlin: Ullstein, 1990), 138-139; Ruth Ludwig to AK, 5/7/42, MS2371/3(?); L.S. (full name unknown), "Der Roman eines Atelier-Abends" (The Romance of a Studio Evening), clipping from unidentified newspaper, Center for the Preservation of Historic Document Collections (CPHDC).

25 *Arrow,* 214–18. Eva Zeisel, unpublished memoir (with permission); letters to AK from Leni Heaton, 5/11/45; Ernst Jaeger, 1/6/46; Lotte Jaeger, 3/25/46; 5/13/48; Marion Alward, 5/1970 and 9/28/78; and from AK to Marion Alward; MS2373/3, 2374/2, 2375/2, 2386/5, and 2391/3.

8. IN THE GALE OF HISTORY

1 Stephen Spender, *World Within World,* 118.

2 Hermann Ullstein, *House of Ullstein,* 193–94. Von Weisl was among the Jewish journalists fired at this time, see *Un pionnier,* 135.

3 Victor Weisskopf, *The Joy of Insight: Passions of a Physicist* (New York: Basic Books, 1991), and author's interview with Weisskopf, op. cit. For the description of Eva's apartment see Lanouette and Silard, 78–79, and Lessard, op. cit.

4 Weisskopf interview; Manès Sperber, *Shards,* 47.

5   AK, Preface in Alexander Weissberg, *The Accused,* ix; Weissberg, 211.

6   See H. R. Knickerbocker, *The German Crisis.*

7   *Arrow,* chaps. 29 and 30.

8   Ibid., 227 and 229; Eva Zeisel interview, 4/26/94; Eva Zeisel, unpublished memoir, 13–14; von Weisl, *Un pionnier,* 135.

9   Author's interview with Otto Bihalj-Merin, 1/7/89; *Arrow,* 234.

10 AK, *The God That Failed,* 23; *Arrow,* 236–37.

11 AK, *Invisible Writing,* 16–17; *The God That Failed,* 24–25.

12 Mendelssohn, 303–4; *Invisible Writing,* 17–20; *The God That Failed,* 37–41; Gustav Regler, *The Owl of Minerva,* 143; Report No. 54, "Kostler, Arthur," Cannon Row Police Station, 11/8/40, TNA: PRO FO 1110/215.

13 Unattributed typescript in the Koestler Archive, with quote from Wilhelm Reich, 95–96, MS2302/4(?).

14 *Invisible Writing,* 25. For "family and fatherland" see Christopher Hitchens, "Eric the Red," a review of Eric Hobsbawm's autobiography, *Interesting Times* (New York: Pantheon, 2003), *New York Times Book Review,* 8/24/03.

15 Axel Eggebrecht, *Der halbe Weg. Zwischenbilanz einer Epoche* (Halfway There: Interim Report on an Era) (Reinbek bei Hamburg: Rowohlt, 1975), 23–24 and 257–58.

16 Ibid., 30; *Arrow,* 227–31; Manès Sperber, *Warning,* 164–65.

17 Ibid.

18 Albrecht Betz, *Hanns Eisler: Political Musician* (Cambridge, UK: Cambridge University Press, 1982), 91–103.

19 Haase, 69; Johannes R. Becher, "Unsere Front" (Our Front), editorial in *Die Linkskurve* (Left Turn), no. 1, 1929, see Dieter Kliche and Gerhard Seidel, eds., *Die Linkskurve, Berlin 1929–1932. Bibliographie einer Zeitschrift* (*Die Linkskurve,* Berlin, 1929–1932, Bibliography of a Magazine) (Berlin and Weimar: Aufbau, 1972), Foreword, 11.

20 AK and Andor Németh, *Wie ein Mangobaumwunder,* and Phil Casoar, "Nachwort" (Afterword), to the same book, 127–60; *Invisible Writing,* 44 and 171; Andor Németh, "A Szélén Behajtva" (Folded at the Corner of the Page), in *Válogatott írások* (Selected Writings) (Budapest: Magvetö, 1973), 649–55, 661–62, 671–72, 691–95; *Wie ein Mangobaumwunder* is in MS2339/6. Some months later the story was translated back into Hungarian and published in Budapest, leading Dr. Barron to claim a portion of the royalties. See also György Tverdota, *Németh Andor, Egyközep-europai értelmiségi a huszadik század elso felében* (Andor Németh, A Central European Intellectual) (Budapest: Balassi, forthcoming).

21 Typescripts are in MS2339/6.

22 AK, *Der Mord im Odeon-Theater* (Murder at the Odéon Theatre), typescript, MS2339/6.

23 *Invisible Writing,* 171; Németh, op. cit.; Eva Zeisel, 13; Lessard, 42; Weisskopf, 53.

24 Johannes Becher to MORP, 7/21/32. Rossiiskii tsentr khranenia i izucheniya dokumentov noveishei istorii (Russian Center for the Preservation and Study of Documents of Modern History—RCPSDMH), Moscow, Fund 541, Folio 1, file 6.

25 *Invisible Writing,* 46; RCPSDMH, 541/1/92; Moses Lutzky to AK, 7/7/51, MS2377/4; Lotte Jäger to AK, 3/25/46, MS2374/2.

9. RED DAYS

1 *Invisible Writing,* 50–51. This is the source of all information about Koestler's stay in Kharkov not attributed to other sources.

2 Weisskopf, 54–56.

3 *Von weissen Nächten,* 81–82; *Invisible Writing,* 67.

4 RCPSDMH, 541/1/6: Willetts, 226.

5 *Von weissen Nächten,* 88.

6 The story of Nadezhda is told in *The Invisible Writing,* 90–107. Baku became the city in which Fedya Nikitin, the protagonist of *The Age of Longing,* spent his childhood and youth—as the son of one of the Baku commissars. In that novel, Fedya is described as Armenian and reads the same works on the Armenian massacres that Koestler had read during his visit to Erevan.

7 *Invisible Writing,* 112 and 114.

8 Langston Hughes, *I Wonder as I Wander,* 113–14.

9 Ibid., 117. Hughes may have been right. Koestler notes in *The Invisible Writing* that the Attakurdov trial was "an exotic and amateurish forerunner of the great show trials in Moscow," but he doesn't signal it as explicitly influencing the novel; see *Invisible Writing,* 120.

10 Hughes, 119.

11 Ibid., 116, and Langston Hughes, *Notebooks,* and Folders JWJ MSS519 and 521/12, Beinecke Library, Yale.

12 Hughes, 114–15 and 119–22.

13 Ibid., 130–31; Hughes, *Notebooks,* and Folders JWJ MSS519 and 521/21, Beinecke Library, Yale.

14 Hughes, *Notebooks,* and Folder 523/15, Beinecke Library, Yale.

15 AK, *The Yogi and the Commissar,* 142–43; AK, untitled fragment of autobiography, two pages, MS2336/3(?).

16 Weisskopf and Zeisel interviews; Weissberg, 212.

17 Zeisel interview; AK, autobiographical fragment; *Invisible Writing,* 53.

18 Ukraine then contained the largest German-speaking minority in the Soviet Union, and Kharkov was the headquarters of the National Minorities Publishing House, including a German section, and a small association of German writers.

19 *Invisible Writing,* 52–53. A copy of the "thin paperbound volume" in German published in Kharkov was found in Koestler's papers after his death and is now in Edinburgh. Koestler writes that he was sent a copy by an unknown American reader in 1947, but the volume in Edinburgh is marked as a gift from Richard Crossman. A further source of confusion is that on page 83 of *Invisible Writing,* Koestler describes the book as having 480 pages. However, the copy in Edinburgh has 180 pages. The "4" must be a typographical error.

20 Ibid., 149–50; Weissberg, 212–13.

21 Eva Zeisel, unpublished memoir, 15.

22 For *Twilight Bar* see AK, "Die Siebente Grossmacht" (The Seventh World Power), unpublished typescript, 9 pages, MS2336/3.

23 AK, "Author's Note" to *Twilight Bar.* Whether from convenience or through an oversight, Koestler later "forgot" the existence of *An Improbable Occurrence* and referred to this early version in both *The Invisible Writing* and his author's note as if it

were the same play. The basis for my discussion of the earlier work is the incomplete typescript of a prose recapitulation of it (it is more than a synopsis), "Unwahrscheinliche Begebenheit," 34 pages, dating from April 1934 in MS2339/6.

10. ANTI-FASCIST CRUSADER

1. Von Weisl, 135. In his autobiography Koestler describes a scene in which he tried to sell some articles to Bruno Heilig, a former Ullstein colleague now editing a Zionist newspaper in Vienna. When they met in the Café Herrenhof, Heilig suddenly asked, "Why are you talking in whispers?" "Am I?" said Koestler. "I thought I was talking normally." "In Berlin you used to yell, and now you whisper," said Heilig. "That is all I want to know about Russia." *Invisible Writing,* 166.

2. Ibid. I have also relied for this scene on an autobiographical passage in Koestler's unpublished 1934 novel for young adults, *Die Erlebnisse des Genossen Piepvogel* (The Adventures of Comrade Dickybird), typescript, 207–8, MS2325/1; interview with Nogradi.

3. Author's interview with Charlotte Ignotus, 2/20/90.

4. *Invisible Writing,* 172–87, and author's note to *Twilight Bar;* Németh, op. cit.; author's interviews with Pál Rézs, 6/10/89 and György Kassai, 1/7/92; Tverdota, op. cit.

5. For József's poem, see Erzsébet Vezér, "Arthur Koestler on Attila József," *New Hungarian Quarterly* 30, no. 114, 1989, 68. According to Tverdota, József was asked to write several songs for the play, but "Happiness" is the only one that has survived.

6. Author's interviews with with Istvan Vas, 6/10/89, Imre Cserepfalvi, 6/12/89, Erzsébet Vezér, 6/21/89, and François Fejtö, 1/13/92. Fejtö states that Koestler was "one hundred percent Stalinist, dogmatic, and arrogant, accepting no contradiction" at this time, and convinced that the Soviet Union was "our only hope." See François Fejtö, *Mémoires.*

7. AK, *Mbo-Mba utnak indul* (Mbo Mba on the Road), 39, MS2343/4. The Hungarian title and some notes and drafts in Hungarian suggest that Koestler began the play in Hungarian, but the final version is in German.

8. Ibid., 39–40.

9. See Phil Casoar, Afterword to AK and Andor Németh, *Au chat qui louche,* 116–19. This is the French version of *The Mango Tree Miracle.* The four stories written in Budapest were reissued as *Nagyvarosi történek* (Big City Stories) in 1997. See also Tverdota, 154–159.

10. AK, *Bricks to Babel,* 321–22.

11. *Invisible Writing,* 205.

12. No one yet knows the truth behind the fire, but Münzenberg set out to prove that the Nazis were to blame, a thesis that has been vigorously contested since then.

13. Gross, *Willi Münzenberg,* 244.

14. *Invisible Writing,* 209–10; Abusch, *Literatur im Zeitalter des Sozialismus; Invisible Writing,* 210; Claud Cockburn, *A Discord of Trumpets* (New York: Simon and Schuster, 1956), 305–6; Koch, *Double Lives,* 83–85; Theodore Draper, "The Man Who Wanted to Hang," *The Reporter,* vol. 8, 1/6/53.

15. Münzenberg, *Reichstag Fire Trial.* See diagrams between pages 308 and 309, and pages 338 and 362.

16. *Invisible Writing,* chap. 19. The work on this project must have been carried out at

phenomenal speed. Koestler and his collaborators all wrote in German, yet the first edition came out in French in late 1933 and the English translation appeared less than six months later as *The Encyclopaedia of Sexual Knowledge*. A later edition was published as *The Practice of Sex*.

17 *Encyclopaedia,* 154 and 226.

18 Alexander Stephan, *Die deutsche Exilliteratur* (German Literature in Exile) (Munich: C. H. Beck, 1979), 58; David Caute, *The Fellow-Travellers,* 151n.

19 *Invisible Writing,* 224 and 227; see also Gross, 244.

20 AK, *Dickybird,* 205, 209, 236–37 and 252–54; *Invisible Writing,* 236–37. The translations from *Dickybird* are mostly mine.

21 Oprecht's organization was called the Büchergilde Gutenberg (Gutenberg Book Guild). For the Association of German Writers in Exile, see Caute, op. cit., 150–51, and Jean-Michel Palmier, *Weimar en Exil,* 426.

22 Otto Bihalj-Merin, "Begegnungen mit Anna Seghers in früher Zeit" (Meetings with Anna Seghers in Earlier Times), in *Über Anna Seghers, ein Almanach zum 75. Geburtstag* (On Anna Seghers: A 75th Birthday Almanac) (Berlin and Weimar: Aufbau, 1975), 65. The description of the Café Mephisto is taken from the same source.

23 *Invisible Writing,* 233–34; Max Zimmering, "Kleine Begegnungen mit einem grossen Menschen" (Small Encounters with a Great Man), in *Servus, Kisch! Erinnerungen. Rezensionen. Anekdoten* (Greetings, Kisch! Memories, Reviews, Anecdotes) (Berlin and Weimar: Aufbau, 1985), 89. Zimmering was present at the discussions of Koestler's novel and describes the novel as "written with talent, with lots of good psychological details" but "smelling of anti-communist and anti-Party tendencies." Kisch had shown his insight by anticipating Koestler's later apostasy.

24 Dorothee was incensed that in *The Invisible Writing* (a book dedicated to her) Koestler had described her eyes as "brown," when they were green. Author's interview with Dorothee Koestler, 12/13/88. Daphne Henrion, an artist, remembers them as "bright blue," which suggests at the very least that their color was unusual. I have settled for "bluish green."

25 Author's interviews with Dorothee Koestler, 12/13/88 and 6/1/89. Bihalj-Merin's adopted daughter, Mirjana, lived at the Maisons Lafitte children's home—she appears in *Comrade Dickybird* as "Little Miss Prickly." A third member of Dorothee's family, her brother Ernst, a doctor, had also joined the Communist Party and moved to Zurich, and after Dorothee's father died, her mother, Elisabeth, moved to London. Speech at memorial ceremony for Dorothee Koestler by Gerhard Schoenberner, 5/11/92; also a curriculum vitae of Dorothee compiled by herself; author's interview with Jean Flack, 1992.

26 *Invisible Writing,* 236; interview with DK, 6/1/89; DK's curriculum vitae. When interviewed some fifty years later, Dorothee couldn't remember the incident of the attempted suicide, but she did remember Koestler saying at the time, "I want to die."

27 Interview with DK, 6/1/89; Phil Casoar to author, 1/11/93.

28 In *The Invisible Writing,* AK calls him "Maros" rather than Merin, presumably to disguise his real identity. At the time AK wrote, Bihalj-Merin was living in Yugoslavia, and AK probably didn't wish to embarrass him.

29 The book was *Exerzierplatz Deutschland* (Germany, Field of Maneuvers) by "S. Erckner," a nom de plume for someone described as "a former officer of the German general staff" (Paris: B. Rosner, 1934). The French translation was called *Allemagne,*

champs de manoeuvres (same publisher). See Dieter Schiller and Regine Herrman, "Kulturelle Tätigkeit deutscher Künstler und Publizisten im französischen Exil 1933 bis 1939" (The Cultural Activities of German Artists and Publicists in French Exile 1933–1939) in Dieter Schiller et al., *Exil in Frankreich* (Exile in France) (Frankfurt am Main: Roderberg, 1981), 228.

30 *Études sur le fascisme, Cahiers mensuels de l'Institut pour l'Étude du Fascisme* (Fascist Studies, Monthly Notes of the Institute for the Study of Fascism), nos. 3–4, July–August 1934. This double issue came out quite soon after Koestler got to INFA; the second, nos. 5–6, was prefaced by an apology for a break in publication "owing to all kinds of difficulties," and the date was given as 1934–35. Koestler claimed that he was responsible for the entire contents of the "first issue" of the bulletin, except for an article on "Conditions in the Ricefields in the Po Valley"; see *Invisible Writing,* 244.

31 Anonymous [AK], "L'Allemagne souterraine, I. Grand Guignol" (Underground Germany, I. Grand Guignol), *L'Intransigeant,* 8/22/34; "II. La naissance du monde souterrain" (II. The Birth of the Underground), ibid., 8/23/34.

32 Author's interview with Georg Glaser, 4/23/93; Casoar interview with Glaser. See also Glaser's autobiographical novel, *Geheimnis und Gewalt* (Secrecy and Power) (Basil: Stremfeld/Roter Stern), 204–31; Manès Sperber, *Shards,* 48–49.

33 Manès Sperber, *Shards,* 48–49; Otto Bihalj-Merin, 63.

34 *Études,* 5–6, back page. The announcement of the exhibition presented it misleadingly as "the initiative of a group of French organizations" desirous of "revealing the essence of fascism" in various ways.

35 Manès Sperber, *Shards,* 49 ff.; Jacques Omnès, "L'Institut pour l'Étude du Fascisme (INFA)," in Gilbert Badia et al., eds., *Les Bannis d'Hitler* (Hitler's Exiles) 195–97. Otto stayed on until the exhibition opened in the spring of 1935 but was obliged to move to Zurich when the French revoked his visa. The exhibition opened on March 9, 1935 in the Galerie de la Boëtie on the Left Bank, and was an instant success, enlivened by right-wing demonstrations in the street and a police raid to remove a cartoon deemed offensive to the king of Italy. Manès Sperber wrote a comprehensive catalogue for it. See letter from Leopold Grünwald to AK, 1/23/73, MS2388/3.

36 Münzenberg's influence had begun to slip in Moscow ever since his relocation from Berlin to Paris. With that move, the German-based International Workers' Aid had lost its raison d'être and was soon folded into the Comintern; see Gross, 244, 260–68; Omnès, 186–87 and 197–98; McMeekin, *Tycoon* (New Haven: Yale University Press, 2003), 275–94.

11. MARKING TIME

1 Interviews with DK, 12/13/88 and 6/1/89; *Invisible Writing,* 247–48; Manès Sperber, *Shards* (this phrase appears on pages 62–63 of the typescript of the English translation of *Shards,* which I was shown before publication, but I cannot find it in the published edition).

2 *Die Saar-Ente* (The Saar Duck), nos. 1–2, 1/6/35, published by the Association of German Writers (a copy is available in the Internationaal Instituut voor Sociale Geschiedenis, Amsterdam). An illustrated poem by Koestler appears on page 3. See also AK, "Sphinx in Saarbrücken" (The Sphinx of Saarbrücken) in *Das Neue Tagebuch,* December 1934. A copy is in MS2338/1.

3 *Invisible Writing,* 276; Willy Aldor to AK, 10/17/50 and 12/15/50; AK to "Paul," New York, 10/30/50, MS2376/5(?).

4 Werner Mittenzwei, *Exil in der Schweiz* (Exile in Switzerland) (Frankfurt am Main: Röderberg, 1981), 75–78; Karl Retzlaw, *Spartakus* (Frankfurt: Neue Kritik, 1971), 370; *Invisible Writing,* 279.

5 *Invisible Writing,* 278, ff.; Hay, *Born 1900,* 52–64 and 109–11.

6 Interview with DK, 6/1/89; Hay, 145–48; text of divorce petition by DK, 3/2/48, in MS2303/3(?).

7 Interview with DK, 12/13/88; *Invisible Writing,* 280–81.

8 Ibid., 218, 281–82, and 285; Willy Aldor to AK, op. cit.; AK to "Paul," op. cit.

9 *Invisible Writing,* chap. 27; Németh, op. cit.; Koestler to Németh (in German), 7/17/35. Although Koestler doesn't say so, both he and Bihalj-Merin went to Switzerland for Maria's funeral. According to the Swiss writer Werner Mittenzwei, who was also there, Maria had divided her estate among the poor émigré writers who had been her guests. Németh was one of the beneficiaries, but Koestler apparently wasn't. See Tvertoda, 176–78, and Mittenzwei, 269.

10 *Invisible Writing,* chap. 28.

11 AK, "Menschen, fern der Gegenwart" (Men Distant from the Present); "Professor Mannheims Bekehrung" (Professor Mannheim's Conversion); "Piscators Fischer von Sankt Barbara" (Piscator's Fishermen of Santa Barbara); all in *Das Neue Tagebuch,* copies in MS2338/1.

12 AK, "Der unbekannte Kisch" (The Unknown Kisch), *Das Neue Tagebuch,* 4/27/35, copy in MS2338/1.

13 AK to John Gheeraert, 8/25/75, MS2389/4; John Gheeraert, *Bericht uit Bredene* (Report from Bredene) (Antwerp: De Vries-Brouwers, 1976), 26–39; Gheeraert to author, 2/2/90, 4/16/90, and undated, 1993; author's interview (by telephone) with Louisa Eisler Fischer, 6/9/93.

14 AK, "The Good Soldier Schweik Goes to War Again," unpublished and unfinished handwritten manuscript (in German), 63–171, in MS2327/1.

12. PRISONER OF FRANCO

1 *Invisible Writing,* 313–16. My account of Koestler's Spanish adventures and imprisonment there follows Koestler's, except where otherwise noted.

2 Ibid., 319.

3 AK, "Fascist Friendships," *News Chronicle,* 9/1/36, 1–2; AK, *Spanish Testament,* 37–40. Strindberg's wife, Utie Strindberg de Vries, later wrote to Koestler to deny that her husband was a spy and to explain the circumstances of his presence in Seville; see *Invisible Writing,* 320–22 and 322 note.

4 For MI5, see The National Archives (TNA), Kew, UK, KV2/1273. This was the first time Koestler had come to the notice of MI5.

5 *Invisible Writing,* 330.

6 Ibid. Lillian Hellman, *An Unfinished Woman* (Boston: Little, Brown, 1969), 103–4.

7 *Invisible Writing,* 330–31; Jean Lacouture, *André Malraux* (London: Andre Deutsch, 1975), 245; Louis Fischer, *Men and Politics: An Autobiography* (New York: Duell, Sloan and Pearce, 1941), 384–85.

8 The address is listed in a divorce petition that Dorothee filed in Paris (under her Resistance name, "Nicole Ascher") on 3/2/48, MS2301/1.

9   *Invisible Writing*, 333–34. It seems unlikely that Willi was solely or even mainly responsible for the photographs. Some of the same pictures appear in *L'Espagne 36–39 vue par Henri Clérisse* (Spain 1936–1939, Seen by Henri Clérisse) (Paris: Georges Ventillard, 1937).

10 AK to Mr. Roberts, 6/3/50, MS2376/3.

11 The initials POUM stand for Partido Obrero de Unificación Marxista (Party of the Workers for Marxist Unification).

12 *Invisible Writing*, 336.

13 Ibid., 155.

14 This line achieved notoriety partly as a result of Orwell's ferocious attack on it soon after its first publication. Auden protested that it had been misunderstood but in any case changed it to read "The conscious acceptance of guilt in the fact of murder"; see W. H. Auden, *The Collected Poetry of W. H. Auden* (New York: Random House, 1966), 184.

15 Cited in *Spanish Testament*, 187–88.

16 AK, *Dialogue with Death*, 18.

17 *Dialogue*, 24–27, and Sir Peter Chalmers Mitchell, *My House in Málaga*, 261.

18 *Testament*, 200–204.

19 *Dialogue*.

20 The dramatic scene at the Villa Santa Lucia that morning has been described by all three of the principal actors involved: Luis Bolin, Sir Peter Chalmers Mitchell, and Koestler. Koestler produced three slightly differing versions of it (in the *News Chronicle*, *Spanish Testament*, and *Dialogue with Death*), as well as a partial fourth in *The Invisible Writing*. Yet another partial account has been provided by Joaquin Vazquez Torres, who assisted Bolin in makin the arrest and later told his son about it. My version is based mainly on Bolin and Koestler, with additional details from the French author Phil Casoar and from Torres's son, as passed on by his cousin by marriage Janetta Parladé. See *Spanish Testament*, 223–27; *Dialogue with Death*, 46–52 and 59–60; *Invisible Writing*, 350; Luis Bolin, *The Vital Years* (New York and Philadelphia: Lippincott, 1967), 248; Chalmers Mitchell, *My House*, 278–85; Phil Casoar to author, 6/6/97; Janetta Parladé to author, 7/27/05 and 12/16/90.

21 Chalmers Mitchell was allowed to board a British battleship and sail to Gibraltar, and then to England; Chalmers Mitchell, *My House*, 285–98.

22 *Dialogue*, 59–61.

23 George Orwell, *Homage to Catalonia*, 45.

24 See AK, *Dialogue with Death* (London: Hutchinson, Danube Edition, 1966), Preface, 5–6.

25 For lessons, see Barry Jones interview with Koestler. In order not to call the Gestapo's attention to himself, and to maintain the fiction of Englishness, Koestler kept his diary in English; see Preface to *Dialogue*, 6.

26 *Dialogue*, 106–7.

27 Ibid., 139.

28 Ibid.

29 *Invisible Writing*, 114 and 358–59.

30 *Dialogue*, 199.

31 *Dialogue*, 215; *News Chronicle*, 5/15/37, front page.

32 *News Chronicle*, 5/17/37; AK's essay (untitled) in Richard Crossman, ed., *The God*

That Failed, 68. Koestler misremembered the origin of this line and mistakenly ascribed it to Goethe. For the telegram to his parents, see Adele Koestler to Dorothee, 5/15/37, in CPHDC, 619/1/2.

13. TURNING POINT

1 George Orwell, "Why I Write," in Richard Rovere, ed., *The Orwell Reader* (New York: Harcourt, Brace, 1956), 394.

2 André Malraux, *Man's Hope* (New York: 1938), 392–93.

3 AK to Thomas Mann, 5/12/37, cited in Buckard, 141–42.

4 The National Archives (TNA), Kew, UK, KV2/1273.

5 *Invisible Writing,* 365–66.

6 Dorothee Koestler, "Vorlaeufiger Bericht ueber den Fall Arthur Koestler" (Preliminary Report on the Case of Arthur Koestler) (unsigned typescript in German), 3/1/37, 1–2 and 4–5, in CPHDC, 619/1/8. The German spelling indicates that the report was composed on an English typewriter.

7 Ibid., 4. Interview with DK, 6/1/89; Chalmers Mitchell, *My House,* 296–98. The initial publicity was so effective that the pro-Falangist *Daily Mail* informed Franco that any harm done to Koestler would injure the Nationalist cause in England.

8 297. See DK, "Vorlaeufiger Bericht ueber Taetigkeit in London vom 8–21.III.37" (Preliminary Report on Activities in London 3/8–21/37), 1-2, CPHDC, Fund 619, Folio1, File 8; DK, "Bericht aus London, vom 29.III–7.IV.1937" (Report from London, 3/29–4/7/37), 1. Also DK's handwritten letter to AK dated 3/9/37, CPHDC, 619/1/1. See also letters from Eleanor Rathbone, M.P., to Viscountess Astor, M.P., 4/12/37, and from Anthony Crossley, M.P., to the Marquis de Moral, 3/14/37, Sidney Jones Library, Special Collections, University of Liverpool, XIV/2/12 (24) and (28).

9 Mary Stott, "Tribute [to Arthur Koestler]," *Journal of the Voluntary Euthanasia Society,* 1983.

10 Letter to DK from Hans Stammreich, 5/3/37, CPHDC, 619/1/2, 3–4.

11 DK to Hans Stammreich, 5/5/37. CPHDC, 619/1/8, 31, 619/1/2, 1–2 and 50–51.

12 See Marcel Junod, *Warrior Without Weapons* (Geneva: International Committee of the Red Cross, 1982), 123–25; *Invisible Writing,* 363–64; Bolin, 294–95; Hugh Thomas, *The Spanish Civil War,* 670–71.

13 Letters from DK to AK, 3/9/37 and 4/15/37, CPHDC, 619/1/1, 3, 5, and 5a.

14 Author's interview with DK, 12/13/88. Dorothee had a bitter little story about the typing. According to her, Koestler had started typing himself but made so many mistakes that he asked Dorothee to take over. When he was revising the typescript, he cursed her for the many mistakes in the opening pages. Only when she reminded him that he had typed them himself did he retract the accusation and apologize.

15 The reference to a possible Moscow assignment appears in Cynthia Koestler's diary some twenty years later; see Cynthia Koestler diary, 11/15/66, MS2305.

16 *Invisible Writing,* 371–73; Thomas Mann, *Tagebücher* (Diaries), 106, cited in Buckard, 142–43; see also AK to the Society for Psychical Research, 2/10/53, MS2379/1.

17 Mrs. Harriet Wallgren to AK, 7/18/63, MS2384/5; *Invisible Writing,* 375–76. In a letter to the "Dear Friends" in Paris dated 4/27/37, DK wrote, "Don't forget the old

K[oestler]s on the 28th, Sziget-u[tca] 38, Budapest, listing me or Carrefour as the sender, but on no account the [Spanish] Agency!" CPHDC, 619/1/8. Adele's letter is in CPHDC, 619/1/2.

18 *Invisible Writing,* 379.

19 TNA, KV2/1273; Buckard, 149.

20 "Palestine the Melting Pot," *News Chronicle,* 12/14/37; "This Is an S.O.S. for Palestine," 12/15/37; "Partition—the Only Solution," 12/16/37. See Buckard, 147–58, for a more detailed account of Koestler's Palestine visit and articles. The original typescripts are in MS 2339/5.

21 *Dialogue,* 103.

22 Ibid., 116–18.

23 Ibid., 204.

24 George Orwell, "Review of *Spanish Testament*" (*Time and Tide,* 2/5/38), and Murray A. Sperber, "Looking Back on Koestler's Spanish War," both in Murray A. Sperber, *Arthur Koestler,* 11 and 109–21.

25 *Invisible Writing,* 350–54.

26 Ibid, 351.

14. THE GOD THAT FAILED

1 Ursula Prutsch and Klaus Zeyringer, *Die Welten des Paul Frischauer* (The Worlds of Paul Frischauer) (Vienna: 1997), 144.

2 *Invisible Writing,* 423.

3 Robert Conquest, *The Great Terror,* 368–69, 382–84 and 398.

4 Dorothee's dismissal from Münzenberg's organization was engineered by Herbert Wehner, an NKVD agent in Paris, as a direct result of her brother's arrest. Ernst Ascher was executed by the NKVD in October; see Reinhard Müller, *Herbert Wehner—Moskau 1937* (Hamburg: Hamburger Edition, 2004), 78–79.

5 Eva Zeisel, unpublished memoir, 16; Lessard, "The Present Moment," *New Yorker* profile of Zeisel, 44 and 46; George Marx, *The Voice of the Martians,* 274–75; AK, preface to Alexander Weissberg, *The Accused,* xi. Eva never did find out the real reason she was released. Alex Weissberg had collected testimonials from his influential scientific colleagues, including Pyotr Kapitza, and the Austrian consul had made official inquiries about her, since Eva and Alex had both retained their Austrian citizenship. Ultimately it seems she was a small cog in the elaborate machinery of the show trials and proved unnecessary to the impresarios in charge of staging them.

6 The letter was dated 6/15/38 and was sent on behalf of both Weissberg and a German colleague in Kharkov, Friedrich Houtermanns, arrested at the same time. A copy of the letter is in AK's papers, MS2374/1. See also Zeisel memoir, 16; AK, Preface to Weissberg, xvii–xix; AK letter to Weissberg, 6/18/46, MS2374/1.

7 *Invisible Writing,* 385–87; Manès Sperber, *Shards* typescript (see chap. 11, note 1), 93.

8 *Invisible Writing,* 388.

9 Müller, op. cit., 54–55. Abusch signed his report to Moscow with his party alias, "Henri."

10 Letter from AK to the Writers' Fraction of the German Communist Party, 4/22/38, RCPSDMH, 495/205/5221.

11 In *The Invisible Writing* (389) Koestler mentions only one letter, and it is clear that he

was thinking of this second, much longer one. He appears to have forgotten the first letter. See also Müller, 48 and 56, and Michael Scammell, "Arthur Koestler Resigns," *New Republic,* 5/4/98.

12 RCPSDMH, 495/205/5221. The letter in the Comintern archives appears to be the original, with Koestler's crossings out and emendations. It does not, however, bear a signature.

13 Müller, 56–57.

15. NO NEW CERTAINTIES

1 See *Invisible Writing,* 261. The original German text of the novel was thought to be lost after the French police raided Koestler's apartment a year later, and when it was published in West Germany after World War II, it was in a back-translation from the English. The German typescript confiscated in Paris can be found in the CPHDC in Moscow, where the book's title is given as *Der Sklavenkrieg;* see CPHDC, 619/1/4–7.

2 AK, *The Gladiators,* Postscript, 310.

3 For reviews see *New York Times,* 7/16/39; *Manchester Guardian,* 3/17/39; *The Spectator,* 3/24/39; AK to Axel Springer, 11/26/47, MS2376/1.

4 *Invisible Writing,* 264; V. S. Pritchett, *"The Gladiators,"* *Christian Science Monitor,* 4/15/39, 10; George Orwell, "Arthur Koestler," in Murray A. Sperber, *Arthur Koestler,* 17.

5 "Arthur Koestler at 65—A Fighter for Men's Minds Now Studies their Brains," *New York Times Magazine,* 8/30/70; AK, untitled essay in *The God That Failed,* 73; *Invisible Writing,* 393.

6 *Invisible Writing,* 267; AK to Heinz Graber, 11/29/71, MS2387/2; Manès Sperber, *Shards,* 134; Alfred Döblin, "Brief an Arthur Koestler" (Letter to Arthur Koestler) in *Schriften zur Politik und Gesellschaft* (Writings on Politics and Society) (Olten und Freiburg im Breisgau: Walter, 1972), 374–79. See also Schiller et al., *Exil im Frankreich* (Frankfurt am Main: Röderberg, 1981), 345 and 350–51.

7 Gross, 295–306 and 313–14. See also McMeekin, *Tycoon,* chapter 16. Writing to Léon Blum in 1939, Willi claimed that he had resigned from his party positions as early as December 1936 and had stayed in the party only till 1937, but it's reasonably clear that he was lying to bolster his reputation. Centre Historique des Archives Nationales—CHAN (Historical Center of National Archives), Paris, Box F7/15125.

8 Alfred Kantorowicz, *Deutsches Tagebuch* (German Diary) (Munich: Kindler, 1959), 59 and 340, and Ludwig Marcuse, *Mein zwanzigstes Jahrhundert* (My Twentieth Century) (Munich: Paul List, 1968), 244.

9 CHAN, F7/15125. The French police archives contain a photograph of prisoners at the detention camp in Gurs posing with a copy of *Zukunft;* see *Die Zukunft,* no. 1, Paris, 10/12/38.

10 *Die Zukunft,* no. 7, 11/25/38 (unsigned draft of editorial in CHAN, F7/15123); AK to Mann, 10/24/38 and 11/17/38, CHAN, F7/15124; Duchess of Atholl to AK, 10/31/38.

11 Siegmund Freud, "Ein Wort zum Antisemitismus" (A Word on Anti-Semitism), in *Die Zukunft,* no. 7. Freud's cover letter to AK was so shakily written that his son, Martin, had to type out a copy. CHAN F7/15123.

12 See Herbert Lottman, *The Left Bank,* 122.

13 Manès Sperber, *Shards,* 134.

14 *Invisible Writing,* 218–22; Frances Aldor to AK, 8/5/46, MS2374/3. See *The Practice of Sex.* According to Koestler, the British edition of this work retained only 46 pages from the 800-plus that he and Manès Sperber had written for the original French edition, but he was mistaken about the British title and also in thinking that his name had been omitted. It appeared (in garbled form) as "Coester."

15 Fischer, "Darkness of Arthur Koestler," op. cit.; Ragna Ragnes to AK, 5/14/46, MS2374/3.

16 Author's interviews with Daphne Henrion (née Hardy), 3/6/89 and 12/8/92.

17 See Ludwig Marcuse, op. cit., 242–43; Robert Neumann, *Ein leichtes Leben* (An Easy Life) (Vienna-Munich-Basel: Kurt Desch, 1963), 57–61; Palmier, *Weimar en Exil,* 291–92.

18 Interviews with Henrion, op. cit. Daphne described their traveling companion as "a rich Hungarian publisher, who (unlike us) stayed in the best hotels."

19 AK to Sperber, 7/17/39, with permission of Jenka Sperber. ÖLA 2/88.

16. DARKNESS VISIBLE

1 Schwarzschild's remark to Koestler is mentioned in Cynthia Koestler's diary entry for 5/16/63, MS2305. For Rubashov see Louis A. Gordon, "Koestler, Zionism and Jabotinsky" in *Studies in Zionism* (Tel Aviv), vol. 12, no. 2 (1991), 157–58 and 158 note.

2 *Invisible Writing,* 394–95.

3 Ibid.

4 AK to Sperber, 7/17/39 (with permission).

5 AK, *Scum of the Earth,* 30; "Arthur Koestler at 65," *New York Times Magazine,* 8/30/70; Henrion interview, 12/8/92.

6 *Scum,* 31 and 35.

7 Gilbert Badia, "Camps répressifs ou camps de concentration" (Internment Camps or Concentration Camps), in Badia et al., *Les Barbelés de l'exil,* 294–95.

8 Daphne Henrion to author, 4/19/99.

9 Koestler was detained under a decree dating from 5/2/38; see Decision of the Ministry of the Interior to revoke Koestler's arrest and detention order signed P. Boursicot, 11/7/46, Archives de la Préfecture de Police de Paris (Paris Police Archives—PPA), Fund GA K4/4. See also police report dated 12/13/45 and sent to Guy de Rothschild in response to his request for information on Koestler's behalf, MS2374/2. See also MI5 memo in TNA, 1110/215. The sole contemporary document referring to Koestler's arrest gives the reason as "political activities." See fragment of document issued by G. Oudard, Chief Commissioner [of Police], 10/11/39, Paris Police Archives, GA K4/12.

10 Valiani, op. cit.; *Scum,* 75 and 99 ff. (Leo appears there as "Mario" and Gustav Regler as "Albert.")

11 "Undesirable aliens" were distinguished from "enemy aliens" by virtue of being undefined by law and therefore subject to harsher conditions. The camps for "enemy aliens" were governed by international conventions and had much better food and accommodations than Le Vernet. See Koestler's testimony on behalf of H. O. Mengers (who sued the German government for impairment of health and loss of freedom after the war), 2/9/53, MS2379/1.

12 *Scum,* 108–10; Regler, 350.

13 Regler, 334.

14 *Scum,* 91.

15 Ibid., 111–12.

16 Valiani, op. cit.

17 According to Valiani, Daphne eventually managed to send Koestler a sleeping bag to place on the straw. The only other person to have a sleeping bag was Valiani. Leo Valiani, "Koestler the Militant," *Encounter,* July–August 1983, 68–72. The umbrella scene was reported to Eva Auer by an Austrian prisoner at Le Vernet, Count Schonborn; author's interview with Eva Auer, 9/17/93.

18 József Román, *Távolodóban* (Ever More Distant) (Budapest: 1990); author's interview with Román, 8/6/89.

19 Correspondence between AK and Walter Öttinghaus (of the Men in Distress Committee), and between AK and unnamed representatives of the Thomas Mann Committee and Spanish Veterans Committee in Paris, December 1938, in MS2312/6. For the activities of the German Communists at Le Vernet, and for their attitude to Koestler, see Frei, *Die Männer von Vernet,* and Sibylle Hinze, *Antifaschisten im Camp Le Vernet* (Anti-Fascists in Le Vernet Camp) (Berlin: Militärverlag der Deutschen Demokratischen Republik, 1988). Also "Newsletter on Contemporary Communism," vol. II, no. 2, February 1947, published by Ruth Fischer, copy in MS2312/6.

20 Henrion interviews 3/6/89 and 12/8/92. Also Münzenberg to A. Berthoin, Secretary General of the Ministry of the Interior, Paris, 10/6/39, in CHAN, F7/15125; and Münzenberg to Léon Blum, 10/13/39, in CPHDC, 619/1/3.

21 Author's interview with Paul Willert, 1990; Noël Coward, *Future Indefinite* (London: Heinemann, 1944), 84–85 and 121; Sam Tanenhaus, *Whittaker Chambers,* 135, 137, 144, 147–49, and 555 note. The suggestion that Willert was a party member was made by Chambers to the FBI and appears in his memoir, *Witness,* 51–55, where Willert is given the pseudonym of "Noel." It also shows up in Koestler's FBI File, in MS2308, while the allegation that Willert worked for British Intelligence is made repeatedly by Stephen Koch in *Double Lives,* 82, 93, 308, 311, and 331, though without documentation. Willert was cited in the charges against Katz as part of the Slansky show trial in Prague in 1952, though that again is hardly conclusive. According to just about everyone who met him, Willert (like Katz) loved to cultivate an air of mystery about his activities. Years later Koestler characterized him as "shifty"; see AK diary, 5/25/53, MS2305.

22 AK diary, 5/25/53, MS2305; Henrion and Paul Willert interviews. Willert's activism in this matter and his concern for Koestler and Regler are confirmed by Regler in his memoirs and by the memories of Daphne Henrion. Malraux's intervention is confirmed by a letter dated 11/27/39, in the French police files and signed by him, attesting to Koestler's "loyalty to France" and offering to act as guarantor in the case of Koestler's release, CPHDC, 619.1.3. Evidently Willy Aldor also sent packages to AK via Dorothee; see Aldor to AK, 12/15/50, MS2377/1.

23 For Nicolson's intervention see MI5 memo, 11/9/40, op. cit.: PRO FO 1110/215. AK was released on 1/23/40. See PPA, Fund GAK4.

24 Daphne Hardy diary (with permission), 14–19; the diary is now in the Koestler Archive, Edinburgh University, reference CLX-A-228; TNA, K7411. AK's visa ap-

plication was again considered by MI5 shortly after the raid on his apartment and re-
fused on the grounds of his alleged affiliation with the International Revolutionary
Marxist Center. The information was supplied to the British authorities by the
Deuxième Bureau of the French police. See TNA, KV2/1273.

25 Hardy diary, 20–21.
26 Ibid., and *Scum,* 151.

17. SCUM OF THE EARTH

1 *Scum,* 172–73. *Scum* is the source for the narrative of Koestler's escape from France,
unless otherwise noted. See also AK, pocket diary, 5/11/40, MS2304, and Balder
Olden to AK, 6/12/45, MS2373/3, and 11/26/46, MS2374/4.

2 AK, "Escape from France." This unpublished handwritten manuscript of five pages
by AK was evidently intended for inclusion in *Scum* but didn't make it, MS2342–
43(?); AK, pocket diary, 5/22/40.

3 Gisèle Freund to AK, 9/29/55, MS2380/2, and 1/17/56, MS2381/1; AK to Freund,
10/5/55, MS2380/3. See also AK's pocket diary, 5/22–24/40, op. cit.; *Scum,* 5; Preface
to the Danube edition of *Scum,* 9; and *Invisible Writing,* 420. See also Noel Riley
Fitch, *Sylvia Beach and the Lost Generation* (New York: Norton, 1983), 398. Adrienne
Monnier later remembered the Stendhal book as being *The Charterhouse of Parma*
rather than *The Red and the Black;* see *Le Littéraire,* 11/2/46.

4 Hardy interviews, 6/3/89 and 5/28/90.

5 AK to DK, 11/12/44, MS2372/4; author's interviews with DK, 6/1/89, and DH
6/3/89.

6 *Scum,* 171 and 191; AK, pocket diary, 6/17/40; DH diary, "From Limoges to Biarritz," 1; AK interview with Jean Duché, *Le Littéraire,* 10/26/46.

7 Fourteen years later, in 1954, Koestler was able to recover some of these papers, including part of the German typescript of *Darkness at Noon* (then still called "The Vicious Circle"), from a later occupant of the house, Monsieur P. Colomb. AK to P.
Colomb, 3/18/54, MS2379/1, and P. Colomb to AK 4/4/54, MS2379/2.

8 DH diary, "Limoges to Biarritz," 9–15; AK, pocket diary, 6/23/40.

9 DH diary, 28–29.

10 G. D. Hacket to AK, 1/10/43, MS2372/2.

11 DH diary, 39–41.

12 AK to Daphne Hardy, 10/17/40. When Olden read about this episode in *Scum of the
Earth,* he surmised that the potassium cyanide must have lost its effect because of its
age. Olden had come close to taking it but managed to escape just in time to Argentina, where Primavera joined him in 1944. Olden to AK, 6/12/45, op. cit.

13 AK pocket diary, 7/3/40–8/1/40.

14 *Scum,* 193 and 214; Père Piprot to AK, 5/5/47, MS2375/1. Piprot is called "Darrault"
in *Scum.*

15 AK pocket diary, 7/3–8/1/40.

16 *Scum,* 247, and unpublished manuscript fragment, "Escape from France," op. cit.,
2–3. Stephen Schwartz has raised the possibility that Benjamin didn't commit suicide but was murdered by Stalin's agents; see Stephen Schwartz, "The Mysterious
Death of Walter Benjamin," *The Weekly Standard,* 6/11/2001, 23–29. The cause of
death on Benjamin's death certificate was given as a "cerebral hemorrhage," which

could have been a cover-up or a genuine diagnosis. Neither version is conclusive, and Koestler's experience when he took his portion of the morphine tablets in Lisbon (see below) and survived could be seen to support either theory.

17 Münzenberg was indeed dead. He was found hanged from a tree in the Midi region of France in October 1940, having been dead since June. According to one theory, it was suicide; according to another, he was killed by two men he was with, presumably on Stalin's orders. See Gross, op. cit., 324–26; Koch, *Double Lives,* 340–44; and McMeekin, *Tycoon,* 304–6. Also *Scum,* 227–28; AK pocket diary, 8/8/40.

18 For Fry's rescue operation see Varian Fry, *Surrender on Demand.* The Emergency Rescue Committee later became the International Rescue Committee. AK to DH, 8/3/40, and DH to AK, 9/5/40.

19 *Scum,* 264–65; AK pocket diary, 8/?/40, MS2304; TNA, KV2/1273. The British soldiers who escaped were Lieutenants Hopkins and McCallum and Staff Sergeant Newman. Koestler doesn't name a fourth who was with them.

20 In his autobiography, Sperber writes that Koestler did give him one pill "to be used if a quick death was the only way out," but that he lost it afterward. It is questionable, however, if one morphine tablet would have done the job. See Manès Sperber, *Shards,* 161 and 183.

21 See François Brigneau, "Arthur Koestler, le proscrit pathétique" (Arthur Koestler, the Pathos of Exile), article 5, *Paris-presse l'intransigeant,* 6/20/59, 10.

22 See preface to the Danube edition of *Scum,* 10–11. Also Rüdiger von Etzdorf, "Diary of a British Agent," in *The Royal United Services Institution Journal,* London, vol. 114, no. 655, September 1969; Brigneau, op. cit., 12; and E. E. Bullen to AK, 9/12/78, MS2391/3. The detail about Koestler's Palestinian passport and the role of the American consul general comes from Koestler's letter "To the British Passport Control Officer," in Lisbon, 9/21/40, copy in MS2414/1. Koestler's emergency certificate is in TNA, KV2/1273.

23 TNA, KV2/1273. For Ellen Hill, Janetta Parladé to author, 9/3/90.

24 See TNA, K7411. Also AK letter to Michael Striker, 10/6/40; Exiled Writers Committee of the League of American Writers, Inc., to AK, 10/24/40, both in the possession of Eva Zeisel. The league did in due course obtain a visa for Koestler, but by then he was already in England; see League to AK, 10/28/40 and 11/28/40; also American Consulate General, Lisbon, to AK 12/13/40, MS2371/1.

25 AK, unpublished handwritten manuscript, "Notizen für Benno Lévy" (Notes for Benno Lévy), MS2414/1(?).

26 AK to DH, 10/17/40 (with permission).

27 AK, *Invisible Writing,* 421–22; AK, transcript of unpublished interview with Iain Hamilton, 3/3/74, MS2436/5; AK, statements to the British Consul-General and the British Passport Control Officer, Lisbon, November 1940, copies in MS2414/1; A. H. W. King to AK, 3/11/53; AK to A. H. W. King, 3/24/53, MS2332/5. See also Brigneau, op. cit. In his autobiography Koestler confused BOAC with the Dutch airline KLM, but it was BOAC.

18. DARKNESS UNVEILED

1 Hamilton, 66; J. N. Owen, Report on interrogation of Koestler, with addendum to "H.M. Chief Inspector" and handwritten postscript, 11/7/40, TNA, KV2/1273.

2 Owen, op. cit.

3 Hamilton, 67; unsigned, "Report No. 54," Cannon Row Police Station, 11/8/40. TNA, 1110/215, unsigned to Major Sinclair, 12/9/40, MS2308/2.

4 J.F.C., Memo to Mr. Wood, MI5, 11/9/40, TNA, 1110/215. Koestler was detained under sections 15 (i) and 1 (iii) (h) of the Aliens Order of 1920.

5 AK to DH, 11/14/40 and 11/20/40.

6 Hamilton interview, 7–8. Years later, Koestler identified the hangman as Albert Pierrepoint and cited Pierrepoint as telling the Royal Commission on Capital Punishment about one of his victims, "He was not an Englishman. He kicked up rough. He was a foreigner." Pierrepoint was not yet the chief executioner he later became but still an assistant. See also AK, *Reflections on Hanging,* 172.

7 AK to DH, 11/20/40, 11/29/40, and 2/12/40.

8 AK to DH, 11/29/40 and 2/12/40; author's interview with DH, 5/28/90; Hamilton interview, 10.

9 DH to AK, 11/7/40; interview with DH, 5/28/90. It was Rupert Hart Davis who suggested to Daphne that the Bible was "always a good source for titles." The verse in question is Job 5:14.

10 For Rubashov models, see AK interview with Cyril Connolly, 44, MS2440/1.

11 Koestler's reliance on Seville led to some minor circumstantial "mistakes," such as the location of the peephole in the cell door, where Soviet practice didn't jibe with the Spanish, but the accuracy of Koestler's larger picture of Rubashov's life in confinement has not been contested.

12 Ivanov's role mimics that of the police inspector, Porfiry Petrovich, in *Crime and Punishment,* while his metaphysical debate with Rubashov in the cell strongly recalls the verbal duel between the Grand Inquisitor and Ivan Karamazov in *The Brothers Karamazov.* Unfortunately, Koestler tips his hand by having Ivanov refer directly to *Crime and Punishment* and Raskolnikov, when the scene would work better without it. The Karamazov parallel is not alluded to directly.

13 Michael Foot, "Arthur Koestler," in *Loyalists and Loners* (London: Collins, 1986), 216. Wickham Steed to AK, 12/25/40, MS2414/1; Kingsley Martin, "Bourgeois Ethics," *New Statesman,* 2/8/41; Strachey to Koestler, 1/23/41, MS2414/1; Anonymous (R. D. Charques), "Tragedy of Logic," *Times Literary Supplement,* 12/21/40.

14 George Orwell, "New Novels," *New Statesman and Nation,* 1/4/41, and "Arthur Koestler," in Murray A. Sperber, *Arthur Koestler,* 13–24; *Catholic World,* August 1941.

15 Hamilton interview, 10. Whittaker Chambers, "Brightest in Dungeons," *Time,* 5/26/41.

16 Author's interview with DH, 6/3/89.

17 *Invisible Writing,* 426; Hamilton interview, 8; Olivier Todd, "Janus, ou les deux faces d'Arthur Koestler" (Janus, or the Two Faces of Arthur Koestler), *L'Express,* 2/3–9/79.

18 Paul Willert to AK, undated, 1941, MS2371/2.

19 AK to Heinz Neumann, 4/2/41, MS2372/1.

20 *Scum,* 16–17.

21 Ibid., 128. Though a goodly number of the refugees Koestler mentioned were Jewish, he was referring here to all the anti-fascists who opposed Hitler. The use of the term *Holocaust* to denote the mass murder of European Jewry didn't come into use until about a decade later.

22 Ibid., 130 and 247.

23 KGG, interview with Arthur Koestler, C.B.E., in series "British Service Camera-men: 1939–1945," Imperial War Museum, Department of Sound Records, Accession No. 005393/03, 12. Nicholson to AK, 4/7/41, MS2371/1.

24 Jonathan Cape to AK, 10/29/41, MS2371/2; Herbert Read, "A Moral Climate," *Spectator,* 9/26/41; Anonymous, "Tale of a Betrayal," *Times Literary Supplement,* 9/20/41.

25 Harold Strauss, "A Searing Story of Concentration Camps in France," *New York Times Book Review,* 10/5/41; Clifton Fadiman, *New Yorker,* 10/4/41; W. H. Chamberlin, "Émigré in France," *Christian Science Monitor,* 11/8/41; Leo Lania, "The Zero Point of Infamy," *Saturday Review of Literature,* 10/18/41; Paul Hutchinson, "The World Gone Mad," *The Christian Century,* 11/5/41.

19. IN CRUMPLED BATTLEDRESS

1 AK to H. S. Latham, 4/3/41, and James Putnam, 5/2/41, MS2356/1; *Invisible Writing,* 424–25. Koestler originally applied to enlist on December 17, 1940; see TNA, KV2/1273.

2 AK to T. R. Fyvel, 4/18/41, MS2372/1; AK to DH, 1/6/41. This and the descriptions of army life that follow are taken from the letters AK wrote to DH from April 1941 to March 1942 (cited with permission).

3 See Mark Lynton, *Accidental Journey* (Woodstock, N.Y.: Overlook Press, 1995), 64–65. Lynton (then Max-Otto Löwenstein) served briefly in the 251st Company at the same time as Koestler.

4 KGG interview with AK, op. cit., 4.

5 AK letters to DH, 5/26/41 and Michael Polanyi 6/1/41, International Association for Cultural Freedom (IACF) Records, University of Chicago Library, Box 198, Folder 1.

6 Lynton, 68; AK to Allen Lane, 6/23/41, MS2372/1.

7 AK to Michael Polanyi, 11/10/41, MS2344/7; list of lecture topics submitted by "Private A. Koestler," no date, MS2363/3. A note in AK's MI5 file, dated June 1942, explains that AK was made "an exception to the general rule that enemy aliens shall not be employed as lecturers to the troops" in view of his "special qualifications" to do so, see TNA, KV2/1273.

8 AK to Paul Willert, 9/4/41, MS2372/1; KGG interview with AK, 8–11; Connolly interview with AK, 14–16; list of Koestler's army lectures for December 1941, op. cit.

9 AK to Willert, op. cit.

10 AK to Paul Willert, 7/1/41, MS2372/1.

11 Willert to AK, 1/20/42, MS2372/1.

12 Copy of "Report on Injuries" (Army Form B117) filed by AK on 9/28/41, MS2307/1; Rees, *A Chapter of Accidents,* 152.

13 Author's interview with Robert Ringel, 10/9/92.

14 AK to DH, 12/28/41; interview with Robert Ringel; Robert Ringel to author, 1/7/93, "Easter Sunday," 1993, and 6/25/93; A. G. Jones to AK, 2/3/57, MS2381/3. Malingering was not uncommon in the APC. Lynton describes a Greek fellow-soldier who managed to doctor his urine. Lynton, a hostile witness, describes Koestler as egotistical and "much disliked" (Lynton, 70 and 92), but letters from other APC members to AK tell a different story.

15 Frank Halliday, *Indifferent Honest* (London: Duckworth, 1960), 160–61; AK to DH,

11/25/41; AK to Major McKay, 12/2/41 and 12/6/41, MS2372/1; Arthur Calder Marshall to AK, 12/12/41, MS2371/2; Richard Crossman to AK, 1/1/42 and 1/28/42, MS2371/3; Bonamy Dobrée to AK, undated [Jan. 1942?], MS2371/3; DH to AK, undated [Jan. 1942?]; Paul Willert to DH, undated [Jan. 1942?], undated [Jan. 1942?], and 1/20/42. Halliday, 161; AK, "Going Native," *Kaleidoscope,* 276.

16 AK to DH, 12/28/41, TNA, KV2/1273.

17 See AK, "The Novelist's Temptations," in *The Yogi and the Commissar,* 28–35.

18 E. M. Forster to AK, 9/28/41, 10/9/41, 10/28/41, 11/13/41, 12/9/41; AK to Forster, 10/1/41, 10/17/41, all in MS2345/1. See also Mary Lago and P. N. Furbank, eds., *Selected Letters of E. M. Forster,* vol. 2 (Cambridge, Mass.: Belknap Press, 1985), 197–98.

19 Hamilton interview, 23 and 81; Peter Lewis, *George Orwell,* 104.

20 AK diary, September 1941–October 1942, MS2305. Daphne had moved to Oxford after Koestler insisted she leave London because it was "too dangerous." Author's interview with Stephen and Natasha Spender, 12/9/88.

21 Hamilton, 76; Connolly to AK, undated postcard and undated letter [1941 or 1942], MS2371/2.

22 Stephen and Natasha Spender interview, and author's interview with Diana Cooke (by telephone), 6/19/03.

23 Shelden, *Friends of Promise,* 84; Peter Quennell to AK, "Sunday," 1941(?), MS2371/2, and AK, "Koestler's Micromemoirs," *Encounter,* op. cit., 58. See also Peter Quennell, *The Wanton Chase* (London: Collins, 1980), 21. Daphne Henrion remembered seeing Koestler don a hairnet during their trip to the south of France. According to her, he would dip his head into a basin of water and then put a hairnet over it so that it would dry flat, but he never slept in it (DH to author, 8/12/92). Skelton's published version states innocuously that when Quennell took Koestler a cup of tea one morning, "he found him sitting up in bed wearing a black hairnet." She adds, less innocuously, "Four times Koestler repeated that he'd cleaned out the bath for us to show what a noble fellow he was." Evidently the hairnet and the bath were paired in everyone's minds at the time. See Skelton, *Tears Before Bedtime,* 48.

24 Author's interview with David Astor, 8/12/88. See also Clive Fisher, *Cyril Connolly,* 223: "Who shall command ze dezert? Wavell, Orvell or Fyvel?" and Cesarani, 191. These anecdotes also had great staying power.

25 Author's interview with George Strauss, 3/23/90.

26 Marie Petworth to AK, 12/42, MS2371/2; AK diary, 10/6/41, 4/8/42, and 1/18/42, MS2305. Koestler's attitude to Englishmen and sex was reflected in his diary, where he coined aphorisms to express his disdain: "their schoolboys are gentlemen and their gentlemen schoolboys"; English intellectuals "need 5–10 years to get over their public school complex—if they ever get over it." Musing on members of the "pink generation," he remarked, "around 30, some (C[yril] C[onnolly]) manage to find the bridge to para-normal sex, but the majority not; and even the minority remain para-normal." "Para-normal" was shorthand for men who had practiced homosexuality at boarding school but turned to heterosexual relations later. Author's interview with Foot, 2/21/90. For general background, see Hewison, *Under Siege,* chaps. 3 and 4.

27 Michael Foot, op.cit., 217, and "The Destroyer," *Encounter,* September–October 1983; Thomas, *John Strachey,* 219–20; John Strachey, *The Strangled Cry,* 12–13 and

18. Strachey to AK, 1/23/41. In later years, Strachey and Koestler would "gush together as they reminisced about the exhilaration they had experienced on their conversion to Marxism and the sense of relief and confidence it had given them"; George Strauss interview.

28 Guy de Rothschild, *The Whims of Fortune,* 164–65; Foot, op. cit.; author's interview with Stephen and Natasha Spender.

29 AK to Paul Willert, 10/2/41, MS2372/1, and 7/19/43[?], MS2372/4.

30 David Astor interview; David Astor, "Crusader," *Encounter,* July–August 1983, 32.

20. THE NOVELIST'S TEMPTATIONS

1 Adele K to AK (in German), 1/4/41, MS2371/1.

2 A.W. Brian Simpson, *In the Highest Degree Odious: Detention Without Trial in Wartime Britain* (Oxford: Clarendon Press, 1992), 258; Miriam Kochan, *Britain's Internees in the Second World War* (London: Macmillan, 1983), 175; Ferenc Aldor to AK (in Hungarian), 12/8/42, MS2371/4; author's interview with Andre Deutsch, 5/31/90; DH to Aldor, CPHDC, MS619/1/3; Aldor to AK, 2/12/41, MS2371/1; AK to Harold Benjamin, 4/28/41, MS2372/1; Benjamin to AK, 5/12/41, 7/8/41, and 8/2/41, MS2371/1. See also *Invisible Writing,* 219.

3 Aldor to AK, 11/23/42, 12/8/42 (both in Hungarian), 12/14/42, MS2371/4; 1/14/43 (in Hungarian), 1/30/43, 2/7/43 (in Hungarian), 5/2/43, MS2372/2; AK to Aldor, 11/30/42, 1/5/43, 2/13/43, MS2372/4; *Invisible Writing,* 218–21; Inge Goodwin to Henry McAdam, 3/20/06; McAdam to author, 9/11/08. The Hungarian-born British publisher Andre Deutsch was interned on the Isle of Man at the same time as Aldor and has confirmed Koestler's description of him, author's interview with Andre Deutsch, 5/31/90.

4. DK to AK, telegram, 7/31/41, MS2301/1; AK to Elizabeth Ascher, 8/7/41 and 9/29/41, MS2372/1; AK to Eva Zeisel, undated [August 1941?], MS2372/1; B. F. Heine to AK, 8/30/41 and 9/20/41, MS2371/1 and 2; Ascher to AK 12/28/41, MS2371/2; Emily Hughes, Friends Service Council, to AK, 3/4/42, and Ascher to AK, 5/27/42, MS2371/3; DK to Ascher, 8/22/42 and 9/4/42, TNA, KV2/1273; AK to Aliens Department, 9/28/42, MS2301/1.

5 Babette Gross to AK, 8/17/41, MS2371/2; Gabriel Hacket to AK (in Hungarian), 1/10/43, MS2372/2. Koestler sought English-language publishers for Valiani and Regler and received a steady stream of refugees from Central Europe looking for sympathy and sustenance; see, for example, AK to Valiani and to Erika Mann, 9/14/42, MS2372/1; AK to Valiani, 6/8/43, and to Regler, 1/21/44, MS2372/4.

6. AK, "The Quarantine Solution" (typescript), and correspondence between AK, David Astor, and Eleanor Rathbone, October 1941–January 1942, MS2413/2.

7 AK, "Scum of the Earth—1942," *Evening Standard,* 6/3/42, and "Scum of the Earth 2—Revolt in the Prison Camp," 6/4/42, reprinted in the second edition of *Scum of the Earth* (London: Cape, 1945), 85–93.

8 Arthur Koestler, *Protective Custody,* broadcast 5/7/42, MS2340/2. All further references to the play are from this script. The words of the Dachau Hymn, which Koestler obtained from the Austrian novelist Robert Neumann, were translated by John Lehmann. Koestler later learned that a second and shorter Dachau hymn existed, with only slight resemblances to the one he used, composed by Leopold Marx; see AK to Marx, 2/13/45, MS2374/1, and Marx to AK, 3/6/45, MS2373/3.

9 Anthony Howard, *Crossman: The Pursuit of Power* (London: Cape, 1990), 6, 33–34, and 51; AK's scripts and letters are in MS2363/2; Crossman to AK, 7/2/42, MS2371/4; invoice from AK to the BBC, April[?] 1942, MS2372/1.

10 AK, "Outline for a Cough Campaign," typescript of a sample script in German, MS2339/5. See also AK to Crossman, 7/11/42, MS2372/1; AK, "Zu Tode gesiegt" (Winning to Death), text of planned leaflet in German, MS2402/5; Tom Bower, *The Perfect English Spy: Sir Dick White and the Secret War, 1935–90* (London: Heinemann, 1995), 46.

11 AK, "Lift Your Head, Comrade," typescript, MS2340/3.

12 KGG, interview with Koestler, op. cit., 12–15; Arthur Calder Marshall to AK, 10/29/43, MS2372/3; *News Chronicle,* 12/12/42.

13 C. K. Lynton-Harris, Films Division, M.O.I., to AK, 11/13/43; film outline, incomplete and undated; untitled typescript, MS2363/2; KGG interview with AK, 15.

14 T. R. Fyvel, "Arthur Koestler and George Orwell," in Harold Harris, ed., *Astride the Two Cultures,* 150; letters from Fyvel to AK, 1/20/41, 2/4/41, and 2/13/41, MS2371/2; *Evening Standard,* Foot to AK, 6/11/42, MS2371/3, and AK to Foot, 7/8/42, MS2372/1; author's interview with Foot, 2/21/90; Foot, *Loyalists and Loners,* 217.

15 AK, "Waiting for the Tube—The Idle Thoughts of Sidney Sound (Your Neighbour on the Underground)," 1–3, *Evening Standard,* 7/10/42, 7/17/42, and 7/25/42, MS2441/2.

16 AK, "The Yogi and the Commissar," *Horizon,* June 1942, and in *Yogi,* 9–20.

17 AK, "Knights in Rusty Armor," *New York Times Magazine,* January 1943, and in *Yogi,* 100–105.

18 AK, "The Fraternity of Pessimists," *New York Times Magazine,* November 1943, and in *Yogi,* 106–12.

19 AK to Polanyi, 3/5/42, MS2366/7.

20 AK, *Arrival and Departure,* 161.

21 Ibid., 126 and 134–49.

22 Ibid., 159–61 and 183–88.

23 AK interview with Pierre Debray-Ritzen and Sven Hasselblatt (in German), 1971, 9, MS2340/1; AK and CK, *Stranger on the Square*, 235–36.

24 Anon (R. D. Charques), "The Idealist," *Times Literary Supplement,* 11/13/43; Philip Toynbee, "New Novels," *New Statesman and Nation,* 12/4/43; Clifton Fadiman, "Arthur Koestler," *New Yorker,* 11/20/43, 105; Harold Rosenberg, "The Case of the Baffled Radical," *Partisan Review,* Winter 1944, 100–103.

25 Rosenberg, op. cit.

26 Orwell, "Arthur Koestler," in *Dickens, Dali and Others* (New York: Reynal and Hitchcock, 1946), reprinted in Murray A. Sperber, *Arthur Koestler,* 21–24.

27 AK diary, 1/22/65, MS2306/1.

21. IDENTITY CRISIS

1 AK, "The Birth of a Myth," *Horizon,* April 1943, republished in a longer version as "In Memory of Richard Hillary" in *Yogi,* 46–67.

2 AK, *Arrival,* 106; Raymond Mortimer, "Arthur Koestler," 133; V. S. Pritchett, 64. For when news of the Holocaust reached the West, see Robert J. Hanyok, *Eavesdropping on Hell: Historical Guide to Western Communications Intelligence and the Holocaust, 1939–1945* (Washington, D.C.: Center for Cryptologic History, National Security Agency, 2005).

3   See Wood and Jankowski, *Karski,* chap. 8. Richard Breitman, *Official Secrets: What the Nazis Planned, What the British and Americans Knew* (New York: Hill and Wang, 1998).

4   Typescript in MS2363/2. See also Edwards, *Victor Gollancz,* 372; Wasserstein, *Britain and the Jews of Europe,* 203.

5   In his letter to Frank Newsome at the BBC, Koestler wrote, "I think the best thing to do is to send you the facts as I heard them from Karski, in the first person singular, and then leave it to your service to write it up in the proper way." See AK to N. F. Newsome, BBC European Service, 6/28/43, and AK to Karski, 10/12/43, MS2372/4; E. Thomas Wood to author, 2/10/93. Wood subsequently discovered that the script had been broadcast on July 7 and 8, 1943, and in at least one version had omitted Karski's name. He also learned that, contrary to Karski's claim, repeated by Cesarani, Koestler did not read the script himself (it was read by Duncan Grinnell Milne); Wood to author, 5/26/93.

6   *Arrival,* 74–85.

7   See Lewis, *George Orwell,* 365.

8   See *Horizon,* December 1943; AK, *Invisible Writing,* 428–29; Wasserstein, 117.

9   AK, "On Disbelieving Atrocities," *New York Times Magazine,* January 1944, and in *Yogi,* 94–99.

10   AK, "In Memory of Richard Hillary," *Yogi,* 60. A much shorter version of the essay appeared as "The Birth of a Myth" in *Horizon,* April 1943.

11   Author's interviews with Michael Foot, 2/21/90, George and Bonita Strauss, 3/23/90, and Daphne Henrion, 5/28/90.

12   George and Bonita Strauss and Daphne Henrion, op. cit.

13   The question of when and to whom Koestler went for analysis is a murky one. Walter Laqueur, who also underwent analysis in London during the war, remembers bumping into Koestler on the way into or out of his analyst's office and remembers that Koestler's analyst was Hungarian. Astor to author, 8/12/88; author's interview with Walter Laqueur, 3/18/92. See also Dr. David Le Vay to AK, 9/6/75, and AK to Le Vay, 9/22/75, MS2389/4. See also *Yogi,* 247.

14   AK diary, 2/29/44–4/15/49, MS2305.

15   Author's interview with DH, 3/6/89.

16   AK diary, op. cit., "Wednesday," 3(?)/22/44, 4/2/44, 4/29/44; author's interviews with DH, 5/28/90 and 8/12/92.

17   AK, "The French 'Flu," *Tribune,* November 1943, and in *Yogi,* 21–27, a review of new books by three writers, Gide, Aragon, and Vercors, who were particuarly popular with English intellectuals; see Cyril Connolly's *The Unquiet Grave* (London: Horizon, 1944), and for background, Hewison, *Under Siege,* 183, and Bergonzi, *Wartime and Aftermath,* 50. Bergonzi actually uses the term *French 'flu* to characterize Connolly's book.

18   AK, "The Intelligentsia," *Horizon,* March 1944, and in *Yogi,* 68–84; Orwell, "Pacifism and the War," *Partisan Review,* September–October 1942, and in Sonia Orwell and Ian Angus, eds., *The Collected Essays of George Orwell,* vol. 3 (New York: Harcourt, Brace and Co., 1968), 230.

19   Hamilton interview, part 4, 17; AK diary, "Wednesday" [2/29/44] and 4/29/44.

20   AK diary, undated [June 1944].

21   Ignotus, *Political Prisoner,* 17–20; Robert Neumann to AK, 3/19/41, MS2371/1; AK

to Neumann, 4/2/41, MS2372/1; AK to Károlyi, 10/25/41, 11/15/41, and 12/6/41, in Károlyi Papers, Central Committee of the Hungarian Socialist Workers' Party, Archive of the Institute for Party History (CCHSWP/AIPH), Budapest; Catherine Kàrolyi to AK, 10/6/43, MS2372/3; Ilona Duczynska to M. Károlyi, 11/30/43, and to Michael Polanyi, undated, Duczynska Papers, CCHSWP/AIPH, 258–59a and 267–67a; AK to unknown recipient, undated, MS2372/1(?).

22 David Astor to author, 9/23/93. "Mesmeric charm" was the phrase used by Robert Boothby, MP, to describe Weizmann's manner.

23 Rothschild, *Whims of Fortune,* 163; A. J. Ayer, *Part of My Life* (New York and London: Harcourt Brace Jovanovich, 1977), 262.

24 Rothschild, 165; AK diary, 4/24/44; author's interview with Guy de Rothschild, 1/10/92; Michael Ignatieff, *Isaiah Berlin, a Life* (New York: Henry Holt, 1998), 120.

25 AK diary, entry for "Wednesday" [March 15?], 1944, MS2305.

26 Gabriel Hackett to AK, 1/10/43; AK to Elizabeth Ascher, 1/11/43, MS2372/2; AK diary, 4/22/44.

27 Hamilton interview, op. cit.; Wasserstein, op. cit., 249–60; Andrew Handler, *The Holocaust in Hungary* (Tuscaloosa: University of Alabama Press, 1982), 22–23. In Teddy Kollek's version of this story, it was Shertok who got the "million Jews" reply from Lord Halifax; see Kollek, *For Jerusalem* (New York: Random House, 1978), 52.

28 "Telegram in Code," unsigned; Irene Aldor to Ferenc Aldor (in Hungarian), 6/1/44; Ferenc Aldor to AK, 7/7/44, all in MS2373/2.

29 AK to Ferenc Aldor, 10/9/44, MS2372/4.

22. COMMISSAR OR YOGI?

1 For meeting, Celia Goodman's diary, 9/25/80 (private collection). For Wilson's praise of Mamaine, see Wilson, *Europe Without Baedeker,* 181–82.

2 AK diary, March 1944, MS2304.

3 AK to Mamaine Paget, "Tuesday night," May 1944; Mamaine Paget's diary, January–May 1944; both cited with permission of Celia Goodman; AK diary, May 1944, MS2304.

4 Author's interview with Celia Goodman, 3/5/90. One of Koestler's failed gambits to Celia was, "What if we were in the desert? You would do it then, wouldn't you?"

5 AK diary, op. cit.; Mamaine Paget's diary, op. cit.

6 AK diary, 5/8/44 and 6/3/44; Mamaine Paget's diary, op. cit.

7 See Michael Ward, "The Development of Spirituality and Ethics in the Work of Arthur Koestler, 1937–1959," doctoral dissertation, University of Edinburgh, 1997, 53–54; AK, "Arrival and Departure II," handwritten MS, 51, MS2317/3.

8 AK to Father Dickinson, February 1944, MS2372/4.

9 AK diary, 3/11/44.

10 Anna Kavan, "The Case of Bill Williams," and review of *The Company She Keeps, Horizon,* February 1944, 96–99 and 140. AK to Connolly, 6/26/44 and 6/28/44; AK to Anna Kavan and to Jonathan Cape, 6/27/44, all in MS2372/4; Lewis, *George Orwell,* 365 note; AK diary, 7/1/44 and 7/10/44.

11 AK diary, 7/11/44.

12 AK diary, 7/11/44 and 7/12/44. AK, confidential draft of memorandum, "The Case for the Bombing of the Extermination Camps for Jews in Upper Silesia and Poland

by the American Air Force," 7/11/44, MS2403/1. Koestler argued that the Jews were condemned to death anyway, but the destruction of the German plant would prevent or at least delay the execution of 300,000 more still left in Hungary. It would also demonstrate the Allies' sympathy for the Jews and their opposition to the death camps. Technically the bombing (from captured bases in Italy) was feasible, and the plan was formally backed by Churchill and Eden, but it was opposed by officials in the Foreign Office and never put into effect; see Wasserstein, 307–20.

13 AK diary, 6/29/44, 7/10/44, and 7/11/44.

14 Author's interviews with Celia Goodman, 12/14/88 and 3/5/90, and with Ariane Bankes, 3/18/03: AK diary, 7/12/44; Celia Goodman to author, 4/1/00.

15 AK Diary, 7/12/44. AK to Mamaine, "Tuesday night" [July 4?], 1944 (with permission of Celia Goodman).

16 AK to Mamaine.

17 AK diary, 7/13/44 and 7/15/44.

18 AK diary, 7/15/44 and 7/17/44; AK to Shertok, 7/19/44, MS2372/4; G. R. Strauss to Shertok, 7/27/44, Weizmann Archives, Rehovot, Israel. The Budapest venture seems fantastic in retrospect but was not outlandish at the time. The pause in deportations came in response to appeals and warnings from President Roosevelt, the International Red Cross, the pope, and the king of Sweden, and it was in July 1944 that the Swedish diplomat Raoul Wallenberg started his heroic efforts to save some of Hungary's Jews by granting them Swedish passports. See Wasserstein, 262–67, and Randolph L. Braham and Béla Vago, *The Holocaust in Hungary Forty Years Later,* 148–53.

19 AK diary, 7/21/44.

20 AK diary, 7/22/44 and 7/25/44; AK to Mamaine, "Wednesday" [August 2?, 1944] (with permission).

21 Mamaine to AK, Wednesday [August 9?, 1944] (with permission). AK diary, 8/25/44; Mamaine's diary, 8/8/44, 8/9/44, 8/19/44. Eichmann was recalled to Germany on August 25, 1944, but Koestler didn't know this at the time.

22 A. D. Peters to AK, 10/3/44 and 11/23/44, MS2373/2; AK to (?) [illegible] Lantz, 9/9/44, MS2372/4; Peggy Ashcroft to AK, undated, MS2373/2(?).

23 AK diary, "Wednesday" [2/23/44].

24 AK to Orwell, 7/28/44, MS2345/2; publishers' letters to Orwell cited in Bernard Crick, *George Orwell,* 312–15.

25 AK, "End of an Illusion," *Yogi,* 201–9.

26 Ibid., 226.

27 Leonard Woolf, "Disillusion," *New Statesman and Nation,* 5/19/45; Robert Pick, "Mr. Koestler Appraises the Currents," *Saturday Review of Literature,* 5/26/45; Anonymous, "A Wounded Idealist," *Times Literary Supplement,* 5/12/45. See also F. O. Mathiessen, "The Essays of Arthur Koestler," *New York Times Book Review,* 5/27/45.

28 Hannah Arendt, "The Too Ambitious Reporter," *Commentary,* January 1946, 94–95; Eric Bentley, "Les Marxistes d'antan" (Marxists of Yesteryear), *Sewanee Review,* vol. 54, winter 1946, 165–69; Harold Laski, "Mr. Koestler," *Manchester Guardian,* 5/9/45; Kingsley Martin, "Books in General," *New Statesman and Nation,* 9/22/45.

29 George Orwell, "Catastrophic Gradualism," *Commonwealth Review,* November 1945. Reprinted in *Collected Essays,* vol. 4, 15–19.

30 Connolly to Edmund Wilson, 3/19/45, cited in Lewis, 364, note.

23. RETURN TO PALESTINE

1 Characteristically, George Orwell was the only other prominent left-wing intellectual to make a fuss about Warsaw, see Orwell, "As I Please," *Tribune,* 9/1/44. For
news of Adele, see AK diary, 8/25/44.

2 AK to Francis Aldor, 7/31/44; Irene Aldor to AK, 8/18/44; AK to Irene Aldor,
8/29/44; Francis Aldor to AK, 10/23/44; AK to Francis Aldor, 10/29/44; all in
MS2302/2.

3 Author's interview with DK, 6/1/89. Hans, too, pretended to be French and was
known as "Jean."

4 AK to DK, 11/12/44, MS2372/4. It was in this letter that AK apologized for his hasty
departure from Paris in 1940 and explained why it was that Daphne, with her
British passport, was able to accompany him without difficulty.

5 The question of Koestler's citizenship was so complicated that when Cyril Connolly
interviewed him in 1965, he refused to answer questions about it. He had held Hungarian citizenship until 1928, when he was issued a Palestinian passport. This expired in 1932, and he reverted to being Hungarian again. In 1940, after escaping
from France, he applied to renew his Hungarian passport, but his Hungarian citizenship was automatically canceled after he joined the Pioneer Corps, since it was
incompatible with service in a foreign army. This service qualified Koestler for
British citizenship, but he declined to apply, writing to the Home Office that he preferred to wait until he could become a citizen "with undivided loyalty," and so on.
See Connolly interview, 6. See also AK to the Hungarian Minister of the Interior (in
Hungarian), 12/22/40, MS2372/1; AK to Norman Bentwich, MP, 1/8/43, MS2372/4.

6 AK to Polanyi, 1/2/[44], IACF Archive, Chicago, Box 197, Folder 11; Lovat Dickson
to AK, 4/27/44, and John Hampden (British Council) to Dickson, 4/28/44,
MS2356/1; J. Linton to AK, 9/22/44, MS2373/2; AK to A. Feuchtwanger (Jewish
Agency for Palestine), 9/30/44, MS2356/1; Hamilton interview, part 5, 6.

7 AK to Mamaine, undated (with permission of Celia Goodman); AK to Mamaine,
"January" 1944, MS2302/2; AK interview (in French) in *Paris-Presse l'Intransigeant,*
6/17/59.

8 AK to Mamaine, undated [January? 1945], MS2303/2.

9 AK, *Thieves in the Night,* 63–64.

10 L., "Arthur Koestler's Visit," *Hephzibah Newsletter* (in Hebrew), 3/9/45.

11 *Ein Hashofet* means "Spring of the Judge" in Hebrew, and the settlement was named
for U.S. Supreme Court Justice Louis Brandeis. The album of photos showing the
settlement is in the Koestler Archive, MS2456/4. The Bible quotation is from II
Peter 10.

12 Anny Bauer to AK, 1/7/48, MS2375/2.

13 AK and Cynthia Koestler, *Stranger on the Square,* 36–38; Menachem Begin, *The Revolt,* 308–10; Thurston Clarke, *By Blood and Fire,* 54.

14 Invitation to AK from the Hebrew Technical College, MS2373/3; von Weisl to AK,
7/22/73, MS2388/3; AK to von Weisl, 7/25/73, MS2388/3; Joseph Nedava, "HaPerek
HaYisraeli Shel Arthur Koestler" (The Israeli Chapter of Arthur Koestler), *Ma'ariv,*
3/28/83.

15 AK to Mamaine, 2/16/45; Hamilton interview, part 5, 12.

16 Hamilton, *Koestler,* 376–77, note.

17 Hamilton interview, part 5, 8. See also *Stranger,* 37.

18 AK to Mamaine, op. cit.; Anny Bauer to AK, op. cit.

19 AK to Daphne Hardy, 2/11/45, MS2301/1.

20 AK to Dickson, 1/17/45, MS2356/1; AK to Mamaine, undated, January 1945, and 2/16/45, MS2303/2.

21 Mamaine to AK, 1/8/45 and 1/19/45, MS2303/2; AK to D. Hardy, 2/11/45 and 5/3/45, MS2301/1; Mamaine to AK, 12/31/45, 1/8/45, 1/19/45, 2/3/45, MS2303/2.

22 Mamaine to AK, 1/8/45, 1/19/45, 2/3/45; AK to Mamaine, 2/16/45, MS2303/2.

23 Mamaine to AK, 3/12/45, 3/29/45, 4/10/45 (telegram), 4/10/45; AK to Mamaine, 4/15–20/45, MS2303/2.

24 Wilson, *Europe Without Baedeker,* 180–84; Edmund Wilson, *The Forties* (New York: Farrar, Straus and Giroux, 1983), 106; Edmund Wilson, *Letters on Literature and Politics, 1912–1972* (New York: Farrar, Straus and Giroux, 1977), 417–23; Mamaine to AK, 4/28/45, MS2303/2. See also Jeffrey Meyers, *Edmund Wilson, a Biography* (Boston: Houghton Mifflin, 1995), 279–82.

25 Mamaine to AK, 5/10/45, 6/15/45, 7/5/45, and 7/26/45, MS2303/2.

26 Mamaine to AK, 6/28/45, MS2303/2.

27 Anny Bauer to AK, 11/24/45, MS2373/4, and 1/7/48, MS2375/2. Hamilton interview, part 5, 9. Anny was not the only object of Koestler's attentions in Palestine. He also had a brief affair with Suzanne Peet, who worked, like Anny, for the Palestine Information Office at the time; see from Peet to AK, undated [1945], MS2373/3.

28 Mamaine's diary, 8/12/45 and 8/13/45 (with permission).

29 Ibid., "Monday" [8/20/45], "Wednesday" [8/15/45], "Saturday" [8/18/45], "Monday" [8/20/45], "Monday" [8/27/45].

24. WELSH INTERLUDE

1 Mamaine's diary, 8/28–31/45.

2 Goodman, ed., *Living,* 23; Mamaine's diary, 8/28-31/45.

3 *Living,* 22–23; Mamaine to Edmund Wilson, 9/7/45, Edmund Wilson Papers (EWP), Yale Collection of American Literature, Beinecke Rare Book and Manuscript Library; Mamaine's diary, 9/13/45, 10/11/45, 10/22/45, 11/2/45, 11/10/45, and 1/10/46; Mamaine to Celia, 11/6/45 (unpublished portion with permission).

4 Neumann, *Ein leichtes Leben,* 141.

5 D. H. to AK, 10/30/45, MS2301/3.

6 Hamilton interview, part 5, 28.

7 Ibid.; George Orwell, "Books," *Tribune,* 11/30/45.

8 AK interview with Rayner Heppenstall, BBC, November 1960, MS2340/2; Hamilton interview, part 5, 29.

9 Mamaine's diary, 1/10/46; Crick, *George Orwell,* 334; Crick interview with AK, 4/30/64, lent by Prof. Crick; Storm Jameson, *Journey from the North* (London: Collins Harvill, 1970), 131.

10 Memorandum by George Orwell, enclosed with Orwell letter to AK, 1/2/46, MS2345/2. Among the names floated for the new body were "Magna Carta League," "Renaissance—a League for the Defence and Development of Democracy," and "League for the Dignity and Rights of Man."

11 AK to Orwell, 1/9/46, MS2345/2; Mamaine's diary, 1/10/46; Mamaine to Wilson, 1/27/46, Beinecke YCAL MSS 187 Box 38, folder 1028–1035; Orwell to AK, 1/10/46, 2/11/46, and 2/27/46, MS2345/2; see also *Stranger,* 41–42.

12 AK to Orwell, 1/9/46, 3/19/46, MS2345/2.

13 AK to Rodney Phillips, 3/14/46; Humphrey Slater to AK, 3/19/46; both in MS2345/2.

14 AK to Celia, 3/21/46 (with permission); Bertrand Russell, "The Atomic Bomb and the Prevention of War," typescript. R. Crawshay-Williams to AK, 1/21/46, MS2345/2; "Draft of a Petition," unsigned typescript in MS2345/2; Mamaine's diary, "Sunday" [4/14/45].

15 Gollancz to AK, 6/18/45; AK to Gollancz, 6/20/46; MS2345/1.

16 Mamaine to Russell, 4/16/45; AK to Russell, 4/26/45; Peter Russell to AK, 4/29/46; Russell to AK, 5/3/45; AK to Russell, 5/6/46; Russell to AK, 5/13/46; MS2345/2. Mamaine to Celia, 4/23/46, in *Living,* 30–31; Mamaine's diary, 4/24/45. There was also a mix-up of the mail, as a result of which Koestler's letter to Russell went to Gollancz and his letter to Gollancz went to Russell; Russell claimed that Koestler had misrepresented him in his letter to Gollancz. The nature of the "misrepresentation" was trivial, but it, too, served as a convenient excuse for Russell to back out of the scheme.

17 Ronald Clark, *The Life of Bertrand Russell,* 499; Mamaine to Celia, 3/24/46 and 4/17/46 (unpublished passages with permission); Celia Goodman to author, 5/3/90; author's interviews with Celia Goodman, 5/3/90, and Joan Lee Thompson, 2/23/90.

18 Peter Russell to AK, 4/29/46, MS2374/3.

19 Mamaine's diary, 4/24/46; Peter Russell to AK, 5/14/46, MS2374/3; *Stranger,* 41.

20 Mamaine's diary, 1/23/46; Mamaine to AK, 1/25/46, 1/26/46, and 2/4/46, MS2303/2; *Living,* 27.

21 Mamaine to Edmund Wilson, 12/9/45, EWP, Yale; Mamaine's diary, "Sunday" [6/21/46].

22 Mamaine's diary, 1/10/46 and 6/18/46.

23 Mamaine to Celia, 8/25/46 (with permission).

24 Plesch to AK, 7/2/46, MS2374/3; Braham and Vago, op. cit., 156.

25 Adele to Irene Aldor (in German), 4/15/45 and 6/29/45, MS2302/1; AK to Irene Aldor, 9/5/45; AK to Geoffrey Dalton (Foreign Office), 9/5/45; T. G. Kemeny-Harding to AK, 10/17/45; Adele to Irene Aldor, undated [January 1946]; Adele to AK, 1/31/46; all in MS2302/2. Hilda Striker to AK, 8/6/46, MS2374/4. Adele's letter from "a friend" is undated, MS2302/2.

26 AK to Adele, 9/5/45; Kenneth B. Cohen to AK, 10/29/45; G. Dalton (Foreign Office) to AK, 11/19/45 and 12/3/45; AK to American Joint Distribution Committee, 11/21/45; T. G. Kemeny-Harding to AK, 11/23/45; AK to G. Dalton, 12/8/45; Adele to AK, 2/27/46, MS2302/2.

27 Author's interview with Charlotte Ignotus, 2/20/90; Paul Ignotus, *Political Prisoner,* 34–37; AK to Paul Ignotus, 3/19/46, Ignotus Papers, Petőfi Trodalmi Múzeum, Budapest; Ignotus to AK (in Hungarian), 3/31/46, MS2374/2.

28 Koestler did examine the possibility of Adele staying in a nursing home in North Wales but decided that she would be too lonely and too far from others who spoke German. The Ashtead home was a better solution, because the Berliners could speak to her in her native language. Adele to AK, undated [June 1946]; Dr. G. Mansell Williams to AK, 7/22/46; Ilse Berliner to AK, 3/7/46; AK to Dr. Berliner, 7/2/46; Dr. Berliner to AK, 7/4/46, all in MS2302/2.

29 Mamaine's diary, 7/15/46, 7/19/46, and 7/27/46; Adele to AK 6/14/46, MS2302/2; Adele's diary, 7/13/46, 7/26/46, 7/27/46, and 8/18/46, MS2302/4.

25. THE LOGIC OF THE ICE AGE

1   AK to Wren Howard, 1/17/45, 4/7/45, 6/10/45; Howard to AK, 2/21/45, 3/21/45, 6/27/45; AK to A. D. Peters, 7/18/45, 9/5/45; Peters to AK, 6/11/45, 6/15/45, 8/1/45; Jonathan Cape to Peters, 6/14/45; Peters to Cape, 6/15/45; Howard to Peters, 10/19/45, all in MS2354/2.

2   Author's interview with Émile Delavenay, 2/4/90.

3   For the recovery of part of *Darkness at Noon,* see AK to Paul Christophersen, 2/5/73, MS 2388/4. There is a voluminous correspondence on the translations of *Arrival and Departure* in MS2373/4 and MS2374/1.

4   Abbott to AK, 3/5/46, MS2374/3; AK to Abbott, 3/11/46, MS2374/1.

5   Abbott to AK, 10/11/45, 10/19/45, 11/27/45, MS2373/4; 1/8/46, 3/5/46, 3/6/46, 3/14/46, and 3/19/46, MS2374/2; AK to Abbott, 11/5/45, 12/18/45, 3/11/46, and 3/25/46, MS2374/1; Abbott to A. D. Peters, 4/?/46, MS2374/3.

6   Anonymous [AK], "The Palestine Problem: I—Political Deadlock Between Jews and Arabs," *The Times,* 9/25/45, 5; "The Palestine Problem: II—New Factors in the Racial Balance of Power," *The Times,* 9/26/45, 5.

7   Hamilton interview, part 5, 10.

8   AK, "Land of Broken Promise," unpublished typescript dated "1945," MS2343/4(?).

9   AK to George Weidenfeld, 3/23/46, MS2374/1; George Weidenfeld, *Remembering My Good Friends* (London: HarperCollins, 1994), 128–29.

10   Gollancz telegram to AK, 10/2/45; AK to Gollancz, 10/3/45, MS2345/1; AK memo to Weizmann (page 2 only), Weizmann Archive, Rehovoth, Israel. Koestler seems to have exaggerated the degree of coolness between himself and Weizmann, since four months later he sent Weizmann another memo outlining the case for a Jewish state and the desirability of partition. Weizmann thanked him profusely and expressed the hope that they would soon meet, signing off "Affectionately yours." Weizmann to AK, 2/8/46 and 2/14/46, MS2374/2; AK to Weizmann, 2/11/46, Weizmann Archive.

11   See also Gollancz to AK, 8/15/45, MS2373/4, and AK to Gollancz, 8/27/45, MS2374/1.

12   J. C. Robertson to Trafford Smith, Colonial Office, 3/1/46; MI5, "Memorandum Re Arthur Koestler," TNA, CO537/1709. I am grateful to Julius Purcell for drawing my attention to these documents; Julius Purcell to author, 1/6/00.

13   Documents in TNA, CO537/1709.

14   Howard, *Crossman,* 114, 116, and 125, note; Jones, op. cit., 146; Mamaine's diary, 6/1/46; AK to Jonathan Kimche, 6/5/46, MS2374/1. See Thurston Clarke, op. cit., for the most comprehensive account of the King David explosion. Also Menachem Begin, chap. 15.

15   Mamaine's diary, 8/15/46; *Living,* 34–35; Richard Crossman, *Palestine Mission,* 202.

16   Mamaine's diary, 9/26/46 (also cited in *Living,* 39); Kollek, *For Jerusalem,* 63; author's interview with Kollek, 5/7/93; Kollek to AK, 7/23/46, MS2374/3.

17   AK, "The Future of Fiction," *New Writing and Daylight,* September 1946. Reprinted as "The Future of the Novel" in AK, *Trail of the Dinosaur,* 95–101. See also John Lehmann to AK, 1/9/46, MS2374/2, and AK to Lehmann, 2/20/46, MS2374/1.

18   Connolly to AK, 8/6/46; Guy de Rothschild to AK, 9/13/46; Randolph Churchill to AK, 9/26/46; Harold Macmillan to AK, 10/28/46; Manès Sperber to AK, 1/24/47;

Kollek to AK, 9/6/46; Eric Mills to AK, 9/27/46, MS2356/1. Orwell to Mamaine, 1/24/47 (with permission).

19 Peters to AK, 2/21/46, MS2374/2.

20 AK, *Thieves in the Night.* R. H. S. Crossman, "The Anatomy of Terrorism," *New Statesman and Nation,* 11/2/46; Edmund Wilson, "Arthur Koestler in Palestine," *New Yorker,* 11/15/46; Anonymous, "Without a Shadow," *Times Literary Supplement,* 10/26/46; Kate O'Brien, "Fiction," *Spectator,* 11/29/46; Richard Watts, "Koestler's Novel of Zionism," *New York Times Book Review,* 11/3/46; G.M.D.P, *Manchester Guardian,* 10/25/46; Marvin Lowenthal, *Weekly Book Review,* 11/3/46; Raymond Mortimer, op. cit.

21 O'Brien, op. cit.; Isaac Rosenfeld, "Palestinian Ice Age," *New Republic,* 11/4/46; Watts, op. cit.

22 *Thieves,* 57; Lovat Dickson to AK, 9/20/46; AK to Dickson, 9/23/46, MS2356/1.

23 *Thieves,* 283.

24 Crossman, op. cit.

25 Wilson, op. cit.; Rosenfeld, op. cit.; Diana Trilling, "Fiction in Review," *Nation,* 11/9/46; DH to AK, 1/4/47; AK to DH, 1/27/47; MS2301/3.

26 See George Orwell, "Catastrophic Gradualism," in *Collected Essays,* vol. 4, op. cit., 17.

26. ADVENTURES AMONG THE EXISTENTIALISTS

1. For Koestler's sales figures, see Randolph Churchill, "Europe Today," Column No. 169, May 23, 1946, distributed by United Press of America. *Darkness at Noon's* popularity was vital to Calmann-Lévy's commercial success, for it was one of two postwar best sellers (the other was *The Little World of Don Camillo*) that restored the financial fortunes of his publishing house after the devastating effects of the war.

2 The first report alluded to a delegation led by Gaston Cogniot, editor of the Communist daily *L'Humanité,* requesting Calmann-Lévy to cease publication, to which Robert Calmann allegedly replied that he had received exactly the same advice four years earlier from "a German sitting exactly where you are now." In a later report, Cogniot metamorphosed into Jacques Duclos, second in command of the French Communist Party, and the message was that the party would tolerate a first edition but would regard a reprint as "an unfriendly act," to which Calmann had replied that the one thing the war had been fought for was the freedom to publish and that he had no intention of stopping. See *Carrefour,* 4/11/46, cited in *Le Libertaire* 30, 5/24/46, and Gérard Blum, "Arthur Koestler et le communisme" in Debray-Ritzen, ed., *Arthur Koestler,* 213. Randolph Churchill (see note 1 above) also referred to a Communist delegation, without saying whom it was led by. When Koestler inquired directly of Calmann about the rumors mentioned by Churchill (AK to Calmann, 6/8/46), the publisher denied them (Calmann to AK, 6/?/46). See also Martine Poulain, "Un best-seller dans la guerre froid: la réception du 'Zéro et l'infini' en France, 1945–1950" (A Bestseller in the Cold War: The Reception of "Darkness at Noon" in France, 1945–1950), 8–9, notes 30 and 31. The report about members of the French buying up copies of the book originated with Mamaine's twin sister, Celia, who was living in Paris at the time; see *Living with Koestler,* 35–36. Manès Sperber, who was working for the French Ministry of Information, told Koestler

that the Communist campaign against *Darkness at Noon* was definitely being coordinated by the Soviet Foreign Ministry. These charges were impossible to prove but struck Koestler as plausible. Silone wrote to inform him of similar pressures on Mondadori in Italy, and it seemed that Gyldendal in Norway had come under Communist pressure too; see Rothschild to AK, 4/28/46, and Sperber to AK, 3/15/46, MS2374/3; Silone to AK, date uncertain.

3 Manès Sperber, op. cit. John Strachey later endorsed Sperber's point. "I knew one man of first-rate powers, but without previous acquaintance with Communist doctrine, who as late as the nineteen-forties was definitely influenced in a *pro-Communist* direction by reading *Darkness at Noon*"; see Strachey, *Strangled Cry,* 18.

4 Louis Parrot, "Le sacrifice et la révolte" (Sacrifice and Revolt), *Les Lettres Françaises,* 1/28/46; Claude Morgan, "Nettoyer devant sa porte" (Cleaning the Front Steps), *Les Lettres Françaises,* 2/1/46; Guy de Rothschild to AK, 4/28/46, op. cit. See L'Herne anthology, 217–29, for a round-up of French critical responses to *Darkness at Noon;* also David Caute, *Communism and the French Intellectuals, 1914–1960,* 132–34. It was also rumored that thanks to Communist pressure, the translator, Émile Delavenay (pen name Jérôme Jenatton), had been persuaded to withdraw his name from the French edition but his name was removed without his knowledge; author's interview with Émile Delavenay, 2/4/90, and Delavenay to author, 5/28/00. For Mauriac's comment see Rothschild to AK, 7/19/46, MS2374/3.

5 *Carrefour* 88, September 1946.

6 It was Raymond Aron who had suggested to Winkler that *Carrefour* might like to publish Koestler's *New York Times* article (though Koestler didn't tell Manès Sperber this, since Aron was Sperber's friend and colleague); see AK to Calmann-Lévy, 2/25/46, MS2374/1.

7 It was not until November 1946 that the 1939 order to arrest and deport Koestler was officially revoked by a Decree of the Ministry of the Interior, Paris, dated 11/7/46, and not until early 1948 that he was informed of the decision; see M. Dupuis, Prefect of Police, to the Minister of the Interior, Paris, 1/16/47 and 2/12/48, Paris Police Archives, Fund GA K4. On Koestler's play, see Anonymous, "Une bouffonnerie pitoyable et deux grandes fresques" (A Pitiful Burlesque and Two Big Frescoes), *Les Lettres Françaises,* 11/8/46; Jean Maury, "Jean Vilar répète 'Le Bar du crepuscule'" (Jean Vilar Rehearses "Twilight Bar"), 9/14/46. Clippings in MS2358/1, source of Maury article not indicated.

8 André Gide, *Journals, Volume IV: 1939–1949,* translated by Justin O'Brien (New York: Knopf, 1951), 267–68; AK, Paris diary, 10/11/46, MS2306/4; Connolly interview, 20.

9 AK to Mamaine, "Wednesday" [10/9/46] (with permission). A shorter version of the letter can be found in *Stranger,* 66–67. Maurice Nadeau, "Arthur Koestler, qui vient d'arriver à Paris nous parle de 'La Tour d'Ezra'" (Arthur Koestler, Who Has Just Arrived in Paris, Speaks to Us About "Thieves in the Night"), *Combat,* 10/3/46.

10 AK to Mamaine, 10/9/46.

11 Koestler first told Németh that he had only half an hour to spare from attending rehearsals of *Twilight Bar.* They had a lunch the following week that Koestler tersely described in his diary as "rather sordid," and the third meeting at the hotel was their last time together; see AK, Paris diary, and Németh to AK (in Hungarian), 2/17/46, MS2374/2.

12 *Living,* 41; AK, Paris diary, 11/2/46; author's interview with Jenka Sperber, 1/2/92.

13 DK to AK, 3/21/45, 6/24/45, 9/13/45, 1/26/46, 4/2/46, 4/6/46, 7/6/46, and 11/5/46 (two letters), MS2301/1 and MS2374/2–4; AK to DK, 5/15/45, MS2374/1; Guy de Rothschild to AK, 12/18/45, MS2373/4, and 1/25/46, MS2374/2; AK to Elisabeth Ascher, 4/5/46, MS2373/3–4, and Paul Willert, 4/9/46, MS2344/7. AK, Paris diary, 10/24/46 and 10/26/46.

14 AK, Paris diary, 10/26/46.

15 *Stranger,* 68.

16 Simone de Beauvoir, *Force of Circumstance,* 108, and *A Transatlantic Love Affair,* 223; *Stranger,* 67.

17 AK, Paris diary, 5/18/46 and 5/20/46; Mamaine's diary, 5/20/46; *Living,* 40; Beauvoir, *Force,* 108–9.

18 Mamaine's diary, 10/31/46; AK, Paris diary, 10/31/46; Mamaine to Celia, 11/1/46 (with permission; a shorter version is in *Living,* 43–44); Beauvoir, *Force,* 109–10.

19 See Deirdre Bair, *Simone de Beauvoir,* 316.

20 Beauvoir, *Force,* 108–9; Bair, op. cit.

21 Simone de Beauvoir, *The Mandarins,* 90–102. Beauvoir later claimed that she and Koestler had been drunk at the time and that their lovemaking "wasn't any good," which was probably true, since Beauvoir didn't experience her first full orgasm until later that year, when she started an affair with Nelson Algren; see Baird, 316 and 333.

22 *Living,* 41–42; Mamaine to Edmund Wilson, 11/1/47, EWP, Yale; AK, Paris diary, 10/25/46.

23 Sperber to AK, 3/15/46, MS2374/2; AK, Paris diary, 10/27/46 and 10/29/46. Albert Camus, *Carnets, janvier 1942–mars 1951* (Notebooks, January 1942–March 1951) (Paris: Gallimard, 1964), 185–186. This meeting has been described in several biographies of Camus, Sartre, and Malraux, and there has been speculation as to whether the meeting was called by Malraux in order to enlist progressive writers in the cause of de Gaulle or whether leftist writers hoped to remind Malraux of his revolutionary past. There seems little doubt that the prime mover was Koestler and that his project for a new human rights organization motivated the meeting. See, e.g., Olivier Todd, *Albert Camus, une vie* (Paris: Gallimard, 1996), 421. Sartre, in speaking of the Circassians, seems to have had in mind all the Caucasian peoples who were deported by Stalin after the war (on the grounds that they had collaborated with their German occupiers), not just the one nation. See also Mamaine to Wilson, 11/1/47, op. cit.

24 *Living,* 60–61.

27. FRENCH LESSONS

1. AK, "Koestler Finds a Trojan Horse in France," *New York Times Sunday Magazine,* 1/5/47, 11 and 41–42; Jean Duché, "Arthur Koestler s'explique" (Arthur Koestler Explains), *Le Littéraire,* 10/26/46, and "Pourquoi l'écrivain de 'Le Zéro et l'infini' juge l'U.R.S.S." (Why the Author of "Darkness at Noon" Condemns the USSR), *Le Littéraire,* 11/20/46. See also Sperber to AK, 2/25/47, MS2375/1; AK to Sperber, 3/7/47, and to Balder Olden, 2/20/47, MS2376/1; *L'Humanité,* 1/31/47; *Le Journal du Centre,* 3/19/47; Claude Morgan, "Nous en Avons Assez!" (We Have Had Enough!), *Les Lettres Françaises,* 2/2/47; Pierre Courtade, "Koestler ou la Venus du Carrefour" (Koestler or *Carrefour*'s Venus), *L'Action,* 1/31/47.

2 Bertrand d'Astorg, "Arthur Koestler, Prix Nobel 1960," *Esprit* 10, October 1946; Anonymous, "Koestler et le Socialisme" (Koestler and Socialism), *Combat,* 11/22/46; Thierry Maulnier in *Concorde,* 1/30/47, cited in Debray-Ritzen, 227–28.

3 Maurice Merleau-Ponty, "Le Yogi et le prolétaire" (The Yogi and the Proletarian), *Les Temps Modernes* 3, December 1946, reprinted in Maurice Merleau-Ponty, *Humanisme et terreur,* 161–91.

4 Merleau-Ponty, 165. See also Raymond Aron, *Memoirs: Fifty Years of Political Reflection,* 215–17; Beauvoir, *Transatlantic,* 224; Aron, *Mémoires,* 312–13 (not in the English translation); Ronald Aronson, *Camus and Sartre* (Chicago: Chicago University Press, 2004), 85–93.

5 Beauvoir, *Force,* 111; see also Patrick McCarthy, *Camus,* 218–19.

6 Hilary Spurling, *The Girl from the Fiction Department, a Portrait of Sonia Orwell* (New York: Counterpoint, 2002), 73–77 and 82; Beauvoir, *Force,* 111; Beauvoir, "Conversations with Jean-Paul Sartre," *Adieux,* 267, cited by Aronson, 259; see also Aronson, 19.

7 Mamaine's diary, 11/3/46; Mamaine to Celia, 11/1/46 (in *Living,* 43–44) and 11/17/46 (with permission).

8 Mamaine to Celia, 10/23/46 and 10/26/46 (with permission).

9 Mamaine's diary, 11/7/46; Mamaine to Celia 11/17/46 and 11/29/46 (with permission). Mamaine's conversations with Camus were in French, and most of what he said to her was left in the original French in both the diary and the letters.

10 Olivier Todd, op. cit., 425–27; Mamaine to Celia, 1/20/47 (with permission); Celia Goodman to author, 7/30/00; Camus to Mamaine, 12/29/46 (with permission).

11 Camus to AK, 12/12/46, and AK to Camus, 12/16/46, Centre de Documentation Albert Camus, Bibliothèque Méjanes, Aix-en-Provence.

12 John Lehmann to AK, 12/11/46 AK to Lehmann, 12/9/46 and ?(date unknown); Malraux to Mamaine, 3/18/47 (with permission).

13 *Living,* 47–50.

14 Ibid., 46–50; AK to James Putnam, 5/31/47, 7/26/47, and 11/8/47, MS2413/4.

15 V. S. Pritchett, op. cit., 55.

16 Mortimer, op. cit., 133.

17 Bertrand d'Astorg and Jacques Brenner, "Deux livres d'Arthur Koestler" (Two Books by Arthur Koestler), unidentified newspaper clipping in Calmann-Lévy archive.

18 See George Mounin, "Le talent ne donne pas raison" (Talent Is No Justification), *Les Lettres Françaises,* 12/27/46; Jean Gacon, "Une arme dangereuse de l'anticommunisme" (A Dangerous Weapon of Anti-Communism), *Cahiers de Communisme* 2, February 1947; Roger Garaudy, "Une littérature de fossoyeurs" (A Literature of Gravediggers), *Éditions Sociales,* 1947, 60. For Laurent Casanova, see Martine Poulain, op. cit.

19 Beauvoir, *Transatlantic,* 71–72 and 75. By the time she came to describe this outing in volume one of her memoir, *Force of Circumstance,* Beauvoir was much more hostile to Koestler and accused him of drawing attention to the small size of Cezanne's and Van Gogh's heads, "like Sartre and me."

20 *Living,* 58.

21 Ibid., 59–60, and AK diary, 10/8/47; Beauvoir, *Transatlantic,* 79; for Kaplan's character see James Atlas, *Bellow, a Biography* (New York: Random House, 2000), 139–40.

22 *Stranger,* 68–70; *Living,* 58–61; Beauvoir, *Force,* 130–31; Ronald Hayman, *Sartre,*

250–51; Todd, 443. Some ten years later Sartre provided a fascinating sketch of Koestler's complex psychology and introverted nature in his preface to *The Traitor* by the French philospher André Gorz, though Koestler is not named in the text; see André Gorz, *The Traitor*, translated by Richard Howard (New York: Simon and Schuster, 1959).

23 Beauvoir, *Transatlantic,* 82–83.

24 AK, "The Heroic Times," unpublished typescript provided by Celia Goodman. Celia Kirwan (later Goodman) to AK, 12/16/47 and 12/17/47, MS2301/2; AK to Winkler, 12/23/47, MS2376/1; Todd, 427–28.

25 Guy Leclerc in *L'Humanité,* 4/7/48.

26 Mamaine's diary, 1/11/48.

27 Ibid.; Beauvoir, *Force,* 140, and *Transatlantic,* 149. Camus's black eye led to a mythical version of this incident that was propagated by Sartre's unofficial secretary, Jean Cau. According to Cau, Camus and Koestler had challenged each other to a race on all fours across the Place Saint-Michel. Koestler won, but Camus accused Koestler of cheating and Koestler gave him a black eye. This version was reproduced by Ronald Hayman in his biography of Sartre but is not true. See Jean Cau, *Croquis de mémoire* (Sketch for a Memoir) (Paris: Julliard, 1985), 133; Hayman, 249.

28 Mamaine's diary, op. cit.; Suzanne Valiches [?] to AK, 1/14/48, MS2375/2; Beauvoir, *Force,* 370, and *Transatlantic,* 153–54; *Stranger,* 70–71.

29 DK interviews, 12/13/88 and 6/1/89; Ruth and Stanley Cohen to author, 3/10/91; E. Schah, Société Française de Propagation du Travail Industriel et Agricole parmi les Juifs, to the Prefect of Police, Paris, 7/23/48, and Certificate of Employment, French Delegation to the International Refugee Organization, 10/27/48, French Police Archives, Fund GA K4.

30 DK's postcards to AK, December 1946–January 1947, MS2375/1; DK's curriculum vitae, 1950's; Odette Valabregue to AK, 3/2/48, MS2303/2.

31 AK, handwritten manuscript fragment, 497–500 (perhaps intended for *Stranger on the Square?*), MS2343/3. Gide noted in his diary that the French translator had gotten even the title of *Scum of the Earth* wrong. *La Lie de la terre* meant "the dregs of the earth," a designation that struck Gide as "inadmissible" (and in effect seemed to side with the French bureaucrats' contempt for the refugee "scum"). See *The Journals of André Gide,* 268 and note.

32 Bernard Berenson, *The Passionate Sightseer, from the Diaries, 1947–1956* (New York: Thames and Hudson, 1988), 62.

33 Mamaine's Italian diary, 6–7, MS2302/2.

34 AK French and Italian diary, MS2305; Jean Lacouture, *Malraux, une vie dans la siècle* (Paris: Le Seuil, 1976), 375.

35 *Living,* 73–74; AK to Sartre, 1/18/48, MS2345/2; Beauvoir, *Force,* 141, and *Transatlantic,* 184–85; Stephen Spender, *The Thirties and After,* 169–70.

36 Condensed and reprinted as "Land of Bread and Wine" in *Dinosaur,* 40–43.

28. DISCOVERING AMERICA

1. Rodney Phillips to AK, 10/9/46, MS2375/4; AK, "London Letter," *Partisan Review,* March–April 1947, 138–45, May–June 1947, 341–345, and January 1948, 32–39.

2 Francis Henson, IRRC, to AK, 4/18/46, MS2374/3; AK to Henson, 4/23/46, and to A. D. Peters, 12/9/46, MS2351/2; Peters to Sheba Strunsky, IRRC, 1/13/47; AK to Pe-

ters, 12/7/47; Peters to AK, 12/13/47; Strunsky to Peters, 12/23/47; IRRC, Announcement, all in MS2314/3.

3 AK's FBI file, obtained by Murray Sperber under the Freedom of Information Act,
see Sperber to AK, 5/30/80, MS2308/2. Peters to AK, 1/1/48, MS2351/4; Anonymous,
"Arthur Koestler," cited in U.S. Government Memo from L. V. Boardman to A. H.
Belmont, 3/10/54, in Koestler's FBI File, MS2308; AK to Leo Valiani, 4/9/50,
MS2376/3; IRRC, "Notes on Arthur Koestler" (draft); A. D. Peters telegram to
IRRC, undated, MS2314/3; AK, French and Italian diary, 14.

4 AK, American diary, 3/17/48, MS2306/4.

5 Ibid., 3/18–25/48; Peters to AK, 12/21/46, MS2351/2; *Celebrity Bulletin,* New York,
3/19/48, MS2413/4; Arnold Beichman, "Arthur Koestler," unpublished memoir
(with permission).

6 AK, American diary, op. cit.; William Phillips, *A Partisan View,* 134; author's interview with Phillips, 6/17/92; Carol Gelderman, *Mary McCarthy* (London: Sidgwick
and Jackson, 1989), 140–43.

7 AK, American diary, 3/20/48; Phillips, op. cit.; Sidney Hook, *Out of Step,* 443.

8 AK, American diary, 3/23/48, 3/25/48, and 3/28/48.

9 Harvey Breit, "A Visit with Arthur Koestler," *New York Times Book Review,* 4/4/48.

10 Phillips, op. cit., 135; author's interview with Phillips; James Putnam to AK, 2/25/52,
MS2356/3; David Martin to author, 2/2/94; I have quoted from the final, revised text
of the lecture, published as "The Babbitts of the Left" in *Life* 24, 5/3/48, 123–29, and
reprinted as "The Seven Deadly Fallacies" in *Dinosaur,* 47–52. The lecture delivered
at Carnegie Hall was considerably less polished than the published text but along the
same lines; interview with Phillips.

11 Roger Baldwin to Sheba Strunsky, 3/26/48, copy in MS2413/3; AK, American diary,
3/20/48; Frances Stonor Saunders, *The Cultural Cold War,* 39.

12 AK, American diary, 3/24/48.

13 Ibid., 3/30/48–4/1/48.

14 Eva Zeisel to AK, 3/29/48, MS2413/3; AK to Eva Zeisel, 3/31/48 (with permission).

15 AK to Mamaine, 4/1/48, MS2302/2.

16 See William L. O'Neill, *A Better World,* 218–20; Stonor Saunders, 71; AK, American
diary, 4/3/48.

17 *Alert,* cited in Alexander Stephan, *Communazis* (New Haven: Yale University Press,
2000), 187; Eva Yates to AK, 4/10/48, MS2413/3; "Highlights" column by Robert L.
Balzer, MS2413/3 and 4; Marion Kreith to author, 4/3/95.

18 AK, American diary, 3/16/48, 4/5/48, and 4/8/48.

19 Ralph Cohn to AK, 4/22/48, MS2413/3; John T. Elliott to AK, 4/17/44, MS2351/1;
Paul Streger to AK, 10/23/45, MS2351/1; AK, American diary, 4/8/48; Everett Freeman to AK, date unknown; A. D. Peters to AK, 12/8/46, MS2351/1; Roy Myers to
Peters, 1/22/47, MS2351/1; Frances Spitz and Irving Reis to AK, undated [January?]
1947, MS3351/1; AK to Peters, 1/31/47, MS2351/1.

20 AK, American diary, 4/7–8/48; AK to the Society for Psychical Research, 2/10/53,
MS2379/1; Langston Hughes to AK, 4/20/48, MS2413/3.

21 AK, American diary, 4/17/48.

22 AK, American diary, 4/24/48.

23 Ibid., 4/26/48 and 4/29/48; author's interview with Marietta Torberg, 9/7/93.

24 Ibid., 5/3/48–5/5/48.
25 Ibid., 5/8/48.

29. FAREWELL TO ZIONISM

1 AK, "Letter to a British Soldier in Palestine," *New Statesman and Nation,* 8/16/47, 126–27.

2 AK to Gollancz, 8/28/47, MS2376/1.

3 The chairman, a Swedish judge, told Teddy Kollek about the influence of Koestler's novel, and Kollek passed this on to Koestler; see AK to Olivier Clément, 7/27/74, MS2389/1. Another curious instance of the influence of *Thieves in the Night* was when a British judge, having condemned the Irgun terrorist Dov Gruner to death, was kidnapped by other members of the Irgun, kept hostage, and given a copy of the novel to read while in captivity. David Leitch, "Explosion at the King David Hotel," in M. Sissons and P. French, eds., *Age of Austerity,* 70.

4 AK to Johann Voigt, 8/12/47, MS2376/1.

5 AK, Palestine diary 1948, 4, MS2306/3. Where no other source is cited, all descriptions of AK's activities in Israel are taken from this diary.

6 AK, *Promise and Fulfilment,* 196–99.

7 Louis Heren, *Growing Up on the* Times (London: Hamish Hamilton, 1978), 63; AK, "Letter to the Editor," *Palestine Post,* 6/15/48, copy in MS2331/3(?); AK, Palestine diary, 51.

8 Author's interview with Gavriel Zifroni, 4/28/93.

9 Shertok changed his name to Sharett after independence.

10 AK, Palestine diary, 24–25.

11 In the summer of 1947 the Irgun captured two British sergeants to hold as hostages in the hope of exchanging them for three of their members sentenced to death by a British military court. When the Irgun men were hanged, the Irgun hanged the two sergeants in reprisal. Deir Yassin was an Arab village near Jerusalem stormed by forces of the Irgun and Lehi shortly before Koestler arrived in Israel. The attackers killed more than 250 of the inhabitants, including many women and children. In *Promise and Fulfilment,* Koestler described "the bloodbath of Deir Yassin" as "the worst atrocity committed by the terrorists in their whole career." See *Promise,* 160, and Heren, op. cit., 75–76.

12 AK, Palestine diary, 55.

13 AK, Palestine diary, 55–56. Jona Janai, "A Letter from One of the 'Thieves in the Night,'" and Zvi Frish, "Thieves in the Night—Again a Failure," both in the Hebrew journal *Youth and Nation,* December 1946. See also Joseph Nedava, ed., *Arthur Koestler: Be-Kvalei HaMa'arav. HaDerech El HaTzionut U-Mimenah* (Arthur Koestler: Bound to the West. The Road to Zionism and Away from It) (Tel Aviv, 1985), 46–59.

14 Ibid., 61–62 and 76.

15 Altalena was the pseudonym Jabotinsky used for many of his writings. The "Altalena Affair," as it came to be known, was one of the most painful and controversial episodes in Israel's struggle for independence.

16 AK dispatch, 6/23/48, typescript in MS2339/5.

17 AK to *Palestine Post,* 6/29/48, copy in MS2331/3; AK, Palestine diary, 98.

18 AK dispatch, 7/5/48, MS2339/5; A. P. Wadsworth to AK, 7/7/48, MS2375/2; AK to

Kollek, 3/25/46, MS2374/1; author's interview with Shlomo Avineri, 5/3/93; AK to Dr. Menzel, 9/21/48, MS2376/1; veterinary inspection certificate, 10/15/48, and pedigree certificate, MS2311/2.

19 See Heren, 64–65; AK, Palestine diary, 104.

20 AK, Palestine diary, 148–51 and 161; *Promise,* 278–79.

21 Interview with Gavriel Zifroni, 4/28/93.

22 AK, Palestine diary, 138–39.

23 Kollek to AK, 3/9/49, MS2375/4.

24 AK, Palestine diary, 136.

25 Ibid., 164–65; AK, "Seen in Daylight," list of characters and handwritten manuscript, MS2343/4.

26 Mamaine to Celia, 7/25/48 (with permission).

27 *Living,* 93–94.

28 Paul Winkler to AK, 10/11/48, MS2376/1; Mamaine to Celia (unpublished portion with permission), 11/8/48; *Living,* 94–95; author's interviews with Betty Winkler, 4/22/93, and Françoise Gilot, 4/13/93; AK diary, 7/30/49. The larger lodge was occupied by Hubert Ripka, a journalist and former minister of foreign trade in the Czech government, who was writing his memoirs for Winkler.

29 For the Kant quotation in its entirety, see *Promise,* viii. See also AK to A. D. Peters, 7/2/48, MS2351/4; AK to James Putnam, 1/19/49 and 1/30/49, MS2356/2.

30 Putnam to AK, 11/3/48 and 2/18/49; AK to Putnam, 11/11/48 and 1/19/49, MS2356/2; *Stranger,* 49; *Living,* 96 and 103–5; Putnam to AK, 11/3/48, 2/18/49, and 3/4/49; AK to Putnam, 11/11/48, 1/19/49, 2/16/49, and 4/16/49; AK to Peters, 4/16/49, MS2356/2.

31 *Promise,* 252–53.

32 Ibid., 332–33.

33 Leonard Woolf, "The Promised Land," *New Statesman and Nation,* 10/29/49; Anonymous, "The Jews in Palestine," *Times Literary Supplement,* 10/28/49; Quentin Reynolds, "The Palestine Story: Past and Future," *New York Times Book Review,* 10/23/49; Marvin Lowenthal, "Mr. Koestler's Promenade in Palestine," *New York Herald Tribune Book Review,* 12/25/49; Leslie A. Fiedler, "Koestler and Israel," *Partisan Review,* vol. 17, no. 1, January 1950.

34 Maurice Carr, "Arthur Koestler's Renunciations," *Jewish Chronicle,* 5/5/50, copy in MS2402/2.

35 Ibid.

30. A MARRIED MAN

1 *Stranger,* 58.

2 Mamaine to Celia, 12/5/48 (unpublished portion with permission).

3 Mamaine and Koestler attributed the shock to an allergic reaction to novocaine on Mamaine's part, but Celia, who had responded similarly to the same drug, later learned that it was the intravenous injection of the drug that caused the shock, not the drug itself. Celia Goodman to author, 7/30/01.

4 *Living,* 106–9; Mamaine to Edmund Wilson, 6/14/49, EWP, Yale; Mamaine to AK, 6/1/49, 6/3/49, 6/4/49, 6/6/49, 6/12/49, and 6/14/49, MS2303/3; AK to Mamaine, 6/12/49 and "Monday" [undated], MS2303/3; AK to F. C. Deller, 7/27/49, MS2376/3.

5 DK to AK, undated [1949], MS2301/1.

6 AK to James Putnam, 3/17/47, MS2356/2.

7 Michael Polanyi to AK, 5/15/41 and undated [1943], MS2344/7; AK to Polanyi, 7/17/43, University of Chicago Library, Michael Polanyi Papers, Box 4, Folder 10; Polanyi to AK, 8/14/43, 8/4/49, and 7/29/70, MS2344/7. Many years later, when Polanyi was suffering from dementia, Polanyi's wife, Magda, accused Koestler of plagiarizing her husband's work and "stealing" his ideas. This does not appear to have been Polanyi's opinion, however. See Magda Polanyi to AK, 8/31/75, 9/1/75, and 8/25/80, MS2344/7.

8 For the genesis of *Insight and Outlook,* see "Interview with Arthur Koestler" in Stanley Rosner and Lawrence E. Abt, *The Creative Experience* (New York: Grossman, 1970), 145; Cynthia Koestler diary, 5/16/63, MS2305; *Arrival,* 176.

9 Miriam Rothschild to author, 7/26/00 and 10/16/00. The extent of Strauss's role in the composition and editing of *Insight and Outlook* is unclear. In the book he is thanked for reading the manuscript and "making many valuable corrections and suggestions," but in a letter to James Putnam at Macmillan, Koestler referred to Strauss as having "edited" his book "without remuneration" and asked Putnam to send Strauss a wire recorder (unobtainable in Britain) as a form of compensation; AK to Putnam, 5/15/48, MS2376/1.

10 Michael Polanyi, *Science, Faith and Society,* see especially 11, 14, 28, 38, and 44–45. For Polanyi's differences with Koestler see Polanyi to AK, 6/24/49, MS2344/7.

11 Koestler hasn't received the credit due to him for his invention of the term *bisociation.* In *The Oxford Companion to the English Language* it is attributed to Tom MacArthur in 1990 (Roy Behrens to author, 7/14/94), and in Merriam-*Webster's* (Third Edition) it is defined but with no attribution given.

12 For Koestler's hopes, see AK to Anny Bauer, 5/10/46, MS2374/1.

13 Paul Kecskemeti, "Koestler as System-Maker," *Partisan Review,* May 1949, 536–39; Herbert Read, "A Cosmic Hedonist," *The Observer,* 6/9/49; A. J. Ayer, "Mr. Koestler's New System," *New Statesman and Nation,* 7/30/49; James R. Newman, "Arthur Koestler's *Insight and Outlook:* The Novelist Formulates a Philosophy Complete with Circuit Diagrams," *Scientific American,* March 1949, 56–59, cited in Murray K. Sperber, 123–32. For kinder views, see Michael Polanyi, "Mr. Koestler," *Manchester Guardian,* 6/28/49, and Michael Oakeshott, "Creative Activity, a Formula," *Spectator,* 7/1/49. Also Anonymous, "Mind and Brain," *Lancet,* 8/20/49: "The value today of a bold attempt to bring together thought and feeling can hardly be overestimated."

14 AK to Eric Strauss, 2/7/50 and 2/21/50, MS2376/3; Strauss to AK, 2/16/50, MS2375/3; AK to James Putnam, undated memo [spring 1949?], MS2356/2.

15 Memo to Putnam. The title was thought up by Enid Starkie to head her compilation of Gide's writings on his disillusionment with communism, and Crossman borrowed it for the entire book; Crossman to AK, 6/17/49, MS2375/4.

16 Richard Crossman, ed., *The God That Failed,* Introduction, 1–2 and 8 note; Crossman to AK, 1/27/48, 1/29/48, 2/19/48, and 9/2/48, MS2375/2, and 6/17/49, MS23754; AK to Crossman, 2/11/48, 11/18/48, and 11/29/48, MS2376/1; AK to Malraux, 11/11/48, and Malraux to AK, 12/16/48, MS2345/1; Hamish Hamilton to AK, 4/11/48, MS2413/3. AK, untitled essay, *God,* 25–82.

17 Rebecca West, "The Roads to Communism and Back," *New York Times Book Review,* 1/8/50. For other views see Arthur M. Schlesinger, Jr., "Dim Views of the Red

Star," *Saturday Review,* 1/7/50; Reinhold Niebuhr, "To Moscow—and Back," *Nation,* 1/28/50; Robert Hatch, "Studies in the Permanent Crisis," *New Republic,* 3/19/50; Anonymous (Peter Calvocoresi), "Two-Way Rebellion," *Times Literary Supplement,* 2/3/50.

18   *Stranger,* 75.

19   Phillips, 135–36; interview with Phillips, 10/10/92.

20   Danielle Hunebelle, "Portrait," in Debray-Ritzen, 12–14.

21   Interview with Pamela Merewether, 3/8/90; Cynthia's diary, 3/9/70, MS2305; "Auntie B" to Cynthia, 11/4/76, MS2390/2.

22   Interview with Betty Winkler, 1/2/92; *Stranger,* 51–61 and 65.

23   Camus to Mamaine, 6/16/49, Camus Estate, Paris; AK to Darina Silone, 7/16/49, MS2376/3.

24   Mamaine to Celia, 5/12/49 (unpublished portion with permission), and *Living,* 109.

25   *Living,* 109–13; Mamaine to Celia, 8/20/49 (unpublished portion with permission).

26   Celia Goodman, "Notes on the MS of Iain Hamilton's *Koestler, a Biography,*" in Celia Goodman to AK, 3/3/78, MS2301/2.

27   Adele's letters are in MS2302/1. Koestler once remarked to Celia how much Sartre adored his mother and how he envied Sartre for that. Author's interview with Celia Goodman, 3/5/90.

28   Adele to AK, 2/19/50; AK to Adele, 2/21/50, MS2305.

29   *Living,* 118.

30   Mamaine's diary, 12/18/49, 12/24/49, and 12/25/49, MS2303/3; AK, "Mini-Memoirs," handwritten MS, 1–7, in MS2332/5; AK, *The Age of Longing,* 256–57.

31   AK to Putnam, 12/26/49, MS2356/2; AK diary, 1/26/50, MS2305; Mamaine's diary, 12/27/49 and 3/1/50, MS2303/3; *L'Humanité,* 12/28/49.

32   Mamaine's diary, 3/10–13/50, MS2303/3; Mamaine to Celia, 3/14/50 (unpublished portion with permission); AK diary, 3/15/50, 3/27/50, 4/3/50, and 4/11/50, MS2305; AK, "A Rebel's Progress," *Observer,* 1/29/50, reprinted in *Dinosaur,* 102–5; AK to Astor, 2/7/50, and to Sonia Orwell, 2/13/50, MS2376/3; Sonia Orwell to AK (undated), MS2376/4.

33   Mamaine's diary, 4/15/50, MS2303/3; AK diary, 4/17/50 ("Saturday got married, had very pleasant lunch at Abbattoires with Winklers"), MS2305; *Living,* 134–35; *Stranger,* 85–86.

34   *Living,* 135.

35   Mamaine's diary, 4/16/50, MS2303/3; AK diary, 4/17/50 and 4/28/50, MS2305. See also *Stranger,* 86.

36   Mamaine to Celia, 4/28/50 (with permission).

31. TO THE BARRICADES

1   When Sartre's play *Les Mains sales* (Dirty Hands) was performed in France in 1948, the Communist critic Guy Leclerc went so far as to call him "Koestler's understudy"; see Caute, op. cit., 249.

2   Greta was the daughter-in-law of the philosopher Martin Buber and sister-in-law of Willi Münzenberg. She had been married to the the German Communist Party leader, Heinz Neumann, and after seeking refuge in the Soviet Union, had been arrested for "left-wing deviationism." Neumann disappeared and was presumed killed. See AK diary, 2/26/49 and 3/2/49, MS2306/1; Antony Beevor and Artemis Cooper,

Paris After the Liberation, 408–13; Tony Judt, *Past Imperfect,* 112–14; and Lottman, *Left Bank,* 266–69; Beauvoir, *Letters to Sartre* (London: Radius, 1991), 445–46.

3 AK to Hamilton, 6/18/46, MS2354/2; AK to Weissberg, 6/11/46, 6/28/46, and 5/18/49; Weissberg to AK, 12/23/47, 5/19/48, 1/25/49, 4/25/49, and 6/2/49. On Weissberg in Paris, author's interview with Jenka Sperber, 1/8/92, and *Living,* 115.

4 Mamaine's diary, 3/17/50; Caute, 183–85; Judt, *Past Imperfect,* 113–14; Lottman, *Left Bank,* 273–74; Hayman, *Sartre,* 273.

5 AK, "Demi-Vierges et anges déchus" (Semi-Virgins and Deceived Angels), *Le Figaro Littéraire,* 7/2/49. Reprinted as "The Little Flirts of St. Germain des Prés" in *Dinosaur,* 60–65 My quotations are from the English version, adjusted in one or two places to bring them closer to the French.

6 AK diary, 4/11/50; *Living,* 128 and 132–33.

7 Hook, *Out of Step,* 382–401; Peter Coleman, *The Liberal Conspiracy,* 7.

8 Burnham to AK, 9/17/49, MS2375/4; AK to Burnham, 9/15/49, MS2376/3; Michael Warner, "Origins of the Congress for Cultural Freedom, 1949–50," *Studies in Intelligence,* vol. 38, no. 5 (Summer 1995), 91–92; Ted Morgan, *A Covert Life,* 196–98.

9 Fischer to AK, 10/4/49, MS2375/4. Lasky had made a name for himself by attending the All-German Writers' Conference in East Berlin and delivering a controversial speech in fluent German on the censorship and persecution of writers in the Soviet Union. This exploit almost got him expelled from the city, but he persuaded the US military authorities to fund a magazine and let him take the cultural fight to the enemy.

10 Warner, 92–94; author's interview with Mel Lasky, 1/6/90; Coleman, 15–19; Saunders, 11–13 and 27–31.

11 Warner, op. cit.; Burnham to AK, 4/10/50, Hoover Institution Archives (HIA), James Burnham Collection, Box 6, Folder 69.

12 Mamaine's diary, 3/17/50; Lasky to AK, 4/19/50, 5/25/50, 6/5/50, 6/8/50, and 6/12/50, and AK to Lasky, 6/16/50, MS2395/3; Burnham to AK, 4/10/50 and 5/26/50, HIA, Burnham, Box 6, Folder 49.

13 When Hamish Hamilton tried to get around the ban by publishing a German-language edition in Britain and seeking a German copublisher, the Foreign Office rejected the plan "for political reasons." An official blandly explained that there was "no censorship" by the Allied Control Commission of books published in the British zone, but if a book was considered "unsuitable," the publishers would be "rapped over the knuckles" and would "get into trouble." This was more than enough to stop the book, for no German publisher could afford to upset the occupation authorities.

14 Mamaine's Berlin diary, typescript; AK's Berlin diary, typescript, both in MS2306/4. Descriptions of the Berlin Congress are taken from these two sources, supplemented by Coleman and Saunders unless otherwise indicated. The characterization of Sartre as a man of goodwill and confusion is from "Arthur Koestler at 65," *New York Times Magazine,* 8/30/70.

15 Pierre Grémion, "Berlin 1950. Aux origines du Congrès pour la Liberté de la Culture" (Berlin 1950. Origins of the Congress for Cultural Freedom), *Commentaire,* vol. 9, no. 34, summer 1986.

16 *Der Monat,* July–August 1950, 339–47.

17 AK, "Two Methods of Action," in *Dinosaur,* 183–85; *Monat,* 355, for Koestler's opening words.

18   Author's interview with Arthur Schlesinger, Jr., 10/9/94.

19   AK, "Berlin Congress," typescript, MS2396/1. The speech appears in a considerably shorter and revised form as "An Outgrown Dilemma," in *Dinosaur,* 186–96.

20   F.H., "Heisse Diskussion im Kulturkongress" (Heated Discussions at the Cultural Congress), *Der Tag,* Berlin, 6/29/50; Hook, op. cit., 436–39.

21   Author's interview with Lasky, 1/6/90.

22   Coleman, 249–51. Manifesto drafts are in MS2395/4; interview with Jenka Sperber, op. cit.

23   Mamaine's diary, "Sunday" [7/2/50].

24   Hook, 443–44.

25   *Living,* 141–42; interview with Lasky; undated typescript of AK interview with RIAS, in German, in MS2396/3. On Brecht, Elizabeth Young's diary (with permission), 7/28/60.

26   *Neue Zeitung,* 6/27/50, copy in the Koestler Archive, MS3204/4; *Living,* 146; Johannes Becher to the Bureau of the Congress for Cultural Freedom, 6/30/50, copy in Koestler Archive, MS2395/3(?).

27   AK, Berlin diary, 1 and 4.

32. THE CONGRESS FOR CULTURAL FREEDOM

1.   AK, memo to Lasky, Silone, Schmidt, Kogon, Rousset, and Brown, 7/4/50, MS; AK to Burnham, 7/12/50, MS2376/3; Mamaine's diary, 4/7/50. Koestler also said that if the congress started its own publishing house, he was ready to transfer all his available books to the firm and recommended that others do the same, on condition that the new company was nonprofit and would plow all its profits into the congress, but this was hardly practicable.

2   Melvin Lasky, "Congress for Cultural Freedom Special Report: Situation and Perspectives," typescript, 7/5/50, MS2396/1; Mamaine's diary, 7/17–21/50.

3   Michèle Barat, *L'Observateur* 13, 7/6/50.

4   André Stil, "Koestler au fouet" (Koestler Cracks the Whip), *L'Humanité,* 7/8/50; Jean Kanapa, "Le traitre et le proletaire, ou l'entreprise Koestler and co. ltd" (The Traitor and the Proletarian, or the Enterprise Koestler and Co., Ltd.), *Éditions Sociales,* Paris, 1950, 4–5 and 51–52; *Action,* 6/26–7/2/50 and 8/?/50.

5   Barat, op. cit.

6   Hugh Trevor-Roper, "Ex-Communist v. Communist," *Manchester Guardian,* 7/10/50; *Economist,* 7/?/50; Peter de Mendelssohn, "Berlin Congress," *New Statesman,* 7/15/50. Lasky published a long letter of rebuttal, but Koestler remained silent; see Hugh Wilford, *CIA, the British Left, and the Cold War,* 195. The notion that Trevor-Roper forced the withdrawal of the words in the teeth of Koestler's opposition has had a long life; see for example, Coleman, Saunders, and, most recently (2003), Wilford.

7   Hamilton interview, part 1, 9, 2/19/74; AK to Mr. Elridge, 7/4/50, MS2395/3.

8   AK, "Talk at Anglo-American Press Association Luncheon, 26 July, 1950," typescript, MS2341/1.

9   Coleman, 140–41.

10   AK to Sperber, 10/24/50 and 10/30/50 (with permission) now ÖLA 2/88; author's interview with Pierre Grémion, 1/2/92.

11 Mamaine's diary, 8/6/50 and 8/10/50; AK to Brown, 8/18/50, MS2395/3; AK, "Proposal for a Coordinated Western European Radio Network Campaign," typescript, MS2395/5. The idea for a radio campaign was eventually adopted by the French Committee of the CCF but was never funded; see minutes of CCF meeting, 8/30/50, MS2395/5. Sperber to AK, 11/9/50 and 12/18/50 (with permission) ÖLA 2/88; author's interview with Grémion, op. cit.

12 AK to Brown, 8/7/50, MS2395/3.

13 Mamaine's diary, 8/8/50 (with permission), cited in part in *Living,* 151.

14 Coleman, 140–41.

15 AK to Father Job Dittberner, 10/11/72, MS2387/4; Hamilton interview, part 3, 3, 2/27/74.

16 Mamaine's diary, 8/17/50 (with permission), cited in part in *Living,* 153–54; AK diary, 10/7/50, MS2306/4; author's interview with Catherine Storr (née Peters), 6/6/00.

17 *Living,* 153–54; AK to Bondy, 8/18/50; AK to Burnham, 8/18/50; Kingsley Arbitration Transcript, 26 and 34, MS2370/1; AK to Kingsley, 8/20/50, MS2376/3.

18 *Living,* 153–54; AK diary, 8/19/50, MS2306/4.

19 *Living,* 154–58.

33. BACK TO THE USA

1 AK diary, 10/10/50; Burnham to AK, 9/2/50, MS2376/3.

2 Burnham to AK, 9/14/50, HIA, Burnham, Box 6, Folder 49; see Burton Hersh, *The Old Boys* (New York: Scribner's, 1992), chap. 16, for Smith and the reorganization of the CIA.

3 AK diary, 10/7/50, MS2306/4; AK to Russell, 9/13/50 and 9/22/50, MS2345/2, and AK to Sperber, 9/21/50, MS2376/3; affidavit by Mamaine Koestler, 7/2/53, MS2376/4. There is some mystery as to how much money was at stake in Koestler's plan for a fund. Koestler had written to Brown to say that he might contribute as much as 10 percent of his entire royalties in addition to the income from the play of *Darkness at Noon,* and he seems to have thought that Greene's promise was for 10 percent of the Continental royalties on all his novels. In her affidavit, however, Mamaine suggests that perhaps Greene had only his latest novel, *The End of the Affair,* in mind. See AK to Brown, 8/18/50, George Meany Memorial Archives, Brown Collection, Box 13, Folder 50; AK to Greene, 9/21/50, MS2376/3; AK to Russell, 9/22/50, op. cit.

4 Memo "From Dorothy Norman," September 1950, MS2397/4.

5 AK, draft of letter to Hemingway, 9/13/50; AK to Hemingway, 10/12/50, MS2302/1; Koestler followed up with a second letter to Hemingway some four months later, again without receiving a response. AK to Hemingway, 3/4/51, MS2302/1. In a letter to Dos Passos, Koestler wrote: "The point is that we are no longer engaged in merely helping individuals but are providing a forum and rallying center for a whole culture in exile"; AK to Dos Passos, 2/26/51, MS2302/1. See also AK to Mamaine, 10/28/50, MS2302/1; AK, Deed of Gift to the Fund for Intellectual Freedom, New York, 12/12/50, MS2398/1.

6 Louis Fischer to AK, 1/1/51, undated [January 1951] and 1/16/51; AK to Fischer, 1/16/51 and 2/7/51; V. Rudolph to FIF, 2/24/51, MS2397/4. The editors of *Literaturny Sovremennik* were Boris Yakovlev, whom Koestler had met at the Congress for Cul-

tural Freedom in Berlin that summer, and the literary critic Vyacheslav Zavalishin. Other prominent writers associated with the magazine included Mark Aldanov and Boris Nicolaevsky.

7 Philip Rahv to AK, 1/6/51, and AK to Rahv, 1/16/51, MS2377/3; see Allen Weinstein, *Perjury,* and, with Alexander Vassiliev, *The Haunted Wood: Soviet Espionage in America—the Stalin Era* (New York: Random House, 1999), for the most exhaustive examination of the question of Hiss's guilt. Also Tanenhaus, *Whittaker Chambers.* For the other side see Tony Hiss, *The View from Alger's Window.*

8 AK, "The Complex Issue of the Ex-Communist," *New York Times Magazine,* 2/19/50, republished as "Chambers, the Villain," in *Dinosaur,* 53–59.

9 AK to Lester Markel, 5/10/51, Markel to AK, 6/18/51, MS2369/2. The information about Markel's letter emerged during the arbitration of Koestler's suit against the dramatist Sidney Kingsley for fraud and breach of promise in his dramatization of *Darkness at Noon.* See tribunal transcript, "In the Matter of Arbitration Between Arthur Koestler and Sidney Kingsley," 2/12/52, 129, MS2370/1.

10 AK, "The European Legion," *New York Times,* 10/8/50, and in *Dinosaur,* with a postscript on Eisenhower, 204–14, and "Appalling Alternatives," *Saturday Review of Literature,* 1/13/51.

11 AK diary, 11/3/50, MS2305.

12 Lester Markel to AK, 1/5/48, MS2375/2; A. D. Peters to AK, 12/19/49, and AK to Peters, 12/22/49, MS2351/5; Mamaine's diary, 8/7/49; *Living,* 154; AK to Kingsley, 8/20/50, MS2369/2; AK diary, 10/17/50; Arbitration Transcript, Morning Session, 21–29, MS2370/1.

13 Arbitration Transcript, 2/12/52, Afternoon Session, 123, MS2370/1; AK to Mamaine, 10/4/50, MS2303/3.

14 Howard Barnes, "Darkness at Noon," *New York Herald Tribune,* 1/15/51; Richard Watts, Jr., "The Grim Tragedy of Revolution," *New York Post,* 1/15/51; John Chapman, "'Darkness at Noon' Is a Powerful and Intellectual Modern Drama," New York *Daily News,* 1/15/51.

15 *Stranger,* 114; AK diary, 1/31/51, MS2305.

16 AK to Putnam, 8/11/49 and 9/24/49, MS2356/2.

17 Richard Rovere, "When the Will to Resist Is Gone," *New York Times Book Review,* 2/25/51; Frederic Morton, "Mr. Koestler's New Novel: A Formidable Polemic of Terrible Urgency," *New York Herald Tribune Book Review,* 2/25/51; Robert Peel, "Contemporary Man as Victor and as Victim," *Christian Science Monitor,* 3/1/51; Anthony West, "Some Conceptions of Man," *New Yorker,* 3/17/51; Alfred Kazin, "Ideology vs. the Novel," *Commentary,* vol. 11, January–June 1951, 398–400; Anonymous, "Allegory of the '50s," *Time,* 2/26/51.

18 Anonymous, "War of Nerves," *Times Literary Supplement,* 4/20/51; Richard Crossman, "Darkness at Night," *New Statesman,* 4/20/51; R. D. Charques, "Fiction," *Spectator,* 4/20/51.

19 AK to Mamaine, 10/30/50, MS2303/3; AK diary, 10/28–29/50, MS2305; *Stranger,* 99; AK diary, 11/9/50 and 11/11/50, MS2305.

20 AK to Mamaine, 10/30/50, op. cit.

21 Mamaine to Edmund Wilson, 10/20/50, EWP, Yale; Mamaine to AK, 10/13/50, 10/21/50, 10/16/50, 11/8/50, and 11/9/50, and AK to Mamaine, 11/12/50, MS2303/3.

22 AK to Mamaine, 11/17/50, MS2303/3.

23 *Living,* 163–65.

24 AK diary, 1/8/51, MS2305; author's interview with Miranda DeKay and Susan Colt, 10/27/02.

25 Author's interview with Miranda DeKay and Susan Colt; *Living,* 171.

26 Mamaine to Celia, 2/4/51 (with permission).

27 Mamaine to AK, 10/21/50, MS2303/3; AK to Cynthia, 2/9/51, and Cynthia to AK, 2/13/51, MS2303/1; *Living,* 174.

34. POLITICALLY UNRELIABLE

1 Saunders, 89; AK, "Message to Bruxelles Conference of Congress for Intellectual Freedom," 11/19/50, MS2395/3; Arthur Schlesinger, letter to members of the ACCF, 12/7/50, MS2395/3; Sperber to AK, 12/18/50, MS2377/23; Nicolas Nabokov to Schlesinger, 7/19/51, JFK Library, Boston, Schlesinger Collection, Folder P-20.

2 AK to Denis de Rougemont, 1/29/51, Jay Lovestone, 1/29/51, and James Burnham, 1/29/51, MS2395/3.

3 Lovestone to Brown, 12/26/50, Meany Archives, Lovestone Collection, RG18-003, Box 11, Folder 12; Burnham to AK, 2/8/51, HIA, Burnham, Box 6, Folder 49; AK diary, 4/16-18/51, MS2305; *Living,* 183.

4 AK Diary, 4/17/51, MS2306/1; Bob Morris to AK, 1/12/51 and 4/3/51, MS2309/5; Mamaine's diary, 3/23/51 (with permission); *Living,* 177 and 182–83.

5 *Living,* 182–83.

6 Burnham, memo to the CIA, 5/31/51, HIA, Burnham, Box 11, Folder 5.

7 AK to Sperber, 4/25/51, MS2377/3; author's interview with Marietta Torberg, 9/7/93; AK to Foy Kohler, 12/5/50; printed program of conference "In Defense of Free Culture"; Pearl Kluger, ACCF, to AK, 4/9/51 and 6/5/51; printed program of ACCF's "Three Meetings in May" at Freedom House; Daniel James, ACCF, to AK, 3/6/52, all MS2395/3; English text of *Que Veulent les Amis de la Liberté?* (What Do the Friends of Liberty Want?), MS2395/4; AK to Nicolas Nabokov, 7/30/51, MS2395/3.

8 AK, "The Shadow of a Tree," *Collier's,* special issue, October 1951; also in *Dinosaur,* 151–76. See also notes (apparently made by Koestler) on a *Collier's* editorial meeting, 3/30/51, MS2377/3(?).

9 Koestler's letter was in response to an exchange between Crossman and Hook on the subject of Koestler's article in the *New Statesman;* see Richard Crossman, "Agreeing to Disagree," *Nation,* 12/16/50; Hook to AK, 3/27/51, and AK to Hook, 4/16/51, MS2377/2.

10 For FIF reports and accounts and correspondence on *Literaturny Sovremennik,* see MS2397/3. See also AK to Winkler, 5/10/51, MS2377/3; Robbins, Green, and Sosnoff memo to Pearl Kluger, undated; and AK to Commissioner of Internal Revenue, Washington, 3/28/52, MS2397/3.

11 AK to Markoosha Fischer, 1/28/51, MS2397/4; AK to Agnes Knickerbocker, 5/29/51, MS2377/2; AK to Hook, 6/27/51, HIA, Hook Collection, Box 17, Folder 42; Graham Greene to Mamaine Koestler, 10/30/50, MS2397/3.

12 Dos Passos to AK, 2/21/51 and 2/8/51, MS2397/4.

13 For a copy of AK's speech (and a similar one he gave in Philadelphia) see MS2341/4. Koestler also sent an appeal to the Brussels meeting of the CCF but with no results, Grémion, 62–63. Financial Statement, Fund for Intellectual Freedom, 6/30/51, is in MS2397/3.

14 AK, *Bricks to Babel,* 263–67; Annual Report, Fund for Intellectual Freedom,

3/15/52, MS2397/3; AK to Albert Einstein and Storm Jameson, 2/26/51, Ivan Bunin to AK, 3/29/51, AK to Bunin, 4/20/51, Nicolas Nabokov to AK, 6/22/51, MS2397/4; Nabokov to AK, 7/30/51, IACF, Chicago, Box 197, Folder 11. In *Bricks to Babel* Koestler candidly admitted that had he known the stage version of *Darkness at Noon* would run so long and amass such large royalties, he might not have been so impulsively generous, but, having made his promise, he stuck to it.

15 Navasky, *Naming Names,* 246; *Living,* 175; AK to Schulberg, 3/13/51; Schulberg to AK, 3/19/51; AK to Schulberg, 4/6/51; Schulberg to AK, 5/30/51, MS2377/3; AK to Schulberg, 10/14/51, MS2378/1; Schulberg to AK, 11/8/51, MS2377/4.

16 See *Living,* 18.

17 See Dorothy Herrman, "The Writers," in George S. Bush, ed., *The Genius Belt* (Doylestown, Pa.: James A. Michener Art Museum and the Pennsylvania State University Press, 1996); author's interview with Ruth Goetz, 6/17/92.

18 Mel Lasky, "Remembering," *Encounter,* Sept–Oct, 1983, 60.

19 *Living,* 189. Eileen Simpson, *Poets in their Youth* (New York: Noonday Press, 1990), 220.

20 *Living,* 189.

21 Author's interview with Diana Trilling, 6/8/92; Edmund Wilson, *The Fifties,* 117; interview with Marietta Torberg, op. cit.

22 Author's interviews with Michael Bessie, 11/17/02, Ruth Goetz, op. cit., and Miranda DeKay, op. cit. The "cryptic comment" appears in Koestler's diary for 8/19/51, MS2305, where he is looking back at the months on Island Farm.

23 Jamison, *Touched with Fire,* 13–14. Jamison quotes Koestler's *Act of Creation* in support of some of her theories but doesn't turn her analytical gaze on Koestler himself; see 103–4 and 115–16.

24 Mamaine's diary, 2/14/51 (with permission).

35. THE LANGUAGE OF DESTINY

1 Mamaine to Celia, 3/16/51, in *Living,* 176, except for the first and last sentences (with permission).

2 Mamaine to Celia, 4/26–27/51 (with permission).

3 *Living,* 168, 178–80, 188. Senate Bill S674, granting Koestler the right to permanent residence in the US, was passed by the Senate on June 21, 1951, confirmed by the House of Representatives on July 19, and became law on August 8. Copy in MS2344/5.

4 Mamaine's diary, 6/29–30/51 and 7/2–13/51 (with permission). Camus later wrote to Mamaine that he was "extremely frustrated" that they were going to be separated by an ocean again. "Please try to come back again. I was happier than I was able to tell you the other evening. That's the way I like to be, and there are few beings with whom I feel so calm and natural"; Camus to Mamaine, 8/3/51, Camus Estate, Paris.

5 Mamaine to AK, 10/9/50, AK to Mamaine, 10/14/50, MS2303/3; Sperber to AK, 3/16/51 and 5/21/51 and AK to Sperber, 3/28/51, MS2377/3; Sperber to AK, 4/12/51 (with permission); AK to Malraux, 8/31/51, MS2378/1. For reviews, see Jean Blanzat, "Les Romans de la semaine: Les Hommes ont soif par Arthur Koestler" (Novels of the Week: *The Age of Longing* by Arthur Koestler), *Le Figaro Littéraire,* 7/28/51; Maurice Nadeau, "Les Livres: Le nouveau roman de Koestler" (Books: Koestler's New Novel), 7/5/51. The play was published by Random House as "a play

by Sidney Kingsley" in large type and "based on the novel by Arthur Koestler" in smaller type; see Kingsley, *Darkness at Noon: A Play; Stranger,* 127–37.

6 Mamaine's diary, 7/13–31/51 (with permission).

7 AK diary, 7/24/51, MS2305.

8 Ibid., 7/24/54 and 8/19/51, MS2305; interview with Betty Winkler, 4/22/93.

9 The reference was to Goethe's lines "A bellyful of this witches' brew / And every wench is Helena to you"; see *Arrow,* 215.

10 AK diary, 8/19/51, MS2305.

11 Ibid., 8/25/51.

12 Paul Graetz to AK, 12/1/49, MS2375/4, 3/28/50 and 5/22/50, MS2376/4; AK to Graetz, 12/8/49 and 4/17/50, MS2376/3; AK diary, 4/3/50 and 4/11/50, MS2306/4; *Living,* 131 and 133; *Stranger,* 150–51; Mamaine to Celia, 4/1/50 (unpublished portion with permission); AK, "Film Project," typescript, MS2343/3.

13 Colin Deane to author, 6/25/08, 6/28/08, and 7/14/08.

14 AK to Mamaine, 8/22/51 and 8/29/51, Mamaine to AK, 8/20/51 and 9/10/51, MS2303/4; Anthony Lousada to Mamaine, 8/20/51 (with permission); AK diary, 9/26/51, MS2305.

15 AK diary, 10/11/51, 10/20/51, and 1/24/52, MS2305; *Stranger,* 146–47.

16 AK diary, 8/19/51, MS2305.

17 Ibid., 1/24/52 and 3/31/52, MS2305. See also *Arrow,* 31, and *Invisible Writing,* 361.

18 AK diary, 9/26/51, 11/5/51, 1/24/52, and 3/17/52, MS2305; author's interview with Miranda DeKay, op. cit.

19 Manès Sperber to AK, 1/5/51 (with permission); AK to Kohler, 5/2/51, MS2377/2; Tribunal Transcript, Morning Session, 13, 80, 90–110, MS2370/1.

20 AK to A. D. Peters, 12/22/49, MS2351/5; Mamaine to AK, 12/5/51, AK to Mamaine, 1/27/52, MS2303/4; Tribunal Transcript, Morning Session, 5–6, 12–13, MS2370/1.

21 Tribunal Transcript, Morning Session, 112; Afternoon Session, 134–38, 141, MS2370/1.

22 *Arrow,* 304.

23 AK diary, 2/26/52, MS2305; Chambers to AK, undated [1952], MS2332/5.

24 AK diary, 3/17/52, MS2305.

25 Ibid., 3/10–14/52 and 3/31/52; *Arrow,* 51.

26 AK diary, 4/19/52, MS2305. Three years after Koestler left Island Farm, the island was flooded by a hurricane, and the farmhouse and bridge were swept away. The island was later purchased by the Pennsylvania Power Company, with plans for a nuclear power station, but the project was abandoned and the empty island, still without a bridge, passed into the hands of the Pennsylvania Department of Conservation and Natural Resources. It is now wilderness.

36. THE PHANTOM CHASE

1 AK diary, 4/22/52, MS2305.

2 Ibid., 4/22/52 and 5/14/52.

3 AK diary, 5/14/52 and 6/6/52, MS2305.

4 Mervyn Jones, *Michael Foot: A Biography* (London: Gollancz, 1994), 125; Cesarani, *Arthur Koestler,* 400–01.

5 Cesarani, 400. Libby Brooks and Stephen Moss, "The Labour Leader's Wife, the Genius and the Unanswered Questions About That Rape," *Daily Mail,* 2/26/99, 11.

6 AK diary, 5/14/52, MS2305; Carl Rollyson, *To Be a Woman: The Life of Jill Craigie* (London: Arum, 2005), 135.

7 Rollyson, 136; AK diary, 5/21/52; there is a photograph of Koestler, Foot, and Craigie at Koestler's birthday party in MS2456/2.

8 Rollyson, 337–38; Salman Rushdie to author, 12/6/04.

9 Anne Robinson to author, 5/9/00 and; author's interviews with Jenny Stringer, 6/5/00, and Anne Robinson, 6/6/00; Jenny Stringer to author [?].

10 Zita Crossman to AK, undated, "Friday" [spring 1952]; Crossman to AK, 7/24/52, MS2378/2; Joan Lee Thompson to author, 4/21/00; Daphne Henrion to author, 12/27/98.

11 Priscilla was the daughter of the Romanian diplomat and close friend of Proust, Prince Antoine Bibesco, and of Elisabeth Asquith, whose father, Herbert Asquith, had been prime minister of Britain. AK diary, 6/6/52, MS2305; author's interviews with Priscilla Hodgson, 1/7/92 and 4/19/93; Priscilla Hodgson to author, 3/8/93. See also Lees Mayall, *Fireflies in Amber* (Salisbury, UK: Michael Russell, 1989), 101–2, for details of Priscilla's wartime adventures.

12 AK diary, 6/15/52, 6/21/52, and 7/10/52, MS2305; Priscilla Bibesco to AK, "Wednesday evening" [1952], MS2378/2; interview with Priscilla Hodgson, 4/19/93.

13 AK diary, 5/30/52, MS2305.

14 AK diary, 7/10/52 and 8/10/52, MS2305.

15 Friedrich Nietzsche, *Beyond Good and Evil,* translated by Walter Kaufmann (New York: Vintage, 1966), 87.

16 Richard Freadman, *Threads of Life: Autobiography and the Will* (Chicago: University of Chicago Press, 2001), 178–79.

17 *Arrow,* 52.

18 Peter Quennell, "Three Koestlers: Clown, Careerist, Philosopher," *Daily Mail,* 10/25/52; AK to Harold Rubinstein, 10/30/52; Michael Rubinstein to AK, 11/3/52, both in MS2332/5; AK diary, 10/27/52, MS2305; Anthony West, "Books," *New Yorker,* 11/1/52; AK, "The Koestler Saga," *New Yorker,* 7/26/52; Marvin Lowenthal, "Arthur Koestler, the Man of Many Causes, Begins a Self-Portrait," *New York Herald Tribune Book Review,* 9/21/52; Charles Rolo, "The Peripatetic Reviewer," *Atlantic Monthly,* October 1952; Stephen Spender, "Koestler's Story of His Fervent Quest for Utopia," *New York Times Book Review,* 9/21/52; V. S. Pritchett, "Books in General," *New Statesman,* 11/8/52; Philip Toynbee, "Patterns of Experience," *Observer,* 10/26/52.

19 AK interview with Gordon Hølmebakk, January 1953, MS2435/5; Bonamy Dobrée to AK, 7/27/53, MS 2378/4; AK diary, 10/10/53, MS2305.

20 AK diary, 11/24/52 and 11/26/52, MS2305; AK postscript to the Danube Edition of *Darkness at Noon;* Curt Riess to AK, 4/1/82, MS2394/1; see also Eugen Loebl, *Stalinism in Prague: The Loebl Story* (New York: Grove Press, 1969), 171–81.

21 Willert to AK, 2/11/53, MS2378/3; AK diary, 5/25/53, MS2305; Chambers to AK, 8/12/52 and 4/20/53, AK to Chambers, 4/15/53, MS2344/2; AK to Malraux, 4/28/53, MS2379/1. Koestler declined to review *Witness* for *The Manchester Guardian* on the grounds that he would not carry weight as an ex-Communist. He also refused similar offers from *The Observer* and *The Sunday Times.* AK to Wadsworth, 4/29/53 and 5/7/53, MS2379/1; Wadsworth to AK, 5/3/53, MS2378/3; *Stranger,* 166–67.

22 AK diary, 12/21/52 and 3/22/53, MS2305; AK to Jack Newsom, 3/8/53, MS2344/6. For the German election poster, see *Invisible Writing,* illustration facing 431.

23 AK diary, 5/8/53, 5/10/53, and 6/14/53, MS2305; George Mikes to AK (in Hungarian), 3/31/53 and 7/27/53, MS2378/4; George Mikes, *Arthur Koestler: The Story of a Friendship* (London: Deutsch, 1983), 5–13.

24 Author's interview with Joan Lee Thompson, 2/23/90.

25 Anonymous, "Qu'est devenu Arthur Koestler?" (What Has Become of Arthur Koestler?), *Magazine Littéraire,* February, 1967.

26 AK diary, 10/4/52, MS2305; unpublished first draft of *Stranger* in MS2332/2.

27 Author's interview with Lena Wickman, 3/22/90.

28 AK diary, 10/16/52, 10/20/52, 11/23/52, 12/9/52, and 1/4/53; interviews with Margaret Stephens and John Russell.

29 *Stranger,* 158–60. Cynthia doesn't name her lover. See also AK diary, 4/20/52 and 11/1/52, MS2305. Author's interviews with John Russell, 6/17/93, Devina and James Thackera, 5/18/90, Pamela Merewether, 8/3/90, and Martyn Beckett, 3/26/90; *Stranger,* 160 and 165.

30 Author's interview with Mark Paterson, 5/16/90; *Stranger,* 165 and 169–71; Cynthia to AK, 8/19/53, MS2303/1.

31 AK diary, 11/2/52, 11/17/52, and 11/23/52, MS2305; author's interview with Margaret Stephens, op. cit.; K. R. Eissler to AK, 9/30/52, MS2378/2.

32 AK diary, 9/21/52, MS2305; author's interviews with Margaret Stephens, op. cit., and Dorothee Koestler, 12/13/88. It's not clear if Dorothee told Koestler on this occasion, but she had received a manipulative letter from Adele, urging her to visit Adele in Swiss Cottage and saying that for Adele, "Dörte" was still *die einzige Schwiegetochter* (the only daughter-in-law) she recognized. Dorothee didn't dare visit Adele for fear of incurring Koestler's wrath. It is interesting to note that Adele defended both Dorothee and Mamaine against her beloved son.

33 AK diary, 5/7/53 and 6/18/53, MS2305; Anthony Lousada to Mamaine, 8/20/51; draft of statement by AK to Messrs. Stephenson, Harwood, and Tatham, 9/10/53; "The Humble Petition of Mamaine Koestler," MS2308/1.

37. I KILLED HER

1 AK diary, 12/29/52, 5/16/53, and 8/16/54, MS2305.

2 Ibid., 6/15/52.

3 Ibid., 3/22/53.

4 Ibid., 7/11/53, 7/14/53, and 7/25/53.

5 Ibid., 5/9/53 and 8/25/53; Janine to AK, 6/8/53, MS2378/3.

6 AK to Jack Newsom, 10/18/53, Janine Graetz to Newsom, 12/17/53, MS2344/6.

7 AK diary, 11/29/53 and 9/18/53 [*sic*—probably a mistake, should be more like 10/18/53], MS2305.

8 Ibid., 10/19/52; Frances Partridge, *Everything to Lose: Diaries, 1945–1960* (London: Gollancz, 1985), 185; author's interview with Janetta Parladé, 9/3/90.

9 AK diary, 1/18–19/53 and 2/5/53, MS2305; interview with Janetta Parladé.

10 Sir Nicholas Henderson to AK, 1/29/54; interview with Parladé; Parladé to author, 5/22/03; AK, "Europe's Serene Outpost," *Observer,* 10/18/59, republished as "Tu Felix Austria" (Thou Happy Austria) in *Drinkers of Infinity,* 135–40. It is not clear if

Koestler found time on this trip for one of his cousins, Eva Somló, who was living in Vienna and asked him to call her; see Eva Somló to AK, 2/12/54, MS2379/3.

11 AK diary, 3/21/54, 3/23/54, 4/6/54, and undated [4/28/54?], MS2305; Parladé to author, 5/22/03.

12 Parladé interview.

13 AK diary, undated [April 1954], 4/29/54, and 5/14/54, MS2305; AK to Mamaine, undated [May 1954], MS2303/4; Christine Newsom to AK and Janine, 4/30/54, MS2379/3.

14 For Koestler's abandoned novel see the typed diary extracts and handwritten notes in MS2342/5; Celia Goodman to AK, 6/2/54, MS2301/2.

15 AK diary, 11/29/53 and 2/4–6/54, MS2305; Mamaine to AK, 4/5/54, 4/20/54, MS2303/4; 4/28/54 (two letters, with permission); Mamaine to AK, 4/30/54 and 5/14/54, AK to Mamaine, 5/14/54, MS2303/4.

16 Mamaine to Sperber, 4/25/54 (with permission). Mamaine had published one of Manès Sperber's novels with Verschoyle and had spent a great deal of time with him after the death of his father in London in the spring of 1954, she comforting him for his loss and he her for her illness.

17 Interview with Russell, op. cit.; AK to Sperber (in German), 6/22/54 (with permission); Csato to AK, undated [June 1954], MS2379/3.

18 AK to Olga [Nabokov?], 11/4/75, MS2390/1; AK to Camus, see note 19 below; interviews with Parladé, 9/3/90, and Diana Cooke (by telephone), 6/19/03.

19 AK to Camus [in French], undated [June 1954]. The letter is handwritten and from its many corrections appears to be a draft. Some form of the letter was sent, because Camus replied on June 16, asking Koestler to get in touch the next time he was in Paris; Camus to AK, 6/16/54, MS2345/1; also Camus to Mamaine, 4/23/54 and 5/2/54 (with permission), AK to Sperber [in German], 6/12/54 (with permission).

20 Camus to AK, 6/16/54, op. cit.; Sperber to AK, 6/17/54, MS2379/3; J. F. Stokes to Csato, 6/2/54, MS2301/2(?); Celia Goodman to AK, 4/22/54, 6/11/54, and 8/9/54, MS2301/2.

21 AK diary, 7/24/54, MS2305.

22 Ibid., 7/24/54.

23 Ibid., 7/29/54, 8/7/54, and 8/9/54.

38. CASSANDRA GROWS HOARSE

1 AK diary, 3/16/53 and 3/22/53; AK to Dr. Jonathan Gould, 3/6/53; Gould to AK, 3/17/53, MS2332/5.

2 *Invisible Writing,* 15.

3 Emanuel Litvinoff, "The Invisible Writing," *Spectator,* 7/2/54; Marvin Lowenthal, "World of Double-Think and Double-Cross," *New York Herald Tribune Book Review,* 10/10/54; Charles Rolo, "Reader's Choice," *Atlantic Review,* October 1954; Stephen Spender, "In Search of Penitence," *New York Times Book Review,* 10/10/54; Reinhold Niebuhr, "The God That Failed," *New Republic,* 10/25/54; Gerald Weales, "Up to Date on Arthur," *Hudson Review,* vol. 8, spring 1955; Anonymous, "Last Train to Nowhere," *New Statesman,* 7/3/54.

4 *Invisible Writing,* 354.

5 Ibid., 352; AK diary, 12/8/52, 12/9/52, 12/21/52, and 6/24/53, MS2305.

6 Ibid., 7/21/53 and 9/18/53; J. B. Rhine to AK, 4/4/49 and 5/18/49, MS2375/3; AK to

Rhine, 4/16/49, MS2376/3; Gerald Heard to AK, 5/22/49 and 8/9/49, MS2375/3–4; AK to Ernest W. Martin, 1/2/47, MS2358/1; AK to Vita Sackville-West, 1/24/50, MS2376/1; Sackville-West to AK, 3/3/50, MS2376/4. AK to Secretary, SPR, 2/10/53 and 2/21/53; W. H. Salter, Hon. Sec. SPR, to AK, 2/13/53 and 2/25/53; Denys Parsons to AK, 4/18/53; all in MS 2309/6. AK diary, 3/23/53; *Stranger,* 164.

7 AK diary, 9/9/52, 10/19/52, 8/20/52, and 7/15/54, MS2305.

8 Ibid., 7/15/54 and 7/22/54; AK to Sperber (in German), 6/22/54 (with permission).

9 AK diary, 8/9/54, MS2305.

10 PEN didn't have much success with the fund, and in 1959 Koestler turned it over to the Congress for Cultural Freedom, where it was administered by the Polish émigré writer Kot Jelénski. See AK to John Hunt, 2/27/59, IACF Records, Chicago, Box 198, Folder 1; AK to Kot Jelénski, 11/28/59 and 6/14/60, MS2383/2 and 5; Jelenski to AK, 6/3/60 and 6/30/60, MS2383/4. For *Encounter* see AK, "A Guide to Political Neuroses," *Encounter,* November 1953; Lee Congdon, *Seeing Red,* 105–7; AK diary, 5/26/53 and 4/27/54, MS2305; author's interview with Irving Kristol, 3/18/92; Kristol to Mel Lasky, 7/14/53, and to Luthy, 7/14/53, IACF Records, Chicago, Box 198/1.

11 AK diary, 7/29/54, MS2305.

12 Ibid., 8/16/54; author's interview with Joan Lee Thompson, 1/3/90.

13 Janine Graetz to AK, 11/14/54, 12/8/54, MS2379/2 and 4; 2/11/55, 3/23/55, MS2380/1; and 10/10/56, MS2381/2.

14 Elizabeth Jane Howard, *Slipstream,* 261. My account of Koestler's relationship with Howard is based both on this book of memoirs and on an earlier and briefer memoir, "Remembering," in *Encounter,* July–Aug. 1983, supplemented by my interview with Howard, 5/23/90. See also Sayre, *On the Wing,* 27–33.

15 Author's interview with Howard, op. cit.; AK diary, 6/15/55, 7/6/55, and 7/8/55 (private collection). In *Slipstream* Howard gives a slightly different version of her pregnancy and ensuing abortion, indicating that she did know about Janine and Koestler's child (270) and saying nothing about her initial desire to have the baby. I have preferred the version given in her interview, if only because it came earlier and was not carefully framed for a wider audience.

16 Howard to AK, undated [June?] 1955, MS2380/1, and Howard, "Remembering," op. cit.

17 Author's interviews with Joan Lee Thompson, 1/3/90, 2/23/90, and 1/28/93. J. Lee Thompson based another movie (*The Weak and the Wicked,* starring Glynis Johns) on Joan's memoir about her prison experience.

18 Interviews with Joan Lee Thompson, op. cit.

19 *Stranger,* 195–96; AK diary, 8/2/55 (private collection).

20 Ignatieff, *Isaiah Berlin, a Life* (New York: Holt, 1998), 183–85.

21 AK diary, 12/19/54, MS2305; AK, "Judah at the Crossroads," in *Dinosaur,* 106–41.

22 Isaiah Berlin to AK, 11/18/54 and 11/30/54, MS2379/4; AK to Berlin, 11/25/54, MS2379/1; author's interview with Isaiah Berlin, 5/25/90; Sayre, op. cit., 28; author's interview with Joan Thompson, 6/8/90.

23 Sperber to AK, 10/11/55, MS2380/2; Bourdet interview with Sperber, op. cit. In later years, Berlin and Koestler agreed to accept their differences and restored amicable relations.

24 AK, "The Trail of the Dinosaur," in *Dinosaur,* 160–61 and 164; AK diary, 12/19/54, MS2305.

39. MATTERS OF LIFE AND DEATH

1 This account of the campaign, unless otherwise footnoted, is based on two main sources: Edwards, *Victor Gollancz,* chap. 24, and John Grigg, "The Do-Gooder from Seville Jail," in Harris, ed., *Astride the Two Cultures,* op. cit., 123–35. Derek Bentley was officially pardoned in 1993.

2 Author's interview with David Astor, 6/2/00; David Astor, "Crusader," *Encounter,* July–August 1983, 31–33.

3 *Stranger,* 196.

4 Ibid., 210; AK diary, 11/9/55, 12/15/55, and 2/2/56 (private collection).

5 AK, *Reflections on Hanging,* 169.

6 AK diary, 2/16/56, 2/22/56, 2/24/56, 2/25/56, and 3/14/56, MS2305; Cynthia's diary, 10/1/69, MS2303/1; AK to Gollancz, 3/14/56 and 3/15/56, MS2400/1; *Stranger,* 219–21.

7 Goodhart cited in Hamilton, 274; Anonymous, "A Life for a Life," *Times Literary Supplement,* 4/20/56; Frank Tannenbaum, "After Murder, a Rope," *New York Times Book Review,* 6/30/57; Reinhold Niebuhr, "Justice and the Death Penalty: *Reflections on Hanging* by Arthur Koestler," *New Republic,* 8/26/57; Richard H. Rovere, "Matter of Life and Death," *New Yorker,* 9/14/57; Ian Gilmour, "The Death Penalty: *Reflections on Hanging* by Arthur Koestler," *Spectator,* 4/13/56.

8 See Albert Camus and Arthur Koestler, *Réflexions sur la peine capitale* (Reflections on Capital Punishment) (Paris: Calmann-Lévy, 1957). The French edition also contained a factual chapter on French experience with the death penalty by the lawyer Jean Bloch-Michel. Manès Sperber to AK, 7/13/55 (with permission), 11/7/55, 6/20/56, and 9/28/56, MS2359/1; AK to Sperber, 10/5/55 and 12/31/56, MS2359/1, and 2/4/57 (with permission); AK to Camus, 3/21/56, MS2359/1(?), and 9/17/58, Camus Estate.

9 Astor to AK, 3/10/56, MS2400/1; AK interview in *Paris-presse l'intranigent,* op. cit.

10 *Stranger,* 190 and 196–201; AK diary, 10/10/55, 10/12/55, 10/13/55, 10/15/55, 10/17–25/55 (private collection); Cynthia's diary, 11/19/70; AK to Robin Maugham, "Thursday" [October 1955], MS2332/5; Griselda Kentner to AK, 10/23/55.

11 AK diary, 5/3/55, 6/25/55, 6/29/55, and 9/5/55 (private collection).

12 *Stranger,* 205–6 and 210–11; AK diary, 10/31/55, 11/7/55, and 11/12–20/55 (private collection).

13 Author's interviews with Elizabeth Jane Howard, op. cit., and Pierre Debray-Ritzen, 1/2/92.

14 *Stranger,* 223–30; AK diary, 4/15/56, 4/21/56, 6/23/56, and 7/4/56 ff. (private collection); interview with Joan Lee Thompson, op. cit.

15 AK diary, 2/4/56, 4/18/56, 9/16–17/56, and 10/27–29/56 (private collection); AK to Sperber, 12/17/56 (with permission).

16 AK diary, 10/24/56 (private collection); Zoltán Szabó, "Kivülröl" (View from Outside) in *Terepfelveres* (The Beating) (Bern, 1981), 154–56 and 160–62; author's interview with Irving Kristol, 3/18/92; Mikes, 17–18.

17 Szabó, op. cit.; CCF cable to AK, 10/27/56, AK cable to CCF, 10/28/56, Chicago, IACF, Box 197, Folder 12.

18 Mikes, 19–20; AK diary, 10/28/56 (private collection).

19 AK diary, 10/29–11/5/56 and 11/7/56–11/13/56 (private collection); Judith Szabó to AK, 11/8/56; Armand Petitjean to AK, 11/11/56; author's interview with János

Kenedi, 6/27/89; Saunders, 302; Coleman, 134; Harold Nicolson to AK, 11/15/56; Storm Jameson to Margot Walmsley, 11/23/56, MS2381/2; AK to Storm Jameson, 12/1/56, MS2380/3.

20 AK diary, 11/16/56 (private collection).

21 Ibid., 12/11–18/56; AK to Sperber, 12/17/56, MS2359/1.

22 Author's interviews with Elizabeth Young, 5/31/00, and George Faludy, 3/4/89; Al Hart to AK, 12/4/58, MS2356/3; Marion Bieber to AK, 7/15/58. The Hungarian Writers Association was formed in London, financed by the CCF, and Koestler got the CCF to support a magazine and an anthology of Hungarian literature in translation. But Ignotus and Faludy fell out over the magazine's political direction, and it proved impossible to find translators for the anthology, so Koestler returned the money and washed his hands of the matter. See Michael Josselson to AK, 9/5/58, AK to Josselson, 9/6/58 and 9/7/58, and Josselson to AK, 9/13/58, Chicago, IACF, Box 197, Folder 12.

23 Author's interviews with Paul Kövesdy, 6/10/92, and Faludy, op. cit. Koestler also helped Kövesdy to meet Pierre Mendès-France in Paris.

24 AK diary, 10/26–29/57, 5/25/58, and 6/18–19/58 (private collection); AK to Josselson, 5/19/58, Marion Bieber to AK, 5/27/58, Chicago, IACF, Box 17, Folder 5. These letters show that the payments to Eva Hay were eventually taken over by the CCF.

25 AK diary, 11/5–28/56 (private collection); *Paris-Presse l'Intransigeant,* 6/15/59. It should be added that Koestler strenuously protested against the publication of this "interview," mainly because his brief conversation with a reporter had been dressed up with extensive excerpts from his autobiographical works to look as if they were all part of a much more serious discussion of his life verbatim. The few snippets of actual conversation were not at issue, however; see AK to Calmann-Lévy (with attachments), 7/1/59, MS2359/3.

26 Lees Mayall, op. cit., 102.

27 Author's interviews with Elizabeth Young and George Faludy, op. cit.; Elizabeth Young's diary, undated [1958] (with permission); *Paris-Presse,* op. cit.; Celia Goodman to unknown correspondent, 12/29/57 (with permission).

40. COSMIC REPORTER

1 *Stranger,* 188 and 191; *Sleepwalkers,* 225; AK diary, 4/29/55, 5/3/55 (private collection). It's possible that Koestler was subconsciously influenced in his choice of title by Hermann Broch's novel of the same name, *The Sleepwalkers,* published in 1931.

2 AK to Eva Auer (in German), 3/18/58 (with permission).

3 AK diary, 10/24–25/58 (private collection); AK to Al Hart, 7/10/58 and 7/22/58, MS2356/3; AK to Herbert Butterfield, undated draft, 1958; Butterfield to AK, 8/8/58. Butterfield was a layman in scientific matters, but his book *The Origins of Modern Science* has since become a classic; see I. Bernard Cohen, *Revolution in Science,* 389–91.

4 *Arrow,* 50–51; *Dialogue,* 50, 103; *Invisible Writing,* 351–54.

5 There may have been a less obvious influence at work on Koestler. Otto Weininger had berated Jewish scientists for concentrating on the "soulless" sciences of chemistry and medecine (which they had reduced to a mere matter of prescribing drugs, according to Weininger) and extolled the noble "Aryan values" that had inspired

Copernicus, Galileo, Kepler, Newton, Faraday, and their successors; see Weininger, op. cit., 314–15. It's curious, in view of Koestler's later book *The Case of the Midwife Toad,* that Weininger included Lamarck in his list of the great "Aryan" scientists. See also Wistrich, op. cit., 530.

6 *Dinosaur,* 246.

7 *The Sleepwalkers,* 237–238.

8 Some forty years later the science historian and Kepler specialist James R. Voelkel asserted that Kepler had "purposely misrepresented his methodology" and had deliberately depicted himself as "having been driven aimlessly to his conclusions." If this was so, Koestler had fallen into Kepler's trap and drawn overly far-reaching conclusions from it. See James R. Voelkel, "Commentary on Ernan McMullin, 'The Impact of Newton's *Principia* on the Philosophy of Science,' " in *Philosophy of Science* 68, September 2001.

9 *Sleepwalkers,* 425–26, 484–86, and 527–29. An obvious influence on Koestler was Michael Polanyi, who had rejected "the ideal of scientific detachment" outside the exact sciences, because "it exercises a destructive influence in biology, psychology and sociology, and falsifies our whole outlook beyond the domain of science." See Polanyi, *Personal Knowledge,* xiii and part I, chap. one, "The Lesson of the Copernican Revolution." Polanyi had first formulated these ideas around the time he became friends with Koestler; see his *Science, Faith and Society.*

10 For the two recent studies of Galileo see Wade Rowland, *Galileo's Mistake,* and William R. Shea and Mariano Artigas, *Galileo in Rome;* also George Johnson, "Contrarian's Contrarian: Galileo's Science Polemics," *New York Times,* 8/12/03, a discussion of these two works that is explicitly framed with reference to *The Sleepwalkers.* See also Mark Graubard, "*The Sleepwalkers:* Its Contribution and Impact," in Harris, ed., *Astride the Two Cultures,* op. cit., 20–36, and Joseph Agassi, "On Explaining the Trial of Galileo," in Agassi, *Science and Society,* 321–51.

11 The CCF's outposts in Bombay, Bangkok, Singapore, Hong Kong, and Tokyo were under intellectual siege from nationalists, neutralists, and fellow travelers, and the CCF felt that Koestler's worldwide reputation as an anti-Communist would strengthen its cause and improve the morale of its local supporters. See Minoo Masani to AK, 8/20/53, MS2378/4; AK to Masani, 8/30/53, MS2379/1; AK diary, 6/22/58 (private collection); David Green to AK, 2/26/58, Herbert Passin to AK, 7/2/58, and John Hunt to AK, 10/31/58, Chicago, IACF, Box 198, Folder 1; AK to Al Hart, 12/13/58, MS2356/3.

12 AK, Asian diary (handwritten MS), 3–5, MS2306/2; AK, *The Lotus and the Robot,* 16–17.

13 AK, Asian diary, 18–21; AK to Cynthia, 1/11/59, MS2303/1; *Lotus,* 57 and 62.

14 AK to Cynthia op. cit, *Lotus,* 52–54; AK to Robert Lusty, 2/5/59, MS2355/1.

15 AK to Cynthia op. cit..

16 *Lotus,* 22–24 and 32–34; AK to Jayaprakash Narayan, 2/8/59, MS2412/1. For Narayan's ideas, see Guy Wint, "Narayan at Oxford," *Encounter,* December 1959, and "Report of a Seminar on the Future of Democracy in India," typescript, St. Antony's College, Oxford, 12/5–6/59, Chicago, IACF, Box 198, Folder 1.

17 *Lotus,* 165–69; Lees Mayall, op. cit., 116; AK to Robin Campbell, 11/18/60, MS2383/5; *Paris-Presse l'Intransigeant,* op. cit.

18 Quentin Crewe, *A Curse of Blossom: A Year in Japan* (London: Weidenfeld and Nicholson, 1960), 150–52; *Lotus,* 272–74.

19 AK to Hoki Ishihara, 2/8/59, MS2412/2.

20 *Lotus,* 223–25; AK to Cynthia, 3/3/59, MS2303/1; *Times,* 3/24/59; Japanese PEN Club to AK, 4/4/59, MS2412/2; Jørgen Schleimann, CCF, to AK, 4/31/59 and 5/5/59, Chicago, IACF, Box 198, Folder 1; author's interview with John Hunt, op. cit. For Josselson's comment and the CCF's problems in Japan, see Coleman, 187–88.

21 AK, "The Last of the Saints," *Observer,* 4/26/59; AK, "The Last of the Saints 2—A Sanskrit Class in Prison," *Observer,* 5/2/59; AK, "The Last of the Saints 3—A Spoonful of Buttermilk," *Observer,* 5/10/59. See also Cynthia Koestler, "Twenty-five Writing Years," in Harris, ed., *Astride the Two Cultures,* op. cit., 141; Barbara Wood, "The Birth of 'Small Is Beautiful,'" *Observer,* 4/24/84; Narayan to AK, 5/2/59; AK to Narayan, 5/8/59; AK to John Hunt, CCF, 5/22/59; Hunt to AK, 10/22/59, Chicago, IACF, Box 198, Folder 1; Wint, "Report of a Seminar," op. cit.

22 AK, "Diary Extracts," 1/4/61, MS2306/1; Burnham to AK, 4/16/61, MS2384/2; *Lotus,* 216. In a series of "tightly controlled laboratory experiments" conducted in China, Japan, Korea, and the United States at the end of the twentieth century, the Michigan social psychologist Richard Nisbett showed that the "cognitive processes" of Easterners and Westerners did in fact diverge radically in many areas and were not at all as unified as some psychologists had supposed. Easterners tended to think more "holistically" than Westerners, paid "greater attention to context and relationship," relied "more on experience-based knowledge than abstract logic," and showed "more tolerance for contradiction." See Erica Goode, "How Culture Molds Habits of Thought," *New York Times,* 8/8/2000.

23 AK, "Yoga Unexpurgated," *Encounter,* August 1960, and AK, "The Stink of Zen," *Encounter,* October 1960, and *Encounter,* Letters to the Editor, January 1961; Mark Amory, ed., *The Letters of Ann Fleming* (London: Collins Harvill, 1985), 270; Reginald Kapp to AK, 12/27/60, MS2384/3.

24 William Empson, "A Full-Blown Lily," *New Statesman,* 10/27/61; AK, *Lotus,* 277–78; D. J. Enright, "The Yogi and Mr Koestler," *Spectator,* 11/4/61; Sidney Hook, "But There Was No Light," *New York Times Book Review,* 3/5/61. For Jung, see AK, "Between the Lotus and the Robot," in AK, *Drinkers of Infinity,* 287; Burnham to AK, 4/16/61, MS2384/2.

41. THE SQUIRE OF ALPBACH

1 AK diary, 8/17/57 (private collection); author's interview with Otto Molden, 9/7/93; AK to Sperber, 7/31/57 (with permission); Fritz Molden, *Der Konkurs: Aufstieg und Fall eines Verlegers* (Bankrupt: The Rise and Fall of a Publisher) (Hamburg: Hofmann und Kampe, 1984), 117–19.

2 Ibid., 8/19/57; author's interviews with Eva Auer, 9/17/93, and Alexandra Terzic-Auer, 9/14/06.

3 AK diary, 8/24–26/57, 9/2-5/57, author's interview with Eva Auer.

4 Author's interview with Eva Auer.

5 Ibid.; AK diary, 10/17–21/57 (private collection).

6 AK to Eva Auer (in German), undated (with permission); AK diary, 11/7/57 and 2/27–3/3/58 (private collection); *Paris-Presse l'Intransigeant,* op. cit.; interview with Eva Auer; Dezső and Tonka Somló to Adele Koestler, 1/10/57, MS2302/2; Agnes Aczel de Aranyi to A. D. Peters, 3/9/83, MS2414–2415.

7 AK to Eva Auer, 4/21/58, MS2383/1; Wolfgang Pfaundler to AK, 5/21/58 and

5/31/58, MS2382/3; author's interviews with Leni Moser and Otmar Radinger, 9/17/93, Otto Molden, op. cit., and Eva Auer, op. cit.; AK diary, 6/8–10/58 (private collection).

8 Quentin Crewe to AK, 9/5/62, MS2384/3; author's interview with Hanna Molden, 9/16/93.

9 Author's interview with Eva Auer.

10 Interviews with Eva Auer and Otto Molden, op. cit.; AK diary, October 1960 (private collection); Janine Graetz to AK, 9/24/60, MS2383/4.

11 Chambers to AK, 7/24/58 and 8/11/59, and to T. S. Matthews, 7/7/59, MS2344/2; AK pocket diary, 6/17–18/59; William F. Buckley, Jr., *Odyssey of a Friend* (New York: National Review Inc., 1969), 249–51 and 271; Tanenhaus, *Whittaker Chambers,* 508–10.

12 Tanenhaus, ibid.; Margarete Buber-Neumann to AK, 4/19/54, MS2379/4, 1/11/57, 2/17/57, MS2381/4; AK to Frederick Warburg, 7/2/59, and AK to Buber-Neumann, 10/27/61, MS2359/3; AK on Chambers, *National Review,* 7/29/61. For Jesenská see Buber-Neumann, *Mistress to Kafka: The Life and Death of Milena,* translated by Ralph Mannheim (London: Secker and Warburg, 1966), with an introduction by Arthur Koestler. The book was later republished under several variations on this title.

13 See Alfred Kantorowicz, *Deutsche Schicksale* and "Abschied von Arthur Koestler" (Farewell to Arthur Koestler) in *Die Geächteten der Republik,* 150–78; AK, "Erwiderung an Abschied von Arthur Koestler" (Rejoinder to "Farewell to Arthur Koestler"), typescript, MS2441/3; Kantorowicz to AK, 9/6/[59], MS2383/2.

14 Author's interviews with Margaret Stephens and Lena Wickman, op. cit.

15 AK to Dr. Mandl, 9/3/60, and AK to Rabbi Jakob Kokotek, 9/3/60, MS2352/3.

16 Rolph, *Further Particulars,* 149–53; Grigg, "The Do-Gooder from Seville Jail," in Harris, ed., *Astride the Two Cultures,* op. cit., 130–32; AK, "Histoire du Prix" (A History of the Prize), in Debray-Ritzen, op. cit., 357–58.

17 Rolph, op. cit.

42. RETREAT FROM RATIONALISM?

1 Dennis Gabor to AK, 3/6/60 and 3/23/60, AK to Gabor, 3/8/60 and 10/21/60, AK to Lance Whyte, 1/17/61, MS2346/3; AK to Sir Cyril Burt, 11/2/61, MS2344/1.

2 Timothy Leary to AK, 3/8/60 and 1/4/61, MS2346/3.

3 J. B. Rhine to AK, 5/11/60, AK to Rhine, 8/23/60, MS2346/3.

4 See AK, *The Ghost in the Machine,* 203–4 and 208, and "Some Aspects of the Creative Process," in Farber and Wilson, eds., *Man and Civilization,* 188–208 and 293–97. AK to Cynthia, "Saturday" and 1/31/61, MS2303/1.

5 AK to Gabor, 11/18/61, MS2346/3; AK, "Mystical Hallucinations Induced by Drugs Are Arousing Controversy in America," *Sunday Telegraph,* 3/12/61, reprinted in AK, *Drinkers of Infinity,* 201–12.

6 AK, "Mystical Hallucinations"; Timothy Leary, *Flashbacks,* 56–57. Leary calls Pollard "Pointsman," but the rest of his account matches Koestler's in all other respects, except that it is slightly racier. According to Leary, the psychologists at Michigan did work for the CIA and were hostile to Leary and his politics. See also "The Art of Fiction LXXX: Arthur Koestler," *Paris Review,* summer 1984, 183–201 (interview by Duncan Fallowell).

7 Leary, 59. For an earlier account of Koestler's visit, see Timothy Leary, *High Priest,* 135–55. Since the book is cast in the form of a journal and much of this chapter is written in the language of a "trip," it is less immediately useful than Leary's later account but does contain some fresh details. See also Robert Greenfield, *Timothy Leary: A Biography* (New York and London: Harcourt, 2006), 131–33.

8 AK, "Mystical Hallucinations"; AK to Dr Hofmann, 3/14/70, MS2347/3.

9 AK, "The Pioneer Beyond the Pale," *Observer,* 5/7/61, reprinted in shortened form in *Drinkers,* 230–34.

10 AK to Leary, 2/17/61, Leary to AK, 4/25/61, Rhine to AK, 5/10/61, Rhine to Leary, 6/5/61, MS2346/3.

11 AK, "Pavlov in Retreat," *Observer,* 4/23/61, "Behold the Lowly Worm," *Observer,* 4/30/61, and "Pioneer," op. cit.; also in abridged form in *Drinkers,* 213–33; AK, "Mystical Hallucinations." Koestler later came to the conclusion that psychotropic drugs did have clinical value and felt that "every psychiatrist should have a session with mescalin or LSD in order to know what a psychosis is like, and what hallucinations are like. It should be part of the psychiatrist's curriculum." See *Paris Review* interview, 187–88.

12 For the correspondence in *The Observer* see Hamilton, 328–29.

13 John Cohen to AK, 5/8/61 and 5/15/61, AK to Cohen, 4/1/61, MS2346/3. Hansel continued to investigate ESP and became a leading critic of its claims; see C.E.M. Hansel, *ESP.*

14 Brian Inglis, "Parapsychologist," *Encounter,* September–October 1983, 53–57, and "Arthur Koestler and Parapsychology," *Journal of the American Society for Psychical Research* 78, July 1984, 269; Cynthia Koestler, "Twenty-five Writing Years," in Harris, ed., *Astride the Two Cultures,* op. cit., 147; Cynthia's diary, 9/28/61, 10/23/61, 12/1/61, and 12/10/61, MS2305. See also Rosalind Heywood to AK, "Thursday" [no date] and 5/1/76, MS2390/2. In 1966 Koestler put the weighing machine up for auction; see Inglis and AK to Messrs. Harrods, 6/7/66, MS2385/3.

15 Alan McGlashan to Cynthia, 7/31/61, MS2393/2.

16 Cynthia's diary, 9/31/61 and 10/14/61; AK to unidentified individual, 10/25/60, MS2356/3.

17 AK, "The Scandal of the Quarantine" and "Dog Quarantine: A Final Word," *Observer,* 4/1/62 and 4/22/62, republished in *Drinkers* as "Animals in Quarantine" and "Dogs, Sticks and Smugglers," 58–73; Cynthia's diary, 1/20/62, 4/9–17/62, and 4/27/62; Grigg, op. cit., 132–35; interviews with David Astor, op. cit. and 6/2/00.

18 Cynthia's diary, 9/30/61 and 11/25/62; anonymous typescript, "Suicide of a Nation," MS2344/3; AK, "When the Daydream Has to Stop," *Observer,* 2/10/63, also in *Drinkers,* 74–83. If Britain didn't join the European Common Market, Koestler told Cynthia, he was more resolved than ever to move to Paris, "have 3 dogs and only a pied-á-terre in London." It was impossible, he said, to live "cut off from Europe."

19 Cynthia's diary, 3/10–16/63.

20 See *Encounter,* July 1963; AK, ed., *Suicide of a Nation?*

21 Jelenski's and Strachey's charges, along with Koestler's answers, are cited in AK, "*Darkness at Noon* and *The Strangled Cry,*" in *Drinkers,* 280–81. Strachey's comments on Koestler appear in his *Strangled Cry,* op. cit., 11–23, and his conclusion about "the task of reason" in ibid., 77. There is a longer version of Koestler's interview with

Urban in G. R. Urban, ed., *Talking to Eastern Europe* (London: Eyre and Spottis-woode, 1964).
22 Urban, 102–4.

43. A NAIVE AND SKEPTICAL DISPOSITION

1 Dr. A. Walzer, Kepler-Gesellschaft, to AK, 7/2/62, MS2384/3; AK to Franz Ham-mer, 9/23/63, MS2384/5; Hans Haber to Nancy Thomas, BBC, 8/26/63, MS2340/2; Cynthia's diary, "September and October," 1963; AK, "The Greatest Scandal in Christendom," op. cit.
2 AK diary, 1/16/61, MS2305; Dennis Gabor to AK, 3/6/60, 3/23/60, 10/27/60, 11/25/61 and 2/19/63, AK to Gabor 3/8/60, 11/18/61, and 12/13/61, MS2344/1; AK to Holger Hyden, 6/24/62 and 8/5/63, Hyden to AK, 9/24/63, MS2344/1; Polanyi to AK, 12/15/61 [*sic;* judging from the rest of Polanyi's correspondence with AK it should have been dated 1960] and 1/21/61, AK to Polanyi, 1/16/61, MS2366/7.
3 Burt to AK, 8/6/63, 8/12/63, 8/17/63, 9/30/63, 10/3/63, and 10/26/63, AK to Burt, 8/12/63 and 10/8/63, MS2344/1. Burt's academic fraud was first exposed by the American psychologist Leon Kamin in 1974 and was exhaustively documented in a biography of Burt by the English psychologist Leslie Hearnshaw in 1979. See Leon J. Kamin, *The Science and Politics of IQ* (Potomac, Va.: Lawrence Erlbaum Associ-ates, 1974), 35–47; R. C. Lewontin, Steven Rose, and Leon J. Kamin, *Not in Our Genes* (New York: Pantheon, 1984), 86–87 and 101–6.
4 AK, *The Act of Creation,* 21–22 and 139.
5 Peter Medawar, "Koestler's Theory of the Creative Act: *The Act of Creation,*" *New Statesman,* 6/19/64; Koestler's reply and Medawar's response, *New Statesman,* 7/10/64; all reprinted in Medawar, *The Art of the Soluble* (London: Methuen, 1967), 85–98. See also Kathleen Nott, "The Bloom and the Buzz," *Commentary* 38, No-vember 1964), 84–88; Stephen Toulmin, "Koestler's Act of Creation: Vision, Theory, Romance," *Encounter,* July 1964, 58–70.
6 Henry David Aiken, "The Metaphysics of Arthur Koestler," *New York Review of Books,* 12/17/64, reprinted in Murray A. Sperber, *Arthur Koestler,* 151–61. See also Carl R. Hausman, "Understanding and the Act of Creation," *Review of Metaphysics,* vol. 20, no. 1, issue 77, 88–112. Koestler's theory of bisociation and its workings in humor led, among other things, to an invitation to write the entry on wit and humor for the fifteenth edition of the *Encyclopaedia Britannica,* and the word *bisociation* now appears in *Webster's Third International Dictionary.*
7 For later works see John D. Barrow, *The Artful Universe;* António Damásio, *Descarte's Error;* António Damásio, *Looking for Spinoza;* and Paul Feyerabend, *Against Method.*
8 Polanyi to AK, 11/9/62, AK to Polanyi, 11/19/62, MS2344/7.
9 AK diary, 1/4/61; Cynthia's diary, 9/18/61, 10/9/61, and 11/17/61. A thick sheaf of the typed menus has been preserved in MS2312/4.
10 Cynthia to AK, 1/25/59, 1/28/59, 2/8/59, and 3/1/59, MS2303/1; Cynthia's diary, 11/22/62 and 11/28–29/62; McGlashan to Cynthia, 9/11/63, MS2384/5.
11 McGlashan to AK, 6/29/[60?], MS2383/4; author's interviews with Joan Lee Thomp-son, 8/6/90, Pamela Merewether, 8/3/90, Elizabeth Jane Howard, 5/23/90, Maurice Cranston, 4/11/90, and John Grigg, 6/1/00; Pamela Merewether to author, 6/19/96.
12 AK to Henry Green, 2/9/60, MS2383/5; AK diary, 1/4/61; Cynthia's diary, 10/30/61;

Joan Lee Thompson to AK 7/12/[62?], MS2384/3; interviews with Janetta Parladé, 9/3/90 and 6/18/03, and Joan Lee Thompson, 2/23/90. Joan Lee Thompson to AK "Friday" [1963?], MS2384/5.

13 Joan Lee Thompson to AK, 5/28/[63?], MS2384/5; author's interviews with Celia Goodman, 3/5/90, and David Astor, 9/24/93.

14 AK to Ignotus, 10/26/60, Ignotus Papers, Petőfi Irodalmi Múzeum, Budapest; AK to Gabor, undated [1960?], and to Mikes (in Hungarian), 7/16/60, MS2383/5; Cynthia's diary, 8/15/61; on visit to Burgenland, see typed excerpt from AK's notebook, 8/15/61, in MS2343/3.

15 Jenő Somló to AK (in Hungarian), undated [November 1964?], 12/27/64, MS2385/1, and 6/17/65, MS2385/2; AK to Somló (in Hungarian), 12/7/64, MS2385/1; Lenke Singer to AK (in Hungarian), 2/3/65 and 4/26/65, MS2385/2; AK to Florence Ignotus, 3/11/65.

16 Celia Goodman to "Peg" (the Princess of Hesse and the Rhine), 1/5/64 (with permission); Ignotus to Josselson, 2/12/63, MS2384/5; Mikes to AK (in Hungarian), 8/21/64, AK to Eva Auer, 8/26/64, MS2385/1; Mikes, *Friendship,* 20–21.

17 Interview with Eva Auer, op. cit.

18 Alexandra Terzic-Auer to author, op. cit.

19 Ibid.

20 AK to Eva Auer, 1/15/63 (with permission); author's interviews with Auer, Karen Duftner, Radinger, op. cit.; Terzic-Auer to author, op. cit.

21 Ibid.; interview with Hanna Molden, 9/16/93.

22 Interview with Eva Auer; Cynthia's diary, 8/20/64.

23 Cynthia's diary, 8/13/64 and 8/22/64; Ernest Gellhorn to AK, 9/24/64, AK to Gellhorn, 10/22/64, AK to Hydén, 11/25/64, MS2346/3.

24 Cynthia's diary, 8/19–21/64 and 9/1/64; AK to Burnham, 11/25/64, MS2346/3; author's interview with William F. Buckley, Jr., 8/12/92; marriage certificate in MS2308/2.

44. SEEKING A CURE

1 Cynthia to her mother (Mrs. Elisabeth Jefferies), 2/9/65, MS2301/4; Cynthia's diary, 3//5/65, 3/13/65, 3/20/65, 3/28/65, and 4/4/65.

2 AK to Gellhorn, 10/22/64, MS2346/3; Hamilton, 343–44; Cynthia's diary, 3/29/65; AK to Gellhorn, 2/4/65, and to Hydén, 3/2/65, MS2346/4.

3 Paul Mishkin to author, undated; Willis Harman to AK, 3/17/65, MS2346/4.

4 Cynthia's diary, 3/18/65, 3/24/65, 3/29/65, 4/9/65, 5/4/65, and 5/14/65; Ernst Hilgard to AK, 11/30/64, AK to Hilgard, 12/7/64 and 2/8/65, MS2346/4; AK to Hydén, 8/17/6, MS2385/1.

5 AK, "Cloudcuckoocamp," typescript, MS2323/1.

6 Cynthia's diary, 4/20/65, 4/28/65, 4/30/65, 5/10/65, 5/12/65, 5/20/65, 5/26/65, and 6/12/65; AK to Karl Pribram, 9/27/65, Pribram to AK, 10/12/65, MS2346/4.

7 AK, "Mistress to Picasso," *Observer,* 3/3/65, reprinted in *Drinkers,* 189–92; author's interview with Françoise Gilot, 4/13/93; Cynthia's diary, 6/20/65.

8 Cynthia's diary, 9/1–3/65; AK to Jerome Bruner, 9/28/65, Alister Hardy, 10/1/65, and Paul MacLean, 10/13/65, MS2346/4.

9 Cynthia's diary, 9/5/65.

10 For correspondence on the Danube Edition, see MS2354/3 and 4. Koestler chose the

name Danube Edition and picked out the colophon for it: a diagram of black and white concentric circles strung with small black and white diamonds to create the illusion that it was a spiral instead of a circle. This optical illusion illustrated the notion, dear to Koestler, that "seeing is not necessarily knowing" but "knowing is seeing"—perception is colored by what we know. See also Connolly interview, 40–41.

11 Connolly interview, 8–12 and 20–22.

12 Cynthia's diary, fall 1965; AK to Pribram, 9/27/65, MS2346/4, and 2/28/66, MS23472; unsigned and undated note from AK to Pribram, MS2347/2; Pribram to AK, 10/12/65, MS2346/4, and 2/23/66, MS2347/2; Hayek to AK, 7/20/65, MS2346/4; AK to Hayek, 4/10/66, MS2347/2; AK to Louis Fischer, 4/18/66, AK to Hydén, 8/17/66, MS2346/4; AK to MacLean, 1/31/66, 8/17/66, and 3/2/67; MacLean to AK, 2/24/67, 3/2/67, and 3/31/67; Seymour Kety to AK, 5/13/66, MS2347/2; Cynthia's diary, 9/1–3/65 and 2/16/67; AK to Hardy, 10/1/65 and 1/4/67, MS2347/2; AK, "Mysterium Tremendum," in *Drinkers,* 166–72.

13 AK to Wolfgang Foges, 5/19/59, with enclosure, MS2359/3.

14 AK, "Of Geese and Men," a review of *On Aggression* by Konrad Lorenz, *Observer,* 9/18/66, also in *Drinkers,* 156–60; Cynthia's diary, 8/16–17/66.

15 Cynthia's diary, 9/23/61, 7/11/62, and 7/4/65.

16 Interview with Eva Auer; Cynthia's diary, 7/11/65, 7/29/66, and 8/4/66.

17 Cynthia's diary, 7/16–26/67; interview with Eva Auer; Terzic-Auer to author, 9/22/03.

18 Cynthia's diary, 7/14/66, 7/22/66, 7/25/66, 7/26/66, 9/26/66–10/2/66, and 2/8/67.

19 AK to Eva Auer, 10/14/65 (with permission); Cynthia's diary, fall 1966; author's interview with Gilot, op. cit.

20 Cynthia's diary, 3/13–19/67, 4/17/67, 4/17–5/20/67, 5/24–7/7/67, and 10/6–9/67; AK diary, 4/5/67; *Evening News,* 3/17/67; correspondence in *Times,* 3/22/67, 3/25/67, 3/28/67, and 3/31/67; AK to Harold Harris, 1/19/67, and AK to Maurice Cranston, 2/6/67, MS2355/2.

21 See Coleman, chap. 14, and Saunders, chaps. 23–26.

22 Caute, *Fellow-Travellers,* 298–300.

23 AK to Michael Josselson, 4/25/67, and to Kot Jelenski, 12/11/67, Harry Ransom Humanities Research Center, University of Texas, Austin, Josselson Papers; Polanyi to AK, 10/31/67, MS2366/7; AK to Polanyi, 11/4/67, University of Chicago Library, Michael Polanyi Papers, Box 4, Folder 10; AK to Father Job Dittberner, 10/11/72, MS2387/4.

24 Cynthia's diary, 1/30/67 and 6/11–25/67; Abram Weinshall to AK, 6/27/67, AK to Weinshall, 8/8/67, MS2385/5.

25 The Countess of Warwick [Janine Graetz] to AK, 9/3/67, MS2385/5. Janine had married Charles Guy Fulke Greville, the seventh Earl of Warwick, in November 1963. She was the earl's third wife and now went by the name of Janine Greville.

26 AK, *Ghost,* 202; Cynthia's diary, 12/8/66.

27 The word *holon* was formed by Koestler from the Greek *holos,* a "whole," and the Greek *on,* meaning a "part." Holon is also the name of an ancient city just south of modern Tel Aviv, and one wonders if Koestler subconsciously remembered this when making his coinage; see AK, *Ghost,* 48 and 56.

28 Ibid., 61, 116–17, 202, 210–11, 215, and 230–32.

29   Ibid., 234 and 267.

30   Ibid., 277–87, 289–90, 296, and 337–39.

31   Stephen Toulmin, "The Book of Arthur," *New York Review of Books,* 4/11/68. A Macmillan internal memo of 2/15/68 reads in part, "The attached Koestler . . . reviews . . . give evidence that our advance publicity maneuvers with the booklet and pills were successful. The reviewers took Macmillan's lead from the pill line, and our total impact will be much greater—publicity, promotion, and advertising. Congratulations! It's fun to see things work." Copy in MS2352/5.

32   For reviews see William Sargant, "Into Orbit," *Spectator,* 10/27/67; John Lear, "A Pill That Elides Evolution," *Saturday Review,* 2/24/68; Leslie Fiedler, "Towards the Freudian Pill," *New Statesman,* 10/27/67; Edwin A. Roberts, Jr., "Mr. Koestler Proposes a Brain Pill to Enable Thought to Curb Emotions," *National Observer,* 3/11/68; Robert Jay Lifton, "Man as Mistake," *New York Times Book Review,* 4/17/68; David Krech, "Assault on the Citadel," *Science,* 5/10/68; Alex Comfort, "Koestler's Proper Study," *Guardian,* 10/20/67; Marvin Mudrick, "Prometheus at Work and Play," *Hudson Review,* summer 1968.

33   Charles Rycroft, "Holons and Hierarchies," *New Society,* 10/19/67.

34   Dennis Polter, "The Ominous Beat of Koestler's Ragged Black Wings," *The Times,* 9/21/67.

35   For later books pro and con Koestler's thesis see Erich Fromm, *The Anatomy of Human Destructiveness* (New York: Holt, 1992), in which Fromm argues against Lorenz's and Koestler's thesis that man is a killer by nature, and Willard Gaylin, *Hatred, the Psychological Descent into Violence* (New York: Public Affairs, 2003). In terms of fingers on the pulse, it may be worth noting that *The Ghost in the Machine* inspired an entire album by the talented rock band The Police, led by Sting; see Robert Sellers, *Sting: A Biography* (London: Omnibus Press, 1989), 44.

36   Fritjof Capra, *The Turning Point* (New York: Simon and Schuster, 1982), 43–44; John Davy, "Scientists Plan for Peace with a Pill," *Observer,* 3/17/68; Gina Kolata, "Scientists Brace for Changes in Path of Human Evolution," *New York Times,* 3/21/98; "Is Depression Productive?" *New Yorker,* 2004.

45. WUNDERKIND

1   Mogens Fog, rector of Copenhagen University, to AK, 1/12/68, MS2352/6; Cynthia's diary, 4/18–21/68; AK, "The Urge to Self-Destruction," in *The Heel of Achilles,* 20.

2   Cyrus Eaton to AK, 5/2/68, MS2352/6; Cynthia's diary, 4/18–21/68, 5/7/68, 6/5/68, and 9/22–25/69; Mikes, 60–61; Dennis Gabor to Iain Hamilton, 5/31/74, MS2430/3.

3   Cynthia's diary, 6/5/68 and 6/6–9/68. See also AK and J. R. Smythies, eds., *Beyond Reductionism,* 1–2, 31–32, 66, 104–13, 118–19, 218–19, and 223–24.

4   *Beyond Reductionism,* 115, 397, 409, 417–20, 426, and 428–34; Cynthia's diary, 6/9–11/68, 6/12–14/68, 9/2/68, and 1/11/70; Anonymous (L. L. Whyte), *Times Literary Supplement,* 11/20/69; David Newth, "A Critique of the Koestler Clique," *New Scientist,* 10/2/69; George Steiner, "Life-Lines," *New Yorker,* 3/6/71. The reference to critics and Teilhard de Chardin is in Steiner.

5   AK, "Diary Extracts," typescript, 10, MS2306/1; AK notebook, 9/10/62, MS2306/7; Cynthia's diary, 11/21/67 and 11/24/67.

6   AK to Polanyi, 10/14/68, MS236/7; AK, "Rebellion in a Vacuum," in *Achilles,* 20–32.

7   Interview with AK in Rosner and Abt, *The Creative Experience,* 133–53; AK's notes

for symposium on "Drugs and Drug Addiction" and program, Zurich, 1/15–16/70, MS2406/4; Elizabeth Hall, "A Conversation with Arthur Koestler," *Psychology Today,* June 1970, 62–65 and 78–84; Kresten Bjerg to AK, 1/22/70, and AK to Berg, 1/30/70, MS2347/3.

8   AK to Peters, 8/19/68, MS2352/6.

9   Cynthia's diary, 11/20–21/68; Barry Jones, memo, "On Arthur Koestler, Amnesty and Communication Failure," 11/26/68, MS2411/1; Anonymous, "Koestler Upset over Mix-up," *Age,* 11/26/68.

10   Cynthia's diary, 11/24/68 and 11/28/68; Jones, "Interview with AK," MS2411/1; Philip Adams, "Obsessed with Disaster," *Australian,* 12/14/68.

11   AK, "A Christmas Story of Christ's Thoughts on the Cross," *Age,* 12/24/68. This story appeared in the December 1968 number of *Encounter* as "The Episode."

12   See Rev. Dr. H. F. Leatherland, "A Dialogue with Arthur Koestler," December 1968, and AK to "John" [Sir John Barry?], 2/15/69, MS2411/1.

13   AK, "Diary Extracts," 9–10 and 12–13.

14   Ibid.

15   AK notebook, 9/2/67 and 5/21/68.

16   AK, "Can Psychiatrists Be Trusted?," paper read to the World Psychiatric Association Symposium, London, November 1969; AK, "Mahatma Gandhi—Yogi and Commissar, a Re-Valuation," *Sunday Times,* 10/5/69. Both essays were republished in *Achilles,* 38–44 and 221–54. See also Hall, op. cit.; Sunanda K. Datta-Ray to AK, 10/15/69, MS2386/3. "Our readership tends to be impatient of any kind of critical analysis," wrote the editor of Calcutta's respected weekly *The Statesman* when turning it down, referring to Hindu-Muslim riots that had resulted after Arnold Toynbee mentioned the prophet Mohammed in an article for the magazine.

17   Polanyi to AK, 7/29/70, MS2344/7; Comfort, op. cit.; AK, "Diary Extracts," 16.

18   Cynthia's diary, 10/4/69, 10/29/69, and 12/15–18/70.

19   Ibid., 10/10/69, 10/23/69, 11/3/69, and 11/8/69.

20   Ibid., 4/17/67, 11/24/67, 6/20/68, 6/24/68, 6/28/68, 6/29/68, 8/5–7/68, 9/20–11/5/68, 1/29/69, 4/23/69, and 11/26/69; AK, "Diary Extracts," 14.

21   The Austrian obituaries are cited in AK, *The Case of the Midwife Toad,* 15–18.

22   Cynthia's diary, 5/17–18/70, 6/18–24/70, 7/8/70, and 7/12/70. Despite his skepticism, Paul Weiss also made some experiments by injecting frog specimens with ink to see if they maintained their dark color and resembled the surviving sample of the toad. The results indicated that Koestler *could* have been correct in suggesting that the ink had been injected *after* Kammerer's visit to Cambridge, but Weiss felt that the results were inconclusive; Weiss to AK, 4/20/71, MS2347/6.

23   *Midwife Toad,* 133.

24   For the *Sunday Times* feature and the BBC program, see AK to Paul MacLean, 8/11/71, and AK to Peter Huppert, 1/24/72, MS2347/1; also materials in MS2320/5–6 and MS2322/4.

25   George Steiner, "Eye of Newt and Toe of Frog," *Sunday Times,* 10/3/71; Richard Holmes, "Koestler's Dramatic Field of Play," *Times,* 9/27/71; Stephen Jay Gould, "Zealous Advocates," *Science,* New Series, vol. 176, no. 4035, 5/12/72, 623–25. Gould's mistakes are noted in a letter to the editor of *Science* from Sigurdur Helgason, a mathematician at MIT, typescript in MS2421/2–3. See also E. J. Steele, *Somatic Selection and Adaptive Evolution* (Toronto: Williams and Wallace International, 1979).

26 Yvan Audouard, "Le Premier qui dit la vérite" (The First to Tell the Truth), *Le Canard Enchaîné*, 2/2/72; Medicus, "Le Crapaud et l'infini" (The Frog and Infinity), *L'Express*, 1/24–30/72; Pierre Debray-Ritzen, "Arthur Koestler réhabilite un crapaud pour rendre justice à un homme" (Arthur Koestler Rehabilitates a Frog in Order to Do Justice to a Man), *Le Figaro*, 2/18/72; D.V., "La Bataille des crapauds" (The Battle of the Frogs), *Le Monde*, 7/19/72; Gérald Messadie, "L'Étreinte du crapaud" (The Frog's Embrace), *Science et Vie*, June 1972; Jean Rostand, "Le 'Byron des crapauds,' était-il un faussaire?" (The "Byron of the Frogs," Was He a Fraud?), *Nouvelles Littéraires*, 3/5/72; Pierre Debray-Ritzen, "Koestler sur deux fronts" (Koestler on Two Fronts), *Le Figaro Littéraire*, 10/1/71; Debray-Ritzen, *Arthur Koestler: Un croisé sans croix*, 200–204.

46. CHANCE GOVERNS ALL

1 The title of Kammerer's book, *Das Gesetz der Serie,* referred to a folk saying in German along the lines of "troubles never come singly," or "it never rains but it pours."

2 Cynthia's diary, 4/11/70, 10/13/70, 10/25/70; John Cutten to AK, 3/2/71, MS2387/2.

3 Ibid., 4/11/70, 10/13/70, 10/25/70, 12/30/70, 3/6–9/71 and 3/22/71; AK, "Marrakech," *Sunday Telegraph Magazine*, 9/8/72. Also in AK, *Drinkers*, 182–93.

4 See AK, *The Roots of Coincidence*, chap. 2, "The Perversity of Physics," 50–81.

5 Ibid., chap. 2, "Seriality and Synchronicity," and chap. 3, "Janus," esp. 105–10 and 140. Koestler found no room for anecdotal evidence in the finished book and invited Renée Haynes to contribute a postscript on "spontaneous phenomena," along with some "qualitative" arguments to balance his "quantitative" arguments for the existence of ESP.

6 Cyril Connolly, "Don't call me . . ." *Sunday Times*, 2/6/72; Michael Foot, "Blow your mind with ESP," *Evening Standard*, 2/8/72; Rupert Strong, "Boggled Minds," *Irish Press*, 2/17/72; Philip Toynbee, "Supernatural Solicitings," *Observer*, 2/6/72. See also Christopher Lehmann-Haupt, "Arthur Koestler in Wonderland," *New York Times*, 8/11/72; Eliot Fremont-Smith, "Peeking at Eternity," *Saturday Review*, 9/30/72; Naomi Bliven, "Head to Head," *New Yorker*, 8/12/72; John L. Hess, "In 2 Koestler Books, a Scientific Challenge," *New York Times*, 2/11/72.

7 AK, "Diary Extracts," 15 and 19; interviews with Leni Moser, Hanna Molden, and Harold Harris, op. cit.; Cynthia's diary, 8/15/70.

8 Cynthia's diary, 3/17/71, 3/21–25/71, 4/19/71, 5/1/71, 5/6–10/71, 6/12/71, 6/30/71, 7/24/71, and 8/30/71; interviews with Fritz Molden, 9/9/93, and Hanna Molden, op. cit.

9 Cynthia's diary, 1/20/69, 2/7/69, 2/17/69, 1/7/71, 12/3/71, 12/6/71, 12/30/71, 1/1/72, 1/8/72, and 1/12–4/25/72; Cynthia Koestler, "Twenty-five Writing Years," op. cit., 144–45.

10 Anonymous, "Irresistible Satire," *Economist*, 10/21/72; Herbert Lomas, "Going off the Motorway," *London Magazine*, December 1972–January 1973; Edmund Fuller, "Warriors on the Symposia Circuit," *Wall Street Journal*, 7/26/73; Mervyn Jones, "A Joke Perhaps?," *New Statesman*, 10/27/72; Gabriel Pearson, "Blind Spots," *Guardian Weekly*, 10/28/72; Anatole Broyard, "Cosmos Without Characters," *New York Times*, 4/3/73; Anonymous, "The Call-Girls," *New Republic*, 5/12/73.

11 Cynthia's diary, 2/2/70 and 10/21/70.

12 Cynthia's diary, 10/17–18/70 and 1/10/71.

13 The letter from Buckingham Palace is in MS2308/2; interview with Sir Martyn Beckett, op. cit.

14 Ibid., 10/21–22/70 and 9/7–9/72; Janine Greville to AK, undated [10/21/70], MS2386/5, and 9/1/72, MS2387/4; AK to Janine, undated [10/22/70], MS2386/5, and 10/2/72, and AK to Cristina Graetz, 10/2/72, MS2387/4.

15 Colin Deane to author, 7/14/08.

16 AK notebook, 2/13/69, 12/16/71, and 9/2/73; Cynthia's diary, 1/24/70, 3/20/70, 11/17/71, and 8/16/72.

17 Cynthia's diary, 10/26/72; AK to Eva Zeisel, 10/18/75, MS2390/1.

18 Cynthia Koestler, untitled typescript, 3/9/70, MS2332/5.

19 Ibid.; Cynthia's diary, 3/7–9/70.

20 Cynthia's diary, 5/2–3/71, 6/11/71, and 9/26–10/1/72.

21 David Pryce-Jones, "Chess Man," *Encounter,* September–October 1983, 25–28; AK, "Reykjavik Notes," typescript, MS2411/2; AK, "Reflections of an Addict" and "A Requiem for Reykjavik," *Sunday Times,* 7/2/72 and 9/3/72, republished as "The Glorious and Bloody Game" in *Achilles,* 206–31.

22 John Beloff and E. D. M. Dean to AK, 7/12/67, Beloff to AK 7/27/67, 11/1/67, and 10/8/71, AK to Beloff, 7/21/67 and 10/27/71, MS2399/3; AK, "Science and Para-Science," *Achilles,* 133–47.

23 Alister Hardy, Robert Harvie, and Arthur Koestler, *The Challenge of Chance,* 12–13; AK to Hardy, 10/17/71 and 3/9/72; Hardy to AK, 2/2/72, AK to Michael Ingrams, 3/3/72, MS2344/4; Cynthia's diary, 4/26/72.

24 Hardy to AK, 10/15/73, MS2344/4; *Chance,* 160 and 209.

25 Cynthia's diary, 2/18/66 and 11/23/66; Brian Inglis, "Arthur Koestler and Parapsychology," *Journal of the American Society for Psychical Research,* July 1984, 266; Norman Moss, "Beyond Our Understanding: Arthur Koestler Investigates the Mysterious World of the Inexplicable," *Sunday Times Magazine,* 11/25/73; Philip Toynbee, "A Sponge in the Post," *Observer,* 11/4/73; Brian Inglis, "It So Happened," *Guardian,* 11/17/73; Hardy to AK, 1/4/74, MS2348/3; Brigid Brophy, "A Classic Non-contribution to Knowledge," *Listener,* 1/3/74; R. H. Thouless, "The Challenge of Chance," *Journal of Parapsychology* 38, December 1974, 423–27; Joseph Rush, "The Challenge of Chance," *Journal of the American Society for Psychical Research* 69, April 1975, 174–77.

26 Montagu Ullman to AK, 9/11/72, AK to John Cullen et al., 8/21/73, Frank Barron to AK, 3/27/73, AK to Frank Barron, 4/9/73, AK to Timothy Leary, 4/9/73, MS2348/2.

27 See www.uri-geller.com; Brian Inglis to AK, 11/25/73, AK to Inglis, 12/3/73, MS2388/3; Arthur Ellison to AK, 12/13/73, MS2348/2; AK to Bob [Joyce?], 11/12/74, MS2389/1; J. B. Rhine to AK, 3/14/75, MS2348/4.

28 Rosalind Heywood to AK, 12/4/73 and 12/9/73, MS2388/3; Heywood to AK, 9/1/74 and "Tuesday" [1974], MS2389/1; Heywood to AK, 3/18/75, MS2390/1; AK to Hardy, 5/21/74, MS2348/3; AK to Rhine, 5/22/74, and to Mr. Gray, 5/24/74, MS2348/3; Celia Goodman to Peg, 8/25/75 (with permission).

47. THE KOESTLER PROBLEM

1 For biography, see Cynthia's diary, 4/23/70 and 10/31/70. Koestler was skeptical about a biography and suggested to Rees that a "triple portrait" of himself, Orwell, and Brecht might work better; see also Hamilton, *Koestler,* xiv, and Frank Barron to

AK, 7/20/73, MS2348/2. Barron had interviewed several writers, including Truman Capote, William Carlos Williams, W. H. Auden, Marianne Moore, Sean O'Faolain, and Norman Mailer, for a book about the creative process. Unfortunately Barron never published his interviews separately and they appear to have been lost, though Barron included snippets from them in *No Rootless Flower: An Ecology of Creativity* (Cresskill, N.J.: Hampton Press, 1995). A young scholar, John A. Miles, Jr., published a two-part article in the journal *Zygon* on Koestler's religious ideas, and a British scholar, Roy Webberley, was completing a lengthy doctoral dissertation entitled "Education and the Work of Arthur Koestler."

2   Trevor-Roper to AK, 3/9/74, MS2348/3; Berlin to AK, 3/27/73, AK to Berlin, 4/7/73, MS2348/2; Berlin to AK, 4/18/73, MS2388/3; Royal Society of Literature to AK, 2/26/74, and Program of the Annual Reception of the R.S.L. for 7/24/74, MS2389/1.

3   AK, "In Memory of A. D. Peters," *Sunday Times,* 2/4/73, also in *Achilles,* 111–13; AK to Peters, undated [1971?], MS2353/1. Koestler was also grateful to Peters for having donated time and money to Koestler's fund to help refugee writers and his campaign against the death penalty, and Peters had served for seven years as chairman of the Koestler Awards for prisoners.

4   Sonia Orwell, Cyril Connolly Fund, to AK, undated, MS2390/1; Magda Polanyi to AK, 8/31/75 and 3/6/76, MS2344/7; Eva Zeisel to AK, 5/27/75, September[?] 1975, and 10/7/75, MS2390/1; AK to Zeisel, 6/2/75 and 9/4/75, MS2390/1, and 10/11/76, MS2390/2. Eva was at pains to get Koestler involved in Polanyi's care partly because Polanyi's elderly wife, Magda, overburdened and sick, was experiencing "all [the] resentments of a neglected wife." These resentments were shortly turned on Koestler himself, when Magda accused him (in a letter greeting his seventieth birthday) of having borrowed his ideas on "holistic biology" straight from Polanyi. A few years later, after the publication of *Janus,* Magda sharpened her accusations, telling Koestler he was well known "for stealing other people's ideas"; see Magda Polanyi to AK, 8/31/75, 1/9/75, and 8/25/80, MS2344/7. Koestler didn't bother to answer the charge.

5   AK, "A Sentimental Pilgrimage," *Kaleidoscope,* 285–305; Cynthia's diary, 2/16–22/73. The title of the article in the *Telegraph* was "Private Dubert's War and Peace," *Daily Telegraph Magazine,* 8/17/73.

6   They turned out to be members of L'Amicale des Anciens Internés du Camp de Vernet-d'Ariège (Association of Ex-Prisoners of the Vernet Camp), established to preserve the cemetery in memory of those who had perished there. L. Menendez, secretary of the Amicale, to AK, 2/24/74 and 3/20/74, MS2389/1–2. There is now a small museum at the site of Le Vernet.

7   AK, "The Lion and the Ostrich: Ten Years On," *Encounter,* October 1973, also as "Going Native" in *Kaleidoscope,* 273–84.

8   Cynthia's diary, 3/3–4/73; AK correspondence with Tim Miller, MS2309/4; AK to Thorpe, 5/19/74; AK to Debray-Ritzen, 6/18/74, MS2348/3. The Bellagio paper was called "The Free Agent in a Hierarchical Context" and was published in a French translation in Debray-Ritzen, 444–53. See also S. A. Mostyn, Moorfields Eye Hospital, to AK, 7/11/73, MS2388/3; Cynthia's diary, 11/1/73; AK to Rebecca West, 8/17/75, MS2390/1.

9   Debray-Ritzen, 262.

10 Rebecca West to AK, 8/12/75 and undated [May 1976], MS2390/1 and MS2390/2; B. I. Grummels to AK, 11/17/75, AK to Grummels, 12/9/75, MS2389/4.

11 AK to Rebecca West, 5/16/76, MS2390/2.

12 AK notebook, 12/25/73.

13 See Harris, ed., *Astride the Two Cultures,* Peter Medawar, "Doing the Honors," *Saturday Review,* 3/6/76; Philip Toynbee, "Homage to Koestler," *Observer,* 8/31/75; George Steiner, "Koestler's Quest," *Sunday Times,* 8/31/75; Jacques Cabau, "Koestler et les étoiles" (Koestler and the Stars), *L'Express,* 3/31/75, and Gérard Guégan, "Koestler et l'Infini" (Koestler and the Infinite), *Le Monde,* 5/16/75.

14 AK telegram to Solzhenitsyn, c/o Heinrich Böll, 2/14/74, MS2389/1; Andrei Kistyakovsky, "Translator's Introduction [to *Darkness at Noon*]," typescript in Russian, MS2323/2; author's interview with Marina Kistyakovsky, 12/13/90. Kistyakovsky was not the first person to translate *Darkness at Noon* into Russian. That distinction belongs to another dissident, Igor Golomstock, who had translated the novel, along with Orwell's *Animal Farm,* some twenty years earlier, in 1956. Koestler particularly approved of Kistyakovsky's Russian title, *Slepyashchaya t'ma,* which in English signifies, very roughly, "Blinding Darkness" but carries the same metaphysical overtones as the original English title. Golomstock's title for the novel, *Mrak v polden',* was a literal translation of the English. Author's interview with Igor Golomstock, 10/15/05.

15 Mikes, op. cit., 21–22; author's interview with Istvan Bart, 6/21/89.

16 Peters to AK, 6/22/71, MS2353/1; AK notebook, 1/29/72, 7/29/72, 12/5/73, 8/24/74, and 12/16/74, MS2305; Olivier Todd, "Janus, ou les deux faces d'Arthur Koestler" (Janus, or the Two Faces of Arthur Koestler), *L'Express,* 2/3–9/79; Cynthia's diary, 10/31/73 and 11/4/73.

17 Cynthia's diary, 10/31/73, 11/4/73, and 11/18/73; AK notebook , 1/29/72, 7/29/72, and 12/5/73; Menachem Begin to AK, 7/2/70, AK to Begin, 7/22/70, MS2386/5. Koestler also declined an invitation to join the British branch of the Zionist Revisionist Organisation, Herut, explaining that while he had "never lost" his admiration for Jabotinsky, the situation was now different. Five years later, Koestler rejected a similar invitation to address the youth Zionist movement Betar. See AK to general secretary, Zionist Revisionist Organisation, 11/6/70, MS2386/5.

18 AK, Notebook, 12/25/73.

19 For the views of Hungarian Jews at the turn of the century I am indebted to Kevin Brook, *The Jews of Khazaria;* and Brook to author, 9/14/00. See also AK, *Thieves,* 23; AK, "Schweik in the Second World War," 91–95; C. K. Lynton-Harris, Ministry of Information, to AK, 11/13/43; AK, untitled typescript ("Race Theory"), 1943, 31 pages. Koestler also referred to the Khazar theory in "The Ubiquitous Presence," his essay written in 1966 to commemorate the tenth anniversary of the abortive Hungarian uprising of 1956; see *Drinkers,* 143.

20 AK, *Bricks to Babel,* 306. Patrick Leigh-Fermor reminded Koestler of the Khazar theory when discussing the work of the Austrian writer Hugo von Kutschera. Author's interview with Leigh-Fermor (by telephone), 6/19/03.

21 AK, *The Thirteenth Tribe,* 224.

22 AK, "The Vital Choice," in Douglas Villiers, ed., *Next Year in Jerusalem: Portraits of Jews in the Twentieth Century* (New York: Viking, 1976), 98–106. The essay's original title was "Views of an Apostate," see typescript in MS2339/5. So nervous was the ed-

itor about Koestler's contribution that he invited a simultaneous response from Berlin, who insisted that Koestler had not done justice to his argument.

23 Ibid.; Naamani, op. cit. I have not been able to track down the Saudi Arabian ambassador's speech to the UN, but when the Swiss bookseller and writer Eugene Schulman met Prince Mohamed al-Faisal on a business visit to Riyadh, the prince showed him a copy of *The Thirteenth Tribe* and said it was proof that Israel had no right to exist; Schulman to author, 5/26/06. For the Israeli ambassador and Jewish libraries see Debray-Ritzen, 269.

24 Hyam Maccoby, "Koestler's Racism," *Midstream* 23, March 1977; Raymond Sokolov, "Origins of the Jews," *Newsweek,* 8/30/76.

25 Wieseltier, op. cit.; Hyam Maccoby, "Jew," *Encounter,* September–October 1983. Koestler's views on the importance of the Khazars weren't entirely without a grain of truth. The Israeli linguist Paul Wexler has suggested that Koestler was right to deduce a "Slavo-Turkic" origin for the majority of Ashkenazi Jews but overemphasized the Khazars at the expense of the Slavs; see Wexler, *The Ashkenazic Jews: A Slavo-Turkic People in Search of a Jewish Identity* (Columbus, Ohio: Slavica, 1993). Some population geneticists have since determined that while most surviving Ashkenazim seem to possess a "Mediterranean lineage," a majority of Ashkenazi Levites bear a different genetic signature, one that might very possibly have originated with the Khazars, though that is still far from certain. See also George Johnson, "Scholars Debate Roots of Yiddish, Migration of Jews," *New York Times,* 10/29/96; Brook, *Jews of Khazaria,* op. cit.; Brook to author, 9/14/00; Nicholas Wade, "Y Chromosome Bears Witness to Story of the Jewish Diaspora," *New York Times,* 5/9/2000; "Geneticists Report Finding Central Asian Link to Levites," *New York Times,* 9/27/03. On the implications for diaspora politics see Franz Knopfelmacher, "Arthur Koestler: The Mole of God," *Quadrant,* October 1982, and Bernard Avishai, "Koestler and the Zionist Revolution," *Salmagundi* 87, summer 1990.

26 A. D. Peters to AK, 6/22/71, MS2353/1.

27 Stephen Toulmin, "Arthur Koestler's Theodicy," *Encounter,* February 1979.

28 Todd, "Janus, ou les deux faces d'Arthur Koestler," op cit.

29 John Heilpern, "Appointment with Janus," *Observer,* 2/26/78.

48. AN EASY WAY OF DYING

1 Eva Zeisel to AK, regretting his decision not to attend her seventieth birthday party in the USA, 1/1/77, MS2335/4; interview with Margaret Stephens. Despite Steiner's repeated attempts to get an appointment with the regular English faculty at Cambridge, he was repeatedly rejected. See also George Steiner, "Le Morte d'Arthur" op. cit.; Julian Barnes, "Playing Chess with Arthur Koestler, *Observer,* 7/3/88.

2 Steiner, "Le Morte d'Arthur."

3 Celia Goodman to Peg, 3/16/80 (with permission); author's interview with Donald Wayne, 5/4/90; interview with Celia Goodman.

4 Obituary of Daphne Hardy Henrion, *Daily Telegraph,* 11/26/03.

5 Author's interview with Ariane Bankes, 5/6/90.

6 Author's interview with Donald Wayne, op. cit., 5/4/90; Anonymous (name removed) to George Mikes, 8/9/83 (provided to the author by Donald Wayne); Barnes, op. cit.

7 Interview with Wayne.

8 Rosalind Heywood to AK, 3/18/75, 4/18/75, and undated [1975], MS2390/1; also 4/29/75, undated [1976], and undated [1976], MS2390/2; Celia Goodman's diary, 9/5/76, and Celia Goodman to Peg, 1/25/77, MS2301/2; Brian Inglis, "Arthur Koestler and Parapsychology," *Journal of the American Society for Psychical Research* 78, July 1984, 263–72; AK to P. G. F. Nixon, 12/19/79, AK to Bloomfield, 8/26/79, Bloomfield to AK, 9/10/79, MS2346/1. Koestler told John Heilpern that he would have liked to be a faith healer; see Heilpern, op. cit.

9 Ibid.; author's interview with John Maddox, 3/29/90. It seems that Koestler did get the offer of a scientific column from *Encounter* but by the time it came along was already too ill to go through with it; see Celia Goodman's diary, 7/30/79.

10 E. J. Steele, *Somatic Selection and Adaptive Evolution,* op cit.; E. J. Steele, "The Evidence for Lamarck," *Quadrant* 364, March 2000, 47–56; AK, *Bricks to Babel,* 9 note; AK to Dr. Huppert, 9/9/80, MS2392/4; E. J. Steele to author, 4/16/05 and 4/26/05; author's interview with Jeffrey W. Pollard, 7/26/05.

11 John Cullen to AK, 11/16/70, MS2399/3; AK, "Postscript," in John Beloff, ed., *New Directions in Parapsychology,* 167.

12 Todd, op. cit.; Celia Goodman's diary, 3/4/79.

13 Celia Goodman's diary; printed invitation to 10 Downing Street, in MS2392/4; Hugh Thomas to AK, 9/17/82, and AK to Thomas, 9/20/82, MS2394/1.

14 David Astor, "Crusader," op. cit. The Koestler Awards continue to flourish to this day.

15 See AK's notes on Hamilton manuscript, typescript, 12/4/78, MS2301/2; Victor Sebesiyen, "Tribute That Turned Sour," *Hampstead and Highgate Gazette,* 4/16/82; Anonymous, "Koestler's Veto on Private Life," *Evening Standard* [date unascertainable]; Celia Goodman's diary, 3/8/80; author's interview with Celia Goodman, 12/14/88; Secker and Warburg catalogue, autumn 1975; AK, draft of letter to Hamilton, 5/8/79, AK to Michael Rubinstein (of Rubinstein Callingham), 6/3/79, and AK to Celia Goodman, 6/4/79, MS2301/2. Michael Rubinstein to Hamilton, 6/7/79, AK to Harold Harris, 3/27/80, Rubinstein Callingham to Oswald Hickson, Collier and Co., 12/4/80, MS2464/6.

16 Francis Huxley, "Thirsting for the Absolute," *Guardian Weekly,* 11/30/80; James Sloan Allen, "Koestler's Monument to Himself," *Christian Science Monitor,* 5/11/81; Mark Czarnecki, "A Prolific Search for the Absolute," *Maclean's,* vol. 4, 3/9/81, 62; Bernard Dixon, "Two Cultures at One," *New Scientist,* 1/8/81; Jim Miller, "Koestler at Twilight," *Newsweek,* 5/4/81.

17 Bernard Crick, "Koestler's Koestler," *Partisan Review,* no. 2, 1982.

18 Max Gallo, "L'Hérétique" (The Heretic), *L'Express,* 5/12/81; Christiane Delacampagne, "Arthur Koestler, témoin lucide et passionné" (Arthur Koestler, Lucid and Passionate Witness), *Le Monde,* 7/17/81; Jean Clémentin, "Et un tombeau pour Arthur, un!" (And a Tomb for Arthur, Just One!), *Le Canard Enchainé,* 8/26/81.

19 Crick, op. cit.

20 Harold Harris, "Introduction," AK and CK, *Stranger on the Square.*

21 Dr. J. Q. Mathias to Dr. I. J. Freedman, 2/20/79, Dr. A. F. Hoffbrand to Dr. Freedman, 3/25/80, Dr. M. Kremer to Dr. Freedman, 1/7/82, MS2307/1; AK to Holger Hydén, 5/23/80, MS2392/4; author's interview with Anne Cutts, 5/4/90.

22 Barnes, "Playing Chess with Arthur Koestler," op. cit.

23 C. R. Sweetingham, Euthanasia Society, to AK, 4/1/69, MS2409/1; AK to Maria La-

certa Finton, 11/25/76, MS2390/2, 7/12/78, MS2391/3, 2/2/80 and 8/13/80, MS2392/4; AK, Preface, in *A Guide to Self-Deliverance* (London: Voluntary Euthanasia Society, 1981).

24 AK, "Whereof One Cannot Speak . . . ?," in Arnold Toynbee, Arthur Koestler, et al., *Life After Death,* 238–60, and in *Kaleidoscope,* 313–38; Cynthia Koestler to "Auntie Beattie," 12/11/76, MS2301/4; Celia Goodman's diary, 4/20/79, MS2301/2.

25 Celia Goodman to Peg, 3/4/79, and Celia Goodman's diary, 3/19/79, MS2301/2.

26 Mikes, 16–47.

27 AK, suicide note, handwritten on two pages, MS2308/1.

28 Celia Goodman to Peg, 9/3/82; Mary Benson, "Arthur and Cynthia," *London Magazine,* June–July 1997, 118–21.

29 Interview with Mary Benson; AK, suicide note.

30 Interviews with Mary Benson and Lady Beckett, 2/15/90; Dr. J. Q. Creightmore to author, 6/12/91; Mikes, op. cit., 3 and 76; author's interview with Pat Kavanagh, 5/24/90.

31 Dr. J. Nossiff to author, 6/13/98; Mikes, p. 76; AK interview with Rayner Heppenstall, 1946(?), 24, MS2340/2; report of postmortem examination, MS2308/1; AK, "Preface", Nora Sayre, op. cit., 35.

32 Julian Barnes, unpublished manuscript (with permission); interview with Harold Harris, 9/4/90; C. E. Robins to author, 8/13/91.

33 AK, *Invisible Writing,* 352 and 370.

EPILOGUE

1 Martin Wainwright, "Koestler and Wife Found Dead," *Guardian,* 3/4/83; John Ezard, "A Brave Journey Through a Dark Century," *Guardian,* 3/4/83; Anonymous, "Obituary, Mr Arthur Koestler, a Major Figure in Modern Literature," *Times,* 3/4/83; Eric Pace, "Arthur Koestler and Wife Suicides in London," *New York Times,* 3/4/83; Walter Goodman, "Arthur Koestler, an Intellectual and a Man of Action," *New York Times,* 3/4/83.

2 Interviews with Harold Harris and David Astor; pamphlet on memorial meeting in MS2461.

3 John Ezard, "Koestler Leaves Bequest for Parapsychology," *Manchester Guardian Weekly,* 6/26/83; Anonymous, "A Chair in the Unpredictable," ibid., 7/3/83. Prof. Colin Blakemore, Oxford University, to John Beloff, 11/21/83; Beloff to Blakemore, 12/2/83, MS2463/5; Beloff to author, 3/19/00; interview with Beloff, op. cit.; Martin Bailey, "Charles Backs Welsh Bid for Koestler Chair," *Observer,* 12/2/84; Our Education Correspondent, "Edinburgh to Get Chair of Para-psychology," *Daily Telegraph,* 2/23/84; interview with Diana Henderson, director, Development Fund, Edinburgh University, 5/2/89(?). When sorted and catalogued, the Koestler Archive filled 140 capacious boxes on every subject under the sun, from Zionism to communism, from Hinduism to Buddhism, from fiction to autobiography, from astronomy and psychology to evolution and parapsychology, with especially valuable material on the politics of the Comintern, the Popular Front, the Spanish Civil War, the foundation of Israel, and the cultural Cold War. For Vizinczey, see Adrian Turpin, "Scepticbusters," *Financial Times,* 4/1/05.

4 *Stranger on the Square.* For reviews see Rosemary Dinnage, "Irascible First Paddle," *Times Literary Supplement,* 3/2/84; Anatole Broyard, "Books of the Times," *Times,*

8/22/84; Geoffrey Wheatcroft, "Darkness at Twilight," *Spectator,* 2/25/84; Godfrey Hodgson, "Two Koestlers," *New Statesman,* 2/24/84; Hilton Kramer, "Casanova of Causes," *New York Times Book Review,* 10/7/84; Goodman, *Living with Koestler,* 194. For comparisons with Cynthia see Edward Pearce, "Life with K," *Sunday Telegraph,* 3/13/85; Robert Nye, "Skirmishes in an Unholy War," *Scotsman,* 2/9/85.

5　George Mikes, "Who Killed Cynthia Koestler?," *Observer,* 8/3/86; Harold Harris (who had consulted Cynthia's doctor just to be sure), Celia Goodman, and the Koestlers' neighbor in Suffolk, Donald Wayne, all wrote to dismiss the rumor of cancer; see Harold Harris, "For the Love of Arthur," *Observer,* 8/10/86, and letters to the editor from Celia Goodman and Donald Wayne, *Observer,* 8/24/86; Bernard Avishai, "The Dangers of Devotion," *New Yorker,* 1/6/97.

6　Cesarani, 5, 400–01, 550, and 562.

7　Anthony Burgess, "The Curse of Koestler," *Daily Mail,* 3/4/83; George Steiner, "Koestler's Quest," *Sunday Times,* 8/31/75; Steiner, "Koestler: A Voyager to Intellectual Frontiers," *Sunday Times,* 3/6/83.

8　Author's interviews with Lady Beckett, op. cit., Pat Kavanagh, 6/17/03, and Pamela Merewether, op. cit.

9　Author's interviews with Pat Kavanagh, Julian Barnes, John Grigg, Pamela Merewether, David Astor, and Lady Beckett, op. cit.

10　Author's interviews with Pamela Merewether and Elizabeth Jane Howard, op. cit.; Pamela Merewether to Harold Harris, 2/8/84, MS2346/4.

11　Cesarani, op. cit., 3; Raphael, op. cit., 29. For evidence of the negative impact of Cesarani's book, see William Pfaff, *The Bullet's Song* (New York: Simon and Schuster, 2004), 273–75. For articles marking the centenary, see Walter Laqueur, "A Bully and a Classic," *Times Literary Supplement,* 11/4/05, and Christopher Hitchens, *"Darkness at Noon,* Arthur Koestler's Milestone Anti-Stalinist Novel," *Slate,* 9/13/05. The first of the two conferences on Koestler in Hungary was organized by the Michael Polyani Liberal Philosophical Association and took place in Budapest. All the papers were presented in Hungarian. The second conference, organized by the *Terrorhaza* (Terrorhouse), a museum devoted to victims of the Gulag and the Holocaust, was also held in Budapest and papers were presented in Hungarian, German, and English.

INDEX

NOTE: AK refers to Arthur Koestler.

ABOUT THE AUTHOR

Michael Scammell is the author of *Solzhenitsyn: A Biography*, which won the *Los Angeles Times* prize for biography in 1985 and English PEN's prize for best biography in 1986. He is the editor of *The Solzhenitsyn Files*, *Unofficial Art from the Soviet Union*, and *Russia's Other Writers* and has translated many books from Russian, including Nabokov's *The Defense* and *The Gift* (in collaboration with the author), *Crime and Punishment* by Dostoyevsky, *Childhood, Boyhood and Youth* by Tolstoy, and memoirs by Soviet dissidents Anatoly Marchenko and Vladimir Bukovsky. Scammell writes regularly for *The New York Review of Books*, *The New York Times Book Review*, *Los Angeles Times Book Review*, *The New Republic,* and *Harper's,* and has also written for *The Times, The Times Literary Supplement, The Guardian,* and *The Observer.* He is the founder and first editor of the London-based human rights journal *Index on Censorship,* a former president of the PEN American Center, and a vice president of International PEN. He teaches nonfiction creative writing and translation in the School of the Arts at Columbia University in New York.

ABOUT THE TYPE

This book was set in Granjon, a modern recutting of a typeface produced under the direction of George W. Jones, who based Granjon's design upon the letter forms of Claude Garamond (1480–1561). The name was given to the typeface as a tribute to the typographic designer Robert Granjon.